KU-612-965

ÖBB
1020.38

46251
BRITISH RAILWAYS

THE GREAT BOOK OF TRAINS

Featuring 300 locomotives shown in over 160 full-colour illustrations and more than 500 photographs

Brian Hollingsworth Arthur Cook

BEDFORD EDITIONS LIMITED
LONDON · NEW YORK

2860

FLYING SCOTSMAN

THE GREAT BOOK OF TRAINS

Featuring 300 locomotives shown in over 160 full-colour illustrations and more than 500 photographs

Published by Bedford Editions Ltd,
52 Bedford Row,
London WC1R 4LR

ISBN 0-86101-327-1

All correspondence concerning the content of this volume should be addressed to Bedford Editions Ltd.

The Authors

BRIAN HOLLINGSWORTH, M.A., M.I.C.E.

Brian Hollingsworth has had an extravagant passion for railways ever since he can remember. After qualifying in engineering at Cambridge University, and after a brief excursion into the world of flying machines, he joined the Great Western Railway in 1946 as a civil engineer. Later, his mathematical background led him into British Rail's computers and also to a heavy involvement with BR's TOPS wagon and train control system.

He left British Rail in 1974 to take up writing and has published eleven major books on various aspects of railways and locomotives (including one on how to drive a loco), including Salamander's 'The Illustrated Encyclopedia of the World's Steam Passenger Locomotives', besides contributing to technical railway periodicals.

He is director of the Romney, Hythe and Dymchurch Railway and civil engineering adviser to the Festiniog Railway. He has a fleet of one-fifth full size locomotives which run on his private railway in his own 'back garden' (actually a portion of a Welsh mountain!), and he actually owns the full-size LMS 'Black Five' Class 4-6-0 No. 5428 *Eric Treacy*, which operates as a working locomotive on the North Yorkshire Moors Railway for tourists and rail enthusiasts.

ARTHUR F. COOK, M.A., M.I. Mech. E.

A lifelong railways enthusiast, Arthur Cook was born in the famous English railway town of Doncaster, Yorkshire. He read Engineering at Cambridge University, and stayed on as a research student. After obtaining his degree he subsequently taught at Southampton University, was Principal of the Macclesfield Technical College, and was Administrator at the County Education Headquarters at Chester. He recently retired from British Rail after many years of service. Mr. Cook has written many technical articles on trains and railway systems, particularly modern rail power, and contributed to Salamander's 'Illustrated Encyclopedia of the World's Steam Passenger Locomotives'.

The Steam Consultant

PATRICK B. WHITEHOUSE, O.B.E., A.R.P.S.

Patrick Whitehouse is the author of some 30 books on railway subjects, and has been editor of and consultant to several national railway magazines. He has also been active in steam preservation, becoming the secretary of the very first British line to be rescued by amateurs, the Talyllyn Railway in North Wales. In addition, he is a patron of the world-famous Ffestiniog Railway and has a direct involvement in the preservation and indeed ownership of several main line steam locomotives.

An Associate of the Royal Photographic Society, Patrick Whitehouse has been taking photographs of railway subjects since the age of eleven, and over the years has built up a picture library of approximately 100,000 railway subjects worldwide. To keep himself up-to-date he sets aside at least a month in every year to travel the world not only to look at the main lines but also to poke into the corners to seek out what is left of steam.

Credits

Editors: Ray Bonds, Anthony Hall

Designers: Philip Gorton, Paul Johnson

Color artwork: © Salamander Books Ltd.: David Palmer, Clifford and Wendy Meadway, Michael Roffe, Dick Eastland, Ray Hutchins, W. A. Conquy, Terry Hadler, and TIGA Ltd.

Picture Research: Diane and John Moore *(full picture credits are given at the back of the book).*

Filmset: Modern Text Ltd.

Color and monochrome reproduction: Rodney Howe Ltd. and Bantam Litho Ltd.

Printed in Hong Kong by Leefung-Asco Printers Ltd.

Acknowledgements

The publishers and authors express their thanks to Christopher Bushell and Peter Kalla-Bishop, who checked the manuscripts, making many valuable suggestions, as well as to Margot Cooper and Llinos Black who undertook the typing.

As regards all the wonderful artwork and often rare photographs in the book, we also pay tribute to the team of artists, in particular David Palmer, to Diana and John Moore, and to all those people and institutions who have scoured their archives and photo collections to help make the book one of the best illustrated on steam locomotives, modern locomotives and self-propelled trains.

Contents

Introduction

The Origins and Development of Railways

Long ago in the dawn of civilisation some unsung hero must have first tried laying strips of wood—still called rails when used in fences—on the ground to allow his horse to pull a heavier load. And if the wheels of his cart were fixed outside the shafts, whose spacing was in turn determined by the width of the animal's buttocks, then the distance apart of these wooden strips would approximate to the width between the rails of most of the world's railways today. After a diversion into 'plateways', using cast-iron flanged plates, there came wrought-iron rails and finally steel rails. At the same time the living horse had to give way to the iron one.

By the early 1800's railways and plateways were quite common in mining areas, whilst steam power was also commonly in use for driving pumping machinery. The marriage of the two and hence the first steam locomotive is attributed to Richard Trevithick, a mine captain who hailed from Cornwall, England. Trevithick's locomotive, built in 1804 at Pen-y-darran in South Wales for a wager, was tried out on a local mine tramway. Whilst it seems to have worked quite well, the cast-iron plates which formed the track were not strong enough to carry its weight.

William Hedley's famous *Puffing Billy* of 1813, which ran on a tramway at Wylam near Newcastle-on-Tyne, was one of the earliest successful uses of steam traction, being practical and reliable enough to continue in use until 1859, well into the photographic age.

The first use of steam on a **public** railway was George and Robert Stephenson's *Locomotion* on the Stockton and Darlington in 1825, but the term public here has a literal meaning; it meant that anyone could run his train on the railway by paying the appropriate toll. A high proportion of S&D traffic, including all regular passenger workings, were hauled by horses supplied and operated by independent contractors, just as if the railway was a canal.

There is a plaque on the wall of the original Stockton railway station, which reads as follows: 'HERE ON 30TH, AUGUST 1825, THE FIRST PASSENGER TO TRAVEL BY RAIL WAS BOOKED, THEREBY MARKING AN EPOCH IN THE HISTORY OF MANKIND'. The claim as stated is not pedantically correct—if 'steam train' was substituted for 'rail', it would be nearer being so—but—the truth remains that the coming of mechanical power on railways did have an immense effect the way people lived.

This is not surprising when one considers that the cost of transport was improved at one stroke by a factor of at least four. No longer would most inland people stay all their lives in the place where they were born and no longer need they live within horse-and-cart range of the land on which their food was grown. This was on the credit side; on the debit side, governments in time found a fatal ability to move armies from place to place in days rather than weeks, detraining the troups reasonably fresh and ready for battle, rather than footsore and weary from continuous forced marches. Yet would William of Normandy have ever got ashore at Hastings in 1066 if King Harold's army had been able to move by train from his victory over the Scandanavians in Yorkshire a few days earlier.

Above: *A Baldwin 2-8-2 of the California Western Railroad, seen here restored at Fort Bragg, California.*

The political and economic power generated by the new railways led to the use of them—either unwittingly or deliberately—for the unification and development of nations. In this way the world found itself the richer, but in the process many green and pleasant lands were spoilt by dark satanic mills.

By 1850 many hundreds of miles of railway had been opened in most of the countries of the civilised world, and, indeed, the speed of extension during the next thirty years took the form of a railway mania. By 1870 the continent of America had been spanned, in 1902—with the opening of the Trans-Siberian railway—came the turn of Asia. Australia had to wait until 1916, whilst Cecil Rhodes' dream of an African Cape-to-Cairo line has yet to be fulfilled. By World War I, in most parts of the world, the network was complete.

But a cloud came up over the horizon in the form of a young man called Henry Ford, who in the early 1900's, had the idea of making motor cars not as playthings for the wealthy, but as cheap transport for such as you and I. By the time Ford Model 'T' production ended in 1927 after fifteen million had been made, plus lesser

Above: *An Amtrak GG1 on the Harrisburg-New York line.*

numbers of other makes, railways were finding their customers coming to them by choice rather than necessity. The same applied to traders and shippers as well as those without cars; they had the alternative of lorries and motor buses

Whilst the effect on the main lines was considerable, that on branch and local railways was catastrophic. A few small countries abandoned railways completely, whilst in others great reductions in mileage were made. In France, for example, 15,000 miles of local interest railways were abandoned and in the USA the slaughter of inter-urban local lines amounted to a similar figure over this period.

Whilst shortage of oil during World War II gained a reprieve, the development of aircraft during that conflict led by the 1960's to the jet airliner. The speed of the big jets far more than compensated for the superior comfort and roominess of long-distance trains.

Thus, between road and air competition the railways suffered greatly; indeed, after just over a century of existence their very survival as providers of general transportation was in doubt. The situation was compounded in many countries by continuing and inflexible systems of regulation dating from monopoly days.

Yet today it seems likely that, for a whole series of reasons, the world about to enter upon a new railway age. 20 years ago, one would have had to make that statement in the form of a speculation, but now it has the firmness of a certainty.

First, exhaustion of the world's oil supplies is an event which is likely to be of concern to people living now; therefore any means of transport which is not tied to oil—or would use less oil than others—is one which should be fostered.

Second, there is recognition that the economies of hauling things about in long trains, which flanged steel wheels guided by steel rails permit, make a railway the cheapest form of land transport; always provided that the trains are long enough and/or frequent enough to pay for the fixed costs of what is after all, a very specialized form of highway.

Third, technology is once again on the side of the railway, with such notions as crew-less automatically operated trains or aircraft-speed passenger trains becoming practical possibilities.

Finally, there is growing concern for the environment and this is encouraging for railways, bearing in mind that one extra freight train on the railway means fifty juggernaut lorries off the roads.

So, more than 160 years on from the first steam railway, the future of railways can be viewed with some optimism. Only a tiny fraction of the world's countries are without railways; and several of these have indicated their intention of shortly becoming members of the railway club.

Glossary

Notes — American Railroad English and British Railway English differ slightly. Where this is the case the fact is noted thus: Bogie (US=truck) or Truck (Br=bogie). Both entries appear but the defiition is given only against the British one.

Where appropriate, items are referenced to the cut-away drawing of steam locomotive below, viz Clack valve or Check valve *72*.

Adhesion — the frictional grip between wheel and rail.

Adhesive weight — the weight on the driving wheels of a locomotive. On its amount depends the frictional grip between wheels and rail and hence the drawbar pull which a locomotive can exert.

Air brake — power braking system with compressed air as the operating medium.

Air cushion — type of spring used in some modern carriage suspension systems with air as the operating medium.

Alternating current (ac) — electric current which reverses its direction flow at rapid and regular intervals.

Alternator — a machine which converts mechanical energy to elecical energy and generates alternating current.

Anti-slide/skid — a device for detecting and automatically correcting wheel slide or skid during braking by a momentary reduction of braking force.

Anti-slip — electrical circuit which detects driving wheel slip on diesel and electric locomotives. The difference in current taken by a particular traction motor when wheel slip occurs causes an illuminated warning to be given to the driver. In addition, an automatic reduction in engine power and/or partial application of the locomotive brakes may be effected.

Arch tubes — tubes connected to the water-space of the boiler provided in and across the firebox in order to add extra high-temperature heating surface. They also serve to support the brick arch or equivalent.

Armature — the rotating part of a direct current electric motor or generator. Contains a number of coils, or windings, which rotate in a magnetic field and are connected to the commutator.

Articulated locomotive — a steam locomotive whose driving wheels are in distinct sets one or more of which are hinged or pivoted. Fairlie, Beyer-Garratt and Mallet types form the subject of individual descriptions which follow.

Articulation — the sharing of one bogie by adjacent ends of two vehicles.

Ash-pan *52* — a feature of a locomotive which has the same form and purpose as the domestic variety, ie., to collect the ashes which fall through the bars of the grate. The only significant difference is the size, measured in feet rather than inches.

Asynchronous — an alternating current electric motor whose speed varies with load and has no fixed relation to the frequency of the supply.

Axlebox *28, 44* — the axle bearings of a locomotive are known as axleboxes. It is usually convenient to make them box-shaped to suit the guides and openings in the frames which should constrain movement in the horizontal plane but allow freedom vertically.

Balancing *88* — the reciprocation and revolving masses of any steam (or diesel) engine need balancing, if it is to work smoothly. Revolving masses can easily be balanced by counterweights, but the balancing of reciprocating

King Class 4-6-0

Great Britain:
Great Western Railway (GWR), 1927

The drawing shows the working parts of a King Class 4-6-0 (see page 122), senior member of a unique family of standard engines. This uniqueness appears on the drawing in many ways: e.g., the mouth of the main steam-pipe (67) is placed at the highest point of the boiler instead of inside a separate raised dome on top of the boiler as is more usual.

(Drawing reproduced with acknowledgements to Railway Wonders of the World.*)*

1 Chimney
2 Blower Connection
3 Smoke-box Door Baffle
4 Door-fastening Dart
5 Smoke-box Door
6 Smoke-box
7 Blast Pipe
8 Steam Port
9 Outside Steam-pipe
10 Steam-pipe from Superheater
11 Superheater Header
12 Regulator Valve
13 Jumper Top
14 Steam Chest
15 Piston Valve
16 Valve Rod
17 Piston
18 Piston Rod
19 Stuffing Gland
20 Front Cylinder Cover
21 Buffer
22 Screw Coupling
23 Life Guard
24 Bogie Frame
25 Cylinder Drain Cocks
26 Cylinder
27 Bogie Wheel
28 Outside Bogie Axlebox
29 Bogie Spring
30 Bogie Side-Control Spring Housing
31 Crosshead
32 Inside Cylinder Steam Chest
33 Valve Spindle Rocker
34 Guide Bars
35 Guide Bar Bracket
36 Bogie Bearing Angle
37 Engine Main Frame
38 Crank Pin
39 Coupling Rod

parts is a matter of compromise and judgement.

Ballast — material placed between the sleepers and formation of railway track to disribute the load of passing traffic, prevent lateral and longitudinal movement of the track, provide effective drainage and a convenient medium for maintaining level and gradient.

Banking — assisting the working of a train, usually when ascending a gradient, by attaching one or more locomotives to the rear.

Bar frames — see frames.

Bearings — the bushing or metal block of anti-friction material which transmits the load via an oil film to a journal.

Bi-current locomotive — designed to operate on two different electric current frequency systems.

Blast pipe *7* — the exhaust pipes of a steam locomotive are arranged so that the steam emerges as a jet though a nozzle in the smokebox below the chimney. This creates a partial vacuum in the smokebox, which draws air through the boiler tubes and through the fire, so enabling combustion to take place.

Blowdown valve — a means of releasing water, plus impurities contained therein, from the lowest water space of the boiler.

Blower *2* — a steam jet in the smokebox or at the base of the chimney which can be used to draw up the fire when the locomotive is not being run under steam.

Bogie (US=truck) *24, 27, 29, 30* — a pivoted truck, usually four wheeled, provided at the front or rear of a locomotive to give guidance and support. Most items of rolling stock are carried on bogies.

Boiler — steam producing unit. Locomotive type consists essentially of fire box surrounded by a water space in which the combustion of fuel takes place, and barrel containing the flue tubes surrounded by water.

Boiler tubes *75* — see fire tubes

Bolster — transverse floating beam member of bogie suspension system supporting the weight of vehicle body.

Brakes — locomotives usually (but not always) have a hand brake and (also usually) some form of power brake. Power brakes can be actuated by compressed air, steam or vacuum. Air and vacuum brakes normally can be applied throughout the train by using the controls on the locomotive.

Air Brake — the commonest form of train brake, using compressed air as the medium of application.

Vacuum Brake — the alternative to an air brake is a vacuum brake. For steam locomotives the vacuum is much simpler than the air brake, mainly because a vacuum can be generated from any steam supply by a simple static ejector, whereas compressed air needs a relatively complex pump. The objection to the vacuum system is that the pressure available is limited to about three-quarters of the atmospheric pressure, that is, some 12psi (0.8kg/cm^2). This means either very large cylinders or a limited brake force.

Brick arch *79* — a brick or concrete baffle provided at the front of a locomotive firebox below the tubes, in order to extend the flame path. Early locomotives burnt coke; provision of a brick arch was necessary before coal could be used without producing excessive smoke.

Brush conductor — usually of carbon providing electrical contact with a sliding surface moving relative to it such as the commutator of a direct current machine.

40 Leading Driving Wheel
41 Connecting Rod
42 Sand-boxes
43 Driving Wheel Springs
44 Axle-box Horns
45 Sand-pipes
46 Brake Blocks
47 Middle Driving Wheel
48 Vacuum Brake Train Pipe
49 Trailing Wheel Spring
50 Covers for Indiarubber Pads
51 Equalizer Guards
52 Ash-pan
53 Fire Bars
54 Damper Doors
55 Ash-pan Damper
56 Cylinder Drain Handle
57 Sand Gear Handle
58 Fire Door Handle
59 Cab Side
60 Footplate
61 Reversing Gear Handle
62 Fire Door
63 Regulator Handle
64 Blower Valve
65 Whistle
66 Regulator Rod
67 Mouth of Steam-pipe
68 Vertical Stays
69 Boiler Casing
70 Internal Steam-pipe
71 Safety Valves
72 Clack Box
73 Water Delivery Trays
74 Longitudinal Stays
75 Fire Tubes
76 Superheater Elements
77 Superheater Flue Tubes
78 Firebox
79 Brick Arch
80 Firebox Back Plate
81 Firebox Crown
82 Firebox Tube Plate
83 Firebox Stays
84 Firebox Throat Plate
85 Expansion Bracket Position
86 Splashers
87 Smoke-box Tube Plate
88 Balance Weight
89 Fusible Safety Plug
90 Foundation Ring
91 Tender Wheel Spring
92 Spring Hanger
93 Brake Block
94 Brake Rod
95 Water Scoop
96 Water Inlet Pipe
97 Deflector Dome
98 Rear Buffer
99 Tender frame
100 Front Tender Buffer
101 Water Scoop Handle
102 Brake Handle
103 Axlebox
104 Vacuum Brake Reservoir

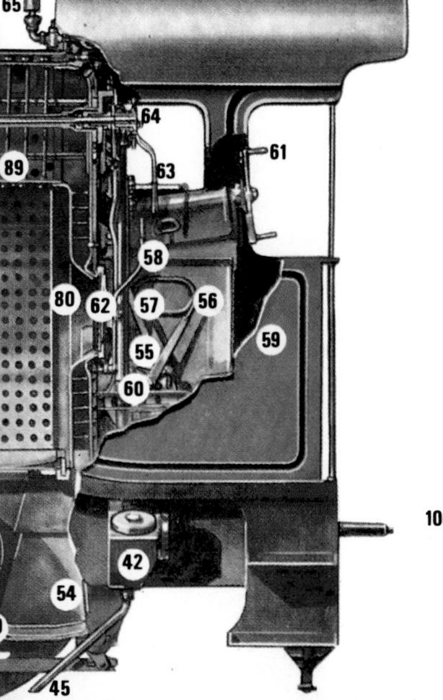

Cam — reciprocating, oscillating or rotating body which imparts motion to another body known as a follower, with which it is in contact.
Camshaft — a shaft which carries a series of cams for operating the inlet valves and exhaust valves of a diesel engine, and contactors in some electric traction control gear systems
Car — American term for a carriage or wagon.
Carriage — passenger-carrying railway vehicle.
Catenary — supporting cable for the contact or conductor wire of an overhead electrification system.
Chimney (US/Smokestack) — the orifice through which the exhaust steam and the gaseous products of combustion are dispersed into the atmosphere.
Circuit breaker — automatic switch for making and breaking an electrical circuit under normal or fault conditions.
Clack valve or Check valve *72* — a non-return valve attached to the boiler at the points where feed water is admitted.
Coal pusher — a steam-operated device in the tender intended to push coal forward to a point where it can be shovelled directly into the fire.
Collector shoe — metal block in contact with conductor rail for collecting current from third rail electrification system.
Combustion chamber — a recessing of firebox tubeplate inside the boiler in order to increase the firebox volume at the expense of reducing the length of the tubes — in order to promote better combustion in long-barrelled boilers.
Commutator — part of the armature of a direct current electrical machine upon which the brushes bear. Cylindrical assembly of copper segmented bars insulated from each other and connected to the coils of the armature winding.
Commuter — holder of railway season ticket. Term now generally applied to a person who travels by public or private transport daily between residence and place of work.
Compensated springing — the inter-connection, by means of equalising levers, of the springs of adjacent axles. The idea is to avoid individual axles being over—or under—loaded by irregularities in the track.
Compound — a compound steam engine has its cylinders arranged so that one or more take high-pressure steam from the boiler as usual, then the remainder take the low-pressure steam exhausted from the high-pressure cylinders and use that to produce further useful work.
Compression stroke — second piston stroke of four-stroke cycle diesel engine during which air charge in cylinder is compressed and heated by piston movement.
Compressor — machine for raising the pressure of air above atmospheric. Provides compressed air for operation of brakes, auxiliaries and so on.
Conductor — see guard.
Conjugated valve-gear — more than two cylinders were often used in order to provide smoother running and also where an adequate total cylinder volume could only be provided in this way. In order to reduce complication, the valves of all the cylinders could be arranged to be worked by conjugating levers from the valve gears of two of term.
Connecting rod (US=Main rod) *41* — these connect the piston rods to the crank pins of the driving wheels or crank-shaft.
Consist — composition or make-up of the train.
Contactor — remotely controlled switch used for frequently making and breaking electrical power circuits on load.
Converter — machine for converting electrical power for alternating current to direct current or vice versa.
Core — iron section around which is wound the coil or wire through which an electric current is passed to produce a magnetic force in an electro-magnet.
Coupler — (Br=Coupling).
Coupling (US=Coupler) *22* — couplings join the vehicles of a train. Non-automatic couplings on passenger locomotives are usually of the screw pattern, formed of to links connected by a screw. Vehicles are coupled by placing the coupling of one over the hook of the other and tightening the screw, so that the buffers are in contact. Automatic couplings are designed to couple when, usually after the jaws have been opened, the vehicles are pushed gently together. The couplings then engage and lock.
Coupling rod *39* — connects together the crank-pins of the driving or coupled wheels on one side of a locomotive.
Counter-pressure brake — using the pumping action of the cylinders to brake the train. Great heat is generated and the cylinders are kept from over-heating dangerously by the injection of water, which instantly flashes into steam, thereby absorbing the energy generated.
Crank — device for converting rotary to reciprocating motion or vice versa. Consist of an arm, one end of which is fixed to a shaft and the other free to rotate about the axis of the shaft.
Crank axles — the inside cylinders of locomotives drive on to axles with sections off-set to form cranks.
Crank-pins *38* — locomotive wheels are driven by rods which transmit the driving force to the driving wheels through these large steels pins fixed in the wheels.
Crosshead *31* — in conjunction with the guide-bars the crosshead guides and constrains the piston rod to keep in line as it moves in and out of the cylinder.
Current — rate of flow of electricity round a circuit.
Cut-off — the point during the cylinder stroke at which steam is cut off by the valves. It is usually expressed as a percentage of that stroke. Typically, a steam locomotive would be set to cut-off at 75% when starting and at between 5% and 40% when running.
Cycle — series of events repeated in a regular sequence. Diesel engines operate on a two or four stroke cycle.
Cylinders *26* — in a steam locomotive the energy contained in steam is turned into mechanical force in the cylinders. Each cylinder contains a piston and the pressure of the steam on this piston produces the force.
Dampers *54, 55* — the amount of heat produced by a fire is governed by the amount of air admitted to it. This can be adjusted by opening or closing damper doors in the ashpan assembly. These are worked by levers in the locomotive cab.
Dead-man's handle — device for cutting off power and applying the brakes in the event of the driver becoming incapacitated whilst driving.
Dead section — length of conductor in an electrified railway system which is not energised.
Deck — see footplate.
Deflector dome *97* — This is provided in or on the tender in connection with the water pick-up apparatus. Water scooped from a set of troughs between the rails is first fed skywards up a vertical pipe; the deflector dome at the top of this pipe then turns the flow downwards so that the tender is filled.
Diesel — compression ignition, internal combustion engine.
Direct current (dc) — electrical current which flows in one direction continuously.
Direct drive — direct mechanical connection between output end of prime mover and driving wheels of locomotive.
Disc brake — braking mechanism utilizing friction pads applied by caliper action to a disc secured to vehicle axle or wheel centre.
Dome — the steam is usually taken from the boiler at its highest point. Where height is available, a chamber known as the dome is provided above the top of the boiler barrel in order to collect the steam.
Double head — to attach a second locomotove to the front of a train.
Down — usually the line of track which carries trains in a direction away form the town or city in which the headquarters of the railway company are located.
Draincocks *26, 56* — when a locomotive is starting from cold the first steam which enters the

Below: *A British Railways driver demonstrates the use of the "dead-man's handle".*

cylinders condenses to water. Draincocks are provided, worked from the cab, to allow this water to escape. Otherwise the cylinder would be burst by the pressure of trapped water when the piston reached the end of its stroke.

Drawbar—horsepower hour — a unit of work done by a locomotive in hauling a train. One of these units represents the exertion of a single horse-power at the locomotive drawbar for an hour.

Driving wheels *40, 47* — the driven wheels of a locomotive, sometimes referred to as coupled wheels.

Drop-grate or **Dump-grate** — when disposing of a locomotive after use the residue of the fire needs removing. Traditionally this was shovelled out through the fire-hole door, but an arrangement to allow the whole grate to be dropped or dumped was sometimes provided.

Dual control — operated or controlled from two seperate positions.

Dynamic braking — system of braking utilizing the braking characteristics of the engine compression, transmission or traction motors.

Dynamic loading — load applied to track or structure by vehicle in motion passing over it.

Dynamo — direct current electrical machine used for charging batteries and providing current for carriage lighting.

Dynamometer car — vehicle with equipment for measuring and recording draw-bar pull, horse-power, speed, and so on, of a locomotive under load.

Earth — electrical connection to complete a circuit.

Eccentric — disc, keyed to a shaft or axle, whose centre does not coincide with that of the axle. It rotates inside a ring, known as an eccentric ring, known as an eccentric strap, to which is attached the eccentric rod, and imparts reciprocating motion to a link for operating the steam distribution valve to the cylinder.

Electric traction — haulage of vehicles by electric-motor-driven unit utilizing electric power obtained form batteries or an external source via conductor wire or rail.

Equalisers — see compensated springing.

Exhaust steam — emmission of steam from the cylinder after completion of the working stroke.

Expansion of steam — increase in volume of steam in the cylinder after the supply has been cut off. The ability to take maximum advantage of the expansive qualities of steam results in economies in the consumption of fuel and water.

Above: *A "multiple unit", with four Denver & Rio Grande Western RR units hauling coal in Rockies.*

Express — fast train stopping at few intermediate stations.

Fairing — structure or cover to provide a smooth surface and reduce air resistance.

Feed-pump — a pump to feed water into the boiler; either driven from the motion or independently by steam from the boiler.

Field — space around a magnet or a conductor carrying an electric current where magnetic lines of force may be detected.

Firebox *80-84* — made of steel or copper and fixed inside the boiler. The box in which the fire burns.

Fire door or Fire-hole door *58, 62* — the entrance to the firebox, through which coal is shovelled is closed by a fire door.

Fire tubes *75* — the hot gases from the fire pass through these fire tubes (often, *boiler tubes* or simply *tubes*) in the boiler between the firebox and the smokebox, so heating the water with which they are surrounded.

Flange — projecting edge or rim on the periphery of a wheel or rail.

Flange lubricators — on sharp curves, wheel flanges bear heavily against the rails. To ease wear and reduce friction, devices to lubricate these flanges are provided on the locomotive. More usually, though, they are attached to the rail.

Flues *77* — large fire tubes, often referred to as superheater flues, which contain the superheater elements.

Footplate *60* — the surface on which a locomotive crew stands. In fact it usually extends all round the engine, but the term is now taken to mean the floor of the driving cab.

Formation — make-up of a train of vehicles.

Foundation ring *90* — the rectangular ring which connects the firebox to the boiler at the lowest point of both.

Four-foot way — space between running rails of standard gauge 4ft 8½in (1.435mm) track.

Frames *37* — often **main frames** — are the foundation upon which the locomotive is built. In British practice the frames are generally formed of plates; USA practice originally favoured bars, but cast-steel was used generally in later years.

Frequency — number of times a second an alternating electric current reverses its direction of flow.

Fusible plugs *89* — a last-ditch defence against the consequences of boiling the top of the firebox dry, consisting of screwed brass plugs with a lead core. If there was no water present the lead would melt and the leakage of steam would (to some extent) douse the fire.

Gap — break in continuity of conductor rail.

Gas turbine — rotary internal combustion machine which is driven by gas flow thus causing varied discs (s) mounted on common shafts to turn at high speed.

Gauge — standard measure; the distance between running edges or inner faces of the rails of railway track.

Generator — electrical machine which changes mechanical energy into electrical energy. Term generally applied to one which produces direct current.

Governor — device for maintaining as closely as possible a constant engine crankshaft speed over long periods during which the load on the engine may vary.

Grade/gradient — slope or inclination to the horizontal of a railway. Expressed in degrees from the horizontal, as a percentage, or unit rise or fall to the horizontal or slope length.

Grade *53* — usually formed of cast-iron bars on which the fire burns.

Gross weight — total weight of train including payload.

Guard, (American conductor) — person in charge of a train.

Guide bars *34* — see crosshead.

Handbrake — means of applying the brake blocks to the wheel treads without power assistnce. Usually in the form of a screwed shaft with a running nut, attached to the gearing.

Headstock — main lateral end member of a carriage or wagon underframe to which the buffers and drawgear may be attached.

Heating of trains — usually effected by one of three methods; steam-fed radiators, electric-resistance heaters, or hot-air circulation from oil-fired combustion heaters.

Heating surface — areas of locomotive boiler exposed to heat on one side and available for water evaporation on other.

Horns *44* — these are guides, attached to the frames, in which the axleboxes can move vertically when running.

Horsepower — a unit of power equal to 75kg metres per sec, 33,000ft per lb per min, or 746 watts.

Hot box — an overheated vehicle axlebox bearing resulting from breakdown of lubricating film between bearing and journal.

Indicated horsepower — the power developed in the cylinders of a locomotive.

Induction — production of an electric current by change of magnetic field.

Injector — a static device for feeding water into the boiler by means of a series of cones. It is driven by a supply of live steam taken from the boiler or (in the case of an exhaust-steam injector) from the locomotive's exhaust when running.

Integral construction — carriage construction where the body and underframe form one stress and load carrying structure.

Journal — area of a shaft or axle supported by a bearing.

Jumper blast-pipe *13* — this device was sometimes attached to the blast-pipe in order to limit the draught when the engine is working hard.

Lead — the amount which a main steam port of a locomotive cylinder is open when the appropriate piston is at its limit of travel.

Life guard *23* — Provided in front of the leading wheels of a locomotive with the idea of throwing aside objects encountered on the rails. Often also called a guard iron.

Light engine — locomotive running without a train.

Lighting of carriages — by axle driven dynamo, capable of generating when rotated in either direction. Also charges the batteries which supply lighting power when the train is stationary or running slowly.

Live rail — electrical conductor for transmitting power to locomotives or train on third-rail electrified lines.

Load factor — the ratio of actual train loading to maximum capacity.

Loading gauge — the limiting dimensions of height and width of rolling stock and loads carried to ensure adequate clearance with lineside structures.

Low-water alarm — an automatic device to warn the crew that boiler-water level is getting dangerously low.

Main rod (BR=connecting rod) — see connecting rod.

Mallet — see Union Pacific 'Challenger', page 164.

Manganese steel liners — hard wearing lining surfaces used to minimise wear on the horns.

Mercury arc — static device employing a mercury pool cathode for converting alternating to direct current.

Metro — underground railway system for mass conveyance of short journey passengers.

Monocoque — vehicle structure with under frame and body designed to form a single unit on aircraft construction principles.

Monorail — railway system where the track consists of a single rail.

Motion — a generic term used to describe the moving parts (other than the wheels and axles) of the engine.

Motor bogie — bogie having driving wheels or motored axles.

Motor generator set — electric motor and generator mechanically coupled for the purpose of converting direct current from one voltage to another.

Motorman — driver of an electric tram, railcar or multiple-unit train.

Multi-system or voltage locomotive — locomotive designed to operate on more than one electrical system.

Multiple unit — two or more locomotives or powered vehicles coupled together, or in a train, operated by only one driver.

Narrow gauge. — railway track of less than the standard gauge.

Nosing — an oscillating movement of a locomotive about a vertical axis.

Notch — intermediate position of electric tractionpower controller; indentation in manual signal box lever frame to hold lever in position.

One-hour rating — 10 per cent above nominal rating which machine should be able to sustain for continuous period of up to one hour without distress.

Out-of-gauge — vehicle or load which exceeds the loading gauge limits.

Overhead — catenary and contact wire of a suspended electrical distribution system.

Over-ride — take precedence over; manual control over a normally automatic operation.

Over-speed trip — mechanism for stopping a diesel engine in event of excessive crankshaft rotational speed.

Packing — oil absorbing material used to assist the lubrication of an axle bearing; also material placed in the gland to maintain a leak free joint when subjected to pressure.

Pantograph — link between overhead contact system and power circuit of an electric locomotive or multiple unit through which the power required is transmitted. Simplest form is spring loaded pivoted diamond frame with copper or carbon contact strip.

Parlor car — American term for luxuriously fitted railway carriage.

Parallel connection — electrical conductors or circuits so connected that the sum of the currents in the individual conductors of circuits is equal to the total current supplied.

Payload — that part of the total weight of the train which is revenue earning; excluding weight of empty vehicles and locomotive.

Peak hour — period of time when traffic levels are greatest.

Pendular suspension — carriage suspension allowing body to tilt to compensate for fast running round curves.

Piston *17* — see cylinders.

Piston rod *18* — the rod connecting the piston to the crosshead.

Piston valve *15* — see valves.

Pony truck — a two-wheel

Nominal rating — full load output of machine capable of being sustained for continuous period of 12 hours without distress.

Nose-suspended motor — traction motor mounted on bearings on axle being driven, with a "nose" resiliently fixed to a bogie cross member to prevent rotation round axle. Gear on axle is in constant mesh with pinion on armature shaft.

pivoted truck provided at the front or rear of a locomotive to provide guidance and support.

Poppet valve *15* — see valves.

Port *8* — see valves.

Priming — this occurs either when the water level in the boiler is too high or when impurities which cause foaming are present. It means that water is carried over down to the cylinders.

Pullman car — railway carriage providing a higher standard of service and comfort than normal and for which a supplementary fare is exacted.

Push-pull — method of operating whereby the locomotive may be other than at the head of the train, although controlled from there.

Rack railway — system used on mountain railways (and occasionally elsewhere) where gradients exist too steep for the normal adhesion between wheel and rail to be effective. A pinion on the locomotive engages in a rack fixed to the track. The rack can consist either of a longitudinal series of steel teeth or of rungs of gear-tooth profile fixed to side memvers like the rungs of a ladder.

Radial axles — provide the effect of a pony truck but without a separate pivoted frame. The horns and axleboxes of a radial axle are made to allow sideways movement and are shaped so that such movement is sensibly radial about a vertical axis.

Railcar — self-propelled passenger-carrying vehicle.

Railroad — American term for a railway.

Rapid transit — system for high-speed urban mass transport.

Rectifier — a device for converting alternating electric current to direct current.

Regenerative brake — electrical braking system whereby the traction motors of direct current electric locomotives work as generators and feed electrical energy back into the supply system.

Registration arm — cantilever which gives contact wire an offset in relation to track centre line in overhead electrification system.

Regulator (US=throttle) *12* — serves the same purpose as the accelerator pedal on a car; in the case of a locomotive, though, it is a large and usually rather stiff steel handle.

Relay — remotely controlled electromagnetic switch for low electrical currents. Used to make and break circuits which in turn may operate power circuits, other relays and so forth.

Resistance — force, opposing motion; that which opposes the flow of current in an electric circuit, measured in ohms. Used to dissipate surplus electrical energy in form of heat.

Return crank — a revolving lever fixed on the end of a driving crank-pin so that it provides the reciprocating motion, of correct magnitude and phase, to drive the valve gear.

Reversing lever — a lever used for the same purpose as the reversing wheel, but not often found on express passenger locomotives.

Reversing station — point where train reverses direction of travel during course of journey. May be at normal dead-end or terminal station layout or on zig-zag section of steeply graded line.

Reversing wheel or handle *61* — the wheel provided to alter the cut-off point of the valve gear and to move it between forward and reverse.

Rheostat — variable resistance for regulating the flow of electric current.

Rheostatic braking — electrical braking system whereby the traction motors work as generators, the resultant electrical being dissipated as heat in resistances.

Rigid wheel base — horizontal distance between the centres of the first and last axles held rigidly in alignment with each other; the coupled wheels of a steam locomotive.

Rocking grate — an arrangement to enable the grate bars to be rocked or shaken, to encourage the residues of combustion to fall down into the ash-pan.

Roller bearing — hardened steel cylinders located in a cage which revolve in contact with inner and outer races.

Rolling stock — carriages and wagons; railway vehicles.

Rotor — rotating part of an electrical (usually alternating current) machine.

Round house — engine shed in which the locomotive stabling tracks radiate from a turntable.

Ruling gradient — limiting gradient (and therefore trainload) for traction and braking capacities.

Running gear — term generally applied to the wheels, axles, axleboxes, springs, frames of a railway vehicle.

Running light — locomotive movement without a train attached.

Safe load — maximum load which may be applied without undue risk.

Safety valves *71* — allow steam to escape if pressure exceeds the safe limit.

Sanding gear *42, 45* — a device to put sand on the rails to improve adhesion, particularly in damp conditions. It is worked from the cab, and the sand is either allowed

to fall by gravity, or is sprayed into position with steam or compressed air.
Scavenge — to remove the products of combustion from an internal combustion engine cylinder by a regulated flow of air.
Secondary winding — output side of a transformer.
Semi-conductor — material used in electric traction rectifiers, whose electrical resistance depends on the direction of the applied voltage. Germanium and silicon are typical examples.
Series connection — electrical conductors or circuits so connected that the same current flows in each conductor or circuit.
Series-parallel connection — method of connecting traction motors whereby individual motors are connected in series to form groups and each group then connected in parallel.
Series motor — direct current electrical machine with ideal traction characteristics. Produces a high torque when the vehicle is started and as the load increases the speed drops.
Service coach — carriage used for railway departmental purposes, not in public use.
Service life — expected working life of a component before replacement required.
Servo — control system whereby a small amount of effort is augmented to do a large amount of work.
Shock absorber — telescopic hydraulic device for damping spring suspensions.
Shoe brake — simple arrangement for applying a retarding or braking force to the periphery of a rotating drum or wheel, by pressure of a block of wood, metal or friction material against it.
Short circuit — point of very low resistance in an electrical circuit usually if accidentally resulting from insulating failure.
Shunt — direct onto a minor track; marshal vehicles into a particular order.
Shuttle — train which gives a frequent return service over a short route.
Side corridor — passenger carrying vehicle with connecting corridor between compartments along one side.
Single-phase — single alternating electric current. One phase of three-phase supply.
Sleeper — steel, wood or precast concrete beam for holding the rails to correct gauge and distributing to the ballast the load imposed by passing trains.
Slide-bars *34* — see crosshead.
Slide valves — see valves.
Slip — loss of adhesion between driving wheel and rail causing wheels to spin; also short curved connecting line joining lines which cross one another on the level; also driving member rotating at a higher speed than in a fluid coupling.
Smokebox *6* — a chamber at the front end of the boiler which serves to collect ashes drawn through the tubes. A partial vacuum formed in the smokebox by a jet of exhaust steam emerging from the blast pipe provides a flow of air from and through the fire.
Snifting valves — have the same function as by-pass valves but function by admitting air to the steam circuit at an appropriate point when a vacuum is formed in them.
Soleplate — longitudinal main frame member of fabricated or built up carriage bogie, usually of standard rolled steel section or pressings. Also a plate inserted between the chairs and the sleeper at a pair of points to maintain the correct gauge and prevent any spreading of the gauge that might occur from the gradual enlargement of the spike holes in the wooden sleepers.
Spark arrester — a device in the smokebox or chimney to prevent sparks being thrown.
Splashers *86* — Provided to cover the portion of large driving wheels if they protrude through the footplate or running board.
Spring hangers *92* — The tips of leaf springs on a locomotive are connected to the frames by links known as spring hangers.
Stall — to come to a stand under power. Occurs when train resistance exceeds tractive power.
Standard gauge — 4ft 8½ (1,435mm), between rails in a country.
Stays *68, 74, 83* — by its nature, the firebox of a locomotive cannot be circular like the front part of the boiler barrel. Its shape, therefore needs retaining and this is done by a mass of rods known as stays connecting the firebox to the boiler shell.
Stub axle — short non-revolving axle which supports only one wheel.
Stuffing gland *19* — where a moving piston rod emerges from a cylinder in which steam at high pressure is contained, a form of gland containing packing is needed to prevent leakage.
Sub-station — point in electricity distribution system where supply is converted or transformed to suit needs of user.
Sub-way — underground passage to give access to platforms. American term for underground railway.
Supercharge — supply air to the

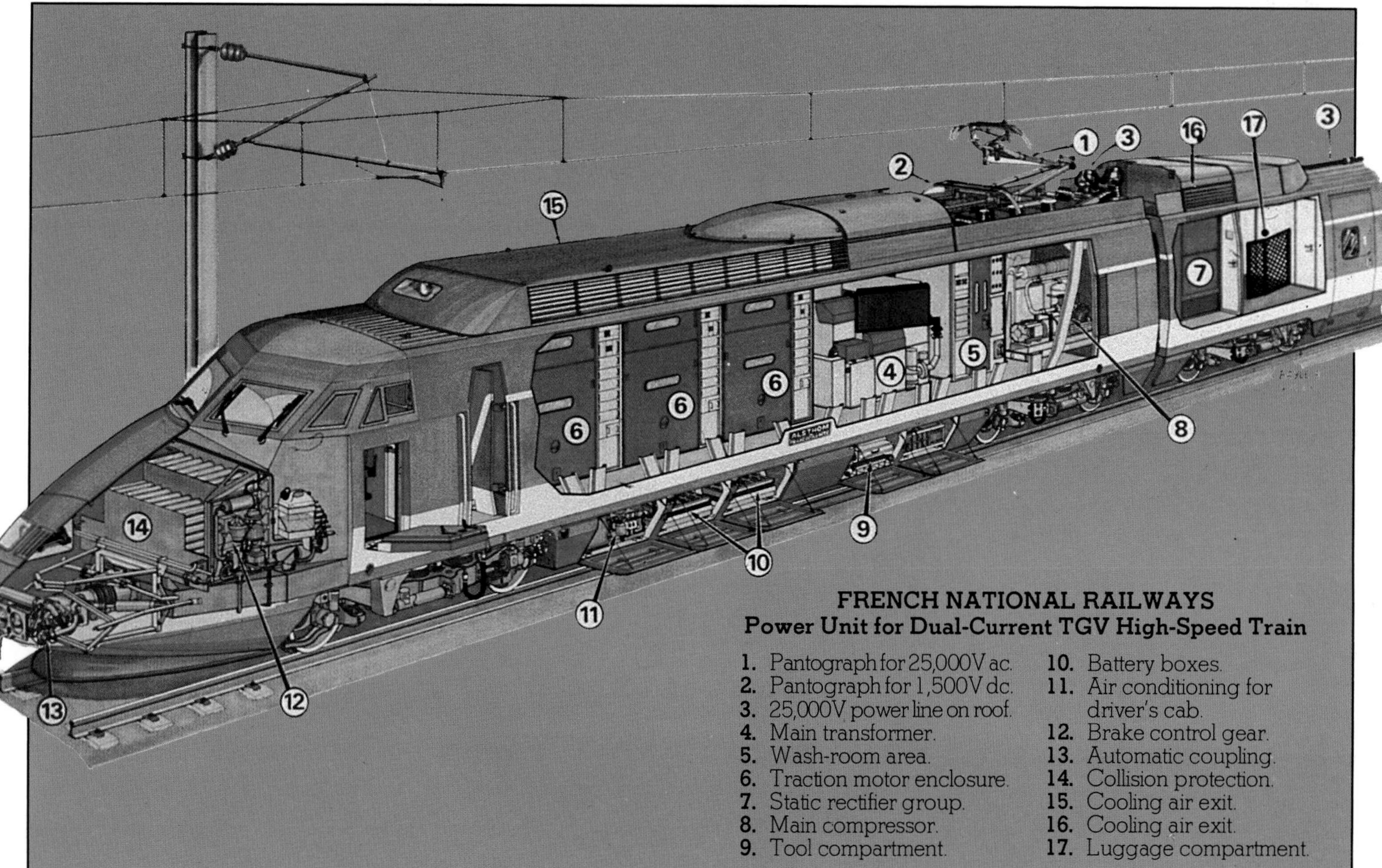

FRENCH NATIONAL RAILWAYS
Power Unit for Dual-Current TGV High-Speed Train

1. Pantograph for 25,000V ac.
2. Pantograph for 1,500V dc.
3. 25,000V power line on roof.
4. Main transformer.
5. Wash-room area.
6. Traction motor enclosure.
7. Static rectifier group.
8. Main compressor.
9. Tool compartment.
10. Battery boxes.
11. Air conditioning for driver's cab.
12. Brake control gear.
13. Automatic coupling.
14. Collision protection.
15. Cooling air exit.
16. Cooling air exit.
17. Luggage compartment.

inlet valves of a diesel engine at above atmospheric pressure.
Superheating — increasing the temperature and volume of steam after leaving the boiler barrel by application of additional heat.
Suspension — connecting system, including springs, between vehicle wheel and body, designed to give best possible riding qualities by keeping unsprung weights to a minimum and reducing shock loadings on track.
Swing-link — metal bar pivoted at each end. Part of suspension system of many bogies and trucks.
Switch — device for opening and closing an electrical circuit.
Switch — American term for points.
Synchronous — electric motor whose speed varies in direct proportion to the frequency of the supply.
Tachometer — instrument giving a continuous indication of rotational speed of diesel engine crankshaft and so on.
Tank locomotive — one which carries its fuel and water supplies on its own main frames.
Tap — intermediate connection between the main connections of an electrical circuit or component.
Tender — a separate carriage for fuel and water attached to a locomotive.
Tender locomotive — one which carries its fuel and/or water supplies in a separate semi-permanently coupled vehicle.
Thermal efficiency — the proportion of the heat value of the fuel consumed which appears as useful work.
Thermic syphon — vertical or near vertical water ducts in the firebox provided with the idea of adding heating surface and improving circulation in the boiler.
Third rail — non-running rail carrying electrical current to electric locomotive or train.
Three-phase — simultaneous supply or use of three electrical currents of same voltage, each differing by a third in frequency cycle.
Throttle — American term for regulator. Valve controlling flow of fuel to diesel engine.
TIA — a form of water treatment, developed by Louis Armand of the French Railways, known as *Traitemant Intégral Armand.* It involved dosing the water in the tenders, regular tests of the acidity or alkalinity of the water in the boilers and decimated boiler repair costs in France and elsewhere.
Top feed — feed water is relatively cold and is best fed into the top of the boiler with clack or check valves fitted there. Hence the term 'top feed'.
Track circuit — section of running line insulated from adjoining sections, into one end of which is fed a low-voltage electrical current with a relay connected across the rails at the other end. When the track section is unoccupied the relay is energised, but the wheel sets of a passing train produce a short circuit which leaves the relay without current. Consequent movement of the relay arm is used to make or break other electrical circuits connected to associated signalling equipment, including illuminated track diagrams, point and signal interlocking automatic colour-light signals.
Tractive effort — this a theoretical figure which indicates how hard a locomotive can pull when 85% (usually) of full-boiler pressure is applied to the pistons.
Train-pipe — continuous air to vacuum brake pipe, with flexible connections between vehicles, through which operation of the train brake is controlled.
TEE (Trans Europ Express) — international European luxury express passenger service conveying only first class passengers at a supplementary fare.
Transformer — device which by electromagnetic induction converts one voltage of alternating current to another.
Transmission — mechanical, hydraulic or electrical arrangement necessary with diesel traction to enable diesel engine to be run whilst locomotive is stationary and provide the necessary torque multiplication at starting. Mechanical transmission usually consists of clutch or fluid coupling, gearbox and final drive/reversing unit. Hydraulic transmissions include one or more torque convertors which may incorporate an automatic gearbox. Electric transmission consists of an alternator or generator directly coupled to the diesel engine which supplies electric current to one or more traction motors driving the locomotive wheels.
Trip — means of release by

Below: *A 1925 Baldwin 2-8-2, formerly of the Denver & Rio Grande Western Railroad.*

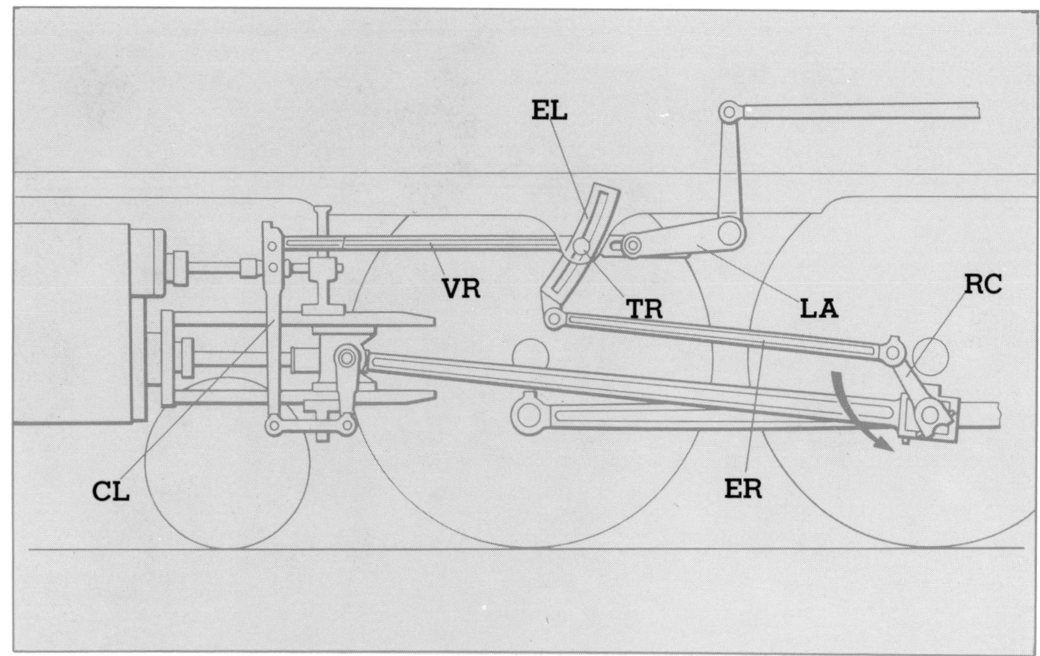

Above and below: *The parts of Walschaerts valve gear. The letters are referred to in the glossary description under* **Valve gears.** *(The diagram was produced from reference © Eleanora Steel.)*

knocking aside a catch.
Trolley — pole mounted on roof of electric vehicle with wheel attached to outer end to pick up electric current from overhead contact wire.
Truck — open railway wagon. American term for bogie on a locomotive or wagon.
Trunk — main route or line of railway from which branch or feeder lines diverge.
Tube — underground railway running in a tunnel excavated by mining methods.
Turbine — rotary machine consisting of one or more sets of blades attached to a shaft; driven by steam or gas flow in railway applications.
Turbo-charger — turbine, driven by the flow of exhaust gases from a diesel engine coupled to a rotary compressor which supplies air at above atmospheric pressure to the engine-inlet valves.
Tyre (American tire) — steel band forming the periphery of a wheel on which the flange and tread profile is formed.
Underframe — framework or structure which supports the body of a carriage or wagon.
Underground — beneath the surface of the ground. Railway built below street level in large cities to avoid congestion.
Up line — line over which trains normally travel towards the headquarters of the railway company concerned.
Up train — one which travels on or in the direction of the up line.
Vacuum — space from which air has been exhausted.
Valves — three types of valves were used on steam locomotives. The **slide valve** was virtually universal during the first 75 years of steam construction. It consisted of a flat valve which slides on flat port face in the steam chest. A recess in the valve face connects the exhaust port with one or other cylinder according to the position of the valve. Also, according to the position of the valve, one or other cylinder port is exposed by its edge as it moves in time with the movement of the piston; steam can then flow into the appropriate end of the cylinder.

In the later years of steam **piston valves** became almost universal. The steam chest is cylindrical; boiler steam and exhaust steam are divided by two pistons which cover and uncover the cylindrical ports as the valves move. The boiler steam can be admitted either in between or outside the pistons; these arrangements are known as *inside admission* or *outside admission* respectively, the former being the most usual one.

A few steam locomotives used **poppet valves,** not dissimiliar to those fitted to the family motor car.
Valve gears — provided in order to move the valves of a locomotive to a precise timing in relation to the movement of pistons. It is necessary to cope with requirements for early and late cut-off as well as forward and reverse working. Numerous linkages have been devised to do this. Walschaert's gear became almost universal in the later days of steam. With reference to the diagram herewith, its working is as follows:-

A return crank RC is fixed to the main crank-pin so that its little end revolves 90° out of phase with the main motion. By means of the eccentric rod ER, a curved slotted link EL is oscillated about a centre TR. A die-block which slides in this link is pivoted to the Valve-Rod VR. It can be lowered by the fore-and-aft movement of the eccentric rod ER is transmitted to the valve rod VR. If LA is raised the movement of VR is reversed. In this way forward and reverse timing of the valve is catered for. By a partial movement of the lifting arm LA a reduced opening of the valve is provided. A combination lever CL serves to bias the opening of the valve towards the beginning of the stroke by, as it were, injecting a dose of the movement of the cross-head into the movement of the valve rod.

Baker valve gear is a version of Walschaerts which replaces the curved slotted link EL with a series of plain links and this was used to some extent in the USA in recent years.

Stephenson's gear would certainly rival Walschaerts if a count of the total number of sets fitted was the criterion. Other gears such as Allan, 'gab' and Gooch were used in small numbers and references are made to these in the body of the book.
Van — covered vehicle for conveyance of luggage, goods or use of guard.
Variable gauge — vehicle or wheelset with facility for operating on more than one track gauge. Achieved by sliding wheel along axle and locking in appropriate position to suit required gauge.
Vestibule — covered gangway giving access between vehicles.
Vigilance device — ensures the continued vigilance or alertness of the driver by requiring him to make a positive action at frequent intervals. Failure to do so results in power being cut off and the brakes applied.
Voltage — electromotive force measured in volts.
Wagon — railway vehicle for the conveyance of goods.
Water gauge — a glass tube fixed to the boiler to allow the water level to be seen — This is the most important indication that there is on a steam locomotive and hence the gauge is usually duplicated.
Westinghouse brake — see air brake.
Working timetable — timetable including all trains running over a particular route or area.
Yard — group of lines or sidings where auxiliary operations to train working are undertaken.

Above: *UP's famous 119 at Golden Spike N.M., Utah.*

STEAM PASSENGER LOCOMOTIVES

STEAM PASSENGER LOCOMOTIVES

Above: *An 1886 advert for the C & NW's Short Line.*

The Development of Steam Power

NO PART of this story is more significant than the development of mechanical motive power. Our story begins in 1830 with the world's first inter-city railway between Liverpool and Manchester. For the first time all the elements of a modern railway came together. The trains ran on metal wheels guided by flanges running inside pairs of rails with 4ft 8½in (1,434mm) between their inside edges. All trains ran to a timetable, were operated by the company, stopping only at its own stations, and were manned by its own staff. And, above all, they were hauled by the great new power of steam. All England held its breath as these little fire chariots began to annihilate space and time at speeds up to 35mph (56km/h). In this way journey times were reduced by a factor of three or more, in comparison with those achieved by road carriages hauled by the flesh-and-blood kind of horse. Within a dozen years even these speeds had doubled, while locomotive weights had trebled, power outputs had quadrupled and a fair degree of reliability had been achieved. In addition, two quite separate lines of development had emerged on either side of the Atlantic Ocean.

Above: *Southern Railway "West Country" class 4-6-2* Blackmore Vale *hauls a train on the Bluebell Railway in 1981.*

Above: *A construction train on the Mexican Railway is pulled across a spindly steel viaduct behind a Fairlie articulated locomotive.*

Even nowadays, when far more wonderful examples of man's mastery over Nature's physical forces are commonplace, we find a working steam locomotive a thrilling sight, but for people living then it must have been awesome indeed. No wonder people expected the cattle to be made barren, the crops to fail, hens to cease laying and fruit to rot on the trees when a steam locomotive thundered by.

None of these things happened but, nevertheless, the coming of the steam locomotive changed the world in a few short years by reducing both the cost as well as the speed of travel again by a factor of three or more. No longer did all but a favoured few among people living in inland regions need to spend all their lives in the same place. Of course, in the wilder parts of the world the coming of steam locomotion often marked the very start of civilisation: the railway actually opened up and built many countries, the United States of America being the most prominent example.

But there is another side to steam on rails and, surprisingly, it was a young actress called Fanny Kemble who is the first person (and both the first and almost the last woman) on record as having realised that here was a new art-form to thrill the senses. On 26 August 1830 she wrote to a friend that "... a common sheet of paper is enough for love but a foolscap extra can alone contain a railroad and my ecstasies". She went on to speak of "this brave little she-dragon ... the magical machine with its wonderful flying white breath and rhythmical unvarying pace" and finally she felt as if "no fairy tale was ever half so wonderful as what I saw". True, not everyone was conducted by George Stephenson personally the first time they met a steam locomotive but, even so, this perspicacious lady really rang the bell in speaking of the iron horse the way she did.

Many of the rest of us are only beginning to realise the value of what we used to have now that it has been or is being snatched away. In most countries one can no longer stand beside the railway line and listen to the *thrum, thrum, thrum* of a steam locomotive as an express train comes up fast towards us, then watch it go by with rods flailing and a white plume of exhaust shining in the sunshine; or maybe stand at the carriage window and listen to the chimney music and the patter of cinders on the roof as a mighty steam locomotive up front pounds up some long hard grade in the mountains.

But this steam locomotive worship thing has much more to it than that and for pointing this out we again owe Miss Kemble our gratitude. Almost without realising it—not being familiar with today's railway locomotives which are just noisy boxes on wheels—she pin-pointed one of the other great charms of the steam locomotive, the fact that most of its secrets are laid bare for those who have eyes to see. Fanny wrote "... she (for they make all

Above: *"Duchess" class 4-6-2* Duchess of Hamilton *leaves York, England, on her first trip after restoration.*

Left: *"A4" class 4-6-2 No.60025* Falcon *bursts from Gasworks Tunnel, Kings Cross with the* Flying Scotsman.

these curious little firehorses mares) consisted of a boiler, a stove, a small platform, a bench . . . she goes on two wheels which are her feet and are moved by bright steel legs called pistons; these are propelled by steam and in proportion as more steam is applied to the upper extremeties (the hip-joints, I suppose) of these pistons, the faster they move the wheels . . . The reins, bit and bridle of this wonderful beast is a small steel handle, which applies and withdraws the steam from the legs or pistons, so that a child might manage it. The coals, which are its oats, were under the bench and there was a small glass tube fixed to the boiler, with water in it, which indicates by its fulness or emptiness when the creature wants water . . ."

Although steam locomotives up to six times larger, forty-six times heavier and with a nominal pulling force sixty times that of Fanny's locomotive

Above: *An Electromotive SD40-2 of Union Pacific, seen here marshalling freight in Green River Wyoming.*

(it was *Northumbrian,* by the way) are included in this book, her enchanting description fits them too. All the elements mentioned are similarly visible to the casual observer in the same way; and whether their maximum speed is 25mph (40km/h) or 125mph (200km/h), their working follows exactly the same principles.

However much the steam locomotive's vital statistics may vary—and this is reflected in extremes of shape as well as size—one thing does not, and that is its degree of attraction for us. Whether it is elaborately painted and lined or just coated with bitumen (or even rust), or whether given a brass-plate complete with romantic name or simply a stencilled-on number, the result is the same—it instills in us a desire to find out everything there is to know about each and every one of these wonderful machines.

In respect of the writing of this book, the most difficult problem has been to select the best examples from among so many well-qualified candidates. Naturally, the first choice has been those that represent major steps along the road of evolution from Stephenson's *Rocket* to such ultimate steam locomotives as, say, the *Niagara* 4-8-4s of the New York Central Railroad.

Efforts have been made to make the geographical coverage as wide as possible; some priority has been given to including examples from all those nations—some of them surprisingly small and agricultural—which built their own steam express locomotives. At the same time the examples chosen are intended to have as wide a coverage as possible in a technical sense: taking express trains across high passes in the North American Rockies needed a different sort of animal to doing high speeds across the Plain of York in England.

Finally, not forgotten have been some brave attempts to advance the technology of the steam express locomotive beyond the original Stephenson concept. Some of the most promising among compound, articulated, condensing and turbine locomotives are included with the sole proviso that the examples chosen did at least run in traffic on important trains, even if they did not represent the main-stream of development.

The Descriptions

The individual descriptions which form the body of the book attempt to look at each locomotive in several different ways. First, one must take a glance at its nuts-and-bolts—that is, weights, pressures, sizes, etc. Second, comes the bare bones of its history—how many there were, when they were built, who designed and built them, how long they lasted and the like. Thirdly, perhaps more interestingly, there are the technical aspects. The steam locomotive came in fascinating variety and, with most of its mechanism being visible, even the smallest details have always attracted attention from professional and amateur alike.

Next comes the tale of what the class of locomotive was built to do as well as how (and whether) if fulfilled its designers' aspirations. Then something has to be said about the way it looks—its success or failure as a work of art if you like.

As regards individual items on the description, the heading of each one begins with the class or class name. Different railways had different systems; many of the designations were designed to tell you something about the locomotive. For example, the British London & North Eastern Railway used a letter which told you the wheel arrangement, followed by a number which identified the actual class within that type. Hence the "A4" class were the streamlined 4-6-2s (of which the record-breaker *Mallard* was the outstanding example), the fourth class of 4-6-2 introduced by the LNER or its predecessors.

Other railways used class numbers which were as random as those applied to some modern aircraft or computers. Yet others (and these included such opposite ends of the spectrum as feudal Great Western of Britain as well as the Railways of the Chinese People's Republic) had names—"King" and

Type Designations for Steam Express Passenger Locomotives

Configuration	British and N. American	Continental European	Name
	0-2-2	A1	–
	2-2-0	1A	–
	2-2-2	1A1	–
	4-2-0	2A	–
	4-2-2	2A1	–
	4-2-4	2A2	–
	0-4-2	B1	–
	2-4-0	1B	–
	2-4-2	1B1	–
	4-4-0	2B	American
	4-4-2	2B1	Atlantic
	4-4-4	2B2	(Jubilee)*
	2-6-0	1C	Mogul
	2-6-2	1C1	Prairie
	2-6-4	1C2	(Adriatic)*
	4-6-0	2C	Ten-wheeler
	4-6-2	2C1	Pacific
	4-6-4	2C2	Hudson, Baltic
	2-8-0	1D	Consolidation
	2-8-2	1D1	Mikado
	4-8-0	2D	(Mastodon)*
	4-8-2	2D1	Mountain
	4-8-4	2D2	Northern (Confederation)*
	4-6-6-4	2CC2	Challenger
	4-6-2 + 2-6-4	2C1 + 1C2	Garratt
	4-8-2 + 2-8-4	2D1 + 1D2	Garratt

* *These names were never frequently used.*

"Castle" for the former and "March Forward" and "Aiming High" for the latter—to distinguish different designs in their locomotive fleet.

There then follows the type, the country of ownership, the railway .....

As regards individual items in the descriptions, in general they are arranged as follows. The heading tells of the class (or name) and type, the country, the railway and the date of introduction of the particular locomotive in question. For steam locomotives, "type" has a special meaning and refers to the arrangement of driving wheels. Many common types have names; others are only referred to by code. The list of types mentioned in this book is given in the table in this introduction.

Steam Locomotive Particulars

Each individual description begins with a list of dimensions, areas, weights, loads, forces and capacities applicable to the locomotive class in question. Naturally these are offered to the reader in good faith, but it must be realised that only one of them—the length of the stroke of the cylinders, is at all precise. Some vary as the engine goes along and coal and water in the boiler and in the tender is consumed or taken on. Others vary as wear takes place and there are one or two which were often deliberately falsified. Usually, too, there are some members of a class which differ from the others in various particulars.

All these things mean that the information is offered with a certain reserve. To emphasise this uncertainty, most of the figures have been suitably rounded. The first figure in each case is given in English gallons, pounds, feet or inches as appropriate; then comes (in brackets) the figure in metric measure. Where capacities are concerned there is an intermediate figure in US gallons. It should be noted that, since both the imperial and the metric figures have been appropriately rounded they are no longer the precise equivalent of one another. This applies particularly in respect of weights; it is a point that the metric ton and the imperial ton differ by far less (2%) than the amount the attributes they are used here to quantify can vary. This will be 10% more. The individual entries are as follows.

Tractive Effort This is a nominal figure which gives some indication of the pulling force ("drawbar pull") which a locomotive can exert. It assumes a steam pressure of 85 per cent of the maximum steam pressure in the boiler acting on the piston diameter. The figure takes into account the leverage implicit in the ratio between the distance from the axle to the crank-pin and the distance from the axle to the rail. In locomotives with more than two cylinders the valve found is multiplied by half the number of cylinders. For compound locomotives none of the formulae available give results that are meaningful in comparative terms, so this entry is omitted in such cases. The value is specified both in pounds and kilograms.

Axle load This figure gives the highest static load applied by any pair of wheels to the rails. For any particular line the permanent way department of the railway places a limit on this value dependent on the strength of the rails and the sleeper spacing. Mechanical departments who control the use of the weighing apparatus usually cheat by understating the amount, but the other side usually specify the limits with some margin to allow for this. Axle load also varies according to the amount of coal and water in the boiler and, in addition, there are the dynamic effects while the engine is moving. The axle load is specified in pounds and tons; but note that the variability is far greater than the difference between imperial tons of 2,240lbs and metric tonnes of 2,204lbs.

Above: *Indian Railways' metre-gauge class "YP" 4-6-2 No.2539 at Agra Fort station.*

Above: *The famous preserved locomotive* Flying Scotsman *near Clapham, Yorkshire, England. Note auxiliary water tender.*

Cylinders The number of cylinders as well as their diameter and stroke are given; the latter can be relied upon for accuracy, but the former will increase as the cylinder is re-bored to counteract wear. When new cylinders or liners are fitted the diameter returns to that specified. Compound locomotives have high-pressure (HP) and low-pressure (LP) cylinders which differ in size and may differ in

Above: *Laying-in continuous welded rail from a special train near Northallerton, Yorkshire, England.*

Above: *A GWR "King" class 4-6-0 rolls a special train alongside the crowded platforms of Snow Hill station, Birmingham.*

Left: *This picture of German Federal Railways 4-6-2 No.001-192-4 shows perfectly the power and glory of steam.*

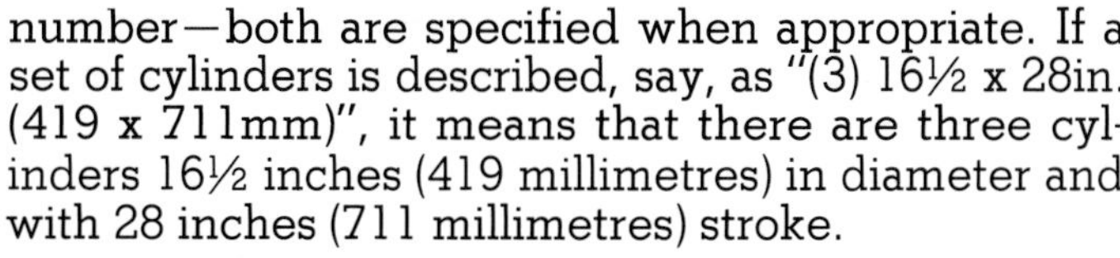

number—both are specified when appropriate. If a set of cylinders is described, say, as "(3) 16½ x 28in. (419 x 711mm)", it means that there are three cylinders 16½ inches (419 millimetres) in diameter and with 28 inches (711 millimetres) stroke.

Driving wheels The diameter of the driving wheels might be thought to be reliable—but they are turned in a lathe from time to time in order to counteract irregular wear. So the actual diameter may be up to 3in (75mm) less than the nominal amount recorded, specified in inches and millimetres. The difference in weight between wheel sets with new tyres and with tyres turned to the permitted limit would reduce the axle-load by ½ ton.

Heating surface The heating surface area of a locomotive (specified in square feet and square metres) is a measure of the size of its boiler and is made up of the surface area of the fire-tubes, of the fire-box and of any water tubes etc. in the firebox.

Superheater The area of the superheater elements is specified in square feet and square metres.

Steam pressure The steam pressure at which the boiler is intended to work is given here. It is also the pressure at which the safety valves should be set to open, but of course at any given moment during a run the steam pressure may be less than this, sometimes considerably less if things are not going well. Steam pressure is specified in pounds per square inch and kilograms per square centimetre.

Grate area This is a particularly important figure because it represents the size of the fire, and the fire is the source of a steam locomotive's power. It is specified in square feet (square metres).

Fuel Unless otherwise stated, the fuel used in a particular locomotive can be assumed to be coal. The nominal amount which can be carried is specified in pounds (lb) and tons. If liquid fuel is used the capacity is specified (with greater confidence than for coal) in British gallons, US gallons and cubic metres.

Water The amount of water carried in tender and/or tanks is specified in British gallons, US gallons and cubic metres.

Adhesive weight A locomotive can only exert the pulling power implicit in its nominal tractive effort if there is adequate adhesion between its driving wheels and the rails. The amount of adhesive weight (often described as "weight on coupled wheels") is specified in pounds and tons. The figure quoted must be regarded as a nominal one.

Total weight The total weight of the engine *and* tender fully loaded is specified in pounds and tons. It is another figure (specified in pounds and tons) whose variability is affected by the same factors as the axle-load.

Overall length This is the length either over the buffers of engine and tender, or over the coupling faces where centre buffers are used, and it is specified in feet and inches as well as in millimetres.

Abbreviations The usual abbreviations are used both in these lists and in the text; lb=pounds, ft=feet, in=inches, sq ft=square feet; gall=gallons, US=United States gallons, psi=pounds per square inch, mph=miles per hour, kg=kilograms, t=tons, mm=millimetres, m=metres, m^2=square metres, m^3=cubic metres, kg/cm^2=kilograms per square centimetre, km=kilometres, km/h=kilometres per hour, hp=horsepower.

A less common measure which appears from time to time is the *chain,* used for specifying the radii of curves. A chain (abbreviated as "ch") equals 66ft, the length of an English cricket pitch, 1/80th mile and, for practical purposes, 20 metres.

Above: *An American engineer at the throttle of a Denver & Rio Grande Western 2-8-2 locomotive.*

Above: *New Zealand Railways class "K" 4-8-4 No.905 near Rotorua on an Auckland express, July 1956.*

How a Steam Locomotive Works

The steam locomotive is often derided for its modest efficiency; yet few realise that its elegant simplicity betokens a *mechanical* efficiency that even today makes it a viable proposition in many circumstances in spite of what those who have a vested interest in its successors have to say. The steam debate continues.

The principle on which the steam locomotive works is that water heated above boiling point tries to become steam and thus expands to a volume 1,700 times greater. Inside the boiler it remains confined and therefore the pressure rises. Once steam is transferred to a cylinder with a piston, therefore, it will push. If the push from the piston is transferred by a system of rods to the wheels, then steam from the boiler will produce movement.

The steam engine consists of these two quite separate parts—the boiler part and the engine part. The boiler is a closed vessel which in most locomotives contains a *fire-box* at the rear and tubes to lead the hot gases from the fire to a *smoke-box* attached at the front. Hundreds of rods called *stays* are provided inside the boiler in order to resist this pressure. A valve, known as the *regulator (throttle)* is provided to control the flow of steam down the main steam pipe to the engine part. Once the steam has done its work there, it is exhausted through the *blast-pipe* into the smoke-box and up the chimney. The so-called blast-pipe is arranged so that the steam issuing from it produced a partial vacuum in the smoke-box and hence draws the fire (in the fire-box) proportionately to the amount of steam being used. Hence the more steam is used the more steam is made. Other types of boiler have from time to time been tried but rarely adopted.

Most steam locomotives are coal-burning and in these the fire burns on a *grate* formed of iron *fire-bars.* As the coal burns, ashes fall through these

Above: *The biggest and most powerful steam locomotive ever used in passenger service—a Union Pacific "Challenger" 4-6-6-4.*

Above: *German Federal Railways class "01" 4-6-2 No.001-187-4 at Neuenmarkt Würzburg with a train to Hof, April 1970.*

Left: *The last steam locomotive built for British Railways, 2-10-0* Evening Star, *at Didcot, Berkshire.*

into an *ash-pan* underneath. Means of putting water into the boiler have to be provided, as well as a store of water to replace that which gets used as steam. If the water tank is on a separate vehicle it is called a *tender* (and the locomotive a tender locomotive). A *tank locomotive* has the tank or tanks on the locomotive.

The engine part consists of *frames* which can be built up from iron or steel plates or bars, or may be a one-piece steel casting. In this are formed slots for *axle-boxes* which carry the *wheel sets* consisting of pairs of wheels mounted on axles. The axleboxes are connected to the frame by a system of springs. The *cylinders* are fixed to the frames and each one contains a *piston*. The piston forces which result from the admission of steam to these cylinders (it is done alternately at either end) are transmitted to the wheels by a system of rods and guides, the latter consisting of *cross-head* and one or more *guide bars.* A circular *piston rod* connects the piston to the cross-head via a steam-tight *gland,* while a *connecting-rod* connects the crosshead to the *driving wheels.* Further pairs of wheels may be driven by means of *coupling rods.*

In order to lead the steam into or out of the end of the cylinder when and—according to the direction and speed of movement—where it is required, a valve or valves are provided. These are linked with the wheels by means of *valve gear.* The types of valves and valve gears used down the years have been many and varied as the narrative to follow bears witness. But all of them exploit the principle that if steam is admitted to one end of a cylinder with a piston inside it, that piston will be pushed with a force dependent on the pressure of the steam and the area of the piston.

Northumbrian 0-2-2

Great Britain: Liverpool & Manchester Railway (L&M), 1830

Tractive effort: 1,580lb (720kg).
Axle load: circa 6,500lb (3t).
Cylinders: (2) 11 x 16in (280 x 406mm).
Driving wheels: 52in (1,321mm).
Heating surface: 412sq ft ($38m^2$).
Superheater: None.
Steam pressure: circa 50psi ($3.5kg/cm^2$).
Grate area: circa 8sq ft ($0.75m^2$).
Fuel (coke): circa 2,200lb (1t).
Water: circa 400gall (480 US) ($1.8m^3$).
Adhesive weight: circa 6,500lb (3t).
Total weight: 25,500lb (11.5t).
Length overall: 24ft 0in (7,315mm).

Above: *1980 replicas of 1829 locomotives.* Rocket *to left,* Sans Pareil *to right.*

Readers might be surprised that Stephenson's immortal *Rocket* does not lead this book's cavalcade of passenger-hauling steam locomotives. The reason for this is that between Rocket's triumph at the Rainhill trials in October 1829 and the opening of the world's first inter-city steam railway on 15 September 1830, there had been as many fundamental changes in steam locomotive design as were to occur over all the years that were to follow. Steam locomotives built in 1982 are no further from those built in 1830 than are those built in 1829—at any rate in fundamentals. Of course they got a little bigger and heavier—by a factor of 40 or thereabouts.

Northumbrian, which hauled the opening train on that disastrous opening day in 1830, had several important things which *Rocket* had not; first, she had a smokebox in which ashes drawn through the boiler tubes could accumulate. Second, the boiler was integrated with the water jacket round the firebox. These two things meant that the locomotive-type boiler, fitted to 99.9 per cent of the world's steam locomotives to be built over the next 150 years, had now fully arrived. The third thing was that the cylinders had now come down to the horizontal position—the axis of *Rocket's* cylinders were fairly steeply inclined at 35° to the horizontal and not surprisingly the out-of-balance forces caused the locomotive to rock badly. Moreover, *Northumbrian's* cylinders were fitted in an accessible position, attached to but outside the wheels although, it is true, still at the wrong end. The *Northumbrian* weighed 7.35 tons less tender, nearly double the 4.25 tons of *Rocket* and her destructive forces were recognised by the provision of a front buffer beam complete with leather buffers stuffed with horse-hair. Another quite important improvement was the use of vertical iron plates as the main frames and a proper tender—rather than a barrel on wheels—was provided.

The features that made *Rocket* a success at the trials were continued in *Northumbrian,* but in larger and stronger form. The multi-tubular boiler—that is to say one which had numerous tubes instead of one big flue for the hot gases to pass through while they exchanged their heat with the water in the boiler. Numerous little tubes have a much greater surface area than one big flue of equivalent size and so heat is passed across to the water at a higher rate; hence such a boiler has high steam-raising capacity in relation to its size.

Below: *An early replica of Rocket before rebuilding.*

The other important feature of *Rocket* was the blast-pipe, once more something that was fundamental to the success of 99.9 per cent of the steam locomotives ever built. By arranging that the exhaust steam was discharged through a jet up the chimney, a partial vacuum was set up at the chimney end. Air would rush in to fill this vacuum and the only way (it was hoped) it could do so was through the fire grate at the other end of the boiler. Hence there was a situation where the amount of air being drawn through the fire and thus the amount of heat produced would depend on the amount of steam being used. More than anything else, this automatic connection between the amount of heat needed and the amount supplied was what gave the Stephensons, father and son, their triumph.

It also says enough that the boiler fitted to *Northumbrian* came to be known as the locomotive-type boiler. Of all the locomotives described in this book, only one (London & North Eastern No.10,000) had another type of boiler and only one (South African Railways' class "25") failed to have the blast-pipe. This was not through the lack of trying for something better, for many attempts were made to introduce new ideas. But only very few prevailed far enough to enter revenue service at all and, of course, none has managed to topple the Stephenson boiler from its throne whilst steam traction exists. Incidentally, credit for suggesting the multi-tubular boiler was attributed by Robert Stephenson to a Mr Henry Booth, treasurer of the L&M Company.

As regards the mechanical part of *Northumbrian,* the principle of having two and only two cylinders outside the frames and directly connected to the driving wheels became more and more the world standard as the years went by. Towards the end of steam this principle became virtually universal, apart from articulated locomotives. Even so, the actual *layout* of Northumbrian's machinery had serious drawbacks.

Because the driving wheels were at the front, the heavy firebox and the heavy cylinders were at the end where the *carrying* wheels were. There was only a box full of smoke at the other end and yet the driving wheels needed all the weight the track could stand to keep them from slipping Moreover, when the

Below: Northumbrian *depicted (so far as is known) in new condition, as the "brave little she-lion" so admired by Miss Kemble.*

Top right: *A contemporary engraving of the Stephenson* Northumbrian. *Note the headlights, and the crew's attire.*

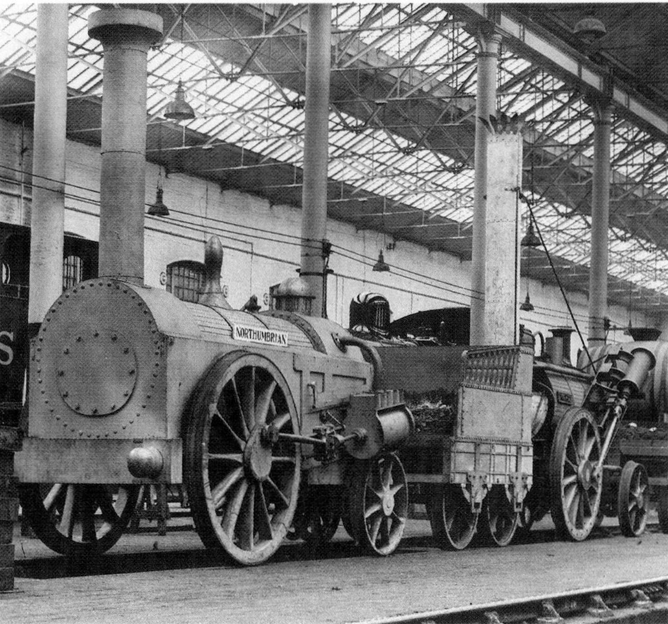

Above: *A dubious wooden replica of Northumbrian constructed in 1930 for the L&M centenary celebrations.*

engine began pulling the force on the drawbar tended to lift the front end of the engine, thereby further reducing the weight available for adhesion.

Another problem arose through the combination of outside cylinders with a short wheelbase. The alternate piston-thrusts tended to swing the engine about a vertical axis so that it proceeded with a boxing motion and in a serpentine manner. It was not until the *Northumbrian* layout was considerably altered by having an extended wheelbase and moving the cylinders to the front that these problems were solved. In the meantime the route of development left the main line for a branch, as we shall see.

A rather dubious feature of *Northumbrian* was the primitive means of reversing. An eccentric —a device to convert rotation to oscillation—was provided on the driving axle in order to move the valve of each cylinder. To reverse the direction of rotation, the eccentric on each side has to be turned nearly 180 degrees relative to the crank. It is easy to leave the eccentrics loose on the axle and provide stops so that they take up the correct position whichever way the wheels turn. The drawback to this simple and excellent valve gear is that it is difficult to devise an arrangement to move the eccentrics upon the axle while the engine is stationary that is not complicated and inconvenient. Otherwise the locomotive can only be reversed by giving a push.

Both *Rocket* and *Northumbrian* had such an arrangement; one snag was that it could not be used while in motion. This was vividly demonstrated on that opening day. When William Huskisson MP, stepped out into the path of *Rocket,* Joseph Locke who was driving had no means of *breaking* (to use the spelling of the day) and the famous accident took place. *Northumbrian* covered herself with glory in rushing the fatally injured man to medical aid, but to no avail.

Northumbrian is regarded as belonging to the "Rocket" class, seven examples of which had previously been delivered to the Liverpool & Manchester Railway in 1829 and 1830. *Rocket's* immediate successors, *Meteor, Comet, Dart* and *Arrow,* were delivered with the cylinders in an almost horizontal position, while *Rocket* was so altered very quickly. *Phoenix* also had a smokebox and so did *North Star. Majestic,* which followed *Northumbrian,* also had all the new features. Only *Rocket's* remains survive, in London's Science Museum, but in fact they come much closer to the later engines than *Rocket* as delivered.

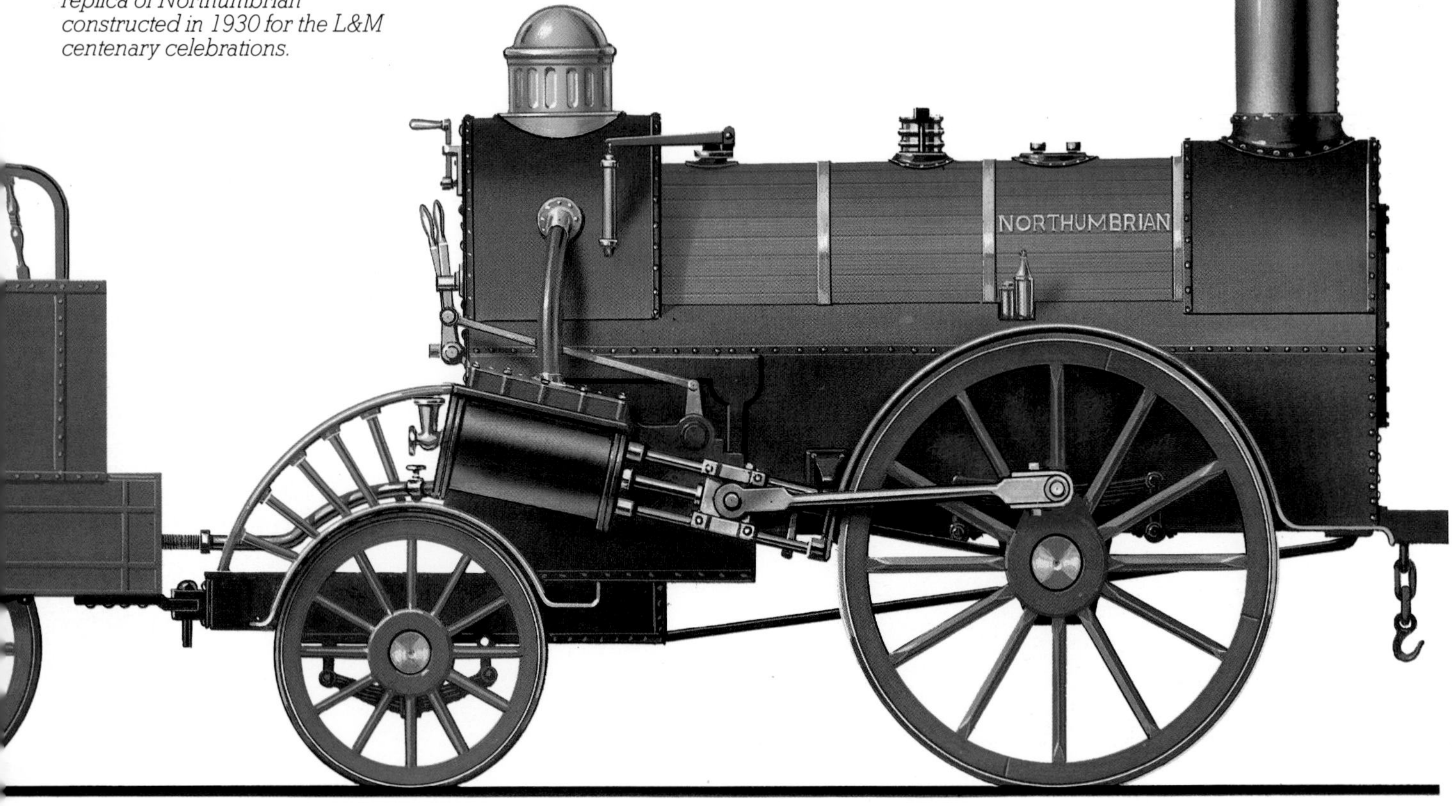

NORTHUMBRIAN

Planet Class 2-2-0 Great Britain: Liverpool & Manchester Railway, 1830

Tractive effort: circa 1,450lb (660kg).
Axle load: 11,250lb (5t).
Cylinders: (2) 11½ x 16in (292 x 406mm).
Driving wheels: 62in (1,575mm).
Heating surface: 407sq ft (38m²).
Superheater: None.
Steam pressure: circa 50psi (3.5kg/cm²).
Grate area: 7.2sq ft (0.67m²).
Fuel (coke): circa 2,200lb (1t).
Water: circa 400gall (480 US) (1.8m³).
Adhesive weight: 11,250lb (5t).
Total weight: 29,500lb (13.5t).
Length overall: 24ft 4in (7,420mm).

Planet arrived on the Liverpool & Manchester Railway in October 1830, soon after it was opened. The Stephensons had changed two things since they completed *Northumbrian* only a few weeks before. The first one was to put the cylinders at the front end instead of the back. This helped to get a good weight distribution; the drive was on to the rear pair of wheels which supported the heavy firebox, and, moreover, 99 per cent of the world's steam locomotives were to have two horizontal cylinders at the front end.

The second thing which was done was aimed at curing the "boxing" motion which plagued the earlier locomotives. This was achieved by putting the cylinders between instead of outside the wheels and connecting them to the driving wheels by making the main axle in the form of a double crank. Crank-axles continued to present a serious technical problem, not only in themselves but also because the big-end bearings of the connecting rods had to be split—and hence weakened—so that they could be removed and replaced. Even so, some 5 per cent of the world's steam locomotives were to have two inside cylinders and crank-axles; Robert Stephenson & Co. supplied some to British Railways as late as 1953.

Planet was quite successful and many of these engines, some with four coupled wheels, were made both by the Stephensons and by others. Outstanding amongst the imitations was a 2-2-0 called *Old Ironsides,* built in Philadelphia, USA in 1832 by a Matthias Baldwin. Starting with this first full-size locomotive Baldwin went on to build up the greatest locomotive manufactory the world has ever known, with a production of 60,000 locomotives during the 130 years of its existence. It is said that Baldwin had such trouble getting payment for his first locomotive that he declared he would build no more! The Stephensons, on the other hand, when they developed *Planet* into their celebrated six-wheel locomotives, decided that this time they would discourage imitators by taking out a patent.

Even so it was *Planet* that finally convinced a sceptical world that a form of reliable mechanical transport had arrived and that the Stephensons

Best Friend of Charleston 0-4-0 Tank United States: South Carolina Railroad (SCRR), 1830

Tractive effort: 453lb (206kg).
Axle load: 4,500lb (2t).
Cylinders: (2) 6 x 16in (152 x 406mm).
Driving wheels: 54in (1,371mm).
Steam Pressure: 50psi (3.5kg/cm²).
Grate area: 2.2sq ft (2m²).
Fuel (coke): not recorded.
Water: 140gall (165 US) (0.64m³).
Adhesive weight: 9,000lb (4t).
Total weight: 9,000lb (4t).
Length overall: 14ft 9in (4,496mm).

History was certainly made on 15th January 1831, the day when the first full-size steam locomotive to be built in the United States went into service. This was *Best Friend of Charleston,* running on the New World's first commercial steam railway, the South Carolina Railroad. This little contraption foreshadowed the building of 170,000 further steam loco-

were the people to provide it. Soon enough it took them from a humble cottage by the Tyne to being millionaires in the £'s of those days, as well as a name that is and will be remembered wherever and while railways exist.

Below: *A drawing of the* Planet *locomotive of the Liverpool & Manchester Railway, Stephenson's first inside-cylinder locomotive.*

motives for service in the USA during the years to come. *Best Friend* was constructed at the West Point Foundry in New York in late 1830. Features included a vertical boiler, a well tank integral with the locomotive, four coupled wheels and two modestly inclined cylinders. It was built at the West Point Foundry in New York to the design of E.L. Miller, engineer of the South Carolina Railroad.

Although, apart from the coupled wheels, none of its principles of design were adopted generally, the locomotive was quite successful, but the next one built for this railroad followed the same principles only as regards mechanical parts—the later version had a horizontal boiler, the first to be built in America. Even so, the original design could handle a train of five cars carrying more than 50 passengers at 20mph (32km/h).

In one rather tragic way, however, the locomotive did contribute to the story of steam traction development. The firemen had become annoyed with the noise of steam escaping from the safety valves and used to tie down the lever which controlled them. One day in June 1831 he did this once too often—and the boiler exploded and he was killed. In due time tamper-proof valves became the rule—people normally need shock before they take action.

Later, the locomotive was rebuilt with a new boiler and re-entered service, appropriately named *Phoenix*. By 1834, the South Carolina Railroad went the whole 154 miles from Charleston to Hamburg, just across the river from the city of Augusta, Georgia. When opened, this was by far the longest railway in the world.

Left: Best Friend of Charleston. *Some contemporary accounts tell of additional cylinders driving the tender wheels.*

Brother Jonathan 4-2-0

United States:
Mohawk & Hudson Railroad (M&HRR), 1832

Above: Brother Jonathan, *a pioneer bogie locomotive.*

Tractive effort: circa 1,023lb (464kg).
Axle load: 7,000lb (3.2t).
Cylinders: (2) 9½ x 16in (241 x 406mm).
Driving wheels: 60in (1,524mm).
Boiler: details not recorded.
Boiler pressure: circa 50psi (3.5kg/cm²).
Adhesive weight: circa 7,000lb (3.2t).
Total weight*: 14,000lb (6.4t).
Length overall*: 16ft 5½in (5,017mm).
**Engine only without tender.*

As regards express passenger trains, certainly one of the great benefactors of mankind was John B. Jarvis, who in 1832 introduced the pivoted leading truck or bogie into the locomotive story, an idea suggested to him by Robert Stephenson when he visited England. Although very few particulars have survived, this little 4-2-0, originally known as *Experiment,* was the vehicle used. This pathfinding design of locomotive was built at the West Point Foundry in New York and delivered to the Mohawk & Hudson River Railroad.

Amongst the features of the locomotive, one notes that the boiler was rather small (copied from Robert Stephenson's "Planet" type) and that there was room for the connecting rods in the space between the sides of the firebox and the main frames, which were situated outside the driving wheels. These in turn were located behind the firebox, as on a Crampton locomotive.

None of these other features became the norm on the world's locomotives, but as regards express passenger locomotives, the four-wheel bogie certainly is much used. It will be found that all the classes of locomotive described in this book have leading four-wheel bogies according to the principle pioneered with *Brother Jonathan.* Incidentally, Brother Jonathan was then an impolite way of referring to the English; no doubt the name was a gesture of triumph at having thrown off any possible continued dependence on English technology.

The idea was to provide guidance by having two wheels pressing against the outer rail of curves as near as possible in a tangential attitude. For any particular radius, or even at a kink in the track, the bogie would take up an angle so that the three contact points between wheel and rail on each side would lie correctly on the curve. This was particularly important on the light rough tracks of the time.

This locomotive demonstrated very clearly that the principle was a sound one and for many years thereafter the majority of American locomotives of all kinds had the advantage of this device. *Brother Jonathan* itself was successful in other ways; converted later to a 4-4-0 it had a long and useful life.

Below: *A replica of* Brother Jonathan, *alias* Experiment.

Vauxhall 2-2-0 Ireland: Dublin & Kingstown Railway, 1834

Tractive effort: circa 1,550lb (700kg).
Cylinders: (2) 11 x 18in (280 x 457mm).
Driving wheels: 60in (1,524mm).
Steam pressure: circa 50psi (3.5kg/cm²).
Overall length: circa 24ft (7,315mm).

George Forrester of Liverpool was a locomotive builder whose name is now hardly known; yet he introduced two fundamental improvements in the mechanism of the steam locomotive, one of which prevailed to the end of steam. The other was also an important move forward.

How *Northumbrian* had two outside cylinders but at the wrong end and how *Planet* had two cylinders at the front but hidden away inside, has already been described. With *Vauxhall*, constructed in 1832 for the Dublin & Kingstown Railway, Forrester built the world's first locomotive with accessible outside cylinders placed horizontally at the leading end. Incidentally, the D&K line was built to the English standard gauge of 4ft 8½in (1,435mm); it was long before the days when the railway gauge in Ireland was standardised at 5ft 3in (1,600mm).

So already the cylinders had reached their final position with this arrangement. Since then it has been applied to most of the world's locomotives built over the subsequent 150 years, even though express passenger locomotives are the ones most prone to being given sophisticated cylinder layouts.

One way in which the Forrester engines differed from modern steam locomotives (except for those built for very narrow gauges) was that the cylinders may have been outside the frames, but the frames were outside the wheels. Separate cranks were provided at the ends of the axles. Even so, in later years this arrangement was much used on locomotives which ran on very narrow gauges, that is, 3ft (914mm) or less.

Forrester's fundamental improvement of the valve gear was also important but as a stepping-stone rather than an arrangement which became much used in the long term. It has been mentioned that the "slip eccentric" valve gear was difficult to reverse from the cab, so Forrester provided a separate eccentric set for each direction for each cylinder—making four in all on the driving axle. The reversing lever could move the eccentric rods (which were set vertically) and engage or disengage the appropriate valve pin by means of V-shaped "gabs" fitted to the ends of the rods. No skill was required as in the previous arrangement, merely enough muscle to move the reversing lever into the appropriate position. But it could not be used while the engine was in motion.

Another feature of the first Forrester locomotives which was not repeated was the substitution of a swing-link parallel motion. This was intended to constrain the joint between the end of the piston rod and the little end of the connecting rod to travel in a straight line, even when the latter was at an angle and therefore trying to force the former out of line. The Stephensons had previously used a cross-head running between slide-bars for this purpose and this simple arrangement has never been displaced from its throne. The only engine apart from *Vauxhall* in this book which did not have it was the "Turbomotive" and that one only because there were no cylinders!

Wide apart outside cylinders combined with a short wheelbase was not a recipe for steady

Bury 2-2-0 Great Britain: London & Birmingham Railway (L&B), 1837

Tractive effort: 1,386lb (629kg).
Axle load: 12,600lb (5.7t).
Cylinders: (2) 11 x 16½in (280 x 415mm).
Driving wheels: 60¾in (1,546mm).
Heating surface: 357sq ft (33.2m²).
Superheater: None.
Steam pressure: 50psi (3.5kg/cm²).
Grate area: 7sq ft (0.65m²).
Fuel (coke): c2,200lb (1t).
Water: c400gall (480 US) (1.8m³).
Adhesive weight: 12,600lb (5.7t).
Total weight: 22,000lb (10.0t).
Length overall: 26ft 9½in (8,168mm).

Edward Bury had a small engineering works in Liverpool and in 1829 he began work on a locomotive with a view to entering it for the Rainhill trials, but it was not completed in time. In the end he supplied the locomotive, which was called *Liverpool*, to the Liverpool & Manchester Railway during 1830. It had two large coupled wheels 72in. (1829mm) in diameter. It had cylinders arranged like *Planet's* but, unlike *Planet*, had frames formed of bars rather than plates. This was a significant innovation, for Bury sold some bar-framed locomotives to America and bar frames for many years became a trademark of engines built on that side of the Atlantic; this went on until bar frames were superseded by cast steel ones. Bury managed to secure the contract for providing locomotives for the London and Birmingham Railway, by far the most important railway to be completed in the 1830s. All 58 of these passenger 2-2-0s had been supplied by 1841.

One problem with these locomotives was their small size and this was a fundamental limitation of the design, rather than something that could be overcome just by a little stretching. Bury considered rightly that pressure vessels should be circular and so his outer firebox was circular in plan and domed on top, attached to a normal cylindrical barrel by circumferential joint. The inner fire-box was D-shaped, with the flat part facing towards the front, to allow the insertion of the tubes at right angles. The trouble was that with the circular shape the length could not be larger than the width. Since the width was also limited, because it had to go between the wheels, the size of the fire (and hence the power output) was strictly limited. Nor could the frames be extended backwards past the round fire-box, so a 2-2-2 development would cause some difficulty.

So in 1837 England's first long-distance trunk railway route out of London was opened, using a fleet of locomotives that were under-powered even by the standards of the day. For

running and by 1836 these 2-2-0s, as well as others supplied to the Liverpool & Manchester, London & Greenwich and other railways had been converted to 2-2-2s. Even so, on the opening day in Ireland, 31mph (50km/h) was achieved; passengers were delighted and amazed that they could read and write with ease while moving at this stupendous speed. Few particulars of this pathfinding engine have survived, but the details missing from the specification above would approximate to those of *Planet* (see page 20).

Left: *George Forrester's* Vauxhall *locomotive built for the Dublin & Kingstown Railway in 1834. Note the horizontal outside cylinders at the front end, a mechanical arrangement which most of the world's locomotive engineers followed in time.*

example, in the same year the London to Bristol railway (then under construction) received a Stephenson 2-2-2 called *North Star* which had double the grate area and double the adhesive weight of a Bury 2-2-0.

The small size and power of these engines had advantages. They were cheap to build and reliable in service—the low stresses on the crank axles brought these always troublesome items more within the scope of the technology of the day. And if heavy passenger trains needed two or three locomotives (or even four) at the head, then so be it. Labour was cheap, while powerful locomotives were expensive as well as relatively untried.

Assuming that Bury was right in thinking like this in 1837—and there are many subsequent examples in locomotive history—his railway had certainly fallen behind the times a few years later.

Below: *2-2-0 No. 1 of the London & Birmingham Railway, the most important line to have been opened during the 1830s. Edward Bury designed these rather small locomotives which tended to be a little underpowered for express passenger work. Even so, they were cheap and reliable and Bury held on to his principles of little-and-often in locomotive design for many years, in fact until he was forced to resign in 1847. This was soon after the LNWR had been formed from the amalgamation of the Grand Junction and London & Birmingham lines.*

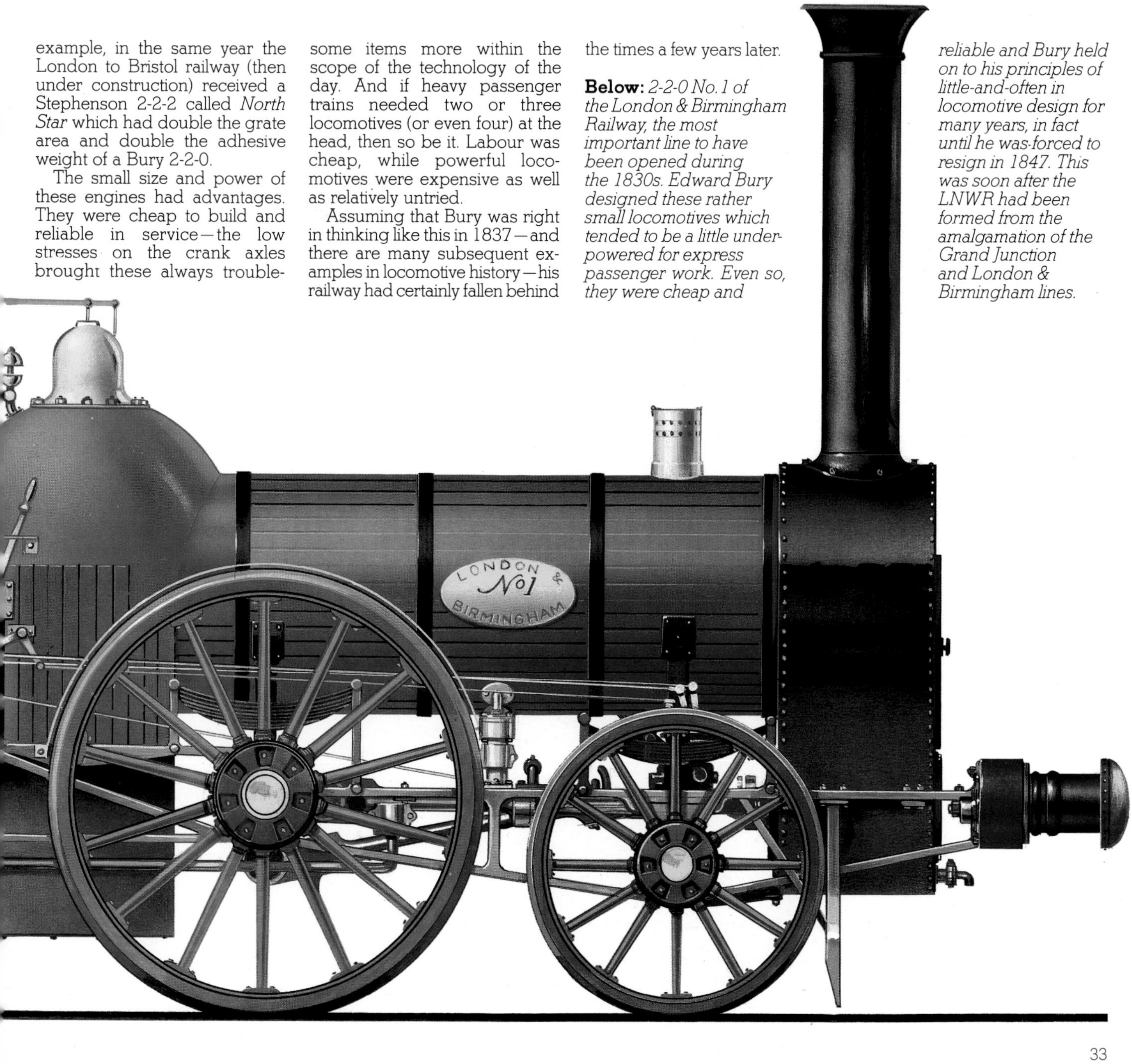

Adler 2-2-2 Germany: Nuremberg-Fürth Railway, 1835

Tractive effort: 1,220lb (550kg).
Axle load: 13,250lb (6t).
Cylinders: 9 x 16in (229 x 406mm).
Driving wheels: 54in (1,371mm).
Heating surface: 196sq ft (18.2m²).
Superheater: None.
Steam pressure: 60psi (4.2kg/cm²).
Grate area: 5.2sq ft (0.48m²).
Adhesive weight: 13,250lb (6t).
Total weight*: 31,500lb (14.5t).
Length overall: 25ft 0in (7,620mm).
**Engine only — tender details not available.*

The first locomotive to be built in Germany was constructed in 1816, but it was unsuccessful, as was a second one built in the following year. It was not until 7 December 1835 that successful steam locomotion was inaugurated in the country, with the opening of the Nuremberg to Fürth railway, known as the Ludwigsbahn, after Ludwig I of Bavaria, who had given his royal assent to the railway in 1834.

The promoter of the railway, Herr Scharrer, tried Robert Stephenson & Co of Newcastle for the supply of material to the line, but Stephenson's prices were considered to be too high, and Scharrer therefore resolved to "buy German". Two Wurtembergers then contracted to supply an engine for the equivalent of £565, "equal to the best English engines and not requiring more fuel". Time passed and Scharrer enquired about the progress of his engine, only to find that the contractors had decamped to Austria. He pursued them there, and was told that the price had doubled. The opening of the railway was approaching, and Scharrer had no alternative but to place an urgent order with Robert Stephenson on 15 May 1835 for a 2-2-2 locomotive, at a price of £1,750 delivered to the line.

Despite the historical importance of this engine, information about it is scanty, even its name being uncertain. Early references are to "Der Adler" (The Eagle), but more recently it has dropped the definite article, and is usually known simply as "Adler". Surviving records of the builder do not record details of the engine, but contemporary illustrations show a locomotive resembling the "Patentee", supplied to the Liverpool and Manchester Railway in 1834, developments of which figure largely amongst products of Stephenson's Newcastle works at this period.

In 1830 Robert Stephenson & Co supplied to the L&MR a 2-2-0 named "Planet", which was notable as being the first engine with inside cylinders and a crank axle. However,the art of forging axles was new, and the combination of the forces from the flanges of the wheels and from the connecting rods soon showed the vulnerability of these delicate forgings. In 1833, therefore, Robert Stephenson designed a 2-2-2 locomotive, in which the driving wheels had no flanges, so that the crank axle was relieved of flange forces. A further advantage of the extra axle was that the axle loading was reduced, a desirable measure, as the axle loading of Stephenson's engines supplied to the L&M had been increasing steadily since "Rocket", which had been built to the severe weight restrictions which the directors of the railway deemed necessary.

The improvements incorporated in the 2-2-2 were patented, and the first engine to incorporate the patents was named "Patentee". This engine weighed 11.45 tons, but the weight of "Adler" was quoted in English sources as 6.6 tons, and in German sources as 14 tonnes, with 6 tonnes on the driving axle. A similar uncertainty applies to the boiler pressure, which has been quoted in an English source as

Campbell 4-4-0 United States: Philadelphia, Germanstown & Norriston Railroad (PG&NRR), 1837

Tractive effort: 4,373lb (1,984kg).
Axle load: 8,000lb (3.6t)..
Cylinders: (2) 14 x 15¾in 9356 x 400mm).
Driving wheels: 54in. (1,370mm).
Heating surface: 723sq ft (67.2m²).
Superheater: None.
Steam pressure: 90psi (6.3kg/cm²).
Grate area: Circa 12sq ft (1.1m²).
Adhesive weight: 16,000lb (7.25t).
Length overall:* 16ft 5½in (5,017mm).
**Engine only — tender details not known.*

Henry Campbell, engineer to the Philadelphia, Germanstown & Norriston Railroad had the idea of combining coupled wheels, as fitted to *Best Friend of Charleston,* with the leading truck of *Brother Johnathan.* In this way he could double the adhesive weight, while at the same time have a locomotive that could ride satisfactorily round sharp or irregular curves. He patented the idea and went to a local mechanic called James Brooks (not the Brooks who founded the famous Brooks Loco Works of Dunkirk, New York) and he produced the world's first 4-4-0 in May 1837.

Although in fact this locomotive was intended for coal traffic, it has its place here as the prototype of perhaps the most numerous and successful of all passenger-hauling wheel arrangements.

The layout of *Brother Johnathan* was followed, the additional driving axle being coupled to the first by cranks outside the frames. The cylinders were thus inside the frames, driving the leading coupled wheels by means of a crank axle, an arrangement which was to become popular on a few railways back in Europe, even if very rarely repeated in America. The high boiler pressure is notable for the time. Whilst this remarkable locomotive demonstrated great potential, the flexibility provided in order to cope with poorly lined tracks was not accompanied with flexibility in a vertical plane to help with the humps and hollows in them. In consequence, Campbell's 4-4-0 was not in itself successful.

Left: *The world's first 4-4-0, designed by Henry R. Campbell, engineer to the Philadelphia Germanstown and Norriston Railroad. It was built in 1837 by James Brooks of Philadelphia.*

60lb/sq in (4.2kg/cm²), and in a German source as 47lb/sq in (3.3kg/cm²). Amongst details of the engine which are known are that it had 62 copper tubes, and that it had shifting eccentrics. The "Adler" was followed by other engines of similar type from Stephenson's. It remained at work until 1857, when it was sold, without wheels and some other parts, for its scrap value.

In preparation of the centenary of the Nuremberg-Fürth Railway, a working replica of the engine was built at the Kaiserslautern Works of DR. This replica is now in the transport museum at Nuremberg. A second non-working replica was made in 1950 for use at exhibitions. Both are based on contemporary paintings.

Left: *This* Adler *replica was built for the German State Railways' centenary celebrations in 1935. It appeared in the ill-starred "der Stahltier" film, whose director was imprisoned by the Nazis for emphasising* Adler's *English origin.*

Below: Adler *was built for the Nuremburg-Fürth Railway in 1835. This was the first railway to be built in what is now known as Germany, but the locomotive was built by the famous firm of Stephenson & Son of Newcastle-upon-Tyne, England.*

Hercules 4-4-0

United States: Beaver Meadows Railroad, 1837

Tractive effort: 4,507lb (2,045kg).
Axle load: circa 10,000lb (4.5t).
Cylinders (2) 12 x 18in (305 x 457mm).
Driving wheels: 44in (1,117mm).
Steam pressure: 90lb/sq in (6.3kg/cm²).
Adhesive weight: circa 20,000lb (9t).
Total weight: *30,000lb (14t).
Length overall:* 18ft 11in (2,564mm).
**Without tender—boiler and tender details not recorded.*

In 1836, the Beaver Meadows Railroad ordered a 4-4-0 from Garrett & Eastwick, in nearby Philadelphia. The workshop foreman, Joseph Harrison, had become aware of the problems encountered by Henry Campbell in keeping all the wheels of his 4-4-0 pressing on the rail, yet he also remembered 4-2-0 *Brother Jonathan* of 1832 which sat on the rough tracks like a three-legged stool on the floor. The saying "right as a trivet" comes vividly to mind, the three legs being, respectively, the two driving wheels and the pivot of the leading bogie or truck. There was also the example of one or two early 4-2-0s by Norris, also of Philadelphia. Harrison had the idea of making his two pairs of driving wheels into a kind of non-swivelling bogie by connecting the axle bearings on each side by a large cast iron beam, pivoted at its centre. The pivots were connected to the mainframe of the locomotive by a large leaf spring on either side.

In this way eight wheels were made to support the body of the locomotive at three points. It was a brilliant notion which solved the problem of running on rough tracks and was the basis of the three-point compensated springing system which was applied to most of the world's locomotives from simple ones up to 4-12-2s.

Hercules was well named and many similar locomotives were supplied. Joseph Harrison was made a partner in the firm which (since Garrett was retiring) became known as Eastwick & Harrison. The famous "American Standard" 4-4-0, of which 25,000 were built for the USA alone, was directly derived from this most innovative engine.

Left: Hercules, *built by Garrett & Eastwick of Philadelphia in 1836, marked an important step forward in locomotive development.*

Lafayette 4-2-0

United States: Baltimore & Ohio Railroad (B&O), 1837

Tractive effort: 2,162lb (957kg).
Axle load: 13,000lb (6t).
Cylinders: (2) 10½ x 18in (268 x 457mm).
Driving wheels: 48in (1,220mm).
Heating surface: 394sq ft ($36.6m^2$).
Superheater: None.
Steam pressure: 60psi ($4.2kg/cm^2$).
Grate area: 8.6sq ft ($0.80m^2$).
Fuel (coke): 2,200lb (1t).
Water: 450gall (540 US) ($2m^3$).
Adhesive weight: 30,000lb (5t).
Total weight: 44,000lb (20t).
Length overall: 30ft 40¼in (9,250mm).

The so-called Norris locomotives have a very important place in locomotive history, being a design which took steam another great step forward.

William Norris had been building locomotives in Philadelphia since 1831. Although a draper by trade, after a few years in partnership with a Colonel Stephen Long, he set up on his own and by the beginning of 1836 had produced some seven locomotives. In that year he built a 4-2-0 for the Philadelphia & Columbia Railroad called *Washington County Farmer*. In arrangement it bore some resemblance to *Brother Johnathan* with leading bogie, but the two cylinders were outside the wheels and frames and the valves were on top of the cylinders. The driving wheels were in front of rather than behind the firebox, so increasing the proportion of the engine's weight carried on them.

In this way the final form of the steam express passenger locomotive had almost arrived. *Northumbrian* had the locomotive-type boiler and two outside cylinders; *Planet* had the cylinders at the front while Forrester's *Vauxhall* had cylinders outside and at the front. Bury's locomotives had the bar frames and *Brother Jonathan* had the bogie. Now we find outside cylinders, bar frames and a leading bogie in combination.

In 1827, the Baltimore & Ohio Railroad was the first public railroad for passengers and freight transport to receive a charter. It was opened for twelve miles out of Baltimore in 1830, but for a number of years horses provided haulage power—although there were trials with steam locomotives. Steam took over in 1834 in the form of vertical-boiler locomotives, known as the "Grasshopper" type.

The Ohio River was reached in 1842 via a route which then included a series of rope-worked inclined planes, but long before this more powerful locomotives than could be encompassed within the vertical-boiler concept were needed. The B&O management were impressed with Norris' *Washington County Farmer* and asked him to build a series of eight similar engines. The first was *Lafayette* delivered in 1837; it was the first B&O locomotive to have a horizontal boiler. Edward Bury's circular domed firebox and bar frames were there and the engine is said to have had cam-operated valves of a pattern devised by Ross Winans of the B&O. It says enough that later members of the class had the normal "gab" motion of the day.

The locomotives were a great success, giving much better performance at reduced fuel consumption. They were also relatively reliable and needed few repairs. The same year Norris built a similar locomotive for the Champlain & St. Lawrence Railway in Canada. This was the first proper locomotive exported from America, and the hill-climbing ability of these remarkable locomotives led to many further sales abroad.

The first Old World customer was the Vienna-Raab Railway and their locomotive *Philadelphia* was completed in late 1837. Before the locomotive was shipped it was put to haul a train weighing 200 tons up a 1 in 100 (1 per cent) gradient, a feat then described as the greatest performance by a locomotive engine so far recorded. Railways in Austria (not the small republic we know today but a great empire also embracing much of what is now Czechoslovakia, Poland, Roumania and Jugoslavia) were the best customers, but even before 1840 Norris had also sent his 4-2-0s to the Brunswick and Berlin & Potsdam Railways in Germany. A large fleet of 15 went to the Birmingham and Gloucester Railway in Britain, where they had some success in easing the problems involved in taking trains up the 1 in 37 (2.7 per cent) Lickey Incline at Bromsgrove in Worcestershire.

The demand for Norris locomotives was so great that the firm was able to offer the design in a range of four standard sizes. Class "C" had a cylinder bore of 9in (229mm), class "B" 10½in (268mm), class "A" 11½in (292mm), class "A extra" 12½in (318mm). Grate areas were, respectively, 6.4, 7.3, 7.9 and 9.5sq ft (0.6, 0.69, 0.73 and $0.88in^2$) while engine weights were 15,750, 20,600, 24,100 and 29,650lb (7.1, 9.4, 10.9 and 13.45t).

The Norris locomotives which came to England were particularly interesting as of course the English railway engineers were more accustomed to sending engines abroad rather than importing them. Seventeen locomotives came over from Philadelphia between March 1839 and May 1842 and they included examples of the three larger out of the four standard Norris sizes. There were nine B's, three A's and five A extras, the latter used as bankers on the heavy grade.

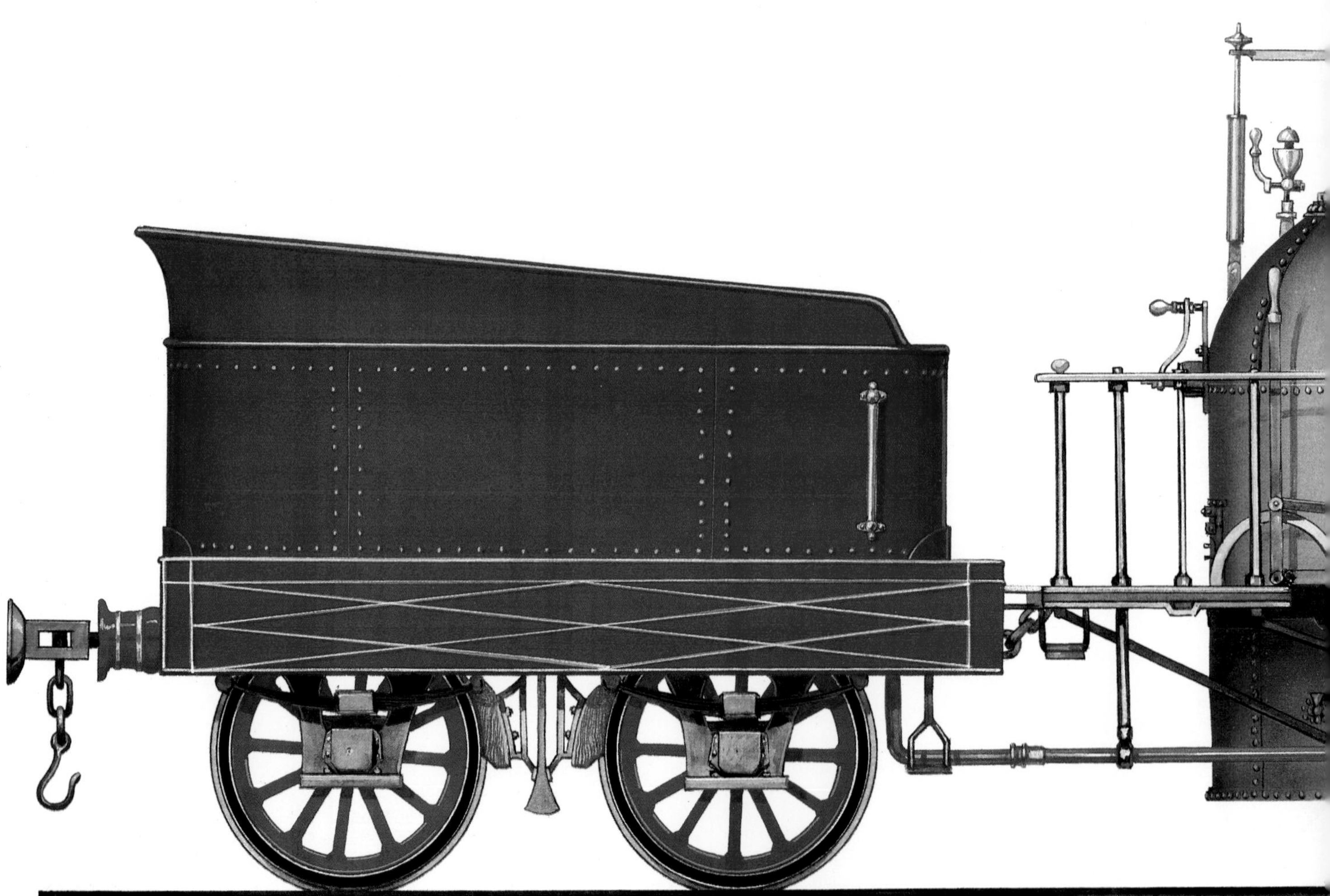

Certain improvements were made to reduce what was originally a very high coal consumption on the arduous banking duties. All five A-extras were converted to tank locomotives and this saved hauling the weight of the tenders. Steam blown from the safety valves and some exhaust steam was turned back into the new saddle tanks. Copper fireboxes replaced iron ones and various other examples of rather shaky workmanship replaced. The result was that a coal consumption of 92lb/mile (26kg/km) in 1841 was reduced by 53 per cent by 1843.

The best of the Norris engines remained in service until 1856.

In his native America, Norris' list of other customers in the 1830s included 27 predecessors of the railroads of the great age of steam, situated in Connecticut, Georgia, Louisiana, Maryland, Massachusetts, New York State, North Carolina, Pennsylvania, Tennessee and Virginia. One of them, the Richmond, Fredericksburg and Potomac Railroad, is even still trading under the same name today. Norris went on to become for a time the largest locomotive builder in the USA, supplying 4-4-0s, 0-6-0s and finally 4-6-0s in addition to the 4-2-0s which made his name. On the other hand the success of these engines in Europe did not bring commensurate prosperity there. Although William Norris and his brother Octavius went to Vienna in 1844 and set up a locomotive building plant, it was other builders who adopted Norris' ideas, produced hundreds of locomotives based on them, and made the money.

The first of the European builders who built Norris-type locomotives was John Haswell of Vienna. Others were Sigl, also of Vienna and Guenther of Austria, Cockerill of Belgium, Borsig, Emil Kessler and his successor the Esslingen Co of Germany. In Britain, Hick of Bolton and Nasmyth of Manchester also built 4-2-0s of this pattern. A 4-2-0 called *La Junta* supplied to Cuba circa 1840, was for many years preserved at the United Railways of Havana station in Havana. No reports have been received either of its survival or destruction. A full-size replica of an early Norris locomotive was constructed in the USA about 1941 and was reported to be preserved on the Tallulah Falls Railway in northern Georgia.

Above: *The gravestones in the churchyard at Bromsgrove, Worcestershire, in memory of a locomotive crew who were killed in a boiler explosion in November 1870. The engine concerned was not a Norris one, but nevertheless the headstones display carvings of locomotives of this type, more typical of the railway at Bromsgrove.*

Below: *A typical standard Norris 4-2-0 locomotive is portrayed in this side view. The elementary controls of a locomotive of the 1840s can all be clearly seen. The horizontal handle behind the firebox is the throttle, while the vertical one alongside the firebox controls the "gad" reversing gear. The spring balance pressure gauge is above the firebox together with the whistle. A brake on the engine was regarded as a luxury.*

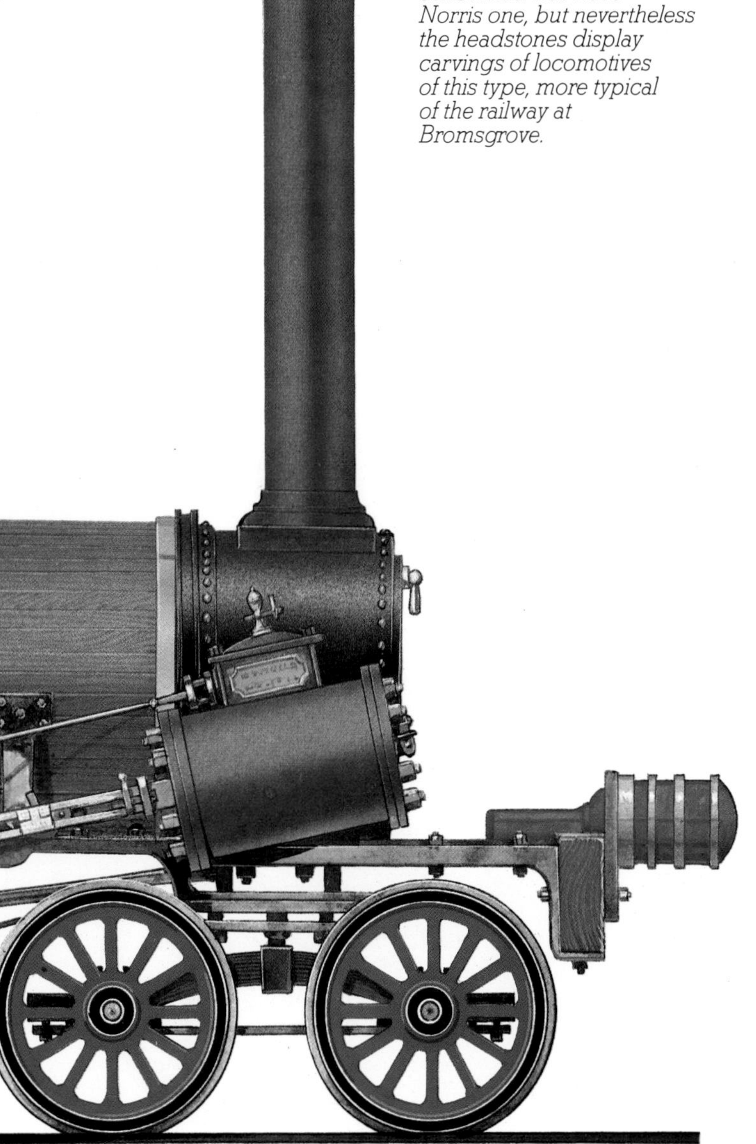

Fire Fly Class 2-2-2 **Great Britain:** Great Western Railway (GWR), 1840

Tractive effort: 2049lb (929kg).
Axle load: 25,000lb (11.2t).
Cylinders: (2) 15 x 18in 381 x 457mm).
Driving wheels: 84in (2,134mm).
Heating surface: 700sq ft (65m²).
Superheater: None.
Steam pressure: 50psi (3.5kg/cm²).
Grate area: 13.5sq ft (1.25m²).
Fuel (coke): 3400lb (1.5t).
Water: 1,800 gall (2,160 US). (8.25m³).
Adhesive weight: 25,000lb (11.2t).
Total weight: 92,500lb (42t).
Length overall: 39ft 4in (11,989mm).

In 1833 Isambard Kingdom Brunel was made engineer to what he referred as "the finest work in England". He was not one to be a follower and he thought little of what he called contemptuously "the coal waggon gauge". He said, "I thought the means employed was not commensurate with the task to be done . . ." and accordingly chose a gauge for his railway almost 50 per cent larger than the one employed by the Stephensons. This 7ft 0¼in (2,140mm) gauge was the largest ever employed by any railway in the world.

When it came to locomotive matters the Great Western Railway was truly great, but this was not so at the beginning. Brunel perhaps a little casually had ordered a series of locomotives from various manufacturers; and it was not one of his best efforts. They were given a free hand within certain almost impossible constraints, that is, that the weight of a six-wheeled locomotive should not exceed 10½ tons and that piston speeds should not exceed 280ft per minute (85m per minute) at 30mph (48km/h). The results were totally unsatisfactory and in its earliest days the GWR had only one locomotive upon which it could rely, the fortuitously acquired Stephenson six-wheel 'Patentee' locomotive *North Star* which weighed 18.2 tons, over 75 per cent above Brunel's stipulated weight. Even the piston speed at 30mph (48km/h) was over the top at 320ft/min (98 m/min).

To take charge of the locomotives Brunel had engaged a young man called Daniel Gooch, a north countryman who had worked with the Stephensons. Following long struggles—often all night—in the running shed at Paddington with the collection of not-too-mobile disasters which formed the GWR locomotive fleet of the time, Gooch formed some very strong views on what should have been done. In the end when it was clear that no sort of timetable could be kept to with things as they were, Gooch had to report over this chief's head upon the situation to the Directors. Brunel was angry but soon made it up and the two remained friends as well as colleagues until the older man's death in 1859.

Eventually Gooch was responsible for drawing up plans and specifications for a wholly practical fleet of more than 100 six-wheeled locomotives, based again on Stephenson's 'Patentees', and including 2-4-0s and 0-6-0s for freight work, as well as 2-2-2s for passenger traffic. Boilers, tenders, motion and many other parts were common to all the types—it was standardisation on a scale the world had never seen before. This time the manufacturers were allowed no latitude—as was to be the case so often in future years, there were only two ways to do things —the Great Western Way and the Wrong Way. As well as drawings, templates were issued to the makers; moreover, the builders were responsible for any repairs needed during the first 1,000 miles (1,600km) running with proper loads. Sixty-two of the locomotives were for express trains and these concern us. The first of these to be delivered was *Fire Fly* which came from Jones, Turner & Evans, Newton-le-Willows, Lancashire, in March 1840, to be followed by *Spit Fire, Wild Fire, Fire Ball, Fire King* and *Fire Brand* from the same firm. On 17 March *Fire Fly* took a special train from Twyford to Paddington in 37 minutes for the 30¾ miles (49.5km). The maximum speed was 58mph (93 km/h). By the end of 1840, for the opening to Wootton Bassett beyond Swindon, a further 25 of these locomotives were available and a timetable worthy of the name could be issued at last.

None of these little fire-horses had their dignity insulted by the attachment of numbers, but there was some attempt at giving related names to the products of each supplier. The results, showing some considerable bias towards the classics, were:

Sharp, Roberts and Co, Manchester: *Tiger, Leopard, Panther, Lynx, Stag, Vulture, Hawk, Falcon, Ostrich, Greyhound.*

Fenton, Murray & Jackson, Leeds: *Charon, Cyclops, Cerberus, Pluto, Harpy, Minos, Ixion, Gorgon, Hecate, Vesta, Acheron, Erebus, Medea, Hydra, Lethe, Phlegethon, Medusa, Proserpine, Ganymede, Argus.*

G. & J. Rennie, Blackfriars, London: *Mazeppa, Arab.*

R.B. Longridge & Co., Bedlington: *Jupiter, Saturn, Mars, Lucifer, Venus, Mercury.*

Stothert & Slaughter, Bristol: *Arrow, Dart.*

Right: *Centaur* was one of Daniel Gooch's famous standard locomotives, and was built by Nasmyth, Gaskell & Co. of Manchester, and delivered in 1841. It ceased work in 1867.

Nasmyth, Gaskell & Co, Manchester: *Achilles, Milo, Hector, Castor, Mentor, Bellona, Actaeon, Centaur, Orion, Damon, Electra, Priam, Pollux, Phoenix, Pegasus, Stentor* (which was the last to be delivered in December 1842).

Incidentally, both the custom of naming as well as the style and shape of the brass letters used persisted for the company's express locomotives until after the railways of Britain were nationalised in 1948. The frames were interesting, being of the sandwich type made from thin sheets of iron enclosing a thick in-filling of oak. The "gab" type valve gear was used. This was later altered in most cases to Stephenson's pattern, so allowing for expansive working of the steam. All the locomotives were coke burners and had large domed "gothic" type fireboxes. Both four-wheel and six-wheel tenders were attached to different members of the class at different times; the dimensions given refer to the use of the six-wheel pattern.

Above: Queen *belonged to the later "Prince" class of 1847. The main difference was the absence of outside frames.*

Phlegethon had the honour of hauling the first Royal Train, provided for Queen Victoria's first railway journey from Slough to Paddington on 13 June 1842. Gooch drove and Brunel was on the footplate with him. The journey of 18½ miles (30km) took 25 minutes and the young Queen was delighted.

Castor hauled the opening train between London and Bristol on 30 June 1841. This was the original full extent of the GWR, but at that time the associated Bristol & Exeter Railway was under construction and *Castor* was able to continue as far as Taunton.

Brunel, as is well known, had the idea of extending the GWR from Bristol to New York and it was on yet another fine summer day, 19 July 1843 that Daniel Gooch took the Queen's husband Prince Albert down to Bristol to launch the famous steamer *Great Britain*, using an unrecorded locomotive of this class. As Gooch records in his diaries, "On the down journey we had some long stops for the Prince to receive addresses, but having no delays on the return journey it was done in 2hrs 4mins. Few runs have been made as quick as this since over so long a distance". In fact, the average speed was 57mph (92km/h) for the 118¾ miles.

There is little doubt that the stability afforded by Brunel's broad gauge tracks with 7ft 0¼in (2,140mm) between the rails, plus the remarkable running qualities of these early standard locomotives led to locomotive performances unequalled in the world at the time.

Another example was on 1 May 1844, the opening day to Exeter, when Gooch personally drove the official party there and back with the locomotive *Orion*. The 194 miles (312km) back from Exeter to London were run in 280 minutes including several stops for water. A year later this journey was being performed by regular express trains with a schedule of 270 minutes, including stops (totalling 13 minutes) at Didcot, Swindon, Bath, Bristol and Taunton.

During the "Battle of the Gauges" in 1845, *Ixion* made test runs on behalf of the broad-gauge faction for the Government's Gauge Commissioners; runs were made from Paddington to Didcot and back. With 60 tons the 53 miles (85km) journey was performed in 63½ minutes with a maximum speed of 61mph (98 km/h), a feat far beyond anything the narrow gauge people could do on their tests between York and Darlington. *Ixion* was the last of these famous locomotives to remain in service, ceasing to run in 1879. The class thus spanned almost 40 years, during which railways grew up as a means of transport. When *Ixion* stopped work the decision to abandon the broad gauge had been taken, although it was not to disappear finally until 13 years later.

By 1879 that young man who had (with the aid of another young draughtsman, also to be famous, called Thomas Crampton) laid out the original *Fire Fly* on his drawing board, had become Sir Daniel Gooch, MP, and Chairman of the Great Western Railway Company.

Lion 0-4-2

Great Britain:
Liverpool & Manchester Railway (L&M), 1838

Tractive effort: 1,836lb (833kg).
Cylinders: (2) 12 x 18in (305 x 457mm).
Driving wheels: 60in (1,524mm).
Superheater: None.
Steam pressure: 50psi (3.5kg/cm²).
Length overall: 33ft 9in (10,287mm).
(Other details not available).

Whilst not strictly an express passenger locomotive, the locomotive *Lion,* built for the Liverpool and Manchester Railway in 1838, has several unusual claims to fame. She was built at a time, almost a decade after the famous locomotive trials at Rainhill, when locomotive design had begun to settle down and one could order engines for specific duties with reasonable confidence *Lion* came from Todd, Kitson & Laird of Leeds and was one of a class of 0-4-2 locomotives named after powerful beasts. It was also a time when the L&M railway began to manufacture its own motive power, a policy that has continued through successive owners of the world's first intercity railway—Grand Junction Railway, London & North Western Railway, London, Midland & Scottish Railway and British Railways—to this day.

A happy chance led to *Lion* being sold to the Mersey Docks & Harbour Board in 1859, for use as a shunting engine. Some years later the Board set her up as a stationary engine. In this guise the engine lasted in commercial service until 1920, when the LMS railway bought the

Right: *Liverpool and Manchester Railway 0-4-2,* Lion *still in running order after 140 years.*

Beuth 2-2-2

Germany:
Berlin-Anhalt Railway, 1843

Tractive effort: 4,120lb (1,870kg).
Axle load; 20,000lb (9.5t).
Cylinders: (2) 13.1 x 22.3 in (330 x 560mm).
Driving wheels: 60¾in (1,543mm).
Heating surface: 500sq ft (47m²).
Superheater: None.
Steam pressure: 78psi (5.5kg/cm²).
Grate area: 8.9sq ft (0.83m²).
Adhesive weight: 20,000lb (9.5t).
Total weight: *41,000lb (18.5t).
Length overall: *20ft 2in (6,143mm).
(—Engine only. Tender details not known).*

The year 1841 was important in the development of the German locomotive-building industry, for in that year three works delivered their first locomotives—Borsig of Berlin, Maffei of Munich and Emil Kessler of Karlsruhe. August Borsig was a man of immense ability and energy, who built an industrial empire which included an iron works and a large water works. At the time of his entry into locomotive building the 4-2-0s built by Norris of Philadelphia were being imported by a number of European railways, and Borsig's first products were 15 engines of this wheel arrangement supplied to the Berlin-Anhalt Railway. They closely resembled the Norris products in having bar frames and a large haycock fire-box, but they included a number of improvements due to Borsig. They were highly successful and further orders followed.

By 1843 Borsig had incorporated further improvements, some of his own devising and some drawn from English practice. This blending of the practices of America, England and Germany was well illustrated in a 2-2-2 locomotive supplied to the Berlin-Anhalt Railway in 1843 and named *Beuth* in honour of August Borsig's former teacher, Professor Beuth of the Royal Industrial Institute of Berlin.

The equal spacing of the axles gave a better weight distribution than in the Norris 4-2-0s. The design was advanced for its day. The flat side valves above the cylinders were driven by the new Stephenson's link motion, which had been first applied in 1842. It was actually an invention of an employee of Robert Stephenson, by name William Howe, whose part in the affair was always acknowledged by his employers.

Like all great inventions it was very simple. Existing valve gears had separate eccentrics for forward and reverse, and "gabs" or claws on the ends of each eccentric rod which could engage or disengage with the valve spindle as appropriate. Howe's idea was to connect the two eccentric rods by means of a link with a curved slot formed in it. In this slot was a die-block to which the valve spindle was connected. The link now just needed to be raised for one direction of travel and lowered for the other; the arrangement worked very well and the majority of the world's steam locomotives over the next 60 years used it.

It was also possible to use intermediate positions to give cut-off of the steam at an early point in the stroke, to allow of more economical working through expansion of the steam. Borsig, however, used an auxiliary slide-valve to control expansion. The fitting of cylinder drain cocks operated from the footplate was an improvement on Norris' engines, in which the drain cocks were operated by levers on the cylinders themselves. The boiler feed pumps were driven by levers attached to the crank pin, and extending back to a position under the cab. As in the Norris engines, bar frames were used. The firebox was elliptical in horizontal section and the upper part formed a capacious steam space. A cylindrical casing on top of the firebox housed the

remains for restoration. In 1930 *Lion* was run at the centenary celebrations of the Liverpool & Manchester Railway and afterwards the engine was preserved to what is now the Merseyside County Museum at Liverpool. *Lion* also ran in the cavalcade to celebrate the 150th anniversary of the L&M, in 1980, and is now the world's oldest working locomotive.

Interesting features of the locomotive include the impressive "haycock" shape firebox and sandwich frames enclosing the wheels.

Lion has also been a film star, playing the title role in that enchanting frolic called "Titfield Thunderbolt", still a favourite.

Right: *140 years of railway progress: Liverpool & Manchester Railway* Lion *of 1841 alongside the Advanced Passenger Train.*

steam pipe and one of the two Salter safety valves. The firebox was finished in bright metal, and the boiler barrel was lagged with wood. The six-wheeled tender had outside frames, and screw-operated brakes acted on both sides of all tender wheels.

This was the 24th engine built by Borsig, and it enhanced his growing reputation as a locomotive builder. Orders flowed in, the works expanded, and by 1846 a total of 120 locomotives had been built, a remarkable achievement for the first five years of a new works. Beuth was typical of many of the products of the works in that period.

The original engine was scrapped, but in 1921 the builders made a full-size replica which is housed in the German Museum.

Below, left: *The locomotive* Beuth *as built for the Berlin to Anhalt Railway in 1843.*

Médoc Class 2-4-0 **Switzerland:** Swiss Western Railway (O-S), 1857

Tractive effort: 8,986lb (4,077kg).
Axle load: 20,150lb (9.2t).
Cylinders: (2) 16 x 24in (408 x 612mm).
Driving wheels: 66¼in (1,686mm).
Heating surface: 1,023sq ft. (95m²).
Superheater: None.
Steam pressure: 114psi (8kg/cm²).
Grate area: 10.75sq ft (1.00m²).
Fuel: 5,280lb (2.4t).
Water: 880 gall (1,050 US) (4.0m³).
Adhesive weight: 40,000lb (18.1t).
Total weight: 88,500lb (40t).
Length overall: 44ft 9½in (13,650mm).

Below: *2-4-0 No.58* Simplon *of the Jura-Simplon Railway, previously No.11 of the Swiss Western Railway. It ran from 1857 to 1901.*

Above: *The "longboilertyp" 2-4-0 of the Swiss Western Railway, later the Jura-Simplon Railway.*

Buddicom Class 2-2-2 **France:** Paris-Rouen Railway, 1843

Tractive effort: 3,100lb (1,460kg).
Axle load: 14,550lb (6.6t).
Cylinders: (2) 12.5 x 21in (318 x 533mm).
Driving wheels: 63in (1,600mm).
Heating surface: 534sq ft (48.5m²).
Superheater: None.
Steam pressure: 70psi (5kg/cm²).
Grate area: 9.5sq ft (0.86m²).
Adhesive weight: 14,550lb (6.6t).
(Original tender details not available).

This locomotive class is the 2nd oldest in this book of which a genuine survivor (not a replica) survies in runnable condition. French National Railways must take the credit (together with their predecessors the Western Railway and the State Railway) because it is their loving care which has enabled this significant and wholly delightful 139-year old creature to be there to give us pleasure today.

The designer, W.B. Buddicom, was one of that band of British engineers who spread the gospel according to Stephenson round the world—though in this case travelling his own different road and one that in the end proved the right one. The Buddicom 2-2-2s represent one more step as regards the European locomotive from *Northumbrian* via *Planet* and *Vauxhall* towards the world standard steam locomotive with two outside cylinders—although it was a close race with very similar and equally famous 2-2-2s built at Crewe to the design of Alexander Allan for the London & North Western Railway in England and known as the "Crewe" type. The motivation behind the new design lay in the constant breakages of the crank axles of inside-cylinder locomotives.

In addition to just two outside cylinders, Stephenson's new link motion was fitted, as well as a deep firebox between the rear two wheels. The results were extremely successful and the engines continued in use for many years. Latterly 22 of them were converted to 2-2-2 tank locomotives, but in 1946 the last survivor, long out of use, was

Above right: *"Buddicom" 2-2-2 as restored to original condition at Bricklayers Arms depot, London, 1951.*

Above: *"Buddicom" 2-2-2 as converted to a tank locomotive.*

The Stephensons pioneered much concerning the locomotive, yet Forrester, Norris, Crampton and others were ahead in adopting what became the final arrangement of the cylinders. The famous 'long-boiler' six-wheeled design offered by Robert Stephenson & Co from 1846 onwards, with two horizontal outside cylinders at the front, was usually combined with an increased length of boiler, in an attempt to extract more of the heat from the hot gases in the tubes. Many of the earlier long-boiler engines had a raised haycock firebox instead of a dome.

The firebox was outside the wheel-base which was proportionately rather short. This led to a tendency for these locomotives to pitch at speed, but their other qualities led to many being built of the 2-2-2, 2-4-0 and 0-6-0 wheel arrangements, both at home and under licence (or not) in many European countries. The word *longboiler* entered the railway vocabularies of several lands.

The example depicted in the artwork below was a late *longboilertyp* of which 15 were built in 1856-58 at Karlsruhe in Germany for the Swiss Western Railway, later the Jura-Simplon Railway. The design was known as the Médoc, an almost standard French type of the period. They all had long and useful lives, the last being withdrawn in 1902.

restored to near original condition.

The preserved engine is No. 33 of the Paris to Rouen Railway, named *Saint Pierre.* It visited England for the 1951 Festival of Britain and was actually steamed and run in the Bricklayers Arms Locomotive Depot, London. It was welcomed into Britain by Miss Buddicom, a descendant of the builder. Normally it is kept at the National Railway Museum at Mulhouse.

Gloggnitzer Class 4-4-0

Austria:
Vienna-Gloggnitz Railway, 1848

Tractive effort: 5,750lb (2,610kg).
Axle load: 16,500lb (7.5t).
Cylinders: (2) 14½ x 23in (368 x 579mm).
Driving wheels: 55¾in (1,420mm).
Heating surface: 760sq ft ($70.6m^2$).
Superheater: None.
Steam pressure: 78psi ($5.5kg/cm^2$).
Grate area: 10sq ft ($0.94m^2$).
Fuel: 4,500lb (2t).
Water: 1,500gall (1,800 US) ($6.8m^3$).
Adhesive weight: 33,000lb (15t).
Total weight: 70,000lb (32t).
Length overall: 42ft 2in (12,853mm).

The story of how the Norris brothers had better-than-average technical insight but less-than-average commercial acumen has already been related. One of those who combined these qualities was a Scotsman called John Haswell who in 1836 went out to Austria to put some locomotives exported from Britain into service. He did this satisfactorily and was asked to stay on in charge of the locomotive department of the 27-mile (43km) Vienna-Gloggnitz Railway. He died in 1897 at the age of 85 having twice been knighted by the Emperor for services to Austria.

One of his most successful designs was for some 4-4-0s based on the Norris layout. They were known as the "Gloggnitzers" even though with the completion of the Southern State Railway over the Semmering Pass in 1857 their sphere of action—except over the pass itself—became extended beyond Gloggnitz to Laibach, 284 miles (460km) from Vienna. Laibach is now known as Ljublana and is situated in Jugoslavia.

Amongst the features of these locomotives should be mentioned the leading bogie, which was arranged to be able to move radially instead of merely to pivot about its centre, as in the Norris engines. Because the coupled wheels were situated close to the bogie, thus constraining the axis of the locomotive, some sideways movement of the bogie was important. Haswell introduced this device well before Levi Bissell of New York (whose name it usually bears) obtained his patent. Also interesting are the gen-u-ine Yankee pattern spark-arresting smoke stack (there was not a Norris factory in Vienna for nothing), the circular-section coupling and connecting rods, and the bundles of brushwood attached to the leading guard irons to sweep the rails clear of stones and other small obstructions.

One of these famous engines has survived and is displayed in the Vienna Railway Museum. This is the *Steinbrück,* which happily in 1860 passed into the hands of the Graz-Köflach Railway, a concern whose kindly reluctance to scrap ancient machinery is greatly appreciated by the locomotive historian.

Below: *Haswell "Gloggnitzer" 4-4-0* Steinbrück *as preserved in the Vienna Railway Museum.*

Crampton Type 4-2-0

France:
Eastern Railway (Est), 1852

Tractive effort: 5,040lb (2,290kg).
Axle load: 27,500lb (12.5t).
Cylinders: (2) 15¾ x 21½in (400 x 500mm).
Driving wheels: 82¾in (2,100mm).
Heating surface: 1,059sq ft (98.4m²).
Superheater: None.
Steam pressure: 92psi (6.5kg/cm²).
Grate area: 15.3sq ft (1.42m²).
Fuel: 15,500lb (7t).
Water: 1,540gall (1,850 US) (7m³).
Adhesive weight: 27,100lb (12.5t).
Total weight: 105,000lb (47.5t).
Length overall: 41ft 9in (12,728mm).

Above: *Crampton 4-2-0 No.170 of the French Northern Railway. Note the huge single pair of driving wheels at the back.*

Thomas Russell Crampton's engines are a legend—the word *Crampton* for a time entered the French language to mean "train"—yet they in no way formed a step forward in the art of locomotive engineering. But they were magnificent.

Crampton was born in August 1816, the same month as Daniel Gooch. He learnt his trade as an engineer under Marc Brunel, father of the Great Western Railway's builder. In due time Crampton joined the GWR himself and worked with Gooch on the design of his celebrated standard locomotives.

In 1842, whilst still working for this company, he applied for a patent for a high-speed express locomotive with a low centre of gravity yet having an adequate-size boiler. The problem was the driving axle—if you used big wheels to permit fast running, then the bottom of the boiler had to clear the revolving cranks and had to be mounted high. So that he could set the boiler low and thus keep the centre of gravity also low Crampton put the driving axle *behind* it. The cylinders were outside the wheels and were mounted well back from the front of the engine. It was a very convenient layout as the machinery was all accessible—in fact, in that respect (but little else) the Cramptons followed the final form of the steam locomotive.

Crampton was working on a broad gauge railway and he must have regarded standard gauge locomotives as having little better stability than the penny-farthing bicycles of the day. In the typical Crampton design illustrated here the height of the centre of the boiler was about the same measurement as the rail gauge, very similar to the same ratio for a conventional design on the 7ft 0¼in (2,140mm) gauge.

He was also concerned about pitching, which affected certain locomotives having a short wheelbase, especially if this was combined with having much of the weight of the engine concentrated on a single central driving wheel. It could be said that the idea was only dubiously original but even so Crampton got his patent and went into business. It was a case of a "prophet not being without honour save in his own country" and the first engine was the 4-2-0 *Namur* for the Namur-Liège Railway in Belgium. The builders were the little known and long vanished firm of Tulk and Ley of Lowca Works, Whitehaven, and since the Belgian line was not complete when the locomotives was ready, trials were held in Great Britain as well as on the Belgian State Railway.

Altogether some 320 Cramptons were built, most of them for various French railways, notably the Northern and Eastern companies. Amongst many notable doings of theirs in that country might be noted the haulage of the last train to leave Paris when it was besieged by the Germans in

Below: *Eastern Railway of France Crampton 4-2-0 No.80 before restoration as the working museum exhibit we know today.*

Pearson 9ft Single Class 4-2-4

Great Britain:
Bristol & Exeter Railway (B&ER), 1854

Tractive effort: 7,344lb (3,330kg).
Axle load: 41,500lb (18.5t).
Cylinders: (2) 18 x 24in (457 x 610mm).
Driving wheels: 106in (2,743mm).
Heating surface: 1,235sq ft (114.8 m²).
Superheater: None.
Steam pressure: 120psi (8.4kg/cm²).
Grate area: 23sq ft (2.15m²).
Fuel: 4,480lb (2t).
Water: 1,430gall (1,720 US) (6.5m³).
Adhesive weight: 41,500lb (18.5t).
Total weight: 112,000lb (49.7t).
Length overall: 30ft 9in (9,372mm).

1870. Another Crampton belonging to the Eastern Railway and rebuilt with a strange double-barrelled boiler, was responsible for breaking the world speed record—not only for trains but for everything—when No.604 was run at 89.5mph (144km/h) with a load of 157 tons, during trials on the Paris-Laroche main line of the Paris, Lyons & Mediterranean Railway on 20 June 1890.

The main drawback of the Crampton design was the limited adhesive weight which could be applied to the rails; with a single driving axle right at the end of the wheelbase this limitation was a fundamental one. Because of this the success of the Cramptons in handling light trains at high speeds was to some extent self-defeating—because of the fast service more people used the trains, more coaches had to be added and the limit of these engines' capacity was soon reached. It is also true to say that, whilst at first sight it would appear that a low centre of gravity would make a locomotive more stable, in fact it is a case where the cure can be worse than the disease. Such locomotives may be less liable to overturn when driven round curves at two or more times the permitted speed, but liability to serious oscillation and consequent derailment from that cause is increased.

Nevertheless, other features made the Crampton engines into sound propositions. Their layout enabled bearings of really adequate size to be applied to the driving axle and this made for long periods of trouble-free running between visits to the shops. Similar advantage sprung from the fact that a rear wheel of a vehicle tends to run with its flanges clear of the rails on curves, leaving the leading wheels to do the guidance. Hence the small (and cheap) carrying wheels bore the brunt of the flange-wear, leaving the large and expensive driving wheels to last longer.

Crampton was also one of the first locomotive engineers to understand and apply the principles of balancing the reciprocating and revolving weights of a locomotive mechanism. This also contributed to the success of his engines, as did his patent regulator or throttle valve. Crampton had clearly a most original mind, although sometimes his ingenuity outran his good sense. In addition to the well-known Crampton layout which was only secondary in the application, his original patent of 1842 claimed the idea of locomotives with a driving axle *above* the boiler. The first (and almost certainly the last) of these, named *Trevithick* after the builder of the world's first steam locomotive, was built in 1847 by the London & North Western Railway at their Crewe Works. It had 9ft (2,742mm) diameter wheels and presented an exceedingly strange appearance. It was not a success.

Crampton took out a further patent in 1849 to cover locomotives provided with an intermediate shaft, either oscillating or revolving, between the cylinders and the driving wheels or axle. Its application to steam locomotives was brief (but not quite so brief as the underslung boiler) but after Crampton had died in 1888 and the patent had expired the idea found extensive use for the drive mechanisms of early electric locomotives.

The considerable mark which Thomas Crampton made in the world of locomotive engineering is recognised by the preservation of 4-2-0 No.80 *Le Continent,* originally of the Paris-Strasbourg Railway, later the Eastern Railway of France. This beautiful locomotive relic, superbly restored and in working order (but only steamed on great occasions) is usually to be found in the French National Railway Museum at Mulhouse. She is the subject of the vital statistics given at the head of this article.

Below: *Crampton 4-2-0 of the Eastern Railway of France as now superbly restored makes one of her rare appearances in steam.*

These remarkable tank locomotives were designed for the broad-gauge Bristol & Exeter Railway by Locomotive Superintendent Pearson and eight (running numbers 39 to 46) were built by Rothwell & Co. of Bolton in 1853 and 1854. They were intended specially for working the B&ER's section of the London to Exeter express route, including the famous train "Flying Dutchman", at that time the fastest train in the world. They had the largest driving wheels ever successfully used on a locomotive and no one has come up with an authentic recording of any higher speed previous to one of 81.8mph (130km/h) made behind a Pearson single while descending the Wellington incline south of Taunton.

Left: *A side view of a Pearson 4-2-4 tank locomotive as used on the broad-gauge lines of the Bristol & Exeter Railway.*

The B&ER had only taken over from the Great Western the working of its own railway in 1849, a bare five years before this very original piece of locomotive thinking was turned into hardware. It says enough of the relationship between the two companies that they were as far as possible removed from the Gooch 4-2-2s first supplied. Most original pieces of thinking in respect of locomotive design spent more time in sidings than on the road, but it was not so with these so-called nine-footers. After 14 years in traffic four of them were rebuilt—to an extent that counted more as a replacement—at the B&ER's own works at Bristol. But the so-original first design was followed.

The engines were guided by a four-wheel bogie at each end, and they were propelled along by that mighty pair of flangeless driving wheels placed more or less centrally between the bogies. As with all locomotives that ran on Brunel's broad-gauge lines, the cylinders and motion were inside the frames.

Water was carried in the tank at the rear as well as in a well-tank between the frames. Pearson's singles were untypical, though, in that they carried no names, only numbers.

In 1876, shortly after the GWR had finally taken over the B&ER, a Pearson single (No.39, renumbered 2001) derailed with loss of life at Long Ashton near Bristol. In consequence the remaining three locomotives were again completely rebuilt on more conventional lines as 4-2-2 singles, regarded by some as the most handsome (this was not hard to achieve) ever to run on the 7ft 0¼in (2,140mm) gauge.

Had the broad-gauge continued into the twentieth century, it would seem as though these rebuilds might have formed the basis upon which development might have taken place. The design of a modern broad gauge 4-6-0 with two large inside cylinders and a power and size similar to that of the *Saint* class 4-6-0s of the GWR would be a fascinating exercise, especially if followed up by a working model.

American Type 4-4-0

United States: Western & Atlantic Railroad (W&ARR), 1855

Tractive effort: 6,885lb (3,123kg).
Axle load: 21,000lb (9.5t).
Cylinders: (2) 15 x 24in (381 x 610mm).
Driving wheel: 60in (1,524mm).
Heating surface: 98.0sq ft ($91m^2$).
Superheater: None.
Steam pressure: 90psi ($6.35kg/cm^2$).
Grate area: 14.5sq ft ($1.35m^2$).
Fuel: (wood) 2 cords ($7.25m^3$).
Water: 1,250 gall (2,000 US) ($5.75m^3$).
Adhesive weight: 43,000lb (19.5t).
Total weight: 90,000lb (41t).
Length overall: 52ft 3in (15,926mm).

Above: *The "General" as currently preserved in working order. The wood "stacked" in the tender hides an oil fuel tank.*

The *General* was built by Thomas Rogers of Paterson, New Jersey in 1855 and it is a wholly appropriate example of the most numerous and successful locomotive design ever to have been built. The reason is that Rogers was responsible for introducing most of the features which made the true "American" the success it was. The most significant development, so far as the U.S.A. was concerned was the general introduction of Stephenson's link motion, which permitted the expansive use of steam. This was in place of the "gab" or "hook" reversing gears used until then, which permitted only "full forward" and "full backward" positions.

In other aspects of design Rogers gained his success by good proportions and good detail rather than innovation. An example was the provision of adequate space between the cylinders and the driving wheels, which reduced the maximum angularity of the connecting rods and hence the up-and-down forces on the slide bars. A long wheelbase leading truck (in English, bogie) allowed the cylinders to be horizontal and still clear the wheels. This permitted direct attachment to the bar frames, which raised inclined cylinders did not.

To allow flexibility on curves, early examples of the breed inherited flangeless leading driving wheels from their progenitors, but by the late 1850s the leading trucks were being given side movement to produce the same effect. Naturally the compensated spring suspension system giving three-point support to the locomotive was continued. Wood-burning was also nearly universal in these early years of the type, and the need to catch the sparks led to many wonderful shapes in the way of spark-arresting smokestacks.

Within two or three years other makers such as Baldwin, Grant, Brooks Mason, Danforth and Hinkley began offering similar locomotives. To buy one of these locomotives one did not need to be a great engineer steeped in the theory of design—it was rather like ordering a car today. One filled in a form on which certain options could be specified and very soon an adequate and reliable machine was delivered.

Speeds on the rough light tracks of a pioneer land were not high—average speeds of 25mph (40km/h) start-to-stop, implying a maximum of 40mph (64km/h), were typical of the best expresses. Although the 4-4-0s were completely stable at high speeds, the increased power required meant that by the 1880s a bigger breed of 4-4-0 as well as "Ten-wheelers" (4-6-0s) were taking over from the "American".

There was another revolution taking place too. The earlier years of the type were characterised by romantic names and wonderful brass, copper and paint work, but the last quarter of the nineteenth century was a time of cut-throat competition, with weaker roads going to the wall. There was no question of there being anything to spare for frills of this kind—so it was just a case of giving a coat of bitumen and painting big white running numbers in the famus "Bastard Railroad Gothic" fount on the tender sides.

For most of the second half of the nineteenth century this one type of locomotive dominated railroad operations in the U.S.A. It was appropriately known as the "American Standard" and about 25,000 of them were built, differing only marginally in design. The main things that varied were the decor and the details. They were simple, ruggedly constructed machines appropriate for what was then a developing country; at the same time a leading bogie and compensated springing made them suitable for the rough tracks of a frontier land.

The subject of the specification above is perhaps the most famous of all the 25,000. The *General* came to fame when hijacked by a group of Union soldiers who had infiltrated into Confederate territory during the American civil war. The idea was to disrupt communications behind the lines, in particular on the 5ft (1,524mm)

Below: *Typical United States "Standard" 4-4-0 illustrating the elaborate decor that was often applied in the early years of American railroading but which was abandoned in the 1880s.*

gauge line 135 miles (216km) long connecting Atlanta with Chattanooga. The Union forces were approaching Chattanooga after their victory at Shiloh and the Confederates were expected to bring up reinforcements by rail. There was a major trestle bridge at a place called Oostenabula and the intention was to steal a train, take it to the site and burn the bridge. A replacement would take weeks to build.

The Union force, twenty in number under the command of a Captain Andrews, having stayed overnight at a place called Marietta and having bought tickets to travel on the train, took over the locomotive at a place called Big Shanty, some 30 miles (48km) north of Atlanta, while the passengers and crew were having breakfast in the depot's eating house. The conductor of the train, whose name was Fuller, gave chase first on a handcart and then on a small private ironworks loco, the *Yonah*.

The raiders' intention was to cut telegraph wires behind them, remove the occasional rail and demand immediate passage at stations they came to in the name of Confederate General Beauregard. A problem Andrews faced was the presence of trains coming the other way on the single line and perhaps the game was lost at Kingston where he had to wait an hour and twenty five minutes until one divided into two sections had finally arrived.

In the end the *Yonah* arrived there only four minutes after Andrews and the *General* had left. Here Fuller took over another "American" 4-4-0, the *Texas* and after this Andrews never got enough time to block the track before what had now become a Confederate posse came within rifle range. In the end, after eight hours and 87 miles the *General* expired when it ran out of fuel; the Union group then scattered into the woods. All were later captured and seven of the senior men shot.

Leaving out the human drama for a moment two qualities of the "American Standards" emerge from this affair. First, in spite of the rough track high maximum speeds of around 60mph (100 km/h) were reached during the chase and both locomotives stayed on the rails. The second thing was that the range between fuel stops was very short. A full load of two cords of wood fuel (a cord is 128cu ft or 3.62m^2) would last for a mere 50 miles (80km).

Both the *General* and the *Texas* (or what purports to be them) have survived. The former, normally in store at Chattanooga, is occasionally run. Oil fuel is used, the tank being concealed under a fake woodpile. The *Texas,* as befits a Confederate conqueror, has an honoured place in Grant Park at Atlanta. Both were converted from the 5ft (1,524mm) gauge of the Western & Atlantic Railroad after the war was over.

The American Civil War was one of the first great wars to be fought using railway transportation, most of which was provided on both sides by this "American" type. The earliest transcontinental railroads were first built and then operated by them; the well-known picture of the last spike ceremony at Promontory, Utah, has placed the Cental Pacific's *Jupiter* and the Union Pacific No.119 second only to the *General* on the scale of locomotive fame. It is said that "America built the railroads and the railroads built America"; substitute "American 4-4-0" for "railroad" and the saying is equally true.

Above: *American Standard 4-4-0, as refurbished to resemble the Cental Pacific RR's* Jupiter, *ready to re-enact the completion ceremony of the first transcontinental railroad at the Golden Spike National Monument, Utah.*

The "American" type was a universal loco; the only difference between those built for passenger traffic and those for freight was between 66in (1,676mm) diameter driving wheels and 60in (1,524mm). It also served all the thousands of railroad companies who then operated America's 100,000 miles (160,000km) of line, from roads thousands of miles long to those a mere ten.

The last "American" class in the U.S.A. did not retire from normal line service for more than a century after Rogers put the first on the rails in 1852. A few survive in industrial use in the remoter parts of the world even today. Numerous examples are preserved in museums and elsewhere all over North American, a few (a very few) perform on tourist railroads, while others are set aside for and occasionally star in western films.

Problem Class 2-2-2

Great Britain: London & North Western Railway (LNWR), 1862

Tractive effort: 9,827lb (4,458kg).
Axle load: 33,000lb (15t).
Cylinders: (2) 16 x 24in (406 x 610mm).
Driving wheels: 93in (2,324mm).
Heating surface: 1,097sq ft ($102m^2$).
Superheater: None.
Steam pressure: 150psi ($8.54kg/cm^2$).
Grate area: 15sq ft ($1.39m^2$).
Fuel: 11,000lb (5t).
Water: 1,800 gall (2,160 US) ($8m^3$).
Adhesive weight: 26,500lb (12t).
Total weight: 133,000lb (60.5t).
Length overall: 43ft 8in (13,310mm).

A working career on top main line expresses lasting more than 40 years is quite exceptional for any locomotive. John Ramsbottom's "Problem" or "Lady of the Lake" class singles, introduced on the LNWR in 1859 managed nearly 50, although a considerable element of luck entered into the achievement.

In the tradition of all the best steam locomotives from *Northumbrian* of 1830 to the Chinese "March Forward" class of 1980, the main characteristic of the "Problem" was simplicity. No one could call the Stirling singles described elsewhere complex, but the "Problem"s were simpler still, having no bogies, the leading axle being carried in the frames like the others.

The first of the 60 built was turned out in 1859, the last in

Right: *A "Problem" class 2-2-2 at speed on the LNWR main line hauling an almost unbelievable 15-coach load.*

Stirling 8ft Single Class 4-2-2

Great Britain: Great Northern Railway (GNR), 1870

Tractive effort: 11,245lb (5,101kg).
Axle load: 34,000lb (15.5t).
Cylinders: (2) 18 x 28in (457 x 711mm).
Driving wheels: 97in (2,463mm).
Heating surface: 1,165sq ft ($108m^2$).
Steam pressure: 140psi ($9.8kg/cm^2$).
Grate area: 17.65sq ft ($1.64m^2$).
Fuel: 7,500lb (3.5t).
Water: 2,900 gall (3,480 US) ($13m^3$).
Adhesive weight: 34,600lb (15.5t).
Total weight: 145,500lb (66t).
Length overall: 50ft 2in (15,240mm).

Above right: *Preserved Stirling No. 1 ready to take part in the Cavalcade celebrating 150 years of main-line railways, August 1975.*

Below: *Stirling 4-2-2 No. 1 of the Great Northern Railway of England, showing the huge single pair of 8-foot diameter driving wheels. Note the domeless boiler and the elegant brass safety valve cover and, on the tender, the gong which was connected to an early form of communication cord. No. 1 is preserved in working order.*

1865. The outside-cylinder inside-valve arrangement was extremely basic, and a further simplification occurred after the first ten had been built when the Giffard injector replaced tiresome pumps for feeding the boiler. A job for which the "Problem" locomotives were noted was the haulage of the Irish mail trains, known as the "Wild Irishmen", from Euston to Holyhead, changing engines at Stafford.

Francis Webb took over from John Ramsbottom in 1871 and he, like other locomotive engineers both before and after, made the mistake of thinking that complexity was the right path. The compound locomotives that resulted were not as reliable as they should have been and in time the LNWR operating department laid down that any express with a load greater than the equivalent of 17 six-wheel coaches (about 270 tons) should be piloted. In this task the "Problem" locomotives, now 30 years old, found a niche and for it they were discreetly rebuilt in the 1890s. The dimensions given in the specifications refer to the final rebuilding, which involved a 25 per cent increase in the total weight over the original. An earlier rebuild had provided the locomotives with cabs and no doubt little remained of the originals of 1859 by the end except their identities. The changes made, however, did little to obviate their worst fault which was the tendency to violent oscillation about a vertical axis at speed.

Left: *"Problem" class No.610* Princess Royal *before being fitted with a cab, but in LNWR's "blackberry black" livery.*

As regards these identities, a hallowed LNWR tradition was closely followed, with numbers and names chosen and allocated at random. Many of the names were evocative, for example, *Erebus, Harlequin, Atalanta, Lady of the Lake, Tornado, Pandora,* but others such as *Problem, Soult, Edith* and *Fortuna,* less so.

The "Stirling 8-foot single" is considered by many to be the epitome of the locomotive regarded as an art form. The graceful lines set off by lovely paint- and brass-work combine to produce a sight that has few rivals for beauty.

Patrick Stirling, Locomotive Superintendent of the Great Northern Railway had the first of them built in 1870 at the line's own Doncaster Locomotive Plant. As was the GNR custom, subsequent numbers were allotted at random, but the prototype was actually No.1 and as such enjoyed considerable fame. It was 23 years before the last and 47th of the class was completed.

The domeless boiler was very apparent to the onlooker; it was both unusual for the time as well as being a Stirling trademark. Mechanically the engine was as simple as can be, with outside cylinders but inside valve chests, the slide valves being driven direct by sets of Stephenson's link motion.

In those days, when trains were formed of six-wheel non-corridor coaches, these engines handled all the crack expresses of the line including the famous 10am Kings Cross to Edinburgh express, known then only unofficially as the "Flying Scotsman". Many authentic recordings were made showing speeds around 75mph (120km/h) with surprisingly heavy loads being hauled by these locomotives, but the coming of such developments as eight- and twelve- wheeled bogie stock, corridor carriages and dining cars spelt their removal to lesser tasks. All had been withdrawn by 1916 except the legendary No.1 which survives at what was the boundary of her home territory at the National Railway Museum at York.

In 1938 Stirling's No.1 was taken out of the museum, restored and used for a publicity stunt in connection with some new rolling stock for the "Flying Scotsman" express. Journalists were invited to Kings Cross for a preliminary run on the Flying Scotsman of 1888, before joining the new luxury train at Stevenage. The event caused a group of railway enthusiasts known as the Railway Correspondence and Travel Society to charter No.1 and its train of six-wheelers for an excursion from Kings Cross to Cambridge. It was the first occasion that a museum piece main-line steam locomotive was run to give steam enthusiasts pleasure, and was the precedent for such activities starting in earnest after World War II.

Class 121 2-4-2 **France:** Paris, Lyons & Mediterranean Railway (PLM), 1876

Tractive effort: 12,225lb (5,545kg).
Axle load: 31,000lb (14t).
Cylinders: (2) 19.7 x 23.7in (500 x 650mm).
Driving wheels: 82½in (2,100mm).
Heating surface: 1,280sq ft (119m^2).
Superheater: None.
Steam pressure: 129psi (9kg/cm^2).
Grate area: 23sq ft (2.2m^2).
Adhesive weight: 61,000lb (27.5t).
Total weight: 109,539lb (49.7t).
Length overall: 56ft 5¾in (1,7215mm).
(Tender details not available).

French steam locomotives always had great distinction and none more so than these enchanting creations which belonged to the famed *Route Imperiale,* otherwise known as the Paris, Lyons & Mediterranean Railway. Previous to their construction the PLM had relied on Crampton-type 4-2-0 locomotives. Finding they needed more power, in 1868 the company built 50 long-boiler 2-4-0s, both their Paris and Oullins shops sharing the work of construction.

Still more power was found to be necessary and in 1876 an enlarged version of these 2-4-0s was produced. It was necessary to go to the 2-4-2 wheel arrangement and, indeed, the earlier

Below: *Paris, Lyon & Mediterranean Railway class "121" 2-4-2 No.90. Note the outside Gooch valve gear, the dome nearly as fat as the boiler, the spring-balance safety valves, the bell to provide communication and the flap to cover the chimney.*

Above: *PLM 2-4-2 locomotive No. 67. Four hundred of this class were built.*

Class 79 4-4-0 **Australia:** New South Wales Government Railways (NSWGR), 1877

Tractive effort: 13,800lb (6,260kg).
Axle load: 32,000lb (14.5t).
Cylinders: (2) 18 x 24in (457 x 610mm).
Driving wheels: 67in (1,702mm).
Heating surface: 1,121sq ft (104m^2).
Superheater: None.
Steam pressure: 140psi (9.8kg/cm^2).
Grate area: 14.75sq ft (1.40m^2).
Adhesive weight: 64,000lb (29t).
Total weight: 133,500lb (60.5t).
(Tender details not available).

An active working life of over 80 years says more for the qualities of these handsome locomotives than pages of print. One of them which was later converted to a 4-4-2 tank locomotive in fact came close to working on its 100th birthday, for it was shunting at the NSWGR Clyde Workshops as late as mid-1972.

In spite of origins as an underground city railway locomotive, these 4-4-0s were intended for top-line express passenger trains. They were based on the layout of some famous and successful 4-4-0 tanks built by Beyer, Peacock of Manchester from 1864 onwards for London's Metropolitan Railway. The original Australian order was for 30, delivered between 1877 and 1879. Later 26 more were supplied by Dübs & Co. of Glasgow (later part of the North British Locomotive Co). A further four came from Beyer, Peacock in 1881 and the final four were built in New South Wales by the Atlas Engineering Pty of Sydney, making 68 in all. It was a pleasant change from so much contemporary locomotive engineering, most of which was to NTA (No Two Alike) standards.

As we have seen and will see again many times throughout this narrative, simplicity was the steam locomotive's trump card and designers who thought to introduce complications, however promising they might seem, did so at their peril. Beyer, Peacock's classic design (the original is attributed to Sir John Fowler), repeated so many times for so many railways, came near the ultimate in this respect. One feature which is hidden from sight is the Allen's straight-link motion which was fitted to these locomotives.

Originally the locomotives had no sides to the cab but later some shelter was provided. The resulting side-sheets had plain circular windows and this is a trade mark of these and other contemporary NSWGR locomotives. Another odd aesthetic feature of the "79"s is the sloping front to the smokebox door, inherited from their Metropolitan progenitors.

The New South Wales railways were notable for a large

Right: *New South Wales Government class "79" 4-4-0 as restored and displayed at the NSW Railway Museum.*

2-4-0s were soon rebuilt with the extra rear carrying axle. This extra pair of wheels gave increased stability when running. Interesting features included a Belpaire firebox, outside Gooch's valve gear (described in connection with Gooch's "Rover" class 4-2-2s) and, later on, big reservoirs on the boiler in connection with the PLM air brake system. Delicious rather than vital were various lesser features. The magnificent chimney, for example, is pure poetry, with that immense *capouchon* and lever-worked flap to close it shut. The sandbox too, whilst a plain rectangle in the side view, is exotically curved when seen from the front. The superb dome with spring-balance safety valves certainly is no anticlimax, while the shape of the cab (if that is the right word for a slightly elaborate wind-shield) is distinctive seen from any direction.

Sixty of this sub-class (to which the dimensions etc given above refer) were built, numbered from 51 to 110, following the 50 earlier 2-4-0s converted to 2-4-2s.

So successful were these engines that between 1879 and 1883 their numbers were increased to 400, all except 40 of this huge fleet, being built "in house" by the PLM. These 40 were built by Sharp, Steward & Co of Manchester. They worked all kinds of passenger trains.

A further development took place in 1888, when yet more 2-4-2s were built. This final version of the design was a watershed of steam development in France. Although in overall weight they were a mere 10 per cent greater than the originals, there were three features incorporated in the design, each of which meant a "Great Leap Forward" in French locomotive design: first, there was Walschaert's valve gear, later to become a world standard for steam locomotives; second the boiler was designed for an unprecedented pressure of 15kg/cm² (214psi), as typical of latter day steam engines the world over and representing a 65 per cent increase over the boiler pressure of the parent design. Thirdly, the design marked a change on the part of the greatest of French railway companies from simple locomotives to compound. This was eventually to lead, in France, to locomotives that beat the world by a big margin in thermal efficiency; that is, in the amount of fuel burnt per unit of power produced.

Other very similar 2-4-2s were built from 1876 onwards for the neighbouring Paris-Orleans Railway. In fact, it seems likely that the PLM copied what they saw being done over the fence by one of the greatest of French locomotive engineers, Victor Fourquenot. In all 126 of the 2-4-2s were built for the P-O and some were even in use 70 years later. One has survived to be restored and displayed in the National Railway Museum at Mulhouse. Not only the PLM copied the P-O. Between 1882 and 1891, forty of the 2-4-2s were built for the Austro-Hungarian State Railway Co. The P-O is said to have had a financial interest in the Austro-Hungarian company.

number of long lightly-laid branch lines serving the farming community. While the crops are growing traffic is minimal and so, long after the "79" class has been superseded on the crack trains of the system, there were the mail trains on these branches needing agile and light-footed locomotives. Hence one finds these 4-4-0s, now re-designated class "Z-12", (between 1885 and 1923 they were known as the "C" class) still at work in the 1960s, 85 years after the design was introduced. One notes, however, one interruption to this peaceful and prolonged old age when, one day in 1932, 7,000 tons of elderly locomotives placed buffer-to-buffer were used to test the Sydney Harbour Bridge.

Duke Class 4-4-0 Great Britain: Highland Railway (HR), 1874

Tractive effort: 12,338lb (5,597kg).
Axle load: 31,500lb (14.25t).
Cylinders: (2) 18 x 24in (457 x 610mm).
Driving wheels: 75½in (1,918mm).
Heating surface: 1,228sq ft (114m²).
Steam pressure: 140psi (9.84kg/cm²).
Grate area: 16.25sq ft (1.51m²).
Fuel: 9,000lb (4t).
Water: 1,800 gall (2,160 US) (8m³).
Adhesive weight: 59,500lb (27t).
Total weight: 161,500lb (73.5t).
Length overall: 51ft 3in (15,621mm.

When they were introduced in 1874 the Highland Railway "Duke" class were the most powerful locomotives in Britain. Although a small concern with fewer than 60 locos on its books the HR needed strong engines to take its trains across the mountains. These ten 4-4-0s, built by Dübs of Glasgow and the first design of newly appointed Locomotive Superintendent David Jones, were the forerunners of several other very similar classes. These were the "Lochgorm Bogie" of 1876, the "Clyde Bogie" of 1886 and the "Strath" class of 1889. The celebrated "Skye Bogie" class of 1882 were also very closely related, but with considerably smaller driving wheels. In all, these engines added up to a very competent fleet of 30 locomotives, which profoundly improved speeds and loads on the Highland lines. That famous HR feature the louvred chimney, intended to throw the exhaust up clear of the cab as well as assist the draughting, appeared for the first time on this class, which also had the graceful double frame arrangement of previous HR locomotives. As befitted a line whose first locomotive chief was Alexander Allan, Allan's straight link valve gear was used.

Another interesting feature was Le Châtelier's counter-pressure brake, by means of which the cylinders could be used to provide the brake force as well as drive the train. The idea was to supplement hand-applied brake-blocks on the long down grades but the equipment never became standard. The principle was very similar to descending a long hill in a motor car by engaging a low gear. The later-fitted front vacuum brake pipe was arranged to fold down to permit the mounting of a wedge-type snowplough. Running numbers were 60 to 69.

Although a ride over the Highland main line was and is one of the finest railway journeys of the world, it has never been one of the fastest. In the early days of David Jones' locomotives the journey from Perth to Inverness 143 miles (230km) took 5¼ hours by the best train, and the continuation on the Wick, a further 162 miles

Right: *David Jones' "Duke" class 4-4-0, depicted in original livery. Later a more sombre green was adopted.*

Gladstone Class 0-4-2 Great Britain: London, Brighton & South Coast Railway (LBSCR), 1882

Tractive effort: 13,211lb (5,993kg).
Axle load: 32,500lb (14.75t).
Cylinders: (2) 18¼ x 26in (464 x 660mm).
Driving wheels: 78in (1,980mm).
Heating surface: 1,492sq ft (139m²).
Superheater: None.
Steam pressure: 140psi (9.8kg/cm²).
Grate area: 20.3sq ft (1.88m²).
Fuel: 9,000lb (4t).
Water: 2,240 gall (2,700 US) (10.2m³).
Adhesive weight: 63,500lb (29t).
Total weight: 153,000lb (69.5t).
Length overall: 51ft 10in (15,800mm).

Above: *"Gladstone" class No. 188* Allen Sarle *at Oxted Surrey, in 1901. Note its spectacular cleanliness.*

Ever since the days of Stephenson's first "Patentee" 2-2-2 it had been taken as a matter of course that express passenger locomotives needed guiding wheels ahead of their driving wheels. So when one of the most able of locomotive engineers introduced 0-4-2 type locomotives to haul the London, Brighton & South Coast Railway's principal expresses, his colleagues won-

(260km), occupied another 8¼ hours. When this fleet of bogie engines had become established, improvements were made, the timings for the two sections of main line coming down to 4 hours and 6 hours respectively. This occurred in 1890.

One of the problems of the HR was that traffic was either a feast—during the beginning and end of the shooting season for example—or a famine. Foxwell (*Express Trains, English and Foreign,* 1895) records the Euston-Inverness mail train leaving Perth one August morning 1888 with two 4-4-0s and *36* carriages, including horseboxes and saloons from companies all over Britain. Not surprisingly and in spite of a banker being provided for the 18 miles (29km) of 1 in 75 (1.3 per cent) from Blair Atholl to Druimachdar Summit, 22 minutes had been lost against the schedule by the time Kingussie was reached. These 4-4-0s stayed in charge of principal Highland expresses until Peter Drummond's bigger 4-4-0s and 4-6-0s arrived at the turn of the century.

David Jones' predecessor at Inverness was William Stroudley, who introduced to the HR his original, handsome and celebrated livery of yellow ochre, more famous for its use on the London, Brighton & South Coast Railway. The "Duke" class first appeared in this colouring although it was not long before David Jones's own green livery was adopted. The only Highland locomotive which is preserved, "Jones' Goods" 4-6-0 No103 of 1894, is (incorrectly) decked out in the yellow colour—this being as near as one can get to a preserved Highland 4-4-0. The last "Duke" to survive was the one which gave the class its name. No.67, *The Duke,* later *Cromartie,* ceased work in 1923; the last of the associated classes (No.95 *Strathcarron*) was withdrawn as London, Midland & Scottish No14274 in 1928, well before the age of preservation.

Above: *"Duke" class No.82* Fife *passing Welch's Cabin at Inverness en route to the south. The lines to the left lead into the departure platforms of the station. Arriving trains both then and now proceed straight on and back into the arrival platforms.*

dered. But there was no need.

William Stroudley had been enticed away from the Highlands of Scotland by the LBSCR directors in 1871 in order to put the Company's then rather messy locomotive affairs in order. He was a man who believed that the best practice was also the most economical, and that good looks were important in locomotives. Stroudley belongs to that handful of locomotive men whose creations stayed in service for more than seventy years.

The last of his masterpieces was the express passenger locomotive class known as the "Gladstone", after the name bestowed on the prototype which first saw the light of day outside the company's own Brighton works in December 1882. Over the next eight years 35 more were built. In 1889 No189 *Edward Blount* crossed the channel and won a Gold Medal at the Paris Exhibition. Once the exhibition was over No189 was tried out on the Paris, Lyons & Mediterranean Railway's Paris-Laroche section of the main line. The locomotive did very well, achieving 69½mph (111km/h) on level road with a heavy train, but, alas, William Stroudley caught a chill during the trials and died in Paris at the early of age of 56. But some of his locomotives (the famous "Terrier" class) were still in service with British Railways in the 1960s.

The success of the "Gladstone" locomotives lay, like that of most of the successful types described in this book, as much in their robustness and simplicity as in their sound design. For example, the slide-valves were placed under the cylinders, but the port faces were inclined when seen in elevation so that the Stephenson's valve gear would work them direct without the intervention of rocking levers. In the absence of guiding wheels in front, springing had special attention with leaf springs on the leading axle and more flexible coil springs on the centre axle. One complication that was considered worthwhile was the installation of equipment to allow the exhaust steam to be condensed in the feed water, some of the waste heat being recovered thereby. Another was air-driven assistance—air was conveniently available from the Westinghouse air brake supply—for the screw reversing gear.

Whilst Stroudley was a man of his time and therefore a strict disciplinarian, the above was an example of his consideration for the men. He also insisted that the driver's name should be painted up in gold paint in the cab of the locomotive he drove; anyone visiting No.216 *Gladstone,* now on display in the National Railway Museum at York, should look for William Love's name. This practice led to a wonderfully high standard of service. Incidentally, *Gladstone* was almost certainly the first main-line express locomotive to be preserved by a private group—in this case the Stephenson Locomotive Society, who bought her in 1927 from the Southern Railway, successor to the LBSCR. They were asked the princely sum of £140 and this included re-boilering and other work to restore the engine to near enough her original appearance. She was painted in that wonderful Stroudley yellow ochre livery and given a home in the London & North Eastern Railway's original museum at York.

As regards their work, the "Gladstone" class worked most of the principal LBSCR expresses including the London-Brighton Pullman trains, predecessors of the famed "Brighton Belle". They were capable of keeping a 60-minute timing with the Brighton Sunday Pullman train, introduced in 1898. The fastest timing today by express electric train is only five minutes less.

Vittorio Emanuele II 4-6-0

Italy:
Upper Italy Railroads (SFAI), 1884

Tractive effort: 15,335lb (6,958kg).
Axle load: 35,500lb (16t).
Cylinders: (2) 18½ x 24½in (470 x 620mm).
Driving wheels: 66in (1,675mm).
Heating surface: 1,720sq ft (124m²).
Superheater: None
Steam pressure: 142lb/sq in (10kg/cm²).
Grate area: 24sq ft (2.25m²).
Fuel: 7,700lb (3.5t).
Water: 2,200gall (2,630US) (10m³).
Adhesive weight: 106,000lb (48t).
Total weight: 184,475lb (83.7t).
Overall length: 54ft 1½in (16,500mm).

The old kingdom of Piedmont, home of Count Cavour, who with King Victor Emmanuel was responsible for ending the Austrian occupation in the north of Italy and going on to create a united Italy, had one of the first important mountain railways in Europe. It connected the capital, Turin, with the port of Genoa, via the Giovi Pass. The 103-mile line was opened throughout in 1853 after a nine-year construction period.

The problem was the crossing of the Apenines at 1,180ft. (360m) altitude, 14 miles (22.5km) from Genoa. The chosen grade up from the port involved an horrendous 1 in 28½ (3½ per cent). 0-4-0 and 0-6-0 saddle tank locomotives, working in pairs back-to-back with one crew, were used by the Piedmont State Railroads with some success for working the incline.

In 1859 Italy was united and in 1865 the Giovi line became part of the Upper Italy Railroads (SFAI), which concern in 1872 set up the first railway locomotive design office in Italy. The last production of this establishment before the SFAI was absorbed into the Mediterranean System in 1885, was this absolutely remarkable machine, Europe's first 4-6-0, No.1181 *Vittorio Emanuele II.*

It was proposed to use this class for working the new and more sensibly graded Giovi diversic. line then under construction, on which (at some cost in extra mileage) the ruling grade would be reduced to 1 in 62 (1.6 per cent). It was opened in 1889, by which time many more 4-6-0s had been completed. By 1896 the class numbered 55. Ansaldo of Genoa, Miani & Silvestri of Milan and Maffei of Munich,

Class X2 4-4-0

Great Britain:
London & South Western Railway (L&SWR), 1891

Tractive effort: 16,426lb (7,453kg).
Axle load: 33,500lb (15.5t).
Cylinders: (2) 19 x 26in (483 x 660mm).
Driving wheels: 7ft 1in (2,160mm)..
Heating surface: 1,350sq ft (126.3m²).
Superheater: None.
Steam pressure: 175psi (12.3kg/cm²).
Grate area: 18.2sq ft (1.7m²).
Fuel: 8,000lb (3.5t).
Water: 3,300gall (4,000 US) (15m³).
Adhesive weight: 65,000lb (29.5t).
Total weight: 182,000lb (82.5t).
Length overall: 53ft 8in (16,383mm).

These lovely engines were the brain-children of William Adams, who, having served his time as a machine engineer and spent a period in charge of the locomotive affairs of the North London Railway, became Mechanical Engineer of the London & South Western Railway in 1878. His masterpiece was a group of 60 express passenger 4-4-0s for the London to Bournemouth and London to Exeter services of the company, constructed over the years 1891 to 1896. In the usual tradition of the day, a few small dimensional differences divided the group into four classes known as "X2", "T3", "T6" and "X6". The main difference lay in the 7ft 1in (2,160mm) driving wheels fitted to the X2s and T6s and the 6ft 7in (2,008mm) ones fitted to the others. All four classes, however, were uniform in giving first class performances. Speeds over 80mph (128km/h) were recorded on many occasions, a reflection on the excellent riding qualities of the Adams own celebrated design of bogie, which gave the drivers confidence to run at these speeds.

The outside cylinders originally had the unusual and spectacular feature of naked tail-rods—that is, the piston rods were extended to pass through glands in the front covers of each cylinder, so the rod could be seen plunging out and in when the engine was in motion. These were removed after Adams had retired in 1895; Adams' elegant store-pipe chimneys were also replaced. The inside slide valves were worked by Stephenson link motion. Running numbers were:— "X2"—577 to 596; "T3"—557 to 576; "T6"—677 to 686; "X6"—657 to 666; there was no change when the L&SWR was absorbed into the Southern Railway.

The coming of corridor coaches and restaurant cars in the early years of the century meant that the Adams 4-4-0s were soon displaced by larger locomotives from normal top-line express work, but in their last years these handsome engines could occasionally be seen on such fast prestige trains as the three- and four-car pullman specials from Southampton to London in connection with Imperial Airways' Empire flying-boat services. Of course, like everything that had wheels in the south of England, the war-time survivors were pressed into moving heavy troop trains at the time of the evacuation from Dunkirk. No.657 starred in the absurd but famous and still shown film "Oh, Mr. Porter", which was shot on the long-closed Basingstoke to Alton line.

Withdrawals began in 1930 and by the outbreak of war in 1939 the Adams 4-4-0s had almost vanished, only a dozen or so examples being left. Most of these were reprieved for the duration but by 1946 all had gone, except No.563 which in 1948 was restored for an exhibition held at Waterloo Station, London, in connection with its centenary. In due time No.563 became part of the national collection and can be seen in the museum at York.

Right: *London & South Western Railway class "X2" 4-4-0 No.563, designed by William Adams, as now restored.*

Bavaria, shared in the construction.

The locomotives had several unusual features including Gooch's valve gear outside the wheels. The working of this gear is explained in connection with Gooch's "Rover" class 4-2-2s, but here its workings are displayed in full view. The gear is actuated by two eccentrics mounted on a return crank, which in turn has its pivot set in line with the centre of the driving axle. It can be seen that when the reversing rod leading from the cab is moved, the valve rod is raised or lowered, rather than the eccentric rods and link, as in the Stephenson's gear.

The rearward position of the cylinders and the forward position of the short-wheel base bogie and smoke-box will be noted. The designers were concerned that the boiler-tubes would be too long to allow the fire to be drawn properly and to obviate this they recessed the firebox tubeplate into the boiler. This reduced the length of the tubes and increased the firebox volume, thereby forming one of the first-ever applications of a very modern feature known as a combustion chamber. The steam pressure was later raised to 156lb/sq in (11kg/cm²).

These engines were very successful and could climb the new Giovi line with 130 tons at a steady speed of 25mph (40km/h). The maximum permitted speed, of course, was double that.

These 4-6-0s had another record—the unenviable one of being the first main-line steam locomotives to be displaced from the work for which they were built by a more modern form of traction. The old Giovi line went over to three-phase electric traction at 3,300 volts, 15 cycles (Hz) in 1910 and the diversion line followed in 1914.

Below: *The "Vittorio Emanuele II" 4-6-0 as built for the Upper Italy Railroads in 1884. These locomotives worked the famous Giovi incline near Genoa.*

Teutonic Class 2-2-2-0

Great Britain:
London & North Western Railway (LNWR), 1889

Axle load: 35,000lb (16t).
Cylinders, HP: (2) 14 x 24in (356 x 610mm).
Cylinders, LP: (1) 30 x 24in (762 x 610mm).
Driving wheels: 85in (2,159mm).
Heating surface: 1,402sq ft (130m²).
Superheater: None.
Steam pressure: 175psi (12.3kg/cm²).
Grate area: 20.5sq ft (1.9m²).
Fuel: 11,000lb (5t).
Water: 1,800gall (2,160 US) (8m³).
Adhesive weight: 69,500lb (31.5t).
Total weight: 158,000lb (72t).
Length overall: 51ft 0¼in (15,552mm).

Above: *A 2-4-0 Webb compound being given an initial starting movement, manually with a pinch bar. Note the single central large low-pressure cylinder.*

The story of Francis Webb, the London & North Western Railway and the compound locomotive is one of the saddest episodes in the whole of locomotive history. Both the man and the railway were of gigantic stature and with good reason. Not for nothing was the LNWR known as "the Premier Line, the largest joint stock corporation in the World", whilst Webb himself made Crewe Works into a manufacturing unit without a rival in its ability to make everything needed by a great railway, starting with raw material. His superb non-compound 2-4-0s (on which his first three batches of compounds were based) included *Hardwicke* which still survives and runs. This locomotive showed what Webb locomotives were capable of when on 22 August 1895, the last night of the famous Race to Aberdeen, she ran the 141 miles (226km) of hilly road from Crewe to Carlisle at an average speed of 67¼mph (107.5km/h) and with a maximum of 88 (141).

In the late 1870s the idea of compounding was in the air and Webb made up his mind that this was a world that he was going to conquer. He first had a Trevithick 2-2-2 *Medusa* converted to a two-cylinder compound 2-4-0 and then in 1882 came his first three-cylinder compound 2-2-2-0 No. 66 *Experiment*. The system Webb adopted was to have two outside high pressure cylinders, 11½in (292mm) diameter driving the rear driving wheels and a great dustbin of a low pressure cylinder 26in (660mm) diameter to drive the front driving axle. There were no coupling rods. Three sets of Joy's valve gear were provided.

Apart from the mechanism of compounding and the three cylinders, the rest of the locomotive was basically a standard LNWR 2-4-0 of which a large number were in use. *Experiment* needed modifications and the first production batch of 29, built in 1883-84, had 13½in (343mm) diameter high pressure cylinders in place of 11½ (292). They were not specially economical and were bad starters—men with pinch bars were needed to give the engines an initial starting movement before they would go. One of the problems was that Webb was an autocrat and anyone who suggested that his beloved compounds were less than perfect was regarded as questioning his superior officer's judgment and hence offering his resignation. So no one told Webb how awful they were even when, inevitably, another 40, the "Dreadnought" class only slightly modified, appeared 1884-88. The only thing his hard-pressed staff could do was to "repair"—actually to *renew* in more powerful form —the fleet of simple express passenger 2-4-0s. By this means 256 new non-compound locomotives were turned out under the Chief's nose between 1887 and 1901.

In 1889 came the best of the Webb compounds, the ten "Teutonic" class; they are the basis of the drawing on this page and their particulars are listed above. The further modification in this case concerned the valve gear of the inside low pressure cylinder. Its Joy's valve gear was replaced by a "slip eccentric", a gear more familiar to manufacturers of steam toys than to full-size builders. In this arrangement a single eccentric is mounted loose on the driving axle. A pin attached to this eccentric and a stepped collar on the axle is arranged to drive it in one position relative to the crank for forward motion, and in another one for going backwards. The cut-off point of steam admission to the high pressure cylinders could be adjusted in the normal way, using the unusual inverted outside arrangement of Joy's valve gear visible in the drawing above. The arrangement worked well except

Below: *L&NWR Webb compound 2-4-0* Jeanie Deans *of the "Teutonic" class.*

for one problem; this typically occurred when a locomotive, having first backed on to its train, tried to start. The slip eccentric gear naturally still would be in reverse, but when the driver opened the throttle, the idea was that the two high-pressure cylinders would taken in the steam and move the train. By the time it had moved forward half-a-revolution of the driving wheels the inside slip eccentrics would have moved round into the forward position; therefore, when the first puff of steam exhausted from a high pressure cylinder into the low, off she would go. Alas, should the engine slip or spin its rear high pressure driving wheels when starting (which, as on all the 2-2-2-0 compounds were not coupled to the front low pressure ones), the low pressure cylinders would still have their valve gear in reverse when they received steam. The result was a stationary locomotive with its two pairs of driving wheels revolving in opposite directions!

Even so, the "Teutonic" locomotives were good once they got going—No.1304 *Jeanie Deans* was famous for regularly working and keeping time on the 2 p.m. Scottish Express from Euston to Crewe during the whole of 1890s. No.1309 *Adriatic* even starred in that legendary final night of racing in 1895, although her run from Euston to Crewe at an average speed of 63.1mph (102km/h) was not quite as great as achievement as that of her simple equivalent *Hardwicke* on the next stage; still it was certainly a very respectable effort. These ten "Teutonic" class which almost managed to approach simple performance, were the pinnacle of Webb's achievement with his compounds. It says little for the management structure of the old LNWR that no one could stop him building a further 140 compound express locomotives before he retired in 1903, none of which approached even the modest abilities of the "Teutonic", and all of which were an embarassment to the operating authorities of the Premier Line.

Rover Class 4-2-2

Great Britain:
Great Western Railway (GWR), 1888

Above: *Great Western Railway broad-gauge "Rover" class 4-2-2 locomotive* Tornado. *Engines of this basic design ruled the broad gauge lines from 1846 until their demise in 1892 and were renowned for their speed and power. Daniel Gooch was the designer.*

Tractive effort: 9,[illegible]9lb (4,370kg).
Axle load: 35,800lb (16.3t).
Cylinders: (2) 18 x 24in (457 x 610mm).
Driving wheels: 96in (2,438mm).
Heating surface: 2,085sq ft (193.7m²).
Superheater: None.
Steam pressure: 140psi (9.8kg/cm²).
Grate area: 24sq ft (22.7m²).
Fuel: 7,000lb (3t).
Water: 3,000gall (3,600 US) (13.5m³).
Adhesive weight: 36,000lb (16t).
Total weight: 160,000lb (73t).
Length overall: 47ft 6in (14,478mm).

As the leaders of the Great Western's broad gauge express fleet, these legendary locomotives were the direct successors to the "Fire Fly" class 2-2-2s, the passenger version of Gooch's famous standard locomotives. The prototype *Great Western* of 1846 was basically a stretched version of the 2-2-2 with the grate area dimension enhanced by 68 per cent and the nominal tractive effort by 36 per cent. The penalty was a 21 per cent increase in weight, the price being paid when *Great Western* broke her leading axle at speed near Shrivenham soon after completion. Alteration to a 4-2-2 followed, but the leading pairs of wheels were held in the frames rather than mounted in a pivoted separate bogie.

Even before this had been done, on 13 June 1846, *Great Western* hauled a 100-ton train from Paddington to Swindon in 78 minutes for the 77½ miles (124km). The design was so sound that it was repeated again and again, each time with slight enlargement and modernisation until the final batch which is the subject of this description appeared in 1888, over 40 years after the prototype was built and only 4 years before the broad gauge was finally abolished. Typically about 24 were in service at any one time, 54 being built altogether.

In order to provide for the expansive use of steam the gab valve gear originally fitted to the standard locomotives was replaced by Gooch's own valve gear, probably devised to get round the Stephenson patent to which the gear related closely. Both valve gears have a pair of eccentrics, one set for forward running and the other for reverse; the little ends of the eccentric rods are connected by a curved link. The curve of the Gooch link, however, faces the opposite way, being concave towards the cylinders instead of convex. The gear is adjusted by lifting or lowering the valve rod and die block, rather than by moving the link and eccentric rod assembly as in the Stephenson gear.

Apart from general sound construction the reasons for the success and longevity of these locomotives lay very much in the broad gauge itself. Most British locomotives of the day carried their cylinders and motion as well as their fire-beds between the frames, which themselves had to be between the wheels; it is therefore not surprising that an extra width of 27¾ inches (705mm) which there was to play with—the difference between the 7ft 0¼in (2,140mm) and 4ft 8½in (1,435mm) gauges—could be used to advantage by designers. For example, the wide firebox, which was later to come as a rightly extolled development at the expense of some complication on standard gauge, had come automatically many years before on the broad. Ample-sized valve chests could be placed between ample-sized cylinders and there was also plenty of room to get at the very sturdy and simple layout that resulted.

For 46 years, then, the Gooch 4-2-2s ruled the Great Western. The "Flying Dutchman" express from Paddington to Newton Abbot was entrusted to one of them in 1892 just as it was in 1848 when it was the fastest train in the world. Later versions naturally had much modification in respect of details and fittings; there were even such mollycoddling devices as exiguous cabs for the enginemen! Right up to the end also, no numbers were carried, only names; and what names, too—*Rover, Swallow, Balaklava, Hirondelle, Timour, Iron Duke, Tartar, Sultan, Warlock, Lightning, Amazon, Crimea, Eupatoria, Inkerman, Courier, Bulkely, Dragon, Great Britain, Emperor, Sebastopol, Alma, Prometheus, Great Western, Tornado. Tornado* was the last broad gauge engine built in July 1888.

E.L. Ahrons, that distinguished observer of late-Victorian train working, described how, in the last years of the broad gauge, he timed *Lightning* running down Wellington bank just west of Taunton at just over 81mph (130 km/h). It was, he said, "his highest speed, not only on the broad gauge but also on any railway until many years afterwards".

Johnson Midland Single 4-2-2 Great Britain: Midland Railway (MR), 1887

Tractive effort: 14,506lb (6,582kg).
Axle load: 39,500lb (18t).
Cylinders: (2) 19 x 26in (483 x 660mm).
Driving wheels: 93½in (2,375mm).
Heating surface: 1,237sq ft (115m²).
Superheater: None.
Steam pressure: 170psi (12kg/cm²).
Grate area: 19.6sq ft (1.82m²).
Fuel: 8,800lb (4t).
Water: 3,500gall (4,200 US) (16m³).
Adhesive weight: 39,500lb (18t).
Total weight: 181,500lb (82.5t).
Length overall: 52ft 7½in (16,038mm).

The Midland Railway of England was noted for having trains which were fast, frequent and, consequently, light. One reason was certainly the fact that at only one town on the system—Kettering in Northamptonshire—did the company not have to face competition. One result was that the Midland was the last railway in Britain to have a fleet of single-driver locomotives and the only one to build them on into the twentieth century.

The first of the single-wheelers of S.W. Johnson, known colloquially as "Spinners", was constructed at the Company's Derby Works in 1887, after an interval of 21 years during which only coupled engines were made. By 1900, there were 95 locomotives in the class, made up of successive batches which differed slightly in main dimensions. Standardisation was then something the Midland left to newer and brasher railways! The dimensions given above refer to the "115" batch of 1897, considered to be the best.

Above: *Midland Railway 4-2-2 No.176 at Bedford station circa 1900. Note the horse-box as the leading vehicle of the train.*

Their elegance was enhanced by a noble crimson lake livery—which was kept unbelievably clean. In fact, it is said that it was the practice for MR shed foreman to feel behind the *backs* of the wheels with white gloves to find if the engines had been sufficiently groomed to be allowed out in traffic. Trays were placed under the engines when on shed in order to collect any oil drips which might sully the clean floor

Class 17 4-4-0 Belgium: Belgian State Railways (SNCB), 1902

Tractive effort: 20,261lb (9,193kg).
Axle load: 40,000lb (18t).
Cylinders: (2) 19 x 26in (482 x 660mm).
Driving wheels: 78¾in (1,980mm).
Heating surface: 1,370sq ft (128m²).
Superheater: See Text.
Steam pressure: 200psi (14kg/cm²).
Grate area: 22.5sq ft (2.1m²).
Fuel: 9,900lb (4.5t).
Water: 4,125gall (4,950 US) (18.5m³).
Adhesive weight: 80,500lb (36.5t).
Total weight: 219,500lb (99.5t).
Length overall: 57ft 4in (17,475mm).

Late in the nineteenth century, the railways of Belgium were specially notable for originality in locomotive design. Some strange-looking 2-4-2s whose appearance was made the stuff of nightmares by the use of *square* chimneys, were to the fore on prime passenger workings; also, of course, the names Alfred Belpaire and Egide Walschaerts are those of two Belgian locomotive engineers whose inventions were used world-wide on the steam locomotive.

So it is rather strange that just before the turn of the century this oldest of nationalised railway systems went overseas to a foreign builder for a foreign design; moreover, one that was among the most simple and conventional and which included among its features neither a Belpaire firebox nor sets of Walschaerts valve gear.

Locomotive engineer J.F. McIntosh of the Caledonian Railway had produced his famous "Dunalaistair" 4-4-0s in 1897 and for many years these engines were the mainstay of express passenger operations on the line in question. Most of those built survived after 1923 into London Midland & Scottish Railway days and some even into the British Railways era after 1948. There were four "marks" (known as Dunalaistair I to Dunalaistair IV) and before 1914 they were bedecked in the superb Caledonian blue livery. All were built at the company's St. Rollox works in Glasgow.

The Caledonian Railway was so proud of their new locomotive giant that they sent her to be displayed at the Brussels exhibition of 1897, from whence the engine returned with a gold medal. An unexpected result was an order from the Belgian State Railways for 5 duplicate locomotives, to be built by Nielson Reid & Co. (a predecessor of the North British Locomotive company), also of Glasgow. Following this, 40 more were built by Belgian firms in 1899 and 1900; all the locomotives were known as Belgian class "17". Subsequently, an enlarged version,

of a Midland loco depot! In such circumstances it is hardly surprising that the quality of maintenance was very high and this was also a factor in enabling low-powered locomotives to handle the traffic satisfactorily. It was also a factor in permitting all the mechanism—two sets of main motion plus two sets of Stephenson's valve gear—to be tucked away out of sight, but not out of mind so far as the fitters and drivers were concerned.

Another reason for the return of the single-wheeler was the invention of the steam sanding gear, which blew sand under the driving wheels just that bit more reliably than the gravity sanding previously used. Air sanding would have been just that bit more reliable still but, alas, the Midland showed a preference for the vacuum rather than the air brake and so compressed air was not available on MR locomotives. Good sanding gear was absolutely essential for a single-driver locomotive with limited adhesive weight.

Express trains of seven or eight bogie carriages weighing between 200 and 250 tons were just right for these celebrated locomotives. In dry calm weather heavier loads could be managed and there are records of trains up to 350 tons being handled and time being kept. They were also certainly very speedy, with maxima of around 90mph (144 km/h) having been recorded. Another role for these beautiful locomotives was that of acting as pilots to the equally celebrated Midland 4-4-0s.

Before a logical system was adopted, numbers were allocated at random, but after 1907 the "Spinners" class occupied Nos. 600 to 694. Naming, like standardisation in those days, was not a Midland thing but, quite exceptionally, one of the last and twentieth-century batch—the ones with the big bogie tenders heavier than the locomotive—was given the name *Princess of Wales.*

One Midland single has survived; No.118 of the batch built in 1897 was set aside in Derby Works after withdrawal in 1928. Beautifully restored and with a fake wooden chimney now replaced by a proper one, she ran in steam at the Rocket 150 Cavalcade in June 1980.

Above: *The restored Midland Railway "Johnson Single" 4-2-2 No.673 as it appeared during the crowd-pulling "Rocket 150" celebrations in 1975.*

Below: *Midland Railway "Johnson Single" 4-2-2 in all the glory of its superb crimson lake livery.*

class "18", was constructed, bringing the total to 185 locomotives by 1905. There was also a 4-4-2 tank engine version, constructed to the tune of 115 examples, which never existed on the Caledonian Railway.

Such continental features as bogie tenders and air brakes were already part of the design and the only obvious modification specified concerned the exiguous cabs of the original Scottish locomotives. These were altered to provide greater protection for the enginemen by the addition of side windows.

Left: *Belgian State Railway class 18 4-4-0 as restored and preserved today.*

Class S3 4-4-0

Germany:
Royal Prussian Union Railway (KPEV), 1893

Axleload: 35,000lb (15.6t).
Cylinders, HP: (1) 18.9 x 23.6in (480 x 600mm).
Cylinders, LP: (1) 26.6 x 23.6in (680 x 600mm).
Driving wheels: 78in (1,980mm).
Heating surface: 1,267sq ft (117.7m²).
Superheater: See descriptive text.
Steam pressure: 171psi (12kg/cm²).
Grate area: 25.0sq ft (2.3m²).
Fuel: 11,000lb (5.0t).
Water: 4,730gall (5,680US) (21.5m³).
Adhesive weight: 69,000lb (30.9t).
Total weight*: 112,000lb (50.5t).
Length overall: 57ft 7in (17,560mm).

*(*engine only)*

Above: *A Prussian class "S3" 4-4-0, the 5,000th locomotive built by the engineering firm of Borsig for the Prussian Railways.*

The passenger engines built by the Royal Prussian Union Railway in the 1880s were 2-4-0s with outside cylinders, but towards the end of the decade the desire for higher speeds and great comfort (and thus greater weight) brought a need for larger locomotives. At that time August von Borries, well known for the system of compounding which bears his name, was locomotive superintendent at Hanover, and the Minister of Public Works sent him on a tour of England and America to study locomotive developments in those countries. Von Borries reported that to carry the larger boiler which would be needed, the engines would need an extra axle, and that the best arrangement would be the American type of 4-4-0. This would give better riding at speed than the existing 2-4-0s with their long front overhang.

In 1890 Henschel built a pair of two-cylinder compound 4-4-0 locomotives to von Borries' design, and in the following year the same firm built four more engines of the same wheel arrangement to the designs of Lochner, the locomotive superintendent at Erfurt, two compound and two with simple expansion. A total of 150 engines were later built to the Erfurt simple-expansion design, but experience with these engines convinced the management of the superiority of von Borries' compounds, and in 1892 he produced an improved version of his design. This was the "S3", the "S" denoting "schnellzuglokomotiv", or express engine, and the digit being the serial number of the type from the introduction of this method of classification. The "S3" was highly successful, and in the period from 1892 to 1904 a total of 1,027 engines of this design were built for the Prussian railways, as well as 46 for other German state railways. The engines eventually worked most of the express trains in Prussia. In addition to the "S3"s, a further 424 locomotives were built to the same design, but with smaller driving wheels, and classified "P4".

The bogie was placed symmetrically under the cylinders and smokebox, and with the leading coupled axle set well back to give as long a connecting rod as possible, the layout showed clearly the influence of von Borries' American visit. Outside Walschaert's (Heusinger) valve gear drove slide valves set at an angle above the cylinders. The engines were rated to haul 320 tonnes at 47mph (75km/h) on the level, and 150 tonnes at 31mph (50km/h) on a gradient of 1 in 100 (1 per cent), and they established a reputation for economy in coal consumption and for smooth riding.

By its sheer size the "S3" class earns a notable place in locomotive history, but it is also important as being the first class to which steam superheating was applied. The need for superheating comes from a physical phenomenon—that water evaporates to steam at a definite temperature dependent on the prevailing pressure; thus at the working pressure of the "S3", 171psi (12kg/cm²), the temperature is 376°F (197°C). With water present in the boiler, the steam temperature cannot exceed that of the water. When

Below: *The class "S3" 4-4-0 was one of the most successful passenger locomotives to run in Germany. Over 1,000 were built around the turn of the century. The class was notable as being the first major application of superheating to steam traction; this offered a major improvement in efficiency at little cost.*

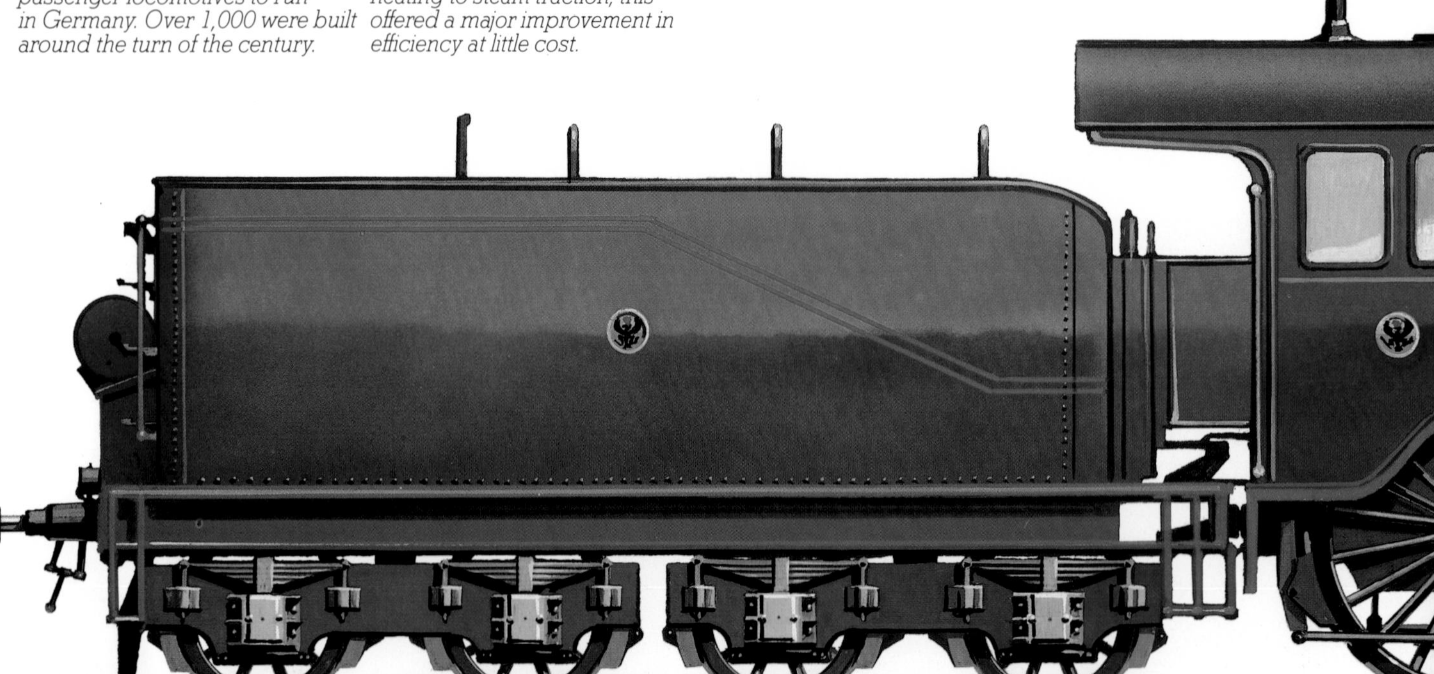

steam is drawn from the boiler it carries some particles of water with it, and when the steam comes into contact with the comparatively cool metal of the valves and cylinders, it loses that, and further particles of water form by condensation. Much of the work done on the piston is by the steam expanding after the valve has closed. Water has no capacity for expanding, and its presence in the cylinder is therefore a loss; it has been heated to the temperature in the boiler to no effect.

If the steam can be heated after it has left the boiler, and is no longer in contact with the mass of water there, the particles of moisture in the steam can be evaporated, making the steam dry. Still further application of heat causes the temperature of the steam to rise, and it becomes superheated. The main advantage of superheated steam is that if it is cooled slightly on making contact with the cool cylinder walls, no condensation occurs until all the superheat has been removed. Superheating is thus a means of eliminating condensation in the cylinder, and thereby making better use of the heat in the steam.

The attractions of superheating had been known to engineers for many years, but it was not until the 1890s that practicable designs of superheater were produced, by far the most important being those designed by Dr Wilhelm Schmidt of Kassel. The various schemes produced had in common that, after leaving the boiler, the steam flow was divided between a number of small tubes, known as "elements", by a distribution box or "header". After being heated in the elements, the steam was collected in another header, and passed through the main steam pipes to the cylinders. In Schmidt's first design, known as the flame tube superheater, a number of the boiler tubes were replaced by a large tube 17.5in (445mm) in diameter, and the elements were inserted into this tube. It was intended that the tube should be sufficiently large for flames to reach the elements (flames from the firebox die out quickly on entering a small tube).

Schmidt found an enthusiastic supporter of his ideas in Robert Garbe, who was chief engineer of the Berlin division of the Prussian railways. With Garbe's support the flame tube superheater was fitted to two 4-4-0 locomotives, an "S3" and a "P4". The "S3" was completed in April 1898, and made its first trial trip on the thirteenth of that month, a notable date in locomotive history. Although the results were encouraging, trouble was experienced with distortion of the large flame tube. Schmidt therefore produced two more designs, in one of which the bundle of elements was housd in the smokebox, and in the other of which a number of the boiler tubes were replaced by tubes slightly larger, and each element made a return loop in one of these tubes.

In 1899 two new "S3" locomotives were fitted with the smokebox superheater, and they were also given piston valves in place of slide valves. With the combination of superheater and well-proportioned piston valves, these engines contained the essential ingredients of the final phase of development of the steam locomotive.

One of these two engines was exhibited at the Paris Exhibition of 1900, and attracted considerable attention. In service a reduction in coal consumption of 12 per cent was achieved compared with a standard "S3", but it was recognised that the temperature of the gases in the

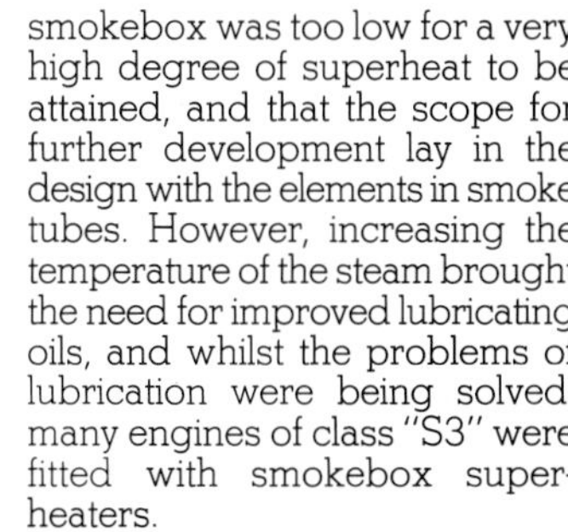

smokebox was too low for a very high degree of superheat to be attained, and that the scope for further development lay in the design with the elements in smoke tubes. However, increasing the temperature of the steam brought the need for improved lubricating oils, and whilst the problems of lubrication were being solved, many engines of class "S3" were fitted with smokebox superheaters.

The intensive development work needed to perfect superheating was largely due to the genius of Schmidt, and in little more than ten years after the first application of the smokebox superheater, the smoke tube design was virtually a standard fitting for large new locomotives; it was first applied to a Belgian Class 35 Caledonian type 4-6-0 in 1903. For a modest outlay, and with little increase in weight, an improvement in coal consumption of up to 20 per cent was obtained, and, equally important in some countries, a similar economy in water. For many engineers the superheater was an alternative to compounding, as it gave a fuel economy similar to that obtained by compounding, but without the mechanical complications of the compound. Others regarded superheating as an extra advantage to be added to that of compounding. Over a period of years after the fitting of the first superheater, both these points of view were apparent on the Prussian railways, and after a succession of superheated simple engines, a four-cylinder compound 4-6-0 was built.

A total of 34 of the "S3" locomotives survived to be incorporated in the stock of German State Railway in 1924.

Below: *The predecessors of the "S3" class were these "S1" class 2-4-0s, of which 242 were built between 1877 and 1885 for the Prussian railway system.*

No. 999 4-4-0 **United States:** New York Central & Hudson River RR (NYC & HRRR), 1893

Below: *The famous record-breaking 4-4-0 No.999 of the New York Central & Hudson River Railroad.*

Tractive effort: 16,270lb (7,382kg).
Axle load: 42,000lb (19t).
Cylinders: (2) 19 x 24in (483 x 610mm).
Driving wheels: 86in (2,184mm).
Heating surface: 1,927sq ft (179m²).
Superheater: None
Steam pressure: 190psi (12.6kg/cm²).
Grate area: 30.7sq ft (2.85m²).
Fuel: 15,400lb (7t).
Water: 2,950gall (3,500US) (13.5m³).
Adhesive weight: 84,000lb (38t).
Total weight: 204,000lb (92.5t).
Overall length: 57ft 10in (17,630mm).

When on 10 May 1893 New York Central & Hudson River Railroad No.999 hauled the Empire State Express at 112.5mph (180km/h) down a 1 in 350 (0.28 per cent) grade near Batavia, New York State, it was not only a world record for steam railways but for any kind of transport. The only problem is that it is not a question of "when" but of "if".

The conductor timed the train (presumably with his service watch) to travel between two marks a mile apart. With four heavy Wagner cars weighing 50-55 tons each, about 2,000 cylinder horse-power would be needed and this would seem to be just a little too much to expect; not so much as regards steam production at a corresponding rate, but in getting that steam in and out of the cylinders in such quantities. A speed of 102.8mph (166km/h) over 5 miles, timed the previous night, is a little more credible, but both must, alas, be regarded as "not proven".

The man responsible for this locomotive's existence was no great railroad tycoon, but an irrepressible patent medicine salesman called Daniels, taken on as the line's passenger agent in New York. He persuaded the management to run this exclusive Empire State Express between New York and Chicago during the period of the Colombian Exposition; the time of 20 hours for the 960 miles (1,536km) was an unprecedented average speed for any journey of similar length.

This combination of speed and luxury was shortly to result in one of the most famous trains of the world, the legendary year-round "Twentieth Century Limited", running daily from New York to Chicago.

No.999 was specially built for the job and the train name was even painted on the tender. The NYC&HRR shops at West Albany turned out this single big-wheeled version of the road's standard 4-4-0s, themselves typical of the US locomotive of their day, with slide-valves, Stephenson's valve gear and more normal 78in (1,981mm) diameter driving wheels.

On account of the record exploit, No.999's fame is worldwide; the locomotive even figured on a US two-cent stamp in 1900. Today, much rebuilt and with those high-and-mighty drivers replaced by modest workaday ones, No.999 is on display at the Chicago Museum of Science and Industry.

Right: *No.999 as preserved for posterity. Although painted in the style of the original as built, the big 86in (2,184mm) diameter driving wheels have been replaced by less distinctive 79in (2,006mm) ones.*

Class 6 4-4-0 **Austria:** Imperial and Royal State Railways (KKStB), 1893

Axle load: 32,000lb (14.5t).
Cylinders HP: (1) 19¾ x 26¾in (500 x 680mm).
Cylinders LP: (1) 29 x 26¾in (740 x 680mm).
Driving wheels: 82½in (2,190mm).
Heating surface: 1,507sq ft (140m²).
Superheater: None.
Steam pressure: 185psi (13kg/cm²).
Grate area: 31sq ft (2.9m²).
Fuel: 16,000lb (7.25t).
Water: 3,650gall (4,400 US) (16.5m³).
Adhesive weight: 63,000lb (28t).
Total weight: 207,000lb (94t).
Length overall: 54ft 1in (16,480mm).

Karl Gölsdorf, head of the locomotive department of the Imperial and Royal Austrian State Railways was an original thinker as well as a first rate engineer and, whilst his ideas never became part of the main stem of development, they not only worked but suited local conditions extremely well.

These little 4-4-0s built at Floridsdorf (a suburb of Vienna) illustrated this very vividly. They were compound locomotives but with only two cylinders, thereby avoiding one of the chief drawbacks of compounding, that is, the complexity that normally results. Of course, with a two-cylinder compound it is absolutely vital to be able to admit high-pressure steam to the low-pressure cylinder when starting, otherwise the locomotive would often never move at all. Even so, the means to do this result in making the engine more difficult to drive, another drawback normally associated with compounding.

Gölsdorf got over this problem by giving the locomotive low pressure cylinder starting ports which were only uncovered by the valves when the valve gear—Walschaert's in this case—was in full gear, as at starting from rest. Once the train was moving, the driver would reduce the cut-off and compound working would commence. In this way the method of driving differed little from that of handling a normal simple locomotive. The permitted axle load on the Austrian railways was very low and these relatively heavy locomotives could only be accommodated by means of another piece of originality. The wheelbase on these engines as in others, was set far back, so that the leading wheel was almost in line with the chimney. By this means the bogie would carry more of the weight than it would if placed in the more usual position, and the maximum axle load was reduced in relation to the total weight.

In service, this class proved itself to be not only powerful but speedy, with a maximum permitted speed of 81mph (130km/h). It was possible to reduce the scheduled time of the best expresses from Vienna to Karlsbad (now known as Karlovy Vary)

from 12 hours to 8. It is no credit to the politicians of Europe that the fastest time between the same two cities today nearly 90 years later is 11 hours 29 minutes.

A striking feature in the appearance of some Gölsdorf locomotives, including these class "6" 4-4-0s, was the pipe connecting the two domes. Technically, this is not so remarkable since in most steam locomotives a main steam pipe runs forward from the point at which steam is collected although it is customary—except in Russia and China—to have it inside the boiler.

Right: *KKStB class "6" 4-4-0. Note the external steam pipe connecting steam dome to throttle*

I-1 Class 4-6-0

United States:
Lake Shore & Michigan Southern Railroad (LS&MSRR), 1900

Tractive effort: 23,800lb (10,800kg).
Axle load: 45,000lb (20.5t)..
Cylinders: (2) 20 x 28in (508 x 711mm).
Driving wheels: 80in (2,032mm).
Heating surface: 2,917sq ft (271m²).
Superheater: None.
Steam pressure: 200psi (14.1kg/cm²).
Grate area: 33.6sq ft (3.1m²).
Fuel: 17,500lb (8t).
Water: 6,000gall (7,200 US) (27.2m³).
Adhesive weight: 135,000lb (61t).
Total weight: 300,000lb (136t).
Length overall: 62ft 3in (18,914mm)..

As has been described, the "American Standard" 4-4-0 hauled most USA passenger express trains from the 1850s

Class D16sb 4-4-0

United States:
Pennsylvania Railroad (PRR), 1895

Tractive effort: 23,900lb (10,850kg)
Axleload: 52,000lb (23.5t).
Cylinders: (2) 20½ x 26in (521 x 660mm).
Driving wheels: 68in (1727mm).
Heating surface: 1400sq ft (130.1m²).
Superheater: 253sq ft (23.5m²).
Steam pressure: 175psi . (12.3kg/cm²).
Grate area: 33.2sq ft (3.1m²).
Fuel: 26,000lb (11.8t).
Water: 4,660gall (5,600US) (21.2m³).
Adhesive weight: 98,500lb (44.7t).
Total weight: 281,000lb (127.4t).
Length overall: 67ft 0in (20,422mm).

By the end of the 19th century the Pennsylvania Railroad had established a reputation for large locomotives, mostly built in own Altoona shops, and characterized outwardly by the Belpaire firebox, a rarity in North America. Its 4-4-0 locomotives were no exception, and the high water mark of the type was reached with the "D16" class, introduced in 1895. With cylinders 18½ x 26in (470 x 660mm) and 185psi (13.0 kg/cm²) boilers, they were large engines for their day, and their appearance was the more impressive because the firebox was placed above the frames, making the boiler higher than was usual at this period.

Two varieties were built initially, one with 80 in (2,032mm) driving wheels for the more level divisions ("D16a"), and the other with 68 in (1,727mm) wheels for the hillier parts of the road ("D16"). The "D16a" engines soon established a reputation for high speed, as they were used in competition with the Atlantic City Railroad on the 58½mile (94km) "racetrack" between Camden and Atlantic

until the 1880s. However, there came a time when loads began to outstep the capacity of locomotives with only two driven axles.

The obvious development was simply to add a third coupled axle, and this is what was done. Some of the best features of the 4-4-0 were retained in the 4-6-0 such as the bogie or leading truck to guide the locomotive, but in other ways problems arose. The ashpan was liable to get mixed up with the rear axle, for example, and the gap between the leading driving wheels and the cylinders, which on the 4-4-0 made the motion so easy to get at, became filled up. Even so, there was a period at the end of the 1800s when the 4-6-0 ruled the express passenger scene in the USA. About 16,000 examples went into service there all told, most between 1880 and 1910.

The high-wheeled example chosen to illustrate this famous type was built by the Brooks Locomotive Works of Dunkirk, New York State in 1900 for the Lake Shore & Michigan Southern Railroad. They were intended to take charge of the prime varnish trains of the Western part of the New York to Chicago main line belonging to what was soon to become the New York Central Railroad.

Kipling wrote of these great days in that evocative short story called ".007" (collected in *The Day's Work*) but in fact they were to be brief. Wide fireboxes, piston valves and superheaters were shortly to replace narrow fireboxes, slide valves and the use of saturated steam, so changing the world of steam for ever. In fact, the paint was hardly dry on these locomotives before the LS&MS ordered some 2-6-2s with wide fireboxes over the trailing pony trucks. However, the propensity of the flanges of the wheels of the leading single-axle pony truck of the 2-6-2s to ride up over the head of the rails at high speeds put these 4-6-0s back in charge of the legendary Twentieth Century Limited service running between New York and Chicago shortly after it was introduced on 15 June 1902.

The timing over the 960 miles (1,536km) between New York's Grand Central Terminal and La Salle Street station in Chicago was 20 hours, an average speed of 48mph (77km/h). This included several stops for servicing and changing locomotives and much slow running in such places as Syracuse, where the main line in those days ran along the main street. Overall the schedule was one of the hardest in the world.

The train originally consisted of a buffet-library car, dining car and three sleeping cars, the last of which had an observation saloon complete with brass-railed open platform. The comforts offered were the equivalent of the highest grade of hotel.

One factor in all this comfort and luxury was the great weight of these 80ft (24.3m) Pullman cars even though there were only five of them. So soon enough it was necessary to increase the amount of accommodation provided and accordingly these 4-6-0s had to be replaced. But even if their days of glory were few, these locomotives with their 80-inch (2,032mm) drivers did wonders with what was then one of the hardest schedules in the world.

Left: *Lake Shore & Michigan Central Railroad "I-1" class 4-6-0 No.604 heads the "Twentieth Century Limited".*

City. On this service one famous driver was credited with covering an eight-mile stretch at 102mph (164km/h). On another occasion the same driver worked a Presidential special over the 90 miles (145km) from Philadelphia to Jersey City at an average of 72mph (116km/h).

The mechanical quality of the design was well demonstrated by engine No.816, which distinguished itself by covering 300,000 miles (483,000km) on the middle division of the PRR in three years and four months, without shopping or other heavy repair. This was a notable feat for its day.

A total of 426 engines were built in five sub-classes of "D16" between 1895 and 1910. Apart from the two driving wheel sizes, their main dimensions were identical as built. With the introduction of Atlantics and then Pacifics in the new century, the "D16"'s were displaced from the best trains, but the class was given a new lease of life from 1914 onwards when nearly half of them were modernised in line with the later engines. Slightly larger cylinders with piston valves were fitted, still with the inside Stephenson's valve gear, and the boiler was given a Schmidt's superheater, with the pressure reduced slightly. Most of the rebuilds were the smaller-wheeled engines, and these became "D16sb" (see the dimensions at the head of this article). In this form they settled down to working numerous branch lines, and three of them were still engaged in this work early in World War II. One of these three, No.1223 built in 1905, was preserved on the Strasburg Rail Road in its native state.

Left: *On the Strasburg Railroad, preserved Pennsylvania RR class "D16" 4-4-0 No.1223 calls at Groff's Drove in July 1970.*

Below: *The superb quality of the restoration work done by the Strasburg Tourist RR is demonstrated by their D16 4-4-0.*

Below: *A head-on view of preserved "D16" class 4-4-0 No.1223 at Strasburg, Pennsylvania, USA.*

Class Q1 4-4-0

Great Britain:
North Eastern Railway (NER), 1896

Tractive effort: 16,953lb (7,690kg).
Axle load: 42,000lb (19t).
Cylinders: (2) 20 x 26in (508 x 660mm).
Driving wheels: 91¼in (2,315mm).
Heating surface: 1,216sq ft (113m²).
Superheater: None.
Steam pressure: 175psi (12.3kg/cm²).
Grate area: 20.75sq ft (1.93m²).
Fuel: Coal, 11,200lb (5t).
Water: 4,000 gall (4,800 US) (18m³).
Adhesive weight: 77,000lb (35t).
Total weight: 206,000lb (93.5t).
Length overall: 56ft 3in (17,145mm).

A racing locomotive! Not just a fast-running locomotive that sometimes went very fast, but one that was specially and uniquely built for the competitive racing of public trains. The intention was to get a trainload of passengers from London to Scotland before a rival one running on a competing line. The East Coast and the West Coast companies had raced each other day after day in 1888 from London (Kings Cross and Euston) to Edinburgh and night after night in 1895 from London to Aberdeen. During the racing the regular timing of about 12 hours was reduced to 8hrs32min from Euston and 8hrs40min from Kings Cross. To put these figures in perspective, the present night trains from Kings Cross take just short of 10 hours for the 525 miles (840km). On the whole in 1895 the West Coast had just the best of it and so their rivals were determined to obtain revenge. How seriously that matter was taken is illustrated by the fact that the North Eastern Railway, otherwise the staidest of companies and which ran the racing trains over (mostly) straight and level tracks from York to Edinburgh, ordered some specially-designed inside-cylinder 4-4-0s to be ready for a resumption of hostilities in 1896. In the event, a derailment at Preston on the West Coast route which, although not connected with the racing, was attributed to high speed, made the competitors lose their taste for the fast running and accordingly only two of the five (Nos. 1869 and 1870) ordered were ever completed. They were known as the Q1 class.

Wilson Worsdell's approach to the problem was to connect quite conventional boiler, cylinders and motion to very large driving wheels which at 7ft 7¼in (2,315mm) were some of the largest ever provided on a coupled engine. Huge wheels might well have meant a very bizarre appearance but the proportions were worked out in such a way as to produce one of the most

Right: *North Eastern Railway "Q1" class 4-4-0 built in 1896 for the railway races.*

Camelback Class 4-4-2

United States:
Atlantic City Railroad (ACR), 1896

Tractive effort: 22,906lb (10,390kg).
Axle load: 40,000lb (18t).
Cylinders: (4) see text.
Driving wheels: 84in (2,134mm).
Heating surface: 1,835sq ft (170m²).
Superheater: none.
Steam pressure: 200psi (14kg/cm²).
Grate area: 76sq ft (7m²).
Water: 3,300 gall (4,000 US) (15m³).
Adhesive weight: 79,000lb (36t).
Total weight: 218,000lb (99t).

The unusual appearance of these strange-looking but path-finding locomotives belied a capability well ahead of their time. The Atlantic City Railroad (ACR) ran them on fast trains which took people from the metropolis of Philadelphia to resorts on the New Jersey coast. It was a 55½ mile (90km) run from Camden (across the river from Philadelphia) to Atlantic City and there was intense competition from the mighty Pennsylvania Railroad which had direct access into the big city. In July and August, for example, it was noted that the booked time of 50 minutes was kept or improved upon each day. On one day the run is reported to have been made in 46½ minutes start-to-stop, an average speed of 71.6mph (115km/h). This certainly implies steady running speed of 90mph (145km/h) or more, but reports of 100mph (160km/h) (and more) speeds with these trains should be regarded as conjecture. The "Atlantic City Flier" was certainly the fastest scheduled train in the world at that time.

Apart from broad-gauge locomotives, here is the first appearance amongst the locomotives in this book of a feature which was in the future to become an integral part of most steam passenger express locomotives—the

beautiful designs ever to run on the rails of the world. Unusually for the time, a large and comfortable cab with side windows and clerestory roof was provided for the comfort of their crews. The slide valves were placed on top of the cylinders and were driven by rocking shafts and Stephenson valve gear. The usual NER Westinghouse air brakes were fitted.

When it was apparent their exceptional services were not going to be needed, the two racers joined their normal-wheeled sisters of Class Q on normal top express passenger work. This continued until the coming of Atlantics in 1903 displaced them on the heaviest trains. A favourite turn was the Newcastle-Sheffield express, which had a remarkable scheduled start-to-stop timing of 43 minutes for the 44¼ miles (71km) from Darlington to York, at 61.7 mph (98km/h) the fastest in the world at that time. Speeds in excess of 80mph (128km/h) were needed to keep time.

In spite of being non-standard, both survived until 1930, long enough to become London & North Eastern class D18 after the amalgamation of 1923; they kept their original numbers although the green livery and polished metalwork had been replaced by plain black long before.

Left: *North Eastern Railway class "Q" 4-4-0. These engines were similar to the racing "Q1" class with normal-size wheels.*

Left: *Atlantic City Railroad "Camelback" class 4-4-2 locomotive No.1027, built in 1896. Note the high- and low-pressure cylinders mounted one above the other, the separate cab for the driver (engineer) on top of the boiler and the ornate decoration on the sides of the tender.*

wide deep firebox, for which the 4-4-2 wheel arrangement is wholly appropriate. In this case it was adopted in order to allow anthracite coal to be burnt satisfactorily, but later it was realised that a large grate was also an advantage with bituminous coal and even with oil.

Two other features of these locomotives are fascinating but to some extent freakish. As can be seen they had pairs of compound cylinders on each side, driving through a common crosshead. The arrangement was named after Samuel Vauclain head of the Baldwin Locomotive Works, and his object was to attain the advantages of compounding without its complexities. In this case the high-pressure cylinders, 13in bore by 26in stroke (330 x 660mm), were mounted on top and the low-pressure ones 22in bore x 26in stroke (559 x 660mm) below. A single set of valve gear and a single connecting rod served both cylinders of each compound pair. Alas, Vauclain compounds soon went out of fashion; as so often occurred, the work done by the HP and by the LP cylinders did not balance, and in the case of this arrangement it meant an offset thrust on the crosshead and consequent problems with maintenance.

The other oddity was the "Camelback" or "Mother Hubbard" cab on top of the boiler for the driver. The fireman, of course, had to remain in the normal position and for him a second and very exiguous shelter was also provided. The object was to improve visibility at the expense of separating the two members of the crew. The Philadelphia & Reading Railroad (later known simply as the Reading RR) which took over the ACR at this time went on to build many "Camelbacks" and the idea spread to other railroads in the area. But it was a practice which never became widely used.

Strangely enough, the name "Atlantic", which even today refers the world over to the 4-4-2 type, did not originate with these remarkable machines. Instead, it was first given to some rather prosaic 4-4-2s (without wide fireboxes) built in 1893 for the Atlantic Coast Line, a railroad which ran southwards towards Florida. Even if the ACR 4-4-2s did not give the type name to the world, the mighty Pennsy took note of the beating its competing trains received at their hands and adopted the principle involved with results described later in this narrative.

Class 500 4-6-0

Italy:
Adriatic System (RA), 1900

Axle load: 32,500lb (14t). (14.5t).
Cylinders, HP: (2) 14¾in x 25in (370 x 650mm).
Cylinders, LP: (2) 23 x 25in (580 x 650mm).
Driving wheels: 75½in (1,920mm).
Heating surface: 1,793sq ft (166.6m²).
Superheater: fitted later.
Steam pressure: 200psi (14kg/cm²).
Grate area: 32sq ft (3m²).
Fuel: 9,000lb (4t).
Water: 3,300 gall (4,000 US) (15m³).
Adhesive weight: 98,000lb (44.5t).
Total weight: 221,000lb (100t).
Length overall: 79ft 2in (24,135mm).

Above: *Italian "500" class back-to-front express engine.*

Even as early as 1825, at the time the Stockton & Darlington Railway was opened, the direction in which a locomotive went and the position from which it was driven had been established. The chimney of *Locomotion,* the S&D's original locomotive, came first in front, while the driver and fireman did their work at the other end of the boiler, that is, to the rear, where the controls and firehole door were situated. Behind them again came the tender which carried supplies of coal and water. Almost all steam locomotives built since then have followed this arrangement.

Questioning what almost seems a natural law is a hard thing to do, but there were some original minds who did so. One was Giuseppe Zara, locomotive engineer of the Italian Adriatic System (Rete Adriatica or RA), in charge of the design office at Florence. He decided that it

Class E3sd 4-4-2

United States:
Pennsylvania Railroad (PRR), 1901

Tractive effort: 27,400lb (12,400kg).
Axleload: 64,500lb (29.3t).
Cylinders: (2) 22 x 26in (559 x 660mm).
Driving wheels: 80in (2,032mm).
Heating surface: 2,041sq ft (190m²).
Superheater: 412sq ft (38m²).
Steam pressure: 205psi (14.4kg/cm²).
Grate area: 55.5sq ft (5.2m²).
Fuel: 34,200lb (15.5t).
Water: 5,660gall (6,800US) (25.7m³).
Adhesive weight: 127,500lb (58t).
Total weight: 363,500lb (165t).
Length overall: 71ft 6in (21,640mm).

In the 19th Century the standard American passenger engine was the 4-4-0, but towards the end of the century the type was reaching the limit of size which was possible on eight wheels, and train loads were still increasing. A move to ten wheels was inevitable, and there were two attractive alternatives, the 4-6-0 and the 4-4-2 or Atlantic. The former could have a greater adhesive weight, but the grate was restricted by the need to fit between the rear coupled wheels. The Atlantic had more restricted adhesive weight, but could have a very large grate. For the Pennsylvania Railroad the Atlantic was the obvious choice. The road was already laying exceptionally heavy rails, which could accept a very high axle load, whilst the locomotives had to be able to burn coal of moderate quality in great quantities.

In 1899 Altoona works produced its first two Atlantics, and they exploited the wheel arrangement to the full, with an adhesive weight of 101,600lb (46.1t) and a grate area of 68sq ft (6.3m²), more than twice that of the largest PRR 4-4-0. However, a third engine had a more modest grate of 55.5sq ft (5.2m²), and it was this size which became standard for all subsequent Atlantics, as well as for many other engines of the same period. With

Above: *a Pennsylvania Railroad class "E2" 4-4-2 at speed with a New York-Chicago express.*

this engine the pattern was set for the construction of 576 more Atlantics, all having the same wheel diameter, boiler pressure and grate area.

Although the basic dimensions were common to all the engines, successive improvements were made. The three prototypes had Belpaire tops to the fireboxes, in accordance with established Pennsylvania practice, but the next two batches, totalling 96 engines, had the more usual round-topped firebox. Thereafter the Belpaire box reappeared, and was used on all subsequent engines. The two batches mentioned above differed only in their cylinder diameter,

would be best to have the driver in front and to that end produced a 4-6-0 with the boiler and cylinders reversed on the frames. Coal was carried in a bunker on one side of the firebox, which itself was above the bogie rather than between the driving wheels. The tender trailed behind the chimney and of course carried water only.

The advantages claimed were, first, that the lookout was excellent, as good as that of any electric or diesel locomotive today. Second, the exhaust was discharged some distance behind the cab and this reduced the smoke menace in tunnels, so far as the crew were concerned.

There were four compound cylinders with an unusual arrangement. The two high-pressure cylinders were on one side, set at 180 degrees to one another; while the low-pressure pair were similarly arranged on the other. Each pair was set at 90 degrees to the pair on the other side, as in a normal locomotive. A single valve and valve chest each side, driven by sets of outside Walschaert's valve gear, controlled the admission of steam into each pair of cylinders. A number of locomotives in Italy had this arrangement of compounding, known as the Plancher system after its inventor. One drawback was that it was difficult to equalise the work done between the high-pressure and the low-pressure cylinders. The result was that a sideways swinging motion was liable to occur.

The prototype was exhibited at a meeting of the International Railway Congress held in Paris. A detail that impressed R.M. Deeley of the Midland Railway was the arrangement whereby a small opening of the regulator admitted live steam to the low-pressure cylinders, essential for starting. When the regulator was opened a little further, the locomotive changed over automatically to compound working. Deeley adopted this arrangement in his successful Midland compounds, but Zara did not use it for his remaining 42 "cab-forward" locomotives, preferring an independently worked valve instead. One reason might have been that it was desirable to use this valve to equalise the work done between the high—and low—pressure cylinders. Normally this would be a pious hope, but in the case of a Plancher compound it would coincide with making the ride more comfortable, since the high—and low—pressure cylinders were on opposite sides of the locomotive. There was therefore some prospect of drivers actually bothering to make this adjustment.

Whilst in France, tests were run with the prototype and 78 mph (126km/h) was reached with a 130-ton train. Back at home these strange locomotivs, which had become Italian State Railways 670.001 to 670.043 after the railways were nationalised in 1905, successfully worked express trains in the Po Valley for many years. They finally ceased work in the early 1940s. Most were later superheated, becoming class 671 when this was done.

Below: *This strange back-to-front steam locomotive was designed for the Italian Adriatic system at the turn of the century, Guiseppe Zara was the engineer responsible.*

class "E2" having 20.5in (521mm) cylinders, and class "E3" 22in (559mm), the intention being to use the "E3"s on heavier work. All these engines had slide valves, but in the next series, starting in 1903, piston valves were used, at first with Stephenson's valve gear, but from 1906 with Walschaert's.

By 1913 a total of 493 engines had been built, all having a boiler with a maximum diameter of 65.5in (1,664mm). By that time the Pacific was well established on the railway, and it seemed that the heyday of the Atlantic had passed. However, Axel Vogt, the Chief Mechanical Engineer, was still averse to incurring the expense of six-coupled wheels if four would suffice, and in 1910 he built a further Atlantic with another type of boiler, having the same grate area as the earlier Atlantics, but a maximum diameter of 76.75in (1,949mm), almost as large as the Pacifics, and with a combustion chamber at the front. The new engine, classified "E6", developed a higher power than the existing Pacifics at speeds above 40mph (64km/h). Two more "E6"s were then built, but with superheaters, and this made the performance even more impressive, and it was possible to increase the cylinder diameter to 23.5in (597mm).

After four years of intensive development work, a production batch of eighty "E6"s were built, having a number of changes from the prototypes, including longer boiler tubes. These engines were built at great speed between February and August 1914, that is, in the same year that the first of the famous "K4s" Pacifics was built. These engines took over the principal express workings on all the less hilly parts of the system, and during World War I they achieved prodigious feats of haulage for four-coupled engines. When large numbers of production "K4s" Pacifics appeared after the war, the "E6s" engines settled down to work on the less busy routes, mainly in New Jersey.

The smaller Atlantic soon established a reputation for high speed, but their full potential was realised in 1905 when the Pennsylvania Special was accelerated to an 18-hour schedule from Jersey City to Chicago, giving an overall average speed of 50.2mph (80.1km/h), with an average of 57.8mph (92.9km/h) over the 189 miles (304km) from Jersey City to Harrisburg. It was on the first westbound run to this schedule that "E2" No.7002 was credited with exceeding 120mph (193 km/h), but the claim was based on dubious evidence. On this service the "E2" and "E3" engines kept time with up to eight wooden coaches, totalling about 360 (short) tons, but with the introduction of the heavier steel stock, double heading became common.

The "E6s" engines were able to handle trains of 800-900 tons on the New York-Philadelphia-Washington trains, but it was on lighter trains that they produced their most spectacular performances. Their greatest distinction was to haul the Detroit Arrow between Fort Wayne and Chicago, for in 1933 this was the world's fastest train, with a start to stop average of 75.5mph (121.4 km/h) over the 64.1 miles (103km) from Plymouth to Fort Wayne and 75.3mph (121.1km/h) over 123 miles (198km) from Fort Wayne to Gary. On this service they hauled five or six steel coaches, weighing 300 to 350 tonnes.

Over the years many of the earlier Atlantics were modernised with superheaters and piston valves, making them into modern engines for light duties. Five of them survived until 1947, and one of them, by now classified "E2sd", was preserved. It was renumbered to 7002, thus purporting to be the engine of the 1905 record. The "E6s" engines survived well into the 1950s, and one of them, No.460, has been preserved. This engine had achieved fame by hauling a two-coach special from Washington to New York carrying news films of the return of the Atlantic flyer Lindbergh. The train averaged 74mph (119km/h); the films were developed en route and shown in New York cinemas before those carried by air.

Claud Hamilton Class 4-4-0

Great Britain: Great Eastern Railway, 1900

Tractive effort: 17,100lb (7,757kg).
Axle load: 41,000lb (18.5t).
Cylinders: (2) 19 x 26in (483 x 660mm).
Driving wheels: 84in (2,134mm).
Heating surface: 1,631sq ft (151m²).
Superheater: none.
Steam pressure: 180psi (12.7kg/cm²).
Grate area: 21.3sq ft (2m²).
Fuel (oil): 715gall (860 US) (3.25m³).
Water: 3,450gall (4,150 US) (16m³).
Adhesive weight: 82,000lb (37.5t).
Total weight: 213,000lb (97t).
Length overall: 53ft 4¾in (16,276mm).

A new century was not yet three months old on the day when a really superb 4-4-0 locomotive, named *Claud Hamilton* after the chairman of the company and appropriately numbered 1900, emerged from the Great Eastern Railway's Stratford Works. Although its inside-cylinder layout was typical of the century that had gone, the large cab with four big side windows and many other features were way ahead of their time. Some of them, such as the power-operated reversing gear and water scoop, were still waiting to be adopted generally when the last steam locomotive for Britain was built 60 years later. Even energy conservation was considered, because the first "Claud"s burned waste oil residues instead of coal; these were available from the company's oil-gas plant. Other equipment very up to date for the day included an exhaust steam injector and a blast-pipe with variable orifice. Two sets of Stephenson's valve-gear filled such space as was left after two sets of main motion had been accommodated between the frames. Before 1914, the livery of polished metal and royal blue was as magnificent as any applied to any steam locomotive anywhere at anytime.

The "Claud Hamilton" class has a complicated history. Eventually 121 of these engines were built between 1900 and 1923. Up-to-date features such as enlarged boilers, superheaters and piston—instead of slide—valves were gradually introduced on successive batches, culminating in the ten "Super-Claud"s of 1923. As these improvements were introduced on new construction, most earlier locomotives of the class were rebuilt to conform. The original "Claud"s suffered several rebuildings and in due time most of them emerged as one or other of the last two sub-classes of "Super Claud". The latest of these varieties of rebuilding, done under the auspices of the London & North Eastern Railway, reverted to the round-topped firebox of the original No.1900, while intermediate construction and re-construction provided for a Belpaire firebox.

Using the LNER classification

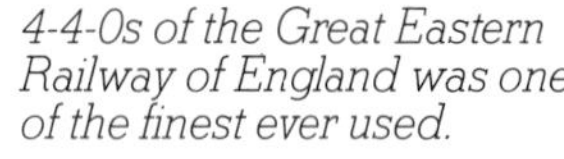

Below: *The glorious royal blue, brass and copper livery of the "Claud Hamilton" 4-4-0s of the Great Eastern Railway of England was one of the finest ever used.*

Grosse C Class 4-4-0

France: Paris, Lyons and Mediterranean Railway (PLM), 1898

Axle load: 38,600lb (17.5t).
Cylinders, HP: (2) 13.4 x 24.4in (340 x 620mm).
Cylinders, LP: (2) 21.3 x 24.4in (540 x 620mm).
Driving wheels: 78.7in (2,000mm).
Heating surface: 2,040sq ft (190m²).
Superheater: None.
Steam pressure: 213psi (15kg/cm²).
Grate area: 26.7sq ft (2.5m²).
Fuel: 11,000lb (5t).
Water: 4,400gall (5,280 US) (20m³).
Adhesive weight: 76,000lb (34.4t).
Total weight: 223,500lb (101.5t).
Length overall: 63ft 0in (19,200mm).

France produced insufficient coal to meet the needs of its railways, and any means of saving fuel was therefore important to French locomotive engineers. In the 19th century the most important fuel-saving development was the introduction of compounding. In a compound engine the steam passes through two sets of cylinders in series. By this means a greater overall expansion ratio is possible than in a "simple" engine, and more work is thus extracted from each cylinder-full of steam. One of the problems facing the designer of a compound locomotive was to even out the stresses in the moving parts of the engine, it was generally agreed that the work done in the high-pressure and in the low-pressure cylinders should be as nearly equal as possible. The ratio of the work done in the cylinders depended partly on the sizes of the cylinders, but also on the "cut-off", that is, the point in the piston stroke at which the admission of steam is shut off. In a full-blooded compound the driver could vary the cut-off in each set of cylinders at will by means of two reversing wheels, but to get the full benefit of this flexibility the driver needed to be very skilled. This was the method used by the Northern. An alternative was the driver having only one reversing wheel to operate.

Above: *Partial encasement of the engine is evident in this PLM 4-4-0 "Coupe-Vent" ("Windcutter") No.220C91.*

The first PLM compound was an adaptation of an existing

LNER class	Description	Number built new	Number of rebuilds	Length of service
D14	Original "Claud Hamilton" as described above	41	0	1900-1931
D15	Belpaire fireboxes introduced	66	9	1903-1933
D15/1	Superheaters introduced	4	70	1911-1935
D15/2	Extended smokebox	0	80	1914-1952
D16/1	Larger boilers ("Super-Claud")	10	5	1923-1934
D16/2	ditto	0	40	1926-1952
D16/3	Coupling-rod splashers removed. Round top boilers again	0	104	1933-1958

system, the details are given in the accompanying table.

During their days as the prime express locomotives of the GER, the original "Claud"s could handle a 14-car "Norfolk Coast Express" non-stop from the Liverpool Street terminus in London to North Walsham. The schedule provided for hauling loads up to 430 tons and running the 130 miles (208km) in 159 minutes, quite an amazing feat for so small a locomotive.

The coming of 4-6-0s in 1913 meant that the top timetable trains of East Anglia were no longer handled by these famous engines. The top assignment of all, however, remained with them for many years, for no heavier locomotives were permitted to run on the line serving Wolferton, the station for Sandringham House, a favourite Royal residence. The frequent Royal Trains from London to Sandringham were handled by either of two specially painted "Royal Claud"s. In the 1930s these superbly-kept engines were a reminder—even if green rather than blue—of the days when Great Eastern engines were indeed a sight for sore eyes.

On railway nationalisation day, 1st January 1948, there were 13 "D15/2"s, 16 "D16/2"s and 88 "D16/3"s. The class just failed to achieve a 60-year working life and also by a sad chance just failed to be represented in preservation. One was so set aside at Stratford works but, alas, was only marked on one side to be spared the torch. Inevitably the foreman of the cutting up gang approached the line of locomotives from the other side. So, alas these famous engines are now but a memory in the minds of their admirers.

design of 2-4-2 locomotive, of which the company possessed 290 examples. The four cylinders were in line, with the inside high-pressure cylinders driving the leading axle and the outside low-pressure cylinders driving the second axle. The valve gears were controlled by a single reversing wheel, on the second system mentioned above. The boiler pressure was 213psi (15kg/cm²), which was the highest in the world. Two locomotives were built to this design, numbered C1 and C2. They were successful, and a new design was therefore prepared, with the firebox between the coupled axles. This produced a more stable engine. The first of the new design, C3, was a 2-4-0, but two more were built with leading bogies, numbered C11 and C12. These also were successful, and a further refinement of the design was produced in 1894.

Forty engines, numbered C21 and C60 were built to this design between 1894 and 1896. The most conspicuous change from the three earlier engines was a partial encasing of the engine to reduce wind resistance. A pointed casing connected the front of the chimney and the smokebox door to the footplating, and the cab front was vee-shaped. As built, the engines had the inside and outside valve gears connected, as in the previous engines, but after a series of tests to determine the most favourable combination of cut-offs for maximum power output, it was decided that there was little benefit in ajdusting the low-pressure cut-off, which was therefore fixed at 63 per cent. The driver's reversing wheel then controlled only the high-pressure cut-off. A valve allowed the driver to admit some live steam to the low-pressure cylinders to assist at starting, but even this refinement was eliminated from some of the engines by giving the high-pressure cylinders the unusually long maximum cut-off of 88 per cent, which was considered to overcome starting difficulties.

These locomotives took over all the principal work on the less steeply-graded sections of the PLM, but train loads were increasing, and when more locomotives were required, a larger boiler was fitted, although the cylinder sizes remained the same. The 120 engines, numbered C61 to C180, were built to this design between 1898 and 1901. The boiler was slightly longer than in the earlier engines, so that the "point" or "beak" of the front of the casing was blunted, but a further casing was fitted between the chimney and the dome. The two classes had the nicknames *compound à bec* (beaked compounds) or *coupe-vent* (wind-cutter), and they were distinguished from one another by the class names "le petit C" and "le grosse C".

The "grosse C" became the standard PLM express engine until the introdution of Atlantics in 1906. They handled the fastest expresses on the *ligne impériale* from Paris to Lyons and Marseilles, including the famous "Côte d'Azur Rapide". With 220 tons they could maintain 53mph (85 km/h) on the 1 in 125 climb to Blaisy Bas, and the overall journey from Paris to Marseilles was covered at a running average of 54mph (87km/h). On test they reached 87 to 93mph (140 to 150km/h) with light trains. This capacity for high speed was credited to the *coupe-vent* casing, but in the light of later work on compound locomotives it is likely that it was as much due to the generous size of steam pipes and ports. No.C145 is preserved.

de Glehn Atlantic 4-4-2

France: Northern Railway, 1910

Axle load: 39,231lb (17.8t).
Cylinders, HP: (2) 13½ x 25¼in (340 x 640mm).
Cylinders, LP: (2) 22 x 25¼in (560 x 640mm).
Driving wheels: 80¼in (2,040mm).
Heating surface: 1,485sq ft ($138m^2$).
Superheater: 420sq ft ($39m^2$).
Steam pressure: 228psi ($16kg/cm^2$).
Grate area: 33.4sq ft ($2.75m^2$).
Fuel: 15,000lb (7t).
Water: 5,070gall (6,080 US) ($23m^3$).
Adhesive weight: 78,500lb (35.6t).
Total weight: 264,500lb (120t).
Overall length: 59ft 10½in (18,247mm).

Above: *Northern Railway of France de Glehn 4-4-2 No. 2.674. These four-cylinder compounds were outstanding.*

In spite of his name—partly French and partly German—Alfred de Glehn was born an Englishman, yet he rose to be Director of Engineering of the Société Alsacienne de Constructions Mécaniques at Mulhouse in the 1870s while still under 30. Together with Gaston du Bousquet of the Northern Railway of France he developed a system of compounding for steam locomotives which stood the test of time. In France a majority of twentieth-century express passenger locomotives were de Glehn compounds.

One major factor in its success was the fact that French locomotive drivers were not promoted from firemen but instead were trained as mechanics. In fact, the actual word used was *mechanicien*. This meant that the man in charge on the footplate could be expected to know the reasons for the complexities of a compound's controls and act accordingly to get the best results.

The de Glehn system was certainly complicated from the driver's point of view—there were *two* throttles and *two* sets of reversing gear, as well as intercepting valves, to control the working. The locomotives could be set tc work in five modes as shown in table 1.

In the A position of the intercepting valve, the exhaust from the HP cylinders was delivered to the receiver and steam chest of the LP cylinders. A safety valve set to blow off at 85lb/sq in ($6kg/cm^2$) in this vessel limited the pressure applied on the LP side.

In the B position, this connection was closed and the HP exhaust sent direct to the blast pipe. Settings IV and V were used only to move the engine under light load, or in an emergency if some problem developed in the LP or HP engines respectively. Setting III could boost the pressure on the LP side up to the 85lb/sq in ($6kg/cm^2$) to which the receiver safety valve was set.

Of course in addition to choosing the correct setting, it was necessary to select the correct combination of cut-offs by adjusting the two independent reversing gears. With all these alternatives to think of, the move from running a simple engine to driving a compound could be likened to moving up from strumming a piano to conducting a whole orchestra!

Du Bousquet and de Glehn began their co-operation in connection with some very successful compound 4-4-0s produced during the 1890s, but their lasting place in the hall of fame was assured when Northern Railway Atlantic No.2.641 was exhibited at the Paris Exhibition of 1900. Outside bearings on the leading bogie and inside ones on the trailing wheels gave an unusual look, but the 4-4-2 was certainly a good-looking example of the locomotive builders' art and the engine was the first of a class of 32 built for the Northern Railway.

The inside LP cylinders were in line with the front bogie wheels and drove the leading coupled

Table 1 Mode	Purpose	Nominal tractive effort developed
I	Normal	16,171lb (7,337kg)
II	Starting	24,069lb (10,921kg)
III	Boost	19,194lb (8,709kg)
IV	LP Isolated	11,125lb (5,048kg)
V	HP Isolated	12,944lb (5,873gk)

Table II Mode	HP Throttle	LP Throttle	Intercepting Valves
I	Open	Shut	A
II	Open	Open	B
III	Open	Open	A
V	Shut	Open	B

Table III Country	Railway	Number ordered
France:	Eastern Railway	2
"	Paris-Orleans	14
"	Midi Railway	34
"	French State Railway	9
Britain:	Great Western Railway	3
Prussia:	Royal Union Railway	79
USA:	Pennsylvania BR	1
Egypt:	State Railways	10

axle whereas the outside HP pair were in the familiar position above the rear bogie wheels and drove the rear pair of coupled wheels. The arrangement had a slight objection in that the both sets of cylinders were attached to the frames at a point where the frames were weakened by a circular cut-out to clear the bogie wheels, but otherwise the only difficulty was the servicing and repair of two complete sets of mechanism in the limited space between the frames. Both bogie and six-wheel tenders were used.

In spite of these drawbacks (which could be lived with) the performances of the Atlantics, on such trains as the boat trains between Paris and Calais on some of the hardest schedules in the world, were remarkable. The economy in coal consumption was considerable and the money so saved was welcome, but this was not the only advantage. The Atlantic had begun to approach the point where the performance was limited not by the capacity of the locomotive, but by the capacity of the man who shovels in the coal. It follows that a locomotive which had better thermal efficiency could also produce more power. And so it proved; trains of 270 tons weight hauled by a 4-4-2 were expected, say, to climb the 1 in 200 (0.5per cent) incline 13 miles long between St. Denis and Survilliers at an average speed above 100km/h (62.5mph).

Orders followed for similar machines, not only from all over France but also from many foreign countries. The tally was as shown in table III.

Some of these were of a slightly enlarged design and others differed quite markedly in details of layout, but all followed the same basic principles. The French railway systems went on to build many classes of 4-6-0, 2-8-2, 4-6-2, 4-8-2 and other types to this basic compound design, while the Great Western Railway of England based all their future express passenger designs on the same mechanical layout, but with four simple cylinders.

As elsewhere in the world, all-steel carriages and more spacious accommodation raised train weights to a point where a minimum of six coupled wheels were required, so the de Glehn 4-4-2s vanished between the wars. Northern Railway No.2.670 has survived and is displayed superbly restored in the National Railway Museum at its own city of origin, Mulhouse in Alsace.

Left: *Nord de Glehn 4-4-2 No.2.670 as restored for the National Railway Museum at Mulhouse, France.*

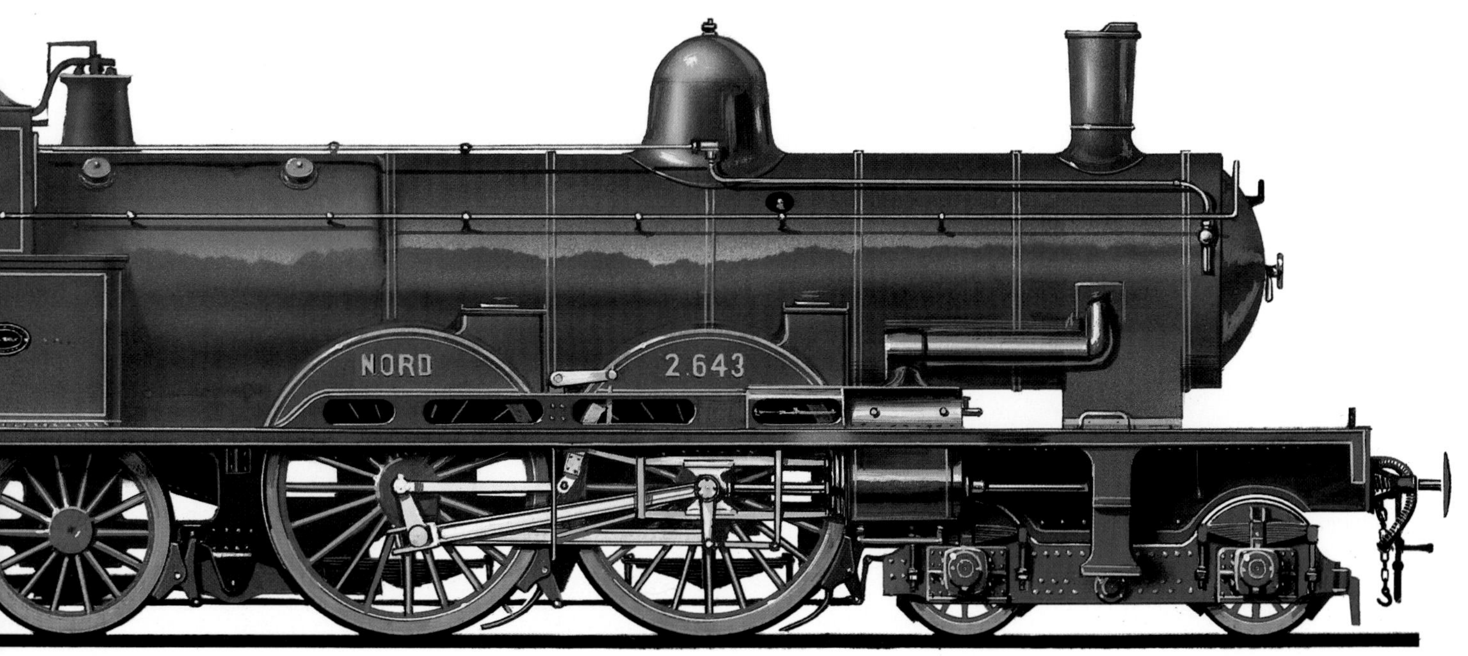

Below: *De Glehn four-cylinder compound 4-4-2 of the Northern Railway of France complete with more modern bogie tender.*

Class Q 4-6-2 New Zealand: New Zealand Government Railways (NZGR), 1901

Tractive effort: 19,540lb (8,863kg).
Axle load: 23,500lb (10.5t).
Cylinders: (2) 16 x 22in (406 x 559mm).
Driving wheels: 49in (1,245mm).
Heating surface: 1,673sq ft (155m²).
Superheater: None.
Steam pressure: 200psi (14kg/cm²).
Grate area: 40sq ft (3.72m²).
Fuel: 11,000lb (5t).
Water: 1,700 gall (2,000 US) (7.7m³).
Adhesive weight: 69,500lb (31.5t).
Total weight: 165,000lb (75t).
Length overall: 55ft 4½in (16,872mm).

The year 1901 was marked by the construction of the first of a famous type—arguably *the* most famous type—of express passenger locomotive, which was to go on being built until the end of steam. And it was not one of the great railway nations which was responsible for conceiving the idea (and to whose order it was built) but tiny New Zealand. A.W. Beattie, Chief Mechanical Engineer of the Government Railways, wanted a locomotive with a big firebox capable of burning poor quality lignite coal from South Island mines at Otago.

American manufacturer Baldwin suggested a "camelback" 4-6-0 with a wide firebox above the rear coupled wheels, but the New Zealander proposed a 4-6-0 with the big firebox carried by a two-wheel pony truck, making a 4-6-2. The 13 engines were quickly completed and despatched across the Pacific Ocean; and in this way a name was given to thousands of locomotives yet to be built. In due time the word "Pacific" entered that dialect of the English language used for describing railways.

Below: *NZGR class "Q"—she was the world's first class of Pacific locomotive when built in USA in 1901.*

Above: *Class "Q" No.343 on the southernmost passenger railway in the world between Invercargill and Bluff, Southland.*

Class F15 4-6-2 USA: Chesapeake & Ohio Railway (C&O), 1902

Tractive effort: 32,400lb (14,696kg).
Axle load: 52,500lb (24t).
Cylinders: (2) 23½ x 28in (597 x 711mm).
Driving wheels: 72in (1,829mm).
Heating surface: 2,938sq ft (273m²).
Superheater: None.
Steam pressure: 180psi (12.7kg/cm²).
Grate area: 47sq ft (4.4m²).
Fuel: 30,000lb (13.5t).
Water: 7,500 gall (9,000 US). (34m³).
Adhesive weight: 157,000lb (71.5t).
Total weight: 408,000lb (185t).
Length overall: 74ft 0in (22,555mm).

The Chesapeake & Ohio Railroad (C&O) can trace its corporate history back to 1785 when the James River Company received a charter. The first President was George Washington in person! Railroad operations did not begin until 1836 when the Louisa Railroad in Virginia was opened.

Only a few weeks after the Missouri Pacific RR got the first of their 4-6-2s, this historic company took delivery from the American Locomotive Company of the prototype of their famous "F15" class Pacifics. This time there was no ambiguity—the standard North American express passenger locomotive of the twentieth century had finally arrived. This path-finding C&O No.147 was also fitted with piston valves, but it still had Stephenson's

A feature which was also to appear on most of the world's steam locomotives built after this time was the type of valve gear used on these engines. Of 105 locomotives yet to be described in this book, 86 have Walschaert's valve gear. The invention was not new—a Belgian engineer called Egide Walschaert had devised it back in 1844 and a German called Heusinger had reinvented it since—but this application marked its entry into general use outside continental Europe. The gear gave good steam distribution, but the main advantage lay in its simplicity, as well as in the fact that it could conveniently be fitted outside the frames in the position most accessible for maintenance. In this case the gear was arranged to work outside-admission piston valves, which piston valves themselves were in the forefront of steam technology at the beginning of the century.

It should be said that this class of engine came closer than ever before to the final form of the steam locomotive. Only two fundamental improvements were still to be applied generally—inside-admission piston valves in place of outside, and superheating.

After some minor modification the "Q" class gave long and faithful service, the last of them not ceasing work until 1957. During their prime, in addition to working the principal trains on the South Island main line, some came to the North Island for use on the Rotorua Express, running between Auckland and the famous hot springs of the same name.

Right: *The splendid New Zealand Government class "Q" 4-6-2 No.343 as running in 1956 when nearing the end of more than 50 years service to this 3ft 6in gauge railway system which had adopted US practice for its locomotives.*

link valve motion between the frames. Naturally no superheater, but her size and power set a new standard. A further 26 followed during the years 1903-11. Most survived until the C&O turned to diesels in the early 1950s and, in a country that was not then given to hanging on to old machinery, that said a great deal for the qualities of the "F15" class. Of course, as the years went by, top-line express work was passed on to their successors, yet there were routes whose weak bridges meant that these comparatively light engines continued being used on prime trains nearly to the end. During the 1920s all the "F15" locomotives were modernised with Walschaert's valve gear, superheaters, larger tenders, different cabs, mechanical stokers, new cylinders and, in some cases, even new frames; in fact, just in the manner of the legendary Irishman's hammer—"a hundred years old, only two new heads and three new handles".

Left: *A latter-day Chesapeake & Ohio 4-6-2 of class "F16", introduced in 1937 and built by Baldwins of Philadelphia. Note that special C&O trademark, the mounting of two duplex air pumps on the front of the smokebox of No.174.*

In addition to setting the style for nearly 7,000 USA 4-6-2s to follow, the "F15" founded a dynasty on their own road. The "F16" 4-6-2s of 1913 represented a 34 per cent increase in tractive effort and a 28 per cent increase of grate area, while for the "F17" of 1914 these increases were 45 per cent and 71 per cent respectively, in each case for a penalty of a 27 per cent increase in axle load. After World War I, classes "F18" and "F19" appeared, notable for 18,000 gallon 12-wheel tenders. These 61 4-6-2s handled all C&O's express passenger assignments until the coming of 4-6-4s in 1941.

It will be noted that these 4-6-2s showed something else. During the age of steam no major system outside North America ever had track strong enough to carry an axle load greater than 22½ tons, so these locomotives were as good an indicator as any that the USA, having come up from well behind, was now starting to go far into the lead in industrial might.

Large Atlantic Class 4-4-2

Great Britain:
Great Northern Railway (GNR), 1902

Tractive effort: 17,340lb (7,865kg).
Axle load: 45,000lb (20.5t).
Cylinders: (2) 20 x 24in (508 x 610mm).
Driving wheels: 80in (2,032mm).
Heating surface: 1,965sq ft (182.5m²).
Superheater: 568sq ft (52.8m²).
Steam pressure: 170psi (12.0kg/cm²).
Grate area: 31sq ft (2.88m²).
Fuel: 14,500lb (6½t).
Water: 3,500 gall (4,200 US). (16m³).
Adhesive weight: 90,000lb (41t).
Total weight: 252,500lb (115t).
Length overall: 57ft 10¼in (17,634mm).

These famous engines introduced the big boiler with wide firebox to Britain; 94 were built between 1902 and 1910. Until the arrival of 4-6-2s in 1921, they ruled the Great Northern Railway's portion of the East Coast main line from London to Scotland, that is, between Kings Cross and York. Even after this, the light formation of the de-luxe all-Pullman expresses introduced in the 1920s was just right for these Atlantics.

By the mid-1930s, new streamlined Pacifics made the older 4-6-2s available for the Pullmans, but the thirty year old warriors found a new and skittish lease of life on the famous high speed light-weight "Beer Trains" between Kings Cross and Cambridge. They also stood by as pilots at places like Peterborough, Grantham and Doncaster, demonstrating on various occasions that in favourable circumstances with a crew willing to 'have a go' they could keep "Pacific" timings with the streamliners as well as 17-coach expresses.

The coming of the "Green Arrow" class 2-6-2s which could stand in on any main line train and, in addition, the war-time lack of light fast trains, was the end for the 4-4-2s. The first one (GN No.1459, LNER No.4459) ceased work in 1943 and the last (GN No.294, LNER Nos.3294 and 2822, British Railways No. 62822) in November 1950. She reached 75mph (121km/h) on her last run. To the British public of 70 years ago they epitomised the romance of the railway; their owners liked them too—at an original price of £3,400 each they could hardly be described as a bad investment. Their crews also liked the ease with which they could be driven and fired, even if the exiguous cabs gave little shelter from the elements.

Like most of the world's greatest steam locomotives they were starkly simple, but yet up-to-date. Cylinders were outside, valves and valve gear (Stephenson's) inside. The first 81 came out unsuperheated, with balanced slide valves. The last ten, built in 1910, had piston-valves and superheaters. In time all were fitted with the latter and most were converted from slide to piston valve. There were also three experimental four-cylinder compounds, but none of them prospered against the standard version. All the 4-4-2s except one of the compounds were built at the company's own Doncaster Plant, to the design of Henry Ivatt.

One starkly simple feature, wholly unusual in the twentieth century for an express passenger locomotive, was the lever or Johnson bar reverse; this was more usually applied to shunting locomotives which ran slowly but needed to change direction frequently. It was difficult to alter the cut-off at speed with the lever—the combined strength of both driver and fireman were needed sometimes. There was certainly no chance of making

Midland Compound 4-4-0

Great Britain:
Midland Railway (MR), 1902

Axle load: 44,500lb (20.5t).
Cylinders, HP: (1) 19 x 26in (483 x 660mm).
Cylinders, LP: (2) 21 x 26in (533 x 660mm).
Driving wheels: 84in (2,134mm).
Heating surface: 1,317sq ft (122.5m²).
Superheater: 272 sq ft (25.3m²).
Steam pressure: 200psi (14.1kg/cm²).
Grate area: 28.4sq ft (2.63m²).
Fuel: 12,500lb (5.75t).
Water: 3,500 gall (4,200 US). (16m³).
Adhesive weight: 89,000lb (40.5t).
Total weight: 234,000lb (106t).
Length overall: 56ft 7½in (17,260mm).

The "Midland Compound" locomotives have a place in any locomotive hall of fame. S.W. Johnson introduced them in 1902; later they were developed by his successor R.M. Deeley, substantially rebuilt (in which form they are portrayed) by Henry (later Sir Henry) Fowler in 1914. They were the only long-term successful application of the compound principle in Britain; and when the Midland Railway was amalgamated with others in 1923 to form the London Midland & Scottish Railway, the "Midland Compound" was chosen (just a little surprisingly) as the standard express locomotive for the new organisation. Eventually 240 of them were built. Their numbers ran from 900 to 939 and 1000 to 1199 in MR and LMS days and most survived to become British Railways' Nos.40900 to 41199.

The LMS examples had wheels 3in (76mm) less in diameter. The last of them ceased work in 1961 only seven years before the "final" finish of steam on BR. Midland No.1000 has been preserved in working order at the York National Railway Museum. Most were built at the Midland's Derby Works but a number of orders went to outside manufacturers in early LMS days.

Unlike the Webb compounds, these locomotives had a *single* high-pressure cylinder and *two* low-pressure ones. The high-pressure cylinder was between the frames and the two low-pressure ones were outside. Also between the frames were *three* sets of Stephenson's valve gear as well as the inside cylinder's motion. When the throttle was in the partly open position, live steam was admitted to the low-pressure cylinders, resulting in "simple" working. This was necessary for starting. At full throttle, the port which allowed this "simple" operation closed and proper "compound" working ensued.

This resulted in an anomaly that confused many drivers from non-Midland depots to which the engines were allocated in LMS days—that is that more steam was used when the throttle was partly closed than when it was fully open. Even so, the long-lived "Midland Compound" locomotives were considered to be reliable and useful machines. For the fast, frequent but short trains of their parent Midland Railway, the "Crimson Ramblers" were found to be adequate and economical.

Right: *"Midland Compound" No.1000 piloting enthusiasts' special at Settle Junction, Yorkshire, in May 1950. The second locomotive is LNER No.4771* Green Arrow.

Above left: *"Large Atlantic" No.4458 at the head of a Pullman Express in pre-World War II days.*

Above: *"Large Atlantic" No.251 as restored to the original Great Northern Railway livery. This locomotive is preserved in the National Railway Museum.*

the fine adjustments *en route* which were behind the lower coal consumption of certain contemporary types. But coal was a cheap part of the cost equation and if the the GN Atlantics did burn a bit more, their overall economics were quite beyond suspicion.

The first of the Ivatt large Atlantics, GN No.251, LNER No.3251 (later renumbered as LNER No.2800) has survived to find an honoured place in the National Railway Museum at York. Whilst stored in the paint shop at Doncaster waiting for a vacancy, it was taken out and in company with preserved "small" Atlantic *Henry Oakley*, was set to run a special train from Kings Cross to Doncaster to celebrate the centenary of the GN loco works. The use of these two locomotives on this "Plant Centenarian" special train of 20 September 1953 was important as it maintained the precedent so far as British Railways is concerned, for the running of museum pieces for entertainment purposes. The veterans did the 156 mile (250km) run in a respectable 192 minutes running time.

City Class 4-4-0

Great Britain:
Great Western Railway (GWR), 1903

Tractive effort: 17,790lb (8,070kg).
Axle load: 41,000lb (18.5t).
Cylinders: (2) 18 x 26in (457 x 660mm).
Driving wheels: 80½in (2,045mm).
Heating surface: 1,351sq ft (126m²).
Superheater: 216sq ft (20.1m²).
Steam pressure: 200psi (14.1kg/cm²).
Grate area: 20.56sq ft (1.91m²).
Fuel: 11,000lb (5t).
Water: 3,000 gall (3,600 US). (13.6m³).
Adhesive weight: 81,000lb (36.75t).
Total weight: 207,000lb (94t).
Length overall: 56ft 2¼in (17,126mm).

The Great Western "City" class 4-4-0s owe their fame to an occasion in May 1905 when a special mail train from Plymouth to Paddington descended the winding alignment of the Wellington incline, just west of Taunton, at a very high speed. That famous train-timer and journalist Charles Rous-Marten, had been invited and he recorded 102.3mph (164 km/h) then a world record for steam in respect of an authentically and independently recorded occasion.

A careful analysis of the timings at successive quarter-mile posts has since suggested that Rous-Marten mistook some other object for one of them and that the actual speed was a little less. Even so, the incident led to the preservation of its heroine No. 3717 *City of Truro*. The series was numbered originally from 3433 to 3442 then renumbered 3710-3719.

There were only ten "City" class proper, all built at the GWR works at Swindon, but a further 27 were created by rebuilding locomotives of the related "Badminton" and "Atbara" classes. They represented something of stop-gap, while the old GWR was making a huge and sudden leap forward from a locomotive fleet that was old-fashioned for the nineteenth century to one that was far ahead of its time for the twentieth. In the meantime this series of locomotives, with inside-cylinders and outside-cranks, as well as both outside- and inside-frames, but with up-to-date boilers, was turned out.

The mechanical layout, superficially at least, was very close to that very earliest 4-4-0 of all, Campbell's 4-4-0 of 1837 for the Philadelphia & Norristown Railroad in the USA. Few others, least of all those in the inventor's native land had built any similar locomotives, but many had been constructed in the last decade of the century for the GWR. There were 60 "Duke" class, 156 "Bulldog" class, 20 "Flower" class, and 40 "Stella" class in addition to "City" and conversions mentioned. The outside-framed 4-4-0 was very much a trademark of the turn of the century GWR passenger locomotive fleet.

In consequence of being stop-gaps, the "City" class had only a short reign on top express work, but even apart from the record had a reputation for fast running. The last of them ceased work in 1931, although *City of Truro* went back into traffic for a short time after World War II so that it would be available for enthusiasts' specials. She now resides in the Great Western Museum at Swindon.

Below: *Great Western No.3717* City of Truro *as preserved, on a train near Hullavington, Wiltshire. This locomotive held the world speed record of 102.3mph (164km/h) for many years and is now preserved in the Great Western Railway Museum at Swindon, Wilts, England.*

Saint Class 4-6-0

Great Britain:
Great Western Railway (GWR), 1902

Tractive effort: 24,395lb (11,066kg).
Axle load: 41,500lb (19t).
Cylinders: (2) 18½ x 30in (470 x 762mm).
Driving wheels: 80½in (2,045mm).
Heating surface: 1,841sq ft ($171m^2$).
Superheater: 263sq ft ($24.4m^2$).
Steam pressure: 225psi ($15.8kg/cm^2$).
Grate area: 27.1sq ft ($2.52m^2$).
Fuel: 13,500lb (6t).
Water: 3,500 gall (4,200 US). ($16m^3$).
Adhesive weight: 125,000lb (56t).
Total weight: 251,000lb (114t).
Length overall: 63ft 0¼in (19,209mm).

Above: *"Saint" class No.2937* Clevedon Court. *The "Courts" were the last batch of the "Saints" built in 1911.*

When, shortly before the turn of the century, a not-so-young man called George Jackson Churchward found himself heir apparent to William Dean, Chief Locomotive Engineer of the Great Western Railway, he (Churchward) had already decided that there would have to be very great changes when he took over Corridor trains and dining cars, as well as the demand for faster schedules meant a whole new express passenger locomotive fleet, for even by nineteenth century standards the then current GWR locomotives were both heterogenous and unsatisfactory. Whilst Churchward was number two under an ageing chief at the Swindon Factory, he was able to test his ideas by causing to be built a number of very strange designs indeed. Because so many peculiar oddments already existed—such as 4-4-0s converted from standard gauge 0-4-4s(!), themselves converted from the broad gauge on its abolition in 1892—they attracted little attention.

But 1902 was the year when a big outside-cylinder 4-6-0 No.100 (later 2900), tactfully named *Dean* (later *William Dean*), saw the light of day. By the standards of the locomotive aesthetics of the period it was one of the strangest looking locomotives of all, though to those few who knew about the design and appearance of the typical North American Ten-wheeler, No.100 was totally familiar, despite being disguised by ornate Victorian brass and paint work. This reflected Churchward's friendship with A.W. Gibbs, Master Mechanic (Lines East) of the Pennsylvania Railroad.

The layout of the American Ten-wheeler prototype was followed exactly. Both cylinders and valve chests were mounted outside the frames in the most accessible possible position; the Stephenson's valve gear inside the frames drove the inside-admission valves via transverse shafts and pendulum cranks. With some refinement the arrangement was used by Churchward and his successors on some 2,000 locomotives. The frame arrangement for Churchward's standard locomotives was a compromise between USA and British practice. Plate frames were used for the main portion in which the driving wheels were held, but the cylinders were in true Yankee style, each together with one half of the smokebox saddle, the front of the locomotive being carried on a short length of bar frame. The domeless boiler had less of the USA and more of Churchward than the engine part about it (but very little previous GWR practice); however, some time was to elapse before the design of this component became fully developed.

At this time Churchward was about to take full charge, not only (as on most British railways) of the building and repairing of locomotives, but also of their running. He would sit round a drawing board together with its incumbent, the incumbent's boss and the Chief Draughtsman and they would discuss the job in question. If doubts arose over manufacture, an expert from the works—the foundry foreman, maybe—would be sent for. If it was a point about the locomotive in service, then the running superintendent would come over. Perhaps Churchward would ask what others did about the problem, in which case the Record Office would quickly produce a book or periodical tabbed to indicate the relevant page. The result was that before long the GWR possessed a locomotive fleet that in many ways had few rivals the world over.

It was a far cry from the ways of some of the autocratic, self-important and "know-all" characters who occupied the chief's chair on a number of other British lines in those days. Churchward did it all, not by cleverness, but simply by listening to others and then applying that rarest of qualities, common sense. Churchward took some time to make up his mind whether to have as his best express power the 77 two-

cylinder "Saint" class 4-6-0s, derived from *William Dean;* or whether the four-cylinder contemporary "Star" class 4-6-0s of similar speed and power, of which there were 60 before Churchward retired in 1921, would be the better. He finally decided on the latter and it does seem to this writer at least that this is one of the very few times when the judgment of one of our greatest locomotive engineers could be seen to be at fault.

The jump from the first-line express power of 1892, the graceful 4-2-2 "Dean Single" to *William Dean* of 1902 involved the following increases in the various measures of power; tractive effort—20 per cent; cylinder stroke—25 per cent (the bore was the same); heating surface—35 per cent; steam pressure—12 per cent; grate area—30 per cent; adhesive weight—204 per cent. In addition to these shocks, there was that arising from the full side nudity of exposing wheels, cylinders and motion.

Although the locomotives came to be known as the "Saint" class, 32 had been built before the first Saint name appeared, No.2911 *Saint Agatha* in 1907. Following on *William Dean,* in 1903 there came a second prototype (No.98, later 2998 *Ernest Cunard*) and then in the same year another (No.171, later 2971, *Albion*). No. 171 was turned out temporarily as a 4-4-2 in order to make direct comparison with a French de Glehn compound 4-4-2 No.102 *La France,* which had been imported as an experiment. The first production batch of 19 (Nos. 172-190, later 2972-90) appeared in 1905, and some of these also had a short period as 4-4-2s; they were named after characters in Sir Walter Scott's Waverley novels. In May 1906 Nos.2901-10 were built, later named after Ladies. No.2901 well named *Lady Superior* was the first British locomotive to have a modern superheater, in this case of the Schmidt pattern and all had been given superheaters (now of Swindon design) by 1912.

In the 20 genuine Saints which followed in 1907, the austere staight lines of the running boards were mitigated by providing the curved drop-ends so much a characteristic of most GWR locomotives built since that time. Finally in 1911 came 25 Courts, all superheated from the outset and with further improvements. Cylinder diameter was increased by ½in and, more obviously, the very characteristic "top-feed" fittings either side of the safety valves on the domeless boiler were added. These came to be very much a GWR trademark.

Churchward's boilers were his greatest triumph and the best among them was this No.1, which was not only fitted to the 77 Saints but also to 74 "Star" 4-6-0s, the 3 "Frenchmen" 4-4-2s, 330 "Hall" 4-6-0s, 80 "Grange" 4-6-0s and 150 "28XX" 2-8-0s.

Amongst the No.1 boiler features were measures to avoid the damage to boiler plates etc. caused by delivering relatively cold feed water straight into the hot boiler water, as was normal before his day. By placing the non-return feed valves (clack valve is the technical term) on top of the boiler and directing the delivery forward, the feed water flowed to the front of the barrel via a series of trays which collected impurities deposited as the water gathered heat. There, now fairly hot, the feed water mixed with that already in the boiler without detriment.

In due time the whole "Saint" class (except the prototype) was brought up to the standards of the last ones to be built. In building these latter, Churchward finally decided on the two-cylinder versus the four-cylinder question because at the last minute he cancelled the final five Courts, yet continued to build four-cylinder "Star" locomotives. Further development of the GWR express passenger locomotive was all based on the "Star" layout; yet the "Saint" was a remarkable engine and able to match anything in the way of performance which its complex four-cylinder sisters could produce.

In 1925 No.2925 *Saint Martin* was fitted with 72in (1,828mm) diameter wheels in place of 80½in (2,045mm). Tractive effort was increased in proportion and maximum speed was very little affected. In this form and described as the "Hall" class, a further 330 "Saint"s were built, most of which went on until dieselisation.

A particularly pleasing feature was the exceptional precision with which all these later engines were built and repaired. This was the main contribution of Churchward's successors, who saw to it that Swindon had the kit—the Zeiss optical setting out apparatus was one item—to achieve dimensional accuracy higher than was normal practice elsewhere. The story that British Railways' standards of fits and tolerances for a locomotive when it was new corresponded to Swindon's standards when they considered it was worn out, was not entirely apochryphal.

No.2920 *Saint David* was the final surivior of the Saints proper when withdrawn in 1953.

Above: *Going and coming. Two views of "Saints" at work. The upper photograph shows that they were far from neglected even in British Rail days. As these views show, most of the "Saints' were altered to have the curved foot-plating of the later batches of these path-finding locomotives.*

Below: *No.2902* Lady of the Lake *as depicted here retains the straight foot-plating of the original members of the class.*

Class P 4-4-2 Denmark: Danish State Railways (DSB), 1907

Axle load: 40,000lb (18t).
Cylinders,HP: (2) 14¼ x 23½in (360 x 600mm).
Cylinders, LP: (2) 23½ x 23½in (600 x 600mm).
Driving wheels: 78in (1,980mm).
Heating surface: 2,072sq ft (192.5m²).
Superheater: None
Steam pressure: 785psi (13kg/cm²).
Grate area: 34.5sq ft (3.20m²).
Fuel: 13,500lb (6t).
Water: 4,650gall (5,550 US) (21m³).
Adhesive weight: 80,000lb (36t).
Total weight: 262,500lb (119t).
Length overall: 60ft 9in (18,515mm).

It could be argued that flat Denmark was uninteresting locomotive country. Nevertheless, Danish steam engines were both distinctive and handsome—and none more so than the "P" class Atlantics, introduced in 1907. Nineteen came from the Hannoversche Maschinenbau AG of Hanover, Germany (Hanomag) and in 1910 a further 14 from Schwartzkopff of Berlin. The second batch was designated "P-2" and had larger cylinders (14½ and 23½ x 25¼in—360 and 600 x 640mm) and higher boiler pressure (213lb/sq in—15kg/cm²).

They were four-cylinder compounds, with the low-pressure cylinders outside the frames and with a single piston-valve spindle serving both high and low pressure valves on each side. Heusinger's (Walschaert's) valve-gear was used, but out of sight inside the frames instead of in the usual position outside. All cylinders drove on the rear coupled axle; the inside ones were raised and their axis sloped downwards towards the rear so that the inside connecting rods would clear the leading coupled axle. Maximum permitted speed was 62mph (100km/h).

Visually the Danish 4-4-2s were very striking; the chimney was adorned with the Danish national colours—red, yellow, red—and there were such details as that near-complete circle described by the injector pipe on the side of the boiler before homing on to the clack valve.

Above and below: *Danish State Railways class "P" 4-4-2. These striking machines were the mainstay of Danish passenger services from 1910 to 1935.*

Class 640 2-6-0 Italy: State Railways (FS), 1907

Tractive effort: 24,810lb (11,256kg)
Axle load: 33,000lb (15t).
Cylinders: (2) 21¼ x 27½in (540 x 700mm).
Driving wheels: 72¾in (1,850mm).
Heating surface: 1,163sq ft (108m²).
Superheater: 361sq ft (33.5m²).
Steam pressure: 171psi (12kg/cm²).
Grate area: 26sq ft (2.42m²).
Fuel: 13,300lb (6t).
Water: 3,300gall (3,940US) (15m³).
Adhesive weight: 98,000lb (44.5t).
Total weight: 197,970lb (89.8t).
Overall length: 54ft 2⅜in (16,530mm).

When the Italian State Railways was formed in 1905, one of the first tasks undertaken by the Chief Mechanical Engineer of the new organisation, Guiseppe Zara, was the design of a standard range of locomotives. He was a man of both ability and an original turn of mind—certainly his smaller express passenger locomotive was full of unusual and interesting features, but in spite of that some are still in use 75 years after the first one took the rails.

The class "640" 2-6-0 appeared in 1907 and the first batch was built by Schwartzkopff of Berlin. Production continued until 1930 and 188 in all were built. The majority were constructed by Italian builders. The class also included 15 rebuilt from class "630" two-cylinder compounds. Class "630" was originally intended as the standard class, but the advent of superheating meant that they were superseded by the "640" almost as soon as they came into service.

It was fairly original to choose the 2-6-0 or Mogul wheel arrangement at all for express passenger work—but combine it with large wheels, *inside* cylinders and *outside* steam chests and valve gear and you really have something that is worth a detour to see.

The reason why 2-6-0s have not often hauled the world's great trains is that the two-wheel leading pony trucks have been suspect for a fast running locomotive. Most express engines have four wheel bogies, yet a 2-6-0, say, has a higher proportion of adhesive weight in relation to total weight, an important advantage in a mountainous country such as Italy. However, Zara had a card up his sleeve—his Zara truck, called in Italy the Italian bogie. The leading coupled wheels are allowed about ¾in (20mm) of side-play in their axle-boxes, spherical journals and bushes are provided on the crank pins and coupling rods so that the coupling of the wheels will still work properly when the wheels are not in line. The leading pony wheels are mounted in a truck which also carries the leading axle, in such a way that both the pony wheels and the leading driving wheels play a

Denmark was a pioneer in the adoption of diesel-electric traction and the first diesel-electric express trains went into service as long ago as 1935. They were known as the "Lyntog" Lightning trains and, whilst there was no threat to steam haulage of heavy expresses, the Atlantics found that their duties on fast light trains were affected. For this reason between 1943 and 1955 a number were converted to rather close-coupled 4-6-2s at DSB's Copenhagen shops. The boiler was lengthened by adding an additional ring, while the original wide firebox was replaced by a narrow one the same size as that belonging to the class "R" 4-6-0s. The original cylinders and motion were retained but new wheels of lesser diameter (68in – 1,727mm) were provided. The new engines were redesignated class "PR".

The forty-year long process of replacing Danish steam with diesel power came to fruition in the end, but a little before this time the last 4-4-2 was withdrawn. This was No.912 in 1968. Denmark is full of steam-lovers and their enthusiasm is recognised by the preservation of two of these superb 4-4-2s (Nos.917 and 931 – the latter is displayed in the museum at Odense) and one (No.908) as rebuilt into a Pacific.

Above: *Pre-war view of a Danish State Railways' class "P" 4-4-2, showing the clean lines before air brakes.*

part in guiding the locomotive round a curve. The device has been very successful and 2-6-0s and 2-6-2s have dominated steam express passenger operations in Italy ever since.

Main line electrification began in Italy before No.640.001 took the rails, so it is not surprising that no further new designs for express passenger work appeared after 1928. But electrification was also a factor in the survival of engines like the "640" – obsolescence would have overtaken them long before if the new engines built had been steam.

Left: *Italian State Railways' class "640" 2-6-0 No.640.004 at Allessandria Locomotive Depot in June 1972.*

BESA Class 4-6-0

India: Indian Railways, 1905

Tractive effort: 22,590lb (10,250kg).
Axle load: 39,500lb (18t).
Cylinders: (2) 20½ x 26in (521 x 660mm).
Driving wheels: 74in (1,880mm).
Heating surface: 1,476sq ft ($137m^2$).
Superheater: 352sq ft ($32.7m^2$).
Steam pressure: 180lb/sq in ($12.7kg/cm^2$).
Grate area: 32sq ft ($3.0m^2$).
Fuel: 16,800lb (7½t).
Water: 4,000gall (4,800 US) ($18m^3$).
Adhesive weight: 118,000lb (54t).
Total weight: 273,000lb (124t).
Length overall: 62ft 3¼in (18,980mm).
(These dimensions refer to later examples with Walschaert's valve gear, outside valves and superheater).

More British than anything that ran in Britain, this archetypal Mail Engine gave over 75 years of service and is still actively in use. This is the British Engineering Standards Association "Heavy Passenger" 4-6-0, introduced in 1905, of which a number (but not one of the originals) are still in passenger service in India at the time of writing.

The railways of India were developed mainly by private enterprise under a concession system whereby the then British Government of India guaranteed a modest return on investment in return for a measure of control, as well as eventual ownership. The government felt that one of their perquisites was to set standards and, having made rather a mess of the gauge question, made up for it with an excellent job of setting out a range of standard designs for locomotives.

The decision to do this was the result of representations made by the British locomotive manufacturers. At a time when there was an explosion of demand for steam locomotives, they found it difficult to cope efficiently with orders for small batches of similar locomotives which differed only in minor detail.

For the broad (5ft 6in—1676mm) gauge there was a "Standard Passenger" 4-4-0, a "Standard Goods" 0-6-0, a "Heavy Goods" 2-8-0 and, finally, a "Heavy Passenger" 4-6-0, all of which were successful enough to be still in use 75 years after the designs were conceived. The "Heavy Passenger" 4-6-0s were still being *supplied* in 1950, well after independence, while the 4-4-0s operate still in Pakistan.

State-owned railways such as the North Western obeyed without question, but some of the others were slower to abrogate their independence in such a sensitive matter as locomotive design. However, the qualities of the standard product in due time spoke for themselves. Of course, it was still possible to specify alternatives in the way of accessories, even if one had to accept the fundamental features of the design.

Above: *Indian Railways BESA 4-6-0 No.24256 now allocated to the Eastern Region, was built by the Vulcan Foundry in 1949.*

Below: *4-6-0 No.24328 of the Western Railway, this is a 1923 product of William Beardmore & Co. of Glasgow.*

The first BESA 4-6-0s were solid hunks of sound engineering, bigger when introduced than almost anything that ran in the same country. Their closest relations at home seem to have been some 4-6-0s built in 1903 for the Glasgow & South Western Railway by the North British Locomotive Co. of Glasgow. NBL were to supply the first standard 4-6-0s to India.

Down the years many more were built there and at the Vulcan Foundry at Newton-le-Willows as well as by Robert Stephenson & Co. A few came from Kitson of Leeds and, shortly after World War I, some were made by William Beardmore of Glasgow, better known for marine engineering than for locomotives. Early examples were non-superheated with outside cylinders, inside slide-valves and Stephenson's valve gear but, early on, outside Walschaert's gear, outside piston valves and superheaters were adopted. The boilers had Belpaire pattern fireboxes. Between the wars a few small batches were turned out with poppet valves. Some later examples had bogie tenders instead of six-wheeled.

When the all-India locomotive numbering system was adopted in 1957 there were 387 broad-gauge 4-6-0s still running in India. More existed in Pakistan, both East (now Bangladesh) and West. All but a very few were either built to the BESA design or close to it. The new running numbers ran from 24,000 to 24,470; the few gaps were for some 4-4-2s and a few non-standard 4-6-2s and 4-6-0s.

The BESA 4-6-0s stayed in top-line work even after their successors, the India Railway Standard (IRS), XA and XB 4-6-2s had arrived in the mid-1920s, because of unsatisfactory qualities amongst the new arrivals. The great success of the BESA designs seems to lie in the fact that they were taken from British practice as it existed, with the difference that both average and maximum speeds in India were 25 per cent lower than at home while loads were about the same. This more than compensated for rougher working conditions; one notes, for example, that in dusty areas, locomotives ran hot so frequently that pipes were provided to trickle cold water on to vulnerable bearings! One factor in the good performance offered by the older engines lay in the extra 9½in (240mm) of space available for the firegrate between the wheels compared with similar engines in Britain, because of the broad gauge track.

Above: *Some of the Indian Railways' surviving "BESA" 4-6-0s have bogie tenders instead of the six-wheel variety originally provided.*

Even so, the coming of the post-war 4-6-2s as well as diesels and electrics did spell out the beginning of the end for the BESA 4-6-0s. By 1980 the number in use had fallen to about 100, but they could still be found at work on passenger trains. And if the importance of trains can be measured by the amount of humanity packed into or clinging on to them, then those in question are important indeed. However, they are a far cry from the days when the "Imperial Indian Mail", hauled by one of these locomotives, provided luxury accommodation for 32 persons only—and their bearers (servants), of course—for the 1,230 mile (1,968km) journey from Bombay to Calcutta.

Below: *The condition of 4-6-0 No.24280, supplied by the North British Loco Co. in 1915, belies its age, approaching 70 years.*

Class P8 4-6-0

Germany:
Royal Prussian Union Railway (KPEV), 1906

Tractive effort: 26,760lb (12,140kg).
Axle load: 39,000lb (17.75t).
Cylinders: (2) 22.6in x 24.8in (575 x 630mm).
Driving wheels: 68.9in (1,750mm).
Heating surface: 1,542sq ft (143.3m²).
Superheater: 634sq ft (58.9m²).
Steam pressure: 170.6psi (12kg/cm²).
Grate area: 27.8sq ft (2.58m²).
Fuel: 11,000lb (5.0t).
Water: 4,700gall (5,700 US) (21.5m³).
Adhesive weight: 114,000lb (52t).
Total weight: 172,500lb (78.5t).
Length overall: 61ft 0in (18,592mm).

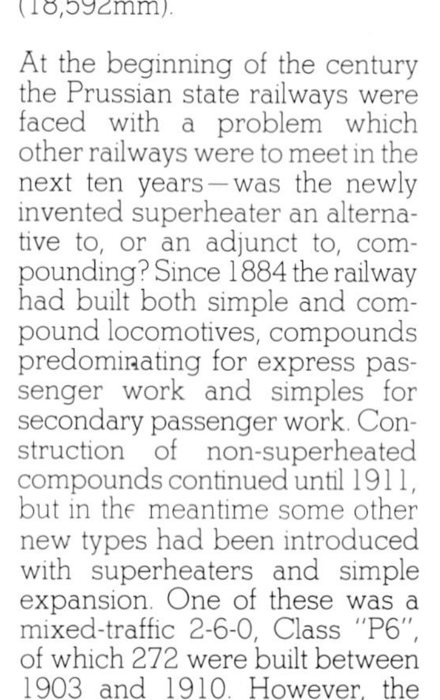

Above: *Class "38" 4-6-0 No. 38.3635 at the head of a German Federal Railways local train at Lippstadt.*

At the beginning of the century the Prussian state railways were faced with a problem which other railways were to meet in the next ten years—was the newly invented superheater an alternative to, or an adjunct to, compounding? Since 1884 the railway had built both simple and compound locomotives, compounds predominating for express passenger work and simples for secondary passenger work. Construction of non-superheated compounds continued until 1911, but in the meantime some other new types had been introduced with superheaters and simple expansion. One of these was a mixed-traffic 2-6-0, Class "P6", of which 272 were built between 1903 and 1910. However, the 63in (1,600mm) driving wheels of these engines were found to be too small for the speeds that had been intended, and there were difficulties with weight distribution.

In 1906 an enlarged design, a 4-6-0 with wheels of 69in (1,750 mm) was introduced. It was originally envisaged that this new engine would have a permissible speed of 68mph (110km/h), and that it could undertake express passenger work on the hilly parts of the system. Unfortunately the first engines of the type proved to be unreliable and unpopular, and suffered many failures in service.

The solution to the problems included a reduction in the cylinder diameter and adjustments to the weight distribution between the axles, but it was also decided that the motion and valve gear was unsuitable for speeds in excess of 62mph (100km/h), and the engines were rated as secondary passenger and mixed-traffic engines, with the classification "P8". Thus a locomotive which originally had been intended for express passenger work on a limited part of the Prussian system became the most widely-used and popular mixed-traffic engine ever built, serving eventually over much of Europe.

Like many of the most successful and popular steam engines, the "P8" was simple in layout, and initially at least, elegant in outline. The round-topped boiler, with a long narrow firebox, was well proportioned, and although at least two variants of boiler were fitted in due course, the basic shape was not changed. In addition to Dr Schmidt's superheater, the engines also had long-travel piston valves, which he recommended as an adjunct to his superheater. The combination of superheater and piston valves, with a well-proportioned Walschaert's valve gear, gave the engines an efficiency which approached the highest that was ever to be attained with simple expansion. Their load rating was 700 tonnes on the level at 50mph (80km/h) and 300 tonnes on 1 in 100 (1 per cent) at 31mph (50km/h).

Once the intitial snags had been cleared from the "P8", it was built in large numbers, its axle load permitting its use over much of the Prussian system. It was also built in small numbers for the state railways of Oldenburg, Mecklenburg and Baden as well as for export. Although nominally a secondary passenger engine, it took a full share in express passenger work on which speed was limited to 62mph (100km/h).

At the end of World War I, by which time 2,350 "P8"s had been built for the KPEV, Germany was required to hand over large numbers of locomotives as reparations, and 628 "P8"s were allocated to other countries. The Belgian railways had been particularly badly affected, and they received 2,000 locomotives, of which 168 were "P8"s. These

Below: *In due time the "P8" class 4-6-0s of the Prussian railways became class "38" of The German State (now Federal) Railways whose smart red-and-black colours are depicted here.*

engines survived a second invasion by the Germans, and, adorned with an elegant lipped chimney, they lasted until the end of steam in that country in 1966.

The loss of "P8"s was partly made good by building more of them, the last being completed in 1928. On the German State Railway the engines became class 38. Under the German State ownership and later there was much reboilering of the engines, but the alterations which affected their appearance were the fitting of full-depth smoke deflectors, feedwater heaters and other external fittings.

World War II saw the "P8"s spreading into Eastern Europe as the Germans moved east, and this resulted in an even wider distribution than before. They worked in Czechoslovakia, Greece, Jugoslavia, Poland, Roumania and Russia, and many of them remained in those countries. In several countries they were modified externally in accordance with national practice, but the basic design was rarely altered. Eventually a total of 3,438 "P8"s were built in Germany, and about 500 in other countries. In addition the Polish railways, which acquired a large number of genuine "P8"s, built 190 engines in which a larger boiler, with wide firebox, was mounted on a "P8" chassis.

After World War II a nominal total of 2,803 "P8"s remained in Germany, but many of them were unservicable. On the formation of the DB and DR (in West and East Germany respectively) the engines were divided between the two systems. On both railways the full-depth smoke deflectors were mostly replaced by the post-war variety. Although difficulties with steaming had never been a weakness of the "P8" class, some of the DR engines were fitted with Giesl exhausts.

Two of the DB engines were converted to quasi tank engines by coupling them to four-wheeled tenders by a coupling which was designed to permit running in both directions. In addition a number of engines were equipped for push-and-pull working with the original tenders. However, the spread of dieselization made rapid inroads into the "P8" class, and by 1968 the total was down to 73, mostly working south of Stuttgart. The rate of withdrawal then slowed, and the last engine survived until January 1975, three years after the last of them on DR had been withdrawn. However, engines of the class remained at work in other countries, and several were still at work in Poland and Roumania in 1979, 73 years after the introduction of the class. Eight are preserved at various sites in Germany.

It is interesting to note that, although the "P8" was built to the Continental loading gauge, the general layout and dimensions were very similar to some 1,500 British 4-6-0s, although the ancestry of the British engines was independent of that of the German ones. The valve events of the "P8" were almost identical with those of the LMS Class 5 Stanier 4-6-0 "Black Fives".

Above: *Royal Prussian Union Railway "P8" class 4-6-0 in its latter days as class "38" on the German Federal Railways.*

Below: *"P8" class 4-6-0 of Prussian design but hauling behind it a train belonging to the Roumanian State Railways.*

Cardean Class 4-6-0

Great Britain:
Caledonian Railway (CR), 1906

Tractive effort: 22,667lb (10,282kg).
Axle load: 41,500lb (19t).
Cylinders: (2) 20¾in x 26in (527 x 660mm).
Driving wheels: 78in (1,981mm).
Heating surface: 1,814sq ft (168.5m^2).
Superheater: 516sq ft (48m^2).
Steam pressure: 200psi (14.1kg/cm^2).
Grate area: 26sq ft (2.4m^2).
Fuel: 11,000lb (5t).
Water: 5,000gall (6,000 US) (22.7m^3).
Adhesive weight: 123,000lb (56t).
Total weight: 294,000lb (133.5t).
Length overall: 65ft 6in (19,964mm).

No engines ever built have a better claim to be regarded as the epitome of the Golden Age of Steam than *Cardean* and her sisters. The complex and beautifully polished Caledonian Railway blue livery as depicted in the illustration speaks for itself, but in many other ways the running of these engines seems now to be like some dream. For example, *Cardean* was allocated to one train and one driver at a time. The legendary David Gibson (described as being "temperamental as a film star") had her from 1911 to 1916. Every weekday she ran the famous "Corridor"—the 2pm from Glasgow to Euston—as far as Carlisle, returning in the evening on the corresponding train from Euston.

There is no doubt that Gibson regarded *Cardean* as his personal property and lavished on his locomotive a concern and a care that nowadays only a very few men give even to their own motor cars. The result was a degree of reliability that is far out of reach of any railway administration today. There were of course occasional happenings and one such took place in April 1909 when a crank axle broke at speed. One of the driving wheels became detached and bowled away down the bank. Although the train parted from the engine, became derailed and was brought quickly to a stand by the automatic Westinghouse brake, the locomotive (now a 4-5-0!) went merrily on but quite amazingly stayed on the rails. This happened during the reign of James Currie, Gibson's predecessor.

Gibson is today remembered almost as well as John Farquharson McIntosh, the designer of

Above: Cardean's *lesser cousins. A class "908" mixed traffic 4-6-0. There were 10 engines of this class, all built at St. Rollox works in 1906.*

Class A 4-6-0

Australia:
Victorian Government Railways (VGR), 1907

Tractive effort: 27,480lb (12,464kg).
Axle load: 39,500lb (18t).
Cylinders: (2) 22 x 26in (559 x 660mm).
Driving wheels: 73in (1,854mm).
Heating surface: 2,048sq ft (190.6m^2).
Superheater: 375sq ft (35m^2).
Steam pressure: 185psi (13kg/cm^2).
Grate area: 29sq ft (2.7m^2).
Adhesive weight: 118,000lb (54t).
Total weight: 263,500lb (119.5t).
(Tender details not available).

The first of these "A" class 4-6-0s, which all followed this now well-established tradition of self-help in locomotive building, was delivered in 1905 from the Victorian Government Railways own Newport Workshops. They were large

these fine engines. The five members of the class were built at the Caledonian Railway's own St. Rollox shops in 1906 and were very conservative in design. Inside cylinders and motion, with Stephenson's valve gear driving slide valves situated on top of the cylinders via rocking levers, was an entirely nineteenth-century arrangement. McIntosh believed that the better riding and aesthetics given with the cylinders and motion inside the frames more than balanced the handicap of inaccessibility, as well as the extra costs involved in making a crank axle. Superheaters were added in 1911-12. Later, vacuum-brake equipment was fitted to enable vacuum-braked trains of other companies to be worked, for the Caledonian Railway was an air-brake line.

A steam servo-mechanism for the reversing gear was a help and large bogie tenders were provided for non-stop runs over such distances as the 150¾ miles (243km) from Carlisle to Perth. Rather oddly, only one of the class was named and it also seems strange that the one chosen should be that of the house in which the Deputy Chairman of the company lived. So all except No.903 *Cardean* had to be content with numbers which ran from 904 to 907.

No.907 perished in Britain's worst-ever railway disaster at Quintinshill near Carlisle on 22 May 1915. The other four survived through the railway grouping of 1923. The last survivor was *Cardean* herself, withdrawn as London Midland & Scottish No. 14752 in 1930. Only one Caledonian feature was adopted by the LMS, and that a few years later, when William Stanier specified the CR's deep-toned "hooter" style whistle for his locomotives.

Below: *Caledonian Railway 4-6-0 No.903* Cardean *in all her glory as running between Glasgow and Carlisle prior to 1914.*

Above: *The sole preserved Caledonian Railway locomotive, 4-2-2 No.123 of 1886, currently on display in Glasgow.*

handsome engines, typical of British practice of the day and seven years later there were 125 of them, all with outside cylinders, and inside slide-valves actuated by Stephenson link motion and bogie tenders. Originally, none had superheaters but these were added gradually over the years, the last being converted in 1949. In 1923, non-superheated engines became class "A-1", superheated ones class "A-2". All the "As" then took the running numbers 816-839.

Some 4-6-0s for freight traffic had arrived from Baldwin of Philadelphia as early as 1879. The famous "DD" class 4-6-0 for mixed traffic was built locally from 1902 onwards and they formed the progenitors of the most numerous and long-lasting express passenger locomotives of the state of Victoria.

Left: *A Victorian Railways' class "A" 4-6-0. These were the principal express passenger locomotives for many years.*

There were a few modifications such as the conversion of 57 to oil-firing during the late 1940s and, earlier, the addition of smoke deflectors. A group of 5 were extensively modernised with new front-ends and "Boxpok" disc wheels, which considerably changed their appearance.

Between 1915 and 1922 sixty more "A2" class engines (Nos. 940 to 999) were delivered and these had Walschaert's valve gear and outside valves. There was no difference in classification between the "Walschaert A2s" and the "Stephenson A2s" and together the 185 locomotives were the mainstay of Victoria's passenger services until after World War II. There were a few modifications such as the fitting of smoke deflectors, conversions to oil firing and a group of five with Boxpok disc wheels. When one considers that there were only some 640 locomotives on the whole Victoria 5ft 3in (1,600mm) gauge railway system, it can be seen that the position the "A2" 4-6-0s occupied was an important one. It was if the London, Midland, Scottish Railway had 2,300 "Royal Scot" 4-6-0s instead of 70.

In 1950 some "R" class 4-6-4s were delivered from Britain and these made numerous class "A1" and "A2" 4-6-0s redundant. Even so, the class lasted until 1963 in normal service. Three have been preserved, No.995 at the Australian Railway Historical Society museum at Newport, No.964 at Edwardes Lakes and No.996 in the public park at Echucha. So ended an era in the history of the state.

4500 Class 4-6-2 France: Paris-Orleans Railway (P-O), 1907

Axle load: 39,000lb (17.5t).
Cylinders, HP (2) 16.5 x 25.6in (420 x 650mm).
Cylinders, LP (2) 25.2 x 25.6in (640 x 650mm).
Driving wheels: 74¾in (1,900mm).
Heating surface: 2,100sq ft (195m^2).
Superheater: 684sq ft (63.5m^2).
Steam pressure: 232psi (16kg/cm^2).
Grate area: 46sq ft (4.27m^2).
Fuel: 13,500lb (6t).
Water: 4,400gall (5,280US) (20m^3).
Adhesive weight: 117,000lb (53t).
Total weight: 301,000lb (136.5t).
Overall length: 68ft 2½in (20,790mm).

(These dimensions refer to the superheated version of the class before rebuilding by Chapelon).

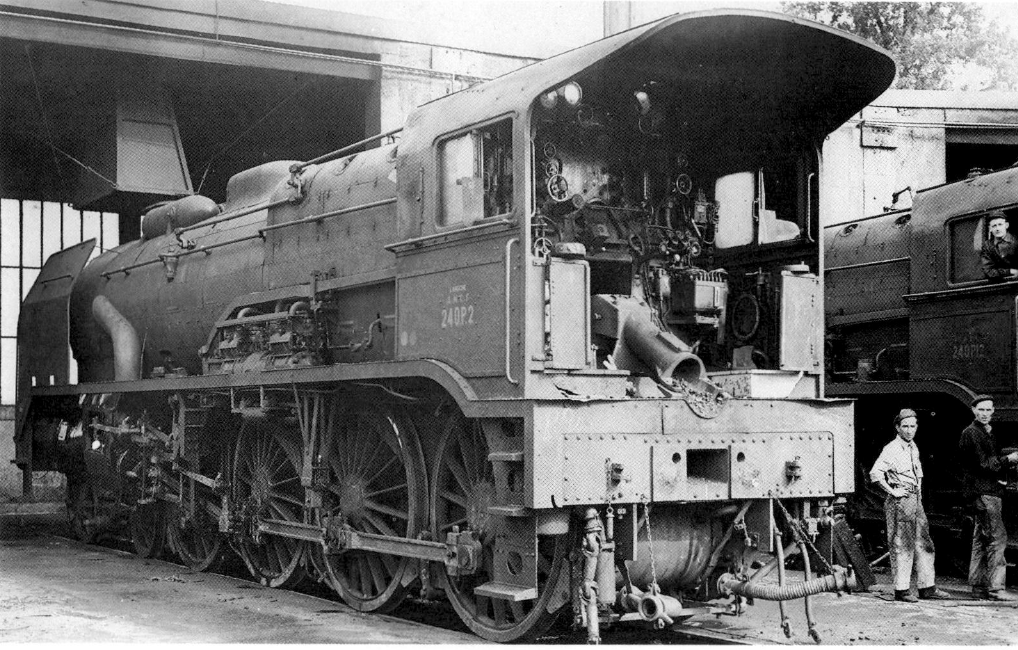

Above: *A Paris—Orleans 4-6-2 rebuilt into a 4-8-0 (No.240P2) for the Paris-Lyons Mediterranean main line in 1940.*

If the number of express passenger locomotives to be included in this book was reduced to a single one then this locomotive might well be the choice. It was by a short head the first Pacific to *run* in Europe (not the first to be built—some were built in Britain for Malaya earlier the same year) and later became not only the most powerful but also the most efficient 4-6-2 ever to run in Europe. It was also certainly the most technically advanced Pacific but also, of course, somewhat complex.

One hundred "4500" Pacifics were built between 1907 and 1910 mostly by French builders but rather strangely including a batch of 30 (Nos.4541-70) by the American Locomotive Co of Schenectady, USA. There were also another 90 of class "3500" which were identical except for wheels 4in (100mm) smaller in diameter. The "3500"s were constructed between 1909 and 1918.

All these Paris-Orleans 4-6-2s were four-cylinder de Glehn compounds. An interesting feature was the trapezoidal grate which was wide at the back in the usual manner of Pacific grates. At the front, however, it was narrow and sat between the frames. Later, examples were delivered with superheaters and some had them fitted later. The high-pressure cylinders had piston valves while the low-pressure ones had balanced slide valves. They were competent but not specially remarkable machines in those days, capable of cylinder horsepowers of around 2000.

In the 1920s the replacement of wooden carriages by steel began to show up the inadequacies of the Pacifics, yet a commitment to electrification absorbed totally any resources there might have been for new construction.

A young man called André Chapelon, who had an appointment as development engineer on the Paris-Orleans Railway, proposed a drastic rebuilding and in 1926, persuaded his superiors—against their better judgement—to put the work in hand in accordance with his ideas. Changes in the administration meant further patient persuasion but eventually in 1929 the transformed No.3566 took the road. A new era in steam traction had begun; there was a 25 per cent increase in power production for the same amount of steam, while the boiler improvements which made more steam available took the possible cylinder horsepower up to 3,700, an 85 per cent increase over the originals.

Chapelon achieved this apparent miracle after a careful analysis of the shortcomings of the original design. He considered the whole process of producing steam power from cold water to exhaust steam and took the following measures to improve it:

(a) Pre-heating the feed-water with waste heat from the exhaust.
(b) Provision of extra heating surface in the firebox, using flattened vertical ducts known as thermic syphons.
(c) Provision of a superheater 24 per cent larger in size and of a more efficient (but also more complicated) design.
(d) Much larger steam pipes to improve steam flow.
(f) Poppet valves to give quicker and larger openings to steam and exhaust, replacing the existing high-pressure piston-valves and low-pressure slide-valves.
(f) An improved exhaust system giving greater draught with less back pressure. This took the form of a double chimney.

The existing Walschaert's valve gears were retained to work the oscillating camshafts of the poppet valves.

The P-O announced that No.3566 had hauled 567 tons

Below: *French National Railways 4-6-2 No.231E23, as rebuilt by Chapelon from the original 1907 Paris-Orleans Railway design.*

from Poitiers to Angoulême, 70.1 miles (113km), start-to stop at an average speed of 67.3mph (107.7km/h); a 1 in 200 (0.5 per cent) gradient was climbed at 77.5mph (124km/h). This was a performance unprecedented in France and caused a sensation in the world of locomotive engineering.

To cover requirements on the P-O, thirty-one further "3500" 4-6-2s were rebuilt. As electrification proceeded, some of the originals became surplus, and other railways in France could not wait to get their hands on these miracle locomotives. Twenty were rebuilt for the Northern Railway and later 23 for the Eastern. Later on a further 20 were built new for the Northern.

In 1932, sixteen further locomotives of the "3500" series were given a rather less drastic rebuilding, in which poppet valves were not provided, but instead a form of twin piston valve head was used. This gave double the amount of port opening for a given amount of movement and was known as the Willoteaux valve after its inventor, an assistant of Chapelon's.

During the same year one of the remaining unsuperheated "4500" class 4-6-2s was rebuilt into a 4-8-0 at Tours. The intention was to provide a locomotive with one-third more adhesive weight, more suitable for the gradients of the line to Toulouse, altogether steeper than those en route to Bordeaux. A different

boiler was needed, having a narrow firebox to fit between the rear driving wheels and one based on those carried by the Northern 4-6-2s was used.

Otherwise the recipe was as before, except that some improvement in detail enabled 4,000 cylinder hp to be developed. Eleven more were rebuilt in 1934 and in 1940 a further twenty-five "4500" were rebuilt for the PLM (now South-Eastern Region SNCF) main line, designated class "240P". This time a mechanical stoker was fitted.

Dimensions etc. of these engines which differed substantially from the originals were as follows:
Axle load: 44,000lb (20t).
Cylinders LP: (2) 25.2 x 27.2in (650 x 690mm).
Heating surface: 2,290sq ft ($213m^2$).
Superheater: 733sq ft ($68m^2$).
Steam pressure: 290psi ($20.4kg/cm^2$).
Grate area: 40sq ft ($3.75m^3$).
Fuel: 26,500lb (12t).
Water: 7,500gall (9,000US) ($34m^3$).
Adhesive weight: 177,500lb (80.5t).

The sort of achievement that these 4-8-0s were capable of included the surmounting of Blaisy-Bas summit between Paris and Dijon with 787 tonnes at 59mph (94½km/h) minimum after several miles at 1 in 125 (0.8 per cent). During the war the "240P" had to manage 28 coaches and could reach 53mph (85km/h) on the level with this load. Alas, after the Paris-Lyons line was electrified in 1952, proposals to use these engines elsewhere in France foundered, for reasons which have never been adequately explained.

In the 1960s the remaining Pacifics of Paris-Orleans design had become concentrated—much to the delight of their many British admirers—at Calais. Their effortless performances with heavy boat trains up, say, the 1 in 125 (0.8 per cent) climb to Caffiers between Calais and Boulogne will long remain in the memory.

In 1956 some tests were made of the behaviour of electric locomotive pantograph current collectors at high speeds, and 110.6mph (177km/h) was reached by 231E19 pushing an equivalent of 220 tons. This was the highest speed achieved by these engines.

Against this was the sad fact that, economical as the Chapelons were in respect of coal consumption, in overall terms they were more expensive to run than the fleet of simple rugged 2-8-2s—the 141R class—supplied from North America at the end of World War II. These could also manage, say, 850 tons on a 1 in 125 (0.8 per cent) gradient at over 52mph (84km/h), even if you would not describe the performance as effortless. So in the end at Calais as elsewhere in France, simple engines out-lasted even these superb compounds. No.231E22 is displayed at the Mulhouse Museum and No.231E41 is being restored at St Pierre-les-Corps. Unrebuilt Paris-Orleans No.4546 is also preserved.

Above: *Calais Maritime Station. Chapelon 4-6-2 No.231E39 has just arrived from Paris with the "Golden Arrow" express. The connecting steamer is on the right.*

Below: *Paris-Orleans Railway 4-6-2 No.4546 shown as restored to original condition for display at the French National Railway Museum at Mulhouse, Alsace.*

Class S 3/6 4-6-2

Germany: Royal Bavarian State Railway (KBStB), 1908

Axleload: 39,500lb (18t).
Cylinders, HP: (2) 16.7 x 24.0in (425 x 610mm).
Cylinders, LP: (2) 25.6 x 26.4in (650 x 670mm).
Driving wheels: 73.6in (1,870mm).
Heating surface: 2,125sq ft (197.4m²).
Superheater: 798sq ft (74.2m²).
Steam pressure: 228psi (16kg/cm²).
Grate area: 48.8sq ft (4.5m²).
Fuel: 18,800lb (8.5t).
Water: 6,030gall (7,240US) (27.4m³).
Adhesive weight: 116,000lb (53t).
Total weight: 328,500lb (149t).
Length overall: 69ft 11in (21,317mm).
(Dimensions refer to the 1923 series)

The locomotives of Bavaria were as different from those of Prussia as were the Bavarian Alps from the stark North German plain. The reason for this was simple: most of the Bavarian engines were designed by A G Maffei, and in the present century that firm's chief designer, Heinrich Leppla, had a flair for locomotive lineaments which was quite lacking in the centrally-controlled designs of Prussia. The supreme achievement of Maffei was the family of Pacifics which originated in 1908, and were supplied over a period of 23 years to the railways of Bavaria and Baden and to the German State Railway.

From 1895 all the passenger engines bought by the Bavarian Railway were four-cylinder compounds, and these included two Atlantics acquired in 1901 from Baldwin of Philadelphia. Contact with these engines seemed to influence Maffei, for it became the first European locomotive builder to adopt the bar frame as standard. Associated with this was the American practice of casting the cylinders in massive blocks which incorporated the smokebox saddle. All four cylinders drove the same axle, which in the Pacifics was the middle one. The inside high-pressure cylinders were steeply inclined to allow the connecting rod to clear the leading coupled axle, and their valves were level with, but outside, the cylinders, which placed them conveniently alongside the outside valves, which were above their cylinders. A simple vertical rocker enabled the outside valve gear to drive the inside valves also, and all steam pipes were contained within the cylinder block.

Above: *A class "S3/6" 4-6-2 at speed. Note right-hand running.*

Top: *The luxurious interior of one of the saloon cars of the Rheingold Express.*

The first engines to this design were supplied in 1908 to the Baden Railway; Bavaria took delivery of its first batch in the following year. By 1911 twenty-three had been built, with driving wheels 73.6in (1,870mm) in diameter and a boiler pressure of 213psi (15kg/cm²). Then came 18 engines with 78.7 in (2,000mm) wheels, and between 1913 and 1924 a further 78 with the smaller wheels. Succeeding batches incorporated detail changes, including the addition of feedwater heaters, an increase in axle load, and an increase in boiler pressure to 228psi (16kg/cm²). All were classified S3/6, which indicated an express locomotive (schnellzuglok) with three driving axles in a total of six. Of these engines 16 went to France and 3 to Belgium as reparations after World War I.

In 1925 the first German State Railway standard Pacifics were built, but these engines had a 20 tonne axleload, and pending the introduction of a smaller version of the class there was a need for more Pacifics with an axle load of 18 tonnes. So impressed were the DR authorities with the power output of the Maffei engines that they ordered a further 40, which were delivered between 1927 and 1931. These were the only engines ordered by DR to a design which originated on a state railway other than the Prussian. The class was then numbered from 18.401 to 18.548, with 8 blanks.

With these extra engines the class spread from its native haunts, and until the introduction of the standard "03" Pacific with 18 tonnes axle load they worked from sheds as far afield as Osnabrück and Berlin Anhalt. But even the "03"s did not

displace them from the Rhine Valley main line, and it was Bavarian Pacifics which worked the prestigious Rheingold express both before and after World War II. So successful were they on this service that 30 of the final batch of 40 engines were given new welded boilers with combustion chambers between 1953 and 1956, as part of the German Federal Railway reboilering programme. These engines were renumbered 18.601-30. When displaced from the Rhine Valley by electrification they retired to Bavaria, and their last duties were the expresses between Munich and Lindau on Lake Constance. The last of them were withdrawn from Lindau shed in 1966.

One engine passed into the hands of the new German State Railway in East Germany, and this also was given a new boiler, and used for high-speed testing. It is scheduled to be amongst the 13 locomotives of the family which are preserved in various places. Amongst them is Bavarian No.3634 of 1912, which is in the Germany Museum in Munich restored to its original livery.

In side view the Bavarian Pacifics had a slender appearance, with "daylight" showing under the boiler and through the bar frames, but head-on the massive cylinder block gave a blunt impression. In DR days small smoke deflectors were fitted, and these helped to mask the bluntness of the cylinder block. At first stovepipe chimneys were fitted, but late chimneys were of a graceful flared shape, which was almost British. Usually modifications made to German designs worsened their appearance, but the Bavarian Pacifics became gradually better looking, although they suffered by losing their original holly green livery with yellow lines and black bands.

Below: *A German State Railway class "S 3/6" 4-6-2 poses with a set of Rheingold Express cars.*

Class 10 4-6-2 Belgium: Belgian State Railway (EB), 1910

Tractive effort: 43,800lb (19,800kg).
Axleload: 43,200lb (19.6t).
Cylinders: (4) 19.7 x 26.0in (500 x 660mm).
Driving wheels: 78in (1,980mm).
Heating surface: 2,500sq ft ($232m^2$).
Superheater: 816sq ft ($76m^2$).
Steam pressure: 199psi ($14kg/cm^2$).
Grate area: 49.2sq ft ($4.6m^2$).
Fuel: 15,400lb (7t).
Water: 5,280gall (6,340US) ($24m^3$).
Adhesive weight: 130,000lb (59t).
Total weight: 352,640lb (160t).
Length overall: 70ft 3in (21,404mm).

Locomotive enthusiasts arriving for their first visit to Belgium might well have suspected a delayed attack of *mal de mer* when they saw a Pacific carrying a boiler apparently intended for an Atlantic. They were indeed seeing one of the most remarkable looking locomotives in Europe, but it was a 2-10-0 rather than an Atlantic which accounted for the shortness of the boiler.

At the beginning of the century the Belgian State Railway was passing through an interesting phase, in which a number of classes of inside cylinder locomotive were built with a close resemblance to the MacIntosh locomotives of the Caledonian Railway of Scotland, but in 1904 a new era of locomotive construction was instituted under the direction of J B Flamme. French compound locomotives were attracting much attention, and one of these was acquired on loan. It showed such an improvement over existing Belgian engines that 12 similar locomotives were built, followed by 57 compound 4-6-0s. The next move was the construction of four 4-6-0s of a new design to compare the application of superheating to simple and compound locomotives. As a result of these tests, Flamme decided that he could revert to the simplicity of the non-compound, but for the largest classes it would be desirable to use four cylinders, to give the improved balancing which had been demonstrated by the four-cylinder compounds.

The outcome of this decision was the introduction of two classes of very large locomotives, a Pacific for express work and a 2-10-0 for freight work. Apart from a small difference in the firebox dimensions, the boilers of the two types were identical, and its length was determined by the weight limitations on the 2-10-0. This boiler would have looked short on any Pacific, but as Flamme arranged his inside cylinders to drive on the leading axle, with a generous length of connecting rod, the effect was accentuated. Even the outside cylinders were ahead of the smokebox, and there was a platform over the inside cylinders and motion protruding far ahead of the smokebox. The boiler itself was unusual for Europe of that time, as it had a very large grate to suit low-grade coal, and to accommodate this without excessive weight, the boiler tapered steeply outwards just ahead of the firebox, giving the outline of boiler known in the United States as "wagon top". Walschaert's valve gear was fitted to the outside valves, with rocking shafts to drive the inside valves.

Twenty-eight of these engines were built between 1910 and 1912, followed by a further 30 in the succeeding two years; the second batch had a slightly smaller grate and shorter rear end, which reduced the weight from 102 to 98 tonnes. These engines, which became Class 10 under a later classification, took over the principal express work on the routes from Brussels to Liège and Luxembourg, and proved very successful.

Under a programme of rehabilitation of the Belgian locomotive stock after World War I, the superheaters of the Pacifics were enlarged, double chimneys were fitted, designed by the then Chief Mechanical Engineer, Legein, the frames were strengthened at the front, and many smaller improvements were made. The process of improvement continued over the years. Smoke deflectors were added and ACFI feed water heaters, so that with the addition of extra fittings the weight gradually crept up. One locomotive was fitted with a mechanical stoker, and another had further shortening of the firebox and rear end to reduce the weight again. Neither of these alterations was repeated. The original six-wheeled tenders were replaced by bogie tenders from Prussian reparations engines.

From 1938 more major improvements were instituted, influenced by Chapelon's work in France. These included larger steam pipes, a still larger superheater, and the replacement of the Legein exhaust by the Kylchap pattern. With the massive chimney of the Kylchap exhaust, and the various extra fittings on the boiler, the engines now had a truly formidable appearance, but the alterations produced the intended improvement in performance. With successive imrovements their loading on the heavily-graded Luxembourg line had been increased from 350 to 500 tonnes. They continued to haul the expresses on that route until electrificaton, and on 30 September 1956 one of them hauled the last steam-worked passenger train on that line. The last of the second series was withdrawn from service in 1956, but the last of the first series remained in service until 1959, 49 years after the introduction of the class.

Below: *The strange-looking front end of Belgian class "10" 4-6-2 No.10045, one of a very successful series.*

1501 Class 4-6-2 **Argentina:** Buenos Aires and Pacific Railway (BAP), 1910

Tractive effort: 26,472lb (12,011kg).
Axle load: 40,000lb (18t).
Cylinders: (2) 21 x 26in (533 x 660mm).
Wheels: 67in (1,701mm).
Heating surface: 1,597sq ft ($148m^2$).
Superheater: 435sq ft ($40.5m^2$).
Steam pressure: 150psi ($10.5kg/cm^2$).
Grate area: 27sq ft ($2.5m^2$).
Fuel (oil): 1,960gall (2,350 US) ($8.9m^3$).
Water: 5,500 gall (6,600 US) ($25m^3$).
Adhesive weight: 118,000lb (53.5t).
Total weight: 361,000lb (164t).
Overall length: 70ft 2¼in (21,392mm).

The four main British-owned railways of Argentina fanned out from the capital, Buenos Aires, across the pampas towards the west. The 5ft 6in (1,676mm) gauge main line of the Buenos Aires & Pacific was the one that went *due* west and at least partly earned its name by reaching Mendoza at the foot of the Andes from where the Transandine railway led across to Santiago on Chile's Pacific coast. The nature of the country served is indicated by the fact that there was a 205-mile (328km) length of straight track en route.

In 1909, the company ordered from the North British Locomotive Company of Glasgow some Pacifics of very distinctive appearance. They were of advanced design for their day and in fact they were the first locomotives supplied by NBL to have superheaters. It is clear that they only barely needed that extra pair of carrying wheels at the rear end. On the broad gauge, of course, the narrow firebox is not so narrow and, furthermore, at less of a disadvantage anyway with oil firing. The hinged buffers were an Argentine specialty, cattle thrown aside by the cowcatcher might get caught on fixed ones; equally unconventional were the decorative shape of the hinges on the smokebox door, and the unusual aspect of the cab.

British-built locomotives of the day, for India say, could easily be confused with those for home use, but these imposing engines had an ambience all their own. Fourteen (Nos.1511-24) were supplied during 1910-11 and these were the last express passenger locomotives ordered for the company before nationalisation in 1948. This was a reflection of the parlous economic situation of the foreign-owned railways in Argentina during that period.

After nationalisation, the Buenos Aires and Pacific Railway became known as the General San Martin National Railroad, but the 4-6-2s soldiered on. They were still in use in the mid-1970s, giving good service on stopping passenger trains after more than sixty years at work.

Right: *After more than sixty years of service, 4-6-2 No.1515 of the General San Martin National Railway, stands at the head of a local train. Note the hinged buffers of European pattern in the folded position above the cowcatcher.*

Class A3/5 4-6-0 **Switzerland:** Swiss Federal Railways (SBB), 1913

Axle load: 18,000lb (16t).
Cylinders, HP: (2) 14¼ x 26in (360 x 660mm).
Cylinders, LP: (2) 22½ x 26in (570 x 660mm).
Driving wheels: 70in (1,780mm).
Heating surface: 1,389sq ft ($129m^2$).
Superheater: 497sq ft ($46.2m^2$).
Steam pressure: 220psi ($15.5kg/cm^2$).
Grate area: 28sq ft ($2.6m^2$).
Fuel: 15,500lb (7t).
Water: 3,900gall (4,700 US) ($17.8m^3$).
Adhesive weight: 106,000lb (48t).
Total weight: 243,000lb (110t).
Overall length: 61ft 2in (18,640mm).

As inhabitants of a small country with two great locomotive designing cultures on their doorstep, the Swiss took basic locomotive principles from neighbouring France and Germany. The Jura-Simplon Railway, which led to the French border, used de Glehn compounds; while the

Gotthard Railway which pointed towards Germany, on the whole favoured the compounding system of Maffei of Munich.

When it came to building the engines, though, the famous Swiss Locomotive Works (SLM) of Winterthur did very nearly all of it. Of their express passenger 4-6-0s, only four out of 200 were not SLM products. To be sure, the Swiss had no 4-6-0s in one sense, because they used their own system of classification—what the Anglo-Saxon world called a 4-6-0 the Swiss would know as an A3/5; that is to say, a locomotive with maximum speed above 75km/h (47mph) and three coupled axles out of five.

It may appear strange that 4-6-0s were thought adequate for a mountainous country, but nearly all the main lines ran in the valleys and an exception the Loetschberg Railway was built as an electric railway. So that left the Gotthard line and here it was convenient to employ 4-6-0s in pairs or a 4-6-0 piloted by a 2-10-0 to haul express passenger trains up the long 1 in 38½ (2.6 per cent) approach ramps to the Gotthard tunnel.

The dimensions given refer to the most common group of Swiss 4-6-0s, of which 109 (Nos. 701-809) were built for the Jura-Simplon and Swiss Federal railways between 1902 and 1909. The superheaters were added between 1913 and 1933.

The Gotthard Railway (GB) began using 4-6-0s in 1894 and by 1905 had 30 de Glehn compounds (GB Nos. 201-30, SBB Nos. 901-30) but the next orders were for Maffei compounds (SBB) Nos.931-38 and 601-49 of which 931-34 actually came from Maffei), distinguishable from de Glehn's by having the drive on to the leading pair of coupled wheels. 4-6-0 No.705 is preserved in running order—it is intended to be displayed in the Lucerne Transport Museum.

Left: *Swiss Federal Railways' preserved "A3/5" class 4-6-0. This locomotive is currently in use for hauling special trains provided for the enjoyment of steam locomotive enthusiasts.*

Class 3700 4-6-0

Netherlands:
State Railway (SS), 1910

Tractive effort: 25,647lb (11,633kg).
Axle load: 37,000lb (17t).
Cylinders: (4) 15¾ x 26in (400 x 660mm).
Driving wheels: 72¾in (1,850mm).
Heating surface: 1,566sq ft (145.5m^2).
Superheater: 441sq ft (41m^2).
Steam pressure: 171psi (12kg/cm^2).
Grate area: 30.3sq ft (2.8m^2).
Fuel: 13,200lb (6t).
Water: 3,960 gall (4,750 US). (18m^3).
Adhesive weight: 110,000lb (50t).
Total weight: 270,500lb (123t).
Length overall: 60ft 8in (18,480mm).

To British eyes the steam locomotives which ran on the continent of Europe were certainly not things of beauty—except in Holland, where the principal express locomotives had a totally familiar style. The only thing that was strange about them was their enormous height; this was partly illusion because they were normally observed from platforms at ground level rather than three feet above the rails and partly because they really were a lot taller—almost 2ft (600mm), in fact. But there they all were—tall, stylish 4-6-0s, with low running boards, splashers, copper-capped chimneys, brass domes and apple green paint. The only un-British things about them were some big elegant oil lamps and an absence of names.

The first batch came from Beyer, Peacock of Manchester in 1910 and 120 were built between then and 1930. Some were built by Werkspoor, the native locomotive builders and others in Germany. Later versions had widened eight-wheel tenders instead of six-wheel ones. There were four cylinders in line, all driving on the leading coupled axle. Two sets of Walschaert's valve gear worked the valves of the outside cylinders direct and the inside ones via rocking levers. Knorr's feed-water heaters and pumps were fitted. In the 1920s two locomotives were the subject of experiments in the use of low-grade pulversided coal, but the results were not successful enough to be perpetuated.

In 1929 a 4-6-4 tank version of the class was built, ten in number, but time was running out for steam in Holland, Electrification proceeded apace during the next few years and,after the war, was resumed with greater urgency. Steam operations came to an end in 1958, but happily the railway administration set aside a 4-6-0 which is now displayed in the Railway Museum at Utrecht; This No.3737 is in running order and has worked steam specials in recent years.

Below: *Netherlands State Railways class "3700" 4-6-0 No.3737. This locomotive has been restored to near its original condition and is on display in the National Railway Museum at Utrecht.*

Fairlie 0-6-6-0

Mexico:
Mexican Railway (FCM), 1911

Tractive effort: 58,493lb (26,533kg).
Axle load: 46,000lb (21t).
Cylinders: (4) 19 x 25in (483 x 635mm).
Driving wheels: 48in (1,219mm).
Heating surface: 2,924sq ft (272mm²).
Steam pressure: 183psi (12.9kg/cm²).
Grate area: 47.7sq ft (4.43m²).
Fuel: 20,000lb (9t).
Water: 3,500 gall (4,200 US). (16m³).
Adhesive weight: 276,000lb (125t).
Total weight: 276,000lb (125t).
Length overall: 50ft 7¾in (15,435).

The Mexican Railway ran 264 miles (426km) from the port of Vera Cruz on the Atlantic Ocean to Mexico City, at an altitude of 7,349ft (2,240m). The summit of the route is at Acocotla, 8,320ft (2,536m), but in 108 miles (174 km) the line climbs to 8,050ft at Esperaza. The maximum gradient is a hideous 1 in 22 (4.5 per cent) and the sharpest curve is 325ft radius or 17½ degrees. Before electrification came in 1923, this superbly scenic but very difficult railway had not unexpectedly something rather special in the way of motive power.

The "Fairlie" articulated locomotive was invented by an English engineer called Robert Fairlie in 1864 and foreshadowed the majority of locomotives (other than steam) in service today by having a generator for the working fluid—steam in Fairlie's case, electricity in modern times—as part of the locomotive body; the body being carried on two power bogies which provided the traction. All the axles were therefore driven, so the total weight was available for adhesion, yet the whole vehicle remained extremely flexible. The arrangement made the locomotive an excellent proposition for sharply curved steeply graded mountain lines. Even so, "Fairlies" were never as popular as the "Garratt" or "Mallet" articulated locomotive types, and their application for this British-owned Mexican line was certainly their greatest both as regard size of individual locomotives and their success as haulage units.

The first "Fairlie" came to Mexico in 1871 and by 1911, a total of 49 had been delivered, of which 18 were still in service in 1923 when electrification made them finally redundant. The last and largest of them was a batch of three supplied by Vulcan Foundry in 1911, carrying running numbers 183 to 185. The advantage of the "Fairlie" is best summed up by comparison with

Right: *A Mexican Railways "Fairlie" locomotive of the batch supplied by the Vulcan Foundry in 1911.*

George the Fifth Class 4-4-0

Great Britain
London & North Western Railway (LNWR), 1910

Tractive effort: 20,066lb (9,102kg).
Axle load: 43,680lb (19.5t).
Cylinders: (2) 20½ x 26in (521 x 660mm).
Driving wheels: 81in (2,057mm).
Heating surface: 1,547sq ft (144m²).
Superheater: 303sq ft (28.1m²).
Steam pressure: 175psi (12.3kg/cm²).
Grate area: 22.4sq ft 92.08m²).
Fuel: 13,440lb (6t).
Water: 3,000gall (3,600 US) (13,640)
Adhesive weight: 85,680lb (38.25t).
Total weight: 212,800lb (95t).
Length overall: 57ft 2¾in (17,445mm).

In 1903 Francis Webb retired (somewhat reluctantly, so rumour has it) from the locomotive chieftainship of the London & North Western Railway. His compound locomotives, as well as the other but outdated engines which had been kept on to bolster up the former's inadequate performance quickly followed. Webb's immediate successors, George Whale and W.J. Bowen-Cooke, restocked over the next ten years with 336 workmanlike 4-4-0s and 4-6-0 express locomotives, all built at Crewe Works. And when one says built at Crewe Works, that is exactly what is meant. Trainloads of coal, iron ore, limestone, copper ingots etc. would roll in at one end of Crewe Works and completed locomotives with evocative names decked out in that wonderful "blackberry black" livery would roll out at the other. For this capability, Francis Webb must take a good deal of the credit, even if he held on too long to funny ideas when it came to locomotive design.

Of the four types of express locomotive built at Crewe during those eventful years, outstanding

a typical British main-line locomotive of the day. Compare, for example, these Mexican Railway locomotives with a LNWR type. For a penalty of 29 per cent in weight and 5 per cent in axleload, one obtained an 114 per cent increase in grate area, 220 per cent more adhesive weight and 190 per cent more tractive effort. The "Fairlie"s were the most powerful locomotives built in Britain up to this time.

Although the speeds of trains on the Mexican Railway's inclines were severely restricted by traction limitations going up, and to 8mph (13km/h) for safety reasons coming down, the "Fairlie"s had excellent riding and tracking qualities at high speeds. This was inadvertently discovered on one or two occasions when runaways occurred; speeds estimated at up to 70mph (113km/h) were achieved on sharp curves without derailment. The motion of these locomotives was quite conventional, with outside piston valve cylinders and Walschaert's valve gear. On the other hand the double boilers were very unusual indeed. The boiler barrels at both ends were nearly similar, but the firebox in the centre was common to both barrels. One big dome in the usual position for one half of the boiler (normally the uphill end) collected the steam for all four cylinders.

The expense involved in this double boiler was almost certainly the main reason why the "double Fairlie" articulated locomotive was never widely used. It is true there were some problems with the flexible pipes and joints which fed the steam from the boiler to the powered bogies, but experience and the improvement of details would have solved them. In fact this is just what has happened on the one railway left in the world that has "double-Fairlie" steam locomotives still in use, the Festiniog Railway in North Wales. Their 40 ton 0-4-4-0 tanks, are, however, a far cry from the 123-ton Mexican monsters.

"Single Fairlie"s, however, went into quite extensive use. These locomotives had a normal boiler, a leading power bogie and a trailing un-powered bogie behind the firebox. An ability to negotiate absurdly sharp curves was the property that appealed and many (under various names, for Fairlie's patent was not recognised in the USA) were used on urban railways, particularly elevated lines which had to negotiate city street corners. But "single Fairlies" were only, as it were, half of what was a good idea.

was the later of the two classes of 4-4-0, the legendary "George the Fifth" locomotives which entered service in 1910. To the solid simplicity of the earlier design, the "Precursors" of 1903, were added piston valves and superheaters with results that today are hard to believe. Ninety "George the Fifths" were built, to which must be added a further 64 conversions from "Precursors" as well as another ten from a group of unsuperheated 4-4-0s known as "Queen Marys". These relatively small locomotives handled the great northbound expresses out of London's Euston station in a competent manner, handling trains of more than 400 tons in weight—shall we say 13 bogie coaches—on the Euston to Crewe schedules which involved average speeds of 55mph (88km/h) between stops and maxima of 75 (120) or so. When a "George" went roaring by hauling one of these long rakes of "plum and spilt milk" carriages, it was an exceedingly fine sight. There were very few railways in the world which at that time confided such exacting loads and timings to four-coupled power. North of Crewe towards Carlisle on steeper gradients the related 4-6-0 "Experiment" or "Prince of Wales" classes were at least in theory the usual motive power, but south of Crewe the most important workings were in the charge of these 4-4-0s.

Left: *A LNWR* "George the Fifth" *class 4-4-0 picks up water at speed.*

The "Georges" had everything of the simplest; note the round top outer firebox wrapper instead of the more complex Belpaire pattern used elsewhere. The cylinders were inside, but the use of Joy valve gear, whose rods and slides were located in the same vertical plane as the connecting rods, meant that all the inside motion was accessible for lubrication and maintenance. Some minor weaknesses marred their performance when in worn condition; for example, the Schmidt type piston valves would start to leak and increase steam and coal consumption by noticeable amounts. And having said that the Joy valve gear was very simple, the version fitted to the "George" was not quite as simple as it might have been. For some reason—one suspects it may have been in order to use the same gear as that fitted to the "Precursors" which had *outside* admission slide valves instead of inside admission piston valves—there was an extra rocking lever between the valve rod and the valve spindle. Wear here was also detrimental to steam consumption. Of course, LNWR locomotives were such that this only meant that as the time came nearer when a visit to Crewe Works was due, "Georges" just needed to be thrashed a little harder than ever to get over the road "right time"; the "Georges" were certainly in the "North-West" tradition of being able to stand it.

In 1923, when the railways of Britain were merged into four groups, all the "Georges" came into the possession of the London Midland & Scottish Railway, ruled largely by Midland Railway men who thought little of any locomotives whose origin was LNWR. It was no surprise, then, that withdrawal of these splendid locomotives began in late 1935 and continued until the last one ceased work in May 1948. With the scrapping of superheated Precursor *Sirocco* in October 1949 the LNWR 4-4-0s (and, indeed, all the LNWR express passenger engines) disappeared. None of the 4-4-0s or the 4-6-0s was preserved, a surprising final piece of spite on the part of the 'Midlanders'.

Class S 2-6-2

Russia:
Ministry of Ways of Communication, 1911

Tractive effort: 30,092lb (13,653kg).
Axle load: see text.
Cylinders: (2) 22½ x 27½in (575 x 700mm).
Driving wheels: 72¾in (1,850mm).
Heating surface: 2,131sq ft ($198m^2$).
Superheater: 958sq ft ($89m^2$).
Steam pressure: 185psi ($13kg/cm^2$).
Grate area: 51sq ft ($4.72m^2$).
Fuel: 40,000lb (18t).
Water: 5,000gall (6,000 US) ($23m^3$).
Adhesive weight: see text
Total weight: 370,500lb (168t).
Overall length: 77ft 10½in (23,738mm).

This handsome design of express passenger locomotive either was just or was just not the most numerous in the world. Construction continued over a period of 40 years, usage over more than 60 and certainly its numbers were the largest in the hands of one administration. Compared with British locomotives, Russian ones can be four feet (1,200mm) higher and two feet (600mm) wider; in terms of weight, though, in steam days locomotive axles could be loaded at most with two tons less each. So there was no temptation towards (or even the possibility of) filling the huge space available with inaccessible ironmongery.

In both Czarist and Communist Russia, steam locomotive design was in the hands of university professors and they studied and tried out many fascinating theoretical possibilities—more thoroughly, perhaps, than elsewhere. But when it came to actual usage out on the road, then these learned gentlemen seemed always to reach the conclusion that Old Geordie (Stephenson) had got it right and the simplest answer was the best.

Another characteristic in which the old regime was far ahead of its time was standardisation; this continued as did locomotive classification, without even a wriggle, over that great watershed in human history the Russian Revolution. In 1955, Britain had, for example, some 20 classes of express passenger locomotives ten or more strong, while the Soviet Union had a mere four; this out of a fleet intended for such traffic approximately the same in number. These class "S" (written "C" in Russian script) 2-6-2s were a standard design ordered by the Ministry of Ways of Communication for general usage amongst the many independent railways. The "S" stood for the Sormovo works at Nijni Novgorod where the class was built. About 900 were turned out before the Revolution.

Very little needs to be said of the design which took very early on the standard final form of the steam locomotive, having two cylinders, Walschaert's valvegear, wide firebox, superheater and compensated springing. The fulcrum points of the latter could be altered to bring extra weight on to or off the driving wheels. For running on lines which had inadequate permanent way, the maximum axle-load could be quickly changed from 18 tonnes to 16 tonnes by a simple adjustment, at the cost of reducing the adhesive weight from 54 tonnes to 48 tonnes.

A modified and enlarged version known as class "Su", was first produced at the Kolomna Works near Moscow in 1926. This sub-class, of which about 2,400 were built during the next 15 years, is the basis of the particulars and of art-work below. The "u" stood for *usilenny*, which means "strengthened"; in Russian script "Su" is written "Cy". The cylinders, wheelbase and boiler were enlarged but, interestingly, the boiler pressure was kept at the same modest level. The adoption of high boiler pressure was so often (like the substitution of diesel for steam 40 years later) a costly matter of "keeping up with the Jones'".

The extra cost of a high-pressure boiler is considerable, especially as regards maintenance, while even its theoretical

Below: *The standard Russian passenger locomotive, the class "Su" 2-6-2.*

Right: *Class "Su" 2-6-2 No. 100-85 outside Sormovo works. This example is equipped for burning oil fuel.*

Class 685 2-6-2

Italy:
State Railways (FS), 1912

Tractive effort: 27,741lb (12,586kg).
Axle load: 35,500lb (16t).
Cylinders: (4) 16½ x 25½ (420 x 650mm).
Driving wheels: 72¾in (1,850mm).
Heating surface: 1,922sq ft ($178.6m^2$).
Superheater: 516sq ft ($48.5m^2$).
Steam pressure: 171psi ($12kg/cm^2$).
Grate area: 38sq ft ($3.5m^2$).
Fuel: 13,500lb (6t).
Water: 4,842gall (4,040 US) ($22m^3$).
Adhesive weight: 103,500lb (47t).
Total weight: 265,362lb (120.4t).
Overall length: 67ft 6in (20,575mm).

The "685" class was developed from 1912 onwards as the standard Italian express locomotive. In total 390 eventually were produced, some by conversion from an earlier non-superheated compound design on the Plancher system (the "680" class) and others built new. The idea was to obtain almost the power of a "690" class 4-6-2, yet not suffer the restricted usage of the latter due to their 19 tons axle load. The "685's used superheated steam and had four cylinders, each pair using a common piston valve. The tortuous passageways intrinsic to that unusual arrange-

Right: *The Italian State Railways class "685" standard express locomotive of which 390 were made.*

advantages are dubious. Of course, some railways had to adopt high-pressures in order to obtain sufficient tractive effort with the largest cylinders that could be squeezed into a tight loading gauge, but Soviet Russia was not one of them. Those university owls again!

After World War II, production was restarted at Sormovo Works (whose location was by then known as Gorki) and continued until 1951, by which time some 3,750 "S" class had been built. Variations included some built in 1915 for the standard gauge Warsaw-Vienna line known as sub-class "Sv" (Cb). There was also a "Sum" (Cym) group, having a system for pre-heating the air used in combustion. A Scotsman named Thomas Urquhart introduced successful oil-burning locomotives to Russia in 1880, since when it became commonplace. Many "S" class used this form of firing.

ment did not assist the "685" class to become the world's most free running engines. A prominent but odd feature of all Italian steam locomotives including the "685" is the Salter's spring-balance safety valve required by law, provided in addition to two normal modern pop valves. The Zara truck described earlier was naturally also a feature.

Arturo Caprotti was of course an Italian and the patent poppet valve gear he devised (which might well have become a world standard if steam had continued) was later fitted to 123 of these engines. The usual problem of maintenance—which stemmed from the Caprotti cam-boxes being precision not blacksmith engineering—was overcome by a unit-replacement system.

Two other names associated with attempts to improve these and other Italian steam locomotives are Attilo Franco and Piero Crosti, whose Franco-Crosti boiler was designed to take the exhaust gases from a conventional locomotive and extract some of the heat from them in large drums, so pre-heating the feed-water. Aesthetically, the result is awful, but five "685" converted in 1940 showed an 18.93 per cent saving in fuel. Even so, those who devised the system had thrown away simplicity, steam's trump card; the remaining 385 were left alone.

Right: *An Italian State Railways class "685" 2-6-2 receives some attention to lubrication from its driver.*

Class 231C 4-6-2

France:
Paris, Lyons and Mediterranean Railway (PLM), 1912

Axleload: 40,500lb (18.5t).
Cylinders, hp: (2) 17.3 x 25.6in (440 x 650mm).
Cylinders, LP (2) 25.6 x 25.6in (650 x 650mm).
Driving wheels: 78.7in (2,000mm).
Heating surface: 2,185sq ft ($203m^2$).
Superheater: 694sq ft ($65m^2$).
Steam pressure: 228psi ($16kg/cm^2$).
Grate area: 45.7sq ft ($4.3m^2$).
Fuel: 11,000lb (5t).
Water: 6,160gall (7,400 US) ($28m^2$).
Adhesive weight: 122,000lb (55t).
Total weight: 320,500lb (145.5t).
Length overall: 65ft 7in (20,000mm).

Above: *"The Flèche d'Or" (Golden Arrow) hauled by a long-serving, efficient ex-PLM "231C" 4-6-2.*

French engineers were early converts to the creed of compounding, and in no other country was compounding pursued more enthusiastically or successfully. Nevertheless, from time to time right up to the last steam designs, occasional doubts entered the minds of French engineers, and a batch of simple expansion locomotives appeared, but the outcome was always a strengthening of the orthodox doctrine.

The Pacifics of the PLM illustrated this process. Between 1890 and 1907 the railway ordered 845 locomotives, of which 835 were compounds, and in the period 1905 to 1907 construction of compound Atlantics and 4-6-0s was in full swing. But in 1907 the first European Pacific appeared, and in 1909 the PLM produced two prototype locomotives of that wheel arrangement, one simple and one compound. Apart from the recurrent desire to ensure that the mechanical complications of the compounds were really justified, there was a further reason for this particular digression into simple expansion. Compound expansion enables a higher proportion of the energy in the steam to be converted into work during expansion, but to get the full benefit of the greater expansion in the compound it is necessary to use a high steam pressure, and high pressure brings higher boiler maintenance costs. At this time there was a new attraction for engineers—the superheater—which offered the possibility of improving the thermal efficiency sufficiently for simple expansion to be acceptable, and with it the possibility of using a lower boiler pressure.

The two PLM Pacifics put this problem to the test, for the compound engine used saturated steam but the simple engine was superheated. The compound had the de Glehn layout of cylinders, with the outside high-pressure cylinders set well back over the rear bogie wheels, but the simple engine had the four cylinders in line, as in the PLM Atlantics and 4-6-0s. The in-line arrangement gave a much more rigid assembly than the de Glehn arrangement. Apart from the differences in cylinders, motion and boiler already mentioned,

Above: *A Paris, Lyons and Mediterranean Railway compound 4-6-2, depicted in SNCF days, receives attention from its crew.*

Below: *The locomotive for the "Flèche d'Or" (Golden Arrow) express backs down from Calais depot to Calais Maritime station.*

the two engines were as far as possible identical, but the compound worked at 227psi (16kg/cm²) and the simple at 171psi (12kg/cm²).

In 1911 the two engines ran comparative trials, and the superheated engine developed higher powers and used 16 per cent less coal than the compound. A natural step would have been to try superheating *with* compounding, but at that time it was not found possible to build a superheated compound within the weight restrictions. Thus 70 more simples were ordered in 1911, but by the following year the design problems of the superheated compound had been overcome, and 20 were built, differing from the prototype in having all four cylinders in line, as in the simple engines. Uncertainty still prevailed, and 20 more simples were next built, but then in 1913 a careful comparison was made between the two varieties of superheated design, and the compound returned a 25 per cent lesser coal consumption and better performance. The issue was finally settled, and the PLM built no more simple Pacifics; the existing simple engines were in due course converted to compounds.

In 1921 a further 230 Pacifics were ordered, and in 1931 55 more, making a total of 462. Successive batches incorporated improvements, mainly to the exhaust arrangements and to the boiler proportions, but the basic layout remained unchanged. Improvements continued to be made, and later still Chapelon's ideas on steam passage and boiler proportions were incorporated in an engine which was rebuilt with a boiler having 284psi (20kg/cm²) pressure. A scheme to apply this boiler widely was initiated, but the incorporation of the PLM into the SNCF resulted in 30 engines only receiving this treatment, the last of them in 1948, but 284 engines received a more modest treatment on Chapelon lines. By this time the sub-divisions of the class were very complicated.

The PLM Pacifics had long and distinguished lives, and the quality of their performance responded directly to the improvements which were made to them, but they never achieved the levels of the Chapelon rebuilds of the Paris-Orleans Pacifics. As electrification displaced them from the PLM main line from 1952 onwards, they spread to other regions. Withdrawal began in the 1950s, but many of the boilers were not worn out, and there was thus a good supply of spare boilers, with which some of the engines were maintained in service until 1969.

Four engines were retained for preservation, including 231K22, a rebuild with partial Chapelon improvements, which is at Steamtown, Carnforth, Lancashire.

Class 310 2-6-4

Austria:
Imperial and Royal State Railway (KKStB), 1908

Axleload: 32,200lb (14.6t).
Cylinders, HP (2) 15.4 x 28.3in (390 x 720mm)
Cylinders, LP: (2) 24.4 x 28.3in (620 x 720mm).
Driving wheels: 82.7in (2,100mm).
Heating surface: 2,077sq ft (193m²).
Superheater: 463sq ft (43m²).
Steam pressure: 213psi (15kg/cm²)
Grate area: 49.7sq ft (4.6m²)
Fuel: 19,000lb (8.5t).
Water: 4,620gall (5,550 US) (21m³).
Adhesive weight: 98,000lb (44t).
Total weight: 322,000lb (146t).
Length overall: 69ft 11in (21,318mm)

Above: *Striking view of Gölsdorf 2-6-4 No.210.01 showing the original member of the class in as-built condition.*

The railways of the Austrian empire were lightly constructed, and in places heavily graded. Locomotives were thus required to have a low axle load, but to be capable of developing high powers at moderate speeds when burning low-grade fuel. From 1897 to 1916 locomotive design in the empire was largely in the hands of Karl Gölsdorf, a designer of fertile imagination, who is credited with some 45 different designs, all branded clearly with his ideas.

After building two-cylinder compounds he reached the stage in 1908 when four cylinders became necessary, but as a means of reducing weight he used a single piston valve to serve the high-pressure and low-pressure cylinders on each side of the engine. This involved tortuous steam ports, which would have imposed a severe limit on power output at high piston speeds.

In that year Gölsdorf produced his masterpiece. When other European railways were just turning to the Pacific, Gölsdorf found that by reversing the Pacific into a 2-6-4, he could support the large firebox which the quality of coal required, and at the same time make the front of the engine lighter in weight than with a leading bogie. To mitigate the disadvantages of his valve arrangement, he used driving wheels 82.7in (2,100mm) in diameter,although the maximum speed was only 62 mph (100km/h). By this means piston speeds were kept low. Every possible device was used to keep the weight down, so that this large engine had a load on the coupled axles of only 32,200lb (14.6 tonnes), a remarkable achievement. At the speeds involved the leading pony truck proved to be no disadvantage.

The proportions of the cylinders, which are critical in a compound, proved to be less than ideal, and despite some modifications to the valves, the locomotives never achieved the power output which the size of boiler merited. Nevertheless they hauled the principal expresses on the easier main lines of old and new Austria until the appearance of 2-8-4 locomotives in 1928.

The first 2-6-4s were saturated and classified "210", but from 1911 superheaters were fitted. Austria had a total of 43 of these "310" class engines, and in addition seven were supplied to Prussia and three to Poland. The last of the Austrian engines was withdrawn in 1957.

Whatever their deficiencies in performance, the 2-6-4s were most imposing engines, and to build such a large locomotive for such a small weight was a masterpiece of design. One of them is preserved at the Vienna Technical Museum.

Below: *A class "210" 2-6-4 in Austrian Federal Railways' days when nearing the end of its life.*

Remembrance Class 4-6-4 Tank

Great Britain:
London, Brighton & South Coast Railway (LBSCR), 1914

Tractive effort: 24,180lb (10,991kg).
Axle load: 44,000lb (20t).
Cylinders: (2) 22 x 28in (559 x 711mm).
Driving wheels: 81in (2,057mm).
Heating surface: 1,816sq ft (167.7m²).
Superheater: 383sq ft (35.6m²).
Steam pressure: 170psi (11.9kg/cm²).
Grate area: 26.7sq ft (2.48m²).
Fuel: 8,000lb (3½t).
Water: 2,700gall (3,250 US) (12m³).
Adhesive weight: 126,000lb (101t).
Total weight: 222,000lb (101t).
Length overall: 50ft 4¾in (15,361mm).

Those great trains of the world which were hauled throughout their journeys by tank locomotives were few and far between. One such was the immortal "Southern Belle", the all-Pullman express which ran non-stop several times a day over the 51 miles between London's Victoria Station and Brighton. Specially associated with this train was a group of seven 4-6-4 or "Baltic" tank locomotives, the most powerful motive power ever owned by the London Brighton and South Coast Company.

Previously, the express trains between London and the south coast had been hauled by a fleet of 4-4-0s, 4-4-2s, and 4-4-2Ts, supplemented by two 4-6-2Ts. The new 4-6-4s were to some extent a stretched version of the latter and were known as class L. Their designer Colonel L. B. Billinton was instructed to produce locomotives capable of running the "Belle" and other fast trains such as the "City Limited" to an accelerated timing of 45 or 50 minutes instead of the even hour. In fact, the 60 minute timing was never improved upon, even by the "Southern Belle's" successor, the electric "Brighton Belle" which replaced the steam train after 1933, but the addition of third-class Pullman cars to the previously all-first formation made the train an increasingly harder haulage proposition.

Conventional practice of the day was followed in most respects but the valve gear arrangement was interesting. Outside Walschaert's valve gear was used,

Below: *4-6-4T No.B333 (later 2333)* Remembrance *at Victoria Station, London in 1930. This was the Southern Railway's War Memorial locomotive and bore special plaques on the side tanks to that effect for many years.*

Class F 4-6-2

Sweden:
Swedish State Railways (SJ), 1914

Axle load: 35,500lb (16t).
Cylinders, HP: (2) 16½ x 26in (420 x 660mm).
Cylinders, LP: (2) 24¾ x 26in (630 x 660mm).
Driving wheels: 74in (1,880mm).
Heating surface: 2,038sq ft (189m²).
Superheater: 732sq ft (68m²).
Steam pressure: 185psi (13kg/cm²).
Grate area: 38.5sq ft (3.6m²).
Fuel: 14,336lb (6.5t).
Water: 5,500gall (6,600 US) (25m³).
Adhesive weight: 105,000lb (48t).
Total weight: 322,000lb (146t).
Length overall: 69ft 9in (21,265mm).

Above: *Swedish State Railways' class "F" 4-6-2. All these engines were sold to Denmark when the Swedish Railways were electrified. This one was returned to Sweden for preservation.*

Sweden is not a country associated in many people's minds with the building of steam locomotives, yet there was and is a locomotive-building industry there. Moreover, the country had its own style of locomotive engineering and this was even occasionally exported. It is a measure of the essential simplicity of the steam locomotive that very small countries (and railway companies) can build their own designs economically. More often, however, the Swedes took orders for other people's designs. Nydquist and Holm of Trollhättan had an order in the 1920s for some 0-10-0s for Russia. The locomotives were duly completed and the builders were instructed that a Soviet ship would call for them at the firm's own quay. They were loaded aboard, whereupon the captain promptly unloaded gold bars to their value on to the quayside.

Nydquist and Holm not only built but also designed Sweden's finest ever class of express locomotive, the class "F" 4-6-2s delivered to the Swedish State Railways in 1914. It will be seen that they were very distinctive and at the same time very handsome machines. The leading bogie had frames outside, partly no doubt for clearance reasons. This feature also facilitated the employment—it is thought for the first time ever—of roller bearings

Above: *"Remembrance" class No.329* Stephenson *is here depicted in its original LB&SCR umber livery. These famous tank locomotives handled the legendary "Southern Belle" all-Pullman express which ran several times a day between Victoria Station, London, and Brighton until in 1933 the steam train was superceded by the all-electric "Brighton Belle".*

actuating inside piston valves between the frames via rocking levers; all this in spite of having the cylinders themselves outside the frames. One reason for this unusual arrangement was the wish to have similar cylinders to the 4-6-2Ts plus the need to provide a well tank between the frames under the boiler, which the existence of valve motion there would preclude. There had in fact been trouble including a derailment, whose cause had been attributed to the swishing of water in half-full tanks plus the high centre of gravity. This occurred soon after the prototype, No.321 *Charles C Macrae* first entered service in April 1914. The solution was on similar lines to the extra dummy funnels on some steamships of the day, that is, adopted so as not to spoil the appearance. It consisted of making all but the bottom 15 inches of the side tanks into dummies in order to lower the centre of gravity of the locomotive. The modifications were successful and speeds as high as 75mph were quite frequently run without any further problems.

A second locomotive (No.328) was completed just before war broke out that autumn and five further examples (Nos.329-333) in 1921-22. Two more received names at that time—No.329 became *Stephenson,* while No.333 was chosen to be the War Memorial for the company's servants killed in the war and so was named *Remembrance.* The later examples of the class were never fitted with the feed-water heaters and steam-operated feed pumps which, unusually in British practice, were fitted to the earlier ones for a time after they were new.

After electrification in 1933, the Southern Railway converted the 4-6-4 tanks into 4-6-0s known as class N15X in which guise they had a long and honourable career on the less exacting longer distance services of the bigger system, lasting well after 1948 into British Railways days. That this was considered worth-while doing demonstrates more than any words the excellent qualities of these extremely handsome locomotives. The last survivor (LB&SCR No.331, SR No.2331, BR No.32331) was withdrawn in July 1957.

(a Swedish speciality) for full-size locomotive axles.

The "F"s also used a system of compounding, of German origin, which attempted to get the advantages of a compound locomotive without the complications. The four cylinders all drove the centre coupled axle and were accordingly fairly steeply inclined at an angle of 6¼° to the horizontal. The two low-pressure cylinders were outside and the two high-pressure ones inside. Each pair was served by a single piston-valve spindle with multiple heads which controlled the admission of steam from the boiler to the high-pressure cylinders, the release of steam from the high-pressure cylinders, its admission to the low-pressure ones and finally the exhaust from the low pressure cylinders to atmosphere. The complicated feature of this arrangement was the labyrinth of passageways inside the cylinder castings, but at least these did not involve moving parts. A single set of Walschaert's valve gear was provided in full view on each side of the locomotive.

Left: *A Swedish "F" class 4-6-2 heads a passenger train near Nyboda in 1927. Note the electrification poles and wires, which were to spell the end of steam traction on the main line expresses of Sweden.*

A "windcutter" cab was fitted, although the permitted speed was only 62mph (100km/h) reflecting, as did the very light axle load (16 tons) track conditions in Sweden at that time. The unusual "bath" shaped tender also made its contribution to the distinctiveness of the design. The "F" class handled the principal expresses on the Stockholm-Gothenburg and Stockholm-Malmö main lines.

An absence of coal deposits combined with the presence of water power induced the Swedish railways to proceed with electrification and in 1936 these big 4-6-2s were declared surplus to requirements. A customer was to hand just across the water and the class "F" 4-6-2s, Nos.1201-11 shortly became Danish Railways class "E" Nos.964 to 974. Their new owners took to their purchase readily, so much so that during and after World War II the Danish locomotive-building firm of Frichs built another 25 to the original drawings.

King Christian of Denmark was a lifelong railway enthusiast and he asked that his funeral train should be hauled by steam. Two "E"s did the duty, although by the time he died diesel traction had taken over generally. Two "E" class are preserved, No.974 (ex SJ 1211) of 1916 and No.999 of 1950. A further two locos (Nos.978 and 996) are also set aside for possible operation.

K4 Class 4-6-2 **United States:** Pennsylvania Railroad (PRR), 1914

Tractive effort: 44,460lb (20,170kg).
Axle load: 72,000lb (33t).
Cylinders: (2) 27 x 28in (686 x 711mm)
Driving wheels: 80in (2,032mm).
Heating surface: 4,040sq ft (375m²).
Superheater: 943sq ft (88m²).
Boiler pressure: 205psi (14.4kg/cm²).
Grate area: 70sq ft (6.5m²).
Fuel: 36,000lb (16t).
Water: 10,000gall (12,000 US) (46m³).
Adhesive weight: 210,000lb (96t).
Total weight: 533,000lb (242t).
Overall length: 83ft 6in (25,451mm).

The Pennsylvania Railroad called itself the Standard Railroad of the World. This did not mean that the system was just average or typical, but rather that the railroad's status was one to which other lines might aspire, but a status that it was extremely unlikely that they would reach. The Pennsy's herald was a keystone, indicating the position the company felt it occupied in the economy of the USA. The famous "K4" 4-6-2s, introduced in 1914 and the mainstay of steam operations until after World War II, might well similarly be given the title Standard Express Locomotive of the World.

There were 425 of them, built over a period of 14 years, and they followed a series of classes of earlier 4-6-2s introduced previously. The Pennsy was normally exceedingly conservative in its locomotive engineering and its Pacific era was ushered in by a single prototype ordered from the American Locomotive Company in 1907, later designated class "K28". By 1910 the railroad felt it knew enough to start building some of its own and in a short time 239 "K2"s were put on the road. In 1912, quite late in the day really, superheating was applied to these engines.

In 1913, the company went to Baldwin of Philadelphia for 30 "K3" 4-6-2s. These were interesting in that they were fitted with the earliest type of practical mechanical stoker, known as the "Crawford" after its inventor, D.F. Crawford, Superintendent of Motive Power (Lines West). This had been in use on the Pennsylvania Railroad since 1905 and by 1914 nearly 300 were in operation—but only 64 on 4-6-2s. Later designs of stoker used a screw feed, but the principle used in the Crawford was to bring forward the coal by means of a series of paddles or vanes, oscillated by steam cylinders, which were feathered on the return stroke like the oars of a rowing boat. The coal was fed into the firebox at grate level, unlike later types of stoker, which feed on to a platform at the rear, for distribution by steam jets.

In addition, there was a further Alco prototype supplied in 1911, larger than the "K28" and designated "K29". There was also the "K1" class, which was an "in house" project, designed but never built.

The prototype "K4" Pacific appeared in 1914; it was considerably larger than the "K2" class, having 36 per cent more tractive effort and 26 per cent more grate area at a cost of a 9 per cent increase in axle loading. The design owed as much to that Apex of the Atlantics, the "E6" class 4-4-2 as to the earlier 4-6-2s.

Top: *Pennsylvania Railroad "K4" class 4-6-2 No.3749 built at Altoona.*

Above: *The "Broadway Limited" leaves Chicago in 1938. The streamline locomotive is "K4" class No.3768, styled by Raymond Loewy.*

The Pennsylvania Railroad was one of the very few North American lines to approach self-sufficiency in locomotive design and construction. It liked to build its own locomotives, designed by its own staff, in its own shops. One aid to this process was a locomotive testing plant at a place called Altoona — a hallowed name amongst the world's locomotive engineers. Altoona was then the only place in North America where a locomotive could be run up to full speed and power on rollers and where instrumentation could pick up exactly what was happening inside. In this way the designers' expectations could be checked under laboratory conditions and corrections applied.

The prototype "K4" was put to the question at Altoona soon after it was built, but few changes were needed as a result for the production version. The oil headlight and wooden pilot (cowcatcher) were not, however, repeated. By 1923, after more than 200 "K4"s had been built, power reverse replaced the hand-operated screw reversing gear of earlier engines. In due time the latter were converted, foreshadowing a date (1937) when hand reversing gear would be illegal for locomotives with over 160,000lb (72.7t) adhesive weight. The same edict applied to the fitting of automatic stokers to locomotives of such size and many (but not all) "K4"s were fitted with them during the 1930s. Before then the power output had been severely limited by the amount of coal a man could shovel. The last five "K4"s had cast steel one-piece locomotive frames. Another interesting box of tricks that also became general in the 1930s, was the continuous cab signalling system. A receiver picked up coded current flowing in track circuits and translated this into the appropriate signal aspect on a miniature signal inside the cab.

One could see signs of Pennsy's conservatism, for example, even in the later "K4"s the ratio of evaporative heating surface to superheater size was as low as 4.3, instead of the 2.2 to 2.5, more typical of the passenger locomotives which other North American railroads were using in the 1930s. There was also the modest boiler pressure, three-quarters or less of what was used elsewhere. It is not being suggested that such a policy was wrong, only that it was different. Low boiler pressures and modest degrees of superheat had a marked and favourable effect on the cost of maintenance and repair; perhaps the Pennsy, who could buy coal at pit-head prices, had done its sums in depth, trading some extra (cheap) coal for less (expensive) work in the shops.

Running numbers were allocated at random between 8 and 8378, although the last batches built during 1924-28 were numbered in sequence from 5350 to 5499. All were built at the PRR's Juanita shops at Altoona, Pennsylvania except Nos.5400 to 5474 of 1927 which came from Baldwin.

Above: *PRR "K4" class 4-6-2 No.5354, built between 1924 and 1928, takes water at a wayside station.*

There were a few "specials" amongst the "K4" fleet. Two engines (Nos.3847 and 5399) were fitted with poppet valve gear, thermic syphons in the firebox, and improved draughting; so equipped they could develop over 4000hp in the cylinders instead of the 3000hp typical of a standard "K4". A number of other engines (designated class "K4sa")had less drastic treatment with the same end in view; in this case the firebox and exhaust improvements were accompanied by larger piston valves, 15in (381mm) diameter instead of 12in (305mm). One engine (No.3768) was fully streamlined for a while; a number of others were partly streamlined and specially painted to match certain streamlined trains. Many types of tender were used, including a few which were so big they dwarfed the engine, but held 25 tons of coal and 23,500 US gallons (107m^3) of water.

Until the coming of the Duplex locomotives after World War II, the "K4"s handled *all* Pennsy's express passenger trains outside the electrified area. During the winter of 1934 the *Detroit Arrow* was scheduled to cover the 64 miles (102km) from Plymouth to Fort Wayne, Indiana, in 51 minutes, an average speed of 75½mph (121km/h) and accordingly for a short time the fastest steam timing in the world. The cylinder limitations of the standard "K4"s did, however, mean much double-heading in driving Pennsy's great "Limiteds" across these long level stretches of the Lines West. The fact that these legendary locomotives were so economical in other ways more than balanced such extravagances as the use of two on one train.

In crossing the Alleghany mountains, such heroic measures as three "K4"s (or even, it is said, sometimes *four)* at the head end were needed to take, say, an unlimited section of the "Broadway Limited" up the 1 in 58 (1.72 per cent) of the Horseshoe Curve. Nowadays such things are only a memory, but a single "K4", presented to the City of Altoona, stands in a little park inside the famous semi-circle curve in remembrance of the monumental labours of one of the world's greatest express locomotives. Another (more accessible) is under cover in the Strasburg Railway's excellent museum in the town of that name.

Below: *One of the famous "K4" class 4-6-2s of the Pennsylvania Railroad. Between 1914 and 1928 425 were built, mostly at the road's own Altoona shops.*

C53 Class 4-6-2 Dutch East Indies: State Railways (SS), 1917

Axle load: 28,000lb (12.5t).
Cylinders, LP: (2) 13.4 x 22.8in (340 x 580mm).
Cylinders, HP: (2) 20.5 x 22.8in (520 x 580mm).
Driving wheels: 63in (1,600mm).
Heating surface: 1,324sq ft (123m²).
Superheater: 463sq ft (43m²).
Steam pressure: 200psi (14kg/cm²).
Grate area: 29sq ft (2.7m²).
Fuel (oil): Not recorded
Water: Not recorded
Adhesive weight: 83,000lb (37.5t).
Total weight:* 147,000lb (66.5t).
Overall length: 68ft 6½in (20,889mm).
*(*Engine only—tender details not recorded).*

Above: *Official works photograph of "C53" class 4-6-2 for Indonesia.*

Java, the densely populated main island of Indonesia, was in pre-World War II days provided by its Dutch rulers with an excellent railway system. There were such things as 12-coupled freight locomotives, colour light signalling, flying junctions and even suburban electrification around Djakarta, then known as Batavia. There were also the fastest narrow gauge trains in the world—and they were steam.

This perhaps may seem a little strange, considering that Indonesians are hardly concerned with such handicaps to the enjoyment of life as worrying over time. But there was a reason; in colonial days it was not considered safe to run trains at night, not by reason of any possible sabotage, but because the natural hazards of tropical railroading in the dark were too much for the careful Dutch—mindful of their orderly native Holland—to contemplate.

Since Java is close to the equator, sunset occurs there sensibly at the same time throughout the year, so the timetable was not too complex; but it did also mean that trains between Batavia and Surabaya, the island's principal cities, could not complete their journeys of 512 miles (820km) between dawn and dusk unless they got a move on. For many years an overnight stop on the way was tolerated—possibly even enjoyed—but in the end measures were taken, including the purchase of new locomotive power, to improve matters.

These magnificent Pacifics were instrumental then in reducing the time for this journey from 29 hours to 12 hours 20 minutes. The overall average speed of 41.5mph (66.4km/h) included 12 stops and there were also intermediate start-to-stop speeds up to 47.4mph (75.8km/h) and maxima as high as 75mph (120km/h). In contrast, the present administration has inhibitions about running its diesels at these sort of speeds, but none about running them at night. So a more sedate 15-hour journey is possible.

There were 20 of these 3ft 6in (1,067mm) gauge four-cylinder compounds, built by Werkspoor in Holland during 1917-21, running numbers 1001-20. During the Japanese régime of occupation they were designated class "C53" and numbered C5301-20. Three survived in use during the 1970s and one of these is reserved for the museum.

Right: *Indonesian Railways' "C53" class 4-6-2 in post-Colonial days.*

Class 231D 4-6-2 France: State Railway (Etat), 1914

Axle load: 40,500lb (18.5t).
Cylinders: HP (2) 16½ x 25½in (420 x 650mm).
Cylinders: LP (2) 25¼ x 25½in (640 x 650mm).
Driving wheels: 76½in (1,950mm).
Heating surface: 2,110sq ft (196m²).
Superheater: 861sq ft (80m²).
Steam pressure: 242psi (17kg/cm²).
Grate area: 46sq ft (4.27m²).
Fuel: 13,500lb (6t).
Water: 4,400gall (5,280 US) (20m³).
Adhesive weight: 121,500lb (55t).
Total weight: 300,000lb (136t).
Length overall: 75ft 4½in (22,974mm).

The Western Railway of France was for many years a by-word for inefficiency and things did not change very much for the better when it was taken over by the State in 1908. However, the one thing the new administration did which was sensible was to provide themselves, from 1914 onwards, with a stud of express passenger Pacific locomotives based on and very similar to those of the Paris-Orleans line. The principal difference lay in the use of a round-top firebox instead of the Belpaire type; this enabled adequate spectacles to be provided in the front of the cab, the top corners of which being heavily restricted by the tight loading gauge of this particular railway. During the first war, some locomotives were even supplied by North British of Glasgow, but after it was over the government adopted the design as a French standard and ordered 400 of them from French builders. Of these 280 went to the Etat lines. In the end the Alsace-Lorraine Railway—only recently back into the French fold—ended up with 100 of the remainder, although the Eastern, Northern and Paris-Orleans railway companies also had some for a time.

In 1928, the rather ramshackle state system began to mend its ways under the direction of Raoul Dautry. The administration took the sensible course of rebuilding on Chapelon principles no less than 269 of their now enormous fleet of 4-6-2s. All the engines got higher superheat, larger steam

Right: *Ex-Western Railway of France 4-6-2 No.231.D.722.*

passageways and double chimneys. Thirty only (Class "231G") had the full treatment with oscillating-cam poppet valves on both the high-pressure and the low-pressure sides. Then there were 134 (Class "231D") with poppet valves on the LP side only, while 23 (Class "231F") had Willoteaux double piston valves also only on the LP side. Finally, 85 (Class "231H") made do with some modest improvements to the geometry of their valve gears. The results were excellent and the engines were just as much at home on fast expresses as on 22-coach wartime trains carrying, say, 2,500 passengers, which were noted as running at up to 62mph (100kph) on level track.

A vivid impression of what it was like to drive and fire one of these fine machines can be gained from Jean Renoir's cinema film *La Bête Humaine*. A plot packed with blood and lust to an extent unheard of for the 1930s (it was based on Zola's 19th century novel) quite failed to steal the show from the chief star, an Etat Class "231D" Pacific.

No.231D596 is intended for the National Railway Museum at Mulhouse, while No.231G558 is preserved also.

Class A1 4-6-2 Great Britain: Great Northern Railway (GNR), 1922

Tractive effort: 29,385lb (13,333kg).
Axle load: 45,000 (20.5t).
Cylinders: (3) 20 x 26in (508 x 660mm).
Driving wheels: 80in (2,032mm).
Heating surface: 2,930sq ft (272m²).
Superheater: 525sq ft (49m²).
Steam pressure: 180psi (12.6kg/cm²).
Grate area: 41.25sq ft (3.8m²).
Fuel: 1,800lb (8t).
Water: 5,000gall (6,000 US) (22.7m³).
Adhesive weight: 134,500lb (61t).
Total weight: 332,000lb (151t).
Length overall: 70ft 5in (2,146mm).

Above: *Preserved ex-London & North Eastern Railway class "A3" 4-6-2* Flying Scotsman *leaves York for the south with an enthusiasts' special.*

The month of April 1922 was a milestone in the history of the railways of Great Britain for that was the month in which the first member of the first whole class of Pacific locomotive went into service. Few designs can match the record of these engines and their derivatives. Seventy-nine were to be built between 1921 and 1934 and they were originally class-designated with great appropriateness "Al".

The Great Northern Railway 4-6-2s were the work of a man called Nigel Gresley (later Sir Nigel Gresley) who became Locomotive Superintendent of the GNR in 1911. Gresley was very much what would now be called a "systems" engineer—by this one means that he was more a master of concepts than of detail.

The concept represented by these famous 4-6-2s was that, overall, a "big engine" (that is, one with ample capacity for the job in hand) was the most economical type. This in spite of the fact that it might cost more to build. The first ten "A1"s cost an average of £8,560 as against £6,840 for the first ten Great Western Railway "Castle" 4-6-0s. The thinking behind the design was also difficult to fault in that Gresley recognised that simplicity was the steam locomotive's greatest asset. At the same time he realised the importance of having perfect balance of the reciprocating forces. The minimum number of cylinders to achieve this was three and, whilst this meant one cylinder and set of motion between the frames, Gresley adopted a "derived" valve gear which meant that there was no more mechanism to crowd out the limited space available there.

Gresley was also an artist and his locomotives were aesthetically very pleasing—and, as will be related, they went as well as they looked. He decked them out in a really attractive livery and gave them evocative names, most being taken from racehorses. They rightly hold their place of honour in any locomotive hall of fame.

In contrast, they were beset with bad details. A stiff "all-or-nothing" throttle combined with the absence of any compensating levers between the rear pony truck and the driving wheels made them liable to slipping their wheels at starting. Rails needed changing because of wheelburn every few weeks at places where Gresley's 4-6-2s habitually started heavy trains from rest! A tendency for the large-ends of inside connecting rods to run hot seemed quite endemic—yet those of other companies' never gave more than occasional trouble. There were also such unforgiveable things as lubricator pipes which, if they broke, could only be replaced by lifting the boiler off the frames. Another problem was drifting steam obscuring the view of signals.

Certainly one cause of these shortcomings was that Gresley in 1923 became Chief Mechanical Engineer of the London & North Eastern Railway (LNER), an amalgamation of the Great Northern, Great Eastern, North Eastern, Great Central, North British and other smaller companies. He removed himself to London and became remote from locomotive development at Doncaster. Gresley has always been given the credit for certain changes to the Pacifics' valve gear made in 1926 which greatly improved their coal consumption at small cost. It has only recently come to light that Gresley was not only not responsible for initiating the changes but furthermore they were devised in the teeth of his opposition.

The situation arose in 1925 when an elegant but smaller and highly decorated 4-6-0 called *Pendennis Castle* from the rival Great Western Railway was tried out on the LNER. She did everything the big Pacifics could do with easy mastery and burned 10 per cent less coal, as well as creating a profound impression whilst doing it.

Why the "Castle" was so good was a bit of a puzzle to the LNER men, but suspicion rested on the detailed geometry of the Walschaert's valve gear. Some minor alterations to the Pacific's valve gear were tried but the results were inconclusive. After this, rather than lose face by asking for a set of drawings, a cloak-and-dagger operation was mounted while another "Castle" was on hand at Darlington after taking part in the Stockton & Darlington

Below: Flying Scotsman *as running before conversion from class "A1" to class "A3" but after the attachment of a corridor tender for long non-stop runs.*

Railway Centenary celebrations later the same year. All the motion was secretly measured and through the enterprise of Bert Spencer, Gresley's Technical Assistant at Kings Cross, some new geometry was worked out and applied to No.2555 *Centenary*. The results were amazing—not the 10 per cent saving in coal which the "Castle" had achieved against the other Pacifics, but twice as much.

After a preliminary period of disbelief, Gresley took a ride on *Centenary*, expressed himself converted and issued instructions for all his Pacifics to be altered as they went through shops. The savings in coal amounted to around 1½ tons on a run from Kings Cross to Newcastle and in fact enabled runs of this length to be worked without engine change. About the same time, boilers designed for a higher working pressure of 225 psi (15.75 kg/cm^2) were introduced, in some cases combined with a reduction of cylinder diameter. Engine weight rose by some six tons, axle load by two tons. Locomotives fitted with these boilers were designated class "A3" instead of "A1" and sometimes as "Super-Pacifics".

The longest non-stop journey in the world was run by these locomotives, over the 392¾ miles (632km) from London to Edinburgh each peacetime summer beginning in 1928. Special corridor tenders were built and attached to certain selected locomotives to enable crews to be changed en route. Pullman-type vestibule connections and automatic 'buck-eye' couplings to match those on standard LNER corridor carriages were provided at the rear of these tenders.

In 1935 No.2750 *Papyrus* made a high-speed run from London to Newcastle preparatory to the introduction of the "Silver Jubilee" express with a 240 minute schedule. The 268 miles (432km) were run off in an amazing net time of 230 minutes, an average of 69.9 mph (112.5km/h). Coming back, 108mph (174km/h) was touched at Essendine north of Peterborough, a speed believed to be still a world record for an unstreamlined steam locomotive. The streamlined version of the Gresley Pacific came into service to run this new high-speed train. This was the event that displaced the non-streamlined 4-6-2s from their prime position on the East Coast main line, but they had no problem in keeping time on the streamliners when called upon to do so in an emergency.

Above: Flying Scotsman *wakes the echoes for a trainload of admirers. The colour change in the smoke from white to black indicates that a round of firing is in progress.*

World War II brought 24-coach trains to the East Coast main line and the "A3" as well as the few remaining "A1"s performances on these and on freight trains were a vindication of their brilliance as a concept, although lower standards of maintenance emphasized their detail weaknesses.

After the war, during which Gresley had died, efforts were made to overcome these troubles. Some success was achieved but progress was somewhat hampered by the deaf ear which the main works were liable to turn towards suggestions from the running sheds, however sensible. The "A3"s appearance was slightly changed when the smoke problem was effortlessly solved (after 25 years of fiddling with it) by the fitting of German pattern smoke deflectors either side of the smokebox but even in the 1960s all were easily recognisable as running mates of the original "A1" class which first saw the light of day 40 years before.

The prototype itself had been rebuilt into what was virtually a new design and one other had been withdrawn in 1959. Otherwise the class remained intact until 1962, still on prime express passenger work, and performing better than ever with the double chimneys which had been fitted 1958-60. The last to go was British Railways No.60041 *Salmon Trout* in December 1965.

In 1934 the running numbers had been (in chronological order) 4470-81, 2543-99, 2743-97, 2500-08. The second of two post-war renumberings had left them as 102-112, 44-100, 35-43 (4470 no longer belonged to this class). In 1948 British Railways had added 60,000 to the numbers so that they became 60035 to 60112.

Happily, a certain Alan Pegler purchased the most famous locomotive in the class (and perhaps in the world), the immortal *Flying Scotsman*. After adventures which have included journeyings as far as the west coast of America, this grand engine is stationed at the Steamtown Museum, Carnforth, and performs with great regularity and panache on main-line steam-hauled special trains on British Railways lines.

Super-Pacific 4-6-2 France: Northern Railway (Nord), 1923

Axle load: 41,500lb (19t).
Cylinders, HP: (2) 17.6 x 26in (440 x 660mm)
Cylinders, LP: (2) 24.4 x 27.2in (620 x 690mm)
Driving wheels: 74.9in (1,900mm).
Heating surface: 2,680sq ft ($249m^2$).
Superheater: 616sq ft ($57m^2$).
Steam pressure: 227psi ($16kg/cm^2$).
Grate area: 37.5sq ft ($3.5m^2$).
Fuel: 15,500lb (7t).
Water: 7,000gall (8,500 US) ($31.5m^3$).
Adhesive weight: 122,500lb (56t).
Total weight: 353,000lb (160t).
Length overall: 70ft 1in (21,350mm).

Above: *A Nord "Super-Pacific" awaits departure from the Gare du Nord at Paris. These locomotives for many years ran the boat trains such as the "Golden Arrow" between Paris and the Channel Ports.*

We have discussed how the Pacifics of the Paris-Orleans Railway were suddenly transformed by André Chapelon from run-of-the-mill locomotives into the most remarkable 4-6-2s ever to run. Another French company, the Nord, used the same methods and came nearly as far, but in easy stages. They began with two strange-looking 4-6-4s built in 1911—which perhaps showed what not to do rather than what should be done.

All except two of the Nord 4-6-2s were de Glehn compounds and a group of 40 quite standard for the day, based on some locomotives built for the Alsace-Lorraine Railway in 1908, was delivered in 1912-13. The war prevented any further development until 1923, when the first 40 "Super-Pacifics" were delivered from Blanc-Misseron of Lille. Improvements in the steam circuits and a modest increase in the steaming capacity of their boilers made them into remarkable engines, equally famous on both sides of the English Channel for their work on such legendary trains as the "Golden Arrow" and the "Calais-Mediterranean" expresses. It says enough that

Hornby, the British toy train makers, chose a "Super-Pacific"

Class P10 2-8-2 Germany: Royal Prussian Union Railway (KPEV), 1922

Tractive effort: 40,400lb (18,200kg).
Axle load: 43,000lb (19.5t).
Cylinders: (3) 20.5 x 26.0in (520 x 660mm).
Driving wheels: 68.9in (1,750mm).
Heating surface: 2,348sq ft ($218.2m^2$).
Superheater: 883sq ft ($82 m^2$).
Steam pressure: 200psi ($14kg/cm^2$).
Grate area: 43.8sq ft ($4.07m^2$).
Fuel: 15,430lb (7.0t).
Water: 6,930gall (8,320 US) ($31.5m^3$).
Adhesive weight: 167,000lb (77t).
Total weight: 243,500lb (110.5t).
Length overall: 75ft 5in (22,980mm).

After World War I large numbers of Prussian locomotives, particularly "P8" 4-6-0s, were distributed throughout Europe as reparations, and in 1919, as part of a programme for making good the losses, design work began on a 2-8-2 locomotive, intended particularly for secondary passenger traffic on the more hilly routes of the country. Post-war difficulties delayed work on the new class, which was designated "P10" and although it was designed as a Prussian engine, the German State Railway had been established by the time that the first one was completed in 1922 by Borsig.

Although much of the design reflected Prussian practice of the previous twenty years, one class had a particular influence on the "P10". This was the "G12" three-cylinder 2-10-0, which had been produced in 1917 to meet the urgent need for a powerful goods engine for lines of medium axle load. For speed of design, the "G12" was based on a locomotive designed by Henschel for the Ottoman Railway, and it introduced some striking novelties for a Prussian design, particularly bar frames and a Belpaire firebox having a trapezoidal-shaped grate set above the driving wheels.

The novel features of the "G12" were carried over to the "P10", which also had three cylinders. With larger driving wheels there was insufficient clearance to position the firebox above the driving wheels, so the grate was constructed in three portions. The front one was parallel and fitted between the rear driving wheels; there was then a taper outwards, and the rear section was parallel at the greater width. Compared with a normal wide firebox behind the driving wheels, the trapezoidal grate brought the firebox further forward, and gave a better weight distribution, with more weight on the driving wheels. The resultant shape of the firebox walls, with double curves in both vertical and horizontal directions, gave trouble with maintenance, and no more Belpaire fireboxes or trapezoidal grates were built for the German railways.

Above: *Class "39" (ex-Prussian Union class "P10") 2-8-2 No.39.001. These powerful locomotives were one of a number of Prussian classes adopted for the new system.*

The derived motion for driving the inside valve from the outside valves, which had been used on previous Prussian three-cylinder engines, was abandoned in favour of three separate valve gears, but there was a novelty in that the drive for the inside valve was taken from a second return crank attached to the return crank of the left-hand valve gear.

Another new feature were the large smoke deflectors, which became standard practice for all large German locomotives until the introduction of a smaller pattern in the 1950s.

Under the German State the "P10"s were classified as "39", and 260 of them were built between 1922 and 1927. They became popular throughout the country, although their sphere of operation was limited by their high axle load. With a maximum permissible speed of 68mph (110km/h) they were able to haul any German express passenger train until the general increase of speed in the 1930s. Although classified as secondary passenger engines, they were true mixed-traffic engines, and they continued to share their time between passenger and freight work until the

plus some blue "Wagon-Lits" cars as the basis for their first train set which had any pretensions to realism. The "Super-Pacifics" had no difficulty in running the 184 miles (296km) from Calais to Paris with 550 tons—and sometimes more—in 184 minutes. This included the 1 in 250 (0.4 per cent) climb to Caffiers as well as other long inclines, yet kept within the legal speed limit of 75mph (120km/h). A handsome brown livery ensured that these magnificent engines looked as well as they ran.

More "Super-Pacifics" were built in 1925 (10) and 1931 (40) and these differed in detail, but all 90 were regarded as interchangeable. A narrow firebox 11ft 9in (3,580mm) long seemed to present no problems to the French *chauffeurs* and the boiler provided ample steam for the two high-pressure cylinders. Some of the early engines had balanced slide-valves for the low-pressure cylinders in place of piston-valves. Two others had poppet valves and two more were rebuilt as two-cylinder simples with Cossart valve gear. One (No.3.1280) was streamlined for a time and this locomotive can be seen in the National Railway Museum at Mulhouse. The others were all withdrawn by 1962.

last was withdrawn in 1967.

After World War II the class was divided between the DB and DR (ie west and east Germany), and 85 of the engines on DR were rebuilt with new boilers, with round-topped fireboxes and wide grates. Their appearance was greatly altered by the fitting of the standard DR feedwater heater, with a trapezoidal tank ahead of the chimney.

The "P10"s were the high-water mark of Prussian design, but they were also important as marking the transition to the German State standard locomotives, experience with the "P10" class being available before the design of the standard locomotives was finally settled upon.

E1/D1 Class 4-4-0

Great Britain: South Eastern & Chatham Railway (SECR), 1919

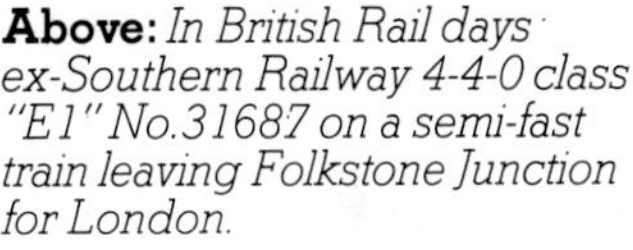

Above: *In British Rail days ex-Southern Railway 4-4-0 class "E1" No.31687 on a semi-fast train leaving Folkstone Junction for London.*

Tractive effort: 17,950lb (8,170kg).
Axle load: 38,000lb (17.5t).
Cylinders: (2) 19 x 26in (483 x 660mm).
Driving wheels: 78in (1,981mm).
Heating surface: 1,276sq ft (119m²).
Superheater: 228sq ft (21m²).
Steam pressure: 180psi (12.7kg/cm²).
Grate area: 24sq ft (2.2m²).
Fuel: 10,000lb (4.5t).
Water: 3,450gall (4,143 US) (15.7m³).
Adhesive weight: 75,000lb (34t).
Total weight: 204,000lb (93t).
Length overall: 55ft 2¾in (16,834mm).

On a journey from London to Paris there could be no greater contrast between the "Super-Pacifics" of the French Northern Railway, and the little 4-4-0s of the South-Eastern & Chatham Railway behind which a traveller of the early 1920s would begin his journey. One factor in their smallness was the difference in weight hauled per passenger—in first class de luxe a Pullman car on the SECR train might weigh 32 tons and carry 16 people, whereas the same passengers across the channel would use first class sleeping cars which might weigh 40 tons and carry only twelve. Since the same variation also occurred in the less luxurious accommodation, a 300-ton boat train on the English side of the channel could become a 500-ton one on the French.

Even so, after the 1914 war was over, the SECR had a problem. Boat train traffic had been transferred from Charing Cross to Victoria but the ex-London Chatham & Dover Railway lines leading there had severe weight restrictions, which precluded the 'L' class 4-4-0s—the most powerful SECR passenger locomotives—from working the new route. Furthermore, plans were afoot to introduce luxurious corridor stock on these boat trains, which would make the problem even worse. At the time neither new locomotives—some 4-6-0s were mooted—or new bridges could be considered and Locomotive Superintendent Richard Maunsell decided to give what might now be called the "Chapelon treatment" to some aged but beautiful 4-4-0s of his predecessor Harry Wainwright.

The immediate result was handsome rather than beautiful. The first conversion was 'E' class 4-4-0 No.179, a new fire box with a 13 per cent bigger grate was added to the existing boiler barrel, and the boiler centre-line was pitched 7in (178mm) higher to give greater depth to the new firebox. Piston valves (with long travel valve-gear which involved revised geometry) and larger superheaters, combined with the improved boilers to transform the performance of what even before were regarded as excellent engines. Success was such that 31 further 4-4-0s of the 'E' and the similar 'D' classes were rebuilt over the next few years, some by Beyer, Peacock and some by the company, and were designated 'E1' and 'D1' classes respectively.

Whilst Southern Railway 4-6-0s soon displaced these 4-4-0s from the principal boat trains, they continued to perform in brilliant style on other routes. They were to the fore on summer holiday extras and forces leave trains even as late as 1958. A swan-song in top-line work occurred when it was found that the London-Paris sleeping car train, introduced in 1938, containing as it did several steel sleeping cars weighing 45 tons-plus apiece, was too much for the a "Lord Nelson" to handle. The solution was to haul this Southern Railway flag train with two 4-4-0s in double harness—a thrilling sight indeed!

Castle Class 4-6-0

Great Britain:
Great Western Railway (GWR), 1923

Tractive effort: 31,625lb (14,182kg).
Axle load: 44,500lb (20.25t).
Cylinders: (4) 16 x 26in (406 x 660mm).
Driving wheels: 80½in (2,045mm).
Heating surface: 2,049sq ft (190 m²).
Superheater: 263sq ft (24.4 m²).
Steam pressure: 225psi (15.8 kg/cm²).
Grate area: 30.3sq ft (2.81 m²).
Fuel: 13,500lb (6t).
Water: 4,000gall (4,800 US) (18m³).
Adhesive weight: 133,500lb (60t).
Total weight: 283,500lb (129t).
Length overall: 65ft 2in (19,863mm).

When Churchward of the GWR produced his first "Saint" largely based on rugged American practice, he also obtained from France a four-cylinder de Glehn compound, later named *La France*. This elegant French lady was put through her paces and compared with the two-cylinder design. Whilst there was not sufficient advantage to justify the complication of compounding, it did seem that the easier running of the compounds' sophisticated mechanical layout was something worth examining further. Hence the building in 1906 of a four-cylinder simple 4-4-2, with the same "No.1" boiler as the "Saint" class, to make direct comparison between a two-cylinder and a four-cylinder mechanism. This 4-4-2 was No.40 (later 4-6-0 No.4000) *North Star*.

The advantages of four-cylinders were, first, that the reciprocating parts could in principle be arranged to be perfectly in balance, whereas the balancing of a two-cylinder locomotive was always a compromise. Second, the forces in the various rods and guides which transmitted the piston force to the wheels would only be half those in the two-cylinder machine. The disadvantages, of course, were the extra costs involved in making nearly twice as much mechanism and also that the moving parts inside the frames would be difficult to reach.

This was compounded in the case of Churchward because, having decided very sensibly to use the same set of Walschaert's valve gear for both the cylinders on one side of the locomotive, he displayed a strange reluctance to expose this gear to the vulgar gaze. Hence the mechanism between the frames became very complex indeed. *North Star* herself in fact had a peculiar "scissors" valve gear, whereby the drive on each side was taken from the cylinder crosshead on the other. This slightly mitigated the complexity between the frames, but there was a problem with R M Deeley of the Midland Railway over patent rights.

Two more French compounds had to be obtained before the simple versus compound issue was finally determined, but construction of "Star" locomotives proceeded to the quantity of eleven in 1907. A batch of ten called Knights followed in 1908, ten Kings (not to be confused with the "King" class of 1927) in 1909 and ten Queens in 1910 and 1911. The year 1913 brought five Princes, 1914 fifteen Princesses and finally there came twelve Abbeys in 1922-23. But all were known generally by the class name of "Star".

By now Churchward had retired and his successor as Chief Mechanical Engineer, Charles Collett ordered his staff to work out the details of a "Star" enlarged to take advantage of an increase in the permitted axle load from 18½ to 20 tons. It had been hoped that the Swindon No.7 boiler, recently introduced for the big "47xx" class mixed traffic 2-8-0s, would suit but the design incorporating it became too heavy. In the end a new No.8 boiler was designed especially for the "Castle" class, with very happy results indeed. The rest of the locomotive was pure "Star" with an extra inch on the diameter of the cylinders; visually, the slightly larger (but still exiguous) cab with its side windows made

Above: *The Great Western Railway honoured its builder with this "Castle" class locomotive in 1935 livery.*

Below: *"Castle" class 4-6-0 No. 5094* Tretower Castle *at speed with a Bristol to Paddington express. These superb locomotives were the mainstay of GWR express services.*

an impact on those who worshipped each separate Great Western rivet. The first "Castle", No.4073 *Caerphilly Castle* appeared in August 1923 numbered consecutively after the last "Star" No.4072 *Tresco Abbey*.

The second "Castle" No.4074 *Caldicot Castle*, was put through a series of coal consumption tests. Afterwards Collett presented a paper to the World Power Conference in which he announced that the result was an overall figure of 2.83lb of coal per drawbar-horsepower-hour. This was received with a certain scepticism by other locomotive engineers who had been apt to give themselves a pat on the back if they got down anywhere near 4lb. Certainly the GWR was then far ahead of its rivals; a major factor was the design of the valves and valve gear, which enabled very short cut-offs to be used; hence expansive use of steam gave most of the advantages of compounding without the complications.

The tenth "Castle" No.4082 *Windsor Castle*, was new when King George V and Queen Mary visited the Swindon Factory in 1924; no doubt the name was held back until then. His Majesty personally drove the engine from the station to the works and a brass plaque was added to the cab side commemorating the fact. No.4082 carried this for many years but not all her days for by an unhappy chance she was under repair when King George V died in 1952. The insignia of No.4082 were quickly transferred to No.7013 *Bristol Castle*, which assumed the identity of this Royal engine for the funeral train. It was perhaps a trifle naïve of the authorities to think they would not be found out, but the row which GWR fans raised in the national press—the differences were easily spotted—was a major embarassment to the then infant (and hated) British Railways.

This time the successive batches kept to the same generic name for the class—fortunately the stormy past of Great Western territory meant that there was an adequate supply of fortified houses therein. Even so, there were a few exceptions such as the 15 converted "Star"s (actually two Stars, one Knight, two Queens and ten Abbeys) and there was a group named after noble Earls, the result of complaints from some aristocratic gentlemen that their names had been given to some rather small and old-fashioned engines. In World War II twelve were given names of famous aircraft and three gentlemen by the names of *Isambard Kingdom Brunel*, *Sir Daniel Gooch* and *G.J. Churchward* amonst others also were remembered.

At the time of its introduction the "Castle" class was the most powerful locomotive design in the country, although far from being the largest. Those sceptical of this claim were convinced during exchange trials in 1925 and 1926 during which a "Castle" was proved to have an economical mastery—with something to

Above: *Preserved Castle class No.7029* Clun Castle. *This locomotive is kept at the Birmingham Railway Museum and is used on mainline enthusiast specials.*

spare—over the hardest schedules the LNER or LMS had to offer, whereas those companies were unable to field a candidate which could do the same on the GWR. The "Castle" class handled the "Cheltenham Flyer" which for some years was the fastest train in the world with a 65 minute schedule for the 77¼ miles (124km) from Swindon to Paddington Station, London. A run with this train on 6 June 1932 with *Tregenna Castle* in 56¾ minutes, an average speed to start-to-stop of 81.7 (131.5km/h), was also a world record for some time after it was accomplished.

The "Castle" class was capable of handling heavy trains. The famous "Cornish Riviera Limited" could load up to 15 of the GWR's 70ft carriages on the by no means easy road from Paddington to Plymouth on a schedule which averaged 55 mph (88 km/h) for the 225.7 miles. For many years this was the longest non-stop run in the country. It is true that carriages were slipped at three points en route but on the last stretch gradients of up to 1 in 37 (2.7 per cent) were encountered.

The last and 171st "Castle" No.7037 *Swindon* appeared in 1950, by which time a few of the earliest had already been withdrawn. The 171 included those fifteen which were converted from "Star" and one (No.111 *Viscount Churchill*) which had originally been that odd-man-out amongst GWR locomotives, Churchward's 4-6-2 *The Great Bear*. These older "Castles" were the first to go.

During the years 1957 to 1960, some time after the GWR had become part of British Railways in 1948, a number of the "Castle" class were modernised with larger superheaters and double chimneys. The results were excellent, but the dieselisation which immediately followed prevented the improvements having any beneficial effect on train working.

Withdrawal began in earnest in 1962 and the last "Castle" ceased running in normal service in July 1965. But this was not to be the end of their history, and it is a measure of the esteem and affection in which they were held that seven have been preserved. The Science Museum had room for one only modern steam engine to illustrate the best in British locomotive engineering and they chose No.4073 *Caerphilly Castle*. This steam locomotive is also the only modern one to appear on a British postage stamp.

Three preserved "Castles" are currently in working order, No. 7029 *Clun Castle* at the Birmingham Railway Museum, No.5051 *Drysllwyn Castle* at the Great Western Society's Didcot Steam Centre, and, so far away and in such a remote part of Australia that its best address is latitude 20°45'S longitude 116°10'E, is No.4079 *Pendennis Castle*.

Class 424 4-8-0 Hungary: Hungarian State Railways (MAV), 1924

Tractive effort: 39,280lb (17,822kg).
Axle load: 32,000lb (14.5t).
Cylinders: (2) 23.6 x 26in (600 x 660mm).
Driving wheels: 63¼in (1,606mm).
Heating surface: 2,230sq ft ($207m^2$).
Superheater: 624sq ft ($58m^2$).
Steam pressure: 200psi ($14kg/cm^2$).
Grate area: 48sq ft ($4.45m^2$).
Fuel: 20,000lb (9t).
Water: 4,620gall (5,550 US) ($21m^3$).
Adhesive weight: 129,000lb (58.5t).
Total weight: 315,000lb (143t).
Length overall: 68ft 10¾in (17,334mm).

It speaks volumes for the qualities of these excellent locomotives that they continued to be built over a period of 32 years and their period of service has now spanned 58 years. As so often, their success stems largely from their being simple and rugged machines in the Stephenson mould. The most unusual feature is the wheel arrangement; by reason of the leading bogie for guidance plus the high proportion of adhesive weight to engine weight, the 4-8-0 type (in North America known as "Mastodon") would seem to be well suited to heavy express trains, yet cases of its use are rare. In this instance the high structure gauge of the Hungarian railway system permitted a deep wide firebox and ashpan to be mounted above the rear coupled wheels, which were given side play of one inch (25mm) either side of centre to ease the running on sharp curves.

They were maids-of-all-work on the MAV, handling top expresses, suburban locals and freight trains with equal facility. Those employed on suburban service could work "push-and-pull"—that is, they were fitted with equipment actuated by compressed air which enabled them to be controlled from a driver's cab at the other end of the train.

The design was developed from an unbuilt 2-8-0 of 1915, without the Brotan boiler of that predecessor, and 27 were built initially by the State Works in Budapest. During the war years a further 218 were built and finally in 1955-6 there were another 120. Numbers ran from 424,001 to 424,365, but not all of these ran in Hungary at the same time. The design has been exported to Slovakia (during World War II when Czechoslovakia was partitioned), and to North Korea. Some were taken over by the Jugoslav State Railways in 1945, and from the same date a few ran in Russia for a time, pending return to Hungary.

Right: *Hungarian State Railways class "424" 4-8-0 No.424.075 on a local passenger train.*

241A Class 4-8-2 France: Eastern Railway (Est), 1925

Axle load: 42,000lb (19t).
Cylinders HP: (2) 17¾ x 28½in (450 x 720mm).
Cylinders LP: (2) 26 x 28½in (660 x 720mm).
Driving wheels: 76¾in (1,950mm).
Heating surface: 2,335sq ft ($21.8m^2$).
Superheater: 996sq ft ($92.6m^2$).
Steam pressure: 228psi ($16kg/cm^2$).
Grate area: 47.7sq ft ($4.4m^2$).
Adhesive weight: 165,000lb (75t).
Length overall: 86ft 2½in (26,275mm).
(Tender details not available).

The de Glehn system of compounding was capable of expansion not only to the 4-6-2 but also to the 4-8-2. The first de Glehn 4-8-2 entered service in 1925; this was No.41001 of the Eastern Railway of France, a line which connected Paris with cities such as Chalons-sur-Marne, Nancy, Belfort and Strasbourg. The loco was built at the company's works at Epernay and, after a four year period of testing and some modification, 41 more were built as the top express locomotive fleet of the line. Soon afterwards, a further 49 were constructed for the State (ex-Western Railway) Railways, but after nationalisation of all the railways in France in 1938, they joined their 41 sisters on the Est lines.

In the meantime, during 1933, some very severe trials were held on the Northern Railway. One test was to haul the Golden Arrow express between Paris and Calais made up with extra carriages to 650 tons. Both the Eastern and the PLM companies supplied 4-8-2s while the Paris-Orleans-Midi line sent one of their famous rebuilt 4-6-2s. The Eastern engines suffered damage to the frames and also showed a higher fuel consumption than the P-O 4-6-2. So far as the Eastern

Below: *Two views of Eastern Railway of France class "241A" 4-8-2s. That on the left shows No.241A.68 in French National Railways livery. The other shows 241-008 as running in Est days.*

was concerned, the result of these very searching tests was that some rebuilt P-O 4-6-2s were acquired and, moreover, the rebuilding of the 4-8-2s on Chapelon lines was put in hand with some success. At a cost of only 6 tons extra weight, the converted engines could produce 3,700hp in the cylinders, a 40 per cent increase. At the same time coal consumption fell by some 15 per cent.

An interesting feature was a six-jet blast-pipe; the amount of draught produced by this could be controlled from the cab. This was one further control to add to the two throttles, two reversing gears and the intercepting valve of the de Glehn system!

The prototype of the class, originally No.41.001 but latterly No.241A1, superbly restored, is displayed in the National Railway Museum at Mulhouse.

4300 Class 4-8-2

United States:
Southern Pacific Railroad (SP), 1923

Above: *Southern Pacific Railroad "4300" class 4-8-2 No.4330. The number "51", carried near the smokestack is the number of the train which the locomotive is hauling.*

Tractive effort: 57,100lb (25,907kg).
Axle load: 61,500lb (28t).
Cylinders: (2) 28 x 30in (711 x 762mm).
Driving wheels: 73½in (1,867mm).
Heating surface: 4,552sq ft (423m²).
Superheater: 1,162sq ft (108m²).
Steam pressure: 210psi (14.8kg/cm²).
Grate area: 75sq ft (7m²).
Fuel (oil): 4,000gall (4,700 US) (18m³).
Water: 13,300gall (10,000 US) (60m³).
Adhesive weight: 246,000lb (112t).
Total weight: 611,000lb (277.5t).
Length overall: 97ft 9in (29,794mm).

The 4-8-2 or "Mountain" type was appropriately named; its origins are a nice illustration of the difference between tractive effort and power. Locomotives with a high tractive effort are often described as powerful, but this is misleading. The 4-8-2 was developed from the 4-6-2 but, whilst the extra pair of drivers meant that a higher tractive effort could be exerted, the power output—which depends on the size of the fire—had to remain limited because there was still only one pair of wheels to carry the firebox.

For climbing mountains a high tractive effort is essential, but high *power* output only desirable. These things were relevant to the Southern Pacific Railroad, for their trains leaving Sacramento for the east had the notorious climb over the Sierras to face, from near sea level to 6,885ft (2,099m) in 80 miles (128km).

So in 1923 SP went to the American Locomotive Co. of Schenectady for the first batch of 4-8-2 locomotives. The design was based on standard US practice, the one feature of note being the cylindrical so-called Vanderbilt tender. A booster engine was fitted, driving on the rear carrying wheels, and this could give an extra 10,000lb (4,537kg) of tractive effort, provided the steam supply held out.

SP impressed their personality on the "4300"s by having them oil-burning and by their trade mark, the headlight mounted *below* centre on the silver-grey front of the smoke box. The 77 engines of the class were very successful, all the later ones being built in SP's own shops at Sacramento. Some of the earlier batches had 8-wheel tenders of lower capacity, instead of 12-wheel ones. None of the class has been preserved.

Class 01 4-6-2

Germany: German State Railway (DR), 1926

Tractive effort: 35,610lb (16,160kg).
Axle load: 44,500lb (20.25t).
Cylinders: (2) 23.6 x 26.0in (600 x 660mm).
Driving wheels: 78.7in (2,000m).
Heating surface: 2,661sq ft (247.3m²).
Superheater: 915sq ft (85.0m²).
Steam pressure: 228psi (16kg/cm²).
Grate area: 47.5sq ft (4.41m²).
Fuel: 22,000lb (10.0t).
Water: 7,500gall (9,000 US) (34m³).
Adhesive weight: 130,500lb (59.2t).
Total weight: 240,000lb (109t) *(without tender).*
Length overall: 78ft 6in (23,940mm).
(These dimensions etc. refer to engines with copper fireboxes, other than the first 10).

In 1922, when the German railways were under Government control, a Central Locomotive Design Section was set up under Dr R P Wagner, an engineer trained on the KPEV, but having a wide knowledge of railways in other countries. After the establishment of the German State Railway in 1922, Wagner's team prepared a scheme for standard locomotives, much influenced by Prussian practice, but taking into account that, in some parts of the country, the engines would have to burn coal of a lower quality than that to which the Prussian engines were accustomed, and that they would have to work in more mountainous country than the North German plain, which dominated the KPEV locomotive designs.

The standard classes therefore had larger grates than their Prussian predecessors, and in the engines with trailing carrying wheels, there was a clear space under the firebox for the entry of air and the removal of ashes, as had been provided, largely under the influence of Maffei of Munich, in the modern passenger engines of the southern German states.

Above: *A German Federal Railways class "01" 4-6-2 makes a fine show crossing a wide-span girder bridge.*

Below: *German "01" class 4-6-2 No.012204-4. The final figure is a check digit for use with a computer system.*

Until this time the maximum axle loading permitted in Germany had been 18 tonnes, but a programme of upgrading of track and bridges to take 20-tonne axle loads had been put in hand, and the first of the new locomotives to be built were two classes of Pacific designed to this increased axle load, and designated "01" and "02". The specification required the engines to haul 800 tonnes at 62mph (100km/h) on the level, and 500 tonnes at 31mph (50km/h) on a 1 in 100 (1 per cent) gradient; the maximum speed was to be 74.6mph (120 km/h).

Of the 139 Pacifics which DR inherited from the railways of the southern states, all but 10 were four-cylinder compounds. It was originally intended that the standard locomotives should all have two cylinders, but in deference to the representatives of the states other than Prussia on the central design committee, the new Pacific was produced in two versions, Class "01" with two cylinders and Class "02" with four compound cylinders. Ten engines of each type were built, and were divided between three locomotive depots for comparison. Trials of the two classes showed a small advantage in fuel consumption to the compounds, but the advantage was considered to be offset by the increased costs of maintaining the latter, and the "01" was adopted as standard for future construction. The use of two cylinders only in the largest passenger class was a clear break with former German practice.

Although the basic layout of the "01" was simple, much of the detailed work was complicated, and there was a full range of auxiliary equipment, including a feedwater heater, with a distinctive heat exchanger buried in the smokebox ahead of the chimney. The use of a round-topped firebox

was a reversion from recent Prussian practice, and, at a time when engineers in many countries were building boilers with a forward extension of the firebox (the so-called "combustion chamber"), Wagner made the front of his firebox almost straight, as he considered that the extra maintenance cost of the combustion chamber was not justified. It was also unusual for a boiler of this size to have a parallel barrel.

The general appearance of the engines owed much to Prussian practice, but with various parts attached to the outside of the boiler for accessibility, there was a distinct North American touch. Of the three apparent domes, the first housed the feedwater inlet, the second was the sand box, and the third housed the regulator. Like the final Prussian designs the engines had bar frames. The long gap between the trailing coupled axle and the trailing carrying axle resulted in the carrying axle having a slightly greater axle load than any of the coupled axles.

The detailed design of the engines was undertaken by Borsig of Berlin, and the first engines were built by that firm and by AEG. Slow progress with upgrading lines for 20-tonne axle loads inhibited the rapid construction of "01"s, but by 1938 a total of 231 had been built, to which were added a further 10 by the rebuilding of the "02" compounds.

Experience with the first engines resulted in later engines having the cylinder diameter increased from 25.6in (650mm) to 26.0in (660mm). The boiler tubes were lengthened, with a corresponding shortening of the smokebox, and later still steel fireboxes were used in place of copper. Improved braking and larger bogie wheels were introduced as part of a programme for increasing the maximum speed of the class to 80.8mph (130km/h).

Above: *This picture shows one of the smaller German class "03" 4-6-2s, No.032180-2. Note the small post-war "Witte" pattern smoke deflectors and, again, the computer check digit.*

In the meantime, in 1930, a slightly smaller version of the "01", designated "03", was introduced for lines still limited to an 18-tonne axle load, and 298 of these were built up to 1937.

Until 1937 the speed limit of most lines in Germany was 62mph (100km/h), so it was not until the general raising of the maximum speed to 120km/h in 1937 that the "01" and "03" had full scope as express engines. However, by 1937 there were already 58 runs daily in Germany booked at start-to-stop speeds of 60mph (97km/h) or more, and the majority of these were worked by the "01" or "03".

When further express engines were built from 1939 onwards, the continued acceleration of passenger trains made it necessary for them to have a maximum speed of 93mph (150km/h), and following experience with the "05" 4-6-4 locomotives, the new engines were given full streamlining and three cylinders. These engines were classed "01^{10}" and "03^{10}", and 55 of the former and 60 of the latter were built between 1939 and 1941; but for the war, the totals would have been 250 and 140 respectively. Apart from two experimental Pacifics made in West Germany in 1957 these were the last new steam express locomotives to be built in Germany.

After the partition of Germany 171 locomotives of class "01" came into the stock of DB in West Germany and 70 into the stock DR in East Germany. Of these 55 of the DB locomotives and 35 of the DR locomotives were rebuilt. The remaining locomotives on DB received the post-war "Witte" smoke deflectors, in place of the full-depth deflectors. Another alteration which affected the appearance of many of the engines was the removal of the sloping plates which connected the side running plates to the buffer beam. The unrebuilt engines on DR retained their original appearance. The last of the DB engines was withdrawn in 1973, but several of the DR engines were still at work in 1981, after being returned to regular service because of the shortage of oil. With their rebuilt sisters they were the last express steam engines at work in Europe.

There was one other German Pacific to be mentioned, which had an unusual history. As part of the experimental work on high-speed steam trains, a streamlined three-cylinder 4-6-6 tank was built in 1939. Like the Class "05" 4-6-4 it had driving wheels 90½in (2,300mm) in diameter, and was designed for a maximum speed of 108mph (175km/h); it was used between Berlin and Dresden. This engine came into DR ownership, and in 1960 parts of it, together with some parts of an experimental high-pressure 2-10-2 locomotive, were used to produce a high-speed Pacific for testing new rolling stock and making brake tests. The all-welded boiler was identical to that used in rebuilding the former Prussian Class "P10" locomotives, DR Class "39". The engine was partially enclosed in a streamlined casing of distinctive shape, with a shapely chimney. The designed speed of the engine was 100mph (160km/h), but it was operated well above this speed into the 1970s, being the last steam engine in the world to exceed the magic speed of 100 miles per hour.

Below: *A German Federal Railways' class "01" 4-6-2, used for handling the principal steam express trains in Germany.*

King Arthur Class 4-6-0

Great Britain:
Southern Railway (SR), 1925

Tractive effort: 25,320lb (11,485kg).
Axle load: 45,000lb (20.5t).
Cylinders: (2) 20½ x 28in (521 x 711mm).
Driving wheels: 79in (2,007mm).
Heating surface: 1,878sq ft ($174.5m^2$).
Superheater: 337sq ft ($31.3m^2$).
Steam pressure: 200psi ($14.1kg/cm^2$).
Grate area: 30sq ft ($2.8m^2$).
Fuel: 11,000lb (5t).
Water: 5,000gall (6,000 US) ($22.7m^3$).
Adhesive weight: 134,500lb (6t).
Total weight: 310,500lb (141t).
Length overall: 66ft 5in (20,244mm).

Above: *In British Rail days, ex-Southern Railway "King Arthur" No.30804* Sir Cador of Cornwall *leaves Bromley, Kent, with a London to Ramsgate train.*

These Knights of the Turntable got their romantic names from the Arthurian legends and this veiled an extreme ordinariness. No doubt the same applied to King Arthur's knights themselves, but in both cases this was no detriment to—indeed it would enhance—the service they gave.

In 1923 Richard Maunsell was made Chief Mechanical Engineer of the Southern Railway newly formed by amalgamating the London & South Western, London, Brighton & South Coast and South Eastern & Chatham

Lord Nelson Class 4-6-0

Great Britain:
Southern Railway (SR), 1926

Tractive effort: 33,500lb (15,196kg).
Axle load: 46,000lb (21t).
Cylinders: (4) 16½ x 24in (419 x 610mm).
Driving wheels: 79in (2,007mm).
Heating surface: 1,989sq ft ($18.5m^2$).
Superheater: 376sq ft ($35m^2$).
Steam pressure: 220psi ($15.5kg/cm^2$).
Grate area: 33sq ft ($3.1m^2$).
Fuel: 11,000lb (5t).
Water: 5,000gall (6,000 US) ($22.7m^3$).
Adhesive weight: 139,000lb (63t).
Total weight: 314,000lb (142.5t).
Length overall: 69ft 9¾in (21,279mm).

When Southern Railway No.850 *Lord Nelson* was new in 1926, she was pronounced the most powerful locomotive in the country—on the slightly spurious basis of tractive effort. So Britain's smallest railway had the strongest locomotive, as well as a publicity department which made the most of it. *Lord Nelson* was the prototype of a class of 16 noble locomotives, named after great seamen of bygone days. Of the other locomotives, seven appeared in 1928 and eight in 1929. Running numbers were 850 to 865. So when latter-day explorers set off to travel to, say, Moscow, Istanbul, Bombay, Athens, Monte Carlo or even Le Touquet, up front at Victoria Station was *Sir Francis Drake* or perhaps *Sir Walter Raleigh,* to speed them on their way.

The "Lord Nelson" class was born out of a need for a more powerful locomotive than the "King Arthur" class in order to handle the heavy holiday expresses, a locomotive with a little more in hand to cover out-of-course delays. The Southern Railway's Civil Engineer was persuaded to allow a ¾-ton increase in axle load on certain principal main lines because of the better balancing implicit in a multi-cylinder locomotive. The result was a magnificent but rather complex four-cylinder 4-6-0, with a Belpaire firebox and a large grate.

An interesting feature of the design was the setting of the cranks successively at 135 degrees to one another, instead of the more usual 90 degrees. The effect of this was to double the number of puffs or beats from four to eight for each revolution of the wheels; the object was to give a more even torque, which would be a help in avoiding slipping the wheels at starting. One adverse effect of the consequent smoothness of running was that coal in the long bogie tenders failed to feed itself forward—as it did when shaken by a rough and rugged "King Arthur"; so "Lord Nelson" firemen who had shovelled all day had to perform near the end of their stints the additional chore of bringing coal forward in the tender.

The "Lord Nelson's" one defect was that they were hard to fire. The even slope of a "King Arthur" grate presented little difficulty, but the "Lord Nelson" one was not only larger (10ft 6in—3,200 mm instead of 9ft—2,743mm) but had a level section at the rear. In consequence, shovelfuls had to be placed very accurately and the front end had to fed with coal thrown all the way, instead of being placed further back to work itself forward. The whole picture was that of a locomotive that needed very skillful firing if it was to steam properly. If that skill was present, the "Lord Nelson" class ran superbly; if not, then time was lost in running and maybe the final disgrace for an engine crew would occur—an out-of-course stop to raise steam. The problem was compounded by the fact that, with only 16 of the class in existence, many crews unfortunately encountered a

Railways. His own SECR locomotive affairs were getting into good shape, but he understandably had doubts about the foreigners. The LSWR ran long-distance expresses to the west country and the front runners in its fleet were twenty 4-6-0s called the "N15" class. Simplicity was the theme of their design with two big 22in x 28in (559 x 711mm) cylinders, outside valves and valve gear, and a parallel boiler with a round-top firebox. Since the LSWR did not have water troughs, big bogie tenders were attached. They ran well but by SECR standards not brilliantly, and Maunsell set about making some improvements to be incorporated in a further batch.

Cylinders on the new locomotives had valves and valve gear which gave events of the kind that had made the "E1" class 4-4-0s such a success on the SECR. More direct steam passages and larger superheaters were used and the ashpan redesigned to improve combustion. A young man called John Elliot, in charge of Public Relations on the SR—a post in which at that time there was plenty of scope—suggested the names and in February 1925 No.453 *King Arthur* left the ex-LSWR works at Eastleigh, to be followed in March by *Queen Guinevere, Sir Lancelot* and eight other knights. Associated names like *Excalibur, Camelot* and *Morgan le Fay* were given to the 20 older locomotives, which also had some of the new technical features applied to them.

At the same time 30 more were ordered from the North British Locomotive Co. of Glasgow while the following year a final 14 were built at Eastleigh. These latter were intended for the Central (ex-LBSCR) section of the SR and had smaller 3,500 gallon six-wheel tenders. So there were now, all told, 74 of the "King Arthur" class and they handled most of the principal SR express passenger assignments until Maunsell's first "Lord Nelson" class arrived in 1927.

The line on which *King Arthur* and his knights rode most often and most nobly into battle was the switchback road beyond Salisbury to Exeter. No.768 *Sir Balin,* travelling eastwards one day in 1934 was observed to regain 6 minutes on a 96-minute schedule with 420 tons, 65 tons more than the maximum laid down for the timing. On this day the maximum speed reached was 86½mph (139km/h) at Axminster but speeds of 90mph (145km/h) and over were not uncommon.

Perhaps the most remarkable run with one of these engines occurred in 1936 when No.777 *Sir Lamiel* regained 17½ minutes in covering the 83¾ miles (134km) from Salisbury to Waterloo in 72¾ minutes an average speed start-to-stop of 69.2mph (111 km/h) with a load of 345 tons.

It is thus appropriate that the "King Arthur" allocated to the National Railway Museum and currently being restored to running order was this same No.777. The "King Arthur" class started to be withdrawn well before steam locomotive preservation became a mania, so none were preserved privately. The saying "happy is the land that has no history" applied to the class, since apart from playing general post with types of tenders, their owners found the "King Arthur" locomotives good enough to remain virtually as they were built, right to the end.

Below: *"King Arthur" class No. 772* Sir Percivale *depicted in the livery adopted by the Southern Railway in 1938, when a brighter green was substituted for the olive green of the 1920s.*

"Lord Nelson" very infrequently.

Eventually, in the late 1930s the problem was solved by improving the air-flow through the firegrate by fitting a multiple-jet blast pipe arrangement known as the Lemaître. Double chimneys were tried at first on two of the locomotives but did not find favour. The tenders were altered so that they were self-trimming, even when attached behind a smooth-running "Lord Nelson" and also, of course, as time went on, expertise needed to make these shy steamers go became more widespread amongst the firemen. In other respects the designers certainly knew their business in that the complex and not too accessible mechanism with two sets of cylinders, motion and the Walschaert's valve gear between the frames, gave little trouble and was not as costly to maintain as might have been expected.

A test with No.850 intended to simulate an enlarged "Atlantic Coast Express", which carried through portions to *six* Devon and Cornwall resorts, and loaded up to 16 coaches, was run on 10 April 1927. It was necessary to schedule the test for a quiet Sunday because the train stretched so far out of busy Waterloo Station that several other platforms would be blocked. Even so, normal schedule time was kept to Exeter, the 171¾ miles (275km) being run in 197 minutes, including a four minute stop at Salisbury and a shorter one at Sidmouth Junction. There were also delays due to weekend engineering works—the leopard had plenty of spots even in those high and far off times. In the end, though, so few "Lord Nelson's" were built that it was not possible to schedule these long trains on a regular basis.

Lord Nelson has survived to be taken into the National Railway Museum collection and is currently doing great things on various special main line excursions. Once or twice, though, it has shown a trace of the old unforgiving spirit towards firemen who thought they were the masters.

Above: *No.850* Lord Nelson, *as preserved and restored to Southern Railway colours, with an enthusiasts' steam Special in 1980.*

Class XC 4-6-2

India:
Indian Railways Standard (IRS), 1927

Tractive effort: 30,625lb (13,895kg).
Axle load: 43,500lb (19.75t).
Cylinders: (2) 23 x 28in (584 x 711mm).
Driving wheels: 74in (1,880mm).
Heating surface: 2,429sq ft (226m²).
Superheater: 636sq ft (59m²).
Steam pressure: 180psi (12.7kg/cm²).
Grate area: 51sq ft (4.75m²).
Fuel: 31,500lb (14.3t).
Water: 6,000gall (7,200 US) (27.25m³).
Adhesive weight: 130,000lb (59.5t).
Total weight: 392,500lb (178t).
Length overall: 76ft 1½in (23,203mm).

The story of the Indian Railways Standard (IRS) 4-6-2 locomotives has not been a happy one. After World War I, a desire to make use of cheaper coal of lower quality than that used formerly led to a specification for locomotives for India provided with wide fireboxes. The passenger engines were the "XA", "XB", and "XC" classes, i.e. light, medium and heavy 4-6-2s. They had maximum axle loads of 13, 17 and 19½ tons respectively. British practice was followed; most were built by the Vulcan Foundry of Newton-le-Willows, Lancashire.

With ample evidence to hand of the first-class qualities of the "BESA" 4-6-0s previously described, the arrival of the first of these locomotives from Britain was awaited with pleasurable anticipation. Alas, they were not satisfactory, being poor steamers, and bad riders to the point not of discomfort but of danger. The valve events were good on paper, but for some reason gave sluggish performance; while the engines were also prone to cracks in the boiler and fractures of the motion and frames.

Although none of the problems were fundamental, nothing was done until in 1937 an "XB" derailed at Bihta on the East Indian Railway, this time with the loss of many lives; this at last got things moving. After an investigation had been made by engineers from France and Britain some of the quite modest modifications required to put the faults right were done. If only the inertia of bureaucracy had not prevented these corrections being made earlier before 284 locomotives had been built and 11 years had elapsed since construction began!

When British India was partitioned in 1947, about 60 "IRS" 4-6-2s went to East and West Pakistan, leaving 76 "XA"s, 81 "XB"s and 50 "XC"s in India proper. In 1957 they were renumbered in the all India list Indian Railways' ("XA" 22001-76; "XB" 22101-81; "XC" 22201-50) although by then occupied on rather menial passenger duties. a few (a very few) survived into the 1980s, the last being withdrawn in 1981.

Right: *Indian Railways class "XB" 4-6-2 No.22104. This was the medium size of the three IRS Pacific designs.*

Class S 4-6-2

Australia:
Victorian Government Railways (VGR), 1928

Tractive effort: 41,100lb (18,643kg).
Axle load: 53,000lb (24t).
Cylinders: (3) 20½ x 28in (521 x 711mm).
Driving wheels: 73in (1,854mm).
Heating surface: 3,121sq ft (290m²).
Superheater: 631sq ft (59m²).
Steam pressure: 200psi (14kg/cm²).
Grate area: 50sq ft (4.7m²).
Fuel: 18,500lbs (8.5t).
Water: 13,000gall (15,500 US) (59m³).
Adhesive weight: 158,000lb (72t).
Total weight: 497,500lb (226t).
Length overall: 85ft 6in (26,060mm).

Above: *Victorian Government Railways "S" class 4-6-2 No. S300 before streamlining.*

These big 4-6-2s were built by the Victorian Railways in 1928 for the principal trains between Melbourne and the New South Wales border at Albury, on the way to Sydney. Their heavy axle load precluded running elsewhere on the VGR and the four constructed were adequate for the needs of the one line on which they were permitted to work.

They were one of the very few classes of steam locomotives in Australia to have three cylinders. The valves of the outside cylinders were actuated by Walschaert's valve gear, while the inside valve was driven via a set of Holcroft-Gresley two-to-one derived gear, as used on the British London & North Eastern Railway. Indeed, with their round-topped boilers and double side-windows, the Australian engines had a definite resemblence to the LNER 4-6-2s. Out of sight, however, were a set of totally un-British cast-steel bar frames. Streamline shrouds were added in 1937; in combination with a blue livery the addition matched a set of new all-steel coaches for the "Spirit of Progress" express. The big 12-wheel tenders dated from this time and enabled the 192 mainly level miles (307km) from Melbourne to Albury to be run non-stop in 220 minutes, an average speed of 52mph (83 km/h). Fairly modest as this might seem, diesel traction today has only meant 8 minutes less journey time. Names of people important in the history of Victoria were given later to these engines, which then became S300 *Matthew Flinders*, S301 *Sir Thomas Mitchell*, S302 *Edward Henty* and S303 *C.J. Latrobe*. They were early victims of dieselisation, being displaced from the "Spirit of Progress" train in 1952; all had been withdrawn by 1954.

Above: *"S" class 4-6-2 No. S302* Edward Henty *heads the air-conditioned "Spirit of Progress" on the Melbourne-Albury run.*

Class Hv2 4-6-0

Finland:
State Railways (VR), 1922

Above: *Finnish State Railways "Hv" class 4-6-0 No.758 at Oulu, Finland. Note spark-arresting smoke-stack.*

Tractive effort: 20,373lb (9,244kg).
Axle load: 29,000lb (13t).
Cylinders: (2) 20¼ x 23½in (510 x 600mm).
Driving wheels: 68¾in (1,750mm).
Heating surface: 1,185sq ft ($110m^2$).
Superheater: 333sq ft ($31m^2$).
Steam pressure: 171psi ($12kg/cm^2$).
Grate area: 20.2sq ft ($2m^2$).
Fuel: 11,000lb (5t).
Water: 3,150gall (3,780 US) ($14.3m^3$).
Adhesive weight: 85,000lb (38.5t).
Total weight: 192,000lb (87t).
Length overall: 51ft 10½in (15,814mm).

Finland's steam locomotives were very tall, very handsome, very distinctive and very few. Many were fired by birch logs and sported spark-arresting smoke stacks in the best traditions of an American Western film. Many were also built at home.

These 4-6-0s of classes "Hv2" and "Hv3" were built in the 1920s and 1930s. Until 4-6-2s arrived in 1937 they were the principal express passenger engines, as indicated by their class letter "H". The second letter is an indication of the axle-load and it is indicative of Finnish conditions that "v" stands for an axle load between 11 and 14 tons and, moreover, that it is not the lowest classification. Some lines of this 5ft (1,524mm) gauge system needed more light-footed locomotives than that!

Interesting features of these engines included by-pass valves —visible as a bump on the side of each cylinder—as an elegant way of avoiding pumping action when coasting. The class held on to cylinder tail-rods long after they ceased to be fashionable elsewhere. A neat air-operated bell was carried in front of the cab and Stephensonian simplicity was not carried so far that the blessings of electric light were not available on board. The "Hv3" class differed only in that they had bogie tenders of higher water capacity instead of six-wheel.

The first native-built "Hv2"s appeared in 1922 from Lokomo of Tampere but a preliminary batch of 15 had been supplied by Schwartzkopff of Germany three years earlier. One (No.680 supplied by Lokomo in 1940) is preserved in the Helsinki Technical Museum.

Below: *Finnish State Railways class "Hv3" 4-6-0 No.782 heads a local train. Note the spark arrester formed of wire mesh at the top of the chimney.*

Royal Scot Class 4-6-0

Great Britain: London Midland & Scottish (LMS), 1927

Tractive effort: 33,150lb (15,037kg).
Axle load: 46,000lb (21t).
Cylinders: (3) 18 x 26in (457 x 660mm).
Driving wheels: 81in (2,057mm).
Heating surface: 1,851sq ft (172m²).
Superheater: 367sq ft (34.1m²).
Steam pressure: 250psi (17.6kg/cm²).
Grate area: 31.25sq ft (2.90m²).
Fuel: 20,000lb (9t).
Water: 4,000gall (4,800 US) (18m³).
Adhesive weight: 137,000lb (62t).
Total weight: 312,500lb (142t).
Length overall: 64ft 11in (19,787mm).

Above: *Preserved Royal Scot No.6115* Scots Guardsman *approaching Chinley with an enthusiast special in November 1978.*

The "Royal Scot"s were another notable class of locomotive that managed more than thirty years on top express work, although a rebuilding which left little of the originals intact halfway through their lives perhaps detracts a little from this achievement. In the mid-1920s the then rather new LMS Railway had to face the fact that there was no locomotive capable singly of hauling the principal train, the 10a.m. Scottish Express from London to Edinburgh and Glasgow, shortly to be known as the "Royal Scot". An ex-LNWR 4-6-0 and 4-4-0 combination would take the train from Euston to Carnforth, while two Midland 4-4-0s would take it on over the hills from there.

A Great Western "Castle" class 4-6-0 was borrowed and demonstrated very effectively in October 1926 that better things were possible. It is said that the LMS made enquiry for 25 "Castles" to be built for the summer service of 1927 but, more practically, the biggest locomotive factory in Britain was given a design-and-build contract for 50 large 4-6-0 express locomotives. The contract with the North British Locomotive Co. (NBL) of Glasgow was not signed until February 1927 and, whilst the first locomotive did not quite go into service in time to help with the summer trains that year, all the "Royal Scot" class were in service by the end of November.

Three cylinders were provided, each with its own set of Walschaert's valve gear and a parallel-barrel boiler with a Belpaire firebox as big as the loading gauge would allow. The locomotives had no technical innovations but were representative of the best practice of the day. In consequence they took to the job they were designed for with the minimum of trouble—and at the same time became much admired by both professionals and the enthusiasts.

Of the 50 locomotives, 25 were given names of regiments and 25 the names of early locomotives. Subsequently, though, all the locomotives were named after regiments of the British Army.

A few minor problems had to be overcome; one was that the piston valves leaked when worn, to an extent that increased steam consumption by nearly half before repairs became due. An accident at Leighton Buzzard in 1931 was attributed to smoke beating down and obscuring the driver's view of signals—this led to the rapid fitting of large smoke deflector plates at the front end, using the pattern developed on the Southern Railway. During the previous year a further 20 "Royal Scot" class had been built, at the old Midland Railway works at Derby; this time the names included a few non-Army titles such as *The Royal Air Force, The Girl Guide* and *The Boy Scout.*

The period was notable for experiments aimed at improving the thermal efficiency of the steam locomotive by increasing the pressure and hence the temperature of the steam. Although it is by no means the only factor involved, steamships and steam power stations use much higher steam temperatures and produce much higher efficiencies, so the prospects were there.

The LMS therefore commissioned from NBL a further "Royal Scot"-like 4-6-0, but with a Schmidt-pattern boiler which generated steam at 1,800psi (and at 325 degrees C) and used that steam to generate more steam, (at 900psi) in a separate circuit (steam pressure 126 and 63 kg/cm²). This new steam was fed to three compound cylinders (one high-pressure, two low-pressure) that were fairly conventionally arranged, except that the feed to the two low-pressure cylinders was supplemented by a steam supply at 250psi (17.5 kg/cm²) from yet another com-

partment in the complex steam generating system.

The locomotive was No.6399 and named *Fury.* Steam at 325 degrees C is very nasty stuff indeed, and when a fire tube burst while *Fury* was on test at Carstairs in February 1930, one man was killed and another seriously injured. After this accident the locomotive was laid aside.

In 1933 the LMS sent a "Royal Scot" locomotive—which changed names with *Royal Scot* for the occasion—to North America, complete with rolling stock, for exhibition at the Chicago World Fair. The train was also exhibited at many places, including Montreal, Denver, San Francisco and Vancouver, on an 11,000-mile (17,700km) tour which followed.

By this time a new locomotive chief had arrived on the LMS scene. William Stanier came from the Great Western Railway, the reputation of which line as the leader in British locomotive practice was then at its zenith. Four things that he did directly affected the "Royal Scot" class. First, he finally eliminated axlebox troubles by initiating a new design of bearing based on GWR practice, which reduced the incidence of "Royal Scot" hot boxes from some 80 to seven annually. Second, he had all the class fitted with new and larger tenders with high curved sidesheets, as used on the other types of locomotive being introduced on the LMS. Third, he took the carcase of *Fury* and rebuilt it into a new locomotive called *British Legion.* The rebuild differed from the others in having a taper-barrel boiler, thereby foreshadowing the shape of things to come. The fourth item was the advent of the Stanier 4-6-2s, which had the effect of displacing the "Royal Scot" class from the very highest assignments.

The effects of well over a decade of hard steaming now began to be felt and in the normal course of things new boilers would be needed, plus other repairs so extensive that the costs would approach that of renewal. The decision was taken to rebuild all the class with taper-barrel boilers of a new pattern, thereby bringing the "Royal Scot" class into line with all Stanier's designs. The rebuilding included new cylinders, in many cases new frames and even new wheel centres only the tenders, cabs and nameplates remained.

Above: *No.6129* The Scottish Horse *shown in the LMS post-war livery.*
Below: *No.46103* Royal Scots Fusilier *in British Rail colours sets out with the "Thames-Clyde Express". Note the horse box coupled next to the tender.*

The first rebuilt "Royal Scot" (No.6103 *Royal Scots Fusilier*) appeared in unlined black livery in 1942, while the last did not come out until 1955. One alteration, fairly insignificant as far as the locomotives were concerned but significant to their public, was the change from the high-pitched Midland Railway whistle to a low-pitched hooter of Caledonian Railway origin, which in Stanier's time was fitted to new LMS locomotives.

The rebuilding was a great success. The new engines stood up to all the abuse of high speed running, heavy loads and wartime neglect better than the originals, and then after the war covered themselves with glory. In the locomotive trials which took place in 1948, shortly after the nationalisation of the main line railways "Royal Scot" representatives performed particularly well.

Although these trials were mounted with great attention to detail by the mechanical side of the railway, there is much evidence in the voluminous report issued afterwards that the results were invalidated by lack of co-operation on the part of the operating authorities and the staff. For example, comparative coal-consumption figures based on a run from Carlisle to Euston of the "Royal Scot" express which included 27 signal checks and stops could be of little use. Such things happened on many of the test runs due to thoughtless controllers allowing a slower train to occupy the line in front.

One thing that did emerge, however, was that the "Royal Scot" 4-6-0s could handle any express train in Britain with something to spare, more economically and just as ably as the bigger and more costly 4-6-2s of nominally much greater power. This surprised many observers, but it is perhaps an indication of the point that these trials were never intended to be taken seriously, and that the one valid conclusion that could be drawn from them, that 4-6-2s could do no more when fired by hand than 4-6-0s, was totally ignored.

The 70 "Royal Scots" disappeared in a very short time once dieselisation was undertaken. The first withdrawal was BR No.46139 (ex-LMS No.6139), *The Welch Regiment* in October 1962. The last ceased work in January 1966, when BR No.46115 *Scots Guardsman* was set aside for preservation. A Mr. Bill acquired her and she is at present on show at the steam centre at Dinting, near Manchester; No.6115 had been out on the main line on various occasions including the Rocket 150 Cavalcade at Rainhill in May 1980. No.6100 *Royal Scot* is also preserved, and can be seen at Alan Bloom's steam centre at Bressingham.

Class A 4-8-4

United States:
Northern Pacific Railroad (NP), 1926

Tractive effort: 61,600lb (27,950kg).
Axle load: 65,000lb (29.5t).
Cylinders (2) 28 x 30in (711 x 762mm).
Driving wheels: 73in (1,854mm).
Heating surface: 4,660sq ft (433m²).
Superheater: 1,992sq ft (185m²).
Steam pressure: 225psi (15.8kg/cm²).
Grate area: 115sq ft (10.7m²).
Fuel: 48,000lb (22t).
Water: 12,500gall (15,000 US) (58m³).
Adhesive weight: 260,000lb (118t).
Total weight: 739,000lb (335t).
Overall length: 105ft 4⅜in (32,125mm).

The King of wheel arrangements at last! It needed 96 years for the 0-2-2 to become a 4-8-4, because all at once in 1927 4-8-4s quickly appeared on several railroads. But by a photo-finish the Northern Pacific's class "A" 4-8-4 was the first and hence the type-name Northern was adopted. The Canadian National Railway, whose first 4-8-4 appeared in 1927 made an unsuccessful play for the name Confederation. Delaware, Lackawanna & Western put forward Pocono for their version. Other early members of the 4-8-4 Club—eventually to be over 40 strong in North America alone—were the Atchison, Topeka & Sante Fe and South Australia, the first foreign member.

The genesis of the 4-8-4 lay in the inbalance between possible tractive effort and grate area of its predecessor the 4-8-2. The Northern Pacific Railroad had a special problem in that its local coal supplies—known rather oddly as Rosebud coal—had a specially high ash content; hence the need for a big firebox and a four-wheel instead of a two-wheel truck at the rear.

And when we say a big firebox, we mean a *really* big one—measuring 13½ x 8½ft (4 x 2½m)—exceeding that of any other line's 4-8-4s. Northern Pacific themselves found their first Northerns so satisfactory they never ordered another passenger locomotive with any other wheel arrangement, and indeed contented themselves with ordering modestly stretched and modernised versions of the originals—sub-classes "A-2", "A-3", "A-4" and "A-5"—right up to their last order for steam in 1943.

The originals were twelve in number and came from the American Locomotive Co of Schenectady. Apart from those enormous grates they were very much the standard US locomotive of the day, with the rugged features evolved after nearly a century of locomotive building on a vast scale. A booster fitted to the trailing truck gave a further 11,400lb (5,172kg) of tractive effort when required at low speeds.

The next 4-8-4 to operate on NP was another Alco product, built in 1930 to the order of the Timken Roller Bearing Co to demonstrate the advantages of having roller bearings on the axles of a steam locomotive. This "Four Aces" (No. 1111) locomotive worked on many railroads with some success as a salesman. The NP was particularly impressed—not only did they buy the engine in 1933 when its sales campaign was over but they also included Timken bearings in the specification when further orders for locomotives were placed. On NP No. 1111 was renumbered 2626 and designated "A-1".

Baldwin of Philadelphia delivered the rest of the Northern fleet. The ten "A-2"s of 1934 (Nos. 2650-59) had disc drivers and bath-tub tenders, and the eight "A-3"s of 1938 (Nos. 2660-67) were almost identical. The final two batches of eight and ten respectively were also very similar; these were the "A-4"s of 1941 (Nos. 2670-77) and the "A-5"s of 1943 (Nos. 2680-89). These last two groups may be distinguished by their 14-wheel Centipede or 4-10-0 tenders of the type originally supplied for Union Pacific.

Below: *Northern Pacific Railroad class "A-4" 4-8-4 No. 2670 was built by Baldwins of Philadelphia in 1941.*

Above: *Northern Pacific Railroad class "A-5" 4-8-4 No. 2680 built by Baldwin in 1943. Note the "centipede" fourteen-wheel tender.*

This final batch is the subject of the art-work above. The amount of stretching that was done may be judged from the following particulars . . .

Tractive effort: 69,800lb (31,660kg).
Axle load: 74,000lb (33.5t)
Driving wheels: 77in (1,956mm)
Steam pressure: 260psi (18.3kg/cm).
Fuel: 54,000lb (24.5t)
Water: 21,000gall (25,000 US) (95m^3).
Adhesive weight: 295,000lb (134t).
Total weight: 952,000lb (432t).
Overall length: 112ft 10in (34,391mm).

Other particulars are sensibly the same as the "A" class.

Northern Pacific had begun well by receiving a charter from President Abraham Lincoln in 1864 to build the first transcontinental line to serve the wide north-western territories of the USA. Through communication with the Pacific coast was established in 1883. By the time the 4-8-4s began to arrive it had established itself under the slogan "Main Street of the North West", and connected the twin cities of St Paul and Minneapolis with both Seattle and Portland.

The flag train on this run was the North Coast Limited, and the 4-8-4s assigned to it, after taking over from Chicago Burlington & Quincy Railroad power at St Paul, ran the 999 miles to Livingston, Montana, without change of engine. This is believed to be a world record as regards through engine runs with coal-fired locomotives. No doubt it was made possible by using normal coal in a firebox whose ash capacity was designed for the massive residues of Rosebud lignite.

Right: *Front end of Northern Pacific Railroad 4-8-4 No.2650. Note the bell and headlight typical of US railroad practice.*

Class Ps-4 4-6-2

United States: Southern Railway (SR), 1926

Tractive effort: 47,500lb (21,546 kg).
Axle load: 61,000lb (27.25t).
Cylinders: (2) 27 x 28in (686 x 711mm).
Driving wheels: 73in (1,854mm).
Heating surface: 3,689sq ft ($343m^2$).
Superheater: 993sq ft ($92.3m^2$).
Steam pressure: 200psi ($14.1kg/cm^2$).
Grate area: 70.5sq ft ($6.55m^2$).
Fuel: 32,000lb (14.5t).
Water: 11,600gall (14,000 US) ($53m^3$).
Adhesive weight: 182,000lb (81t).
Total weight: 562,000lb (255.0t).
Length overall: 91ft 11⅞in (28,038mm).

Hundreds of classes of Pacific locomotives ran in America; to illustrate them the first choice was the earliest proper 4-6-2, of the Chesapeake & Ohio. Second choice was the Pennsylvania RR class "K4", as the 4-6-2 design built in the largest numbers. This locomotive, our third choice, is without any doubt the most beautiful amongst the Pacifics of America.

The history of the Southern Railway's Pacifics began in World War I, when the United States Railroad Administration, which had taken over the railroads for the duration, set out to design a standard set of steam locomotives to cover all types of traffic. One of these was the so-called USRA "heavy" 4-6-2. Based on this design, the American Locomotive Company built the first batch of 36 Class "Ps-4" 4-6-2s in 1923.

In 1925 President (of Southern Railway) Fairfax Harrison, visited

King Class 4-6-0

Great Britain: Great Western Railway (GWR), 1927

Tractive effort: 40,300lb (18,285kg).
Axle load: 50,500lb (23t).
Cylinders: (4) 16¼ x 28in (413 x 711mm).
Driving wheels: 78in (1,981mm).
Heating surface: 2,201sq ft ($204m^2$).
Superheater: 313sq ft ($29.0m^2$).
Steam pressure: 250psi ($17.6kg/cm^2$).
Grate area: 34.3sq ft ($3.19m^2$).
Fuel: 13,500lb (6t).
Water: 4,000gall (4,800 US) ($18m^3$).
Adhesive weight: 151,000lb (69t).
Total weight: 304,000lb (138t).
Length overall: 68ft 2in (20,777mm).

In 1926, the Great Western Railway decided that more powerful locomotives were needed—the "Castle" class 4-6-0s were stretched to their limits on some duties. At the same time a 20 year programme of strengthening bridges was nearing completion; furthermore, the report of an official body known as the Bridge Stress Committee, then recently published, had recommended that for locomotives which had low "hammer-blow" higher axle loads could be allowed. All of this added up to making it practical to build a four-cylinder 4-6-0 with a 22½ ton axle load; just as the "Castle" class had been a stretched "Star" class so the new locomotives were to be a stretched "Castle".

In enlarging the "Castle" class, the original principles were followed exactly. The domeless taper-barrel boiler, with Belpaire firebox was there, and so was the four-cylinder arrangement with the insde cylinders driving the leading coupled axle. Walschaert's valve gear, also inside the frames, drove the valves of the inside cylinders driving the those of the outside ones through rocking shafts. Problems with clearances at the front end of the locomotive led to a unique design of bogie with outside bearings to the leading wheels and normal inside bearings to the trailing ones—this rather striking feature was very much a trademark of the newly named "King" class.

Some slight subterfuges were indulged in so as to bring the tractive effort above 40,000lb. Cylinders designed to be 16in (406mm) diameter were bored out to 16¼ (413) whilst the driving wheel diameter was reduced from the hallowed GWR standard of 6ft 8½in (2,045mm) to 6ft 6in (1,981mm). With the increased boiler pressure the required target was reached and the GWR's capable publicity department could once again claim the possession of Britain's most powerful express passenger locomotive. Tractive effort is no measure of locomotive capability at speed but in the "King" class it was backed up by adequate steam-raising power, inlcuding a firebed 10ft 9in (3,277mm) long. But even without that, a high drawbar pull was an advantage on those steep South Devon inclines, of which the most notorious was the long stretch of 1 in 42 (2.4 per cent) at Hemerdon, east of Plymouth. A "King" was rated to take 360 tons unaided up here, 45 tons more than a "Castle".

The prototype, No.6000 *King George V* which appeared from the works in June 1927, was sent off to the USA when only a few weeks old, to appear at the Baltimore & Ohio Railroad's centenary "Fair of the Iron Horse" held at Baltimore in August. No.6000 led the parade each day and attracted much attention with the famous green livery lined out with black and orange, and with brasswork, name and copper-capped chimney. It must be remembered that American locomotives of the day were much bigger but relatively drab.

Later, a train was worked between Baltimore and Philadelphia; with 544 tons (representing only seven American cars instead of 16 British ones) a speed of 74 mph (119km/h) was reached on level track and a gradient of 1 in 80 (1.25 per cent) was surmounted satisfactorily during the 272 miles (438km) return jour-

his line's namesake in England and was impressed with its green engines. He determined that his next batch of 4-6-2s would make an equal if not better showing. He naturally chose a style very similar to the English SR except that a much brighter green was used together with gold—the small extra cost paid off quickly in publicity. Coloured locomotives were then quite exceptional in North America. A little later the earlier batch of locomotives appeared in green and gold also.

The 1926 batch of 23 locomotives had the enormous 12-wheel tenders illustrated here, in place of the USRA standard 8-wheel tenders on the earlier engines, and a different and much more obvious type (the Elesco) of feed water heater involving the large transverse cylindrical vessel just in front of the smokestack. Some locomotives from each batch had the Walschaert's gear, others had Baker's. A final batch of 5 came from Baldwin in 1928. These had Walschaert's valve gear and 8-wheel tenders of large capacity. All were fitted with mechanical stokers.

Southern had what it called an "optional equipment policy" whereby drivers were allowed to adorn their locomotives in various ways, ways in fact that were similar to those of 70 years earlier. Eagles could be mounted above the headlights, themselves flanked by brass "candlesticks"; stars were fixed to cylinder heads, brass rings to smokestacks. Some locomotives were named after and by their regular drivers. A lot of this might be considered mere nonsense, but the end effect was that few steam engines anywhere were better maintained.

Of the 64 locomotives built, 44 were allocated to the Southern Railway proper, 12 to subsidiary Cincinnati, New Orleans & Texas Pacific and 8 to the Alabama Great Southern, although "Southern" appeared on the tenders of all. Running numbers were as follows:

SR proper—Nox.1366 to 1409.
CNO&TP—Nos.6471 to 6482.
AGS—Nos.6684 to 6691.

The CNO&TP engines had a device known as a Wimble smoke duct, by which the exhaust which otherwise would issue from the chimney could be led backwards to level with the sand dome and discharged there. The CNO&TP was a line with many timber-lined tunnels and a direct close-up vertical blast would have played havoc with the tunnel linings.

The "Ps-4" class was the last steam passenger locomotive type built for the Southern and they remained in top-line express work until displaced by diesels in the 1940s and 1950s. No.1401 is preserved and is superbly displayed in the Smithsonian Museum, Washington, D.C.

Alas, this involved erecting the display building around the locomotive, thereby preventing its use on special trains for railfans, a Southern speciality.

Left: *One of the Southern Railway's superb "Ps-4" 4-6-2s in action. This particular loco is the one preserved in the Smithsonian Museum.*

Below: *The glorious green and gold beauty of the livery applied to the Southern Railway (of USA) "Ps-4" class Pacific is superbly depicted below.*

ney. *King George V* came back with medals, a large bell (still carried) and much honour.

Five more "King" class appeared during 1927, then 14 during 1928 and the last ten in 1930. As a result of early experience, including the derailment of a pair of leading wheels at Midgham near Newbury, modifications were made to the springing and other details affecting the riding. Once these things were corrected the "King" class performed in accordance with expectation and seven minutes were cut from the schedule of the *Cornish Riviera Limited* between London and Plymouth, the new 4 hour timing being attained with heavier loads.

One thing that seems to have been ignored was the fact that the capacity of the locomotive was increased but not that of the human link in its power cycle, that is the fireman who shovelled the coal. The "King" class boiler certainly had the potential of steaming at rates which corresponded to coal consumption maybe 30 per cent greater than the 3,000lb (1,360kg) or so per hour a man could be expected to shovel. Even so, no attempt was made to fit mechanical stokers.

As an illustration of the potential that was available and after some modifications to increase the superheater heating surface by 56 per cent and also to improve the draughting, tests were made using two firemen. An enormous 25-coach load was hauled between Reading and Stoke Gifford near Bristol at an average speed of over 58 mph (93km/h). Later, further improvements were made which involved the fitting of double chimneys. It was with the first locomotive so equipped, No.6015 *King Richard III* that the highest ever speed with a "King" class was recorded, 108½mph (175km/h) near Patney with the down *Cornish Riviera Limited* on 29 September 1955. All the "King" class had double chimneys by the end of 1958.

Time, however, was running out for the "King" class. Their end began early in 1962 when No.6006 *King George I* was withdrawn. It was complete early in 1963, when the last was taken out of service.

Left: *Great Western Railway "King" class No.6010* King Charles I *passing Corsham at speed on Brunel's original main line between Bath and Bristol.*

Class J3a 4-6-4

United States: New York Central Railroad (NYC), 1926

Tractive effort: 41,860lb (19,000kg).
Axleload: 67,500lb (30.5t).
Cylinders: (2) 22½ x 29in (572 x 737mm).
Driving wheels: 79in (2,007mm).
Heating surface: 4,187sq ft (389.0m²).
Superheater: 1,745sq ft (162.1m²).
Steam pressure: 265psi (18.6kg/cm²).
Grate area: 82sq ft (7.6m²).
Fuel: 92,000lb (41.7t).
Water: 15,000gall (18,000 US) (68.1m³).
Adhesive weight: 201,500lb (91.5t).
Total weight: 780,000lb (350t).
Length overall: 106ft 1in (32,342mm).

Above: *"J1" 4-6-4 No.5280 hauling the Empire State Express at Dunkirk, New York State, in February 1950.*

Some locomotive wheel arrangements had a particular association with one railway; such was the 4-6-4 and the New York Central. In 1926 the Central built its last Pacific, of Class "K5b," and the road's design staff, under the direction of Paul W Kiefer, Chief Engineer of Motive Power, began to plan a larger engine to meet future requirements. The main requirements were an increase in starting tractive effort, greater cylinder power at higher speeds, and weight distribution and balancing which would impose lower impact loads on the track than did the existing Pacifics. Clearly this would involve a larger firebox, and to meet the axle loading requirement the logical step was to use a four-wheeled truck under the cab, as was advocated by the Lima Locomotive Works, which had plugged engines with large fireboxes over trailing bogies under the trade name of Super Power. As the required tractive effort could be transmitted through three driving axles, the wheel arrangement came out as 4-6-4. Despite the Lima influence in the design, it was the American Locomotive Company of Schenectady which received the order for the first locomotive, although Lima did receive an order for ten of them some years later. Subsequent designs of 4-6-4s took over the type-name Hudson applied to these engines by the NYC.

Classified "Jla" and numbered 5200, the new engine was handed over to the owners on 14 February 1927. By a narrow margin it was the first 4-6-4 in the United States, but others were already on the production line at Alco for other roads. Compared with the "K5b" it showed an increase in grate area from 67.8sq ft (6.3m²) to 81.5sq ft (7.6m²), and the maximum diameter of the boiler was increased from 84in (2,134mm) to 87⅝in (2,226mm). The cylinder and driving wheel sizes were unchanged, so the tractive effort went up on proportion to the increase in boiler pressure from 200psi (14.1 kg/cm²) to 225psi (15.8kg/cm²). The addition of an extra axle enabled the total weight on the coupled axles to be reduced from 185,000lb (83.9t) to 182,000lb (82.6t), despite an increase in the total engine weight of 41,000lb (22t). Improved balancing reduced the impact loading on the rails compared with the Pacific.

The engine had a striking appearance, the rear bogie giving it a more balanced rear end than a Pacific, with its single axle under a large firebox. At the front the air compressors and boiler feed pump were housed under distinctive curved casings at either side of the base of the smokebox, with diagonal bracing bars. The boiler mountings ahead of the cab were clothed in an unusual curved casing.

No.5200 soon showed its paces, and further orders followed, mostly for the NYC itself, but 80 of them allocated to three of the wholly-owned subsidiaries, whose engines were numbered and lettered separately. The latter included 30 engines for the Boston and Albany, which, in deference to the heavier gradients on that line, had driving wheels three inches smaller than the remainder, a rather academic difference. The B&A engines were classified "J2a", "J2b" and "J2c", the suffixes denoting minor differences in successive batches. The main NYC series of 145 engines were numbered consecutively from 5200, and here again successive modifications produced sub-classes "Jla" to "Jle". Amongst detail changes were the substitution of Baker's for Walschaert's valve gear; the Baker's gear has no sliding parts, and was found to require less maintenance. There were also changes in the valve setting.

From their first entry into service the Hudsons established a reputation for heavy haulage at high speeds. Their maximum drawbar horsepower was 38 per cent more than that of the Pacifics, and they attained this at a higher speed. They could haul 18 cars weighing 1,270 tonnes at an average speed of 55mph (88 km/h) on the generally level sections. One engine worked a 21-car train of 1,500 tonnes over the 639 miles (1,027km) from Windsor (Ontario) to Harmon, covering one section of 71 miles (114km) at an average speed of 62.5mph (100.5km/h).

The last of the "J1" and "J2" series were built in 1932, and there was then a pause in construction, although the design staff were already planning for an increase in power. In 1937 orders were placed for 50 more Hudsons, incorporating certain

Below: *Standard Hudson or 4-6-4 of class "J3" design. The Railroad had 275 engines of this type in passenger service and they monopolised the road's express trains for twenty years.*

improvements and classified "J3". At the time of the introduction of the first Hudson, the NYC, like the German engineers of the time, were chary of combustion chambers in fireboxes because of constructional and maintenance problems, but by 1937 further experience had been gained, and the "J3" incorporated a combustion chamber 43 in (1,092mm) long. Other changes included a tapering of the boiler barrel to give a greater diameter at the front of the firebox, raising of the boiler pressure from 225 psi (15.9kg/cmm²) to 275psi (19.3km/cm²) (later reduced to 265psi), and a change in the cylinder size from 25 x 28in (635 x 711mm) to 22½ x 29in (572 x 737mm). The most conspicuous change was the use of disc driving wheels, half the engines having Boxpok wheels with oval openings, and the other half the Scullin type with circular openings.

The final ten engines were clothed in a streamlined casing designed by Henry Dreyfus. Of all the streamlined casings so far applied to American locomotives, this was the first to exploit the natural shape of the locomotive rather than to conceal it, and the working parts were left exposed. Many observers considered these to be the most handsome of all streamlined locomotives, especially when hauling a train in matching livery. Prior to the building of the streamlined "J3"s, a "J1" had been clothed in a casing devised at the Case School of Science in Cleveland, but it was much less attractive than Dreyfus' design, and the engine was rebuilt like the "J3"s; while two further "J3"s were given Dreyfus casings for special duties.

The "J3"s soon showed an improvement over the "J1"s both in power output and in efficiency. At 65mph (105km/h) they developed 20 per cent more power than a "J1". They could haul 1,130 tonnes trains over the 147 miles (236km) from Albany to Syracuse at scheduled speeds of 59mph (95km/h), and could reach 60mph (96km/h) with a 1,640 tonne train. The crack train of the NYC was the celebrated 20th Century Limited. At the time of the building of the first Hudsons this train was allowed 20 hours from New York to Chicago. This was cut to 18 hours in 1932 on the introduction of the "Jle" series, and in 1936 there was a further cut to 16½ hours. Aided by the elimination of some severe service slacks, and by the "J3" engines, the schedule came down to 16 hours in 1938, which gave an end-to-end speed of 59.9mph (96.3km/h) with 900-tonne trains, and with seven intermediate stops totalling 26 minutes. On a run with a "J3" on the Century, with 940 tonnes, the 133 miles (214km) from Toledo to Elkhart were covered in a net time of 112½ minutes, and the succeeding 93.9 miles (151km) from Elkhart to Englewood in 79½ minutes, both giving averages of 70.9mph (114km/h). A speed of 85.3mph (137km/h) was maintained for 31 miles (50km), with a maximum of 94mph (151km/h). The engines worked through from Harmon to Toledo or Chicago, 693 and 925 miles (1,114 and 1,487km) respectively. For this purpose huge tenders were built carrying 41 tonnes of coal, but as the NYC used water troughs to replenish the tanks on the move, the water capacity was by comparison modest at 18,000 US gallons (68.1m³).

Above: *The prototype New York Central class "J1" No.5200 on test-train of 18 heavyweight cars at Albany in 1927.*

Above: *The streamline version of the New York Central's famous Hudson. The designer was Henry Dreyfus.*

Eventually the engines allocated to the subsidiaries were brought into the main series of numbers, and with the removal of the streamlined casings in post-war years, the NYC had 275 engines of similar appearance numbered from 5,200 to 5,474. It was the largest fleet of 4-6-4 locomotives on any railway, and constituted 63 per cent of the total engines of that wheel arrangement in the United States.

Although the Hudson had their share of troubles, they were generally reliable, and the "J3"s ran 185,000 to 200,000 miles (297,000 to 321,000km) between heavy repairs, at an annual rate of about 110,000 miles (177,000km).

After World War II the Niagara 4-8-4s displaced the Hudson from the heaviest workings, but as that class numbered only 25 engines, the Hudsons still worked many of the 150 trains daily on the NYC booked at more than 60mile/h (96km/h) start-to-stop. Despite rapid dieselisation the engines lasted until 1953-6, apart from an accident casualty.

Schools Class 4-4-0

Great Britain: Southern Railway (SR), 1933

Tractive effort: 25,133lb (11,400kg).
Axle load: 47,000lb (21t).
Cylinders: (3) 16½ x 26in (419 x 660mm).
Driving wheels: 79in (2,007mm).
Heating surface: 1,766sq ft ($164m^2$).
Superheater: 283sq ft ($26.3m^2$).
Steam pressure: 220psi ($15.46kg/cm^2$).
Grate area: 28.3sq ft ($2.63m^2$).
Fuel: 11,000lb (5t).
Water: 4,000gall (4,800 US) ($18m^3$).
Adhesive weight: 94,000lb (42t).
Total weight: 245,500 (110t).
Length overall: 58ft 9¾in (17,926mm).

British locomotive engineers command respect for their mastery of the processes involved in producing and assembling the many components that go to make a steam express passenger locomotive. In some cases, though, one is more cautious when appraising their theoretical approach to design. This slight reluctance to do sums often produced surprises, usually unpleasant. But sometimes they were pleasant ones, as witness the excellent "Schools" class first put into service by the Southern Railway in 1930. The "Schools" locomotives were originally intended as small engines for lesser services but the engineering staff got a pleasant surprise when it was found that in many ways their capability was on a level with the SR's bigger "King Arthur" class as well as with the much bigger but rather disappointing "Lord Nelson" class.

A shortened "King Arthur" boiler was the basis of the design and since it was the barrel rather than the firebox which was reduced in length, it was the big fire plus the hottest part of the heating surface that remained and so steam raising was hardly affected. The bigger ashpan possible because of the wide space between the coupled axles was also a help. Most 4-4-0s with outside cylinders were notorious for the "boxing" effect—i.e. oscillation about a vertical axis—caused by the impossibility of counter-balancing all the reciprocating parts in a two-cylinder engine.

Three cylinders were chosen therefore for the new locomotives, all driving on the leading coupled axle. Each cylinder had its own set of Walschaert's valve gear, but access to the inside motion is much easier on a 4-4-0 than on a 4-6-0 or 4-6-2 as we have seen already in the case of the "American Standard" 4-4-0.

The design was a great success from the start and very few changes were needed over the years. A few locomotives were later fitted with multiple-jet blastpipes and large diameter chimneys, but otherwise the main

Class 500 4-8-4

Australia: South Australian Government Railways (SAR), 1928

Tractive effort: 51,000lb (23,133kg).
Axle load: 49,500lb (22.5t).
Cylinders: (2) 26 x 28in (660 x 711).
Driving wheels: 63in (1,600mm).
Heating surface: 3,648sq ft ($339m^2$).
Superheater: 835sq ft ($77.5m^2$).
Steam pressure: 200psi ($14.1kg/cm^2$).
Grate area: 66.5sq ft ($6.2m^2$).
Fuel: 2,4500lb (11t).
Water: 7,000gall (8,400 US) ($32m^3$).
Adhesive weight: 196,500lb (89t).
Total weight: 498,000lb (226t).
Length overall: 83ft 1½in (25,641mm).

South Australia is by no means easy locomotive country. For example, when South Australian Railways' trains leave the capital, Adelaide, for Melbourne, they have to face a long 1 in 45 (2.2 per cent) climb into the Mount Lofty ranges. In spite of this their motive power sixty years ago was on the small side. In the early 1920s the latest and largest express passenger power was the class "S" 4-4-0 of 1894, with 12,700lb (5,762kg) of tractive effort and 17½sq ft ($1.6m^2$) of grate area.

The State government was not happy about the state of its 5ft 3in (1,600mm) gauge railway system and so adopted the idea of inviting a senior executive from a USA railroad to be the Railway Commissioner. In due time a certain Mr. W.A. Webb, who hailed from the Missouri-Kansas-Texas Railroad—the famous "Katy"—arrived in Australia. His plans for SAR were to include some very large locomotives indeed.

The most notable of Webb's two passenger designs were the ten "500" class 4-8-2s, which had over four times the tractive effort

event was the addition of 30,000 to the numbers upon nationalisation in 1948.

The names of famous schools in SR territory were chosen for the locomotives, in spite of the drawback that many of them had the same names as SR stations and people occasionally confused the nameplate with the train's destination boards. No.900 *Eton* appeared in March 1930, the first of a batch of ten built at Eastleigh Works that year. Five more appeared in 1932, ten in 1933 (including a series commencing with No.919 *Harrow*, named after schools away from the SR), seven in 1934 and eight in 1935, making 40 in all.

One requirement was to permit running through the below-standard-size tunnels on the Tonbridge to Hastings line and to this end the sides of both cabs and tenders had an upper sloping portion. This certainly added to the neat and compact appearance.

Their greatest work was done on the Bournemouth line, on which they regularly hauled the crack *Bournemouth Limited* express, scheduled to run the 116 miles (186km) in 120 minutes non-stop. Cecil J. Allen noted an occasion when a 510-ton train was worked by No.932 *Blundells* from Waterloo to Southampton at an average speed of 61mph (98km/h) and another when with 305 tons No.931 *King's Wimbledon* ran from Waterloo to a signal stop outside Salisbury at an average of 66mph (106½ km/h), 90mph (145km/h) being just touched at one point. Neither of these feats would disgrace a Pacific.

The class was withdrawn in 1961 and 1962 but three examples have been preserved. No.925 *Cheltenham* belongs to the National Railway Museum and is currently in main-line running order. No.928 *Stowe* is with the Bluebell Railway and No.926 *Repton* is in the USA, currently at Steamtown, Bellows Falls, Vermont, although it is understood a move is pending.

Above: *"Schools" class No. 30934* St Lawrence *on an up troop special at Folkestone Warren, Kent, England.*

Below: *"Schools" Class loco No.919,* Harrow, *depicted in the Southern Railways' pre-war livery. A superb locomotive, it suprised even its designers with its efficiency and power.*

Left: *Two views of 4-8-4 No. 500 on a special farewell run from Adelaide to Victor Harbour, Victoria, in March 1962, just before withdrawal from service.*

of the previous top-line passenger locomotives plus other attributes in proportion! Although typically American in design, these monsters were built in 1926 by the English armaments firm, Armstrong-Whitworth of Newcastle-upon-Tyne. In 1928 the locomotives, apparently still not regarded as sufficiently strong pullers, were further enhanced by a booster giving an additional 8,000lb (3,640kg) of tractive effort. This was accommodated in a four-wheel truck, thereby giving Australia the honour of having the world's first 4-8-4 outside North America; the pony truck had previously had an axle loading of over 22 tons.

Another later addition was a pair of elegant footplate valances bearing the "Overland" motif. This reflected the labours of these magnificent locomotives on "The Overland" express between Adelaide and Melbourne. The 1 in 45 of the Mount Lofty incline could be negotiated at 15mph with 550 tons—this with booster in action. It must have been worth listening to—but then so would be *three* of the "500"s 4-4-0 predecessors on the 350-ton Melbourne express of a few years earlier.

The "500"s and the other Webb classes were not multiplied, mainly because heavy axle-loadings precluded their use on all but the principal main lines. Diesel-electric locomotives appeared in South Australia from 1951 on and in 1955 the first "500" was withdrawn. By 1962 all had gone, except No.504, which is preserved at the Australian Railway Historical Society's museum at Mile End, near Melbourne.

KF Type 4-8-4

China: Chinese Ministry of Railways, 1935

Tractive effort: 36,100lb (16,380kg).
Axle load: 38,000lb (17.5t).
Cylinders: (2) 21¼ x 29½in (540 x 750mm).
Driving wheels: 69in (1,750mm).
Heating surface: 2,988sq ft (278m²).
Superheater: 1,076sq ft (100m²).
Steam pressure: 220psi (15.5kg/cm²).
Grate area: 68.5sq ft (6.4m²).
Fuel: 26,500lb (12t).
Water: 6,600gall (8,000 US) (30m³).
Adhesive weight: 150,000lb (68t).
Total weight: 432,000lb (196t).
Length overall: 93ft 2½in (28,410mm).

Twenty-four of these magnificent locomotives were supplied by the Vulcan Foundry of Newton-le-Willows, Lancashire, to China in 1935-6. They were paid for out of funds set aside as reparations for damage done in China to British property in the so-called Boxer riots of 1910. Although British built as well as designed by a Briton, Kenneth Cantlie, the practice followed was American—except in one respect, that is, the limitation of axle load to 16½ tons. Twice that would be more typical of United States locomotive.

The typical American locomotive was directly in line with the original simple Stephenson concept of a locomotive having just two outside cylinders, but it was very fully equipped in other ways. Hence these "KF" locomotives, destined for what was in those days and in material things a rather backward country had, for example, electric lights, while crews of the last word in passenger steam locomotives back in Britain had to make do with paraffin oil. British firemen had to use a shovel to put coal in the firebox, while Chinese ones had the benefit of automatic stokers.

Above: *Chinese class "KF" 4-8-4 locomotive awaiting departure from Nanjing station.*

Other equipment included a supply of superheated steam for certain auxiliaries, and a cut-off control indicator to advise the driver on the best setting for the valve gear. In the case of some of the locomotives, the leading tender bogie was fitted with a

Right: *4-8-4 locomotive (later class "KF") as built by the Vulcan Foundry for the Chinese Ministry of Railways in 1936.*

Class K 4-8-4

New Zealand: New Zealand Government Railways (NZGR), 1932

Tractive effort: 32,740lb (14,852kg).
Axle load: 30,500lb (14t).
Cylinders: (2) 20 x 26in (508 x 660mm).
Driving wheels: 54in (1,372mm).
Heating surface: 1,931sq ft (179m²).
Superheater: 482sq ft (45m²).
Steam pressure: 200psi (14.1kg/cm²).
Grate area: 47.7sq ft (4.4m²).
Fuel: 17,500lb (8t).
Water: 5,000gall (6,000 US) (22.7m³).
Adhesive weight: 122,000lb (55t).
Total weight: 306,000lb (139t).
Length overall: 69ft 8in (21,233mm).

It is always a surprise to think that far-off and remote New Zealand should have one of the finest railway systems in the world. Furthermore, in steam days this sheep-raising country of a mere 1.6 million population produced its own motive power not only in one but in both the main islands. Amongst many fine locomotives designed and built there, the "K" class 4-8-4s were outstanding.

Apart from the cab (which had to accommodate full size New Zealanders) the "K"s appeared as scaled-down versions of typical North American 4-8-4s, with their dimensions reduced in proportion to the narrower 3ft 6in (1,067mm) gauge standard in New Zealand. Even so, the designers certainly had all their buttons on to produce a locomotive of such power within the limitations of an 11ft 6in (3,480 mm) overall height and a 14-ton axleload.

In all 71 "K"s were built between 1932 and 1950, all in NZGR's own workshops. There were three sub-classes, "K", "Ka" and "Kb" numbering 30, 35 and 6 respectively. Running numbers were 900 to 970. The first group had roller bearings to the guiding and tender axles, while the remainder had all axles so fitted. Class "Kb" were built at Hillside workshops, Dunedin, South Island, and the remainder at Hutt, near Wellington, North Island.

The "Kb"s, intended for a transverse line which crosses the mountain spine of the South Island, had boosters which gave an extra 8,000lb (3,640kg) of tractive effort. Originally the "Ka"s and "Kb"s had a boxed-in front end, looking for all the world like the front end of a modern "hood-unit" diesel locomotive, but these ugly attachments were removed immediately after World War II. Two "Ka"s Nos.958 and 959 had Baker's valve gear in place of Walschaert's.

Baker's valve gear was a patented USA arrangement, very much akin to Walschaert's, which did away with the curved link and die-block. In its place there was an ingenious arrangement of levers and simple pin-joints which produced the same effect. The use of Baker's valve gear outside the USA was minimal but even on its home ground it never showed signs of superseding Walschaert's in any general sense. A number of applications are illustrated elsewhere in this book—the patent gear *did* have more of an advantage when it came to the long valve-travel associated with fast-running passenger locomotives.

In the late 1940s the "K"s and "Ka"s, all of which were built for and remained on the North Island lines, were converted to oil-burning, while the "Kb"s on the South Island remained coal fired. This seems to have been the only major modification which occurred—and of course it was one which was dictated by external circumstances rather than by any shortcomings of these

Right: *NZGR class "K" 4-8-4 crosses a temporary bridge of steel girder and timber trestle.*

booster engine; two axles of the six-wheel truck were coupled, so that the booster drive was on four wheels. The booster gave an additional 7,670lb (3,480kg) of tractive effort while in operation. These engines were allocated to the Canton-Hankow railway, while the others were divided between that line and the Shanghai-Nanking railway. One interesting feature was that the Walschaert's valve gear was arranged to give only half the amount of valve travel needed. A 2-to-1 multiplying lever was provided to give the correct amount. The piston valves were 12½in (320mm) in diameter, an exceptionally large size. Running numbers were 600 to 623.

When locomotive-building firms set out to build locomotives bigger than were used in their native land they were not always a success, but this case was an exception, and the class gave excellent service. During the war years exceptional efforts were made to keep these engines out of the hands of the Japanese and to some extent the efforts were successful. It has been reported that 17 out of the 24 survived World War II, which for China lasted over ten years and was exceptionally devastating.

After the communists gained control, the class was designated "KF"—in Roman not Chinese characters—and renumbered from 1 upwards. The letters KF seem to correspond with the English word Confederation; other class designations of what are now non-standard Chinese types lend support to this supposition. The prime position given to these engines in the renumbering is some indication of the regard in which they were held.

Above: *Class "KF" 4-8-4 No.7 at Shanghai in 1981 awaiting shipment back to England for the National Railway Museum.*

Dieselisation of the Chinese Railways is proceeding slowly, priority being given to long distance passenger trains. Trains entrusted to these 4-8-4s were early targets for dieselisation and no 4-8-4 has been seen by Western visitors since 1966, although it is reported they were in use in the Shanghai area as late as 1974.

In 1978, the Chinese Minister of Railways, while on a visit to Britain promised one to the National Railway Museum at York, as a prime example of British exports to the world. This was to happen when a "KF" was taken out of use; accordingly in 1981 No.KF7 was shipped from Shanghai back to the country from whence it came.

wonderful engines. An exception was the replacement of feedwater heating equipment by exhaust steam injectors on the "Ka" and "Kb" batches.

For many years the whole class performed with great distinction on the principal passenger trains and speeds of up to 69mph (110km/h) have been recorded. As regards famous ascents such as the Raurimu spiral incline, they could maintain 20mph (32km/h) with 300 tons on the 1 in 50 (2 per cent) grade, uncompensated for curvature.

Proportionate to the population, New Zealanders have a passion for steam locomotives unmatched even in Britain; this is reflected in the preservation of five of these engines. No.900 is with the Pacific Steel Co. of Otahuhu, No.935 at Seaview, near Wellington and Nos.942 and 945 are at Paekikari, all in the North Island. No.968 is at the Ferrymead Museum of Science and Industry near Christchurch in the South Island.

Class P2 2-8-2 **Great Britain:** London & North Eastern Railway (LNER), 1934

Tractive effort: 43,462lb (19,715kg).
Axle load: 44,800lb (20t).
Cylinders: (3) 21 x 26in (533 x 660mm).
Driving wheels: 74in (1,880mm).
Heating surface: 2,714sq ft ($252m^2$).
Superheater: 777sq ft ($72m^2$).
Steam pressure: 220psi ($15.5kg/cm^2$).
Grate area: 50sq ft ($4.6m^2$).
Fuel: 18,000lb (8t).
Water: 5,000gall (6,000 US) ($23m^3$).
Adhesive weight: 177,000lb (80t).
Total weight: 370,000lb (168t).
Length overall: 74ft 5⅝in (22,692mm).

In thinking of the London & North Eastern Railway's East Coast main line from London to Scotland, one is liable to forget that it extends 130 miles (208km) beyond Edinburgh to Aberdeen. This final section was much more severe than the rest of the line. The ruling gradient north of Edinburgh was 1 in 74½ (1.34 per cent), in place of 1 in 96 (1.05 per cent) on the line south of the Scottish capital.

The standard "A1" and "A3" class 4-6-2s were overtaxed by trains such as the "Aberdonian" sleeping car express and it was decided to build some locomotives with some 20 per cent more adhesion weight than the Pacifics. The result was the first (and only) class of eight-coupled express locomotives to run in Britain, of which the prototype was built in 1934, a handsome 2-8-2 called *Cock o' the North* and numbered 2001. To match the high adhesive weight, the tractive effort was the highest ever applied to an express passenger locomotive working in Britain.

Amongst many unusual fea-

Class V 4-4-0 **Ireland:** Great Northern Railway (GNR (I)), 1932

Axle load: 47,000lb (21.5t).
Cylinders: (3) see text.
Driving wheels: 79in (2,007mm).
Heating surface: 1,251sq ft ($116m^2$).
Superheater: 276sq ft ($25.6m^2$).
Steam pressure: 250psi ($17.6kg/cm^2$).
Grate area: 25sq ft ($2.3m^2$).
Fuel: 13,200lb (6t).
Water: 3,500gall (4,200 US) ($16m^3$).
Adhesive weight: 92,000lb (42t).
Total weight: 232,000lb (105t).
Length overall: 55ft 3½in (16,853mm).

Beginning in 1876, the Great Northern Railway of Ireland owned and operated the main line railway connecting Dublin to Belfast. For many years the steel viaduct over the Boyne River 32 miles north of Dublin presented a severe limitation on the size of locomotives; but once it was stengthened in 1931, the way was clear for some really powerful express locomotives to use it, and the distinctive Irish Class Vs were among the first.

The five Class 'V' compound 4-4-0s were supplied by Beyer, Peacock of Manchester; the tenders were built by the company at their own Dundalk Works. They were three-cylinder compounds on the Smith principle—similar to those built for the Midland Railway of England. The high-pressure inside cylinder was 17¼in (438mm) diameter, whereas the two outside low-pressure ones were 19in (483 mm) diameter; all were 26in (660mm) stroke. Three sets of

tures of this three-cylinder locomotive were the use of poppet valves actuated by a rotating camshaft and a specially-shaped front end, whose external contours were designed to lift smoke and steam clear of the cab in order to improve visibility. The internal contours of the front end, which included a double chimney, were also designed to obtain adequate draught for the fire with the minimum of back pressure. A second 2-8-2 (No.2002 *Earl Marischal*) was built with the normal (for the LNER) arrangement of piston valves driven by two sets of Walschaert's valve gear and the Gresley-Holcroft 2-to-1 motion. This standard arrangment was preferred for the final four members of the class, built in 1936, which externally looked more like the streamline "A4" class 4-6-2s of 1935.

Alas, despite the increase in the size of the P2 compared with the Pacifics, double-heading could not be entirely eliminated. Inadequate bearing surfaces and a lack of guiding force in the leading pony truck caused heavy wear on the sharp curves of the Edinburgh-Aberdeen line, and the engines proved to be heavy in maintenance costs. In 1943-44, therefore, the 2-8-2s were 'rebuilt' as 4-6-2s of class "A2/2", although the lack of continuity of LNER locomotive policy at that time meant these "P2" conversions also remained non-standard. So the objective of doing the conversion remained unattained, while a group of fine-looking locomotives were turned into some of the ugliest ones ever to run on a line renowned for the good looks of its motive power.

Left: *A handsome-looking class "P2" 2-8-2 No.2005* Wolf of Badenoch *works an Aberdeen to Edinburgh train.*

Stephenson's link motion filled what space remained between the frames. The LP cylinders originally had balanced slide valves but these were soon altered to piston valves as on the HP cylinder.

The new locomotives were used to provide faster train services, including a run over the 54¼ miles (138km) from Dublin to Dundalk in 54 minutes, the fastest anywhere in Ireland at that time. The timing for the 112½ miles (286km) between Dublin and Belfast was 148 minutes but this included five stops as well as customs examination at the border. In terms of net time this is still the fastest ever scheduled between the two cities; but it lasted only a short time, for the slump combined with a disastrous strike led in 1933 to drastic economies which included decelerations and, in the case of these locomotives, to a reduced boiler pressure.

The simple yet handsome lines of the five compounds were enhanced by the beautiful blue livery and the names *Eagle, Falcon, Merlin, Peregrine* and *Kestrel*. Running numbers were 83 to 87. *Merlin* is preserved and is at present being restored to running condition under the auspices of the Railway Preservation Society of Ireland.

A further five similar locomotives (Class 'VS') with three simple cylinders and Walschaert's valve gear were built in 1948. These were numbered 206 to 210 and were named *Liffey, Boyne, Lagarn, Foyle* and *Erne*, after Irish rivers.

The last "V" class 4-4-0 was withdrawn in 1961 and the last "VS" in 1965; both classes outlasted the GNR which was dismembered in 1958.

Left: *Great Northern of Ireland class "VS" 4-4-0 built in 1948 by Beyer Peacock & Co. These locomotives differed from the original batch in having Walschaert's valve gear and being non-compound.*

Below: *One of the original class "V" 4-4-0s built by Beyer Peacock in 1932.*

Turbomotive 4-6-2

Great Britain:
London, Midland & Scottish Railway (LMS), 1935

Tractive effort: 40,000lb (18,150kg).
Axle load: 54,000lb (24t).
Cylinders: None.
Driving wheels: 78in (1,981mm).
Heating surface: 2,314sq ft (215m^2).
Superheater: 653sq ft (61m^2).
Steam pressure: 250psi (17.6kg/cm^2).
Grate area: 45sq ft (4.2m^2).
Fuel: 20,000lb (9t).
Water: 4,000gall (4,800 US) (18m^3).
Adhesive weight: 158,000lb (72t).
Total weight: 367,000lb (166.5t).
Length overall: 74ft 4¼in (22,663mm).

Turbines had been for many years the normal motive power for ships and electric generators so why not, reasoned so many engineers, try one on a locomotive. In 1932 William Stanier, then the newly appointed Chief Mechanical Engineer of the London Midland & Scottish Railway, saw a Swedish turbine freight locomotive at work and resolved to try a turbine loco himself. Turbine locomotives had already been tried on the LMS experimentally sometime before, but these were condensing locomotives of a very different concept. The Swedish design avoided the complications of a condenser and Stanier was particularly impressed with the simplicity achieved. Valves and valve gear were entirely eliminated and because there were no reciprocating parts perfect balance could easily be achieved. Three prototype 4-6-2s—the forerunners of the "Duchess" class—were in hand at Crewe and so promising did the idea seem that one of these was earmarked to become a guinea pig for an experiment in turbine propulsion, which came to fruition in 1935.

A multi-stage Metropolitan-Vickers turbine of about 2,000 horsepower was mounted more or less where the left-hand outside cylinder would have been. It drove the leading coupled axle through a three-stage gear train totally enclosed in an oil bath; the reduction ratio was 34:1, so that at 70mph (113km/h) the turbine would be doing 10,000 rev/min. To control the locomotive, rather than throttle the steam which would effect the turbine's efficiency, any number of the six separate nozzles could be "switched in" by being given steam. It was all an exceedingly simple arrangement and on test this No.6202 proved to be more efficient than a conventional 4-6-2. A small turbine was provided on the right-hand side to move the locomotive in reverse at low speed, engaged through a dog-clutch and a fourth gear train. This feature was, sadly, not to prove entirely foolproof.

Unlike most steam locomotive experiments which had the temerity to challenge Stephenson's principles, the so-called "Turbomotive" gave good service—300,000 miles of it, in fact. Her regular turn was the "Liverpool Flyer" up to London in the morning and back in the afternoon, for several years the fastest train on the LMS. Inevitably there were problems but there was also promise; alas, the war came, then nationalisation.

People who were not concerned with the original experiment were in charge and, following a failure of the main turbine in 1947, the locomotive was set aside at Crewe. In 1951 it was rebuilt into a normal reciprocating 4-6-2 named *Princess Anne* but perished in the triple collision at Harrow a very short time after re-entering service.

So ended one of the most promising attempts to produce a turbine-powered express passenger locomotive. A similar story could be told about others such as the Zoelly turbine locomotives tried in Germany, or the enormous 6,000hp one made by Baldwin of Philadelphia for the Pennsylvania Railroad in the USA.

Below: *The "Turbomotive", LMS No.6202, works its usual turn from Euston to Liverpool.*

Andes Class 2-8-0 **Peru:** Central Railway of Peru (FCC), 1935

Tractive effort: 36,600lb (16,600kg).
Axle load: 36,500lb (16.5t).
Cylinders: (2) 20 x 28in (508 x 711mm).
Driving wheels: 52in (1,321mm).
Heating surface: 1,717sq ft (160m²).
Superheater: 341sq ft (32m²).
Steam pressure: 200psi (14.1kg/cm²).
Grate area: 28sq ft (2.6m²).
Fuel: (oil) 1,465gall (1,760 US) (6.7m³).
Water: 2,650gall (3,180 US) (12m³).
Adhesive weight: 146,000lb (66t).
Total weight: 250,000lb (113t).
Length overall: 61ft 11¼in (18,879mm).

"Highest and Hardest" wrote Brian Fawcett in *Railways of the Andes*. He was describing the Central Railway of Peru—a line in whose service he spent much of his life—which climbed from sea level near Lima to 15,693ft (4,783m) altitude at the Galera Tunnel, a bare 99 miles (158km) from Lima, en route for the copper mines high up in the mountains. For many years it was said that the necessarily slow passenger service remained invulnerable to air competition, because none of the airlines operating on the Pacific coast had an aircraft which could go as high as the trains!

Most of the climbing, much of it at between 1 in 22 and 1 in 25 (4.5 and 4 per cent), is concentrated in the final 74 miles (118km) to the top; some of the most spectacular engineering in the world takes the trains via six 'Z' double-reversals up to the summit. Oxygen is provided for passengers, but curiously enough steam locomotives become more rather than less efficient as the atmospheric pressure drops. Even so, the task of lifting traffic up this railway staircase was an horrific one and it was only after many years of traumatic experience that a class 2-8-0 was evolved, combining rugged North American design features with the best British Beyer, Peacock workmanship, which could do the job satisfactorily.

A short boiler was essential because of the heavy grades which meant quick alterations of slope relative to water at each zig-zag. On the other hand a narrow firebox between the wheels was no detriment with oil firing and on such gradients it was an advantage that as many as four out of the five pairs of wheels should be driven. The existence of ample water supplies over the mountain section meant that only a very small quantity

Class 5P5F 4-6-0 **Great Britain:** London Midland & Scottish Railway (LMS), 1934

Tractive effort: 25,455lb (11,550kg)
Axle load: 40,700lb (18.5t).
Cylinders: (2) 18½ x 28in (470 x 711mm).
Driving wheels: 72in (1,829mm).
Heating surface: 1,938sq ft (180m²).
Superheater: 307sq ft (28.5m²).
Steam pressure: 225psi (15.8kg/cm²).
Grate area: 28.65sq ft (2.7m²).
Fuel: 20,200lb (9t).
Water: 4,000gall (4,800 US) (18m³).
Adhesive weight: 119,000lb (56t).
Total weight: 285,000lb (129t).
Length overall: 67ft 7¾in (20,618mm).

The Black Fives! Arguably the best buy ever made by any railway anywhere, in respect of engines capable of handling express passenger trains. These legendary locomotives formed not only the most numerous but also the most versatile such class ever to run in Britain.

In spite of being modestly dimensioned mixed-traffic locomotives, on many occasions they demonstrated that they could handle and keep time on any express passenger assignment ever scheduled on LMS or ex-LMS lines. In its first months of service during 1934, Cecil J. Allen reported the doings of the prototype on the LMS flag train "Royal Scot", loaded to 15 coaches and 495 tons gross. No.5020 was a last-minute deputy for a "Princess" 4-6-2 or "Royal Scot" 4-6-0, the greater complexities of which made them that much the more liable to fall sick, but the smaller engine kept the "Special Limit" timing to Crewe with the maximum allowed load. Excellent valve events and a well-tried boiler lay behind the surprising qualities of these famous locomotives.

In later years, with "Black Fives" on the route of the "Royal Scot" allocated to sheds at Camden, Willesden, Rugby, Crewe, Warrington, Wigan, Preston, Carnforth, Carlisle, Carstairs and Glasgow, it was a great comfort to the operators to know that so many understudies of similar abilities were waiting in the wings when the *prime donne*

need be carted up the mountain—hence the small tender.

The arrangements for sanding were vital because hideous gradients are usually combined with damp rails. Since both gravity and steam sanding gear had been found wanting, the "Andes" class were fitted with air sanding. The quantity of sand carried was also important and on later versions of the class a vast box on the boiler-top held supplies of this vital element in Andean railroading. It also incorporated the steam dome, thereby keeping the sand warm and dry.

By law, a "counter-pressure" brake had to be fitted, but was not normally used because of the damage that was caused to piston and valve rings when it was used. The double-pipe air braking system used avoids the necessity of releasing the brakes periodically during the descent to re-charge the reservoirs—something that might well lead to a runaway in Andean conditions.

As a locomotive that would need to be driven "wide-open" for hour after hour on the ascent, the "Andes" class was very robustly constructed indeed. That the class gave a satisfactory performance on the world's hardest railway is indicated by the fact that the company came back for more, eight times, no less, between 1935 and 1951. Finally there were 29, numbered 200 to 228. Neighbouring railways had some too—the Southern of Peru (under the same ownership) had 20 with slightly larger driving wheels, while the Cerro de Pasco Railroad (which connected with the Central) had a further five. These latter were the last "straight" steam locomotives to be built by the great firm of Beyer, Peacock.

Alas, no longer does steam rule the mountain section, but the 6-hour timing of the old days has not been improved upon. Maybe a 22mph (35km/h) average speed does not seem much but the ascent certainly justified the inclusion of the daily train over the mountain section amongst the Great Trains of the World. No.206 is preserved at Lima.

Below: *One of the world's hardest-working locos, a Central Railway of Peru "Andes" class 2-8-0 depicted in the company's handsome green livery.*

of the route showed signs of the temperament for which they were traditionally celebrated.

It is fair to say, though, that the LMS four-cylinder 4-6-2s did ride more smoothly at speed. At 90mph (145km/h) downhill it was fairly exciting in the dark (no headlight!) on a "Duchess", but on a "Black Five" it could be called a Total Experience. Another advantage of the bigger engines lay in the much larger ash-pan; whilst No.5020 mentioned above did as well as a 4-6-2 was normally expected to do from Euston to Crewe, the 4-6-0 could hardly have continued to Glasgow without the fire becoming choked with the end-products of combustion. Of course, the 4-6-2s also had the *potential* of higher power output; but in order to realise the potential either a super-man or more than one fireman had to be carried, and this was not normally the practice.

North of Perth on the Highland lines, "Black Fives" were the heaviest and largest locomotives permitted, and here they handled most trains of significance from the 550-ton "Royal Highlander" downwards. A pair of them, driven wide open, took such trains up the 20-mile ascent (32 km), mostly at 1 in 60 (1.66 per cent), from Inverness to the 1,300ft (400m) summit at Slochd. Steaming was usually rock-steady, the sound magnificent, and the firemen's task proportionately onerous as the tonnage moved over this and other neighbouring inclines.

William Stanier came to the LMS from rival Great Western in 1932. Under his direction, a design for this two-cylinder mixed-traffic 4-6-0 was produced in 1933 as a replacement for numerous ageing medium-sized 4-6-0s of the LMS constituent companies. The concept was derived directly from the "Hall' class of Stanier's native line, but really only the taper-boilers and the axleboxes of the new engine were based on those of the GWR. Much of the rest seemed to reflect the choice of the best practice from amongst the various areas of the LMS; Lancashire and Yorkshire Railway cylinders, Walschaert's valve-gear and cab, for example; Midland boiler fittings; and Caledonian hooter-type whistle.

London & North Western thinking showed in the arrangements for repair and maintenance of the "Black Five" fleet, which was eventually to number 842 engines and which took eighteen years to build. LMS works at Crewe, Derby and Horwich all contributed with 231, 54 and 130 respectively. Under a pre-war Government scheme to provide work for depressed areas, two outside firms built the remainder; Vulcan Foundry of Newton-le-Willows produced 100 and Armstrong-Whitworth & Co of Newcastle-upon-Tyne 327. Running numbers went from 4758 to 5499, those below 5000 being newer than those above. One hundred more were built under British Railways, the class then being numbered 44658 to 45499. Few changes in design were found necessary, but earlier engines had less superheat originally than the later ones.

On the last batches numerous experiments were tried, such as roller bearings, rocking grates, double chimneys, Caprotti poppet valves, even outside Stephenson's link motion on one engine; but the only major modification that "took" was the installation of renewable high-manganese steel liners to the axlebox guides. This was successful in increasing considerably the mileage between overhauls.

The "Black Fives" based on Preston were the last steam locomotives to haul timetabled express passenger trains on British Railways. It was as late in the day as January 1967, only 20 months before the end, that No.44917 achieved the highest-ever recorded speed for the class. This was 96mph (155km/h), reached north of Gobowen between Chester and Shrewsbury. Fifteen have been preserved and, of these, four can currently be seen from time to time, either individually or in pairs, on main-line steam specials.

Left: *A Stanier "Black Five" 4-6-0 leaves a wayside station in the Scottish Highlands with a local train in tow. North of Perth these versatile locomotives had a near-monopoly of service.*

Class A 4-4-2

USA: Chicago, Milwaukee, St. Paul & Pacific Railroad (CMStP&P), 1935 (see fold-out, page 142)

Tractive effort: 30,685lb (13,920kg).
Axle load: 72,500lb (33t).
Cylinders: (2) 19 x 28in (483 x 711mm).
Driving wheels: 84in (2,134mm).
Heating surface: 3,245sq ft (301.5m²).
Superheater: 1,029sq ft (96m²).
Steam pressure: 300psi (21kg/cm²).
Grate area: 69sq ft (6.4m²).
Fuel (oil): 3,300galls (4,000 US) (15m³).
Water: 10,800gall (13,000 US) (49.5m³).
Adhesive weight: 144,500lb (66t).
Total weight: 537,000lb (244t).
Length overall: 88ft 8in (27,026mm).

Class F7 4-6-4

USA: Chicago, Milwaukee, St. Paul & Pacific Railroad (CMStP&P), 1937

Tractive effort: 50,295lb (22,820kg).
Axle load: 72,250lb (33t).
Cylinders: (2) 23.5 x 30in (597 x 762mm).
Driving wheels: 84in (2,134mm).
Heating surface: 4,166sq ft (387m²).
Superheater: 1,695sq ft (157m²).
Steam pressure: 300psi (21kg/cm²).
Grate area: 96.5sq ft (9.0m²).
Fuel: 50,000lb (22½t).
Water: 16,700gall (20,000 US) (76m³).
Adhesive weight: 216,000lb (98t).
Total weight: 791,000lb (359t).
Length overall: 100ft 0in (30,480mm).

"Fleet of foot was Hiawatha" wrote Longfellow... Intensive competition for the daytime traffic between Chicago and the Twin Cities of St. Paul and Minneapolis was the inspiration for the "Hiawatha" locomotives and trains, the fastest-ever to be run by steam. Three railroads were involved in the competition; first, there was the Chicago & North Western Railway; this line had a 408½ mile (657km) route which its "400" expresses traversed in 400 minutes. The "400"s were formed of conventional equipment of the day, but specially refurbished and maintained. The Chicago Burlington & Quincy Railroad pioneered some stainless steel lightweight diesel—propelled "Zephyr" trains—fairly noisy in spite of their name—over a route 19 miles (30km) longer than the North-Western one.

Lastly—and to us most importantly—there was the Chicago, Milwaukee, St. Paul and Pacific Railroad, whose management decided to enter the lists with special matching high-speed steam locomotives and trains designed to offer a 6½ hour timing for the 412-mile (663km) route. For the first time in the history of steam locomotion a railway ordered engines intended

Top: *Class "F7" 4-6-4 No.103 towards the end of its days; a forlorn sight after some use as a source of spares.*

Above: *With boiler lagging and driving wheels removed, a class "F7" 4-6-4 awaits the ungainly end.*

for daily operation at 100mph (160km/h) and over.

The American Locomotive Company of Schenectady, New York, responded with two superb oil-fired and brightly coloured streamlined 4-4-2s. They were known as class "A" and received running numbers 1 and 2. In service they earned this prime designation by demonstrating that as runners they had few peers. They could develop more than 3000 horsepower in the cylinders and achieve 110mph (177km/h) on the level. It says enough about that success of these locomotives that they were intended to haul six cars on a 6½-hour schedule, but soon found themselves handling nine cars satisfactorily on a 6¼-hour one. These schedules included five intermediate stops and 15 permanent speed restrictions below 50mph (80km/h).

The design was unusual rather than unconventional; the tender with one six-wheel and one four-wheel truck, for instance, or the drive on to the leading axle instead of the rear one, were examples. Special efforts were made to ensure that the reciprocating parts were as light as possible—the high boiler pressure was chosen in order to reduce the size of the pistons—and particular care was taken to get the balancing as good as possible with a two-cylinder locomotive. Another class "A" (No.3) was delivered in 1936 and a fourth (No.4) in 1937.

Further high-speed locomotives were ordered in 1938 and this time the six 4-6-4s supplied were both usual *and* conventional. This time also the class designation "F7" and running numbers (100 to 105) were just run-of-the-mill. The 4-4-2s were superb with the streamliners but not at all suited to the haulage of heavy ordinary expresses. This restricted their utilisation; hence the 4-6-4s which combined heavy haulage powers with high-speed capability. The main concession to speed in the design were the big driving wheels, whilst the main concession to general usage was a change back to coal-burning, in line with most Milwaukee steam locomotives. This in its turn necessitated a high-speed coal hopper and shoots at New Lisbon station, which enabled an "F7" to be coaled during the 2-minute station stop of the "Hiawatha" expresses there. The "F7"s were also very successful engines, capable of 120 mph (193km/h) and more on

level track with these trains.

Test running showed that such speeds could be maintained with a load of 12 cars, a load of 550 tons, and this makes the feat an even more remarkable one. There are also reports of maximum speeds of 125mph (200km/h) and it is a great pity that these cannot be authenticated, since if true would be world records. One did occur in 1940: a speed-up and retiming produced the historic fastest start-to-stop run *ever* scheduled with steam power—81¼mph (130km/h) for the 78½ miles (126km) from Sparta to Portage, Wisconsin. This was on the eastbound "Morning Hiawatha", for by now a second daily run in each direction was operated. Also in 1940 came the "Mid-West Hiawatha" from Chicago to Omaha and Sioux Falls and it was to this train that the 4-4-2s gravitated, although one was usually held in reserve against a 4-6-4 failure on the Twin Cities trains.

Dieselisation came gradually; diesel locomotives made their first appearance on the "Hiawatha" trains in 1941, while steam did not finally disappear from the "Twin Cities Hiawatha" until 1946. The 4-4-2s held on two years longer on the Mid-West train. The last of both types were withdrawn—after a period on lesser workings or set aside—in 1951. It is a matter of considerable regret that none of these record-breaking steam locomotives has been preserved, especially now that the whole Milwaukee Road from Chicago to the Pacific is following them into oblivion.

Even so, models and memories keep these wonderful locomotives alive in the minds of those who admired them in their prime.

Above: *In a cloud of coal smoke, and towards the end of its days, a Milwaukee Road class "F7" 4-8-4 sets forth.*

Below: *A builder's view of the original "F7" class 4-8-4 supplied to the Chicago, Milwaukee, St. Paul & Pacific Railroad in 1938 for working the "Hiawatha" expresses.*

Class F-2a 4-4-4

Canada:
Canadian Pacific Railway (CPR), 1936

Tractive effort: 26,500lb (12,000kg).
Axle load: 61,000lb (28t).
Cylinders: (2) 17¼ x 28in (438 x 711mm).
Driving wheels: 80in (2,032mm).
Heating surface: 2,833sq ft ($263m^2$).
Superheater: 1,100sq ft ($102m^2$).
Steam pressure: 300psi ($21kg/cm^2$).
Grate area: 55.6sq ft ($5.2m^2$).
Fuel: 27,000lb (12t).
Water: 7,000galls (8,400 US) ($32m^3$).
Adhesive weight: 121,000lb (55t).
Total weight: 461,000lb (209t).
Length overall: 81ft 2⅞in (24,762 mm).

In 1936 the Canadian Pacific Railway introduced four trains which were announced as a High-Speed Local Service. In each case the formation consisted of a mail/express (parcels) car, a baggage-buffet and two passenger cars. By North American standards they counted as lightweight, the weight being 200 tons for the four-coach train. Most American railroads would have found some hand-me-down locomotives discarded from first-line passenger service to work them, but that was not the CPR way. They ordered five new 4-4-4 steam locomotives, designated the "Jubilee" type, from the Montreal Locomotive Works to work these trains—although spoken of as streamlined, they are better described as having a few corners nicely rounded. Running numbers were 3000 to 3004.

The new services for which this equipment was ordered comprised the "Chinook" in the West between Calgary and Edmonton (194 miles—310km—in 315 minutes including 22 stops) and the international "Royal York" between Toronto and Detroit (229 miles—366km—in 335 minutes with 19 stops) and two others between Montreal and Quebec. It was the sort of service for which a home-based British company might field a 100 ton 4-4-0 with perhaps 25sq ft ($2.3m^2$) of grate area, but these "small" 4-4-4s weighed some 90 per cent more than this and had a fire-grate 120 per cent bigger.

Even if it was a case where the trans-Atlantic love of bigness might have been misplaced, the "F-2a"s were certainly magnificent. They had such sophisticated features as mechanical stokers, feed-water heaters and roller bearings. One feature that was important for operation in Canada was an all-weather insulated cab, able to provide comfortable conditions for the crew in a country where the outside temperature could easily drop to minus 40°F (−40°C), 72 Fahrenheit degrees of frost.

A further series of similar and slightly smaller 4-4-4s, numbered from 2901 to 2929, were built in 1938, designated class "F-1a". The second series was easily recognisable by the drive on to the rear coupled axle, instead of on to the front axle as with the "F-2a". Nos.2928 and 2929 of this later series are preserved at the National Railway Museum at Delson, Quebec, and (currently but with future undecided) at Steamtown, Bellows Falls, Vermont, USA, respectively.

Below: *Class "F2a" 4-4-4 No. 3003 leaves Montreal with a "High-Speed Local Service".*

A4 Class 4-6-2

Great Britain:
London & North Eastern Railway (LNER), 1935 (see fold-out, page 138)

Tractive effort: 35,455lb (16,086kg).
Axle load: 49,500lb (22.5t).
Cylinders: (3) 18½ x 26in (470 x 660mm).
Driving wheels: 80in (2,032mm).
Heating surface: 2,576sq ft ($240m^2$).
Superheater: 749sq ft ($70m^2$).
Steam pressure: 250psi ($17.5kg/cm^2$).
Grate area: 41sq ft ($3.8m^2$).
Fuel: 18,000lb (8t).
Water: 5,000gall (6,000 US) ($23m^3$).
Adhesive weight: 148,000lb (67t).
Total weight: 370,000lb (170t).
Length overall: 71ft 0in (21,647mm).

Above: *Preserved "A4" class 4-6-2 No.4498 Sir Nigel Gresley with an enthusiast's train.*

Right: *An "A4" class 4-6-2 bursts from Gas Works tunnel shortly after leaving Kings Cross station, London, for Scotland.*

If British railway enthusiasts were to vote for one express passenger locomotive that they considered to be the best, there is little doubt that this one would be elected. For one thing, it would be difficult to ignore the claims of the all-time holder of the world's speed record for steam locomotives.

The Class "A4" streamlined 4-6-2 came in direct descent from the Class "A1" or "Flying Scotsman" 4-6-2s. The LNER management had taken note of a two-car German diesel train called the "Flying Hamburger" which in 1933 began running between Berlin and Hamburg at an average speed of 77.4mph (124km/h) for the 178 miles (285km). The makers were approached with the idea of having a similar train to run the 268 miles (429km) between London and Newcastle, but after an analysis had been done and the many speed restrictions taken into account the best that could be promised was 63mph (102km/h), that is, 4¼ hours. The train was surprisingly expensive for two cars, as well. On 5 March 1935, standard "A3 4-6-2 (No.2750 *Papyrus*) showed what steam could do by making the run with a six-coach train in 230 minutes, thus demonstrating that a four hour timing was practicable.

In this way was born the concept of a streamlined matching locomotive and train to be called "The Silver Jubilee". The LNER Board authorised the project on 28 March 1935 and the first of the four streamlined locomotives No.2509 *Silver Link* was put into steam on 5 September.

The new train, bristling with innovations, was shown to the press on 27 September. Unkind people might compare this with the recent gestation period of British Railways' celebrated High Speed Train, not dissimilar in appearance, concept and in degree to which it extended beyond the bounds of current performance. This was six *years* not six *months*.

On this press trip the British speed record was broken with a speed of 112½mph (180km/h) at Sandy. The locomotive rode superbly and 25 miles (40km) were covered at a speed above 100 mph (160km/h), those aboard being sublimely unconscious of the terror they were inspiring in the lively-sprung articulated carriages behind. Even so, three days later "The Silver Jubilee" went into public service, achieving an instant and remarkable success. In spite of a supplementary fare, the down run at 5.30 p.m. from Kings Cross, with a first stop at Darlington, 232½ miles (374km) in 198 minutes and due at Newcastle 9.30 p.m., was fully booked night after night.

The new locomotives did not bristle with innovations like the trains, but those they had were important. The internal streamlining and enlargement of the steam passages from the regulator valve to the blastpipe made them particularly free-running, while extra firebox volume in the form of a combustion chamber helped steam production. Evocative three-chime whistles gave distinction to the voice of the "A4"s.

The "A4"s were so good that 31 more were built between 1936 and 1938, not only for two more streamline trains ("Coronation" and "West Riding Limited") but also for general service. A few were fitted with double blastpipes and chimneys and it was with one of these (No.4468 *Mallard*) that on 4 July 1938, the world speed record for steam traction was broken with a sustained speed of 125mph (201 km/h), attained down the 1 in 200 (0.5 per cent) of Stoke bank north of Peterborough. Driver Duddington needed full throttle and 45 per cent cut-off and the dynamometer car record indicated that 126mph (203 km/h) was momentarily reached. Equally impressive was an occasion in 1940 when No.4901 *Capercaillie* ran 25 level miles (40km) north of York with 22

Above: *Class "A4" No.2510* Quicksilver *when new in 1935. Note the footplate valences which were later removed.*

coaches (730 tons) at an average speed of 76mph (122km/h).

At first a distinction was made between the original "silver-painted" locomotives, those in LNER green with bird names for general service, and those in garter blue livery with Empire names for the "Coronation". Also in blue were *Golden Fleece* and *Golden Shuttle* for the "West Riding Limited". By 1938, blue had become the standard colour and very nice it looked—not only on the streamlined trains but also with the varnished teak of ordinary stock.

After the war, during which the "A4"s had to cope with enormous loads and one (No. 4469 *Sir Ralph Wedgwood)* was destroyed in an air raid on York, they were renumbered 1 to 34, later becoming British Railways Nos.60001 to 60034. In the famous locomotive exchange trials of 1948, the "A4"s proved to be substantially the most efficient of all the express engines tested, but their proneness to failure also showed up on three occasions during the trials.

Although by no means the most recent LNER large express passenger locomotives, they were never displaced from prime workings, such as the London to Edinburgh non-stop "Elizabethan", until the diesels came in the early 1960s. The reliability problem—one serious weakness was over-heating of the inside large-end—was resolutely tackled and to a great extent solved.

Since the last "A4" was withdrawn in 1966, six have been preserved—No.4498 *Sir Nigel Gresley,* No.60009 *Union of South Africa* and No.19 *Bittern* privately; No.4468 *Mallard* is in the National Railway Museum, No.60010 *Dominion of Canada* is in the Canadian Railway Museum at Delson, Quebec, and No.60008 *Dwight D. Eisenhower* is in the USA at the Green Bay Railroad Museum, Wisconsin. Nos.4498 and 60009 currently perform on special trains, thereby giving a new generation of rail fans just a hint of what these magnificent locomotives were like in their prime.

Below, left: *London & North Eastern Railway class "A4" 4-6-2* Empire of India *one of the batch built in 1937 to work the "Coronation" express.*

Below: *Class "A4" No.60024* Kingfisher. *The locomotives of this class built ostensibly for "general service" were named after birds.*

No.10000 4-6-4

Great Britain:
London & North Eastern Railway (LNER), 1930

Axle load: 47,000lb (21.5t).
Cylinders, HP: (2) 10 x 26in (254 x 660mm).
Cylinders, LP: (2) 20 x 26in (508 x 660mm).
Driving wheels: 80in (2,032mm).
Heating surface: 1,986sq ft ($184m^2$).
Superheater: 140sq ft ($13m^2$).
Steam pressure: 450psi ($32kg/cm^2$).
Grate area: 35sq ft ($3.25m^2$).
Fuel: 20,000lb (9t).
Water: 5,000gall (6,000 US) ($23m^3$).
Adhesive weight: 140,000lb (63.5t).
Total weight: 372,000lb (169t).
Length overall: 74ft 5in (22,682mm).

The tale of LNER No.10000, the "hush-hush" locomotive, is the story of a promising experiment which failed. It was mounted in great secrecy—hence the name—and executed with considerable flair and ability but, like so many attempts before and some afterwards, the principles laid down by Stephenson in *Northumbrian* proved in the end to be the victor.

It is a fundamental law of physics that the efficiency of a heat engine is proportional to the ratio between the upper and lower temperatures reached by the "working fluid"—in this case steam—during its working cycle. The upper temperature depends on the working pressure as well as the amount of superheat; if the pressure could be substantially increased, then there would be a gain in efficiency.

Alas, the conventional locomotive-type boiler is not suitable for very high pressure—there are too many flat surfaces, for one thing. Ships and power stations can make steam at higher pressures in various types of boiler made entirely of tubes and drums and Nigel Gresley held discussions with Messrs. Yarrow of Glasgow to see if anything on these lines could be adopted.

A scheme for a four-cylinder compound was evolved, with a five-drum water-tube boiler pressed to double the normal pressure. There was a long steam drum at the top connected to two pairs of lower water drums, by 694 small-diameter water tubes. The two low-pressure outside cylinders and much of the outside motion was standard with the "A1" class 4-6-2s. Two high-pressure inside cylinders were close to the centre-line; their valves were driven by a rocking shaft from the outside Walschaert's gear sets. The rocking shafts had an arrangement designed so that the valve travel of the HP cylinders could be varied independently of the LP ones by a separate control. The locomotive was built at the Darlington shops of the company.

Once teething troubles had been overcome, No.10000 worked from Gateshead shed for several years. Alas, any fundamental saving in coal consumption there may have been was swamped by extra costs of maintenance and loss of heat through small faults in design. Hence it was no surprise when in 1937 the "hush-hush" engine was rebuilt on the lines of an "A4" class streamliner, remaining the sole member of Class "W1" and the only 4-6-4 tender engine to run in Britain.

Below: *The London & North Eastern Railways' "Hush-Hush" high-pressure compound 4-6-4 No.10000 on a test run hauling the company's dynamometer car.*

Class 05 4-6-4

Germany: German State Railway (DR), 1935

Tractive effort: 32,776lb (14,870kg).
Axle load: 43,000lb (19.5t).
Cylinders: (3) 17¾ x 26in (450 x 660mm).
Driving wheels: 90½in (2,300mm).
Heating surface: 2,750sq ft (256m²).
Superheater: 976sq ft (90m²).
Steam pressure: 284psi (20kg/cm²).
Grate area: 51sq ft (4.71m²).
Fuel: 22,000lb (10t).
Water: 8,200gall (9,870 US) (37m³).
Adhesive weight: 127,000lb (56t).
Total weight: 475,064lb (213t).
Length overall: 86ft 2in (26,265mm).

Above: *Class "05" locomotive No.05.001, as built in streamline form, depicted on a run in March 1935 when the speed record for steam was broken.*

In 1931 the general speed limit on the German railways was only 62 miles per hour (100km/hr) but in that year the first of the high-speed diesel railcars was introduced, with a maximum speed of 100 miles per hour (160km/hr), and suddenly Germany leapt from a backward position in world rail speed to be the world leader. However, the twin railcars had limited accommodation, and their immediate popularity was a challenge to the steam engineers to produce a locomotive which could attain similar speeds when hauling a longer train of conventional coaches. It was calculated that a steam locomotive and train having a seating capacity of 50 per cent more could be built for half

Dovregrubben Class 2-8-4

Norway: Norwegian State Railways (NSB), 1935

Axle load: 34,000lb (15.5t).
Cylinders, HP: (2) 17½ x 25½in (440 x 650mm).
Cylinders, LP: (2) 25½ x 27½in (650 x 700mm).
Driving wheels: 6¼in (1,530mm).
Heating surface: 2,742sq ft (255m²).
Superheater: 1,092sq ft (101m²).
Steam pressure: 240psi (17kg/cm²).
Grate area: 55.55sq ft (5m²).
Fuel: 18,000lb (8t).
Water: 6,000gall (7,200 US) (27m³).
Adhesive weight: 138,000lb (62.5t).
Total weight: 334,000lb (151.5t).
Length overall: 72ft 2in (22,000mm).

The 2-8-4 was a very unusual wheel arrangement outside the USA but the railways of Norway, a surprisingly small country to be a builder of its own locomotives, made it one of their principal express locomotive types. Norway is a long thin mountainous country measuring 1,150 miles (1,850km) from north to south but only an average of 110 miles (177km) wide. The building of a trunk line up the spine of the country has been in progress for many years, the current terminus being Bodø, 797 miles (1,282km) from Oslo. The southern half of this line, the 345 miles (553km)

Right: *Norwegian State Railways "Dovregrubben" (Dovre Giant) class 2-8-4 locomotive depicted when new.*

the cost of a railcar set.

In 1932, therefore, in accordance with normal German practice, private locomotive builders were invited to submit proposals for a locomotive to haul 250 tons at 93mph (150km/h) in normal service, with the capacity to reach 108mph (175km/h) with this load if required. In the meantime wind tunnel work was conducted at the research establishment at Göttingen to determine the possible benefits of streamlining, and it was found that full streamlining of the engine could reduce by 20 per cent the power required to haul 250t at 93mph.

From the 22 proposals submitted, a scheme by Borsig of Berlin for a 3-cylinder 4-6-4 was selected. The detailed design, produced under the direction of Adolf Wolff, incorporated standard DRG features as far as possible, but the overall concept of a locomotive to develop very high speeds with limited loads called for a boiler larger than those of the existing Pacifics, but with the possibility of a smaller adhesive weight. The 4-6-4 wheel arrangement was chosen because a bogie at each end was thought necessary for stability at high speed. Aids to high speed included large driving wheels 90½in (2,300mm) diameter, and very large valves and steam passages. For good balance at speed three cylinders were fitted. The boiler pressure of 284psi (20kg/cm²) was the highest so far used on a conventional German locomotive. Special attention was paid to braking, all axles being braked, with two blocks on all wheels except the leading bogie wheels. Tender was also of record size, with five axles and weighing 86 tons fully loaded. The casing enveloped the engine and tender almost down to rail level, and access to the motion was achieved through roller shutters.

Three engines were ordered, two arranged for conventional coal firing, but the third equipped for burning pulverised fuel, and arranged with the cab leading. The first two engines, 05001/2 appeared in March and May of 1935, and in their highly-finished red livery they made a great impression. For more than a year they were subjected to intensive testing, partly on the road and partly on the locomotive testing plant at Grunewald. In the most notable of the road tests, on 11th May, 1936, 05002 reached a speed of 124.5mph (199km/h) on the level with a load of 197 ton. On another test run with the 169 ton, a speed of 118mph (189km/h) was maintained for 26 miles (42km), requiring an indicated horsepower of 3409, an exceptional figure at that speed.

In October 1936, 05001/2, working from Hamburg Altona depot, entered regular service on trains FD 23/4 from Hamburg to Berlin and back. For the 178.1 miles (285km) from Hamburg to Berlin Lehrter the time allowed was 144 minutes on the outward journey and 145 on the return, giving average speeds of 74.2 and 73.7mph (118.7 and 117.9 km/h) the normal maximum running speed being 94 mph (150 km/h). These were then the highest speeds by steam in Europe, although allowing for the gradients, the locomotive work required was no heavier than with the LNER "Silver Jubilee". The engines often demonstrated their ability to recover time lost by engineering works.

The war brought these high-speed schedules to an end, and after a period of use on ordinary trains, the engines were laid aside until 1950, when they were rebuilt by Krauss-Maffei of Munich into non-streamlined engines with new boilers. The experimental pulverised fuel firing on the third engine, 05003, was not successful, and it was rebuilt as a conventional engine in 1944/5, but it saw little service until it too was further rebuilt by Krauss-Maffei in 1950. In their rebuilt form the three engines worked for seven years on the fastest steam workings then in force on Deutsche Bundesbahn, but the tide of electrification then overtook them. 05002/3 were scrapped, but 05001 was restored to its original streamlined condition, and in 1961 it was placed in the German National Railway Museum in Nürnberg.

Below: *Class "05" locomotive No.05.003, originally designed for the burning of pulverised fuel, in shop grey finish after rebuilding in normal form.*

between Oslo and Trondheim is called the Dovre Railway and it was for this line that these "Dovregrubben" (Dovre Giants) were built.

Messrs. Thune of Oslo built three of these fine locomotives in 1935 and 1936; running numbers were 463 to 465. During the war two more (Nos.470 and 471) were supplied by Krupp of Essen in Germany and later a further two (Nos.472 and 473) were built. They were four cylinder compounds with low-pressure cylinders inside the frames, and high-pressure cylinders outside. A single set of Walschaert's valve gear mounted outside each side served both HP and LP cylinders on that side, the higher valves being driven via rocking shafts.

There were a number of features unusual to Norwegian or European practice. Two regulators were provided, one in the dome and one in the "hot" header of the superheater. There were thermic syphons in the firebox and a "Zara" truck (so named after its Italian designer) which connected the front pony wheels and the leading coupled wheels. The cylindrical frameless tender with covered coal bunker alone would make these engines notable, but perhaps the most remarkable thing of all about them is the successful creation of such a powerful machine within so restricted an axle-loading.

Right: *A Norwegian State Railways "Dovre Giant" 2-8-4 in action on an Oslo to Trondheim express in 1935.*

Class I-5 4-6-4

United States: New York, New Haven & Hartford (New Haven), 1937

Tractive effort: 44,000lb (19,960kg).
Axle load: 65,000lb (29.5t).
Cylinders: (2) 22 x 30in (559 x 762mm).
Driving wheels: 80in (2,032mm).
Heating surface: 3,815sq ft ($354m^2$).
Superheater: 1,042sq ft ($97m^2$).
Steam pressure: 285psi ($20kg/cm^2$).
Grate area: 77sq ft ($7.2m^2$).
Fuel: 32,000lb (14.5t).
Water: 15,000gall (18,000 US) ($68m^3$).
Adhesive weight: 193,000lb (87.4t).
Total weight: 698,000lb (317t).
Length overall: 97ft 0¾in (29,585mm).

These handsome engines were the first streamlined 4-6-4s in the USA to be delivered. They were also very much an example to be followed in that firstly, the desire to streamline was not allowed to interfere with access to the machinery for maintenance and secondly, they followed in all essential respects the simple Stephenson concept.

The New Haven Railroad ran the main line from New York to Boston. This was electrified as far as New Haven, leaving 159 miles (256km) of steam railroad from there to the "home of the bean and the cod". Trains such as "The Colonial" or the all-Pullman parlor car express "The Merchants Limited" heavily overtaxed the capacity of the existing class "I-4" Pacifics and, in 1936, after a good deal of research and ex-

Class 16E 4-6-2

South Africa: South African Railways (SAR), 1935

Tractive effort: 40,596lb (18,414kg).
Axle load: 47,000lb (21.3t).
Cylinders: (2) 24 x 28in (610 x 711mm).
Driving wheels: 72in (1,830mm).
Heating surface: 2,914sq ft ($271m^2$).
Superheater: 592sq ft ($55m^2$).
Steam pressure: 210psi ($14.75kg/cm^2$).
Grate area: 63sq ft ($5.8m^2$).
Fuel: 31,000lb (14t).
Water: 6,000gall (7,200 US) ($27m^3$).
Adhesive weight: 134,000lb (61t).
Total weight: 375,000lb (170t).
Length overall: 71ft 8¼in (21,850mm).

High-speed locomotives are rare in most of Africa. Driving wheels as large as 60in (1,524mm) diameter were exceptional and larger ones were unknown except in the countries bordering the Mediterranean coast. Most of Africa is narrow-gauge country, it is true, but that is no reason for low speeds, provided the track is well aligned and maintained. During the 1930s South African Railways perceived this fact and, with a view to accelerating such schedules as 30 hours for the 956 miles (1,530km) from Cape Town to Johannesburg (average speed 32mph—51km/h), they ordered five high speed locomotives from Henschel & Son of Kassel, Germany, to be known as class "16E"; running numbers were 854 to 859.

Driving wheel diameter was increased by 20 per cent compared with the "16 DA" class, which previously had handled such crack expresses as the famous "Blue Train". This involved a boiler centre line pitched very high (9ft 3in—2,820mm) above rail level—2.6 times the rail gauge of 3ft 6in (1,067mm). This in its turn made necessary a domeless boiler, steam being collected by pipes with their open end placed as high as possible in the boiler barrel. Aesthetically the effect was most imposing and it all worked well too.

The valve gear was interesting, being more akin to that usually found in motor cars than in steam locomotives. As in nearly all car engines, the "16E" class had poppet valves actuated by rotating cams on camshaft. Naturally there had to be a set of valves at each end of each cylinder, steam locomotive cylinders being double acting; in addition, since steam engines have to go in both directions without a reversing gearbox, and in order to provide for expansive working, the cams were of some length and coned longitudinally. The camshaft could be moved laterally by the driver, so that the cam followers engaged different cam profiles, and thus caused the poppet valves to open for longer or shorter periods to vary the "cut-off" for expansive working, while a still greater lateral movement reversed the locomotive. The "RC" poppet valve gear gave wonderfully free running and, moreover, its complexities gave little trouble in SAR's competent hands.

On various special occasions (it can now be told) the "16E"s have shown abilities to reach safely and easily—but illegally according to the SAR rule-book—what by African standards

Above: *South African Railways' "16E" class 4-6-2 No.858* Millie *on "Sunset Limited" at Kimberley*

Left: *During the late 1930s many USA railroads introduced streamlined trains. Here is the Lehigh Valley RR's "Black Diamond".*

Above: *The New York, New Haven & Hartford Railroad class "I-5" 4-6-4, which was built for running fast trains from New Haven to Boston.*

periment, ten 4-6-4s were ordered from Baldwin of Philadelphia. Running numbers were 1400 to 1409.

This "I-5" class with disc driving wheels, roller bearings and Walschaert's valve gear went into service in 1937. They certainly met the promise of their designers in that they showed a 65 per cent saving in the cost of maintenance compared with the 4-6-2s they replaced and, moreover, could handle 16-car 1100-ton trains to the same schedules as the Pacific could barely manage with 12.

Another requirement was met in that they proved able to clear the 1 in 140 (0.7 per cent) climb out of Boston to Sharon Heights with a 12-car 840-ton train at 60mph (97km/h). But, alas, the "I-5"s were never able to develop their no doubt formidable high speed capability because of a rigidly enforced 70mph (113 km/h) speed limit. For this reason and because the line was infested with speed restrictions, the schedule of the "Merchants Limited" never fell below 171 minutes including two stops, representing an average of 55mph (89km/h). Forty years "progress" and a change from steam to diesel traction since the days of the "I-5"s has only succeeded in reducing this time to 170mins today.

were very high speeds indeed. Alas, these locomotives never had an opportunity to demonstrate their high-speed abilities in normal service. South African Railways—the only railway to *fly* into London's Heathrow Airport—has also operated the national airline since its inception and early on it seemed reasonable to encourage anyone in a hurry to travel by aeroplane. So the rail schedules remained unaccelerated and the five handsome "16E"s remained unduplicated.

Four of the five were withdrawn in the 1960s and 1970s, but one (No.858) named *Millie,* is kept on hand in order to work special trains for steam enthusiasts. These are very much a speciality of SAR and often last for ten days or so, the train being stabled each night while its occupants sleep on board. The run behind this beautiful engine, polished like a piece of jewellery and at speed up to about 70mph (110km/h) is always one of the high spots of the trip.

Right: *A pair of beautifully polished South African "16E" class 4-6-2s handle a special train for steam enthusiasts.*

231-132BT Class 4-6-2 + 2-6-4

Algeria: Paris, Lyons & Mediterranean Co (PLM), 1937

Tractive effort: 65,960lb (29,920kg).
Axle load: 40,500lb (18.5t).
Cylinders: (4) 19¼ x 26in (490 x 660mm).
Driving wheels: 71in (1,800mm).
Heating surface: 2,794sq ft (260m²).
Superheater: 975sq ft (91m²).
Steam pressure: 284psi (20kg/cm²).
Grate area: 58sq ft (5.4m²).
Fuel: 24,000lb (11t).
Water: 6,600gall (7,900 US) (30m³).
Adhesive weight: 241,000lb (111t).
Total weight: 47,500lb (216t).
Length overall: 96ft 6⅞in (29,432mm).

Should there ever have been a requirement for a reciprocating steam locomotive to emulate the performance of Britain's new diesel-electric HST125 trains, this locomotive of British concept but French execution would be a reasonable starting point.

One day in 1907, an engineer by the name of H.W. Garratt visited a firm of locomotive manufacturers in Manchester called Beyer, Peacock. Garratt was then working as an inspector for goods manufactured in Britain for the New South Wales Government, but he came to discuss with them an idea which he had patented for articulated locomotives built to the same basic format as mobile rail-mounted guns. The main result in due time was some hardware in the form of two little 0-4-4-0 compound locomotives, hinged twice in the middle, for far-off Tasmania.

This Garratt layout consisted of taking two conventional locomotive chassis or engine units, of whatever wheel arrangement was preferred, and using them back-to-back as bogies a certain distance apart. A boiler cradle was then slung between them, tanks and fuel bunkers being mounted on the engine units.

The reason for the Garratt's success when compared with rival types of articulated locomotives such as the "Mallet", was mainly due to the elegance of its geometry. For example, when swinging fast round curves, the boiler and cab unit moved inwards like a bowstring in the bow of the curve, thereby countering an overturning effect of centrifugal force.

Another advantage of the Garratt arrangement was that there was no running gear (so vulnerable to grit) immediately under the fire-grate; just lots of room and plenty of the fresh air so necessary to ensure good combustion. More important, the absence of running gear beneath the boiler gave complete freedom in respect of the design of this important component. Although a Garratt gives the impression of great length and slenderness, in fact, the boiler can be relatively short and fat. For fundamental reasons short fat boilers are considerably lighter and cheaper than long thin ones, for a given steam raising capacity.

Although many were sold for freight and mixed traffic use, the excellent riding qualities of Beyer-Garratts were seldom exploited for express passenger work, until 1927 when a group of 2-6-2+2-6-2s—later altered to 4-6-2+2-6-4s—with 5ft 6in (1,676mm) diameter driving wheels, were built for the 5ft 3in (1,600mm) gauge Brazilian San Paulo Railway. With them 70mph (113km/h) was achieved, with excellent stability. In 1931 the Spanish Central Aragon Railway obtained six 4-6-2+2-6-4s with 5ft 9in (1,753mm) driving wheels, and these were equally satisfactory; these latter locomotives were built by Euskalduna of Bilbao under licence from Beyer, Peacock.

In 1932 the Paris, Lyons & Mediterranean Company ordered an experimental Garratt-type locomotive from the Franco-Belge Company of Raismes, France, for the Algerian lines. This 4-6-2+2-6-4 was successful,

Below: *The magnificent class 231-132BT Beyer-Garratt locomotives built in France for the Algerian railways.*

Class 142 2-8-4

Roumania: Roumanian State Railways (CFR), 1935

Tractive effort: 44,050lb (19,980kg).
Axle load: 41,000lb (18.5t).
Cylinders: (2) 25.6 x 28.4in (650 x 720mm).
Driving wheels: 76½in (1,940mm).
Heating surface: 3,002sq ft (280m²).
Superheater: 774sq ft (72m²).
Steam pressure: 213psi (15kg/cm²).
Grate area: 51sq ft (4.72m²).
Fuel: see text.
Water: 6,500gall (7,800 US) (29.5m³).
Adhesive weight: 161,000lb (74t).
Total weight: 406,000lb (184t).
Length overall: 74ft 9in (22,784mm).

Another example of a small country building its own express-passenger locomotives, and 2-8-4s to boot, was Roumania. The firms Malaxa and Resita built 58 and 27 respectively between 1936 and 1949. They continued in use until the 1960s. In fact they were copies, built under licence, of the greatest of Austrian steam locomotives, the "214" class. In their home country the history of the class was overshadowed by events; 13 only were built and this unlucky number certainly justified its reputation. First came the German takeover which turned the proud Federal Austrian Railway into a mere division of the German State Railway. Then the war, Russian occupation and finally electrification. All of these traumatically affected the Vienna to Salzburg main line for which the 2-8-4s were built but their cousins in Roumania (called "142"s) flourished and multiplied.

Like so many large locomotives of the time, the genesis of the type lay in a desire to avoid the indignity of double-heading on their owners' principal expresses, in this case between Salzburg and Vienna. Loads had outstripped the haulage capacity of the excellent class "210" 2-6-4s.

Above: *The Austrian "214" class 2-8-4 locomotives adopted as the standard express locomotive design by Roumania.*

A prototype was built in 1931, together with a three-cylinder version for comparative purposes. Poppet valves actuated by oscillating cams driven by Walschaert's valve gear were used, except for one which was fitted with Caprotti gear. The Roumanian copies had the former arrangement, except for a batch which were built in 1939 with Caprotti and later altered to standard.

An unusual feature of these

both at fast running as well as at climbing over the mountains, to a point where further express Garratts of an improved design were ordered. When the PLM lines in Algeria had been amalgamated with the Algerian State Railways (CFAE) an initial order for 10 was later increased to 29 by Algerian Railways (CFA).

Amongst many interesting features of a design which kept wholly to the standard Garratt layout was the Cossart valve gear. This unusual gear drove cam-operated piston valves and enabled the locomotive to use very early cut-offs indeed, in the range of 5 per cent to 7 per cent. If normal valve gears such as Stephenson's or Walschaert's are arranged so they can be linked up to give cut-offs as early as this, it is impossible to arrange the geometry so that the exhaust ports would then open for an adequate fraction of the return stroke. Such a locomotive would experience a checking influence at speed—generally speaking 15 per cent or 17 per cent is the limit with conventional gears, and any more fully expansive working is not possible. The valve gear was also interesting in that it was operated electrically.

Other equipment included duplicate controls at the rear of the cab for running hind end first, a feed water heater, and a turbo-fan for ventilating the cab. There were drench pipes to the ashpan and smokebox, a soot blower to clean the boiler tubes on the run, and a recording speedometer. A double chimney and double variable blast-pipe was provided; unusually the two orifices were placed side by side instead of end-on. A coal-pusher assisted in bringing coal forward ready to be fed to the fire. The tanks and bunker were arranged to correspond in shape with the boiler. The ends were streamlined and the result aesthetically most impressive.

On test on the Northern Railway between Calais and Paris, it was found that the engine rode steadily and could develop cylinder horse-power up to 3,000. In service on the Algiers-Constantine main line, which included gradients as steep as 1 in 38½ (2.6 per cent), the running time for the 288 miles (464km) was reduced from 12½ hours to 8½. Between Algiers and Oran the new timing of 7 hours for the 262 miles (422km) represented an acceleration of 2 hours.

Until the war came to Algeria the express Garratts gave good service but, alas, the electrical valve gear did not stand up to the inevitable neglect when the fighting began. Soon after the war there was an opportunity to dieselise and by 1951 these 30 superb locomotives were out of use.

Perhaps the most interesting point is that, whilst conventional "straight" locomotives in express passenger service have certainly been stretched up to the limit as regards various critical dimensions, the Garratt had still some way to go. Larger wheels could easily be combined with a larger boiler of much greater power output. For example, that hypothetical steam replacement for the HST 125 could have 7ft 6in (2,286mm) driving wheels combined with a 7ft 6in (2,286mm) diameter boiler, all inside the British loading gauge 9ft wide by 13ft high (2,740mm by 3,300mm).

A grate-area of 80sq ft. (7.5m²) would make a steady output of 5,000 horsepower in the cylinders feasible. The large space vacant beneath the firebox would provide space for an adequate ash-pan to contain the residue left behind when the considerable quantities of coal involved had been burnt. The Da Porta combustion system described in connection with the South Africa class "25" 4-8-4s would be a possibility. A turbo-generator could provide electric power for heating and air-conditioning the present carriages of the HST 125 trains, to which little or no modification would be needed. But, alas, such a magnificent means of locomotion must remain haulage power for the Dreamland Express, and hence live entirely in our imagination.

and other Roumanian locomotives is the coal-plus-oil firing system. The coal fire provides the base supply of steam, while the oil supplement covers periods of exceptional demand.

For many years these imposing locomotives covered their share of Roumania's top express passenger assignments. Very unusually for a small country, Roumania has its own diesel and electric locomotive industry; being dependent on modest production from this source, the change to new forms of motive power was sure rather than fast. Even so, the "142"s had ceased work by the end of the 1960s; No. 142.008 is set aside at Bucharest's Grivita depot and 142.072 is displayed at the Resita Locomotive Museum.

Right: *A humble use in this pastoral Roumanian scene for a class "142" 2-8-4 locomotive of the state railway system.*

Duchess Class 4-6-2

Great Britain: London, Midland & Scottish Railway (LMS), 1939

Tractive effort: 40,000lb (18,144kg).
Axle load: 52,500lb (24t).
Cylinders: (4) 16½ x 28in (419 x 711mm).
Driving wheels: 81in (2,057mm).
Heating surface: 2,807sq ft (261m²).
Superheater: 856sq ft (79.5m²).
Steam pressure: 250psi (17.6kg/cm²).
Grate area: 50sq ft (4.6m²).
Fuel: 22,400lb (10t).
Water: 4,000gall (4,800 US) (18m³).
Adhesive weight: 147,500lb (68t).
Total weight: 362,000lb (164t).
Length overall: 73ft 10¼in (22,510mm).

Above: *Ex-London Midland & Scottish Railway 4-6-2 No.46236* City of Bradford *on the down "Royal Scot" in the Lune Gorge near Tebay, Lancashire.*

The most powerful steam locomotive ever to run in Britain! This was demonstrated in February 1939, when No.6234 *Duchess of Abercorn* was put to haul a 20-coach 605-ton test train from Crewe to Glasgow and back. An authentic recording of an indicated horse-power of 3,330 was made and this power output from a steam locomotive has never been matched in Britain. It occurred coming south when climbing the 1 in 99 (1.01 per cent) of Beattock bank at a steady speed of 63mph (102 km/h). This feat was, however, a purely academic one, not because of any limitations on the part of the locomotive but because the power developed corresponded to a coal-shovelling rate well beyond the capacity of one man. Two firemen were carried on the occasion of the test run, which certinaly equalled anything achieved later with diesel traction before the recent arrival of the High Speed Train.

It remains a pity that none of the "Duchess" class 4-6-2s were tried with oil firing or mechanical stoking, not so much because a somewhat academic record might then have been pushed higher, but rather that the faster train services which followed dieselisation might have been achieved years earlier with steam.

Incidentally, the "Duchess" locomotives were fast runners as well as strong pullers and even held the British rail speed record for a short period, although it was not an occasion for any pride. This was because in order to obtain the 114mph (182km/h) maximum, steam was not shut off until the train was so close to Crewe that the crossovers leading into the platforms and good for only 20mph (32km/h) were taken at nearly 60 (96km/h). Minor damage was done to the track and much to the crockery in the kitchen car, but the train and the newsmen aboard survived. The practical features of the design which saved the day were a credit to the engineers concerned, but this was cancelled out by a typical disdain for theory, which could so easily have established the point at which steam should have been shut off and the brakes applied so that the safety of the train should not have been endangered.

Completely unshaken by this incident, with the down train, the imperturbable Driver J.T. Clarke using the same locomotive then proceeded to take the party back to London in 119 minutes at an average speed of 79.5mph (127km/h) with several maxima over 90mph (144km/h) and the magic 100 (160) maintained for some distance near Castlethorpe.

Enough has been said to show that the "Duchess" class represented something close to the summit of British locomotive engineering. Simplicity was not the keynote of the design, but sound conventional engineering made these locomotives the success they were. The designer was William Stanier who had come to the LMS from the Great Western Railway in 1932; he was a worthy product of the Churchward tradition and at the age of 52 far from being a young man. He had one great advantage over his predecessors on the LMS—a direct line to Lord Stamp, President of the company, who had recruited him personally over lunch at the Athenaeum Club. Previous locomotive engineers had been dictated to even over such details as axleboxes by the operating department of the railway—and then blamed for the consequent failures.

So Stanier was able without interference to initiate design work on an excellent range of standard locomotives; the results took the LMS from a somewhat backward position into an enviable one so far as their locomotive stud was concerned. His first

Below: *No.46251* City of Nottingham *depicted in LMS-style British Railways livery, but with the streamline pattern tender originally attached.*

4-6-2 was the *Princess Royal* which appeared in 1933; her cylinder layout was similar to the Great Western "King" class, except that two more independent sets of Walschaert's valve gear were fitted outside the wheels for the outside cylinders. At first the taper boiler did not steam as well as it should and several quite considerable successive internal alterations had to be made, which were applied new to later "Princess Royal" class locomotives as they came out and retrospectively to those already built. One of these locomotives was the "Turbomotive".

A decision to run a streamlined high-speed express from Euston to Glasgow in 1937 was the opportunity to apply all that had been learnt from the 12 locomotives of the "Princess Royal" class for these 4-6-2s were far larger than anything the LMS had had before. The train and the first of the five new locomotives built for it took the names *Coronation Scot* and *Coronation* respectively.

This time the cylinder layout was moved well away from that of the GWR. The centre lines were inclined upwards at a slope of 1½ degrees, while the outside cylinders were brought forward from the original position in line with the rear bogie wheel. The outside valve gears were made to work the valves of the inside cylinders as well as the outside by rocker arms just to the rear of the outside cylinders. A similar arrangement had been fitted to No.6205 *Princess Victoria*. Both wheel and cylinder diameters were slightly larger on the "Coronation" class than on the "Princess Royal" class. An interesting gadget in the tender was the steam coal-pusher which helped the fireman bring coal forward from the back of the tender when supplies at the front got used up.

The boiler was notable for an 11 per cent larger fire grate area and a 133 per cent increase in superheater heating surface, compared with the original *Princess Royal*—although subsequent "Princess Royal" class locomotives had bigger superheaters, none were as large as that. Not many people liked the sausage-shaped streamlined shroud that enveloped the locomotive, but the new blue and silver livery was lovely. The other four locomotives were named after members of the royal family—*Queen Elizabeth, Queen Mary, Princess Alice* and *Princess Alexandra*.

The 6½-hour schedule of the "Coronation Scot" from London to Glasgow with only a 270-ton load was not too demanding for these great locomotives but, quite aside from this, they were found to be excellent heavy artillery for general express passenger use on this West Coast main line. Accordingly, a further ten were ordered of which only the first five were streamlined. All ten were named after duchesses (in fact, the whole class is now usually referred to by that name) and it was No.6230 *Duchess of Buccleuch* that first demonstrated how extremely handsome these engines were when unclothed.

More streamlined engines of an order for 20 (named after cities) placed before the war were delivered gradually over the war years 1939-43. After 18 of them had been completed construction continued with non-streamlined examples, and in 1945 instructions were issued for the streamline casings to be removed from locomotives fitted with it. This was not completed until 1949 by which time the last and 38th "Duchess" (No.6257 *City of Salford*) had been complete for a twelve-month.

The success of the class is measured by the minimal number of changes that were made over their years of service from 1937, until electric and diesel locomotives took over in 1964. Nos.6256 and 6257 had some modification, but these were more in the nature of experiments than cures for recognised ills. In contrast, the number of livery changes were legion—blue and gold streamline, standard LMS maroon, maroon and gold streamline, plain wartime black, lined post-war black, experimental gray, BR dark blue, BR medium blue, BR green and finally LMS maroon with BR insignia as shown in the painting below.

Three have been preserved—No.6229 *Duchess of Hamilton*, in charge of the National Railway Museum, and currently restored to main line running condition; No.6233 *Duchess of Sutherland* in Alan Bloom's collection at Bressingham, near Diss, and No. 6235 *City of Birmingham* in the Birmingham Science Museum.

Above: *The second-from-last and considerably modified "Duchess" No.46256 was named* Sir William A Stanier FRS *in honour of her designer.*

Below: *In London Midland & Scottish Railway days and as originally built in streamline form, No.6225* Duchess of Gloucester *passes Rugby.*

Class GS-4 4-8-4

United States: Southern Pacific Railroad (SP), 1941

Tractive effort: 71,173lb (32,285kg).
Axle load: 68,925lb (31.25t).
Cylinders: (2) 25½ x 32in (648 x 813mm).
Driving wheels: 80in (2,032mm).
Heating surface: 4,887sq ft ($454m^2$).
Superheater: 2,086sq ft ($194m^2$).
Steam pressure: 300psi ($21.1kg/cm^2$).
Grate area: 90.4sq ft ($8.4m^2$).
Fuel (oil): 4,900galls (5,900 US) ($22.3m^3$).
Water: 19,600gall (23,500 US) ($89mm^3$).
Adhesive weight: 276,000lb (125.5t).
Total weight: 883,000lb (400.5t).

Above: *Southern Pacific's tough-haulage class "GS-4" 4-8-4 No. 4456 at San Francisco, California, in May 1952.*

The "Daylight" express of the Southern Pacific Railroad was the third of three famous train services worked by matching streamlined express locomotives and coaches over a similar distance. The "Hiawatha" trains of the Milwaukee line between Chicago and the Twin Cities and the "Coronation" of the British London & North Eastern Railway between London and Edinburgh have been noticed elsewhere. Each of the three trains introduced new standards of speed, comfort and decor, and each train was spectacularly successful in attracting new traffic.

The 470-mile route between Los Angeles and San Francisco was much the hardest as well as the longest of the three. For example, there was nothing on either of the other lines to compare with the 1 in 45 (2.2 per cent) gradient of Santa Margharita Hill, north of San Luis Obispo. The "light-weight" 12-car "Daylight" express weighed 568 tonnes, nearly double the weight of the British train—though it must be said that as regards weight hauled per passenger carried, the latter came out at 15 per cent less than the former.

Because of the severe curvature of the line as well as the heavy gradients the 48.5mph (78km/h) average speed of the "Daylight" train was considerably less than that of the other two, although the lessening of running times represented by all three of the new trains were roughly even. The gradients encountered by the "Daylight" nicely balanced out with the "Hiawatha" faster running, but certainly the "Daylight" was a far tougher haulage proposition than the British train. The motive power provided reflected this.

Eight-coupled wheels were needed and enabled the resulting "Daylight" 4-8-4 to have (with booster) 124 per cent more tractive effort than the LNER "A4" 4-6-2. As regards grate area, that is, the size of the fire, the increase was 119 per cent. The SP already had fourteen 4-8-4s (class "GS-1"), which came from Baldwin of Philadelphia in 1930. As with the LNER's but unlike the Milwaukee's, the SP's new locomotives (class "GS-2") were from a mechanical point of view based very closely on their immediate predecessors. Of course, the decor was something else again and it gave these four black, silver and gold monsters from the Lima Locomotive Works of Lima, Ohio, an appearance which could hardly be described as less than superb.

Like so many large North American locomotives of the time, the success of the "Daylight" type was due to the application of the excellent standard of US practice of the day. Amongst a few special features worth recording was one that has almost no steam traction parallel elsewhere, that is the provision of electro-pneumatic brake equipment. With other forms of traction, the electro-pneumatic brake is commonplace today, especially for multiple-units. Application of the brakes on a normal air-brake system relies on a pressure change travelling down the brake pipe from the locomotive to switch on the brakes under each successive car. This involves a flow of air towards the driver's brake-valve and in consequence a delay of several seconds occurs before the brakes are applied to the wheels of. the rear car. In contrast, with EP braking the signal to apply the brakes goes down the train with the speed of electric current. The thinking was that these few seconds—during which the train would travel several hundred feet—might in the case of a high-speed service be the difference between an incident and a disaster.

The curvature of the route was recognised by the provision of spring-controlled side-play on the leading coupled axle. In this way the wheels could "move-over" on a curve and allow the flange force to be shared between the two leading axles, with benefits to the wear of both rails and tyres. The hilliness of the line gave rise to a series of water sprays to cool the tyres on engine and tender wheels during braking on the long descents. Air sanding gear was provided, fed from a tank under that boiler-top casing, which held a full *ton* of sand! With booster cut in, the "GS"s could manage the standard "Daylight" consist on the 1 in 45 grades (2.2 per cent); but if any extra cars were attached a helper was needed.

Although the "Daylight" type held to the simple and world-standard concept of a two-cylinder locomotive with outside valve gear, the host of equipment provided did add a certain complexity. There were three turbo-generators, for example, and a feed-water heater and pump as well as injectors. It must be said that virtually all of this complication was made up of items of proprietary equipment each of which, as it were, came in a box and could be bolted on. Such fittings were apt to work well because competition kept the suppliers

Below: *One of the original batch (class "GS-2") of Southern Pacific's "Daylight" 4-8-4s as delivered from the Lima Locomotive Works, Ohio, in 1937.*

on their toes; and if problems arose a replacement could be fitted quickly. Even so, an electro-magnetic gadget—inside the boiler!—which sensed foaming and opened the blow-down cocks automatically, did not last.

Like most SP steam locomotives, the "Daylight"s were fired with oil—indeed, SP were the United States' pioneers in this area—economy being achieved with a device called a "locomotive valve pilot" which indicated to the engineer what cut-off he should set to suit any particular speed and conditions of working.

Streamlined trains, worked by further batches of these magnificently-equipped locomotives, spread to all parts of SP's system and thus served such far distant places as Portland in Oregon, Ogden in Utah and New Orleans. Details of the 60 locos were as shown in the table.

The War Production Board refused to sanction the "GS-6" batch, but on being told that "GS" now stood for "General Service" rather than "Golden State", they accepted the proposal. Of an order for 16, six went to Western Pacific Railroad.

The first "GS" to be withdrawn was No.4462 in 1954 and in October 1958 No.4460 (now displayed at the Museum of Transportation at St. Louis, Missouri) brought SP steam operations to a close with a special excursion from Oakland to Reno, Nevada. No.4449 also survived to haul the "Freedom Train" several thousands of miles across the USA in connection with the bi-centennial of independence in 1976. The locomotive is still able to run and has recently been restored to the original superb "Daylight" colours.

Designation	Date	Running Nos	Features
GS-2	1937	4410 to 4415	Driving wheels 73½in (1,867mm) dia instead of 80in (2,032mm)
GS-3	1937	4416 to 4429	
GS-4	1941-2	4430 to 4457	Fully enclosed cabs began with this batch
GS-5	1942	4458 to 4459	As GS-4 but with roller bearings
GS-6	1943	4460 to 4469	No streamlining—plain black

Top: *Southern Pacific's "Daylight" express from Los Angeles to Chicago being pulled at speed behind a class "GS" 4-8-4, which was originally built to haul this particular train.*

Above: *Southern Pacific unstreamlined class "GS-6" 4-8-4 at Dunsmuir, California, with the "Klamath" express in June 1952.*

Royal Hudson Class 4-6-4

Canada:
Canadian Pacific Railway (CPR), 1937

Tractive effort: 45,300lb (20,548kg).
Axle load: 65,000lb (29.5t).
Cylinders: (2) 22 x 30in (559 x 762mm).
Driving wheels: 75in (1,905mm).
Heating surface: 3,791sq ft ($352m^2$).
Superheater: 1,542sq ft ($143m^2$).
Steam pressure: 275psi ($19.3kg/cm^2$).
Grate area: 81sq ft ($7.5m^2$).
Fuel: 47,000lb (21t).
Water: 12,000gall (14,400 US) ($54.6m^3$).
Adhesive weight: 194,000lb (88t).
Total weight: 659,000lb (299t)..
Length overall: 90ft 10in (27,686mm).

To be both Royal and North American is almost a contradiction in terms but, forty years ago, the Canadian Pacific Railway was as much British as it was Canadian. It had been incorporated by an Act of the British Parliament, and its east-most terminal was situated at Southampton, England. It was here in 1939 that King George VI and Queen Elizabeth set sail in the Canadian Pacific liner *Empress of Britain* for a tour of their largest Dominion. Once ashore, their home for much of the visit was a Royal train, at the head of which was a new 4-6-4, No.2850, specially turned out in royal blue and silver with stainless steel boiler cladding. The royal arms were painted on the tender and a replica crown was mounted on the running board skirt just ahead of the cylinders; later this crown was affixed to all 45 of CPR's famous 4-6-4s built between 1937 and 1945.

The genesis of these fine locomotives lay in a wish to improve upon the class "G-3" 4-6-2s which before 1931 had been the top-line power of the system, by increasing their steam-raising capacity a substantial amount. A fire-grate 23 per cent larger was possible if the 4-6-4 wheel arrangement was adopted and the boilers of the new locomotives were based on this. But in other ways, such as tractive effort or adhesive weight, the new locomotives were little different to the old. Their class designation was H-1 and the running numbers were 2800 to 2819.

The boilers had large superheaters and combustion chambers (the latter an addition to the firebox volume, provided by recessing the firebox tubeplate into the barrel), as well as front-end throttles which worked on the hot side of the superheater. This enabled superheated steam to be fed to the various auxiliaries. There were arch tubes in the firebox and, necessary with a grate of this size, a mechanical stoker.

The first effect of the new locomotives was to reduce the number of engine changes needed to cross Canada, from fourteen to nine. The longest stage was 820 miles (1,320km) from Fort William, Ontario, to Winnipeg, Manitoba; experimentally a 4-6-4 had run the 1,252 miles (2,015km) between Fort William and Calgary, Alberta, without change.

For five hectic months in 1931 the afternoon CPR train from Toronto to Montreal, called the "Royal York" became the world's fastest scheduled train, by virtue of a timing of 108 minutes for the 124 miles (200km) from Smith's Falls to Montreal West, an average speed of 68.9mph (111km/h). The record was wrested from the Great Western Railway of England, whose "Cheltenham Flyer" then had a timing of 70min for the 77¼ miles (124km), an average speed of 66.3mph. The 4-6-4s were normally assigned to this train. Subsequently the GWR dropped 3 minutes from their timing and took back the record.

An interesting feature, later provided on one of the "H-1"s, was a booster engine working on the trailing truck. One of the problems of a 4-6-4 was that only six out of 14 wheels were driven; this was no detriment while running at speed but starting was sometimes affected by the limited

Below: *Ex-Canadian Pacific "Royal Hudson" class No.2860 progresses gently along the shore of Howe Sound, B.C.*

adhesion. The extra 12,000lb (5,443kg) of tractive effort provided by the booster came in very handy; the mechanism cut out automatically at 20mph (32km/h).

The 1930s were the period when streamlining was in fashion but when the time came to order some more 4-6-4s, H.B. Bowen, the CPR Chief of Motive Power, decided to compromise. He came to the conclusion that the shrouds which enveloped many contemporary designs made the mechanism inaccessible to an extent which smothered any savings attributable to reduced air resistance. On the other hand, he accepted that the public liked their trains hauled by locomotives which were a little easier on the eye than was then customary.

The result in 1937 was another batch of 30 Hudson type, Nos. 2820 to 2849 designated "H-1c", (the earlier ones had been delivered in two batches of ten, "H-1a" and "H-1b") which had not only softer lines but also sported a superb coloured livery, as our artist has tried to show. Very few mechanical changes needed to be made—although there were certain improvements or changes such as power-operated reversing gear, domeless boilers and a one-piece cast locomotive frame, while boosters were fitted to five of the locomotives. A further ten 4-6-4s, designated "H-1d" were delivered in 1938, while the last batch of five ("H-1e"), Nos.2860 to 2864 of 1940, differed from the others in being oil burners. All the "H-1e"s and five of the "H-1d"s had boosters.

The last batch of 4-6-4s were intended to operate in the far west, between Vancouver and Revelstoke, British Columbia, where oil firing had been the rule for many years. After the war, when the big Canadian oil fields were being exploited, all the "H-1"s operating over the prairies were also converted. This was made easier by the fact that it was customary to allocate a particular locomotive to a particular depot when they were built and they would then remain there for many years. This unusually stable approach to locomotive allocation also allowed the booster-fitted locomotives to be rostered for sections of line where their extra push was needed. For example, booster fitted "H-1c"s allocated to Toronto could take the 18-car 1,300-ton "Dominion" express up the Neys Hill incline on Lake Superior's north shore unassisted with booster in operation; otherwise a helper engine would have been an obvious necessity.

Above: *A head-on view of 4-6-4 No.2860 as preserved and now running on the British Columbia Railway.*

Like other lines which had excellent steam power, well maintained and skilfully operated, the Canadian Pacific Railway was in no hurry to dieselise and, in fact, it was not until 1956 that the first 4-6-4 was scrapped. By mid-1960 all were out of service, but five have survived the scrap-men's torches. Standard Hudson No. 2816 is (at the time of writing) at Steamtown, Bellows Falls, Vermont, USA. Of the "Royal Hudson" types, No.2839 has recently been seen in operation in the USA on the Southern Railway, a line which regularly operates special steam trains for enthusiasts. No.2850 is in the Canadian Railway Museum at Delson, Quebec, No.2858 is on display at the National Museum of Science and Technology at Ottawa and, most famous of all, No.2860 works regular tourist trains on the British Columbia Railway between Vancouver and Squamish. No.2860 has visited Eastern Canada as well as steaming south as far as Los Angeles, hauling a show train intended to publicise the beauties of British Columbia.

Below: *The beautiful red livery of preserved 4-6-4 No. 2860 was basically the same as used on these engines in Canadian Pacific Railway days.*

Class U-4 4-8-4 Canada: Canadian National Railways (CN), 1936

Tractive effort: 52,457lb (23,794kg).
Axle load: 59,500lb (27t).
Cylinders: (2) 24 x 30in (610 x 762mm).
Driving wheels: 77in (1,956mm).
Heating surface: 3,861sq ft (322.5m²).
Superheater: 1,530sq ft (142m²).
Steam pressure: 275psi (19.5kg/cm²).
Grate area: 73.7sq ft (6.8m²).
Fuel: 40,000lb (18t).
Water: 11,700gall (14,000 US) (35m³).
Adhesive weight: 236,000lb (107t).
Total weight: 660,000lb (300t).
Length overall: 95ft 1in (28,990mm).

During the steam age the longest railway in America was not located in the USA, for Canadian National Railways held the title. Around 60 years ago Canada suffered from the sort of railway problems that the United States is in the throes of now and the Government had perforce to take over 24,000 miles of bankrupt lines. The task ahead was formidable and one of the most remarkable railwaymen of all time was engaged to take charge. This was Sir Henry Thornton, who had learnt his trade on the Pennsylvania Railroad and its notorious subsidiary, the Long Island Railroad. In 1914 he was appointed general manager of the British Great Eastern Railway. During World War I he became a brigadier-general in charge of rail movement in France, and received a knighthood.

It was a far cry from 0-6-2 tanks on Thornton's famous jazz service which so much eased the lot of commuters homeward bound from London's Liverpool Street station, to the Trans-Canada Limited running 2,985 miles (4,776km) across a great continent, but he took it in his stride. Adequate tools for the job was very much a Thornton principle. It should, therefore, have been no surprise that CN was right in the vanguard of roads in ordering that ultimate of passenger types, the 4-8-4.

The Canadian Locomotive Company delivered No.6100—named *Confederation* to celebrate the 60th anniversary of the Canadian Confederation—just seven months after Northern Pacific received its 4-8-4s. By the end of the year, CN and its US subsidiary Grand Trunk Western, had a fleet totalling 52 of these great machines. This made CN by far the greatest 4-8-4 owner in the world, a position which was retained until the USSR took the lead in the mid-1950s. Running numbers were 6100-39 and 6300-11, classes "U2" and "U3", for CN and GTW respectively.

Further batches, generally similar, built in 1929 and 1936 brought the numbers up to 77 and then in 1936-38 a high-speed streamline version was built. This "U-4" class, the subject of the dimensions given on this page, had larger driving wheels and a less than typically ugly shroud, but was also very much the same locomotive basically. Running numbers were 6400-4 (CN) and 6405-11 (GTW).

Yet more standard 4-8-4s followed in 1940 and 1944 until finally the total reached 203. All the CN locomotives were built in Canada either by the Montreal Locomotive Works or by the Canadian Locomotive Company also of Montreal, while (no doubt because of import duties) those for GTW were built by US builders.

It is no disparagement to say that the CN engineers were not keen on innovation, and so the class was very much the standard North American product. CN's trade marks were the cylindrical Vanderbilt tenders and, on those built up to 1936, a prominent transverse feed-water heater placed just in front of the chimney. Naturally, such improvements as roller bearings and cast-steel locomotive frames were adopted as they became available.

One locomotive (No.6184) was

Right: *No.6218, a fine specimen of CN's class "U-2".*

Class Ul-f 4-8-2 Canada: Canadian National Railways (CN), 1944

Tractive effort: 52,500lb (23,814kg).
Axle load: 59,500lb (27t).
Cylinders: (2) 24 x 30in (610 x 762mm).
Driving wheels: 73in (1,854mm).
Heating surface: 3,584sq ft (333m²).
Superheater: 1,570sq ft (146m²).
Steam pressure: 260psi (18.3kg/cm²).
Grate area: 70.2sq ft (6.6m²).
Fuel: 40,000lb (18t).
Water: 11,500gall (9,740 US) (53m³).
Adhesive weight: 237,000lb (107.5t).
Total weight: 638,000lb (290t).
Length overall: 93ft 3in (28,426mm).

It was in 1923, very soon after the formation of Canadian National Railways, that eight-coupled locomotives were first introduced into passenger service there. This was the original "U1-a" a batch consisting of 16 locos, built by the Canadian Locomotive Company. Then 1924 and 1925 brought the "U1-b" and "U1-c" batches of 21 and five from Canadian and from Baldwin respectively. The latter were for CN's Grand Trunk Western subsidiary in the USA. In 1929 and 1930 there followed five "U1-d" and 12 "U1-e" from Canadian and from the Montreal locomotive works.

Thus in seven years, fifty-nine 4-8-2s, numbered from 6000 to 6058, became available, although by now the class had become overshadowed by the 4-8-4s introduced in 1927, described on this page. There were also four 4-8-2s acquired by the Central Vermont

tried with poppet valves and in later years when Canada struck oil, many 4-8-4s changed over to that method of firing. Withdrawals began on a small scale in 1955 and grew slowly until the final holocaust of the last 159 took place in 1960. The sadness felt by Canadian railwaymen at the 4-8-4s departure from the scene is well expressed by Anthony Clegg and Ray Corley, in their excellent book *Canadian National Steam Power*, by quoting the following verse chalked on a withdrawn 4-8-4:

"In days gone by this junk pile now
Was a grand sight to behold
On threads of steel it dashed along
Like a Knight in armour bold. . . ."

For a period Canadian National operated certain 4-8-4s in excursion service. This has now finished, but eight have survived; two, including streamliner No. 6400, are on display at Ottawa in the National Museum of Science and Technology.

Railway, another CN subsidiary but one which did not then number or classify its locos as part of the main CN fleet. It did use the CN method of classification, though, so these 4-8-2s were also Class "U1-a". In fact they were rather different in design, having been acquired from amongst a flood of 4-8-2s which the Florida East Coast Railroad had ordered but found itself unable to pay for.

The 6000s performed with *élan* on the then highly competitive express trains between Montreal and Toronto; speeds up to 82mph (131km/h) have been noted with 700 tons or so. Later, the same engines operated well in pool service in conjunction with Canadian Pacific.

In 1944, a further twenty 4-8-2s were delivered from Montreal, of the "U1-f" batch illustrated here. They were brought up to date by having cast-steel locomotive frames, disc wheels and other improvements. Some were oil-burners and all had Vanderbilt cylindrical tenders and outside bearings on the leading bogies. Most significant was a major simplification consisting of the replacement of the boiler feed pump and feed-water heater, by a device called an exhaust steam injector. Injectors are usually tucked away tidily under the side of the cab but in this case the device was hung outside the driving wheels, the large pipe which supplied the exhaust steam adding to its conspicuousness.

Like other injectors but more so, exhaust steam injectors are remarkable conjuring tricks in the application of natural laws. It is difficult to believe that exhaust steam at, say 10psi (0.7kg/cm²) could force water into a boiler containing steam and water almost 30 times that pressure. However, an arrangement of cones turns a high velocity jet of low pressure steam into a low velocity high-pressure flow of water, which has no difficulty in forcing its way past the non-return clack valves into the boiler.

With just a few exceptions, CN steam locomotives were totally utilitarian, but with these excellent engines, efforts were made to make them good looking too. Side valences, a flanged British-style smokestack, green and black livery, brass numbers and placing the dome and sand container in the same box all contributed to the clean lines. The result is so good that one can almost forgive the designers that bullet nose to the smokebox!

Canadian National is amongst that superior class of railway administrations who offer steam for pleasure, as exampled by the fact that a total of six of these locomotives are preserved. No. 6060 of class "U1-f" does the honours and in addition No.6069 is displayed at Bayview Park, Sarnia and No.6077 at Capreol, Ontario. Of the elder CN Mountains, No.6015 is at the Museum at Delson, Quebec, No.6039 (Grand Trunk Western) was at Steamtown, Bellows Falls, Vermont, and No.6043 at Assinboine Park, Winnepeg.

Left: *Canadian National Railways class "Ul-f" 4-8-2 No.6060 depicted in mint condition as delivered.*

Below: *Canadian National Railways class "Ul-f" 4-8-2 as originally built in 1944.*

V2 Class 2-6-2 Great Britain: London and North Eastern Railway (LNER), 1936

Tractive effort: 33,730lb (15,304kg).
Axle load: 49,500lb (22.5t).
Cylinders: (3) 18½ x 26in (470 x 660mm).
Driving wheels: 74in (1,880mm).
Heating surface: 2,431sq ft (225.8m²).
Superheater: 680sq ft (63.2m²).
Steam pressure: 220psi (15.5kg/cm²).
Grate area: 41.25sq ft (3.86m²).
Fuel: 17,000lb (8t).
Water: 4,200gall (5,040 US) (19m³).
Adhesive weight: 146,000lb (66t).
Total weight: 323,000lb (146.5t).
Length overall: 66ft 5in (20,244mm).

These remarkable locomotives were a sympton of the trend apparent during the 1930s for producing all-purpose locomotives. Because the diameter of the wheels had to be a compromise between those previously thought right for freight trains and those appropriate for passenger trains, at full speed they had to turn faster. A better understanding of the best way to balance the reciprocating parts, excellent valve gears to get the steam in and out of the cylinders quickly enough and (in this case) the use of more than two cylinders helped to make this feasible.

In June 1936 the first of Sir Nigel Gresley's (he was knighted that very year) famous "V2" 2-6-2s appeared from Doncaster Works. It was to be the master designer's last major class, for he died in 1941.

The locomotive was named *Green Arrow* after a system of registering freight consignments—from a single packing case to a train-load—just introduced at the time and it was finished in the apple-green passenger livery of the company. Before war broke out the class numbered 86; subsequent building brought the total up to 184. Only a few had names but (with reason) they came to be known (in LNER territory) as the "engines that won the war". In order of construction, their running numbers were 4771-4898, 3653-64, 4899, 3641-3654, 3665-3695. After the war they became (more sensibly) 800 to 983 and in BR days 60800-60983.

As one might have expected with a fire-grate sensibly the same in size, the V2s were virtually as good as the 4-6-2s when it came to express passenger work. A V2 was noted running at 93mph (149km/hr) on the "Yorkshire Pullman". Express fully-braked freight trains were the class's speciality and these engines could manage over 60mph on the level on such trains as the famous "Scotch Goods" (sic) with 600 tons. On occasion, they were pressed into service on the streamliners and no difficulty was found in keeping time, while wartime trains of up to 25 packed carriages were also well within their capabilities.

On the debit side was the fact that whilst the V2s were general-purpose locomotives in the sense that they could haul anything, they were by no means go-anywhere locomotives. An axle-load as heavy as 22 tons meant that only some 40 out of every 100 miles of the LNER system was open to them. Indeed two prototypes of a miniaturised version (class "V4") appeared in 1941 to fill this gap, but Gresley's successor had other ideas and no more were built.

Two other question marks hung over details of the class; the Gresley conjugated valve gear

Right: *Preserved ex-LNER "V2" class 2-6-2 No. 4771* Green Arrow *at the Birmingham Railway Museum depot.*

Below: *The apple green LNER "V2" or "Green Arrow" class 2-6-2, completed in 1936.*

Class E4 4-6-4 United States: Chicago and North Western Railway (C&NW), 1938

Tractive effort: 55,000lb (24,798kg).
Axle load: 72,000lb (32.7t).
Cylinders: (2) 25 x 29in (635 x 737mm).
Driving wheels: 84in (2,134mm).
Heating surface: 3,958sq ft (368mm²).
Superheater: 1,884sq ft (175m²).
Steam pressure: 300psi (21kg/cm²).
Grate area: 90.7sq ft (8.4m²).
Fuel (oil): 5,000gall (6,000 US) (22.7m³).
Water: 16,500gall (20,000 US) (75.5m³).
Adhesive weight: 216,000lb (98t).
Total weight: 791,500lb (359t).
Length overall: 101ft 9¾in (31,033mm).

These handsome locomotives of advanced design have the unhappy distinction of being the first to be superseded by the diesel-electric locomotive from the job for which they were built. The Chicago & North Western Railway had its own way of doing things; not for nothing did its trains run on the left-hand track, whereas most North American trains take the right. When, in 1935, the gloves came off for the fight between the Milwaukee, Burlington and C&NW companies for the daytime traffic between Chicago and the twin cities of St Paul and Minneapolis, the last-named was first into the ring with the famous "400" trains—named because they ran (about) 400 miles in 400 minutes. The C&NW stole this march over their competitors by running

which worked the valves of the middle cylinder was one which has already been mentioned in connection with other LNER locomotives. The other query has also been referred to elsewhere; this was the usual one associated with the 2-6-2 wheel arrangement, viz the tracking qualities of the leading pony truck. All went well until 1946, when two derailments on wartime quality permanent way took place. After investigation the original swing-link self-centring suspension of the leading pony truck was replaced by a side control system which used transverse springing and no further trouble was experienced.

These matters apart, the V2s were superb engines and the last one was not withdrawn until late 1966 when the class was finally overtaken by dieselisation. Happily, the original *Green Arrow* has been preserved and is now restored to working order as part of the national collection.

Left: *Gone, but not forgotten, the original class "E4" 4-6-4 No.4001 of Chicago and North Western Railway in action.*

refurbished standard rolling stock hauled by a modified existing steam locomotive, instead of trains brand new from end to end.

Soon enough, though, the C&NW had to follow their competitors' example. They chose to copy the style of the Milwaukee's "Hiawatha" rather than the Burlington's diesel "Zephyr" and accordingly the American Locomotive Company was asked to supply nine high-speed streamlined 4-6-4s.

The new locomotives, designated "E4" and numbered 4000 to 4008, were delivered in 1938, but in the meantime the C&NW management decided it had backed the wrong horse and went to General Motors Electromotive Division for some of the first production-line diesel locomotives. These took over the new streamlined "400" trains, leaving the new 4-6-4s to work the transcontinental trains of the original Overland Route, which the C&NW hauled from Chicago to Omaha.

Because of the arithmetic of design the basic physical statistics of the "E4" were very close to the "Hiawatha" 4-6-4s, yet it is very clear that lesser differences between the two meant two separate designs. So we have two classes of six and nine locomotives respectively, intended for the same purpose, built by the same firm at the same time, which had few jigs or patterns in common. Such was the world of steam railway engineering.

Amongst the advanced features of the "E4" may be mentioned Baker's valve-gear, oil firing, roller bearings throughout and, particularly interesting, a Barco low water alarm. Boiling dry such a large kettle as a locomotive boiler is a very serious matter indeed and on most steam locomotives there is no automatic guard against the crew forgetting to look at the water-level in the gauge glasses.

Brash styles of painting were not the C&NW's way, and thus it is particularly sad that, when the time came in the early 1950s for the "E4"s to go to the torch, none *of them was preserved. So, therefore, only in imagination is it possible to feast our eyes on their green and gilded elegance.*

Class 56 4-6-2

Malaysia:
Malayan Railway (PKTM), 1938

Tractive effort: 23,940lb (10,859kg).
Axle load: 28,560lb (12.9t).
Cylinders: (3) 13 x 24in (330 x 610mm).
Driving wheels: 54in (1,372mm).
Heating surface: 1,109sq ft ($103m^2$).
Superheater: 218sq ft ($20.25m^2$).
Steam pressure: 250psi ($17.5kg/cm^2$).
Grate area: 27sq ft ($2.5m^2$).
Fuel (coal): 22,000lb (10t).
Water: 3,500gall (4,200 US) ($16m^3$).
Adhesive weight: 86,000lb (39t).
Total weight: 226,000lb (102.5t).
Length overall: 61ft 1⅜in (18,628mm).

These metre-gauge Pacific locomotives were one of the most elegant of all the British colonial designs and they worked on one of the best colonial systems. Before it turned to diesels, the Malayan Railway operated the majority of both its passenger and freight trains with this one class of 66 neat Pacific locomotives. The PKTM had long been a "railway of Pacifics", since the days when railways back home in Britain were still building 4-4-0s as top line express power. In fact, the first Malayan Pacific,the initial member of a run of 60 known as Class "H", was built for what was then the Federated Malay States Railways (FMSR) back in 1907 by Kitson of Leeds. Others were supplied by Nasmyth, Wilson of Manchester and Robert Stephenson of Darlington. Another 79 Pacifics of four more classes followed during the next 30 years.

In 1938 the North British Locomotive Co. of Glasgow supplied some remarkable Pacifics which were to be the ultimate in Malayan steam power. Before the war and Japanese occupation 28 were supplied, and 40 immediately afterwards. They were extremely neat and handsome little machines both in their looks and in their design. One feature was the excellent balance of the moving parts, and consequent absence of hammer blow to make them suitable for lightly laid track, obtained by the use of three cylinders, all driving the middle coupled axle. Another was the use of rotary-cam poppet valve gear; on other railways which tried this promising arrangement it failed to offer any savings, because of the better use of steam in the cylinders, to compensate for its extra cost and additional maintenance expenses. All credit, then, to the FMSR (and later the PKTM), which made enough of a success of this sophisticated system for it to become standard on the railway. No other railway administration in the world managed it—only this one, run by a combination of British, Chinese, Indian and Malay staff, succeeded.

Originally the class was designated "O" and the running numbers were 60 to 87. After the war they were redesignated class "56" and the various batches supplied were numbered 561.01—11, 562.01—06, 563.01—11, 564,01—40. Of these 561.09 and 562.01 were scrapped after war damage and not replaced.

In the late 1950s there was a period when locomotives were painted and lined out in Great Western Railway colours, but before this as well as afterwards, a smart black livery was used. Malayan names were applied to all the motive power at this period—Malay script is used on one side of the locomotive, Roman on the other.

In 1955 there was a proposal to run faster trains in Malaya and two "56" class locos were tested up to 70mph (112km/h) a re-

800 Class 4-6-0

Ireland:
Great Southern Railways (GSR), 1939

Tractive effort: 33,000lb (14,970kg).
Axle load: 47,000lb (21t).
Cylinders: (3) 18½ x 28in (470 x 711mm).
Driving wheels: 79in (2,007mm).
Heating surface: 1,870sq ft ($174m^2$).
Steam pressure: 225psi ($15.8kg/cm^2$).
Grate area: 33½sq ft ($3.10m^2$).
Fuel: 18,000lb (8t).
Water: 5,000gall (6,000 US) ($23m^3$).
Adhesive weight: 141,000lbs (64t).
Total weight: 302,500lbs (137t).
Length overall: 67ft 6in (20,550mm).

The 450 or so broad-gauge (5ft 3in—1,600mm) locomotives of Ireland that existed between the wars were of amazing age and variety, divided as they were into over 80 classes. Some of the last single-wheelers to remain in service in the world were running between Waterford and Tramore as late as 1932. All the companies which did not cross the border into the six counties known as Northern Ireland, had been grouped into the Great Southern Railways in 1925. The economics of the GSR did not allow for any significant new construction of any type of locomotive, let alone new express passenger power.

Aside from a group of ten 4-6-0s inherited from the old Great Southern & Western Company, the GSR relied on 26 locomotives of South Eastern & Chatham Railway design, 2-6-0s put together from parts made at Woolwich Arsenal after World War I and obtained cheaply as surplus stores from the British government. Whilst the need was there for something better for the heavy Mail expresses on the hard road between Dublin and Cork, it seemed most unlikely that anything could be done.

As is well known, in Ireland the unlikely can always be relied upon to happen, but it was still a surprise when three large and handsome three-cylinder 4-6-0s, as up-to-date as any locomotive in Europe, emerged from the Inchicore Works of the Great Southern Railway. They had taper boiler-barrels, Belpaire fireboxes, three independent sets of Walschaert's valve gear and resembled very closely in appearance, size and layout the rebuilt "Royal Scot" class of the London Midland & Scottish Railway—at least they would have done if the rebuilt "Scot"s had then existed. The running numbers were 800 to 802 and the locomotives received the names of the Irish queens *Maeve, Macha* and *Tailte,* complete with nameplates in Erse script. They were the only express passenger locomotives to be built in an independent Ireland, all subsequent ones having been imported.

This illustrates the nice thought that quite small and agricultural nations can set out to design and build steam locomotives of top quality with success and economy; and also the less nice thought that the diesel locomotives which superseded steam can only be built economically by large industrial nations.

The "800" class had just time to prove itself in service that summer of 1939. *Maeve* was timed by O.S. Nock on a journey from Cork to Dublin, when extra carriages added for passengers from a trans-Atlantic liner had swelled the usual load of about 300 tons to 450. A remarkable

markable speed for the metre gauge. The tests were completely satisfactory but nothing came of the proposal and the speed limit remained at 45mph (72½km/h) Malayan Railway's trains, in those days anyway, made up for speed with comfort. Luxury comparable to the "Night Scotsman" or to the "Blue Train" was a feature of the "Golden Blowpipe" express; this used to come as a pleasant surprise to people making their first trip up country after arriving from Europe.

During the same period all Malayan locomotives were converted to burn oil instead of the local coal for which their wide fireboxes were eminently suitable. But there were no problems with the new fuel and Malayan rail travel suddenly became much cleaner.

In 1957 the first diesels arrived and by 1972 only half the Class "56" 4-6-2s were still in service. In 1981 the only steam locomotives left are a pair (No.564.33 *Jelebu* and No.564.36 *Temerloh*) stationed at Kuala Lumpur—where the main works of the system is situated—and used mainly to haul charter trains for tourists plus an occasional service run in some emergency.

Left: *Malayan Railways preserved class "56" 4-6-2 No.564 36* Temerloh *leaves Kuala Lumpur on a private excursion to Batu Caves in September 1979. This locomotive is one of two kept aside after the end of steam in Malaya. The Railway Administration can arrange special trains using one of these two steam locomotives at short notice and and at surprisingly modest cost.*

Below: *Malayan Railways class "0" 4-6-2 No.71* Kuala Lumpur *(later class "56" No.56201) in pre-1941 livery.*

23mph (37km/h) was maintained with this big load on the severe 1 in 60 (1.66 per cent) gradient out of Cork. Later in the journey the ability to run fast was demonstrated with 79mph (126km/h) near Newbridge.

A chronic shortage of fuel persisted long after the war and there seemed little time in the short interregnum before diesel traction took over to see more of the work of these fine locomotives. The first one to go was *Tailte*, withdrawn in 1957; the other two lingered on without seeing much use until 1964. *Maeve* is preserved in the Belfast Transport Museum.

Right: *The Irish Great Southern Railways (later Coras Iompair Eirann) 4-6-0 No.800* Maeve *as preserved. The locomotive is currently on display at the Irish Transport Museum in Belfast.*

FEF-2 Class 4-8-4 United States: Union Pacific Railroad (UP), 1939

Tractive effort: 63,800lb (28,950kg).
Axle load: 67,000lb (30.5t).
Cylinders: (2) 25 x 32in (635 x 813mm).
Driving wheels: 80in (2,032mm).
Heating surface: 4,225sq ft (393m²).
Superheater: 1,400sq ft (130m²).
Steam pressure: 300psi (21kg/cm²).
Grate area: 100sq ft (9.3m²).
Fuel: 50,000lb (23t).
Water: 19,600gall (23,500 US) (90m³).
Adhesive weight: 266,500lb (121t).
Total weight: 908,000lb (412t).
Length overall: 113ft 10in (34,696mm).

The origin of the class occurred during the late 1930s, when rising train loads began to overtax the 4-8-2s which were then the mainstay of UP passenger operations. One day in 1937 a "7000" class 4-8-2 had the temerity to demonstrate the lack of steaming power inherent in the type, on a train with UP President William Jeffers' business car on the rear. Even while the party was waiting out on the prairies for rescue, a dialogue by telegram went on with the American Locomotive Company (Alco) in far-off Schenectady, with a view to getting something better.

The result in due course was this superb class of 45 locomotives of which 20, numbered 800 to 819, were delivered in 1938. A further 15 (Nos.820 to 834) with larger wheels and cylinders as well as 14-wheel centipede tenders—instead of 12-wheel ones—came the following year and it is to these that the dimensions etc given above apply. This second batch was designated "FEF-2", the earlier ones becoming class "FEF-1". FEF stood for Four-Eight-Four!

A final batch of ten almost identical to the second one except for the use of some substitute materials, appeared in 1944. These were known as "FEF-3"s and were the last steam power supplied to UP. All the "800"s came from Alco.

The "800"s as a whole followed—like Northumbrian 108 years earlier—the standard recipe for success in having two outside cylinders only, the simplest possible arrangement. That king of passenger locomotive wheel arrangements, the "Northern" or 4-8-4, was adopted and misgivings originally felt regarding the suitability of eight-coupled wheels for very high speeds were found not to be justified. The negotiation of curves was made easier by the fitting of Alco's lateral motion device to the leading coupled wheels.

The basic simplicity of so many US locomotives was often spoilt by their designers being an easy touch for manufacturers of complicated accessories. The UP managed to resist most of them with the pleasing result that the locomotives had a delightfully elegant uncluttered appearance, unmarred by any streamline shroud. On the other hand, they rightly fell for such excellent simplifications as the cast-steel locomotive frame, which replaced many separate parts by one single casting. Another example was the use of a static exhaust steam injector instead of a steam-driven mechanical water-pump and feed water heater. A complication resisted by the UP was the provision of thermic syphons in the firebox; they held the view that on balance these quite common devices were more trouble than benefit. Even so, both common sense as well as Uncle Sam's rules meant power reversing gear and automatic stoking, whilst electric lighting was something that certainly paid off in helping "800" crews to see what they were doing.

Perhaps the most original feature and one which contributed a good deal to the success of the "800"s was the main motion. Aesthetically, the main rods were pure poetry but there was a great deal more to it than that. Because of the speeds and forces involved, current technology was taken beyond the then accepted limits; at the same time, the magnitude of the stresses to

Below: *Preserved Union Pacific "FEF-3" class 4-8-4 No.8444 with a special train run for hundreds of enthusiasts a year.*

Left: *An "FEF-1" class 4-8-4 of the Union Pacific Railroad ready to leave Denver, Colorado. These locomotives had the smaller 12-wheel tenders.*

Above: *The last steam locomotive built for the Union Pacific Railroad, class "FEF-3" 4-8-4 No.844 (renumbered to 8444 to avoid confusion with a diesel unit).*

which those whirling rods were subject are very different to evaluate with any degree of confidence.

What a triumph for the designers, then, that these lovely tapered coupling and connecting rods were a resounding success even though frequently moved at revolutions corresponding to running speeds above the 100mph (160km/h) mark. The main principle of the new design was that the pulls and thrusts were transmitted from the connecting rods—and hence to three out of the four pairs of wheels—by separate sleeve bearings instead of via the main crankpins in accordance with convention. The result was that separate knuckle-joints in the coupling rods were replaced by making the centre pair of rods forked at both ends and combining the roles of crank-pins and knuckle-pins.

The results were superb and there are many reports of speeds being run up to the design limit of 110mph (176km/h). After the war there was a period when coal supplies were affected by strikes and, in order to safeguard UP passenger operations, the "800"s were converted from coal to oil burning; a 6,000gall (27m³) tank was fitted in the bunker space. Otherwise only minor modifications were needed over many years of arduous service, a fact which is also much to the credit of the designers.

Normally the 4-8-4s were entrusted with the many expresses formed of the then conventional heavyweight stock, but the new engines' arrival on UP coincided with the introduction of diesel-electric streamline trains on much faster timings. In those early days the new form of motive power was not too reliable and "800" class locomotives frequently found themselves replacing a multi-unit diesel at the head end of one of UP's crack trains. They found no problem in making up time on the tight diesel schedules sufficient to offset extra minutes spent taking on water.

The last service passenger train hauled by an "800" was caused by such a failure; it occurred when in autumn 1958, the last one built took the "City of Los Angeles" over the last stretch of 145 miles (232km) from Grand Island into Omaha. No.844 gained time on the streamliner's schedule in spite of the crew's lack of recent experience with steam. A year later there came a time when all were out of service awaiting scrapping; it was a sad moment for all who admired these superb locomotives.

Since then No.844 (renumbered 8444 to avoid confusion with a diesel unit) has been put back into service by a publicity-conscious Union Pacific and frequently performs for her fans. No.814 is displayed across the Mississippi river from Omaha, at Dodge Park, Council Bluffs, and Nos.833 and 838 are also believed still to be in existence, the latter as a source of spares for No.8444.

Below: *A second section of "The Gold Coast" train behind class "FEF-1" (which appeared before "FEF-2"s) 4-8-4 No.826.*

Class 12 4-4-2 **Belgium:** Belgian National Railways (SNCB), 1939

Tractive effort: 26,620lb (12,079kg).
Axle load: 52,000lb (23.4t).
Cylinders: (2) 18⅞ x 28⅜in (480 x 720mm).
Driving wheels: 82¾in (2,100mm).
Heating surface: 1,729sq ft (161m²).
Superheater: 678sq ft (63m²).
Steam pressure: 256psi (18kg/cm²).
Grate area: 39.8sq ft (3.7m²).
Fuel: 17,500lb (8t).
Water: 5,280gall (6,300 US) (24m³).
Adhesive weight: 101,000lb (45.8t).
Total weight*: 188,500lb (89.5t).
Length overall: 69ft 6¼in (21,190mm).
*(*engine only without tender)*

Most modern steam locomotives trace their descent more from *Northumbrian* than *Planet;* but here is an exception; and, moreover, one that was good enough for a world record for scheduled start-to-stop speed. Whilst the Belgian class "12" 4-4-2s were totally conventional as regards principles, the layout of their machinery was unusual if not unique—but then what other than original thinking would be expected of a country that produced both Alfred Belpaire and Egide Walschaert?

The concept was to operate frequent lightweight high-speed

Above and below: *Two views of the Belgian National Railways' class "12" high-speed 4-4-2 locomotives, built in 1938 to haul lightweight expresses between Brussels and Ostend.*

520 Class 4-8-4 **Australia:** South Australian Government Railways (SAR), 1943

Tractive effort: 32,600lb (14,800kg).
Axle load: 35,000lb (16t).
Cylinders: (2) 20½ x 28in (521 x 711mm).
Driving wheels: 66in (1,676mm).
Heating surface: 2,454sq ft (228m²).
Superheater: 651sq ft (60.5m²).
Steam pressure: 215psi (15.1kg/cm²).
Grate area: 45sq ft (4.2m²).
Fuel: 22,000lb (10t).
Water: 9,000gall (10,800 US) (41m³).
Adhesive weight: 140,000lb (63.5t).
Total weight: 449,500lb (204t).
Length overall: 87ft 4½in (26,622mm).

trains, of three cars only, over the 71 miles (121km) between Brussels and Ostend in the even hour, including a stop at Bruges. Between Brussels and Bruges the timing was to be 46 minutes, giving an average speed of 75.4 mph (121.3km/h). The speed limit of this almost level route was specially raised for these trains to 87mph (140km/h). It was decided that four coupled wheels were adequate, whilst the power needed for the high speeds contemplated was best provided by a wide firebox. A leading bogie was certainly desirable and, to avoid oscillations inside cylinders were preferred, made reasonably accessible by the use of bar rather than plate frames. All this added up to the world's last 4-4-2s as well as the world's last inside-cylinder express locomotives. The tenders were second-hand, with streamlining added, and the locomotives were built by Messrs Cockerill of Seraing, Belgium.

Alas, the high-speed trains only ran for a few months before war broke out in September 1939. One of the 4-4-2s (No.1203) has, however, survived and is preserved at the SNCB locomotive depot at Louvain. The best timing by electric traction today between Brussels and Ostend is 11 minutes longer with one extra stop—an 18 per cent *increase* in journey time when steam gives way to electric traction is possibly yet another record achieved by these remarkable locomotives.

Above: *SNCB Class "12" 4-4-2 No.12.004, one of the world's last 4-4-2s.*

South Australia certainly became 4-8-4 country in 1943 when the ten "500" class were supplemented by twelve "520" class. But there the resemblance ends because the "500"s had a lot of wheels in order to give brute force but the "520"s were many-wheeled so that they could tread delicately on the light 60lb/yd (30kg/m) rails of the remote branches in the State. This they did with great success.

All the locomotives were built at the SAGR's Islington shops between 1943 and 1947. The style of their streamlining was clearly based on that of the "TI" class 4-4-4-4s of the American Pennsylvania Railroad. Unlike the contemporary "TI"s though, they were starkly conventional under their shrouds—and, also unlike the "TI"s had useful lives of up to 18 years. In 1948 all the locomotives of this class were converted to burn oil fuel.

Two "520"s are preserved; No.520 *Sir Malcolm Barclay-Harvey* is occasionally run. The other, No.523 *Essington Lewis,* is displayed at the Australian Railway Historical Society's site at Mile End near Adelaide.

Left: *Showing a fine plume of smoke, a "520" class 4-8-4 makes good time with an enthusiasts' special.*

Right: *One of the preserved class "520" locomotives* Sir Malcolm Barclay-Harvey *as built in 1943.*

Class C38 4-6-2

Australia:
New South Wales Government Railways (NSWGR), 1943

Tractive effort: 36,200lb (16,425kg).
Axle load: 51,000lb (23.5t).
Cylinders: (2) 21½ x 26in (546 x 660mm).
Driving wheels: 69in (1,753mm).
Heating surface: 2,614sq ft (243m²).
Superheater: 755sq ft (70.2m²).
Steam pressure: 245psi (17.25kg/cm²).
Grate area: 47sq ft (4.4m²).
Fuel: 31,500lb (14.5t).
Water: 8,100gall (9,700 US) (37m³).
Adhesive weight: 150,500lb (68.5t).
Total weight: 451,000lb (205t).
Length overall: 76ft 4½in (23,279mm).

The last and best of Australian express passenger locomotives were the thirty "C-38" Pacifics of the New South Wales Government Railways, built between 1943 and 1949. They had been planned before the war but the majority were not completed until after it was over. The first five, built by the Clyde Engineering Co of Sydney, were streamlined. The remainder were not streamlined and built at the railways own shops at Cardiff and Eveleigh. The designers had not lost sight of the fact that simplicity was the steam locomotive's greatest asset and that its greatest handicap was the manual labour involved in keeping it running. Hence only two cylinders, valve gear outside, all mounted on a cast steel locomotive frame with integral cylinders, air reservoirs, brackets, saddles, stays etc. All axles had roller bearings and there were rocking and dumping elements in the grate, power reverse and air sanding.

The "C-38" class could give

Above: *Class "C38" 4-6-2 No. 38.01 hauling the "Western Endeavour" transcontinental special en route from Sydney to Perth. Note extra water tanks in the train.*

Right: *4-6-2 No.38.06 on Sydney to Brisbane Day Express at Hawkesbury.*

Class T1 4-4-4-4

United States:
Pennsylvania Railroad (PRR), 1942

Tractive effort: 64,700lb (29,300kg).
Axle load: 69,000lb (31.5t).
Cylinders: (4) 19¾ x 26in (501 x 660mm).
Driving wheels: 80in (2,032mm).
Heating surface: 4,209sq ft (391.0m²).
Superheater: 1,430sq ft (131.9m²).
Steam pressure: 300psi (21.1kg/cm²).
Grate area: 92sq ft (8.5m²).
Fuel: 85,000lb (38.5t).
Water: 16,000gall (19,000 US) (72.5m³).
Adhesive weight: 273,000lb (124t).
Total weight: 954,000lb (432.7t).
Length overall: 122ft 10in (37,440mm).

In the 1930s there was a notable increase in the use of 4-8-4 locomotives in the United States, both for freight and passenger service. There were, however, some problems with the very high piston thrust in these engines, and the resultant stresses in crank pins, while the balancing of the heavy reciprocating parts for high speeds also caused difficulties. All the problems could be solved, but R.P. Johnson, chief engineer of The Baldwin Locomotive Works suggested that they could be avoided by dividing the driving wheels into two groups in a single rigid frame, with separate cylinders for each, thus making the engine into a 4-4-4-4. Compared with the 4-8-4, piston loads were reduced, and it was easier to provide valves of adequate size, but the rigid wheelbase was increased by the space required to accommodate the second set of cylinders. This increase was in itself sufficient to discourage some roads from further consideration of the proposal.

The first road to build a duplex engine was the Baltimore and Ohio, which made a 4-4-4-4 with an experimental water-tube firebox in 1937, but it was the Pennsylvania which first built a locomotive with a conventional boiler to this layout. In 1937, with the principal passenger services still worked by the "K4" Pacifics of 1914 design, the road's engineers embarked on the design of a locomotive to haul 1,090 tons at 100mph (160km/h), which was well beyond the capacity of any existing 4-8-4.

Johnson put the case for the duplex engine, and this appealed to the PRR men, but for the size of the engine required 16 wheels were insufficient, and the PRR took one of its most spectacular steps by adopting the 6-4-4-6 wheel arrangement. The locomotive was designed and built at Altoona, and it was the largest rigid-framed passenger engine ever built. It was numbered 6100 and classified "S1", and with driving wheels 84in (2,134mm) in diameter, a grate area of 132sq ft (12.3m²), and a boiler some 15 per cent greater than that of any 4-8-4, it was essentially an engine for developing high power at high speed. With a streamlined casing design by the fashionable stylist Raymond Loewy, its appearance was a striking as its dimensions.

No.6100 appeared early in 1939, but it spent much of 1939 and 1940 on display at the New York World Fair and it was not until December 1940 that it entered revenue service. Although intended for use throughout the main line from Harrisburg to Chicago, in the event its great length led to its prohibition from the curved lines in the east, and this prohibition was further extended because the maximum axle load came out at 73,880lb (33.5t), against the figure of 67,500lb (30.5t) which had been stipulated to the designer.

As a result the engine was limited to the 283-mile Crestline to Chicago division, on which it proved capable of hauling 1225 tons at an average speed of 66mph (106km/h). With smaller loads it achieved very high speeds, and although the PRR and its official locomotive historian were silent on the subject, it was widely believed to have exceeded 120mph (193km/h) on many occasions. There were, however, problems, particularly with slipping, not helped by the fact that only 46 per cent of the total engine weight was carried on the driving wheels, compared with 65 per cent in a "K4" Pacific.

Despite the limited and variable experience gained so far with the "S1", the PRR ordered two more duplex locomotives from Baldwin in July, 1940. The performance requirement was reduced to the haulage of 880 tons at 100mph (160km/h) and this could be met by a 4-4-4-4, with 80in (2,032mm) driving wheels, and a grate area of 92ft (8.5m²). The maximum

Above: *Class "T1" No.5537 leaving Fort Wayne, Indiana, with the eastbound "Fast Mail" express en route from Chicago to New York.*

substantially higher power output than the "C-36" class 4-6-0s which the larger engines replaced. They were capable of taking the Melbourne Express loaded to 450 tons unassisted up the 1 in 75 (1.33 per cent) inclines of the main line to Albury. Their heavy axle-loading limited them to the principal routes of the state, but this still left ample scope for the class to perform with great ability on the majority of New South Wales' top passenger trains.

Withdrawal began in the mid-1960s and the class just lingered on in normal service until 1970. Several have been preserved and one or two are occasionally put into steam to give pleasure. The longest run of this kind ever made—or ever likely to be made—was when No.38.01 crossed the continent from Sydney to Perth and back on the "Western Endeavour" special train, to celebrate the day in 1970 when 4ft 8½in (1,435mm) metals became available over the whole 2,461 miles (3,961km) between the two cities.

axle load was 69,250lb (31.4t) compared with 73,880lb (33.5t) of the "S1". The two engines, classified "T1" and numbered 6110 and 6111 differed only in that 6111 had a booster. Apart from the inclusion of certain PRR standard fittings, Baldwin was given a free hand in the design. Franklin's poppet valves were fitted at PRR insistence, as these had produced a notable increase in the power of "K4" Pacific. Roller-bearings, light-weight motion, and disc wheels were amongst the modern equipment and the engine was clothed in a casing designed by Raymond Loewy, but quite different from that of No.6100. They were delivered in April and May 1942.

In 1944, No.6110 was tested on the Altoona testing plant and it produced a cylinder horsepower of 6,550 at 85mph (137 km/h) with 25 per cent cut-off. In service the engines worked over the 713 miles between Harrisburg and Chicago, but despite these long runs they built up mileage slowly and spent an undue amount of time under repair. Slipping was again the main trouble, although in these engines 54 per cent of the total weight was adhesive.

At this point the road took a fateful step. Ignoring its old policy of testing and modifying a prototype until it was entirely satisfactory, it ordered 50 almost identical engines. Nos.5500-24 were built at Altoona and 5525-49 by the Baldwin Works and delivered between late 1945 and early 1946.

With a shorter rigid wheelbase than the "S1" and a smaller maximum axle load, the "T1"s were allowed over the full steam-worked part of the PRR main line from Harrisburg to Chicago, and they worked through over the whole 713 miles. They took over all the passenger work on this route, including the 73.1mph (117.5km/h) schedule of the Chicago Arrow over the 123 miles (198km) from Fort Wayne to Gary, and four other runs at more than 70mph (112.5km/h). At their best they were magnificent, with numerous records of 100mph (160km/h) with 910-ton trains, including a pass-to-pass average of 100mph over 69 miles of generally falling grades with a load of 1,045 tons. They rode smoothly, and when all was well they were popular with the enginemen, but slipping remained a major hazard, not only slipping at starting but violent slipping of one set of wheels at high speed.

Below: *Pennsylvania Railroad class "T1" 4-4-4-4 duplex locomotive No.5511, built at Altoona.*

At this time the motive power department of the PRR was at a low ebb, both in equipment and in morale, and compared with the simple and well-known "K4" Pacifics, the "T1" was a complex box of tricks, particularly its valve gear. Maintenance of the big engines proved to be a difficult job, and their appearances on their booked workings became less and less regular. The faithful "K4"s were out again in force.

Various modifications were made to ease maintenance, mainly by the removal of parts of the casing, but one engine was rebuilt with piston valves. Eight engines had their cylinder diameter reduced in an attempt to reduce the tendency to slip but the problem was never solved. As time passed, the worsening financial state of the railroad led to the ordering of mainline diesels.

It was intended that the "T1"s should have a full economic life before succumbing to diesels. In the event, the serious and intractable problems with them had the effect of accelerating dieselisation, and by the end of 1949 most of them were out of service. So ended the most expensive locomotive fiasco of the century.

Challenger Class 4-6-6-4

United States: Union Pacific Railroad (UP), 1942

Tractive effort: 97,400lb (44,100kg).
Axle load: 68,000lb (31t).
Cylinders: (4) 21 x 32in (533 x 813mm).
Driving wheels: 69in (1,753mm).
Heating surface: 4,642sq ft ($431m^2$).
Superheater: 1,741sq ft ($162m^2$).
Steam pressure: 280psi ($19.7kg/cm^2$).
Grate area: 132sq ft ($12.3m^2$).
Fuel: 56,000lb (25.4t).
Adhesive weight: 406,000lb (184.3t).
Total weight: 1,071,000lb (486t).
Length overall: 121ft 11in (37,160mm).

On virtually all counts this locomotive was the largest, heaviest, strongest and most powerful one which ever regularly handled express passenger trains. Its existence was only possible because it was an articulated locomotive, that is, there was a hinge in the middle.

Articulated locomotives were introduced early in locomotive history, but it was not until the full flowering of the narrow-gauge railway late in the 19th century that they were built in quantity. Many designs were tried, but the most popular was that of Anatole Mallet, a French consulting engineer. Mallet was an early advocate of compounding, and from 1876 a number of two-cylinder compound locomotives were built to his designs. In 1884, to cater for larger locomotives, he proposed an articulated design in which the rear set of driving wheels were mounted in the main frame, which supported the firebox and the rear part of the boiler. The front set of driving wheels were in a separate frame, the rear end of which was hinged to the front of the main frame. The front of the boiler rested on the hinged frame, and as the boiler swung across this frame on curves, a sliding support was needed. The high-pressure cylinders drove the rear set of wheels and the low-pressure cylinders the leading set. High-pressure steam was thus entirely on the rigid part of the locomotive, and hinged steam pipes were needed only for the steam to and from the low-pressure cylinders.

The European engines built to this design were mostly for narrow-gauge railways. However, in 1903 the first American Mallet was built. Here the aim was to get the maximum adhesion, and as there were difficulties in designing a locomotive with six driving axles in a rigid frame, articulation was an attractive proposition at this stage. The American engine was an 0-6-6-0 built for the Baltimore and Ohio Railroad. It was the largest locomotive in the world and thereafter that distinction was always held by an American member of the Mallet family.

More American Mallets followed, at first mainly for banking duties, but then for road work. However, with their huge low-pressure cylinders and the tortuous steam pipes between the cylinders, these engines were unsuitable for speeds above 30-40mph (40-50km/h). Above these speeds oscillations of the front frame developed leading to heavy wear on locomotive and track.

In 1924 the Chesapeake and Ohio Railroad ordered twenty 2-8-8-2 locomotives with four simple expansion cylinders. Although the main reason for this was that the loading gauge of C&O could not accommodate the large low-pressure cylinders of a compound, the change brought the further benefit that more adequate steam pipes could be provided, and the engines were capable of higher speeds. Some intensive work was needed to develop flexible joints suitable for carrying high-pressure steam to the leading cylinders.

From this time onwards American interest centred on the four-cylinder simple Mallet and successive improvements were made which upgraded the type from banking duties to main line freight work and, eventually, on a few roads, to express passenger

Below: *"Challenger" class 4-6-6-4 No.3985 at Cheyenne awaiting restoration to working order in 1981.*

work. Amongst changes introduced were longer travel valves and more complete balancing of the moving parts, but most important were the changes made to the connection between the leading frame and the main frame, and to lateral control of the leading wheels. It was these latter alterations which eliminated the violent oscillations which had limited the speed of earlier Mallets.

The Union Pacific acquired 70 compound 2-8-8-0s with 59in (1,500mm) driving wheels between 1918 and 1924. These were essentially hard-slogging, modest speed engines and in 1926, for faster freight trains, the railroad introduced a class which was remarkable in several respects. It was a three-cylinder 4-12-2 with 67in (1,702mm) driving wheels, and was the first class with this wheel arrangement. It was also one of the few American three cylinder engines and the only one to be built in quantity, a total of 88 being built. They were highly successful, but with their long rigid wheelbase and heavy motion they were limited to 45mph (72km/h), and with growing road competition a twelve-coupled engine was needed capable of higher speeds than the 4-12-2.

Experience with the compound Mallets had led to the decision to convert them to simple expansion and the way was then set for the railroad to make another important step forward in 1936 by ordering 40 simple-expansion 4-6-6-4s with 69in (1,753mm) driving wheels. They were numbered from 3900 to 3939 and designated "Challenger". The leading bogie gave much better side control than a pony truck and the truck under the firebox assisted the fitting of a very large grate. The engines were distributed widely over the UP system and were used mainly on fast freight trains, but the last six of the engines were ordered specifically for passenger work. The most obvious difference between these earlier "Challenger" locomotives and those depicted in the art-work above was the provision of much smaller 12-wheel tenders. Much of the coal which the UP used came from mines which the railroad owned.

In 1942 pressure of wartime traffic brought the need for more large engines and the construction of Challengers was resumed, a total of 65 more being built up to 1944. A number of changes were made, notably an enlargement of the grate from 108sq ft ($10.0m^2$) to 132sq ft ($12.3m^2$), cast steel frames in place of built-up frames, and an increase in the boiler pressure to 255psi ($17.9kg/cm^2$) accompanied by a reduction in cylinder size of one inch, which left the tractive effort unchanged.

A less obvious but more fundamental change from the earlier engines was in the pivot between the leading unit and the main frame. In the earlier engines there were both vertical and horizontal hinges, but in the new engines, following the practice adopted in the "Big Boy" 4-8-8-4s, there was no horizontal hinge. The vertical hinge was now arranged to transmit a load of several tons from the rear unit to the front one, thus evening out the distribution of weight between the two sets of driving wheels, and thereby reducing the tendency of the front drivers to slip, which had been a problem with the earlier engines. With no horizontal hinge, humps and hollows in the track were now looked after by the springs of each individual axle, as in a normal rigid locomotive.

All the engines were built as coal-burners, but in 1945 five of them were converted to oil-burning for use on passenger trains on the Oregon and Washington lines. Trouble was experienced with smoke obstructing the driver's view so these five engines were fitted with long smoke deflectors, and they were also painted in the two-tone grey livery which was used for passenger engines for a number of years, as depicted above.

Above: *Union Pacific's "Challenger" 4-6-6-4 No.3964 takes on coal from an overhead coaling plant.*

A favourite racing ground for these monsters was the main line, mostly across the desert, between Salt Lake City, Las Vegas and Los Angeles, where they regularly ran at up to 70mph (112km/h) on passenger trains.

In 1952 coal supplies were interrupted by a strike and a crash programme for further conversions to oil-burning was put in hand, but the strike ended after eight engines had been converted. Rather perversely, in 1950 ten of the original series had been converted back to coal-firing, but in less than a year had been changed yet again to oil. Dieselisation gradually narrowed the field of operation of the "Challengers", but they continued to take a major share of steam working up to 1958 when the delivery of a large batch of diesels rendered them redundant.

The numbering of the Challengers was extremely complicated due to the practice of renumbering engines when they were converted from coal-burning to oil-burning or vice versa. Thus the original engines were renumbered from 3900-39 to 3800-39 and the three batches of the second series were numbered successively 3950-69, 3975-99 and 3930-49, so that 3930-9 were used twice but 3970-4 not at all. Furthermore, eighteen of the second series which were converted to oil-burning were renumbered from 3700-17.

Several other roads bought engines of the 4-6-6-4 wheel arrangement, generally similar to the "Challenger" and they also were used on some passenger work, but it was on the UP that the articulated locomotive had its most important application to passenger work, and a "Challenger" hauling 20 or more coaches was a regular sight. Fortunately one of the engines, No.3985 was preserved as a static exhibit, but in 1981 it was restored to working order, making it by far the largest working steam engine in the world.

Below: *Union Pacific Railroad "Challenger" 4-6-6-4 depicted in the two-tone grey passenger livery used in the late 1940s.*

Class J 4-8-4

United States: Norfolk & Western Railway (N&W), 1941

Tractive effort: 80,000lb (36,287kg).
Axle load: 72,000lb (33t).
Cylinders: (2) 27 x 32in (686 x 813mm).
Driving wheels: 70in (1,778mm).
Heating surface: 5,271sq ft (490m²).
Superheater: 2,177sq ft (202m²).
Steam pressure: 300psi (21kg/cm²).
Grate area: 107.5sq ft (10m²).
Fuel: 70,000lb (31.75t).
Water: 16,700gall (20,000 US) (76m³).
Adhesive weight: 288,000lb (131t).
Total weight: 873,000lb (396t).
Length overall: 100ft 11in (30,759mm).

"Of all the words of tongue and pen, the saddest are 'it might have been'." In the USA, there was just one small (but prosperous) railroad that, on a long-term basis, came near to fighting off the diesel invasion. This was the Norfolk & Western Railway, with headquarters in Roanoke, Virginia, and a main line then stretching 646 miles (1,033km) from ocean piers at Norfolk, Virginia, to Columbus in Ohio. It had branches to collect coal from every mine of importance across one of the world's greatest coalfields. In the end steam lost the battle on the N&W and big-time steam railroading finally vanished from the United States—so dealing a fatal blow all over the world to the morale of those who maintained that dieselisation was wrong. But the Norfolk & Western's superb steam locomotives came close to victory; so let us see how it was done.

The principle adopted was to exploit fully all the virtues of steam while, rather obviously, seeking palliatives for its disadvantages. It was also a principle of N&W management that the maximum economy lay in maintaining the steam fleet in first-class condition, with the aid of premises, tools and equipment to match. All this is well illustrated by the story of the "J" class, Norfolk & Western's own design (and own build) of express passenger super-locomotive.

Around 1940 the company's locomotive chiefs felt that it should be possible to have something better than the standard United States Railroad Association's design of 4-8-2 upon which N&W passenger expresses then relied. Very wisely, they accepted that Robert Stephenson had got the thermal and most of the mechanical principles right with the *Northumbrian,* but what needed attention was the cost and time involved in servicing and maintenance. This meant, for example, roller bearings to the axleboxes and throughout the motion, while an unparalleled number of subsidiary bearings, over 200 in fact, were automatically fed with oil by a mechanical lubricator with a 24-gallon (110-litre) tank, enough for 1,500 miles (2,400km). Even the bearings of the bell were automatically lubricated!

There was another large lubricator to feed high-temperature oil for the steam cylinders; this is normal but the feeds from this lubricator also ran to the steam cylinders of the water and air pumps and the stoker engine. Hence the labour involved in filling separate lubricators at each of these was avoided. The basic simplicity of the two-cylinder arrangement with Baker's valve gear also had the effect of minimising maintenance costs.

Huge tenders enabled calls at fuelling points to be reduced to a minimum. Together with the usual modern US features such as a cast-steel locomotive frame, all these things added up to a locomotive which could run 15,000 miles (24,000km) per month, needed to visit the repair shops only every 1½ years and had a hard-to-believe record of reliability.

During the period when steam and diesel were battling for supremacy on United States railroads, it was typically the case that brand new diesel locomotives were being maintained in brand new depots while the steam

Below: *A class "J" 4-8-4 of the Norfolk & Western Railway takes a fast express passenger train round a curve in the hills of Virginia.*

Above: *The superb lines of the Roanoke-built new Norfolk & Western class "J" 4-8-4 are exemplified in this artwork.*

Top: *New class "J" 4-8-4 No.605, built at Roanoke in 1943, heads the streamliner "Powhattan Arrow".*

Above: *Another "J" built at Roanoke, No.607. Six of these locomotives originally ran unstreamlined.*

engines with which they were being compared were worn out and looked after in tumble-down sheds. Often much of the roof would be missing while equipment was also worn out and obsolete. The filth would be indescribable.

On the Norfolk & Western Railroad during the 1950s, locomotives were new and depots almost clinically clean, modern, well-equipped and well arranged. A "J" class could be fully serviced, greased, lubricated, cleared of ash, tender filled with thousands of gallons of water and many tons of coal, all in under an hour. The result was efficiency, leading to Norfolk & Western's shareholders receiving 6 per cent on their money, while those of the neighbouring and fully-dieselised and electrified Pennsylvania Railroad had to be content with ½ per cent.

In the end, though, the problems of being the sole United States railroad continuing with steam on any scale began to tell. Even a do-it-yourself concern like N&W normally bought many components from specialists and one by one these firms were going out of business. In 1960 this and other factors necessitated the replacement of steam and the "J"s plus all the other wonderful locomotives of this excellent concern were retired.

One feels that the "J"s were the best of all the 4-8-4s, but that is a matter of opinion; in matters of fact, though, they had certainly the highest tractive effort and, as well, the class included the last main-line steam passenger locomotives to be constructed in the United States. They were built as follows, all at N&W's Roanoke shops: Nos. 600 to 603, 1941; 604, 1942; 605 to 610, 1943; 611 to 613, 1950.

No.604 had a booster engine on the trailing truck.

Nos.605 to 610 were originally unstreamlined and ran for two years as chunky but attractive locomotives in plain garb.

In spite of having driving wheels which were on the small side for a passenger locomotive, speeds up to 90mph (144km/h) were recorded in service and 110mph (176km/h) on test. The latter was achieved with a 1,000 ton trailing load of 15 cars and represented the development of a remarkable 6,000hp in the cylinders.

With such power and speed capability available, the fact that overall speeds were not high reflected the hilly nature of the country served. For example, the coach streamliner "Powhattan Arrow" needed 15hr 45min for the 676 miles (1,082km) from Norfolk, Virginia to Cincinatti, Ohio, an average speed of 43mph (69km/h). Whilst this train was not a heavy one, the overnight "Pocahontas" which carried through cars from Norfolk to Chicago via Cincinatti and Pennsylvania Railroad, could load up to 1,000 tons which had to be handled on ruling grades up to 1 in 62 (1.6 per cent).

Norfolk & Western also acted as a "bridge road" and their 4-8-4s hauled limiteds such as the "Tennessean" and the "Pelican"—the original Chattanooga Choo-choos—between Lynchburg and Bristol, on the famous journeys from New York to Chattanooga and points beyond. No.611 was preserved at the Transportation Museum in Roanoke, Virginia, but in 1982 it was being restored to working order.

2900 Class 4-8-4

United States:
Atchison, Topeka & Santa Fe Railway (AT&SF), 1944

Tractive effort: 79,960lb (36,270kg).
Axle load: 74,000lb (33.5t).
Cylinders: (2) 28 x 32in (711 x 813mm).
Driving wheels: 80in (2,032mm).
Heating surface: 5,313sq ft ($494m^2$).
Superheater: 2,366sq ft ($220m^2$).
Steam pressure: 300psi ($21kg/cm^2$).
Grate area: 108sq ft ($10m^2$).
Fuel (oil): 5,830galls (7,000 US) ($26.5m^3$).
Water: 20,400gall (24,500 US) ($93m^3$).
Adhesive weight: 294,000lb (133t).
Total weight: 961,000lb (436t).
Length overall: 120ft 10in (36,830mm).

Above: *Atchison, Topeka & Santa Fe Railway class "3700" 4-8-4 No.3769 climbing the Cajon Pass, California, with the first part of the "Grand Canyon Limited", in June 1946. Note that the chimney extension is in the fully raised position.*

The Atchison, Topeka & Santa Fe Railway (Santa Fe for short) was remarkable in that it was the *only* railroad company which connected Chicago with California. Odder still perhaps that it was named after three small places in the southern Mid-West, while so many railroads with Pacific in their titles never got there. Even now it remains as it was in the great days of steam—solvent, forward-looking and with its physical plant in first-class condition. With a main line stretching for 2,224 miles (3,580km) across America (or 2,547 miles (4,100km) if you let the Santa Fe take you as far as San Francisco Bay) together, once upon a time, with some of the world's finest and most prestigious passenger services, you might think that the company's steam power must have been remarkable—and you would not be wrong.

Nearly all Santa Fe's steam locomotives came from Baldwin of Philadelphia. At one time it included briefly such exotic items as 2-4-6-2 and 2-6-6-2 superheated express Mallet locomotives with 73 and 69in (1,854 and 1,753mm) diameter driving wheels respectively. Six of the class of 44 of the 2-6-6-2s even had *boilers* with a hinge in the middle! Experience with these and a few other wild ideas brought about a firm resolve to stick to the Stephenson path in the future and almost without exception all subsequent steam locomotives built for Santa Fe were "straight" (ie non-articulated) "simple" (ie non-compound) and with two cylinders only. The results of the slow-and-steady policy were magnificent.

The Santa Fe main line crossed the famous Raton Pass in the New Mexico with its 1 in 28½ (3½ per cent) gradient, as well as the less impossible but still severe Cajon Pass in eastern California. East of Kansas City across the level prairies 4-6-2s and 4-6-4s sufficed until the diesels came, but for the heavily graded western lines Santa Fe in 1927 took delivery of its first 4-8-4s. It was only by a small margin that the Northern Pacific Railroad could claim the first of the type as its own. These early 4-8-4s (Nos. 3751 to 3764) were remarkable for having 30in (762mm) diameter cylinders, the largest both in bore or volume in any passenger locomotive, apart from compounds.

This first batch burnt coal, subsequent 4-8-4s being all oil-burners. More 4-8-4s (Nos.3765 to 3775) came in 1938 and a further batch was built in 1941. The final group (Nos.2900 to 2929) on which the particulars given in this description are based, were constructed in wartime. Quite fortuitously, they also became the heaviest straight passenger locomotives ever built, because high-tensile steel alloys were in short supply and certain parts—in particular the main coupling and connecting rods—had to be much more massive when designed to be made from more ordinary metal. They managed this feat by a very small margin, but when those immense 16-wheel tenders were included and loaded there were no close rivals to this title. The big tenders were fitted to the last two batches; and as well as being the heaviest passenger locomotives ever built, they were also the longest.

It must be said that Santa Fe would have preferred diesels to the superb last batch of 4-8-4s, but wartime restrictions prevented this. The company had been early into the diesel game with the now legendary streamlined light-weight de luxe "Super Chief" train, introduced in 1937, as well as the equally celebrated coach-class streamliner "El Capitan". But thirty years ago there were still trains such as the "California Limited", "The Scout" and the "Grand Canyon Limited" and, of course, the original "Chief", still formed of standard equipment. They were often then run in two or more sections each and all needed steam power at the head end.

Apart from the early diesel incursions, these 4-8-4s that totalled 65 ruled the Chicago-Los Angeles main line from Kansas City westwards. It was normal practice to roster them to go the whole distance (1,790 miles—2,880km—via Amarillo or 1,760 miles—2,830km—via the Raton Pass); in respect of steam traction these were by far the longest distances ever to be scheduled to run without change of locomotive. Speeds up in the 90-100 mph (140-160km/h) range were both permitted and achieved.

This journey was not made without changing crews. In this respect feather-bedding union rules based on the capacity of the "American" 4-4-0s of fifty years earlier applied and crews were changed 12 times during the 34 hour run. Water was taken at 16 places and fuel nearly as often, in spite of the enormous tenders.

Below: *Santa Fe "2900" class 4-8-4. Note the chimney extension in the raised position, the handsome tapered connecting rods and the enormous tender with two eight-wheel bogies. Eight of these magnificent engines survive, but none is now steamable.*

Above: *Atchison Topeka & Santa Fe Railway class "3700" 4-8-4 No.3787 hauling the streamline cars of the legendary "Chief" express amongst the mountains of the Cajon Pass in California. This train ran daily over the 2,225 miles (3,580km) of Santa Fe metals between Chicago and Los Angeles.*

Left: *The impressive front end of a Santa Fe "2900" class 4-8-4.*

These magnificent examples of the locomotive builder's art were conventional in all main respects. One unusual feature was the 'hot hat' smoke-stack extension shown on the picture above; absence of overbridges and tunnels over many miles of the Santa Fe route meant that this could be raised for long periods with beneficial effect in keeping smoke and steam clear of the cab. Another detail concerned a modification to the Walschaert's valve gear on some of the 4-8-4s. To reduce the amount of swing—and consequent inertia forces—needed on the curved links, an intermediate lever was introduced into the valve rod. This was so arranged as to increase the amount of valve travel for a given amount of link swing.

Santa Fe was generous in handing out superannuated 4-8-4s as not always properly appreciated gifts to various on-line communities. These included Modesto and San Bernadino, California; Pueblo, Colorado; Fort Madison, Iowa; Kingsman, Arizona; Alburquerque, New Mexico; and Wichita, Kansas. No.2903 is displayed in the Chicago Museum of Science and Industry, while No.2925 is still in the roundhouse at Belen, New Mexico. There was a rumour a year or so ago that Santa Fe might have intentions of entering the steam-for-pleasure business with this locomotive, like neighbour Union Pacific, but nothing came of the proposal.

West Country Class 4-6-2

Great Britain: Southern Railway (SR), 1946

Tractive effort: 31,046lb (14,083kg).
Axle load: 44,500lb (20.2t).
Cylinders: (3) 16⅜in x 24in (416 x 610mm).
Driving wheels: 74in (1,879mm).
Heating surface: 2,122sq ft (197m²).
Superheater: 545sq ft (50.6m²).
Steam pressure: 280psi (19.7kg/cm²).
Grate area: 38.25sq ft (3.55m²).
Fuel: 11,000lb (5t).
Water: 5,500gall (6,600 US) (25m³).
Adhesive weight: 131,000lb (59.5t).
Total weight: 304,000lb (138t).
Length overall: 67ft 4¾in (20,542mm).

Above: *"Merchant Navy" class 4-6-2 No.34002* Union Castle. *Note red-and-cream coaches of early BR days.*

When Oliver Bullied from the London & North Eastern Railway was appointed Chief Mechanical Engineer of the Southern Railway in 1937 he affirmed his intention of contributing a major forward step in the art of steam locomotive design. He was a man of charm, ability, education and integrity and had never allowed the many years spent under Sir Nigel Gresley to blunt an extremely keen and original mind. The result so far as express passenger traffic was concerned was the building of 140 4-6-2s, which collectively were some of the most remarkable machines ever to be seen on rails. Bullied's locomotives were amazingly good in some ways yet almost unbelievably bad in others.

He began from the premise (often forgotten by others) that the prime task of the Chief Mechanical Engineer (C.M.E.) was to build locomotives which could run the trains to time, regardless of quality of coal, bad weather and the presence on board of the least skilled of qualified engine crews. On the whole he succeeded, except perhaps for the need of a certain specialised expertise on the part of the driver; the fireman, on the other hand, just needed to throw the coal in.

Bullied also went to considerable pains to meet what should be the C.M.E.'s second objective: that the first objective should be met at minimum cost. Here one must say that despite the very considered and original approach adopted, these locomotives were disastrously more expensive than their rivals in first cost, maintenance cost and fuel consumption.

A third objective was achieved, however. Bullied belied his name by being most considerate toward the men who worked for him. He was an example to many of his peers through the care he took to add a number of far from costly features to the locomotives in aid of the convenience and comfort of his crews. They repaid him by doing their very best with the strange and unfamiliar engines he created.

Bullied's 4-6-2s all had three cylinders with three sets of patent chain-driven valve gear inside an oil-filled sump between the frames. Outside-admission piston valves were used, driven from the centre via transverse oscillating shafts. A large boiler was provided, with a wide firebox tapered on the base line.

The first ones to be built were called the "Merchant Navy" class; the prototype of the 30 built took the rails in 1941. With the experience gained, some smaller 4-6-2s known as the "West Country" class were introduced in 1945. Over the next five years 109 more were built, making them the most numerous Pacifics in Britain. Southern Railway running numbers were 21C101 upwards; British Railways allocated Nos. 34001-34110. Names of west country locations were given to the first 48; most of the remainder were given names associated with the Battle of Britain and were sometimes known as the "Battle of Britain" class—but there was no technical distinction between the two series.

Other features included a multiple-jet blastpipe known as the Lemaître, disc type wheels with holes rather than spokes, and a so-called air-smoothed casing. Innovations (for the SR) appreciated by the crews included rocking grates, power (steam) operated fire-hole door and reverser, rocker grate and electric light. A French system of water treatment known as *Traitment Intégral Armand*—which really kept the boilers free of scale even in chalky SR country—was used later. All except six were built at Brighton Works, an establishment that, apart from a few locomotives built during the war, had not produced a new one for many years. The odd six were built at Eastleight Works.

The very best features of the 4-6-2s were the boilers. They bristled with innovations so far as the Southern Railway was concerned—they were welded instead of rivetted, fireboxes were made of steel instead of copper and their construction included water ducts called thermic syphons inside the firebox. Yet in spite of these new features the boilers were marvellous steam raisers as well as being light on maintenance, thereby reflecting enormous credit on Bullied and his team.

An elaborate high pressure vessel, holding a mixture of water and steam at 280psi (19.7kg/cm²)

had been found easy, but one to hold oil a few inches deep proved to be difficult. The feature that did not work out was the totally enclosed oil-filled sump between the frames in which the inside connecting rod and three sets of chain-driven valve gear lashed away. Bullied expected that as in a motor car the lubrication drill would consist solely of a regular check of oil level with occasional topping-up. The motion would be protected against dust, dirt and water while wear would be small. Alas, it did not quite work out like this—the sumps leaked and broke and the mechanisms inside also bristled with so many innovations that they were never made trouble-free. The motion also suffered severe corrosion as the oil became contaminated. Hence there were appalling maintenance problems, never properly resolved in spite of many years of unremitting efforts to solve the difficulties.

Stretching of the chains which drove the miniature valve gears, plus the effect of any wear, all of which was multiplied when the motion was transferred to the valve spindles through rocking shafts, played havoc with the valve settings. This explained the heavy steam consumption. Oil leaking from the sump went everywhere, making the rails slippery and even adding a fresh hazard to railway working—the danger of a steam locomotive catching fire. This happened several times.

With outside motion in full view, drivers often spotted some defect before it had gone too far and something broke. But on these engines the first sign of trouble was often some extremely expensive noises, followed possibly by the puncturing of the oil bath as loose bits forced their way out. Incidentally, the price of all this complexity was very great even when development costs had been paid; the production cost of a "West Country" was £17,000 at a time when even such a complicated locomotive as a Great Western "Castle" 4-6-0 cost under £10,000.

Above: *An unkempt "West Country" 4-6-2 No.34017 lays down a fine trail of smoke on a cold snowy day near Weald, Kent.*

An unhandy throttle was another handicap and this, combined with the absence of any equalisation between the rear pony wheels and the drivers, made the locomotives liable to driving wheel slip both at starting and while running. On the other hand the performance which the Bullied Pacifics gave once they got going was superb.

Both classes were good but since the smaller "West Country" class seemed to be able to equal anything the larger "Merchant Navy" could do, one's admiration goes more strongly to the former. During the locomotive exchange trials which took place soon after nationalisation of the railways in 1948, they put up performances equal or superior to any of their larger rivals from other lines. It is clear that the SR people knew their candidates were going to come out bottom in coal consumption anyway, so they were determined to show that they could perform instead. Elsewhere than on the SR punctuality in Britain at that time was dreadful and one cites a run on which No.34006 *Bude* regained 11 minutes of lateness on the level route in the short distance (about 40 miles, 64km) between Bristol and Taunton.

On another occasion in the Highlands of Scotland over 13 minutes time was regained in the famous ascent from Blair Atholl to Dalnaspidal; a drawbar horsepower approaching 2,000 was recorded on this occasion. The coal burnt per mile compared with the normal 4-6-0s on this line was 28 per cent more and the amount burnt per horsepower-hour developed was 22 per cent higher. It is also recorded that the consumption of lubricating oil was not 7 per cent more but *seven times* more; but that was untypical—three times that of a normal engine was more usual! And remember that a normal locomotive was *intended* to be lubricated on a "total loss" system.

On their home territory the "West Country" locomotives were used on almost every Southern steam-hauled main line passenger working from the "Golden Arrow" continental express from Victoria to Dover, down to two and three coach local trains in Cornwall. Their maintenance problems were less apparent because the 140 Bullied 4-6-2s represented a huge over-provision of motive power.

Furthermore, in 1957-60, sixty "West Country" class were rebuilt with new conventional cylinders and motion; in this form and for the short period left to steam they were unambiguously amongst the very best locomotives ever to run in Britain. During 3 to 9 July 1967, the last week of steam on the Southern, these rebuilds worked the luxury "Bournemouth Belle" on several days.

Several both rebuilt and unrebuilt have been preserved and restored; for example, unrebuilt No.21C123 *Blackmore Vale* on the Bluebell Railway and No. 21C192 *City of Wells* on the Keighley & Worth Valley Railway.

Below: *The impressive SR "Battle of Britain" class 4-6-2* Sir Winston Churchill *now on display at Didcot.*

Niagara Class 4-8-4 United States: New York Central Railroad (NYC), 1945

Tractive effort: 61,570lb (27,936kg).
Axle load: 70,000lb (32t).
Cylinders: (2) 25½ x 32in (648 x 813mm).
Driving wheels: 79in (2,007mm).
Heating surface: 4,827sq ft (4.48m²).
Superheater: 2,060sq ft (191m²).
Steam pressure: 275psi (19.3kg/cm²).
Grate area: 100sq ft (9.3m²).
Fuel: 92,000lb (42t).
Water: 15,000gall (18,000 US) (82m³).
Adhesive weight: 274,000lb (124t).
Total weight: 891,000lb (405t).
Length overall: 115ft 5½in (35,192mm).

Above: *A New York Central "Niagara" 4-8-4 on a westbound passenger train of standard heavyweight stock at Dunkirk, New York State, in March 1952.*

Something has already been said of the New York Central Railroad's speedway from New York to Chicago, arguably in steam days the greatest passenger railway in the world, in terms of speeds run and tonnage moved. By the 1940s these speeds and loads were beginning to be as much as the famous Hudsons could cope with and the Central's chief of motive power, Paul Kiefer, decided to move on a step. He proposed a 4-8-4 with above 30 per cent more adhesive weight and tractive effort than the 4-6-4, together with a fire grate 25 per cent bigger. His aim was a locomotive which could develop 6,000hp in the cylinders for hour after hour and could do the New York-Chicago or Chicago-New York run of 928 miles day after day without respite.

The American Locomotive Company at Schenectady, proposed what was to be the last really new design of passenger locomotive to be produced in the USA. It owed something to the Union Pacific's "800" class; dimensionally, the two designs were very close and, in addition, the design of the 14-wheel Centipede or 4-10-0 tender was certainly based on the UP one. The NYC engines had something else unusual for America, in common with the "800"s—a smooth and uncluttered appearance but with no false streamlining or air-smoothing.

Because the NYC structure gauge only allowed rolling stock to be 15ft 2in (4,623mm) tall instead of 16ft 2in (4,928mm) as on the UP, the smokestack had to be vestigial and the dome little but a manhole cover. There were other differences such as Baker's valve gear instead of Walschaert's but in general the adoption of standard American practice led to similarities.

Naturally, the foundation of the design was a cast steel integral locomotive frame—nothing else could have stood up to the punishment intended for these engines. Also, as one might expect, all axles, coupling rods and connecting rods had roller bearings. Baker's valve gear has the advantage that it has no slides, so all its moving parts could, as in this case, be fitted with needle bearings. While speaking of the valves, an interesting detail was that the edges of the valve-ports were sharp on the steam side, but slightly rounded on the exhaust side. This eased the sharpness of the blast beats, thereby evening out the draught on the fire.

Although fundamentally the same design as that fitted to the UP locos, the tender had some interesting differences. The fact that the NYC was one of the very few American railroads equipped with track pans (in Great Britain water troughs) meant that less water could be carried conveniently, leaving more capacity for coal. This in its turn enabled the New York-Chicago run to be done with just one intermediate coaling, while an improved design of power-operated pick-up scoop reduced delays by allowing water to be taken at 80mph (128km/h). Special extra venting avoided bursting the tenders (there had been cases!) when some 1,600cu ft (45m³) of incompressible fluid enters the tank all in a few seconds. Incidentally, the overhang of the tank over the running gear at the rear end was to allow the engines to be turned on 100-foot turntables by reducing the wheelbase.

Allocating the number 6,000 to a locomotive whose target was that amount of horse-power as well as that number of miles run per week might seem to be tempting providence, but all was well. The prototype had the subclass designation "Sla", while the 25 production models (Nos. 6001-6025) were known as "S16" and there was also a single poppet-valve version known as "Slc" (No.5500). This greatest of steam locomotives got the classname "Niagara" and when the word is uttered, no steam man worthy of the name ever thinks of a waterfall! Both targets were achieved—6,700hp on test and an average of 26,000 miles run monthly.

The original idea was that the prototype should be tested and then a production order confirmed, but before work had gone very far instructions were given for all 27 to be put in hand. This was reasonable because in fact the Niagaras were very much a standard, if slightly stretched, product of the industry, whereas what really needed attention was the ground organisation to enable the mileage target to be met. And this, of course, could not be tested until a fleet was available.

By an ordinance of the City of New York, steam locomotives were not allowed inside city limits. Trains therefore left Grand Central Station behind third-rail electric locos for Harmon, 32 miles out in the suburbs. It was here, then, and at Chicago that the Niagaras were, in their great days, kept in first-class condition for what was without doubt one of the hardest services ever demanded of steam, or for that matter, of any motive power.

World records are not achieved without extreme efforts, but excellent organisation allowed quick and thorough servicing. The

Below: *Regarded by many as the Ultimate Steam Locomotive, the last of the Niagara 4-8-4s of the New York Central Railroad.*

power production part of the locomotives had to be just-so to give such a remarkable performance out on the road and to achieve this the fire was first dropped with the engine in steam. Than a gang of "hot men" in asbestos suits entered the firebox—the size of a room—and cleared tubes and flues, did any repairs required to the brick arch, grate etc. Good water treatment ensured that no scale built up in the heating surface, preventing the heat reaching the water inside the boiler. On many railways steam locomotives were allocated one "shed day" each week for these things to be done, but running the 928 miles from Harmon to Chicago or *vice versa* each night, the Niagaras needed to do a week's work in one 24-hour period.

In those days there were 12 daily trains each way just between New York and Chicago—the Chicagoan, the Advance Commodore Vanderbilt, the Commodore Vanderbilt, the Advance Empire State Express, the Empire State Express, the Lake Shore Limited, the Mohawk, the North Shore Ltd, the Pacemaker, the Water Level, the Wolverine and, greatest of all, the 16-hour Twentieth Century Limited.

Even the most fanatical steam enthusiast would admit that other factors have contributed, but nevertheless the Day of the Niagaras did mark a peak. So low have things fallen that the best time by diesel traction today on this route between New York and Chicago is 19hr 50min and there is only one train.

The Niagaras also demonstrated once again that modern well-maintained steam power could be more economical than diesel. Alas, in those days, coal supplies controlled by miners' leader John L. Lewis were less reliable than oil supplies; moreover, most of New York Central's steam power was neither modern nor well-maintained. So, having run more miles and hauled more tons in their short lives than most locomotives which run out their term to obsolescence, the Niagaras went to their long home. None have been preserved.

Below: *New York Central Railroad "Niagara" No.6001 leaves Albany, New York State, for the south in April 1952.*

Right: *"Niagara" No.6018 leans to the curve at Peekskill, New York, with "The Missourian" from St. Louis to New York.*

242 A1 4-8-4

France:
French National Railways SNCF, 1946

Axle load: 46,500lb (2,1t).
Cylinders, HP: (1) 23.6 x 28.3in (600 x 720mm).
Cylinders, LP: (2) 27 x 29.9in (680 x 760mm).
Driving wheels: 76¾in (1,950mm).
Heating surface: 2,720sq ft (253m²).
Superheater: 1,249sq ft (120m²).
Steam pressure: 290psi (20.4kg/cm²).
Grate area: 54sq ft (5m²).
Fuel: 25,000lb (11.5t).
Water: 7,500gall (9,000 US) (34m³).
Adhesive weight: 185,500lb (84t).
Total weight: 496,000lb (225t).
Length overall: 58ft 3½in (17,765mm)..

Above: *A view of Chapelon's masterpiece, French Railways' 4-8-4 No.242.A.1, rebuilt from a pre-war 4-8-2.*

By every competent authority it is agreed that André Chapelon should be included in the shortest of short lists of candidates to be considered as the greatest locomotive engineer of all. And this magnificent locomotive was his greatest work.

What is now the Western Region of the French National Railways had had a bad experience with a large 4-8-2 locomotive designed by a Government-appointed central design committee. It was a three-cylinder simple, but with poppet valve gear intended to give an expansion ratio equivalent to a compound. Alas, the mechanism never managed to achieve this, and moreover, there were other defects in the engine which caused bad riding and a tendency to derail. No.241.101 was laid aside after tests, an embarassment to all, particularly as it had been announced with tremendous fanfare as marking a new era in steam locomotive construction.

Chapelon had long wished to get his hands on this machine and to do to it what he had done before to the Paris-Orleans 4-6-2s. Official opposition took some years to overcome, but in 1942 his plans were agreed to, with a view of building a prototype for express passenger locomotives to be constructed when the war was over. The work was put in hand by the Société des Forges et Aciéres de la Marine et d'Homecourt.

The chassis needed substantial strengthening and the extra weight involved in this and other modifications meant the need for an extra carrying wheel—hence France's first 4-8-4 tender locomotive. The de Glehn arrangement with two low-pressure cylinders inside would have involved a crank axle with two cranks and rather thin webs (since there was no room for thick ones) and it is admitted that this was a source of maintenance problems. So the new engine was to have a single high-pressure cylinder inside driving the leading main axle and two low-pressure cylinders outside driving the second axle. All were in line between the bogie wheels.

Chapelon also moved away from poppet valves and used double piston-valves to give adequate port openings, as in his last batch of 4-6-2 rebuilds. The outside cranks were set at 90 degrees to one another, as in a two-cylinder engine; the inside crank bisected the obtuse angle

Below: *An overall view of the only standard-gauge European 4-8-4 steam locomotive, SNCF No.242.A.1.*

between the other two cylinders, being set at 135 degrees to each. The Walschaert's valve gear for the inside cylinder was mounted partly outside—the eccentric rod was attached to a return crank on the 2nd left-hand driving wheel. The bad riding was tackled with a roller centreing device for the front bogie as well as Franklin's automatic wedges to take up wear in the axlebox guides. Both were of USA origin.

The boiler had two thermic syphons in the firebox, concentric (Houlet's) superheater elements and a mechanical stoker. A triple Kylchap chimney and exhaust system was provided. When completed in 1946, the rebuilt locomotive (now No.242A1) indicated under test that it was by far the most powerful locomotive existing outside North America—the omission of the word steam is deliberate. It could develop a maximum of 5,500hp in the cylinders, compared with 2,800hp before rebuilding. This power output is similar to that of which a typical USA 4-8-4, perhaps 50 per cent, heavier than No.242A1, was capable of as a maximum when driven hard.

This sort of power output enabled then unheard-of things to be done. A typical performance was to haul a 15-car train of 740 tons up a steady gradient of 1 in 125 (0.8 per cent), at a minimum speed of 71mph (114km/h). A 700-ton train was hauled from Paris to Lille in 140 minutes for the 161 miles (258km), while the electrified line from Paris to Le Mans (131 miles—210km) was covered in 109 minutes with a test train of 810 tons weight; well under the electric timings even with this huge train. On another occasion a speed of 94mph (150km/h) was reached; this was also a special test, as there was a 120km/h) (75mph) legal speed limit for public trains in France at that time.

Alas for the future of No.242A1, the top railway brass of France were even more embarrassed by its outstanding success than they were by its previous failure. They were engaged in trying to persuade the French government, at a time when the resources were at a premium, to underwrite a vast programme of electrification; and here comes a young man (Chapelon was only 58) with an engine which (a) could outperform any electric locomotive so far built and (b) was so economical in coal consumption as to nullify any potential coal saving through electrification. And *both* of these items were the corner-stones of the railways' case for electrification.

So it is not hard to understand why this great locomotive was never duplicated. In fact it was quietly shunted away to Le Mans depot where, turn and turn-about with lesser engines, it took over express trains arriving from Paris by electric traction. The potential of the 4-8-4 was still appreciated by its crews. When such trains were delayed they could use its great performance in earning themselves large sums in bonus payments for time regained.

There was another potential question mark standing over a future for a production version of 242A1. It has been mentioned that the rugged American 2-8-2s showed an overall economy over the compounds because low maintenance costs more than balanced the cost of the extra coal burnt. Ironically, some of this was due to Chapelon himself, who had improved the valve events and reduced the cylinder clearances of the 141R so that the amount of this extra coal used was reduced from some 20 per cent to 10.

It should really then be no surprise that as revealed by Baron Gerard Vuillet in his authoritative *Railway Reminiscences of Three Continents*, there was an alternative proposal in the form of a two-cylinder simple 4-6-4 with cast-steel locomotive frame, roller bearings, mechanical stoker and a grate area of 67sq ft (6.2m²). Vuillet remarks, "this 147-ton locomotive would not have been much more powerful at the drawbar than the best French Pacifics weighing 104 tons, but would have had a higher availability."

Chapelon was countering with proposals for three-cylinder compound 4-6-4s and 4-8-4s for express passenger work. He also had in mind a triple-expansion compound 4-8-4 with four cylinders, using steam at 584psi (41kg/cm²) generated in a boiler with a water tube firebox. The locomotive was intended to be capable of developing 8,000 hp. Confidently with the former, and it was hoped with the latter, Chapelon expected that maintenance costs of these modern compounds could be brought down close to those of simple locomotives. Alas, all this is now academic—the great 4-8-4 was withdrawn in 1960 and quietly broken up. Nothing now remains but models, memories and deep regrets for what might have been.

Above: *French Railways 242 A 1 4-8-4 by Chapelon, a steam locomotive which, when it was built in 1946, outperformed any electric or diesel in existence.*

Below: *Chapelon's magnificent 242 A 1 4-8-4, which was the most powerful steam locomotive to run in Europe.*

C62 Class 4-6-4 Japan: Japanese National Railways (JNR), 1949

Tractive effort: 30,690lb (13,925kg).
Axle load: 36,500lb (16.5t).
Cylinders: (2) 20½ x 26in (521 x 660mm).
Driving wheels: 69in (1,750mm).
Heating surface*: 2,640sq ft (245m²).
Superheater: included above.
Steam pressure: 228psi (16kg/cm²).
Grate area: 41.5sq ft (3.85m²).
Fuel: 22,000lb (10t).
Water: 4,850gall (5,820 US) (22m³).
Adhesive weight: 142,500lb (64.5t).
Total weight: 356,000lb (101.5t).
Length overall: 70ft 5½in (21,475mm).
*(*including superheater)*

Before they became world leaders in so many branches of technology, the Japanese were famous as imitators. In some ways—railway safety and signalling was one—they took British ways as their model, but as regards steam locomotives the basis of their practice was American. This has applied ever since Baldwin of Philadelphia supplied Japan with some 2-8-2s in 1897, thereby giving the type-name Mikado to the most prolific of the world's wheel arrangements.

So in recent years Japanese locomotives have usually been neat and elegant miniature versions, to a scale of about three-quarters, of the typical US two-cylinder locomotive, to suit the 3ft 6in (1,067mm) gauge. The last word in express passenger locomotives in Japan were these forty-nine 4-6-4s of the "C-62" class and they were no exception to the rule; yet in details they

Above: *A pair of Japanese National Railways' "C62" class 4-6-4 locomotives head an express train in Hokkaido island.*

Below: *The bold lines of one of the Japanese railways "C62" class 4-6-4s, popularly known as the "Swallows".*

Pt-47 Class 2-8-2 Poland: Polish State Railways (PKP), 1947

Tractive effort: 42,120lb (19,110kg).
Axle load: 46,500lb (21t).
Cylinders: (2) 24¾ x 27½in (630 x 700mm).
Driving wheels: 72¾in (1,850mm).
Heating surface: 2,476sq ft (230m²).
Superheater: 1,087sq ft (101m²).
Steam pressure: 214psi (15kg/cm²).
Grate area: 48.5sq ft (4.5m²).
Fuel: 20,000lb (9t).
Water: 7,000gall (8,500 US) (32m³).
Adhesive weight: 184,000lb (83.5t).
Total weight: 381,500lb (173t).
Length overall: 79ft 7in (24,255mm).

In their short life of 60 or so years the railways of Poland have seen far too much history, yet their locomotive history shows a surprising continuity. The eight-coupled express passenger locomotive appeared early on in the form of the three "Pu-29" 4-8-2s built by the Cegielski Works of Poznan in 1929. The number in the class designation indicates the date of construction; the "P" stands for *Pospieszny* (Passenger) and the "u" means 4-8-2, "t" means a 2-8-2 and so on.

Since general usage of these lengthy locomotives would mean the renewal of many short turntables, second thoughts prevailed over making this 4-8-2 a standard class. It was considered that a 2-8-2 would do as well; the result

were very distinctive. They were the results of a rather substantial rebuilding of some Mikados of Class "D52"—a heavier version of the standard "D51" class—constructed during World War II. The work was done by outside firms, Hitachi, Kawasaki and Kisha Seizo Kaisha.

One suspects that this way of doing things was to circumvent some government or accountant's restriction on building new passenger motive power—little of the machinery could have been re-used and the saving of actual folding money must have been negligible. But such things are a familiar feature of locomotive practice the world over and, anyway, no one can complain about the results, which were superb in both practical and aesthetic terms. Train worship is even more of a religion in Japan than it is in America or Britain and the "C62"s, "Swallows" as they seem to have been (rather strangely) sometimes known, were certainly enshrined at the summit in this respect.

Features worthy of note provided as standard on the larger Japanese steam locomotive include electric light and a feedwater heater complete with steam pump. There are disc wheels all round, the driving wheels having rather prominent lightening holes. The steam dome is inside the sand dome, the latter keeping the former warm and dry. There is no footplate at the front end of the tender—the cab overhangs the leading pair of wheels, while a shovelling plate extends forward from the tender into the cab.

Twenty years ago they could be found hauling the top trains—such as the *Hatsukari* or Migratory Goose Express—out of Tokyo's main station, but now not only has steam locomotion disappeared from these narrow (3ft 6in—1,067mm) gauge lines but long-distance daytime passenger trains as well. They have migrated to the standard gauge electric Shin Kansen network on which the famous bullet trains provide 100mph (160km/h) service start-to-stop several times each hour.

The 4-6-4s, however, for a number of years found a haven in Japan's main northern island, Hokkaido, working—often in pairs and occasionally in threes—the main expresses out of Hakkodate, the ferryboat port at its southern tip. When this finally came to an end two of these giants were set aside for preservation. One (No.C62-2) is on display at the Umekoji Museum Depot at Kyoto, on the Japanese main island, while the other (No. C62-3) is kept at Otaro on the northern island of Hokkaido and run on special occasions.

Above: *An express passenger train being double-headed by a pair of Japanese National Railways' "C62" class 4-6-2 "Swallows".*

was the "Pt-31", which had the same cylinders, wheels and boiler pressure. Like most Polish locomotives, they were simple unrefined but rugged two-cylinder machines reflecting a country in which coal is plentiful, so that the pay-off of complicated refinements is at a minimum.

The German invasion of 1939 came before the whole 110 had been completed and the last 12 appeared as German State Railway class "39" Thirty of the "Pt-31"s stayed in the area taken over by Russia. After the war Poland again became independent but not all the surviving 2-8-2s came back into Polish hands. Many remained in the territory permanently ceded to Russia, while others worked in Austria for several years.

The recipe was so effective that further similar 2-8-2s were introduced in 1947. These were the class "Pt-47", of which 120 were built by the locomotive building enterprise Chrzanow of Warsaw and 60 by Cegielski. The main changes were from a rivetted to a welded firebox, from a separate steam and sand dome to a combined one and from hand stoking to automatic stoking. The new locomotives were as handsome as the old ones and soon took over the haulage of Poland's principal express trains on non-electrified lines. All the 2-8-2s had a Krauss-Helmholtz leading truck, which to some extent has the effect of making the leading driving wheels part of the guiding system when running on curved track. Without some device of this kind, the riding qualities of locomotives with only a single leading guiding wheel have always been regarded as having a question mark applied to them—a number of serious derailments having occurred.

During the dawn of railways in their country, the Russian occupiers of Poland were responsible for not only the now defunct broad gauge there but also for a tall structure gauge. Hence the "Pt-47" has an overall height of 15ft 4in (4,668mm), representing extra space which gave a welcome degree of freedom to the designers.

At the time of writing and by a factor of several times, Poland has more operational steam locomotives than any other country outside Africa or Asia. No doubt one factor in this decision to electrify gradually while keeping steam, lies in a preference for a transport system dependent on Polish coal rather than some other nation's oil, but another factor is certainly the overall economy and reliability of one of mankind's most faithful friends, the steam locomotive in its simplest form.

Left: *A Polish State Railways "P-47" class 2-8-2 at the head of a local passenger train. An interesting feature is the set of double-deck coaches, in order to maximise the seating capacity for a given length of train.*

Class A1 4-6-2 Great Britain: British Railways (BR), 1948

Tractive effort: 37,400lb (16,900kg).
Axle load: 49,500lb (22.5t).
Cylinders: (3) 19 x 26in (482 x 660mm).
Driving wheels: 80in (2,032mm).
Heating surface: 2,461sq ft (228.6m²).
Superheater: 680sq ft (63.2m²).
Steam pressure: 250psi (17.6kg/cm²).
Grate area: 50sq ft (4.6m²).
Fuel: 20,000lb (9t).
Water: 5,000gall (6,000 US) (22.7m³).
Adhesive weight: 148,000lb (67t).
Total weight: 369,000lb (167t).
Length overall: 73ft 0in (22,250mm).

When Sir Nigel Gresley died suddenly in office in 1941, The London and North Eastern Railway had 115 Pacifics and some 600 other three-cylinder engines of his design, all fitted with his derived motion, in which the inside valve took its drive from the two outside valve gears. In peace time this derived motion had been prone to failure, but under wartime conditions of maintenance the problem had become much more serious.

Gresley was succeeded by Edward Thompson, one of his most senior assistants, who had a particular interest in maintenance. Thompson foresaw that a large programme of locomotive building would be needed after the war to make good the arrears of locomotive construction, and in formulating this programme he was particularly concerned to eliminate the derived motion, in the large engines by fitting a third valve gear, and in the smaller ones by eliminating the third cylinder. As he was already aged 60 when promoted, he also felt the need to apply his ideas with urgency.

The opportunity to build a Pacific to his ideas arose from the poor availability of Gresley's "P2" class 2-8-2 locomotives, one of whose troubles was heavy wear of axleboxes due to the long rigid wheelbase on the sharp curves of the Edinburgh-Aberdeen line. By rebuilding these as Pacifics he hoped to improve their performance, and also to gain experience for further new construction. Elimination of

Above: *A Darlington-built British Railways "A1" class 4-6-2 No.60149* Amadis *ready to depart from Kings Cross station, London.*

Below: *British Railways "A1" class 4-6-2 No.60161* North British, *portrayed in experimental blue livery during BR's early days.*

Class WP 4-6-2 India: Indian Railways (IR), 1946

Tractive effort: 30,600lb (13,884kg).
Axle load: 45,500lb (20.7t).
Cylinders: (2) 20¼ x 28in (514 x 711mm).
Driving wheels: 67in (1,705mm).
Heating surface: 2,257sq ft (286.3m²).
Superheater: 725sq ft (67m²).
Steam pressure: 210psi (14.7kg/cm²).
Grate area: 46sq ft (4.3m²).
Fuel: 33,000lb (15t).
Water: 6,000gall (7,200 US) (27m³).
Adhesive weight: 121,500lb (55t).
Total weight: 380,000lb (172.5t).
Length overall: 00ft 00in (00,000mm).

Of only three classes of express locomotive amongst those described in this book can it be said (with much pleasure) that most remain in service, doing the job for which they were made. One of them is this massive broad-gauge (5ft 6in—1,676mm) American-style 4-6-2, the standard express passenger locomotive of the Indian Railways. Class "WP" comprises 755 locomotives, built between 1947 and 1967, with running numbers 7000 to 7754.

The prototypes were a batch of 16 ordered from Baldwin of Philadelphia in 1946, well before Independence, so the decision to go American was not connected with the political changes. It was taken as a result of the satisfactory experience with the American locomotives supplied to India during the war, coupled with unsatisfactory experience with the Indian standard designs of the 1920s and 1930s.

Naturally, the locomotives supplied were built to the usual rugged simple basic USA standards. The provision of vacuum brakes, standard in India, made them even simpler, because a vacuum ejector is a vastly less complicated device than a steam air-pump. An air-smoothed exterior was provided for aesthetic rather than aerodynamic reasons, giving a solid dependable look to some solid dependable locomotives.

The original batch were designated "WP/P" (P for prototypes) and the production version differed in minor details. During the next ten years further members of the class were supplied from foreign countries as follows:

USA—Baldwin	100
Canada—Canadian Locomotive Co	100
Canada—Montreal Locomotive Works	120
Poland—Fabryka Locomotywim, Chrzanow	30
Austria—Vienna Lokomotiv Fabrik	30

There was then a pause until 1963, when India's own new Chitteranjan locomotive building plant began production of the remainder. Some further small modifications to the design were made to facilitate production at this works.

the Gresley gear involved arranging the inside cylinder to drive the leading axle, and as Thompson insisted on all the connecting rods being of the same length, an awkward layout was arrived at, with the leading bogie ahead of the outside cylinders.

Trouble was experienced with flexing of the frame, and loosening and breakage of steam pipes, but nevertheless the arrangement was applied to the "P2"s and to a further 19 mixed-traffic Pacifics with 74in (1,880mm) driving wheels. Before this programme was completed, Thompson also took in hand Gresley's original Pacific, *Great Northern,* and rebuilt it similarly, with separate valve gears, larger cylinders, and a grate area of 50sq ft (4.6m²), in place of the 41.3sq ft (3.8m²) grate with which all the Gresley Pacifics were fitted.

Before Thompson's retirement, his successor designate, Arthur Peppercorn, put in hand quietly in Doncaster drawing office a further revision of the Pacific layout, in which the outside cylinders were restored to their position above the middle of the bogie, and the inside connecting rod was shortened to make the front of the engine more compact. Fifteen new Pacifics with 74in wheels were built to this design, classified "A2", and then 49 more with 80in (2,032mm) wheels were ordered, classified "A1". The *Great Northern* was absorbed into this class under the sub-classification "A1/1".

These engines were not built until after nationalisation, in 1948-49, Nos.60114-27/53-62 at Doncaster, and Nos.60130-52 at Darlington. They all had Kylchap double blastpipes, and five of them had roller bearings to all axles. At first they had stovepipe chimneys, but these were replaced by chimneys of the normal Doncaster shape. They had assorted names, including locomotive engineers, the constituent railways of the LNER, some traditional Scottish names, some birds and some racehorses.

Above: *"A1" class 4-6-2 No. 60139 makes a fine show with the "Yorkshire Pullman".*

The "A1"s proved to be fast and economical engines, and they took a full share in East Coast locomotive workings, except for the Kings Cross-Edinburgh non-stops, for which the streamlined "A4"s were preferred. Their maintenance costs were lower than those of other BR Pacifics, and they achieved notable mileages. Over a period of 12 years they averaged 202 miles per calendar day, the highest figure on BR, and the five roller bearing engines exceeded that average, with 228 miles per day. Their riding was somewhat inferior to that of the "A4", as they had a tendency to lateral lurching on straight track, but nevertheless they were timed at 100mph plus (160+km/h) on a number of occasions.

These engines were a worthy climax to Doncaster Pacific design, but unfortunately they came too late in the day to have full economic lives. By the early 1960s dieselisation of the East Coast main line was well advanced, and the "A1"s were all withdrawn between 1962 and 1966. None of them was preserved.

The fleet of "WP"s work in all parts of the broad gauge network and find full employment on many important express passenger trains, although they have been displaced from the very top assignments by diesels and electrics, also Indian-built. Enormous trains, packed with humanity, move steadily across the Indian plains each headed by one of these excellent locomotives. A crew of four is carried (driver, two firemen and a coal-trimmer) but even with two observers on board as well there is ample room in the commodious cab.

Left: *An Indian Railways class "WP" 4-6-2. The letters "CR" on the tender indicate it is allocated to the Central Railway.*

Class 241P 4-8-2

France: French National Railways (SNCF), 1948

Axle load: 45,000lb (20.5t).
Cylinders, HP: (2) 17.6 x 25.6in (446 x 650mm).
Cylinders, LP: (2) 26.5 x 27.6in (674 x 700mm).
Driving wheels: 79.1in (2,010mm).
Heating surface: 2,633sq ft (244.6m²).
Superheater: 1,163sq ft (108m²).
Steam pressure: 284psi (20kg/cm²).
Grate area: 54.4sq ft (5.1m²).
Fuel: 22,000lb (11t).
Water: 7,480gall (8,980 US) (34m³).
Adhesive weight: 180,900lb (82t).
Total weight: 472,500lb (214t).
Length overall: 89ft 11in (27,418mm).

During the period in which André Chapelon was achieving unprecedented results by his rebuilding of Paris-Orleans Railway Pacifics, the total construction of new engines in France was small in proportion to the size of country. During World War II plans were prepared for a new fleet of high-powered steam engines, which it was confidently expected would be needed in large numbers to make good the arrears of new construction, and to provide for increase in the speed and weight of trains. For the heaviest express work a 4-8-4 was proposed, but construction of an experimental prototype by the rebuilding of an old 4-8-2 was slow. In the meantime construction of a modernised version of a PLM 2-8-2 was undertaken, and large numbers of 2-8-2s were ordered from North America.

Unfortunately in 1946 a national coal shortage caused the government to instruct SNCF to reduce its coal consumption, and the way was paved for a policy decision to electrify all main lines. Further development of steam engines was cancelled, but a case was made for the construction of a limited number of large passenger engines, particularly to cope with increasing loads on the old PLM main line to Marseilles, on which Chapelon 4-8-0s

L-2a Class 4-6-4

United States Chesapeake & Ohio Railway (C&O), 1948

Tractive effort: 52,1000lb (23,639kg).
Axle load: 73,500lb (33.5t).
Cylinders: (2) 25 x 30in (635 x 762mm).
Driving wheels: 78in (1,981mm).
Heating surface: 4,233sq ft (393m²).
Superheater: 1,810sq ft (168m²).
Steam pressure: 255psi (17.9kg/cm²).
Grate area: 90sq ft (8.4m²).
Fuel: 60,000lb (27.5t).
Water: 17,500gall (21,000 US) (80m³).
Adhesive weight: 219,500lb (100t).
Total weight: 839,000lb (381t).
Length overall: 108ft 0in (32,918mm).

It was a case of "last orders please" when in 1947 the Chesapeake & Ohio Railway went to Baldwin of Philadelphia for five 4-6-4s and to the Lima Locomotive Co of Lima, Ohio, for five 4-8-4s. They were to be the last steam express passenger locomotives supplied for home use by any of the big USA constructors, although naturally neither the customer nor the builders realised it at the time.

The C&O divided its routes into mountain and plains divisions and the eight-coupled engines were for the former, the six-coupled ones for the latter. There was, therefore, scope for the 4-6-4s, both north-west of the Allegheny mountains on the routes to Louisville, Cincinatti, Chicago and Detroit, as well as south-east of them in the directions of Washington and Richmond, Virginia.

In 1947 a man called Robert R. Young was in charge at C&O headquarters at Richmond and he believed the passenger train had a future. The Chessie ran through the big coalfields and at that time hauled more coal than any other railroad. It was therefore unthinkable that anything but coal-burning power should be used. Amongst his plans was one for a daytime streamline service actually to be known as The Chessie—and three steam-turbine locomotives with electric drive and 16 driving wheels were built in 1947-48 to haul it on the main stem and over the mountains. Conventional steam was to haul connecting portions and provide back-up. Alas, those whose concept it was had thrown away the steam locomotive's best card, that is simplicity, and in a short two years the turbo-electrics (Class "M-1", Nos.500-502) had been scrapped as hopelessly uneconomic.

In the meantime the whole C&O streamline project had been scrapped, but not before some older 4-6-2s (the "F-19" class) had been converted into streamlined 4-6-4s to handle the new train over part of its route. Furthermore, in the grand manner of a great and prosperous railroad, C&O considered hand-me-downs not be good enough for a prestige train and so had ordered these "L-2a" Hudsons, intending them to be streamlined. Running numbers were 310 to 314 and fortunately they were as trouble-free as the turbines had been troublesome.

On various important counts the 4-6-4s were the top six-coupled locomotives of the world—in engine weight, at 443,000lb (201t), 7½ per cent above those of the nearest rival, Santa Fe. In tractive effort, both with and without their booster in action, the latter worth 14,200lb

of Class "240P" were achieving prodigious feats of haulage. However, to reach this standard of performance with a grate of 40sq ft (3.7m²) required a high standard of fuel, and it was clear that for post-war conditions an engine with a much larger grate was desirable. Furthermore, the ex-PLM engineers who now influenced policy on SNCF favoured the simplicity of piston valves, rather than the poppet valves which were used in most of the Chapelon 4-8-0s. Authority was therefore given for the construction of thirty-five 4-8-2s, in place of the last forty 2-8-2s on order.

Time was short for the production of a completely new design, and Chapelon's 4-8-4 was not even completed, still less tested, so the only possibility was to modify an existing design. The design chosen was an ex-PLM 4-8-2 of a type of which one only had been built in 1930, but which gave the right basic layout and boiler size for the new class. This engine had the high-pressure cylinders inside the frames between the first and second coupled axles, and driving the third axle. The low-pressure cylinders were outside driving the second axle. The high-pressure and low-pressure valves on each side were driven from a common valve gear on the von Borries principle. Into this design were incorporated as many as possible of Chapelon's ideas on large superheaters and generous steam pipes and ports, whilst at the same time the PLM frame structure was strengthened in places where it was known to be weak. Mechanical stoker, feed water heater, and the French TIA system of water treatment in the tender were fitted; the TIA system increased greatly the time between boiler washing out.

Nevertheless the design was a compromise, a number of the parts which it inherited from the old design were overloaded at the power outputs which were now possible, and the mechanical performance left something to be desired. Despite the measures taken to accelerate production of the new class, which was numbered from 241P1 to 241P35, the engines were not delivered until 1948-9, by which time electrification of the ex-PLM main line was well in hand. Initially they worked on the former PLM and on ex-Northern main lines from Paris to Lille and Belgium. As electrification advanced, some of them moved to the Western Region, where they took over the heaviest trains to the Brittany coast from Le Mans onward. Under the enthusiastic regional mechanical engineer they were driven to their limits on these services, on trains which could load to 950 tons at busy times. With loads of 650 tons they could achieve 60mph (96 km/h) from start to stop on short runs, and could reach the speed limit of 74mph (120km/h) with this load in six minutes. Their other speciality was the Bourbonnais line of the old PLM, on which they worked loads of up to 800 tons until displaced by diesels in 1968.

Although their power output in relation to their size never equalled that of the Chapelon 4-8-0s, it was at its best magnificent. They were worked more intensively than previous French passenger engines, and two of them once ran 19,900 miles (32,000km) and 18,578 miles (29,874km) in a month on trains averaging 585 tons, whilst working from Lyons Mouche depot.

The 241Ps managed a working life of nearly twenty years before they were finally displaced by diesels. Four of the engines have been preserved, including No. 241P16 in the French National Railway Museum at Mulhouse where the locomotive is one of the main exhibits.

Left: *French National Railways class "241P" 4-8-2, a design based on some older 4-8-2 PLM locomotives of the same type.*

Below: *The complexity of the impressive SNCF class "241P" is well brought out in this superb drawing.*

Left: *Although seemingly complicated, the C&O class "L-2a" 4-6-4 was fundamentally simple.*

(6,443kg) of thrust, and adhesive weight, the figures are records. The massive qualities of C&O track are illustrated by the fact that their adhesive weight is also unmatched elsewhere.

Technically the engines represented the final degree of sophistication of the American steam locomotive that came from nearly 120 years of steady development of practice and details upon the original principles. The "L-2a" class was developed from the eight "L-2" class 4-6-4s of 1941 (Nos.300-307) and differed from them mainly in having Franklin's system of rotary-cam poppet valves instead of more conventional Baker's gear and piston valves. These locomotives also were notable for having unusually clean lines. The C&O once even had liked to hang a pair of air-pumps in the most prominent possible position on the smokebox door; now even the headlight was cleared away and mounted above the pilot beam.

The advantages of poppet valves have been mentioned elsewhere in this narrative, as have the problems involved in their maintenance. It would appear, though, as if manufacturers on both sides of the Atlantic had begun in this respect to offer a viable product—now that it was just too late to affect the outcome of steam's struggle for survival.

By 1953 Chessie's passenger service had become 100 per cent dieselised. Accordingly there was little work for the new 4-6-4s and all had gone for scrap before their seventh birthday.

Class 01.^{10} 4-6-2 **Germany:** German Federal Railway (DB), 1953

Tractive effort: 37,200lb (16,830kg).
Axle load: 44,500lb (20.2t).
Cylinders: (3) 19.7 x 26.0in (500 x 600mm).
Driving wheels: 78.7in (2,000mm).
Heating surface: 2,223sq ft (206.5m^2).
Superheater: 1,035sq ft (96.2m^2).
Steam pressure: 227.6psi (16kg/cm^2).
Grate area: 42.6sq ft (3.96m^2).
Fuel: 22,000lb (10.0t).
Water: 8,400gall (10,000 US) (38m^3).
Adhesive weight: 133,000lb (60.4t).
Total weight: 244,000lb (110.8t) (without tender).
Length overall: 79ft 2in (24,130mm).

Above: *Recently re-coaled German "01" class 4-6-2 surges through the countryside.*

Left: *German State Railway rebuilt class "01" 4-6-2 ready to leave Hamburg with a cross-border express for Dresden.*

At the end of World War II in 1945 the railways of Germany were devastated, and a large proportion of the express passenger locomotives were out of service. By the end of the decade services were largely restored, but by that time the partition of Germany had been formalized, and the railway system of the Federal Republic had adopted the name German Federal Railway, whilst that of the German Democratic Republic used the old name of German State Railway. The locomotive stock was divided between the two systems on the basis of where the locomotives were located at the end of hostilities.

By 1950 it was clear that both systems would extend their electrified networks, and introduce diesel traction on non-electrified lines, but both systems also made plans for limited construction of new steam locomotives for the interim period. In the event, new construction was confined to mixed-traffic and freight locomotives, and only two completely new express passenger engines were built. These were two three-cylinder Pacifics completed by DB in 1957, by which time the progress of electrification was so rapid that it was clear that there was no prospect of the class being extended.

Steam-hauled passenger trains therefore continued to be worked by the stock of pre-war Pacifics. To prolong their lives, many of these on both systems were rebuilt to varying degrees. Although each railway adopted its own scheme of rebuilding, they had much in common, and where any renumbering was involved, it was arranged that there was no duplication between DB and DR.

The first engines to be altered were the 55 three-cylinder Pacifics of Class "01.^{10}", all of which came into DB ownership. These engines had been built in 1939 and 1940 with full streamlining, but by the end of the war parts of the casing had been removed, and many of the engines lay derelict for up to five years. Between 1949 and 1951 the class was given heavy repairs, in the course of which the streamlined casing was removed, and the engines acquired an appearance in accordance with post-war standards. Compared with the non-streamlined pre-war Pacifics, there was no sloping plate connecting the side running boards with the buffer beam, and the full-depth smoke deflectors were replaced by the small Witte pattern on the upper part of the smokebox. Removal of the casing around the smokebox revealed that the cylinder of the feedwater heater was mounted externally in a recess in the top of the smokebox, instead of being buried in the smokebox as in the "01" and "03" engines. The North American touch in the lineaments of the engines was thereby increased. Various parts which had been made of substitute materials during the war were replaced by normal parts.

The next rebuilding involved fitting new welded fireboxes with combustion chambers to five of the "01" Pacifics, the existing parallel barrel being retained. The original fireboxes without combustion chambers had been troublesome to maintain, despite Dr Wagner's intentions. The modified boiler could be detected by extra firebox washout plugs, but even more conspicuous was the fitting of Heinl feedwater heaters, with a raised casing ahead of the chimney.

Deterioration of the alloy-steel fireboxes of the "01.^{10}" and "03.^{10}" Pacifics then led to the design of a new all-welded boiler with tapered barrel, suitable for fitting to all the large Pacifics; a smaller version of the same boiler was produced for the "03" and "03.^{10}" classes. This new boiler was fitted to all the "O1.^{10}" engines between 1954 and 1956, and to the 26 "03.^{10}" engines which had come into DB ownership between 1956 and 1958. At the same time new front end systems, with larger chimneys, were fitted, and a Heinl feedwater heater, with its tank concealed within the smokebox. The outline of the boiler was simplified compared with the pre-war types, as there was only one dome, and the sandboxes were on the running plates. The dimensions given above refer to these rebuilds.

The rebuilt "01.^{10}" engines became the mainstay of heavy steam passenger workings on DB. As electrification spread northwards, they too moved north, and most of them ended their days at Rheine, where they

Below: *German Federal Railway converted oil-burning class "012" 4-6-2 No.012077-4.*

were amongst the last DB steam engines to finish work in 1975. To increase the availability of the engines, 34 of them were converted to burn oil in 1957-58. These engines became class "012" under the 1968 renumbering, whilst the remaining coal-burners were "011". In the latter days of steam operation on the Hamburg-Bremen line, these engines were hauling 600-tonne trains at speeds up to 80mph (130km/h), and were achieving monthly mileages of 17,000 (27,000km).

It was planned to fit the same type of boiler to 80 of the "01" Pacifics, but due to the increasing pace of electrification, only 50 were converted. Externally the engines were conspicuous by the large-diameter chimney, but as these engines worked over lines with a more restricted loading gauge than those on which the "01.^{10}"s worked, the chimney was much shorter, and gave the engines a very massive appearance.

In East Germany, too, the slower pace of electrification led to the extensive rebuilding of 35 "01" Pacifics between 1961 and 1965. New all-welded boilers were fitted, but whereas on DB the new boilers had slightly smaller grates than their predecessors, those on DR had larger grates to cope with inferior coal. The external appearance of the engines was changed greatly by the fitting of a continuous casing over the boiler mountings, and a deep valancing below the footplating (later removed). Eight of the rebuilds were given Boxpok driving wheels, and 28 of them were later converted to burn oil. The rebuilt engines were classified "01". The rebuilding was so extensive that little of the original engine remained. They took over the heaviest DR steam workings, which included the international trains into West Germany, and they could be seen alongside the DB variants of Class "01" at Hamburg and Bebra.

Class 231U1 4-6-4

France: French National Railways (SNCF), 1949

Axle load: 51,000lb (23t).
Cylinders, HP: (2) 17¾ x 27½in (450 x 700mm).
Cylinders, LP: (2) 26¾ x 27½in (680 x 700mm).
Driving wheels: 78½in (2,000mm).
Heating surface: 2,100sq ft (195m^2).
Superheater: 690sq ft (64m^2).
Steam pressure: 286psi (280kg/cm^2).
Grate area: 55.7sq ft (5.17m^2).
Fuel: 20,000lb (9t).
Water: 8,370gall (10,000 US) (38m^3).
Adhesive weight: 152,000lb (69t).
Total weight: 467,500lb (212t).
Length overall: 87ft 4½in (26,634mm).

This great engine was the result of the Northern Company's desire to improve upon their Chapelon 4-6-2s. An attempt was made to overcome the weakness of the plate frames by adopting cast steel bar-type ones. A higher power output was envisaged and this was taken care of by a wide firebox (instead of trapezoidal!) and a mechanical stoker. Eight streamlined and partly experimental 4-6-4 locomotives were planned, four compounds (class 232S), three simples (class 232R) and one turbine. The idea was to work 200-ton trains at speeds up to 100mph (160km/h). Before the engines were completed in 1940 the railways had been nationalised and a disastrous war with Germany had begun, so the light high-speed trains envisaged for these locomotives to pull were replaced by immense slow ones. The turbine locomotive was never completed.

After the war the performance of the 4-6-4s was re-assessed. In the case of the compounds the designers had unfortunately tried to re-invent the wheel and had not been completely successful.

The rotary-cam poppet valve gear (instead of the oscillating-cam gear used by Chapelon) was troublesome and failed to meet its promise as regards economy in the use of steam. Even so, France was reluctant to abandon the compound principle and it was decided to finish off the chassis originally intended for the turbine locomotive in this manner. The result was the "232U1", completed in 1949 by the firm of Corpet-Louvet.

The purposeful clutter that was the Chapelon outline had been covered by a streamline shroud. Beneath it poppet valves had been replaced by piston valves. The four sets of valves were worked by two sets of outside Walschaert's valve gear. In an effort to reduce maintenance costs roller bearings had replaced plain ones on the axles, grease lubrication had largely replaced oil and again cast bar-type frames were used. The engine was successful; it was able to develop 4,500hp measured at the cylinders, about half way between that for a Chapelon 4-6-2 and the ultimate power of his "242A1" class 4-8-4. One drawback was the heavy axle load; this effectively confined the locomotive (and its fellow streamliners of the "232R" and "232S" classes) to the Paris to Lille main line. Although the engines were designed for better things, the maximum permitted speed was kept at the standard French value of 75mph (120 km/h).

Efforts had also been made to simplify the controls—the complications of those implicit in the de Glehn system of compounding have been referred to earlier. In the "232S" and "232U" locomotives the changeover from simple working (used at starting) to compound was arranged to happen automatically, according to whether the reversing lever was set to give more or less than 55 per cent cut-off. So perhaps the supply of footplate wizards able to cope with the complexities of the typical French express passenger locomotive was not so inexhaustible as their admirers across the Channel thought!

By the time the virtues of the design had been assessed and the question of a repeat order arose, French Railways had turned to electrification. So No. 232U1 remained a solitary and is now displayed in superbly restored condition at the National Railway Museum at Mulhouse.

Below: *SNCF class "232U" 4-6-4 232U1 at the Gare du Nord, Paris in October 1959.*

Below: *French National Railways 4-6-4 No.231U1 as restored for display in the museum.*

P36 Class 4-8-4 USSR: Soviet Railways (SZD), 1953

Tractive effort: 39,686lb (18,007kg).
Axle load: 41,000lb (18.5t).
Cylinders: (2) 22½ x 31½in (575 x 800mm).
Driving wheels: 72¾in (1,850mm).
Heating surface: 2,617sq ft (243m²).
Superheater: 1,537sq ft (142m²).
Steam pressure: 213psi (15kg/cm²).
Grate area: 73sq ft (6.75m²).
Fuel: 51,000lb (23t).
Water: 10,000gall (12,000 US) (46m³).
Adhesive weight: 163,000lb (74t).
Total weight: 582,000lb (264t).
Length overall: 94ft 10in (29,809mm).

Above: *A class "P36" 4-8-4 of the Soviet Railways "on shed" somewhere in Russia.*

Having by 1930 established an excellent class of passenger locomotive—the "S" class—and built about 3,000 of them, the Soviet Railways could sit back and consider the future of long-distance passenger traffic at leisure. Passenger traffic had so far always taken second place to freight but it was recognised that in due time higher speeds and more comfortable (and therefore heavier) trains would be needed for those whom the Soviet government permitted to travel in the future.

The first prototype came in 1932 and it was a logical enlargement of the 2-6-2 into a 2-8-4, combining an extra driving axle to give extra tractive effort and an extra rear carrying axle to give extra power from a larger firebox. The class was given the designation "JS" (standing for Joseph Stalin) and some 640 were built between 1934 and 1941. None is working today but a freight equivalent with the same boiler, cab, cylinders, tender and other parts was the "FD" class 2-10-2, many of which are still in service in southern China, after conversion from 5ft (1,524mm) gauge to standard.

Right: *Two class "P36" 4-8-4s stand nose-to-nose in a locomotive depot in icy Siberia.*

The episode was typical of a sensible and logical attitude towards the needs of the railway system, in respect of which the new socialist regime hardly differed from the old Czarist one. One small prestige extravagance did follow, however, with the building in 1937-38 of the first three of a class of ten high-speed streamlined 4-6-4s for the Red Arrow express between Moscow and Leningrad. It was hoped to raise the average speed for the 404-mile (646km) run from about 40 to 50mph (64 to 80km/h). The first two had coupled wheels 78¾in (2,000mm) diameter, but the third had them as large as 86½in (2,197mm). The latter machine again had boiler, cylinders and much else standard with the "FD" class. In the end the war put an end to the project, but not before the first prototype had achieved 106mph (170km/h) on test, still a record for steam traction in Russia.

World War II for the Russians may have been shorter than it was for the rest of Europe, but it was also a good deal nastier. So it was not until five years after it ended that the first of new class of passenger locomotive appeared from the Kolomna Works near Moscow. This prototype took the form of a tall and handsome 4-8-4, designated class "P36". The new locomotive was similar in size and capacity to the "JS" class but the extra pair of carrying wheels enabled the axle loading to be reduced from 20 to 18 tons. This gave the engine a much wider possible range of action, although this was never needed, as we shall see.

Whilst the locomotive was very much in the final form of the

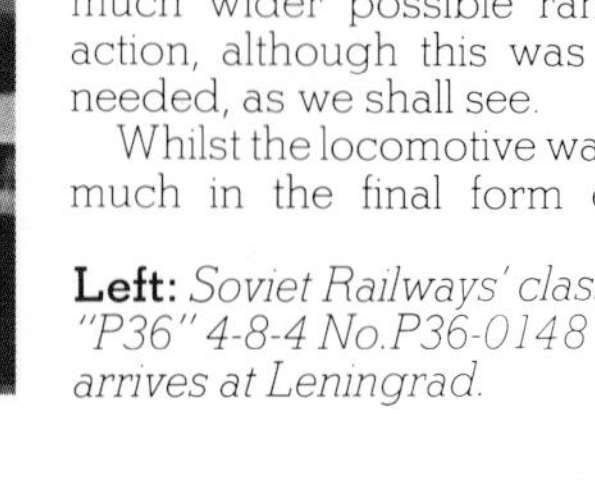

Left: *Soviet Railways' class "P36" 4-8-4 No.P36-0148 arrives at Leningrad.*

steam locomotive, one feature which it had in common with many modern Russian engines was particularly striking and unusual; this was an external main steam pipe enclosed in a large casing running forward from dome to smokebox along the top of the boiler. This arrangement, excellent from the point of view of accessibility, is only made possible by a loading gauge which allows rolling stock to be 17ft 4in (5,280mm) above rail level. Roller bearings were fitted to all axles—for the first time on any Russian locomotive—and there was a cab totally enclosed against the Russian winter, as well as a mechanical stoker for coal-fired examples of the class. Many of the 4-8-4s, however, were oil-burning, particularly those in the west of the country.

After a cautious period of testing, production began at Kolomna and between 1954 and 1956 at least 249 more were built, making them the world's most numerous class of 4-8-4. Of course, compared with other classes in Russia, which numbered from more than 10,000 examples downward, the size of the class was miniscule.

In contrast, though, their impact upon Western observers was considerable because they were to be found on lines visited by foreigners, such as Moscow-Leningrad and between Moscow and the Polish frontier. Some of the class were even finished in the blue livery similar to the streamlined 4-6-4s, but most looked smart enough in the light green passenger colours with cream stripes and red wheel centres.

For some 15 years the "P36" handled the famous Trans-Siberian express, the legendary Russia, from the end of electrification to the Pacific Ocean shore. The run took 70 hours and there were 19 changes of steam locomotive, so Siberia was paradise to at least one class of humanity. Steam enthusiasts had to show some subtlety in recording the objects of their love on film; the use of miniature cameras was very dangerous, but some success was achieved by people who set up a huge plate camera on its tripod, marched up to the nearest policeman and demanded that the platform end be cleared.

Steam enthusiasm was not without its dangers for those at home. In 1956 Lazar Kaganovitch, Commissar for Transportation and Heavy Industry, who had long advocated the retention of steam traction with such words as "I am for the steam locomotive and against those who imagine that we will not have any in the future—this machine is sturdy, stubborn and will not give up", was summarily deposed and disappeared. Steam construction immediately came to an end in the Soviet Union. Some twenty years later steam operation of passenger trains also ended and with it the lives of these superb locomotives.

Above: *A head-on view demonstrates the striking appearance of the "P36" class 4-8-4s, the last word in Soviet steam locomotion.*

Below: *Soviet 4-8-4 No.P36-0223 at the head of a local train (of the Trans-Siberian line) from Blagovetshensk, Siberia, to Vladivostok in November 1970.*

Gelsa Class 4-8-4 Brazil: National Railways, 1951

Tractive effort: 29,857lb (13,547kg).
Axle load: 29,000lb (13t).
Cylinders: (2) 17 x 25¼in (434 x 640mm).
Driving wheels: 59in (1,500mm).
Heating surface: 1,826sq ft (169.5m²).
Superheater: 721sq ft (67m²).
Steam pressure: 284psi (20kg/cm²).
Grate area: 55.5sq ft (5.4m²).
Fuel: 40,000lb (18t).
Water: 4,850gall (5,850 US) (22m³).
Adhesive weight: 115,000lb (52t).
Total weight*: 205,000lb (93t).
Length overall: 81ft 7in (24,870mm).
**without tender*

When it was formed in 1948, the Brazilian National Railways consisted of a grouping of various previously independent lines. Of a total route length of 24,000 miles (38,500km) existing in 1950, metre gauge accounted for 93 per cent. Two world wars and a long period of slump between them meant that much of the locomotive stock on these lines were obsolescent.

In 1949 a consortium of French locomotive manufacturers known as GELSA *(Groupment d'Exportation des Locomotives en Sud-Amerique)* was formed to tender for replacements and, having obtained a contract for 90 large metre-gauge locomotives, they engaged André Chapelon to take charge of design.

When it appeared that 24 of the locomotives were to be two-cylinder 4-8-4s, two treats were in store. First, of course, there was looking forward to seeing what the master rebuilder of compound locomotives would do when he tackled a brand new simple one. Second, there was to be the pleasure of seeing the world's first metre-gauge 4-8-4 locomotive in action.

Very great care was taken not only with the theoretical design but also with practical points such as the need to include many parts standard with existing spares and stores already used and in stock in Brazil.

The Belpaire type boiler was intended to provide steam for a power output of 2000 hp while burning Brazilian coal of low calorific value—about half that of best Welsh steam coal—and with large ash content. The ash-pan floor had to be steeply inclined and there were four exterior chutes as well as a normal one in the middle to dispose of the amazing amounts of clogging residue formed. A mechanical stoker was needed.

Other equipment included power reverse, Worthington's feed water heater and pump and a double Kylchap blast-pipe and chimney. According to the practice of the particular line on which they were to work the engines were fitted either with steam brakes with vacuum for the trains or, alternatively, with air brakes. Rail greasing apparatus

Class YP 4-6-2 India: Indian Railways (IR), 1949

Tractive effort: 18,450lb (8,731kg).
Axle load: 23,500lb (10.7t).
Cylinders: (2) 15¼ x 24in (387 x 610mm).
Driving wheels: 54in (1,372mm).
Heating surface: 1,112sq ft (103m²).
Superheater: 331sq ft (31m²).
Steam pressure: 210psi (14.8kg/cm²).
Grate area: 28sq ft (2.6m²).
Fuel: 21,500lb (9.75t).
Water: 3,000gall (3,600 US) (13.6m³).
Adhesive weight: 69,000lb (31.5t)
Total weight: 218,500lb (99t).
Length overall: 62ft 7½in (19,088mm).

Above: *Indian Railways' class "YP" 4-6-2 No.2630. Note the four-man engine crew leaning out of the cab.*

A total of 871 of thes beautifully proportioned and capable locomotives were built between 1949 and 1970 for the metre-gauge network of the Indian Railways. The newest members of the class, which still remains virtually intact, were the last express passenger locomotives to be built in the world.

It could be said that whilst Britain's principal achievement in India was the construction of the railway network the greatest fault in what was done was the division of the system into broad and metre gauge sections of not far off equal size. Even so, 15,940 miles (25,500km) metre-gauge railways, including many long-distance lines, required to be worked and power was needed to do it.

The strictures rightly applied to the standard "XA", "XB" and "XC" 4-6-2s of the 1920s and 1930s were not deserved by their metre-gauge counterparts, the handsome "YB" 4-6-2s supplied between 1928 and 1950. Nevertheless Indian Railways decided to do what they had done on the broad gauge and go American. Jodhpur, one of the princely states, in those days had still its own railway, and they had received ten neat 4-6-2s from Baldwin of Philadelphia in 1948. Baldwin was asked to produce

was provided, automatically coming into use on curves, which could be negotiated down to 2,624ft (80m) radius (22 degrees).

The prototype was tested in Brittany on the heavily engineered metre-gauge lines of the Brittany system. Brake locomotives were used to simulate the design loads and both French and Brazilian coals were tried. The results were excellent and by the end of 1952 all the locomotives had been delivered. In the meantime, Chapelon himself had visited Brazil—and been appropriately feted as the high priest of steam—to see the new locomotives into service.

Since that time all has been silence—and such small pockets of steam operation using large engines as now exist in Brazil seem to favour older US-built power, possibly just that bit more rugged than these otherwise superb and technically further advanced French machines.

Above: *4-8-4 No.242N4 on test in Brittany with brake-test loco behind the tender.*

---

20 prototypes of class "YP", similar to those locomotives but slightly enlarged. The new locos were also a little simpler, with plain bearings instead of roller ones and 8-wheel instead of high-capacity 12-wheel tenders.

Production orders for the "YP" were placed overseas. Krauss-Maffei of Munich and North British Locomotive of Glasgow got production orders for 200 and 100 respectively over the next five years, but the remainder were built by the Tata Engineering & Locomotive Co of Jamshedpur, India. Running numbers are 2000 to 2870, but not in chronological order. The engines could be regarded as two-thirds full-size models of a standard USA 4-6-2. If one multiplies linear measurements by 1.5, areas by 1.5^2 or 2.25, weights and volumes by 1.5^3 or 3.375 the correspondence is very close. Non-American features include the use of vacuum brakes, chopper type automatic centre couplers in place of the buckeye type, slatted screens to the cab side openings and the absence of a bell.

With so many available, these locomotives can be found in all areas of the metre gauge system; this stretches far and wide from Trivandrum, almost the southernmost point of the Indian railways, to well north of Delhi, while both the easternmost and westernmost points on Indian Railways are served by metre gauge lines. Recent allocation was as follows; Central Railway—9; Northern Railway—101; North-Eastern Railway—235; Northern Frontier Railway—98; Southern Railway—199: South Central Railway—72; Western Railway—155. The two missing engines were withdrawn after accident damage.

Diesel locomotives are now arriving on the metre-gauge network of India, but the "YP" class still hauls important trains.

Above: *An Indian Railways' class "YP" 4-6-2, allocated to the Southern railway system, lays down a fine pall of black smoke at the head-end of a metre-gauge express train.*

Below: *Indian Railways' class "YP" 4-6-2, the last express passenger-hauling steam locomotive to be built in the world.*

Class 11 4-8-2 Angola: Benguela Railway (FCB), 1951

Tractive effort: 36,100lb (16,375kg).
Axle load: 29,000lb (13t).
Cylinders: (2) 21 x 26in (533 x 660mm).
Driving wheels: 54in (1,372mm).
Heating surface: 1,777sq ft (165m²).
Superheater: 420sq ft (39m²).
Steam pressure: 200psi (14.1kg/cm²).
Grate area: 40sq ft (3.7m²).
Fuel (wood): 650cu ft (18.5m³).
Water: 5,000gall (6,000 US) (25m³).
Adhesive weight: 116,000lb (53t).
Total weight: 295,000lb (133½t).
Length overall: 69ft 3in (21,107mm).

The Benguela Railway of Angola was one of the most remarkable (although not one of the most rapid) feats of railway-building in the world. It was the result of the enterprise of an Englishman called Robert Williams, who saw that a railway from the Atlantic port of Lobito Bay was the best way of transporting the copper mined in Katanga (in what is now called Zaïre), instead of sending it east across to the Indian Ocean at Beira for shipment.

Work began at Lobito Bay in 1904 and the 837 miles (1,340 km) to the border at Dilolo was completed in 1929. Through communication with the rest of the 3ft 6in (1,067mm) gauge southern African network was established in 1931; by this route Lobito Bay is 2,464 miles (3,965 km) from Cape Town.

Steam traction was (and largely is) used. In order to provide fuel, the Benguela railway planted eucalyptus forests close to suitable wooding points. These trees, imported from Australia, grow well in Angola and a sufficient area was planted to keep up a continuous supply of logs to fire the locomotives.

As in the case of other southern African lines, the first miles out of the port are the worst, concerned as they are with scaling the African plateau at a height of 5,000-6,000ft (1,500-2,000m). The steep grades of this section came to involve the use of Beyer-Garratt locomotives, but there was also a requirement for some smaller locomotives for the easier sections, particularly for hauling the passenger trains. In the early days 4-8-0s had been used, but in 1951 the Benguela Railway went to the North British Locomotive Co. of Glasgow for six 4-8-2 passenger locomotives, designated class "11".

The requirements were that trains up to 500 tons should be hauled up gradients of 1 in 80 (1.25 per cent) and that curves of 300ft (90m) radius could be negotiated. Axle loading was not to exceed 13 tons. This specification was met by taking the standard South African Railways "19C/19D" class 4-8-2 and making some modifications, mostly in connection with the burning of wood. The smokebox was fitted with an efficient spark arrester—for once without spoiling the elegant simplicity of the appearance of the front end—and a Kylala-Chapelon (Kylchap) exhaust system was provided. The boiler is pitched 7in (178mm) higher than on the SAR prototype, as permitted by the Benguela Rly loading gauge, and this gives room for a larger ashpan, for which drenching pipes are fitted. There was a large timber-holding cage on top of the tender.

That such sophisticated fittings were provided for an African railway may come as a surprise to people used to the primitive equipment provided as late as the 1950s on new locomotives for BR back home in Britain.

Selkirk Class 2-10-4 Canada: Canadian Pacific Railway (CPR), 1949

Tractive effort: 76,905lb (34,884kg).
Axle load: 62,240lb (28.25t).
Cylinders: (2) 25 x 32in (635 x 813mm).
Driving wheels: 63in (1,600mm).
Heating surface: 4,590sq ft (426m²).
Superheater: 2,055sq ft (191m)m²).
Steam pressure: 285psi (20kg/cm²).
Grate area: 93.5sq ft (8.7m²).
Fuel (oil): 4,100gall (4,925 US) (18.6m²).
Water: 12,000gall (14,000 US) (54.5m³).
Adhesive weight: 311,200lb (141t).
Total weight: 732,500lb (332t).
Length overall: 97ft 10⅝in (29,835mm).

Ten-coupled locomotives were used in most parts of the world for freight movement; in fact, the only steam locomotives in quantity production in the world today are 2-10-2s in China. Because the length of a rigid wheelbase has to be limited, five pairs of coupled wheels implies that they are fairly small ones and this in turn means (usually) low speeds. It is true that British Railways had some superb 2-10-0s that were occasionally used on passenger trains "in emergencies" and, in spite of having only 62in (1575mm) dia meter wheels, were timed up to 90mph (145km/h) whilst so doing, but these were exceptional. Perhaps the ten-coupled engines with the best claim to be considered as express passenger locomotives were the 2-10-4 "Selkirk" class of the Canadian Pacific Railway. Not only were they streamlined (in the way CPR understood the term) but the coloured passenger

steam operation that had become chronic in Britain.

The Benguela line had the good fortune for many happy years to carry (mostly) one commodity, copper, from one source to one destination. Railways that do this tend to be prosperous and this was reflected in the fact that the locomotive fleet was well looked after and kept in first-rate condition, both mechanically and visually. Hence the fleet was very economic to run and so did its bit to make the concern even more prosperous—a benevolent rather than a vicious circle, in fact.

Independence from Portugal was followed by a civil war which is still continuing in 1981 and this has for some years now halted the copper traffic. Forestry operations have also been halted by guerilla activity; such trains as do run are mostly hauled by oil-fired steam locomotives, since the country does at least have its own oil supplies.

Above and below: *Two views of the class "11" 4-8-2 of the Benguela Railway in Angola. The photograph above shows that the appearance of these engines in normal service came close to the ideal as drawn below.*

They included a pyrometer to check the steam temperature and a power reversing gear of the Hadfield steam-operated type. The firedoor was also steam operated, electric lights were fitted and there was a recording speedometer. Particularly important was the compensated springing; this feature avoided the trailing wheels stealing adhesive weight from the driving wheels at small track irregularities and so causing slipping—a facet of

livery was also used for them; also, of course, they handled CPR's flag train, then called the "Dominion", across the Rockies and the adjacent Selkirks.

The overall story was very similar to that of the CPR "Royal Hudson". First came the slightly more angular "T-la" batch; 20 (Nos.5900 to 5919) were built in 1929. A further ten ("T-lb") with softer and more glamorous lines were built in 1938 and, finally, another six ("T-lc") came in 1949. No.5935 was not only the last of the class but the last steam locomotive built for the company and, indeed, for any Canadian railway. The "Royal Hudson" boiler was used as the basis, but enlarged and equipped for oil-burning, since all locomotives used on the mountain division had been fired with oil since 1916.

Left: *A Canadian Pacific Railway "Selkirk" class 2-10-4 runs alongside a turbulent river on the fabled Kicking Horse Pass route.*

When one crossed Canada by CPR the whole 2,882 miles (4,611km) from Montreal to Vancouver was reasonably easy going apart from a section along the north shore of Lake Superior and, more notably, the 262 miles (420km) over the mountains between Calgary and Revelstoke. Until the 1950s CPR's flag train, the "Dominion", could load up to 18 heavyweight cars weighing some 1,300 tons and to haul these up the 1 in 45 (2.2 per cent) inclines required some fairly heroic measures. There was very little difference in the timings and loadings of the various types of train, even the mighty "Dominion" made 23 stops over this section.

The 2-10-4s were permitted to haul loads up to about 1,000 tons on the steepest sections. Typically when hauling a capacity load up a bank of 20 miles mostly at 1 in 45, (2.2 per cent) the average speed would be 10mph. The booster would be cut in if speed fell below walking pace and cut out when the train had reached the speed of a man's run. Fuel consumption would be of the order of 37 gallons per mile up grade.

In the mountains downhill speeds were limited to 25-30mph (40-50km/h) by curvature, frequently as sharp as 462ft (140m) radius, but passengers hardly found—or find—this portion of the journey tedious having regard to the nature of the views from the car windows. On the few straight sections of line 65mph (108km/h) could be achieved by these locomotives.

The 2-10-4s were able to negotiate these sharp curves by dint of widening the gauge on the curves from 4ft 8½in to 4ft 9¾in (1,435mm to 1,469mm), an exceptional amount, and by giving the leading axle nearly an inch (25mm) of side-play each way as well as providing it with a pair of flange lubricators. In other ways standard North American practice was applied, including a fairly early application of the cast steel one-piece locomotive frame, and the class stood up well to robust usage.

In 1952 diesels took over the running across the mountains and after the 2-10-4s had done a stint on freight haulage across the prairies, they were withdrawn. The last one was cut up in 1959, except for No.5931 (numbered 5934) in the Heritage Park, Calgary, and No. 5935 at the Railway Museum at Delson, Quebec.

Class 8 4-6-2 **Great Britain:** British Railways (BR), 1953

Tractive effort: 39,080lb (17,731kg)..
Axle load: 49,500lb (22.5t).
Cylinders: (3) 18 x 28in (457 x 711mm).
Driving wheels: 74in (1,880mm).
Heating surface: 2,490sq ft (231m^2).
Superheater: 691sq ft (64m^2).
Steam pressure: 250psi (17.6kg/cm^2).
Grate area: 48.5sq ft (4.5m^2).
Fuel: 22,000lb (10t).
Water: 4,325gall (5,200 US) (20m^3).
Adhesive weight: 148,000lb (67.5t).
Total weight: 347,000lb (157.5t).
Length overall: 70ft 0in (21,336mm).

Above: *"Britannia" class 4-6-2 No.70039 climbing Shap in September 1965 with a Liverpool to Glasgow express.*

Below: *"Britannia" class 4-6-2 No.70020* Mercury *hauling the eastbound Capitals United Express in May 1959.*

The railways of Britain became British Railways on 1 January 1948 and naturally there was much speculation concerning the kind of locomotives that would succeed the "Duchess", "King", "Merchant Navy" and "A4" classes of BR's illustrious predecessors. In early 1951 it was announced that none was planned but instead, the first full-size Pacific for any British railway to have only two cylinders was unveiled. This locomotive class was intended to displace such second-eleven power as the "Royal Scot", "Castle" and "West Country" classes rather than the largest types.

Britannia was a simple, rugged 4-6-2 with Belpaire firebox and roller bearings on all axles, as well as many other aids to cheap and easy maintenance. It was designated class "7", and had a capacity to produce some 2,200 hp in the cylinders, at a very fair consumption of coal, amounting to some 5,000lb/h (2,270kg/h). This was well above the rate at which a normal man could shovel coal on to the fire but the large firebox enabled a big fire to be built up in advance when some big effort of short duration was required.

A total of 55 "Britannia"s were built between 1951 and 1953. They met their designers' goal of a locomotive that was easy to maintain, and also showed that they were master of any express passenger task in Britain at that time. They were allocated to all the regions, but the one that made the best use of the new engines was the Eastern. Their "Britannia"s were allocated to one line and put to work on a new high-speed train service specifically designed round their abilities. During the 1950s in most of Britain it could be said that 20 years progress had meant journey times some 20 per cent longer. On the other hand the new 4-6-2s working this new timetable between London and Norwich meant a 20 per cent *acceleration* on pre-war timings, in terms of the service in general.

In spite of being simple engines in both senses of the world, the "Britannia"s displayed economy in the use of steam. In fact they were right in the front rank yet there was always the nagging fact that the great Chapelon compounds across the Channel could on test do about 16 per cent better. This figure would be diluted in service by various

factors but even so it was considerable, especially as within almost exactly the same weight limits they could develop nearly 1,500 more cylinder horsepower. There was, however, certain reluctance in Britain to go compound, because for one thing there was no counterpart to the French works-trained *mechanicien* drivers to handle such complex beasts. Past experience had also shown the extra maintenance costs implicit in the complexity to have over-ridden economies due to the saving of fuel.

A point was perhaps missed, though, that since the upper limit of power output was a man shovelling, a more economical machine would also be a more powerful one. And since more power involves faster running times and faster running times more revenue, a more efficient locomotive might be both a money saver and a money earner. But there is another way of obtaining some of the advantages of compounding and that is to expand the steam to a greater extent in simple cylinders. This in its turn means that the point in the stroke at which the valves close to steam (known as the cut-off and expressed in terms of per cent) must be very early. However, the geometry of normal valve-gears precludes cut-offs less than, say, 15-20 per cent. This is because, if the opening to steam is limited to less of the stroke than that, the opening to exhaust (the same valve being used for both) is also limited on the return stroke. This means steam trapped in the cylinders and loss of power. The solution is to have independent valves for admission and exhaust and the simplest way of doing this is to use poppet valves actuated by a camshaft. Alas, it cannot be too simple because the point of cut-off has to be varied and, moreover, the engine has to be reversed. Both these things are done by sliding the camshaft along its axis, bringing changed cam profiles into action according to the position of the reversing control in the cab.

Permission was obtained in 1953 to build a prototype for future BR top-line express passenger locomotives. As a two-cylinder machine, the cylinder size came out too big to clear platform edges so, in spite of a yen for simplicity, three cylinders had to be used. Now it is a point concerning poppet valves that much of the mechanism is common, however many cylinders there are. So poppet valves of the British-Caprotti pattern were specified for this sole example of the British Railways class "8" locomotive. On test, No.71000 *Duke of Gloucester* showed a 9 per cent improvement over the "Britannia" class in steam consumed for a given amount of work done. It was a world record for a simple locomotive.

Alas, although the boiler was of impeccable lineage, being based on the excellent one used on the LMS "Duchess" class, there was some detail of its proportions which interfered with economical steam production at high outputs. It would have been easy to correct the faults with a little investigation. Unfortunately (in the words of E.S. Cox, then Chief Officer (Design) at BR headquarters), "there were some in authority at headquarters, although not in the Chief Mechanical Engineer's department, who were determined that there should be no more development with steam"; so nothing was done and no more class "8" locomotives were built.

So No.71000 spent its brief life as an unsatisfactory one-off locomotive. After it was withdrawn the valve chests and valve gear was removed for preservation, but that has not prevented a more than usually bold preservation society from buying the rest of the remains.

Above: *Class "8" 4-6-2 No.71000* Duke of Gloucester. *Note the shaft which drives the rotary-cam poppet valve gear.*

Below: *British Railways' ill-fated, one and only class "8" 4-6-2, Duke of Gloucester, No.71000.*

Class 25 4-8-4 **South Africa:** South African Railways (SAR), 1953

Tractive effort: 45,360lb (20,575kg)
Axle load: 44,000lb (20t)
Cylinders: (2) 24 x 28in (610 x 711mm)
Driving wheels: 60in (1,524mm).
Heating surface: 3,390sq ft ($315m^2$).
Superheater: 630sq ft ($58.5m^2$).
Steam pressure: 225lb/sq in ($15.8kg/cm^2$).
Grate area: 70sq ft ($6.5m^2$).
Fuel: 42,000lb (19t)
Water: 4,400gall (5,300 US) ($20m^3$).
Adhesive weight: 172,000lb (78t).
Total weight: 525,000lb (238t).
Length overall: 107ft 6¼in (32,772mm).

Two successful departures from the fundamental Stephenson principles in one class of locomotive! South African Railways had a problem in operating the section of their Cape Town to Johannesburg main line across the Karoo desert. For many years they had lived with it, facing the expense of hauling in water for locomotive purposes in tank cars during the dry season, as well as the expense of maintaining deep wells, pumps and bore-holes in dry country.

For a long time steam locomotive engineers had toyed with the idea of saving the heat which was wasted in steam exhausted from the chimney. In power stations and ships this steam is condensed back to water and much less heat is wasted. The problem is that condensing equipment is bulky and complex; numerous experimental condensing locomotives had been built but savings in fuel costs were always swamped by higher maintenance costs.

In this case there were not only fuel costs, but there were also heavy water costs to be considered, so the SAR decided to look into the idea of condensing locomotives for the Karoo. Messrs Henschel of Kassel, Germany, had built a quantity of condensing locomotives during the war and in 1948 they were asked to make a class "20" 2-10-2 into a condensing locomotive. The condenser was mounted on a greatly extended tender, while a special turbine-driven fan took care of the draught, now that there was no exhaust blast to induce it directly in the Stephenson manner.

Test indicated that the apparatus saved 90 per cent of the water normally used and 10 per cent of the coal, results that were promising enough to warrant SAR embarking on an unprecedented programme of introducing condensing locomotives. To that end came the class "25" 4-8-4 described on this page.

The 4-8-4s were up-to-date in all respects. Roller bearings were used not only for all the main bearings but also for the connecting and coupling rods. As can be seen, the latter were arranged as individual rods between adjacent crank pins thereby doing away with knuckle joints. The cylinders were cast integrally with the frames, using a one-piece locomotive frame—a similar one supported the equipment in the tender. The boiler was the largest possible within the SAR loading gauge and as a result the chimney and dome were purely vestigial.

In all 90 condensing locomotives were supplied, Nos.3451 to 3540, all except one Henschel prototype by the North British Locomotive Co. of Glasgow, Scotland. A further 50 non-condensing "25"s were also supplied, known as class "25NC" and numbered 3401 to 3450. Ten came from NBL and 40 from Henschel. The tenders hold 18 tons of coal and 12,000 gallons

Above: *Class "25NC" 4-8-4 takes water en route from De Aar to Kimberley on the main line from Jo'burg to Capetown. This loco was of non-condensing type when originally built.*

Below: *This superb drawing of a class "25" condensing locomotive gives a vivid impression of the extreme length of this "Puffer which never puffs".*

($54.5m^3$) of water and were somewhat shorter than those attached to the condensing locos.

Once in service the class was in most respects very successful, but that usually fatal departure from the Stephenson principle of using the jet of exhaust steam to draw the fire—the Achilles heel of all condensing locomotives—at first nearly caused disaster. The fan blades of the blower that was used in place of the blast-pipe wore out rapidly, due to the ash and grit in the exhaust gases. Eventually with Henschel's help, the problem was overcome. As had been intended, over the "dry" section of the Cape Town to Johannesburg main line, between Beaufort West and De Aar, these condensing locomotives enabled a number of costly watering points to be closed down as well as obviating the need to haul in water at others. Over this section they dealt with everything from the famous "Blue Train" to train loads of coal. It is a strange sensation to watch a "25" starting a heavy train; there is complete silence apart from the whine of the blower fan. The condenser silently absorbs those tremendous blasts of steam that so fascinate and thrill the ferro-equinologist.

Left, above: *A class "25" 4-8-4 with condensing tender.*

Below: *Class "25NC" No.3530 lays down a fine trail of smoke with a freight near Modder River in April 1979. The unusual shape of tender indicates where the condensing equipment was removed by conversion.*

By the 1970s, a better solution was on hand for the waterless Karoo—the diesel locomotive. So these strange "puffers that never puff" lost their justification for existence. It was therefore decided to convert the condensing engines to non-condensing, the main alteration consisted of converting the original condensing tenders to rather strange-looking long low water-carts. Currently only one condensing locomotive remains, kept really as a working museum-piece. It is a reminder of what is one of the very few unconventional steam locomotive classes ever successfully run in service and consequently a remarkable *tour de force* of locomotive engineering.

The fleet of non-condensing "25"s, however, remain, with the original 50 now increased to 139. They are now largely grouped at Beaconsfield Shed, Kimberley. At the present time they still work the main line south from there to De Aar, and also east to Bloemfontein and north-west to Warrenton. Many of them have regular crews and with official encouragement are specially polished, decorated, and in some cases named.

More amazing than one could imagine at this late stage in the history of steam locomotion, is the fact that a South African class "25" is undergoing fundamental further development. The honoured name of André Chapelon is the source of a new way of burning coal in a locomotive firebox. The basis of the idea is to divert a proportion of the exhaust steam back into the fire. At the same time a high proportion of the air needed for combustion is led in through short large-diameter tubes just above the fire. The result is that the firebed, behaving more like a chemical reaction than a furnace, reacts to give off producer gas, which mixes with the air being drawn into the firebox and burns cleanly there. The result—no more fire-throwing black smoke or clinker forming, coupled with a substantial decrease in coal consumption. And all for the very minimum of expenditure.

The system suggested by Chapelon was used by a certain South American engineer called Da Porta on the locomotives of a coal-hauling line not far from Cape Horn; after years of successful use there, a small South African class "19D" was converted in 1979. During 1981, class "25NC" No 3450 was rebuilt to class "26" on the same lines as the class "19D". Success has been such that there is even a prospect that the use of these gas-fired locomotives might arrest the decline of steam in this, one of its last strongholds.

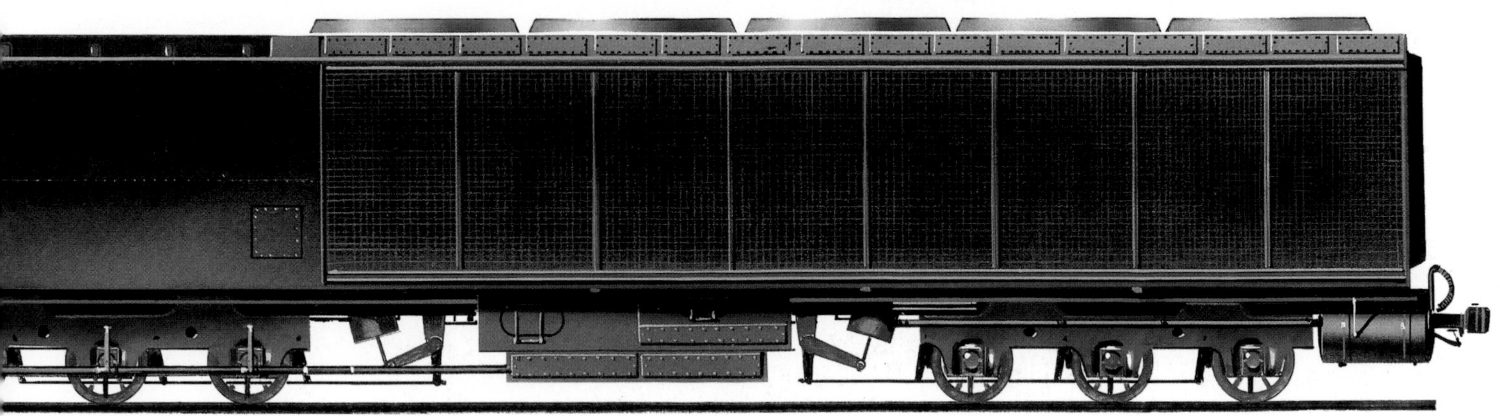

Class 59 4-8-2+2-8-4 Kenya: East African Railways (EAR), 1955

Tractive effort: 83,350lb (38,034kg).
Axle load: 47,000lb (21t).
Cylinders: (4) 20½ x 28in (521 x 711mm).
Driving wheels: 54in (1,372mm).
Heating surface: 3,560sq ft ($331m^2$).
Superheater: 747sq ft ($69.4m^2$).
Steam pressure: 225psi ($15.8kg/cm^2$).
Grate area: 72sq ft ($6.7m^2$).
Fuel (oil): 2,700gall (3,250 US) ($12m^3$).
Water: 8,600gall (10,400 US) ($39m^3$).
Adhesive weight: 357,000lb (164t).
Total weight: 564,000lb (256t).
Length overall: 104ft 1½in (31,737mm).

Often in this narrative British climbs like Shap and Beattock have been spoken of with awe. Shap has 20 miles (32km) of 1 in 75 (1.3 per cent) but what would one say about a climb 350 miles (565km) long with a ruling grade of 1 in 65 (1.5 per cent)? But such is the ascent from Mombasa to Nairobi, up which every night the legendary "Uganda Mail" makes its way.

The building of the metre-gauge Uganda Railway, begun in 1892, was a strangely reluctant piece of empire building, violently opposed at home, yet successful. One of its objectives was the suppression of the slave trade and that was quickly achieved; the second objective was to facilitate trade and that also was successful to a point where the railway was always struggling to move the traffic offering. By 1926 a fleet of 4-8-0s were overwhelmed by the tonnage and the Kenya & Uganda Railway (as it then was) went to Beyer, Peacock of Manchester for 4-8-2 + 2-8-4 Beyer-Garratts, with as many mechanical parts as possible standard with the 4-8-0s. It was the answer to mass movement on 50lb/yd (24kg/m) rails.

As the years went by, other Garratt classes followed and the K&UR became East African Railways. In 1954 with the biggest backlog of tonnage ever faced waiting movement, the administration ordered 34 of the greatest Garratt design ever built. Whilst their main role was the haulage of freight, these giant "59" class were regarded as sufficiently passenger train oriented to be given the names of East African mountains. Also, of course, they bore the attractive maroon livery of the system.

Above: *East African Railways class "59" 4-8-2+2-8-4 No.5904* Mount Elgon.

By British standards their statistics are very impressive—over double the tractive effort of any

Class 15A 4-6-4+4-6-4 Rhodesia: Rhodesia Railways (RR), 1952

Tractive effort: 47,500lb (21,546kg).
Axle load: 34,000lb (15.5t).
Cylinders: (4) 17½ x 26in (445 x 660mm).
Driving wheels: 57in (1,448mm).
Heating surface: 2,322sq ft ($216m^2$).
Superheater: 494sq ft ($46m^2$).
Steam pressure: 200psi ($14.1kg/cm^2$).
Grate area: 49.6sq ft ($4.6m^2$).
Fuel: 27,000lb (12t).
Water: 7,000gall (8,400 US) ($32m^3$).
Adhesive weight: 178,000lb (81t).
Total weight: 418,000lb (190t).
Length overall: 92ft 4in (28,143mm).

A railway linking Cape Town up the whole length of Africa to Cairo was the impossible dream of an English clergyman's son called Cecil Rhodes, who eventually was to give his name to Rhodesia, now known as Zimbabwe. "The railway is my right

locomotive ever employed in passenger service back home, coupled with a grate area nearly 50 per cent greater. Oil-firing was used but provision was made for a mechanical stoker if coal burning ever became economic in East African circumstances. There was also provision for an easy conversion from metre gauge to the African standard 3ft 6in (1,067mm) gauge, as well as for fitting vacuum brake equipment, should the class ever be required to operate outside air-brake territory in Tanzania.

All the latest and best Beyer-Garratt features were applied, such as the self-adjusting main pivots, the "streamlined" ends to the tanks, and those long handsome connecting rods driving on the third coupled axle. Four sets of Walschaert's valve gear were worked by Beyer's patent Hadfield steam reverser with hydraulic locking mechanism. The virtues of the short fat Garratt boiler, with clear space beneath the firebox, made 14 or 15 hours continuous hard steaming no problem. Later, Giesl ejectors were fitted to the class, with results that were controversial operationally, and quite unambiguously awful aesthetically.

One feature which did not work out was the tapered axle loadings, which gave successive axle-loads in tons when running forward of 15.4, 15.4, 19.0, 20.9, 20.8, 18.8, 15.3; 15.5, 19.0, 21.0, 21.0, 19.0, 15.3, 15.3. The idea was that the gradual rise in axle-load should permit operation on 80lb/yd (38.6kg/m) rail north and west of Nairobi in addition to 95lb/yd (45.7kg/m) rail which was by then general between Nairobi and the coast.

The results of fresh motive power were very impressive, the backlog of traffic was quickly cleared and the new engines soon found themselves the largest and most powerful steam locomotives in the world. That they remained that way for 25 years was due to the economical use of well-maintained steam power long preventing any case being made out for a change to diesel traction.

Even so the diesel did win in the end, displacing the "59"s from the mail trains quite early on and gradually from the freights between 1973 and 1980. In addition a proposed "61" class 4-8-4+4-8-4 with 27-ton axle-loading, 115,000lb (52,476kg) tractive effort and 105sq ft (9.8m²) fire grate was shelved indefinitely.

Above: *East African Railways class "59" 4-8-2+2-8-4 No. 5916* Mount Rungwe.

Below: *East African Railways Beyer Garratt No.5928* Mount Kilimanjaro, *depicted in the superb crimson lake livery of the original.*

hand, the telegraph my voice" said Rhodes at the height of his power. When Rhodes died in 1902 his Cape-to-Cairo line had reached the River Zambesi, 280 miles (450km) north of Bulawayo, but there was sufficient impetus to reach Bukama, 2,700 miles (4,345km) from Cape Town in what is now Zaïre, by 1914.

In 1930, for working a 484-mile (778-km) stretch of this Cape-to-Cairo line between Mafeking and Bulawayo, what had now become Rhodesia Railways ordered four 4-6-4+4-6-4 Beyer-Garratts from England. They were typical sound solid chunks of Beyer, Peacock engineering; they also showed the whole objective of the Garratt concept by having a tractive effort greater than and a grate area equal to the largest "straight" locomotive ever to run back in Britain, but within an axle-load limit 30 per cent less. Delays in completing bridge strengthening works denied the Cape-to-Cairo route to the new locomotives (known as the "15th" class) so they went into service on the Bulawayo to Salisbury main line; the haulage of the celebrated "Rhodesia Express" was entrusted to them. In service the class proved to be excellent runners and very light on maintenance. They played a large part in converting the RR management to the idea of a mainly Garratt-operated system and so, immediately after the war, a further 30 were ordered as all-purpose locomotives for the railway. Between 1949 and 1952 yet another 40 with slight modifications were delivered, known as class "15A", and to which the particulars given here apply. A final 10 came from Messrs. Franco-Belge of France, Beyer, Peacock being then swamped with Garratt orders.

The resulting 74 locomotives were the largest class ever acquired by the RR. They were also the second most numerous design of Beyer-Garratt, as well as being the first Garratts to have the "streamlined" front tanks. On a 50mph (80km/h) locomotive, streamlining could only be for show, but the improved lines greatly ameliorated the rather severe looks of previous Garratts.

Their most notable assignment was the British royal family's tour in 1947, when two "15th" class decked out in royal blue handled the 730-ton "White Train". Not until 1963 was the class able to take over the work for which they were originally bought, and for the next ten years the "15" and "15A" classes monopolised the traffic between Bulawayo and Mafeking, through what is now Botswana. The Bulawayo-Cape Town and Bulawayo-Johannesburg expresses were part of these duties; long-distance trains of this kind were worked on the caboose system, whereby two crews would operate the train, one in the cab on duty and the other taking their ease in a comfortable sleeping and eating van (the caboose) marshalled next the engine. The 970 mile (1,556km) round trip from Bulawayo to Mafeking and back would take three days and two nights.

When the railways in northern Rhodesia became Zambian Railways, a number of "15"s were allocated north of the Zambesi. A few others have been withdrawn, but some 50 remain. It is a pleasure to write not only that most of these are still in service but also that a policy has been adopted by oil-poor but coal-rich Zimbabwe to rebuild their fleet of Garratts. In this way these fine locomotives should be good for many more years of service.

Above left: *Class "15A" Beyer-Garratt 4-6-4+4-6-4 No.400 of Rhodesia Railways (now National Railways of Zimbabwe) under steam test at Bulawayo Works after overhaul.*

Left: *Rhodesia Railways Beyer-Garratt 4-6-4+4-6-4 No. 358. This class "15" is running bunker first on the Victoria Falls to Bulawayo train.*

Class 498.1 4-8-2 **Czechoslovakia:** Czechoslovak State Railways (CSD), 1954

Tractive effort: 41,920lb (19,018kg).
Axle load: see text.
Cylinders: (3) 19¾ x 26¾in (500 x 680mm).
Driving wheels: 72in (1,830mm).
Heating surface: 2,454sq ft ($228m^2$).
Superheater: 797sq ft ($74m^2$).
Steam pressure: 228psi ($16kg/cm^2$).
Grate area: 52sq ft ($4.9m^2$).
Fuel: 33,000lb (15t).
Water: 7,700gall (9,200 US) ($35m^3$).
Adhesive weight: see text.
Total weight: 428,500lb (194t).
Length overall: 83ft 11½in (25,594mm).

These remarkable locomotives in their handsome blue livery were some of the finest steam passenger express locomotives ever to be placed on the rails. Anyone with a gift for arithmetic could tell quite a lot about them by merely glancing at the number, which has the class designation as a prefix. The first figure gives the number of driving axles; take the middle figure, add 3, multiply by 10 and the answer is the maximum permitted speed in km/h; then take the last figure, add 10 and that gives the axle load to the nearest ton. So the 498.1 class had four driving axles, a maximum speed of 120 km/h (75mph) and a maximum axle load of between 18 tons and 19 tons. Fifteen were built by the famous Skoda Works during 1954-55.

Amongst things one can hardly tell from a glance would be the existence of a third inside cylinder, whose axis is inclined at 1 in 10 to the horizontal, driving, like the outside cylinders, on the second coupled axle. Roller bearings were fitted to all the main axle bearings and also to the motion. Most remarkably the centre big end was also a roller bearing; the designers had sufficient confidence to wall up this bearing between the webs of the crankshaft.

Other sophisticated equipment included powered reversing gear, mechanical stoking, a combustion chamber, arch tubes and thermic syphons in the firebox, as well as axle load adjustment from 41,000lb (18.5t) to 37,000lb (16.8t) with corresponding reduction in adhesive weight from 164,000lb (74t) to 148,000lb (67.5t). The effect of this change was to transfer weight from the driving wheels to the leading bogie and rear pony truck. The alteration would enable the locomotives to be employed on the country's secondary main lines which would only accept the lower axle-loading, once the principal routes had become electrified. The change involved moving the position of the pivot points of the compensating levers, provision being made to do this without making any physical modifications. Incidentally, the three domes are, respectively from the front, for top feed, sand and steam. Amongst other unusual features are the ten-wheel tenders with one six-wheel and one four-wheel bogie. The three sets of Walschaert's gear are conventional except that the drive to the inside set is taken from a return crank mounted outside on the third coupled-wheel crankpin on the left-hand side.

This arrangement is similar to

Right: *A conspicuous red star decorates the front end of a Czechoslovak State Railways' class "498.1" 4-8-2.*

242 Class 4-8-4 **Spain:** Spanish National Railways System (RENFE), 1956

Tractive effort: 46,283lb (21,000kg).
Axle load: 42,000lb (19t).
Cylinders: (2) 25¼ x 28in (640 x 710mm).
Driving wheels: 74¾in (1,900mm).
Heating surface: 3,161sq ft ($293m^2$).
Superheater: 1,125sq ft ($104.5m^2$).
Steam pressure: 228psi ($16kg/cm^2$).
Grate area: 57sq ft ($5.3m^2$).
Fuel (oil): 3,000gall (3,600 US) (13.5^3).
Water: 6,200gall (7,440 US) ($28m^3$).
Adhesive weight: 167,500lb (76t).
Total weight: 469,500lb (213t).
Length overall: 88ft 0¾in (26,840mm).

These magnificent locomotives, built to a gauge of two Spanish yards or 5ft 5.9in (1,674mm), were the final European express passenger locomotive class, the only *class* of 4-8-4 in Western Europe and the ultimate achievement of Spanish steam locomotive engineering. They were descended from a long line of 4-8-2s dating from 1925. Those built before 1944 were compounds, but since then the world standard form of a two-cylinder simple has prevailed. In the case of these 4-8-4s the only departure from this has been the use of the Lentz system of poppet valves, with an oscillating camshaft actuated by a set of Walschaert's valve gear each side.

The ten locomotives were supplied by the Maquinista Terrestre y Maritima of Barcelona in 1956 and were numbered 242.2001-10. Details included a feed-water heater, equipment for the French TIA water-treatment system, a cab floor mounted on springs, and a turbo-generator large enough to supply current to light the train as well as the engine. Lights on the locomotive included one just ahead of the Kylchap

that found on Chapelon's "242A1" 4-8-4 and it reflects a good deal of contact between him and the CSD before politics put an end to such interchanges. It is interesting to find amongst the progenitors of the "498.1" class a group of three three-cylinder compound 4-8-2s very much in the French tradition. These were built in 1949.

It was found, though, that the simple locomotive was better on an all-round basis and the "498.1" class followed directly on previous 4-8-2s, that is, the nine "486" class of 1933-38 and the forty "498.0" class of 1946-49. The new 4-8-2s, known as the "Albatross" class by their crews, were excellent performers both on heavy international expresses and lighter faster trains. On test speeds up to 93mph (149km/h) were achieved and in normal running the maximum permitted speed of 75mph (120km/h) was often achieved.

Steam traction has recently come to an end in Czechoslovakia. It is understood that 4-8-2 No. 498.106 has been set aside for preservation but it is not known if the work has been completed.

Below: *A fine view of class "498.0" 4-8-2 No.498.82. Note the unusual design of tender with one four-wheel and one six-wheel bogie.*

double chimney, so that at night as well as in the daytime the fireman could judge by the colour of the exhaust whether he had adjusted the oil-firing controls correctly. All axleboxes had roller bearings. A special green livery —lesser Spanish steam locomotives were painted plain black —set off a truly superb appearance.

The 4-8-4s were built to work the principal expresses over the unelectrified section of the main line from Madrid to the French border at Irun, that is, from Avila to Miranda del Ebro. They had no problems in keeping time with such trains as the "Sud Express" loaded up to 750 tons, although really fast running was precluded by an overall speed restriction of 68mph (110km/h). Even so, the "242" class demonstrated on test an ability to run at 84mph (134km/h) on the level with 480 tons, as well as to develop 4,000hp in the cylinders. In service they could maintain a speed of 35mph (55km/h) with 600 tons along 1 in 100 (1 per cent) gradients. The tenders of the 4-8-4s were absurdly small for such a huge locomotive. No doubt the size of turntable available prevented any larger ones being attached, but in the absence of water troughs there was no possibility of making long non-stop runs in the face of a need for some 70 gallons (0.3m³) per mile with less than 6,200 gallons (28m³) available.

Steam has now been eliminated in Spain for normal use. Whilst various steam locomotives have been seen on special excursion trains, they have not so far included a "242", although one (No.242.2009) is set aside in the depot at Miranda del Ebro.

Left: *Note the small tender on this Spanish class "242" 4-8-4.*

Right: *Spanish National Railways class "242" 4-8-4 No.242.2001.*

RM Class 4-6-2 **China:** Railways of the People's Republic, 1958

Tractive effort: 34,597lb (15,698kg).
Axle load: 46,284lb (21t).
Cylinders: (2) 22½ x 26in (570 x 660mm).
Driving wheels: 69in (1,750mm).
Heating surface: 2,260sq ft (210m^2).
Superheater: 700sq ft (65m^2).
Steam pressure: 213psi (15kg/cm^2).
Grate area: 62sq ft (5.75m^2).
Fuel: 32,000lb (14.5t).
Water: 8,700gall (10,400 US) (30.5m^3).
Adhesive weight: 137,750 (62.5t).
Total weight: 38,349lb (174t).
Length overall: 73ft 5½in (22,390mm).

Above: *Brand new "Forward" class steam locomotive No.QJ 3404 on test at the People's Locomotive factory at Datong, China, in October 1980.*

This unusual but neat-looking 4-6-2 is thought to be the final design of steam express passenger locomotive in the world. There is another reason why it is treated as the last word in this book and that is because the country which produced it is also the last in the world to have steam locomotives in production. Those now being built are basically freight locomotives but are used for express passenger trains on certain mountain lines in the People's Republic of China. With many new lines under construction it is possible in China to ride a 1980s railway behind a 1980s steam locomotive.

The "RM"—"Ren Ming" or "People" class—4-6-2s are descended from some passenger locomotives supplied by the Japanese to the railways of their puppet kingdom of Manchukuo, otherwise Manchuria. The older engines in pre-liberation days were known as class "PF-1" ("PF" stood for "Pacific") but afterwards they became redesignated "SL" standing for "Sheng-Li" or "Victory". Locomotive construction to Chinese design did not begin for several years after the Communist victory of 1949, but by 1958 the construction of the "RM" class was under way at the Szufang (Tsingtao) Works. It was an enlarged version of the "SL" class, capable of a power output 12½ per cent greater.

The main difference between the "RM" and "SL" class—and indeed between the "RM" class and virtually all other steam locomotives outside the USSR—was in the position of the main steampipe. This normally ran forward from the dome inside the boiler, but in these engines there was room for it to be situated much more accessibly in well-insulated trunking above the boiler. An interesting detail shared with other Chinese steam power, is the provision of an air horn, in addition to a normal deep-sounding dragon-scaring steam chime whistle. In other ways, though, these fine engines followed what had been for many years the final form of the steam locomotive. Thus we find two cylinders only, using outside-admission piston-valves driven by Walschaert's valve gear, coupled with a wide firebox boiler with no frills except a big superheater and a mechanical stoker. Apart from this last feature British readers could reasonably regard the "RM" class as what a class "7" 'Britannia' 4-6-2 might have been if the designers had had similar axleload limitations but another 3ft of vertical height with which to play.

Visitors to China report that these engines can frequently be encountered travelling at speeds

Below: *The world's final steam express design, a "People" class 4-6-2 No.RM 1201 near Jinan, December 1980.*

around 65mph (105km/h) on level routes hauling 600 ton passenger trains. There is reason to suppose that about 250 were built during the years 1958 to 1964 and that the numbers run from RM1001 to RM1250. Wide variations in the insignia and slogans which decorate present day Chinese steam locomotives introduce some variety into the plain (but always clean) black finish used. An "RM" class, specially painted in green, was used to haul the inaugural train across the great new bridge across the Yangtse River at Nanking.

The type of locomotive still being produced (and used on trains in the mountains) in China is the standard 2-10-2 freight locomotive of the "Qian Jing" or "March Forward" class. Even in 1982 they are still being produced at a rate of about 300 per year at a special factory at Datong in Northern China. Various reasons are given for this continued construction of steam locomotives, unique in the world and recently reprieved indefinitely, but the basis seems to be a combination of cheap indigenous coal and traffic rising at some 10 per cent per year. The construction of diesel locomotives in China absorbs five times as many skilled man-hours as steam locomotives of equal capacity so one can understand the reluctance of the Chinese railways to dispose of this cheap and reliable way of coping with their ever-increasing haulage problems.

It is very pleasant indeed to be able to end this book on such a satisfactory note, indicating a real possibility that our beloved steam locomotive might even now be brought back from brink of extinction. South Africa, India, Poland, Zimbabwe are, as we have seen, other places where the forces which toppled steam from its throne may yet be contained. But is there a possibility of any reconquest by steam in places where it had seemingly vanished from the commercial railway scene forever?

Britain, where steam began, is a poor prospect; a new and huge oilfield, combined with coal supplies that are expensive because of the small seams and old-fashioned pits from which it is mined, make it so. Any return to steam (apart from steam for pleasure) seems likely to take the form of steam turbines on the ground generating electricity for electric trains. It is some compensation to Britons though, that nostalgic steam activities exist in their country to an extent proportionately unparalleled elsewhere. The United States, on the other hand, presents a different aspect—indigenous oil supplies are now inadequate and, not only that, coal production and costs in a vast land are responding in an excellent style to characteristic American drive and know-how. Having demonstrated in the recent past that the steam locomotive can match the diesel in performance and availability for service (see New York Central Railroad's "Niagara" class) and ease of servicing (see Norfolk & Western's "J" class) and being fully aware that it is now practical to make steam environmentally acceptable—as well as more efficient—by means of the producer-gas firebox (see South African Railways's class "26"), it is not surprising that an American consortium is going ahead with the development of a steam locomotive for the 21st century.

Shall we in conclusion then, wish success to American Coal Enterprises, Inc., without being really sanguine that one day in the future steam could be found at the head of a luxury Twenty-First Century Limited running between New York and Chicago.

Above: *Displacing a fine plume of steam, "People" class 4-6-2 No.RM 1019 heads north through an autumnal snowfall from Harbin, Manchuria, with a passenger train in October 1980.*

Below: *A view of a beautifully cleaned "People" class 4-6-2, No.RM 1049 at Changchun Shed, northeast China, 1980.*

Above: *The world speed record holder: France's TGV.*

MODERN LOCOMOTIVES

MODERN LOCOMOTIVES

Above: *Three Units of the ATSF, pictured at Amarillo.*

Today's Motive Power

THE MOTIVE power of a modern railway is almost always diesel or electric. Considerable numbers of steam locomotives also exist, as well as some trains driven by gas-turbines, while trains that are moved by petrol engines, cables, sail-power or even flesh-and-blood horses can also still occasionally be found. After iron horses such as *Puffing Billy* and his like took over from the hay-burners on the world's railways—such as they were—in the early 1800s, steam power ruled effectively, but not unchallenged, for more than a century.

The first serious challenge came in early Victorian times from the atmospheric system. Lineside pumping stations evacuated the air from pipes placed along the centre of the tracks. Trains hauled by piston carriages were thus sucked along, the pistons inside the pipes being attached to the carriages by arms which passed through a longitudinal valve.

The most celebrated installation was that of Isambard Kingdom Brunel along the south Devon coast between Exeter and Newton Abbot, but it only lasted in public service a few months. The least unsuccessful was a less ambitious project installed in Ireland between Kingstown (now Dun Laoghaire) and Dalkey, and this lasted from 1844 to 1854. It could be argued that atmospheric railways were also steam railways in the sense that they depended on steam-driven engines generating the power, but of course that also applies to the majority of electric railways today. Even nuclear power stations are also steam-driven!

Electric Traction

Experiments in true electric traction began in 1835, a bare six years after *Rocket* took to the rails, notably by a blacksmith called Thomas Davenport who came from Vermont, USA. He patented his electric motor as early as 1835, although others—Daniel Gooch of Britain's Great Western Railway was one—also constructed small demonstration motors powered by electricity. Davenport built a model electric railway which still survives.

In 1842 a Scotsman called Robert Davidson built a full-size electric locomotive which actually ran slowly but successfully when tried on the metals of the Edinburgh & Glasgow Railway, although it was clearly not a practical means of traction. The problem really was to find an adequate source of power.

Wet primary batteries such as Leclanché cells were totally inadequate for the purpose and the tale of the modern locomotive really begins with an Italian called Antonio Pacinotti who in 1860 built the first dynamo. Pacinotti's machine could also be used as an electric motor and his creation is the basis of the vast majority of locomotives and trains today.

So our book begins in 1879, appropriately with the first electric locomotive in public service. Incidentally, even the majority of diesel locomotives are more pedantically but correctly described as electric locomotives of the self-generating type.

As readers will see from the history of development portrayed in the pages which follow, it was many years before the kind of current to be used was settled. The trouble was that, while direct current (dc) was best for traction motors, alternating current (ac) was better for transmission. Some railways preferred expense and complications on the locomotives; others preferred to have them in the supply system. Many lines compromised by using special alternating current of such a low frequency that it was almost dc. In the last few years, however, the question has been resolved by the development of simple ways of conversion on the locomotives, so that the supply systems can be ac and the motors dc.

In those early days, long before electricity supply networks came into existence, electric railways used direct current supplied from their own power stations. Most of them were closely related to street tramway lines and were low-key operations using vehicles rated

Above: *Typical North American railroading ... a pair of standard diesel-electric road-switcher units head a Canadian Pacific freight.*

Right: *With 125mph (200km/h) capability, Britain's HST 125s are the world's fastest diesel trains. This is today's "Flying Scotsman".*

Above: *20,000-tonnes-plus in a single load: three Class 9E electric locos haul an iron ore train to Saldanha Bay, South Africa.*

Below: *At 77.4mph (124.6km/h) from Berlin to Hamburg the "Flying Hamburger" was the world's fastest train before World War II.*

at only a few horsepower output. Indeed, often they replaced literal "horsepower" rather than steam. It was very early on that electric railway carriages began to incorporate motive power within themselves and so do away not only with steam locomotives but with locomotives altogether. Now, a hundred years later, people travelling from Paris to Marseilles, London to Cardiff or Edinburgh, and Tokyo to Hiroshima, for example, no longer go to the head of the train to look at the locomotive—for one very good reason: it hasn't got one.

An early line—at Portrush, in what is now called Northern Ireland—began in 1883 to use "white coal", that is, electricity generated by water power, and 1890 saw the application of electric traction to the world's first electric underground railway or subway. This was the City & South London Railway, nowadays part of London Transport's Northern line. By now, the principles of electric traction were well established, although all the applications were for relatively light railway operations.

In 1895 came the first successful "heavy" application of electric power, on the Baltimore & Ohio Railroad's new line, mainly in tunnel, serving a new station in the centre of Baltimore. This was a very bold step into the unknown, because the haulage power of the locomotives was increased by a factor of several times over that of those then existing in regular service. The installation was completely successful and opened the door to a whole new field of heavy-duty electric railroading.

Three further significant steps were taken close to the turn of the century. A German consortium of electrical suppliers, with the co-operation of the government, carried out some trials with large, heavyweight, streamlined motor-coaches, as well as a locomotive. Speeds over 100mph (160km/h) were attained in 1901, and two years later these were raised to an amazing 130½mph (210km/h), using one of the motor coaches. For Germany, this record stood for over 70 years.

Then in 1906 came the electrification of the Giovi incline, connecting the Italian port of Genoa with its hinterland. This put some of the elements together to show that a line which was impossible to run satisfactorily with steam locomotives—because of a combination of heavy traffic, extreme gradients and smoky tunnels—presented no difficulty for electric traction.

Lastly, in 1907, the New York, New Haven & Hartford Railroad electrified a section of its main line using single-phase alternating current overhead catenary current supply with simple double-bogie (Bo-Bo) locomotives and self-propelled passenger trains—just the way railways do it now.

In just over a quarter of a century, electric traction had demonstrated superiority over steam in power, speed, absence of pollution, convenience—all the qualities needed or desirable in the running of a railway, in fact. It had demonstrated a quite remarkable reliability and ease of maintenance and servicing. So why did not its tide come in like a flood?

The reason, of course, was the great expense involved. Compared with steam, electric locomotives were more expensive by a factor of two or three and, in addition, there was also the cost of the conductor rails or wires, transmission lines and sub-stations and often the power stations themselves to be added. In general terms (and greatly over-simplifying the considerations involved), one could talk of the cost of equipping an electric railway costing four to six times the amount needed to equip a steam railway for the same traffic. So no wonder electrification was then seldom resorted to except when there was really no alternative.

Above: *Electric locomotive building at General Electric's plant at Erie, USA. Note running gear ready to receive the bodyshell.*

Below: *A giant Great Northern Railway Class W1 electric locomotive nearing completion by General Electric in 1946.*

Diesel Traction

The diesel engine in the form in which it is now universally used is much less the work of Doctor Rudolph Diesel, of Germany, than of a Briton called Ackroyd-Stuart. In the 1880s he demonstrated an internal combustion engine in which the fuel was injected into the cylinder at the end of the piston stroke. This engine was turned into a practical proposition by Richard Hornsby & Co., of Grantham, England, later Ruston & Hornsby. Dr. Diesel's engine, demonstrated in 1898, used a high compression ratio typical of present day engines to obtain a big increase in thermal efficiency, but the fuel had to be injected by a blast of compressed air at some 1,000psi (65kg/cm^2). This involved heavy ancillary equipment.

In 1896 a small diesel locomotive, the first in the world and which one might more reasonably call an Ackroyd-Stuart locomotive, was built at Hornsbys. It was used for shunting purposes in the works. The first recorded use of a compression-ignition locomotive in public service seems to have occurred in Sweden, when a small railcar with a 75bhp (56kW) engine and electrical transmission was put into service on the Mellersta & Södermanlands Railway in 1913. Of course, this was hardly a greater output than would nowadays be installed in a medium-sized family car,

Above: *Steam for the future? South African Railways' Class 26 "steam" locomotive with gas-generator firebed, in August 1981.*

Below: *General Motors' dominance of the diesel market is illustrated by this Class X45 locomotive in Victoria, Australia.*

Above: *It is a sign of the times that the number of this German locomotive has an extra figure for assisting in computer entries.*

and went no distance towards proving the diesel engine as suitable for rail traction.

As we all know from our motor cars, the problem of using internal combustion engines for traction is—in lay terms—that they need to be going before they will go. This is in contrast to steam engines and electric motors which can produce a force while still at rest. For low powers, the familiar gear-box and clutch in the motor car can be used, but for hundreds—and certainly for thousands—of horsepower something more sophisticated is needed.

Experiments with a diesel engine driving an air compressor and feeding compressed air to a normal steam locomotive engine and chassis were not successful, although the scheme was a simple one. The use of hydraulic fluid as a transmission medium has been reasonably satisfactory, but by far the majority of diesel locomotives ever built have, and have had, electric transmissions. A diesel engine drives an electric generator or alternator which feeds current to the motors of what amounts to an electric locomotive.

The story of compression-ignition power in this book begins therefore with the first diesel-electric locomotive of more than very modest power to run successfully in commercial service. It was put into service by the Ingersoll-Rand, the General Electric and the American Locomotive companies in 1924, and it is a pleasure to write that GE at least still supplies diesel locomotives to the world from its plant in Erie, Pennsylvania.

Because the concept of this first commercially-successful diesel locomotive involved building, to start with, an electric locomotive complete with traction motors and control gear, and then adding to that a diesel-driven generator to supply current for the electric locomotive, it was not only expensive but complex. Furthermore, electrical equipment is not happy living in close company with the vibration and oil-mist which surrounds even the best-maintained diesel engines. Accordingly, in most places and for many years, diesel locomotives—however economical they might be as regards fuel consumption and however efficient operationally—led rather unfulfilled and unhappy lives.

The key to what amounted almost to a complete take-over of the un-electrified railways of the world was the entry into the locomotive field in the 1930s of US General Motors, the world's greatest road vehicle manufacturers. They did not solicit orders until they had a product upon which they could rely and which was sold, complete with a spare parts and repair service—just like one of their motor cars, in fact. Also, just as it was with their motor cars, customers had to buy the models offered, not the ones they thought they wanted.

In this way mass-production and standardisation were able to reduce the cost of a diesel-electric locomotive to a reasonable level. Furthermore (and unlike anybody's motor car) all GM's diesel units were intended to be used on a building-block basis: couple up four units to make a super-power loco, then three, two or perhaps only one for lighter duties, only one crew being needed because of the remote-control facilities (known in railroad parlance as "multiple-unit" working). Individual units were compact enough and light enough to go anywhere a freight car could go and this did away with any need for special types of locomotive for special duties.

It is only a slight exaggeration to say that to take charge of a railroad's motive power procurement at that time it was not necessary to be an expert in the niceties of locomotive design, so long as one could read a manufacturer's catalogue. The policies adopted added up to a stupendous story of success, as the pages which follow reveal.

The following pages also reveal the converse. Those railways—British Railways being perhaps the most notorious example—which were unable to ditch habits of motive power acquisition formed in steam days (that is, of ordering separate custom-built designs for the different duties) found the going exceedingly hard for many years. In some ways, also, the one nation which applied some of General Motors' diesel thinking to steam finds the end result now entirely to their satisfaction, although the Chinese could not have foreseen the big change in the cost of oil relative to coal on the world markets to which this satisfaction is due.

Above: *A Chinese-built BJ "Beijing" diesel-hydraulic locomotive for passenger train haulage, seen when brand new in 1980.*

Below: *The driver's view: an AMTRAK engineer at the controls of a diesel-electric passenger locomotive at Ogden, Utah, USA, in 1980.*

Other Forms of Traction

Gas-turbine locomotives are wholly practical, even with direct drive, but suffer from the fact that their efficiency falls off badly when running at any power output different from their rated one. Trains make highly variable demands on their motive power so it is not surprising that this form has not become common, although there have been sufficient successful applications to justify the inclusion of several turbine-driven entries in this book.

The authors in no way accept the notion that the

Above: *A British Railways standard Class 87 Bo-Bo electric locomotive hauls a passenger train through the northern hills.*

Left: *An all-purpose loco, Swedish State Railways' Class Rc4 electric unit by ASEA, seen in a typical Scandinavian setting.*

Above: *These Japanese high speed "Bullet" trains were the first in the world to offer 100mph (160km/h) start-to-stop average speeds.*

terms "steam" and "modern" are mutually exclusive, and accordingly a sprinkling of steam locomotives which look towards the future, in spite of being steam, have been included. There is even a prospect of steam traction making a come-back in certain countries in the not too distant future.

Of other forms of modern power successfully applied to rail transport over the years, steam-turbine-electric traction is noted in one entry and so is movement dependent on energy stored in a heavy rotating fly-wheel. Gas-generator machines with free pistons driving turbines or reciprocating engines have been tried but have hardly succeeded. Rail movement by muscle power (animal and human) or cable traction is excluded, although a few examples of the former and a great many of the latter can be found. Wind-and-sail power, on the other hand, really has disappeared from the serious railways of the world, and accordingly has (with great regret) no place in this book.

High Speeds

To some, the eclipse of steam traction in recent years has made railways a whole lot less exciting, but this has been amply compensated for by the really startling speeds now being run. The promise of those high-speed trials of 1903 in Germany was at last fulfilled with the electric "Bullet" trains in Japan in 1966 and the diesel-electric HST125 trains in Britain in 1978, as well as more isolated runs in France, Germany and elsewhere. City-to-city speeds of 100mph (160km/h) and running speeds up to 125mph (200km/h) have now become commonplace.

The French have just gone a further stage ahead with a new Paris to Lyons railway, purpose-built for very high speeds indeed. The electric TGV (*Train à Grande Vitesse*) trains used on this line run at up to 162mph (260km/h) to provide a frequent service between these two great cities of France in two hours only for the 266 miles (426km). Hardly time for a meal, at least not a French one!

Other railways, unable to afford new lines, have attempted to build trains which would negotiate the curves of a steam-age railway at these electric-age speeds. It is no disgrace that British Railways found its 150mph (240km/h) Advanced Passenger Train, which tilted to provide built-in super-elevation or banking, just a little bit too difficult. The Italians, the Spanish,

Below: *ATSF's Bi-Centennial engine, number 5700. This specially painted EMD GP seen at the ATSF shops in Texas.*

Above: *A French National Railways Class 15000 Bo-Bo electric locomotive heads the Paris-Strasbourg rapide "Le Stanislas".*

Below: *Indian Railways' WDM Class Co-Co diesel-electric loco No. 17521 brings the "Andhra Pradesh Express" through Dhaulpur.*

the Canadians, the Germans, the Swiss, as well as others, have also encountered problems with this promising idea. The Japanese, on the other hand, have successfully put tilting trains into service, but these have not been for running, say, 150mph (240km/h) trains on 75mph (120km/h) alignments but for having 80mph trains (128km/h) on 40mph (64km/h) alignments on mountain routes. In this way Japan has been able to solve its tilting problems in isolation from the high speed ones.

With 162mph (260km/h) trains in service, one can ask whether rail travel could go even faster. There do seem to be indications that the speed is near the limit possible in practice for flanged steel wheels running on steel rails. While higher speeds might be possible with hover-trains or a magnetic levitation system, this would almost certainly preclude through running on to conventional railway tracks.

For example, the TGV trains enter and leave central Paris on conventional tracks (with a different system of electrification) and extend their runs to Marseilles and into Switzerland (with yet another electrification system) without any special provision other than relatively simple current conversion equipment installed on the trains themselves.

What might happen is that TGV-type railways should appear elsewhere. Some are contemplated in France, of course, but many other countries could find suitable routes. The long-heralded extinction of oil supplies will give a significant uplift to the prospects of new electric railways and it does seem that the excellent hardware described in the later pages of this book will be available when the call finally comes.

It is an illustration of how quickly information concerning railway development can be over-shadowed that since most of this book went to press, the speed limit of the French TGV trains has been raised from 162mph (260km/h) to 168mph (270km/h).

Modern Traction Particulars

Each description is headed by the appropriate class, name or number followed by its wheel arrangement code. An illustrated explanation of the meanings of these codes is given separately.

The actual text begins with tabulated details as follows....

Type: The purpose and kind of locomotive or train under discussion.

Gauge: The distance between the inner edges of the rails, given in feet and inches and in millimetres.

Propulsion: A brief *resumé* of what makes the wheels go round. The power output is usually included here; the one-hour value is specified in horsepower and kilowatts.

Weight(s): Both the adhesive and the total weight of the locomotive in running order, are specified in pounds and in tonnes. If the adhesive weight equals the total weight, one pair of figures only is given.

Max. axleload: This is the heaviest weight carried by any individual axle and again is specified in pounds and tonnes.

Overall length: This is the length of the locomotive or train measured between buffer or coupler faces, specified in feet and inches and millimetres.

Tractive effort: This is the maximum theoretical drawbar pull which a locomotive can exert, specified in pounds and kilo-Newtons. This entry is omitted as inappropriate in the case of a self-propelled train.

Max. speed: An arbitrarily specified speed limit applied to the locomotive or train in question, for safety reasons, specified in miles per hour and kilometres per hour.

As regards the text itself, more emphasis is placed on differences from the norm than on similarities. The reader is also warned that, although the information given is carefully researched and set down in good faith, the figures must be interpreted with reserve. For example, the performance of an electric locomotive depends directly on the voltage of the supply and this can vary within wide limits according to the currents being drawn from the system at any particular moment. Weights can vary quite considerably from those in specifications—and only the honest Chinese admit that they do! The power output of diesel engines can vary according to the precise adjustment of fuel pumps and so on. Even the track gauge is not entirely reliable, for spikes sometimes work loose on even the best regulated railways.

The following abbreviations are used in the tables and text....

ac =alternating current; **ch** =chains (of 66 feet/ 20,117mm); **dc** =direct current; **ft** =feet; **hp** =horse power; **Hz** =hertz or frequency per second; **in** =inches; **km** =kilometres (km/h=kilometres per hour); **kN** =kilo-Newtons (1kN=225lb/147kg force)*; **kW** =kiloWatts; **lb** =pounds; **m** =metres; **max** = maximum; **mm** =millimetres; **mph** =miles per hour; **t** =tonnes **V** = volts

*Note: the only one of these terms not in lay use is the kilo-Newton. Although we may be content to measure both a force and a mass in the same units, pounds or kilograms as convenient, a purist is not content with this, as it takes no account of any possible variation in the force of gravity, which is the connection between a mass and the force it can exert. Hence the Newton, appropriately named after the discoverer of the laws of motion. For our purposes, 1,000 Newtons or one kilo-Newton can be taken to be 225lb (147kg)—but when we come to build railways on the Moon a different conversion value will apply!

Below: *Ship-hauling locomotives prepare to take a US ambulance ship through the canal locks, Pedro Miguel, Panama, June 1919.*

Above: *Today's fastest! A French* Train à Grande Vitesse, *or TGV, set now permitted to run at 168mph (270km/h).*

Above: *A British cross-country express from Newcastle to Cardiff passes Ousdon Junction, Co. Durham, with a Class 45 diesel-electric.*

Below: *German Federal Railway Class ET 403 high-speed four-car electric train now used on airport-city-airport link service.*

Wheel Arrangements

Diagram 1

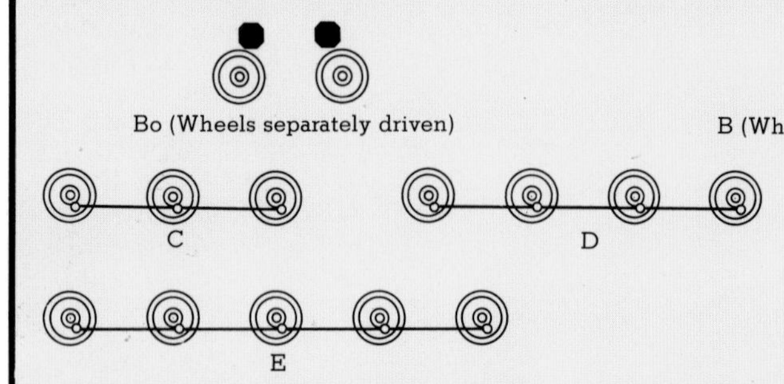

Locomotives both old and new are usually described by their wheel arrangement code. In the case of modern locomotives the basis is the number of axles. The number of driven axles are indicated by A = 1, B = 2, C = 3, D = 4, and so on. Hence the first locomotive entry in this book is described as "B". This also implies that the wheels are connected by gearing or rods: if they are separately driven, as is normally the case nowadays, then the suffix "o" is added to the letter.

Diagram 2

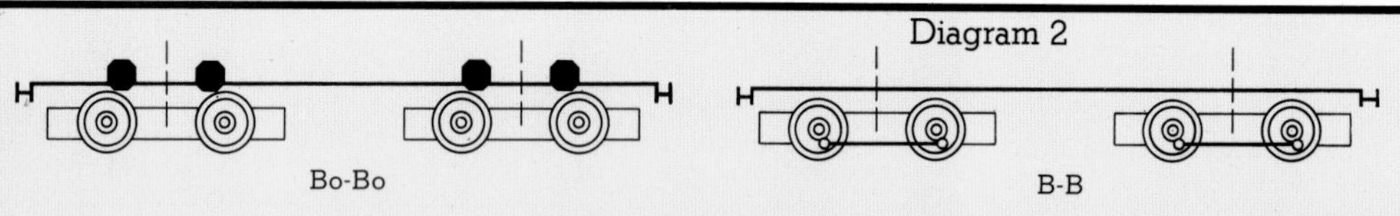

Three-quarters of all modern locomotives and almost all the power cars of self-propelled trains are of the arrangement shown in the left-hand figure, consisting of two two-axle "bogies" or "trucks".

Diagram 3

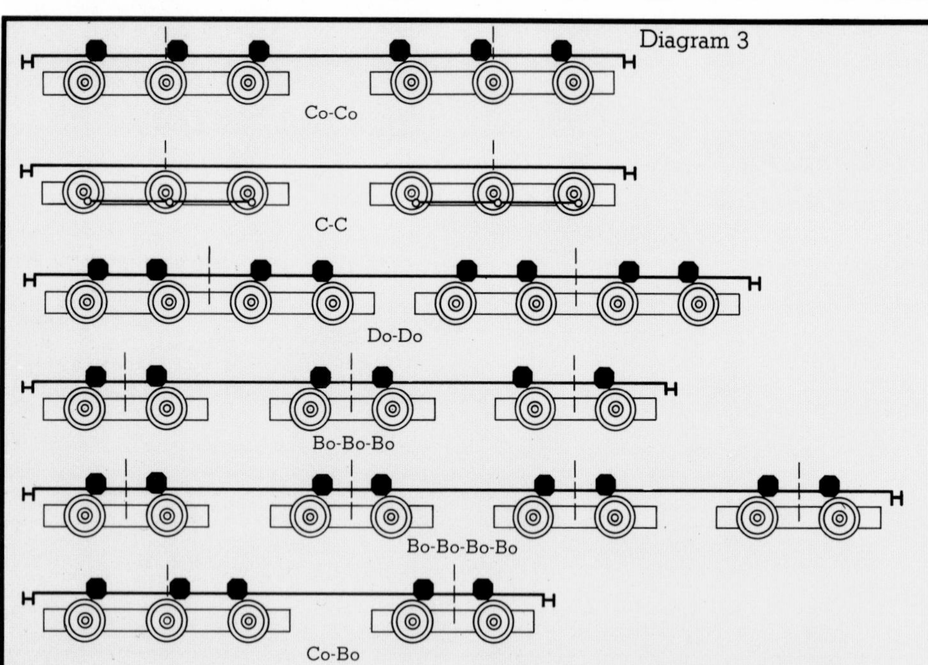

The bogie arrangement is often extended to include three-axle and four-axle bogies. More than two bogies are occasionally used and unsymmetrical combinatons can also be found in rare cases. Bogie locomotives having wheels connected with rods are nowadays never built and rarely found, but the arrangement with bogie wheels connected by gearing is reasonably common. Even so, the fact that the overwhelming majority of locomotives, both diesel and electric, have axles individually driven by separate electric motors means that the suffix "o" and even the hyphen can be dropped. A Bo-Bo becomes therefore and BB. Whatever the wheel arrangement used, though, the principle involved is that each bogey is separately described as in diagram 1 above, and then combined with hyphens.

Diagram 4

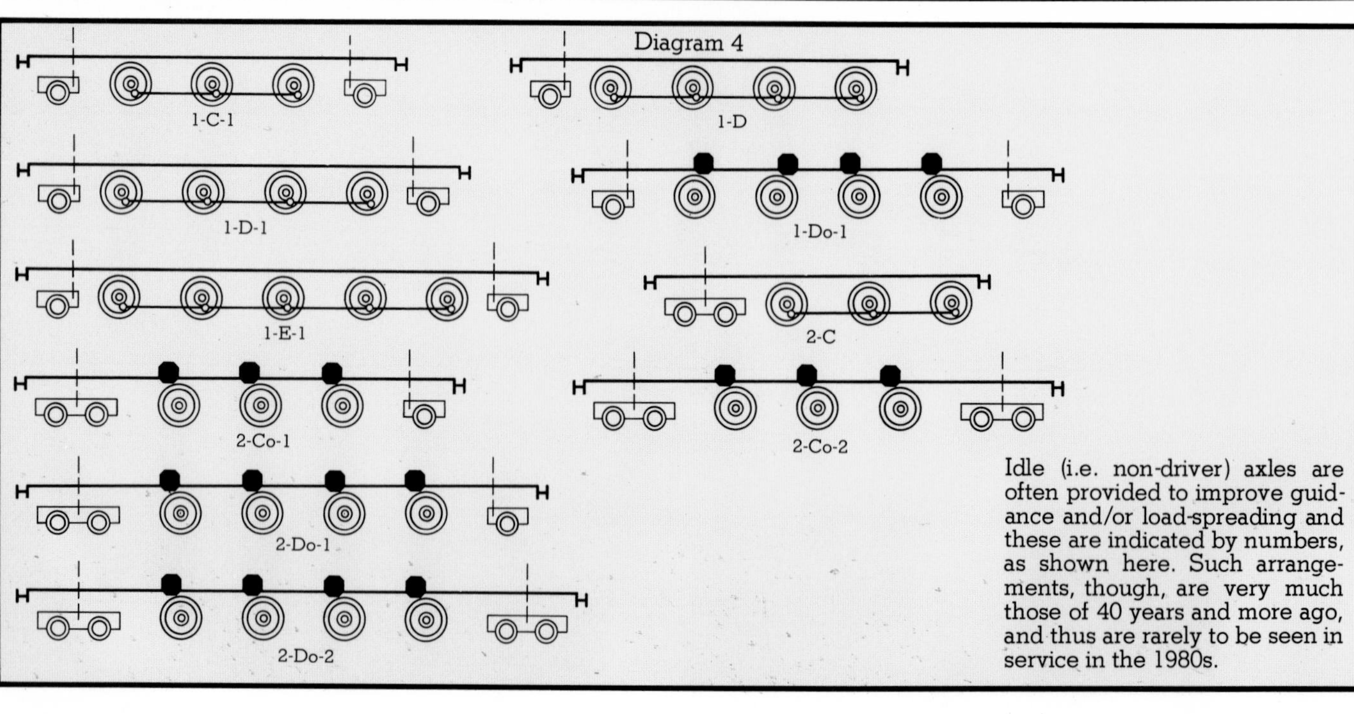

Idle (i.e. non-driver) axles are often provided to improve guidance and/or load-spreading and these are indicated by numbers, as shown here. Such arrangements, though, are very much those of 40 years and more ago, and thus are rarely to be seen in service in the 1980s.

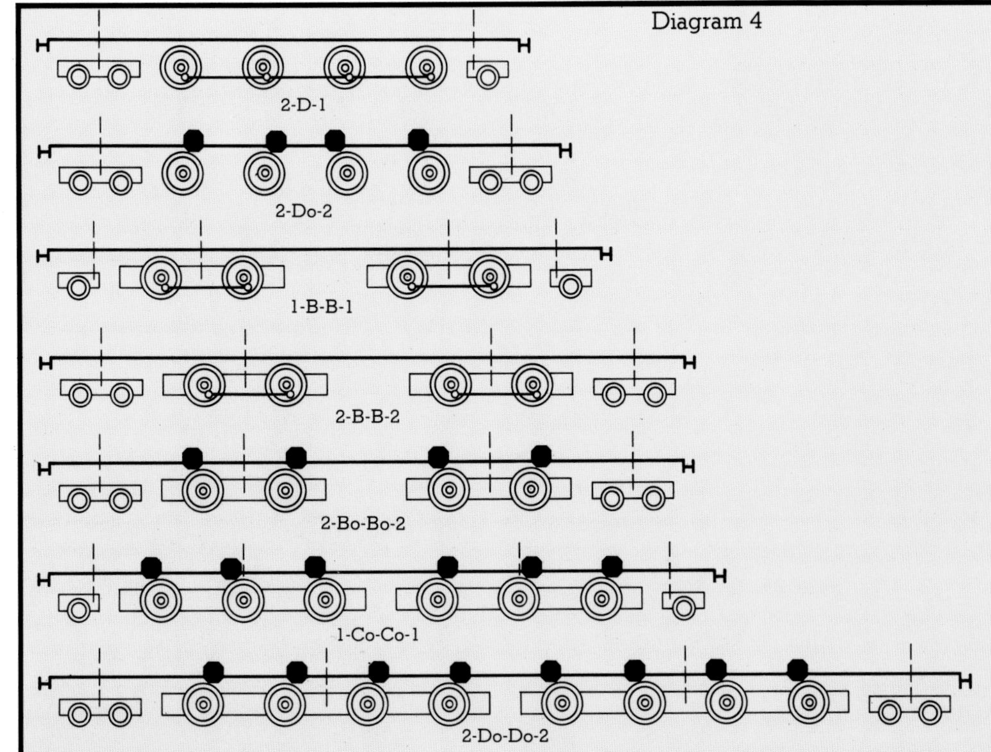

It is also a point that this notation can be used (and often was, particularly by the countries of continental Europe) to describe steam locomotives, as well as diesel and electric ones. Such steam locomotives as appear in this book are here delineated in this manner.

The power of cars of self-propelled trains, which play such a large part in modern railway operation, are not usually described in this way. Almost without exception they are of the Bo-Bo, BB, Bo-2 or B-2 wheel arrangement and therefore need only to be described by stating whether there are one of two motored bogies in the layout.

In contrast and in days gone by, electric locomotive wheel arrangements were often extremely complicated, as shown here and below. It was really for this reason that the simpler Whyte system (used traditionally for steam traction, whereby, for example, a 2-D-1 was described as a 4-8-2) was found inadequate.

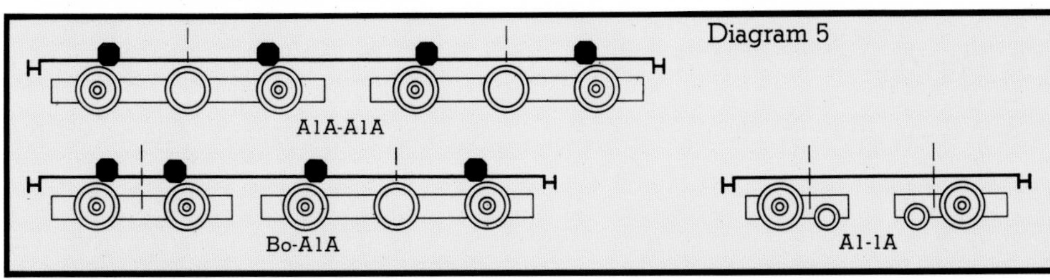

Driven and non-driven wheels are sometimes included in the same bogie or main frame, as shown here, usually to provide better load-spreading rather than guidance.

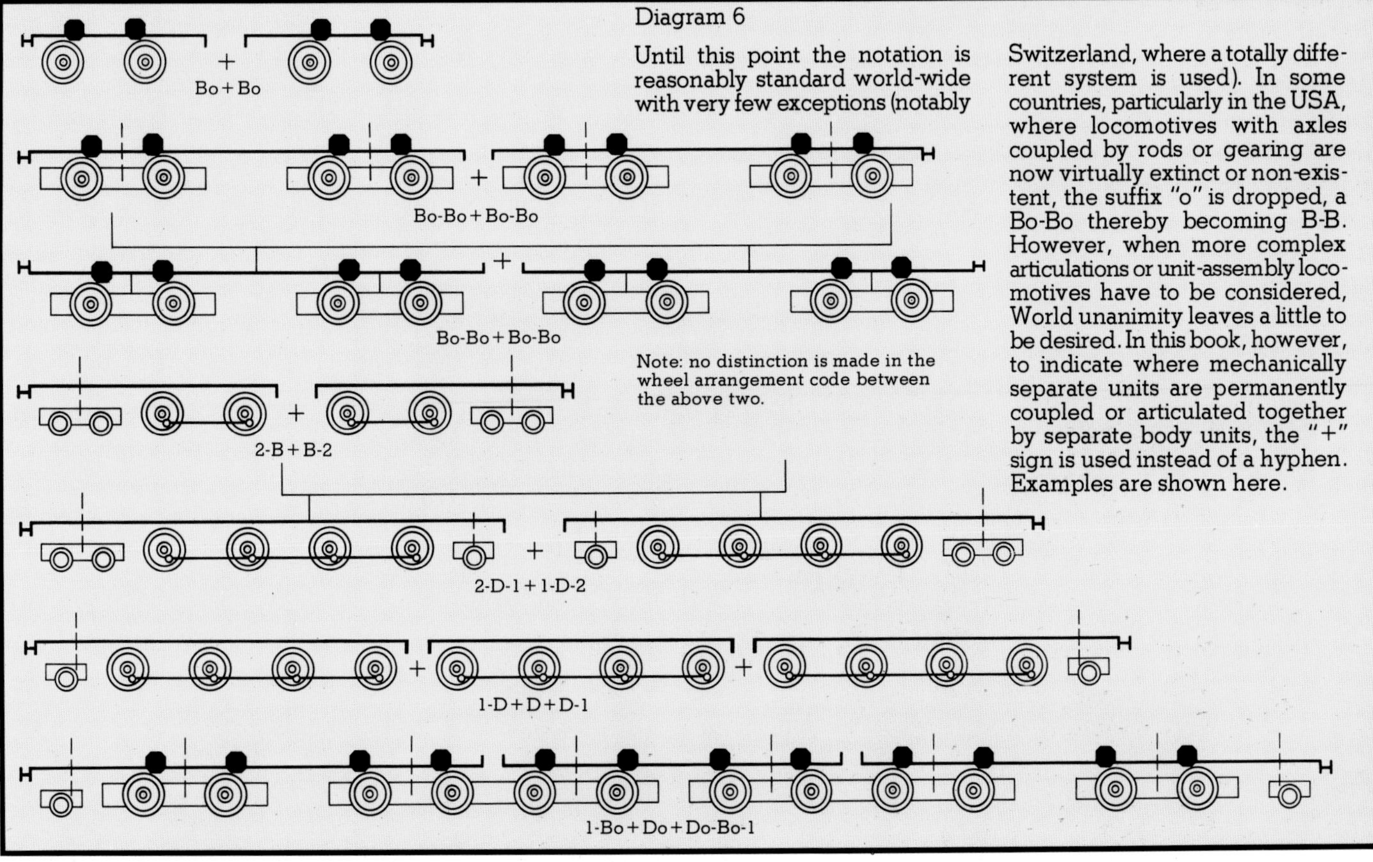

Until this point the notation is reasonably standard world-wide with very few exceptions (notably Switzerland, where a totally different system is used). In some countries, particularly in the USA, where locomotives with axles coupled by rods or gearing are now virtually extinct or non-existent, the suffix "o" is dropped, a Bo-Bo thereby becoming B-B. However, when more complex articulations or unit-assembly locomotives have to be considered, World unanimity leaves a little to be desired. In this book, however, to indicate where mechanically separate units are permanently coupled or articulated together by separate body units, the "+" sign is used instead of a hyphen. Examples are shown here.

Siemens' Original B

Germany: Berlin Trades Fair, 1879

Type: Demonstration electric locomotive.
Gauge: 1ft 5¾in (450mm).
Propulsion: Direct current fed at 150V via a raised centre conductor rail and liquid control resistance to a 5hp (3.75kW) motor connected by gearing to the driving wheels.
Overall length: 5ft 2in (1,570mm).
Max. speed: 8mph (13km/h).

This little tractor represented the first successful use of electric power for the haulage of a train on a public railway. Accounts vary as to its length, but it seems the railway was only about ¼ mile (0.4km) long and in the form of a circle. It was first laid as a demonstration line at the Berlin Trades Fair of 1879 (the outfit was also demonstrated eleswhere), but its use led directly to a second public electric line in a Berlin suburb soon after the exhibition closed. (In fact, it was a tramway and so outside the scope of this book.) The Siemens locomotive was successful and in this way, on May 31, 1879, came into being the future method of traction of many of the world's most important railways.

Attempts had been made to produce an electric locomotive even before the dynamo had been developed during the 1860s, but the problem of producing sufficient current was not easily solved by such means as batteries of primary cells. A Scotsman called Robert Davidson demonstrated a crude battery tractor on the railway between Edinburgh and Glasgow in 1842. The "motors" consisted of wooden cylinders mounted on the axles to which iron bars were fixed. Electromagnets were switched on and off to attract these bars in such a way as to produce rotation. Although the locomotive worked, it was clearly not a practical proposition. In spite of many other attempts, 35 years were to elapse before success was achieved.

It was the dynamo, used to generate current and also adapted as a motor to produce torque, that gave Werner von Siemens this success in Berlin. A small steam-driven power station produced direct current at 150V. The locomotive was started and controlled by a liquid resistance (*see glossary*). Current was collected from a central third rail, its return

Below: *The world's first electric train carrying a load of passengers on a short circular track at the Berlin Trades Fair, May 1879.*

Siemens' Single railcar

Great Britain: Volk's Electric Railway, 1884

Type: Electric railcar.
Gauge: 2ft 8½in (825mm).
Propulsion: Direct current at 460V fed via a central third rail and rheostatic control to two 8hp (6kW) motors with link-belt drive to the wheels.
Weight: 14,326lb (6.5t).
Overall length: 30ft 0in (9,144mm).
Max. speed: 10mph (16km/h).

August 3, 1883 was the day when a short electric pleasure railway was opened along the seafront at Brighton and the date is notable in two ways. This little railway was the first electric line in the world to achieve any sort of permanent existence, for it still runs today having carried some 60 million passengers. Furthermore, it was a pointer to the situation a century later when most electric passenger trains would be self-propelled and no longer need locomotives. It was also the first electric railway in Britain, although another in what is now called Northern Ireland was to open five weeks later. This was the Giant's Causeway Tramway at Portrush, the first railway in the world to run on hydro-electricity, using its own power station.

The Brighton line also originally had its own generating station but using a gas engine as the source of power. Later, power was taken in a way much more typical of the future, from Brighton Corporation's public supply via a substation, an arrangement that was facilitated by the fact that Magnus Volk, who promoted the line, was also the Corporation's electrical engineer. Volk has given his name to the railway.

The scale of the initial operation can be judged from the fact that the original temporary car was built, a ¼-mile (0.4km) of 2ft (610mm) gauge track laid and the generating plant installed all within three weeks. The first season's operation was in the nature of an experiment and by April 1884 the line, which originally ran only from Aquarium Station to the Old Chain Pier, was extended and rebuilt to run from the Palace Pier to Black Rock, a distance of 1¼ miles (2km). The gauge was also altered to 2ft 8½in (825mm), an apparently peculiar figure no doubt chosen because it was exactly two English feet less than standard gauge. The details of the cars built for the permanent line are those given above.

Currently, the line is operated during the summer season by nine 32-seat cars, seven of which are indigenous, the other two having come recently from the now closed Southend Pier Tramway. It is still as popular as ever, and traffic is not discouraged by the fact that an excellent view of Brighton's famous nude bathing beach is available from the cars. A further extension along the beach to Rottingdean laid with a four-rail track to 18ft 0in (5,486mm) overall gauge, on which a car on stilts ran through the sea at high tide, did not last very long.

Left and right: *Views of single electric cars of Volk's Electric Railway at Brighton, England, the oldest existing electric railway in the world, which in 1983 celebrated its centenary. The line is now run by the Brighton Corporation.*

path being via the wheels and running rails.

The train could carry some 30 passengers seated back to back on three four-wheel cars at a speed of 4mph (6.5km/h). The mechanical design of the locomotive was quite complex by present day standards. The armature shaft was mounted longitudinally under the driver's seat, while the field windings protruded each side above the wheels.

The motor was enormous compared with the size of one of similar power today. Torque was transmitted via three spur gears (with an intermediate shaft!) to the longitudinal driving shaft between the wheels, thence via bevel gears to a transverse shaft. There were two pairs of bevel gears arranged so that either pair could be put into mesh by means of an external handle—requiring the driver to dismount—to give forward and reverse. The two driving axles were turned by further spur gears meshing with a gear wheel on the transverse shaft.

The locomotive can be seen today in the Deutsches Museum, Munich, West Germany.

Right: *Werner von Siemens' pioneer electric locomotive demonstrated in Berlin, Germany, in May 1879.*

Nos. 1-3 B_o+B_o

USA:
Baltimore & Ohio RR (B&O), 1895

Type: Main line electric locomotive.
Gauge: 4ft 8½in (1,435mm).
Propulsion: Direct current at 675V fed via a rigid overhead conductor to four gearless motors of 360hp (270kW) each.
Weight: 192,000lb (87t).
Max. axleload: 48,488lb (22t).
Overall length: 27ft 1½in (8,268mm).
Tractive effort: 45,000lb (201kN).
Max speed: 60mph (96.5km).

The world's first main line electrification was installed on this section of the first public railway in America; it ran through the city of Baltimore and in particular through the 1¼-mile (2km) Howard Street tunnel, adjacent to a new main passenger station at Mount Royal. The tunnel was on a gradient of 1-in-125 (0.8 per cent) and trouble with smoke and steam therein was anticipated. The solution adopted was electrification carried out by General Electric of Schenectady, New York State.

More remarkable than anything was the boldness of the decision —these B&O locomotives were over nine times heavier and nine times more powerful than their nearest rivals. It was upon such an enormous leap forward as this that the success of the whole vast investment in the new line was dependent, because a very different construction would have been necessary for steam traction.

Gearless motors were again used, but not mounted direct on the axle, although concentric with it. Torque was transmitted to the wheels through rubber blocks; this flexible drive was yet another feature many years ahead of its time. Each four-wheeled tractor unit was mechanically quite separate, although two were permanently coupled to form one locomotive. There were three double locomotives in all.

The locomotives were quite successful and had no problems hauling 1,630t (1,800 US tons) trains up the gradient. The load including the train's steam engine, which did no work in the tunnel. Trouble was encountered with corrosion of the unusual conductor arrangements; a brass shuttle ran along a Z-section overhead rail, the shuttle being connected to the locomotive by a one-sided tilted pantograph. A conventional third rail mounted outside the running rails replaced this amazing overhead system in 1902.

These locomotives stopped work in 1912, but one was laid aside for many years—in fact, until B&O's centennial "Fair of the Iron Horse" in 1927, at which it was exhibited. Alas, scrapping followed and so the first-ever main-line electric locomotive is no longer to be seen. Electric traction continued in use on the B&O using more modern power until 1952 when electric locomotives of the self-generating type—that is, the all too familiar diesel—took over.

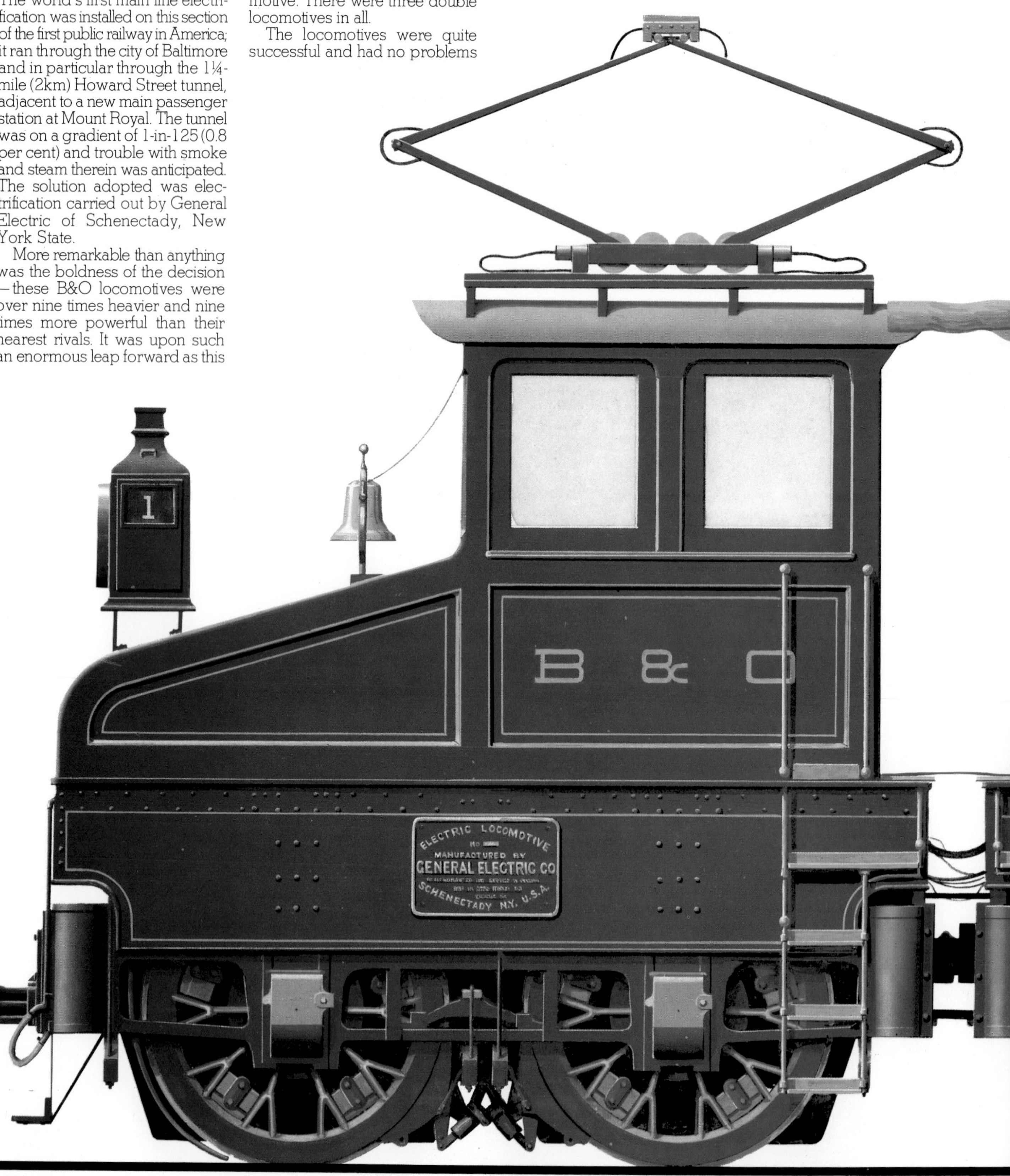

Nos. 1-16 B

Great Britain:
City & South London Railway (CSLR), 1880

Type: Underground railway electric locomotive.
Gauge: 4ft 8½in (1,435mm).
Propulsion: Direct current at 500V fed via a central conductor rail to two 50hp (37.3kW) gearless motors with axle-mounted armatures.
Weight: 20,700lb (9.4t).
Overall length: 14ft 0in (4,267mm).
Max. speed: 25mph (40km/h).

The first electric underground railway in the world was the City & South London line, opened on December 18, 1880. Sixteen locomotives were constructed by Beyer Peacock of Manchester, with electrical equipment supplied by Mather & Platt, also of Manchester, and Siemens of Berlin, for the 3½-mile (5.6km) line, which ran from King William Street Station in the "city" area of London to Stockwell south of the Thames.

The locomotives were completely satisfactory and operated the line for more than 30 years until it was reconstructed in the early 1920s. It now forms part of London Transport's Northern Line, and all except the final few yards at the city end is included in 17¼ miles (27.8km) of continuous tunnel which was for very many years the longest railway tunnel in the world.

Above: *City & South London Railway four-wheeled electric locomotive, as built in 1880.*

In contrast to the Siemens locomotive of 1879, these machines were very simple. The armatures were wound direct on the axles—no gearing or other complications. The braking system also had a simplicity never achieved later. Westinghouse air brakes were used, but there was no compressor. Instead a reservoir was provided and this could be recharged from compressed air supplies provided at the terminal stations.

Another interesting feature (which in contrast, was unnecessarily complex) was the conductor rail mounted on glass insulators. The top of this rail was *below* the level of the running rails, and at points and crossings a ramp was provided to lift the collecting shoes clear of the running rails. This also lasted until reconstruction in 1920, when the usual third and fourth conductor rail arrangement was provided.

One of these locomotives (No.1) is on display at the Science Museum in South Kensington, London, while one of the strange little windowless cars it hauled can be seen at London Transport's museum at Covent Garden.

Left: *Pioneer electric main-line locomotive, put into service on the Baltimore & Ohio RR in 1895.*

Nos. 1-4 He 2/2 Switzerland: Gornergrat Railway (GGB), 1898

Type: Rack-and-pinion mountain railway locomotive.
Gauge: 3ft 3⅜in (1,000mm).
Propulsion: Three-phase current at 550V 40Hz fed via twin conductors and the running rails to two 90hp (68kW) motors geared to the driving pinions.
Weight: 25,356lb (11.5t).
Length: 13ft 6½in (4,130mm).
Tractive effort: 17,632lb (78kN).
Max. speed: 5mph (8km/h).

Electric traction came very early to the pleasure railways of the world—in those days smoke and steam were not thought of in terms of enjoyment—and mountain lines were particularly suitable for electrification. Enabling geriatrics as well as athletes to enjoy the glories of the Alps had long been a possibility under steam power, but when it came to climbing up from Zermatt to see the Matterhorn from that great belvedere the Gornergrat, three-phase electric traction was chosen.

At this time, several railways in Europe and North America were already operated by dc traction, and as Switzerland had no coal but an abundance of water power there was considerable interest there in the new mode of traction. In particular two engineers, C.E.L. Brown and W. Boveri, seeking to improve on the low efficiency of early dc schemes, applied themselves to the problems of three-phase traction. This offered the possibility of eliminating commutators, reducing weight, and allowing braking by regeneration on down gradients.

In 1895 a tram driven by a motor of their design, and manufactured by the newly-formed Brown Boveri Company, was tested successfully between Lugano and Paradiso. This system required two overhead wires with separate current collectors, whilst the third line of supply was taken through the running rails. Encouraged by this success, the engineers offered to produce three-phase rack locomotives for the Gornergrat line and a railway proposed to carry tourists to the top of the Jungfrau.

Left: *Gornergrat Railway train with original-type locomotive, leaving Riffleberg for Zermatt. The Matterhorn in background.*

AEG Single railcar Germany: Study Group for Electric High Speed Railways (StES), 1901

Type: High-speed experimental railcar.
Gauge: 4ft 8½in (1,435mm).
Propulsion: Three-phase current at a voltage variable between 10,000 and 14,000 and a frequency variable between 38 and 48Hz, fed via a triple overhead side-contact wire and a step-down transformer to six gearless synchronous motors each capable of 750hp (560kW) for short periods.
Weight: 132,250lb (60t).
Max. axleload: 13,225lb (10t).
Overall length: 72ft 6in (22,100mm).
Max. speed: 130.85mph (210km/h).

Around the turn of the century the two principal German electrical contracting firms, Siemens & Halske and Allgemeine Elektrische Gesellschaft (AEG) formed, with the support of the Prussian government and various banks, a consortium known as the Studiengesellschaft fur Elektrische Schnellbahnen (Study Group for Electric High-speed Railways).

In 1901, the use of a 14.5 mile (23km) military railway near Berlin was obtained and triple overhead contact wires erected at the side of the track. A railcar built by Siemens was the first test vehicle to be tried out, but the light rail (65lb/yd—32.5kg/m) and shallow ballasting proved inadequate. The swaying and pitching was alarming and finally a derailment occurred at a speed of 100mph (160km/h), putting an end to the trials for the time being. The track was then relaid and strengthened with 85lb/yd (42kg/m) rail, new closely-spaced sleepers and deep ballasting. The minimum curve was eased to 100 chains (2,000m) radius, while the wheelbase of the six-wheel bogies of the cars was increased from 12ft 6in (3,800mm) to 16ft 5in (5,000mm) to improve stability. An interesting point was that the speed to be reached on any particular run was set by arrangement beforehand, as it would depend on the frequency of the supply controlled from the power station.

In 1903, after all this had been done, further attempts were made and 130.5mph (210km/h) was reached smoothly, demonstrating the practicability—only recently

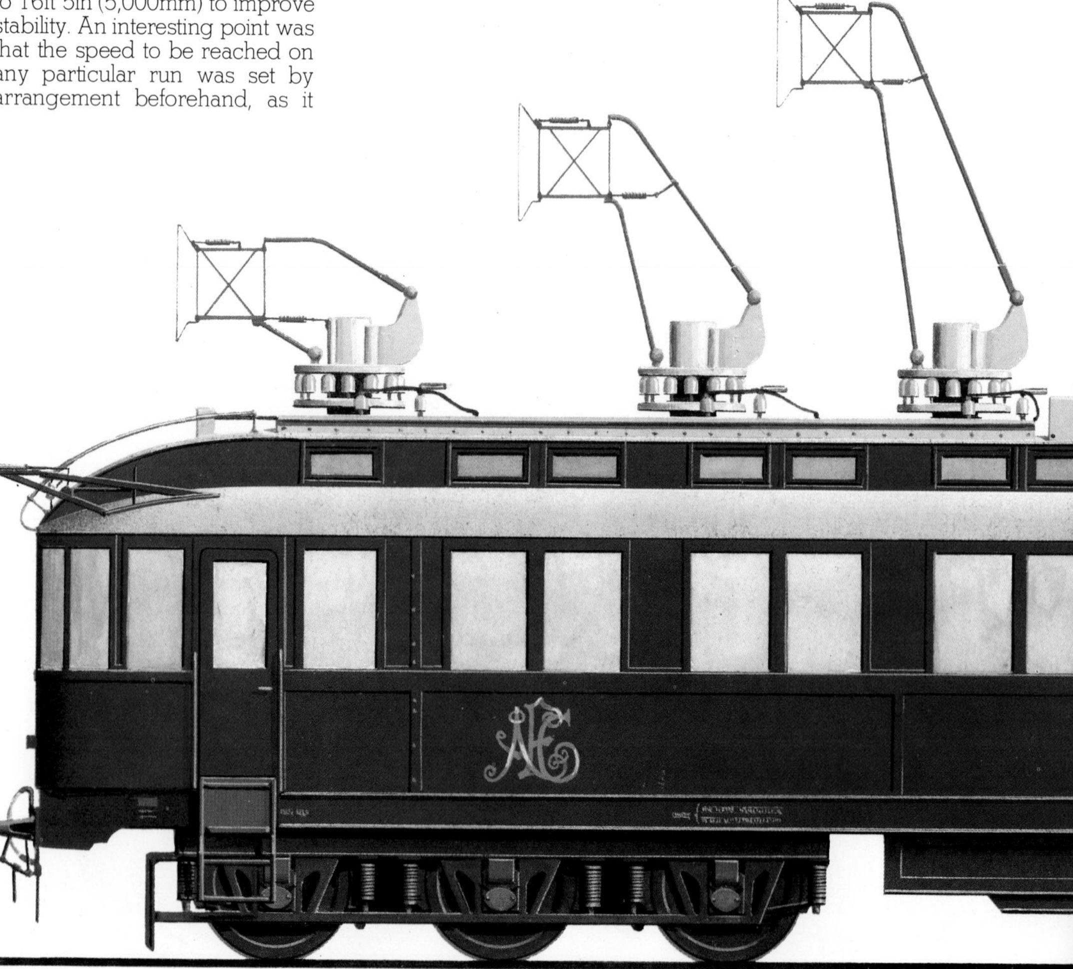

In a distance of 5.8 miles (9.3km) the Gornergrat line rises 4,872ft (1,485m) to an upper terminus at 10,134ft (3,089m), and the maximum gradient is 1-in-5 (20 per cent). Construction began in 1896 and on November 24, 1897 the first trial was made with the world's pioneer three-phase locomotive. Initial tests were successful, and the railway opened in 1898 with three trains, a fourth being added in 1902. The same stock was still in use in 1930, when the locomotives were converted to operate on the standard frequency of 50Hz at 755V.

Choice of three-phase traction had overwhelming advantages for such a railway. Most significant was the fact that as long as the motors remained connected their speed of rotation was governed wholly by the frequency of supply. This automatically governed train speed, a feature that was most important on the descent. By contrast, the complications associated with the need for two independent overhead conductors were not significant on the simple track layouts of a rack-and-pinion line. Special arrangements could be made for a situation when—typically in the late afternoon—all the trains were descending and pumping electricity back into the power station.

Above: *Propelling skiers up to the Gornergrat. Note the wagon for skis at the head of the train.*

The Gornergrat locomotives are *true* rack engines; that is to say the drive is only on the cog wheels, the rail wheels being idlers. The rack system used was Abt's, with a pair of cog-wheels meshing with a double rack on the ground. The teeth on one side were out-of-phase with those on the other, as this smoothed out the thrust. Power came from a hydro-electric plant generating at 5,400V 40Hz, which was transformed to 550V for traction.

These machines originally belonged to that select club of timber-built locomotives. They had two motors of 90hp mounted on the body, each connected to a rack wheel through gearing. Two sets of double pantographs were mounted on the roof. Like most Swiss locomotives, the mechanical parts were made at the Swiss Locomotive Works at Winterthur, while electrical equipment was naturally by Brown Boveri. One end of a coach rested on the frame of the locomotive, and the other end was supported on a bogie. This combination normally propelled a second coach with four wheels; the whole assembly carrying 110 passengers.

The slow walking pace of these trains was just right for summer sightseers; but when Zermatt developed as a winter resort after World War II, the vast commuting crowds of skiers found these repetitive journeys painfully slow. The first of a new series of motor coaches arrived in 1947, halving the journey time, and soon took over all passenger workings. Even so, three out of the four original locomotives survive, much rebuilt and renumbered 3001-3. It is remarkable that these octogenarians—the world's first three-phase locomotives—should have had such long lives, outliving most of the later three-phase main line systems.

---

become a reality—of really fast self-propelled electric express trains. Writing 30 years later Dr-Eng Walter Reichel (who participated in the trials) commented dryly "It is probable that 230km/h (143mph) could have been reached had not caution outweighed a thirst for knowledge."

In addition to this AEG railcar, Siemens & Halske ran both a high-speed railcar which reached 128.5mph (207km/h) and a locomotive which with a train was able to achieve 81mph (130km/h).

Left: *The high-speed experimental railcar constructed by the German General Electric Co., which reached 130½mph (210km/h) in 1903. Note the separate current-collecting bows for each end and each contact wire.*

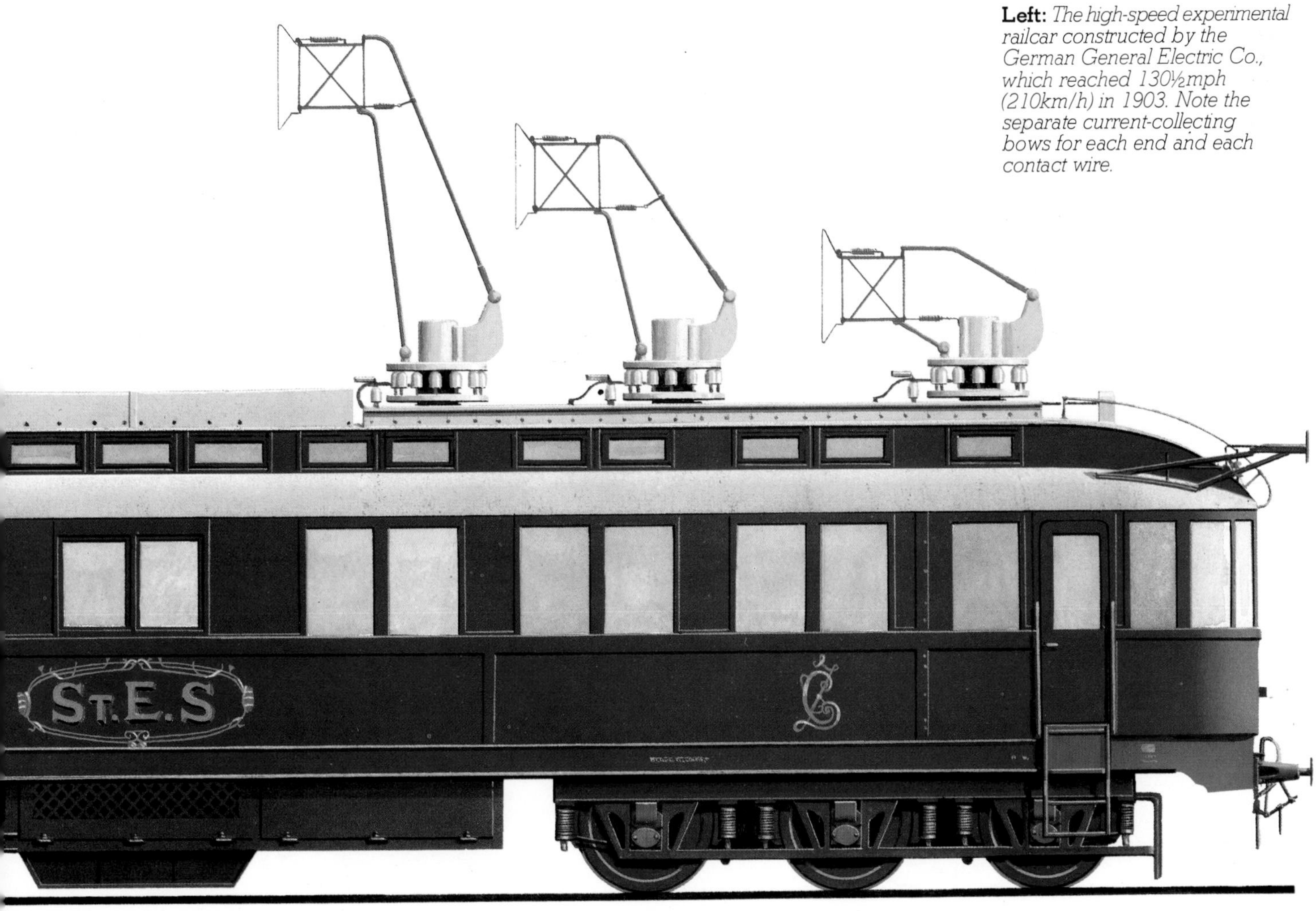

Class S 1-D$_o$-1

United States:
New York Central & Hudson River Railroad (NYC&HR), 1904

Type: Electric passenger locomotive.
Gauge: 4ft 8½in (1,435mm).
Propulsion: 660V direct current collected from under-contact third rail supplying four 550hp (410kW) frame-mounted gearless traction motors with armatures on the axles.
Weight: 142,000lb (64.4t) adhesive, 200,500lb (91t) total.
Max. axleload: 35,500lb (16.1t).
Overall length: 37ft 0in (11,277mm).
Tractive effort: 32,000lb (145kN).
Max. speed: 70mph (113km/h).

A major development in electric traction occasioned by a collision between two steam trains—such was the electrification of New York Central's Grand Central terminal in New York and the surrounding lines. The smoke nuisance in this major city location had long brought criticism upon the railway, but it was the 2-mile Park Avenue tunnel on the approach lines which constituted an operating hazard. At busy times the tunnel was choked with smoke, and sighting of signals was impeded. After several collisions in the tunnel, the climax came in January 1902, when a train ran past a red signal and collided with a stationary train, causing 15 deaths.

The New York Legislature thereupon passed an act prohibiting the use of steam south of the Harlem River after July 1, 1908. Since 1895 the Baltimore & Ohio had operated the Baltimore Belt line with electric traction, including the Howard Street tunnel, so the legislation was not unreasonable, but it had the additional effect of forcing the issue of a major rebuilding of the terminal station.

The railroad adopted the third-rail system at 660V dc with under-contact current collection, and General Electric was appointed contractor. The great pioneer of electric traction, Frank Sprague, was one of the engineers to the project, and for commuter services on the electrified lines Sprague's multiple-unit system of control was applied to 180 cars. For haulage of long-distance trains, GE's engineer Asa Batchelder designed a 1-Do-1 locomotive of massive proportions, which incorporated a number of novelties of his devising. The principal feature of the design was the use of bi-polar motors, with the armature mounted on the axle and the two poles hung from the locomotive frame. The continuous rating was 2,200hp, and the short-term rating of 3,000hp gave a starting tractive effort of 32,000lb (145kN), which enabled the locomotive to accelerate a train of 800 US tons at 1 mile per second per second (0.45m/s^2), and maintain 60mph (97km/h) with 500 tons. The locomotives were fitted with Sprague's multiple-unit control, so that they could operate in pairs with one driver, and they were the first locomotives to be so equipped.

The frames were outside the wheels to allow room for the armatures. The body had a central cab with a good all-round view, and with little more than the air compressors above floor level, the cab was very roomy. Other equipment was housed in the end hoods, including an oil-fired train-heating boiler.

The prototype locomotive, No. 6000, was completed late in 1904, and was tested exhaustively on a 6-mile (9.6km) stretch of the NYC main line near the GE works at Schenectady, which was electrified for the purpose. The test included side-by-side comparative runs with the latest steam engines, in which the steam engine usually gained an early lead, but was then overtaken and handsomely beaten by the electric.

The success of No. 6000 was followed by orders for 34 similar locomotives, classified "T", which were delivered in 1906. One of them hauled the first electrically-worked train from the partially-completed Grand Central Station in September 1906. Full electric

Below: *The prototype 1-Do-1 electric locomotive, as built for the New York Central & Hudson River Railroad in 1904.*

working was instituted in 1907, but unfortunately three days later a train hauled by two "T" class locomotives derailed on a curve, causing 23 deaths. Although the cause of the derailment was not established definitely, the locomotives were rebuilt with end bogies, thus becoming 2-Do-2, and they were reclassified "S".

In regular service the electric locomotives showed savings in operating and maintenance costs compared with steam varying between 12 per cent in transfer service to 27 per cent in road service. In 1908-09 a further 12 locomotives were delivered. The entire class survived through half-a-century of service, ending their days on switching and empty coaching stock working. No. 6000 went to a museum after 61 years' service. Some of the class were still at work for Penn Central in the 1970s.

Left: *After rebuilding as a 2-Do-2 and more than 70 years service Class S No. 113 is on show at the St Louis Transport Museum.*

Class E550 E

Italy: Italian State Railways (FS), 1908

Type: Electric mountain locomotive.
Gauge: 4ft 8½in (1,435mm).
Propulsion: Three-phase current at 3,400V 15Hz fed via twin overhead wires and the running wheels to two 1,000hp (750kW) motors connected to the wheels by jackshafts and coupling rods. Control by liquid resistances.
Weight: 138,850lb (63t).
Axleload: 27,990lb (12.7t).
Overall length: 31ft 2in (9,500mm).
Tractive effort: 22,040lb (100kN).
Max. speed: 31mph (50km/h).

Being a land possessing no supplies of coal but having ample areas of mountainous country, Italy was a natural possibility for electric traction. As regards expertise, it perhaps says enough that Volta of the volt was an Italian, while the maker of the world's first dynamo/electric motor was another, Pacinotti by name. It is then no surprise that, as regards electrification, Italian railways came in early and have progressed further and more quickly than most others.

In 1901 a local railway north of Milan, running 16 miles (26km) from Colico to Chiavenna, had been electrified experimentally, the work being done free of charge by Ganz & Co of Budapest, of whom more will be heard later. The three-phase system used had twin overhead wires which, together with the running rails, gave the three conductors necessary. The supply was at 3,400V 15.8 Hz. The trials were successful and in 1902 the system was extended to the 50-mile (80km) Lecco-Colico-Sondrio line on a permanent basis. So Italian electrification became established on a line with light traffic.

A particularly difficult line to work by steam, because of its gradients, its heavy traffic and its tunnels, was the Giovi incline which connected the port of Genoa with its hinterland. The original line, built in 1853, involved a climb of 4½ miles (7.2km) at 1-in-28½ (3.5 per cent) followed by a 2-mile (3.2km) tunnel. A diversion with easier grades of 1-in-62 (1.6 per cent) and a 4-mile summit tunnel was opened in 1889, but by 1905, when Italian State Railways (FS) was formed, the traffic offering was such that the combined capacity of both the old and the new lines was insufficient.

The experience gained on the Lecco-Colico-Sondrio line gave the infant FS enough confidence to tackle the Giovi line using the same principles, the work being completed in 1908. The locomotives supplied were these ten-coupled tractors, capable of taking 400t (440 US tons) up the 1-in-28 (3.5 per cent) gradient, at their fixed top speed of 31mph (50km/h). An alternative fixed speed of 14mph could be obtained by connecting the motors in cascade. The reason for the low-frequency supply lay in the fact that designers were unhappy about transmitting the heavy forces involved through such

Class 1099 C-C

Austria: Lower Austria Local Railway (NOLB), 1910

Type: Electric mountain locomotive.
Gauge: 2ft 6in (760mm).
Propulsion: Single-phase medium-frequency current at 6,500V 25Hz, fed via overhead wire and step-down variable transformer to two 300hp (225kW) motors, one on each bogie, connected to the driving wheels by jackshafts and coupling rods.
Weight: 103,590lb (47t).
Max. axleload: 17,632lb (8t).
Length: 36ft 2in (11,020mm).
Tractive effort: 10,150lb (45kN).
Max. speed: 31mph (50km/h).

73 years young and still no successors in sight! These fine early examples of the electric locomotive-builder's art have worked virtually all the services on what is now Austrian Federal Railways' narrow-gauge branch from St Pölten—on the Vienna to Salzburg main line—south through the mountains a distance of 56 miles (91km) to Mariazell and Gusswerk ever since electrification was completed in 1911. The line was built in 1898 by the local provincial authority as the Lower Austria Council Railway (*Niederoesterreichische Landesbahn*—NOLB), which was also responsible for the electrification. In 1921 the NOLB system was absorbed into Austrian Federal Railways.

Simplicity was the keynote of the locomotives' design and this has no doubt contributed much to their exceptional longevity. For example, in spite of the long and steep gradients, electric braking is not provided. Some complexity is involved, however, in the drawgear which is mounted on the bogies. This comprises combined central buffer and link-and-pin couplings as well as screw couplings on each side. A single pantograph now replaces the two unusual current collectors originally provided, each consisting of a small pantograph mounted on what for all the world looked like the frame of a step-ladder.

It is quite common to find ancient locomotives looking more or less the same as they did when they left the builders' works, but which have been fundamentally re-equipped as regards their working parts. The Class "1099s" are the opposite—internally they are virtually the same, but brightly-painted modern bodywork has replaced the original drab brown box-like exterior. In spite of wars, economic troubles and various foreign occupations, all 16 still

Left: *Ten-coupled three-phase locomotive, built in 1908 for the electrification of the Giovi incline out of Genoa, Italy.*

gearing as was then available. Low-frequency synchronous motors can conveniently have a suitably low corresponding rate of revolution, thereby doing away with the need for gearing.

Incidentally the designation "E550" has the following significance: "E" = electric, first "5" = 5 driving axles, second "5" = the service on which the locomotive is to be used (in this case heavy freight), and the final "0" is the sequential number of the class within the same type and service.

Success attended all the efforts made and the electrification was rapidly extended to other main lines in that part of Italy, the Mont Cenis tunnel and the French frontier being reached in 1912.

The fleet of "E550s" rose by leaps and bounds, and by 1921, when they were superseded by the similar but more powerful "E551" class, the total had reached 186. They were then by far the most numerous class of electric locomotive in the world. One of these famous machines survives in Milan, on display at the Leonardo da Vinci Museum of Science & Technology, as befits a class of locomotive that was the first to show that electricity could do what steam could not.

survive—Nos. 1099.01-16. The mechanical parts were built by Krauss Works at Linz, Austria, and the electrical equipment by Siemens-Schuckert of Nuremberg, West Germany.

Right: *Austrian Federal Railways' Class 1099 600hp (450kW) electric locomotive, built in 1910 for the metre-gauge Mariazellerbahn in Lower Austria, heads a train from St. Polten to Gusswerk. All 16 of these locomotives still miraculously survive, although new bodywork recently fitted to the whole Class gives them a changed appearance.*

Be 5/7 1-E-1 **Switzerland:** Berne-Lötschberg-Simplon Railway (BLS), 1912

Type: Heavy-duty mixed-traffic electric locomotive.
Gauge: 4ft 8½in (1,435mm).
Propulsion: Single-phase current at 15,000V 16⅔Hz fed via overhead catenary and step-down transformer to two 1,250hp (933kW) motors connected to the wheels by gearing, jackshafts and coupling rods.
Weight: 172,353lb (78.2t) adhesive, 231,420lb (105t) total.
Max. axleload: 36,586lb (16.6t).
Overall length: 52ft 6in (16,000m).
Tractive effort: 39,670lb (176kN).
Max. speed: 47mph (75km/h).

Above: *Bern-Lötschberg-Simplon pioneer Be 5/7 electric locomotive of 1912 at Brig, July 1954.*

When the Simplon tunnel route from Brig, Switzerland, to Domodossola was opened in 1906, businessmen in the Swiss capital Berne, found themselves a mere 52 miles (85km) away from the northern portal of this channel of trade, yet separated from it by the great mountains of the Bernese Oberland. As the Swiss Federal Railways system (then occupied in digesting its recently-absorbed component parts) offered no assistance, it was a case of self-help; with a commendable lack of delay, construction of the Berne-Lötschberg-Simplon Railway began in 1906.

The project was a bold one involving construction of a third major Swiss Alpine tunnel, the Lötschberg, 9.1 miles (14.6km) in length. There were long ascending ramps at 1-in-37 (2.7 per cent) including many further bores, both spiral and otherwise. Whilst this combination of tunnelling and gradient was ideal for electric traction, it needed courage amounting almost to rashness to adopt it for a project of this magnitude at this time. But the engineers had a starting point. Three-phase electric traction had been used in the Simplon tunnel from its opening and, as we have seen, it had also been adopted in Italy for the Giovi and other lines. However, the Swiss electrical firm of Oerlikon realised (as it has turned out with remarkable foresight) that this form of electrification had limited potential for other than specialised lines.

Accordingly, in 1905, Oerlikon went so far as to electrify at their own cost as a demonstration Swiss Federal Railways' 14 mile (22.5km) branch from Seebach to Wettingen. They used their own system of 15,000V 16⅔Hz single-phase low-frequency alternating current developed by their Chief Engineer Dr-Eng Huber-Stockar. By using a low frequency (so low that lamps lit by this current can be seen to flicker strongly), it was possible to overcome the difficulties of using alternating current in a variable-speed motor. At the same time, the current could be fed to the locomotives at high voltage, with a convenient step-down transformer to produce the much lower and variable voltage suitable for the driving motors. The electrification was a technical but not a commercial success and was dismantled after the demonstration was over.

So the first major main line to be built as an electric railway came into being, and to work it 13 of these handsome ten-coupled locomotives were built—the most powerful in the world. The electrical equipment naturally came from Oerlikon, while equally naturally the mechanical parts came from the Swiss Locomotive Works at Winterthur. The locomotives achieved their objective by being

Right: *These giant locomotives of the Lötschberg Railway were the most powerful in the world in 1912.*

Nos. 1-67 HGe 2/2

Panama Canal Zone:
Panama Canal Company, 1912

Type: Rack-and-adhesion electric canal mule locomotive.
Gauge: 5ft 0in (1,524mm).
Propulsion: Three-phase current at 200V 25Hz fed via twin outside conductor rails to two 150hp (112kW) motors with pole-changing arrangements to give the fixed speeds. The rack pinions driven through gearing and the adhesive driving wheels via friction clutches.
Weight: 99,180lb (45t).
Overall length: 31ft 6½in (9,617mm).
Tractive effort: 28,600lb (127kN).
Max. speed: 5mph (8km/h).

Whilst handling ships passing through the Panama canal, these unique and fascinating machines for 50 years pulled heavier loads than any other railway locomotive in the world (as do their somewhat similar successors). They also climbed the steepest gradient of 1-in-1 (100 per cent) on the steps abreast of the lock gates—but not under load, as ships would at that moment be stationary in the lock. Elsewhere the running lines are level; the trackage extends to 20¼ miles (32km) of which 12 miles (19.3km) is equipped with Riggenbach "ladder" rack of a specially heavy pattern.

The braking system also has sufficient force to deal with the massive inertia of an ocean-going ship as well as being able to stop the locomotive in 10ft when descending a 1-in-1 (100 per cent) gradient at 3mph (4.8km/h). Locomotive power has to be provided at each of the four "corners" of a ship and there is a complex control system for the winch set between the cab units. Such is one of the most remarkable locomotive types ever built.

Above: *Flexibility is the name of the game: a Panama Canal ship-hauling electric loco.*

able to handle 300t (330 US ton) trains up the 1-in-37 (2.7 per cent) grade at 31.25mph (50km/h).

There were serious problems in the early days, both electrical and mechanical. Sudden surges of high voltage occurred under certain conditions and this damaged equipment. More serious was the harmonic vibration to the point of failure of the massive triangular connecting pieces joining the driving pins to the two drive shafts to those of the central driving wheel. Before long the causes of the problems were identified and cures found, and it says enough that Norway, Sweden, Germany and Austria all adopted the same voltage and frequency for their main-line electrification, while the locomotives gave more than 40 years of good service. Today Lötschberg "Be 5/7" No.151 has a well-deserved place in the Swiss Transport Museum at Lucerne.

Above: *Ten-coupled electric locomotive No. 151 of the BLS Railway on test between Speiz and Brig, Switzerland, in 1912.*

Nos. 21-28 C

Switzerland:
Bernese Oberland Railway (BOB), 1914

Type: Electric rack-and-adhesion locomotive.
Gauge: 3ft 3⅜in (1,000mm).
Propulsion: Direct current at 1,500V fed via twin contact wires to two 400hp (298kW) traction motors. One motor drives the railwheels via gearing, jackshaft and connecting rods; the other motor drives the rack pinion via gearing.
Weight: 80,445lb (36.5t).
Max. axleload: 27,550lb (12.5t).
Overall length: 27ft 0½in (8,240mm).
Tractive effort: 13,225lb (59kN) adhesion, 26,450lb (118kN) rack-and-adhesion.
Max. speed: 25mph (40km/h) on adhesion sections, 7.5mph (12km/h) on rack sections.

The little Bernese Oberland Railway (the "BOB" to its many loving British friends) is the first stage of an amazing Swiss mountain railway system which by two routes and two changes of gauge takes people to the Jungfraujoch, highest railway station in Europe. Since 1890, it has connected with the main line at Interlaken and served directly the resorts of Grindelwald and Lauterbrunnen. Included in the system are several rack-and-pinion sections equipped with the Riggenbach or ladder rack.

Everything was done by steam in the early days, but in 1914 the 14.7 mile (23.5km) system was electrified. For working the trains, these eight neat locomotives were supplied by Oerlikon and the Swiss Locomotive Works. Two identical motors were fitted, one driving the main cog-wheel for operation on the rack, and the other driving the rail wheels and used both on the rack and off it. On the wholly adhesion sections, 125t (137 US tons) can be hauled up the maximum grade of 1-in-40 (2.5 per cent) from Interlaken to the junction at Zweilütschinen, while the 1-in-8.3 (12 per cent) rack sections up to Grindelwald and 1-in-11.1 (9 per cent) up to Lauterbrunnen limit loads to 60t and 90t (66 and 99 US tons) respectively.

No chances can be taken with the brakes on such grades and five independent systems are provided. First, a normal air brake works on both the rail wheelrims and on a separate braking rack wheel, riding free on one of the axles. There is also a handbrake arranged to come automatically into play when the normal speed is exceeded by 20 per cent. Furthermore, there are two separate screw handbrakes working

Below: *BOB electric locomotive ready to leave Lauterbrunnen Station, Switzerland, with a freight train for Interlaken.*

Right: *BOB rack-and-adhesion electric locomotive. In earlier days the livery was grey and later black was used.*

Nos. 1-13 B_o-B_o

Great Britain:
North Eastern Railway (NER), 1914

Type: Electric freight locomotive.
Gauge: 4ft 8½in (1,435mm).
Propulsion: Direct-current at 1,500V fed via overhead catenary to four 275hp (205kW) nose-suspended traction motors.
Weight: 166,660lb (76t).
Max. axleload: 41,665lb (19t).
Overall length: 59ft 0in (17,989mm).
Tractive effort: 28,800lb (128kN).
Max. speed: 40mph (64km/h).

The principal reason for building the Stockton & Darlington Railway, the first steam public railway in the world, was to haul coal from coalfields near Bishop Auckland to tide-water at Stockton. The route chosen just happened to run via Darlington. This first steam railway was a prime example of what was to become the classic use for them—bulk movement of minerals. Today it is the only use which enables new railways to be justified upon purely financial considerations.

For many years fortune smiled on the S&D and traffic rose to a point where a by-pass (known as the Simpasture line) had to be built to avoid the congestion of Darlington, and other parts of the line had to be increased from two to four tracks. The route was also a very early candidate for electrification, not because of any of its physical characteristics nor because of the need to increase capacity or avoid pollution, but entirely on the basis of reducing running costs.

Electrification of the 18-mile (29km) route from Shildon Yard (the collecting point for coal from the various collieries concerned) to Newport Yard, the distribution point for the numerous coal-consuming customers and shipping staithes in the Stockton-Middlesbrough area, began in 1914 and was completed in 1917. Because of the complexities of the lines, 50 miles (80km) of track were involved. Technical innovation was not a feature; instead, simplicity and economy were the keynotes of the equipment. For example, the locomotives had no train braking equipment. Fortunately, the public power supply system in a major industrial area was by then already adequate to take on the heavy and highly variable demands involved, so one major complication—construction of a purpose-built generating station—was avoided. Incidentally, the power company contracted for the supply of the actual traction current, building and owning the two substations.

Some features were found to be too simple; for example, hand-worked knife switches on these locomotives had to be replaced by power-worked equipment—a combination of hundreds of amps with over a thousand volts was too much for operation by hand. Also, the distance of 200ft (61m)

on the rail wheels and the braking rack-wheel respectively. Finally, provision is made for electric braking, dissipating the energy generated in the process by a bank of blower-cooled resistances.

Since World War II, most BOB passenger trains have been worked by trailer-hauling railcars, but a number of these neat locomotives are retained for freight haulage, service trains and summer peaks, and accordingly join the select ranks of 70-year old locomotives still in use.

Right: *BOB No. 22 at Wilderswil with a freight in August, 1982. Note the standard-gauge wagon on metre-gauge transporter.*

Left: *North Eastern Railway No. 9 Bo-Bo electric locomotive as built for the Shildon to Middlesbrough line to the design of Vincent Raven by the railway's own shops at Darlington in 1914.*

between structures supporting the overhead wire on straight lengths of track was found to be too great when the wind blew, and intermediate stay poles had to be added. Otherwise success was achieved.

As intended, 1,400t (1,640 US tons) trains of unbraked loaded coal hopper wagons—without even brake vans—could be hauled and, more importantly, held to a reasonable speed on gradients of 1-in-100 (1 per cent). Primitive bearings on the wagons made the former more difficult but gave modest assistance with the latter!

Commercial success was, however, short-lived. In the 1930s, coal production in the West Auckland field fell to a low level. Moreover, the overhead conductor system needed a good deal of renewal; the wood poles in particular had reached the end of their short lives. Accordingly, these locomotives were laid aside, hopefully for re-use on the electrification soon to be started from Manchester to Sheffield. However, the war delayed this project and before it was completed in the 1950s, all except one of the Newport-Shildon locos were scrapped

DD1 2-B+B-2 USA: Pennsylvania Railroad (PRR), 1909

Type: Electric passenger locomotive.
Gauge: 4ft 8½in (1,435mm).
Propulsion: Direct current at 600V fed via outside third rail (or by overhead conductors and miniature pantographs at places where third rail was impractical) to two 1,065hp (795kW) motors, each driving two main axles by means of a jackshaft and connecting rods.
Weight: 199,000lb (90.2t) adhesive, 319,000lb (145t) total.
Max. axleload: 50,750lb (23t).
Overall length: 64ft 11in (19,787mm).
Tractive effort: 49,400lb (220kN).
Max. speed: 80mph (129km/h).

The Pennsylvania Railroad gained entry to New York City and its new Pennsylvania Station by single-track tunnels, two under the Hudson River and four under the East River, and for the operation of these tunnels electrification was essential. The third-rail system at 650V was chosen, and between 1903 and 1905 three experimental four-axle locomotives were built, two B-Bs at the Pennsy's Altoona shops and a 2-B by Baldwin. The B-Bs had a separate motor for each axle, whilst the 2-B had a single 2,000hp (2,680kW) motor mounted on the main frame midway between the coupled axles. The motors of both types of locomotive drove through quills, an early version of the drive which was to be used a quarter of a century later on the "GG1" electrics.

Test were made to determine the forces exerted on the rails by the two types of locomotive and by the most recent steam designs, and it was found that the 2-B, with its higher centre of gravity, exerted less than half the force of the B-B, with its low-slung motors. However, the force due to the 2-B was still twice as great as that from the heaviest steam engine. The next two electric locomotives therefore had the 2-B wheel arrangement, but to give the required power each one comprised two units permanently coupled back-to-back, giving the combined wheel arrangement 2-B-B-2. The important change in design from the experimental locomotive was in the drive to the axles, which incorporated a jackshaft mounted in bearings in the main frame of the locomotive, with connecting rods from the motor to the jackshaft and from the jackshaft to the driving wheels. The technical problems with the quill drive were left for solution at a later date.

With 72in (1,829mm) driving wheels, each half of the unit resembled the chassis of an express 4-4-0 steam locomotive. This similarity to steam design was apparent in a number of early electric engines, for example in Prussia, but unusually for such designs the Pennsylvania's was highly successful. It was capable of

Class T B_o-B_o+B_o-B_o United States: New York Central Railroad (NYC), 1913

Type: Express passenger electric locomotive.
Gauge: 4ft 8½in (1,435mm).
Propulsion: Direct current at 660V collected from under-contact third rail supplying eight 330hp (246kW) gearless traction motors mounted on the bogie frames, with armatures on the axles.
Weight: 230,000lb (104.3t).
Max. axleload: 28,730lb (13.0t).
Overall length: 55ft 2in (16,815mm).
Tractive effort: 69,000lb (307kN).
Max. speed: 75mph (120km/h).

In 1913 the New York Central Railroad completed its Grand Central terminal, and in the same year it also completed an extension of electrification along the Hudson River main line to Harmon, 33 miles (53km) from Grand Central. The heaviest expresses would

80mph (129km/h), and there was no appreciable clanking of the rods. Maintenance costs were very low, and were helped by the design of the body. The whole casing could be removed in one unit to give access to the motors and control equipment. This feature was repeated in all subsequent PRR electric designs. A small pantograph was fitted to allow overhead current collection on complicated trackwork.

The first two rod-drive units appeared in 1909-10, the individual half-units being numbered from 3996 to 3999. They were followed in 1910-11 by a further 31, numbered from 3932 to 3949 and from 3952 to 3995. The Pennsylvania classified its steam locomotives by a letter, denoting the wheel arrangement, followed by a serial number, letter "D" denoted 4-4-0. For electrics the road used the same system, the letter being doubled when appropriate, so that the 2-B+B-2, being a double 4-4-0, was a DD. The main production batch of 31 units was classified "DD1", and the two prototypes "odd DD".

The Pennsylvania Station project required seven years, from 1903 to 1910, for its execution, and electrification then extended from Manhattan Transfer, near Newark, New Jersey, to the carriage yards at Sunnyside, Long Island, a total of 13.4 route miles (21.5km). At Manhattan Transfer the change was made to or from steam for the 8.8 miles (14.2km) between there and Pennsylvania Station. The heaviest gradient on the descent to the tunnels was 1-in-52 (1.93 per cent).

The "DD" locomotives worked all the express passenger services on this section of line until 1924 when newer types began to appear, but they continued to share the work until 1933 when overhead electrification reached Manhattan Transfer from Trenton, and the remaining section into Pennsylvania Station was converted to overhead. Third-rail current collection was retained between Pennsylvania Station and Sunnyside, because the Long Island Rail Road used this system.

After 1933 "DDs" continued to work empty trains between Pennsylvania Station and Sunnyside for many years. After the arrival of newer power in 1924, 23 of the "DD1s" were transferred to the Long Island Rail Road, and these remained in service until 1949-51.

The "DDs" were a landmark in electric locomotive design, with exceptionally high power and unusual reliability for their day, but at the same time their design was conservative. Simplicity of design and the flexibility of the "double 4-4-0" chassis contributed greatly to their success.

Below: *Pennsylvania Railroad Class DD1 direct-current 2-B+B-2 electric locomotive.*

now have some 20 miles of fast running with electric haulage, and a new type of locomotive was therefore commissioned, which would be both more powerful than the "S" class 2-Do-2 and also kinder to the track at high speed.

The new class was designated "T", thereby taking the letter vacated by the earlier locomotives when they were rebuilt. The most important change was adoption of an articulated layout in which every axle was motored, but at the same time the whole chassis was more flexible than in the earlier class. There were two sub-frames, each with two four-wheeled trucks pivotted to it. The trucks were connected by arms, and the sub-frames were hinged together at their inner ends and carried the couplers at the outer ends. The body rested on two pivots, one on each sub-frame, and one pivot had some end play to allow for changes in geometry on curves. The whole assembly was therefore flexible, but with restraining forces on all its elements to discourage the build-up of oscillations. The wheel arrangement was Bo-Bo+Bo-Bo, and it was equivalent to two Bo-Bo locomotives hinged together.

Nominal power of the original motors fitted to Class "S" was 550hp (410kW), but in Class "T" the motor size was reduced to 330hp (246kW). This enabled the weight of the motors to be reduced, with a corresponding reduction in the forces on the track and with an improvement in riding. The new class was therefore allowed 75mph (121km/h), later reduced to 70 (113), compared with 60mph (97km/h) on Class "S". The motors were of the same bi-polar type as before, with almost flat pole faces to allow for the vertical movement of the axle (and armature) on its springs.

Left: *A Class T Bo-Bo+Bo-Bo electric locomotive of the New York Central Railroad.*

Another change from Class "S" was that the motors had forced ventilation, which involved some complications of ducting to the bogies. As in the earlier units, in addition to pick-up shoes for the third rail, a small pantograph was fitted. This was used on complicated track layouts where there were long gaps in the third rail, and overhead wires were installed locally. There was an oil-fired train heating boiler, with supplies of water and oil. It seemed anomalous on an electrification introduced to eliminate the smoke nuisance that the locomotive should carry a small stack on its roof emitting oil exhaust!

The first locomotive was completed in March 1918; this was Class "T1a". Nine more, classified "T1b", were delivered later in the year. Sub-class "T2a" of 10 units came in 1914, a further 10 designated "T2b" in 1917, and a final batch of 10 in 1926; these were "T3a". Successive batches differed mainly in the size of train-heating boiler and its fuel supplies, but the "T2s" and "T3s" were 20in (508mm) longer than the "T1s". The bodies of successive batches were a little longer, and the end overhang slightly less.

With a continous rating of 2,610hp at 48mph (77km/h), they were powerful locomotives for their day, and they were highly successful. They continued to work single-headed all express trains out of Grand Central until 1955, when some locomotives surplus from a discontinued electrification in Cleveland began to displace them. They could handle trains up to 980 US tons at 60mph (97km/h).

These locomotives established the practicability of the all-adhesion machine for high-speed work, and they showed that it was possible to avoid the heavy and complicated rod drives of many of their contemporaries.

Class EP-2

"Bi-polar" 1-B-D-D-B-1

USA: Chicago, Milwaukee, St Paul & Pacific Railroad, (CM St P&P), 1919

Type: Express passenger electric locomotive.
Gauge: 4ft 8½in (1,435mm)
Propulsion: Direct current at 3,000V fed via overhead catenary to twelve 370hp (275kW) gearless motors mounted directly on the axles.
Weight: 457,000lb (207t) adhesive, 530,000lb (240t) total.
Max. axleload: 38,500lb (17.5t).
Overall length: 76ft 0in (23,165mm).
Tractive effort: 123,500lb (549kN).
Max. speed: 70mph (112km/h).

Above: *A "Bi-polar" in service under the 3,000 volt catenary wires of the Chicago, Milwaukee St Paul & Pacific Railroad.*

When the Chicago, Milwaukee, St Paul & Pacific Railroad was opened to Tacoma, Washington State, in 1909 (through passenger service did not begin until 1911) it was the last railway to reach the West Coast from the east. As a newcomer, then, the company had to try harder, and one of the ways in which it did this was to work the mountain crossings by the clean new power of electricity.

Catenary wires mounted on timber poles started to go up five years after the line was opened, and early in 1917 electric working began over the Rocky Mountain and Missoula divisions, between Harlowton and Avery, Montana, a distance of 438 miles (705km). Many miles of 100,000V transmission lines had to be built through virgin territory from hydro-electric power plants to rotary substations along the right-of-way. By 1919 the 230-mile (370km) Coast Division from Othello to Tacoma, Washington State, had been electrified also.

Electrification measured by the hundreds of miles was something quite new in the world, and the North American railroad top brass watched with baited breath for the results. Technically, they were totally satisfactory: much heavier loads could be worked than with steam, energy costs were lower, faster running times—and hence better productivity—could be achieved. The system was reliable and one could have been forgiven for thinking that other railroads would quickly follow. Alas, the enormous costs involved proved too frightening at a time when railroads were beginning to feel the effects of competition from road transport. So, with one notable exception, in the USA main line electrification schemes were confined to shortish lengths of line.

The Milwaukee Railroad itself went bankrupt in 1925, and this caused a further ebb of confidence, although it was claimed that the onset of bankruptcy was *delayed* rather than *caused* by the $24 million spent on electrification.

The original passenger locomotives (Class "EP1"), delivered from 1915 onwards by The American Locomotive Co and General Electric, were the same as those for freight, except that they had higher gearing and oil-fired train-heating boilers. They were formed as twin units, permanently coupled, of the 2-Bo-Bo+Bo-Bo-2 wheel arrangement and produced 3,440hp (2,570kW) for a weight of 288 tons. Their plain "box-car" style belied their ability to pull and go in an unprecedented manner. Thirty freight and 12 passenger locos were supplied.

When the wires were going up over the Cascade mountains in 1918, something more exotic was proposed; the result was these legendary "Bi-polars", created by General Electric. The name arose from using two-pole motors. The

reason for this lay in a desire to simplify the mechanics of an electric locomotive. The ultimate in simplicity is to put the armatures of the motors actually on the driving axles, thereby doing away altogether with gearing, but it is then necessary to cater for vertical movement. Hence there can only be two poles, one on either side in a position where the critical air gap between poles and armature is not affected by vertical movement. The price of doing it this way is that the power of each motor is limited, partly because it runs at the low speed of the wheels and partly because two-pole motors are less powerful than those with a more usual number of poles anyway.

The result was that, for a power output virtually the same as the "EP1s", the "EP2s" had half as many more driving wheels. The body was articulated in three parts, connected together by the four-axle trucks. All this made for a lot of locomotive, but the effect of size on the public was nothing compared with the impact of very impressive styling. The electrical equipment was contained in round-topped bonnets at each end of the locomotive and this simple change was what gave these engines that little extra the others hadn't got.

The designers were sensible enough to put the train-heating boiler, fuel and water tanks—all items that do not mix well with electricity—in the separate centre section. All things considered, the Cascade Division in 1918 found itself in possession of a reliable class of five locomotives that could haul 900t (1,000 US tons) trains up the long 1-in-45 (2.2 per cent) grades at 25mph (40km/h), as well as hold them back coming down. Some rather fine publicity stunts were arranged showing a "Bi-polar" having a tug-of-war with two big steam engines (a 2-6-6-2 and a 2-8-0) on top of a huge trestle bridge. The electric had no difficulty in pulling backwards the two steam engines set to pull full steam ahead.

Ten more passenger engines (Class "EP3") were delivered in 1921 by rival builders Baldwin and Westinghouse, and these were more orthodox. Even so, 20 per cent more power was packed into a locomotive with only half the number of driving wheels, the wheel arrangement being 2-C-1 + 1-C-2. Their appearance was fairly box-like, although not quite as severe as that of the "EP1s".

So the "Bi-polars" were outclassed as well as outnumbered by nearly five-to-one soon after they were built, yet these legendary locomotives demonstrated very clearly the value of cosmetics, because they are the ones remembered and regarded as epitomising this longest amongst North American electrification schemes. The great engines gave excellent service, though, and soldiered on through the years. In the late 1950s they were moving the road's crack "Olympian Hiawatha" luxury express over the 438 miles (705km) of the Rocky Mountain Division in 10hr 40min, compared with 15 hours scheduled when the electrification was new.

Some modern electric locomotives of even greater power, built for the USSR but undeliverable on account of the so-called "Cold War", became available at this time. These "Little Joes" as they were known, were further nails in the coffins of the now ageing "Bi-polars". In spite of a rebuild in 1953 which included the addition of multiple-unit capability, all five were taken out of service between 1958 and 1960. One (No. E2) is preserved at the National Museum of Transport in St Louis, Missouri, but the others went for scrap.

In 1973, all electric operations on the Milwaukee came to end, a favourable price for scrap copper being one of the factors. The escalation in the price of oil which followed might have saved the day, although the existence of the whole railroad was soon to be in jeopardy, there being just too many lines in the area. It was no surprise, then, when in 1980 all transcontinental operations over the one-time electrified tracks ceased, and most have now been abandoned.

Below: *"Bi-polar" No. E-2 as preserved at the National Museum of Transport, St Louis, Missouri.*

Below: *The Chicago, Milwaukee St Paul & Pacific Railroad's Class EP-2 "Bi-polar", one of the most impressive locomotives of any form of traction ever to have been built.*

Nos. 1-20 B_o-B_o

Great Britain:
Metropolitan Railway (Met), 1920

Type: Electric passenger locomotive.
Gauge: 4ft 8½in (1,435mm).
Propulsion: Direct current at 600V fed via third and fourth rails to four 300hp (224kW) nose-suspended motors geared to the driving axles.
Weight: 137,760lb (62.5t).
Max. axleload: 34,440lb (15.4t).
Overall length: 39ft 0in (11,887mm).
Max. speed: 65mph (104km/h).

When a railway which has hitherto been confined to short rapid-transit operations within a great metropolis suddenly starts to run out into the country, it is apt to behave as if it owned a transcontinental. The Metropolitan Railway's extension for 50 miles (80km) from Baker Street Station to Aylesbury and beyond was (among more mundane things) part of a grandiose plan for running trains from such places as Manchester, Sheffield, Nottingham and Leicester to Paris, Berlin and Rome. The Channel tunnel was to be the link between Britain and the rest of Europe, while that between the north and the south of London was the Metropolitan Railway.

Alas, it never happened that the "Orient Express" called at Baker Street to pick up secret agents, but the Met did its best to compensate with such delights as Pullman parlour cars on its longer-distance suburban trains, taking commuters from what became known as Metroland to earn their daily bread in the city. At the head of them were these handsome, named and beautifully painted electric locomotives.

Electrification had come to the surface lines of London's underground railways around the turn of the century. In 1904, and again in 1906, a batch of 10 electric locomotives was built to work the trains on country extensions as far as the the limit of electrification, which was Harrow-on-the-Hill for a time and later Rickmansworth. These early machines were reconstructed in 1920 by Metropolitan-Vickers to an extent that amounted to replacement, the result being these outwardly magnificent but basically very conventional electric locomotives.

The usual problems caused by the inevitable gaps in the conductor system were solved by providing collecting shoes and a power line, not only for the Metropolitan trains used on the main line but also on the Great Western services which ran through via Paddington, and were electrically worked from there to Liverpool Street. Vacuum as well as air brake equipment was provided, so that stock which was normally steam-hauled could be handled also.

In 1960 electrification was extended from Rickmansworth to Amersham, and London Transport (into which the Met had been absorbed in 1933) ceased running trains between Amersham and Aylesbury. After this, little work could be found for these engines, and the majority were withdrawn; however, No. 5 *John Hampden* is preserved in the London Transport Museum at Covent Garden and No. 12 *Sarah Siddons* in working order at London Transport's Neasden depot.

Above: *One of the Metropolitan Railway 1920 electric locomotives enters Baker Street station.*

Right: *No. 12* Sarah Siddons, *preserved at Neasden Depot, at Wembley Park, on a special to Watford in September 1982.*

Below: *No. 8, appropriately named* Sherlock Holmes, *who supposedly lodged in Baker Street just opposite the Metropolitan station.*

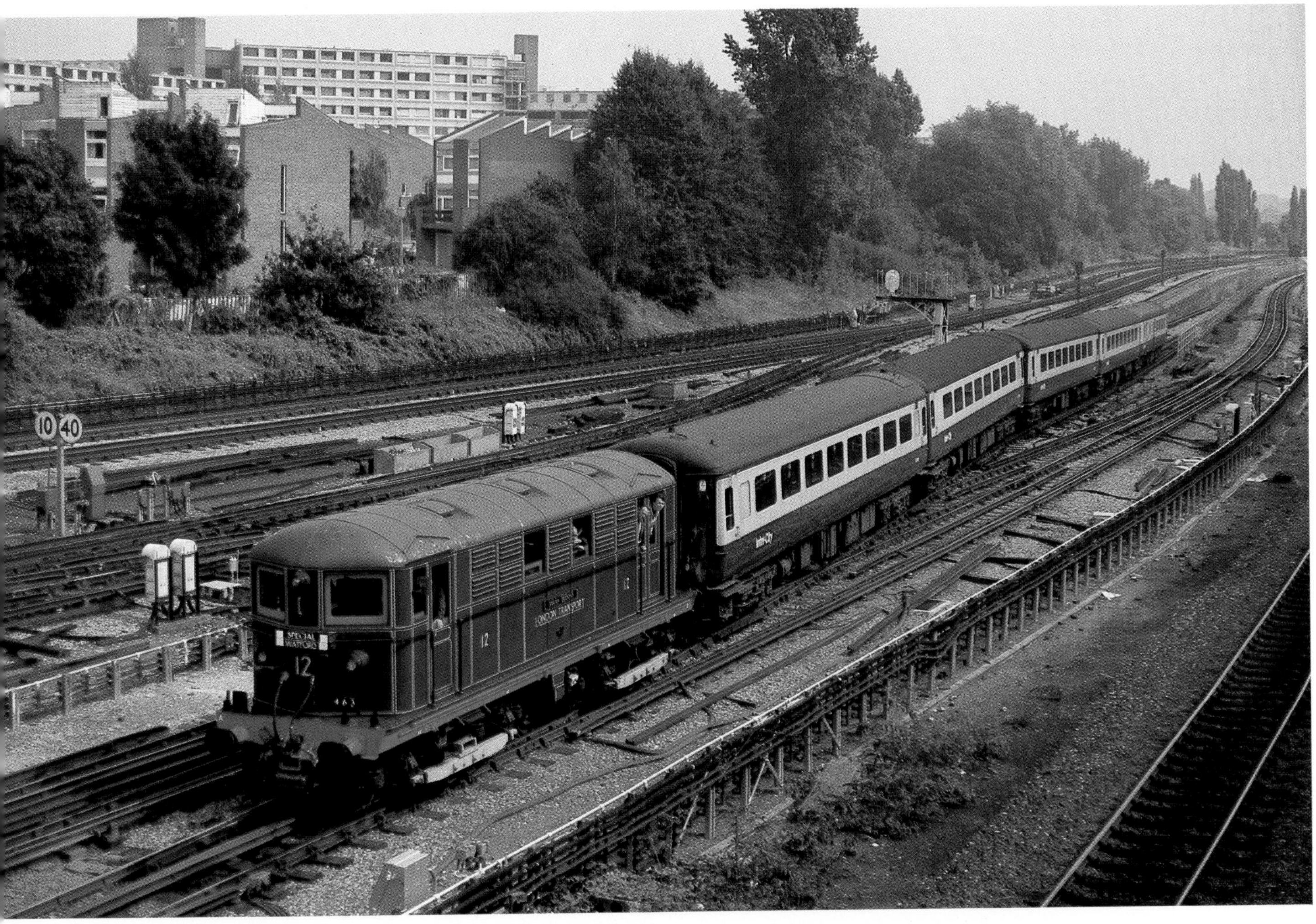
10
40
SPECIAL
WATFORD
12

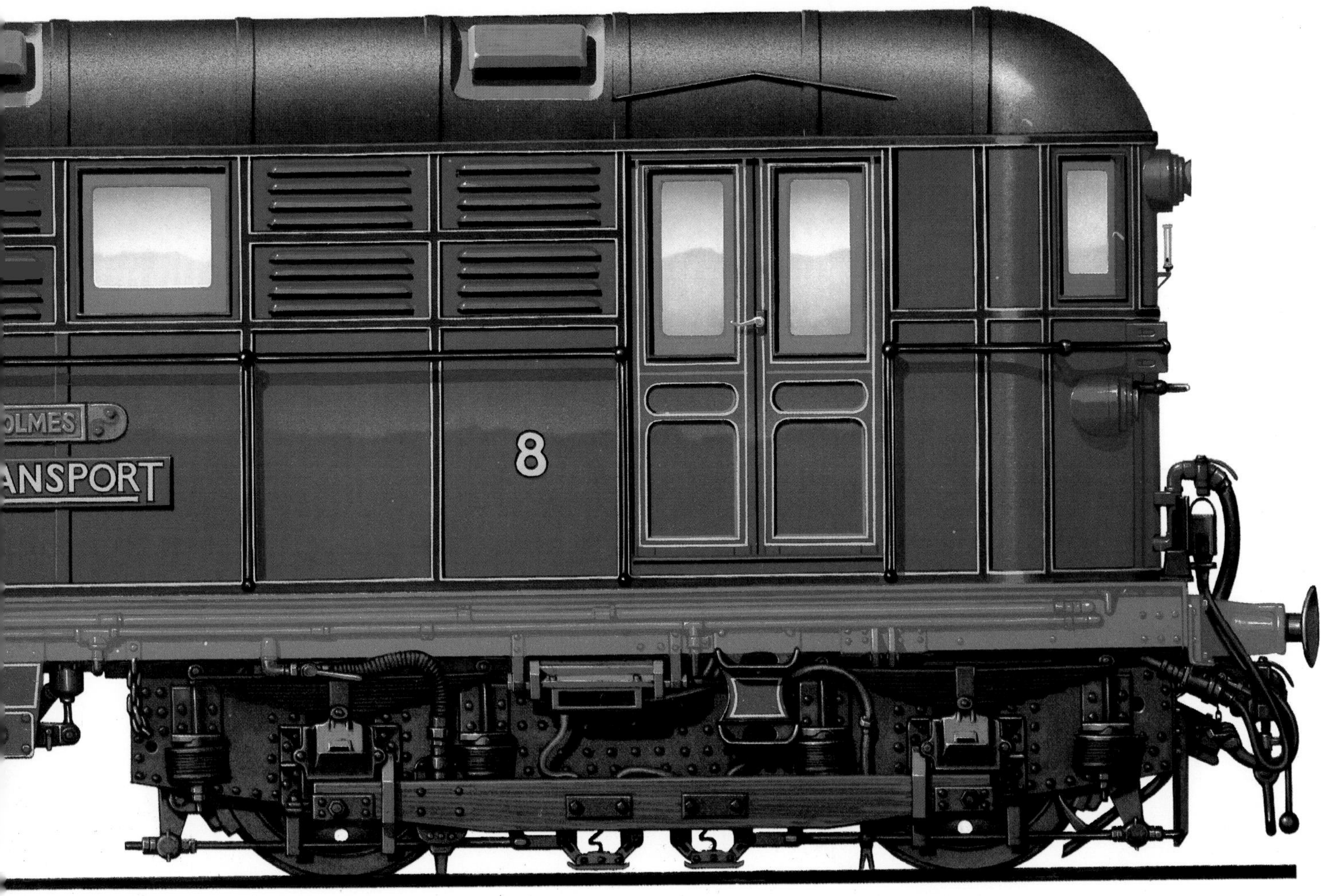
OLMES
ANSPORT
8

Class Ge 6/6 "Crocodile" Switzerland: Rhaetian Railway (RhB), 1921

Type: Electric mountain locomotive.
Gauge: 3ft 3⅜in (1,000mm).
Propulsion: Single-phase current at 11,000V 16⅔Hz fed via overhead catenary and step-down transformer to two 313hp (420kW) motors, each connected to three driving axles by jackshafts and coupling rods.
Weight: 145,460lb (66t).
Max. axleload: 24,240lb (11t).
Overall length: 43ft 7½in (13,300mm).
Tractive effort: 39,600lb (176kN).
Max. speed: 34mph (55km/h).

One of the most famous as well as one of the most spectacular railway systems in the world is the metre-gauge line which serves the Swiss resorts of Davos and St Moritz. Connections with the main standard-gauge railway are made at Landquart and Chur, at around 500ft (150m) altitude, whilst the two main objectives of the line are reached via summits at 5,700ft (1,737m) and 5,980ft (1,823m) respectively. The line from Landquart to Davos was laid out in 1896 with a ruling gradient of 1-in-22½ (4.5 per cent) while the Chur to St Moritz route, completed in 1902, was built to 1-in-29 (3.4 per cent) maximum including four spiral tunnels and the 3.6-mile (5.9km) Albula tunnel connecting the Rhine and Danube watersheds.

Even though curvature as sharp as 328ft (100m) radius is the rule rather than the exception, it was not possible to avoid some of the most expensive and spectacular railway engineering in the world. In steam days, operation was fairly traumatic and the thoughts of Rhaetian Railway engineers turned to this new-fangled power called electricity, which could be generated by the ample water-power available in the district.

Mountain railway electrification in Switzerland had until then tended to follow tramway practice in using low-voltage direct current, but the Rhaetian problem was more that of a main line railway.

When in 1910 construction began of a branch down the Engadine Valley to the Austrian border at Schuls-Tarasp, opportunity was taken to build the line as an electrified railway. The engineers used what was to become the Swiss standard main-line system of 16⅔Hz alternating current, but at the nominal lower voltage of 11,000 instead of 15,000. One reason for this was the tight clearances for the overhead wires in RhB's numerous tunnels. Some box-like tractors of the 1-B-1 wheel arrangement were built for local traffic on the lower Engadine line, but also in 1913-14 came eight experimental (and rather longer) 1-D-1 boxes intended as possible main-line power for the RhB. They incorporated various solutions to the problem of obtaining adequate starting torque from a single-phase alternating current motor.

Above: *Rhaetian Railway Class Ge 6/6 No. 410 leaving Davos-Dorf Station with a Landquart to Davos-Platz train.*

A desperate shortage of fuel during the 1914-18 war (the Swiss had no coal of their own) turned this desire to electrify into an iron resolve. After the war was over, experience with the pre-war electric engines suggested that something completely different would be preferable; and that led to the magnificent locomotives described here.

No.401, the first of 10 C-C electric locomotives, was delivered in June 1921 and this event marked the beginning of an uninterrupted rule of 26 years as the prime power on this spectacular and exacting railway. Two more were built in 1925 and a further batch of three came in 1929. As with most Swiss locomotives, the mechanical parts were supplied by the Swiss Locomotive Works; the electrical equipment was shared by Brown Boveri and Oerlikon.

A timing of 4 hours from Chur to St Moritz (89km) in steam days was improved to 2hr 45min with electrification. In addition, it was possible in due course to provide more comfortable rolling stock (reflected in an increase in weight per seat provided) and such amenities as restaurant cars, for what was still a fairly long journey. Furthermore, a large increase in traffic could be handled without difficulty, considering that the trailing load for one locomotive had increased from 90t to 200t of the RhB's light bogie coaches averaging 20t each.

The design incorporated two jackshaft and rod-drive six-coupled units, each with a large single-phase motor, set some distance apart. These units were connected (in the exact manner of a Beyer Garratt steam locomotive) by a body section which carried the main transformer—always very heavy in the case of a low-frequency supply—as well as

Right: *Rhaetian Railway Class Ge 6/6. Note the big snowplough as carried in winter and spring until about 1960, when small permanently-fixed ones were fitted at both ends.*

all the switchgear and auxiliaries, the two sets of controls and, on the roof, the two pantograph current collectors. The driver looks out from the windows of this central section over the bonnets of the articulated motor units. A similar layout was used for some standard-gauge locomotives (known as the "Crocodiles") built at the same time for the newly-electrified Gotthard line of Swiss Federal Railways.

Interesting accessories included flange-lubricating gear to assist in negotiating the almost continuous curvature, and there was a vacuum exhauster to provide power for RhB's vacuum brakes. For winter use there were transformer tappings to provide a supply of train-heating current and a massive snowplough for attachment at one end. In later years two smaller ploughs were permanently fixed, which saved turning the engines.

Regenerative braking was a possibility, but a problem arose while RhB's low-frequency power supplies remained self-contained. All the trains on the line *could* be running downhill, and without any load on the system (or special provision for such conditions) braking effect would not be forthcoming with dire results. Accordingly, a system of electric braking was adopted which is similar to that provided on many modern diesel-electric locomotives; the power generated by braking is dissipated in a bank of resistances.

A pleasing feature is the brown livery with elegant brass insignia which has been retained despite the fact that after World War II RhB began applying a rather drab dark green colour with chromium-plated *sans serif* lettering and numbering to its new electric tractors.

After these more conventional Bo-Bo locomotives came along in 1947, the "baby-crocs" (as the "Ge 6/6s" were sometimes known) began to be displaced from the prime assignments but continued to give good service on lesser trains. Even though 20 Bo-Bo and seven Bo-Bo-Bo machines are now available, all the baby-crocs except No.401 (which lost an argument with some avalanche debris at Cavadurli near Klosters in 1973) are still in service at the time of writing.

News that further locomotives are at last on order to replace these superb vintage examples of the locomotive-builder's art saddens those for whom they have for so long been part of the landscape of a favourite holiday area. The RhB management has, however, kept two steam locomotives to satisfy the demands of old train lovers, so perhaps they will apply themselves to the less onerous problem of keeping a baby-crocodile or two in running order with the same end in view.

Above: *Rhaetian Railway Class Ge 6/6 No. 405 comes off the 1-in-22½ (4.5%) ascent at Laret Station above Klosters in the heart of the famous Parsenn skiing area.*

Be 4/6 1-B-B-1 Switzerland: Swiss Federal Railways (SBB), 1919

Type: Electric mountain passenger locomotive.
Gauge: 4ft 8½in (1,435mm).
Propulsion: Single-phase current at 15,000V 16⅔Hz fed via overhead catenary to two pairs of 510hp (380kW) motors, each pair driving four wheels by jackshaft and coupling rods.
Weight: 169,710lb (77t) adhesive, 234,730lb (106.5t) total.
Max. axleload: 42,427lb (19.25t).
Overall length: 54ft 1½in (16,500mm).
Tractive effort: 44,080lb (196kN).
Max. speed: 47mph (75km/h).

The Gotthard Railway, one of the world's greatest mountain railways and which must take the lion's share of the blame for giving Switzerland's rail routes the nickname "Turntable of Europe", was opened in 1883. The mountain section was double track including the 9¼ mile (14.8km) St Gotthard tunnel, as well as 19 miles (30km) of lesser bores. The ruling grade of 1-in-38½ (2.6 per cent) applied to both the northern and the southern ascents. Even so, heavy traffic was worked satisfactorily by a fleet of well-built compound 2-10-0 and 4-6-0 steam locomotives.

World War I, during which Switzerland was neutral, posed serious problems because coal supplies—mostly originating from Germany—became minimal. Wood-burning was no substitute and even while the war was on plans were afoot to work the railways with Switzerland's only indigenous form of power, that is, electricity produced by water power, the 'white coal' of the Alps.

Proven technology was available, resulting from five years experience with the Lötschberg Railway and now that the will—and the money—was there, there were no obstacles to rapid and confident progress. On May 29, 1921 the main Gotthard line from Erstfeld

Above: *Swiss Federal Railways' Class Be 4/6 electric locomotive shown in the original brown livery, as built for the inauguration of electric working over the Gotthard line.*

No. 13 2-C$_o$-2 Great Britain: North Eastern Railway (NER), 1922

Type: Express passenger electric locomotive.
Gauge: 4ft 8½in (1,435mm).
Propulsion: Direct current at 1,500V fed via overhead catenary or under-contact third rail to three pairs of 300hp (224kW) motors, each pair driving a main axle by gearing and spring drive.
Weight: 114,240lb (52t) adhesive, 228,480lb (104t) total.
Max. axleload: 38,080lb (17.25t).
Overall length: 53ft 6in (16,307mm).
Tractive effort: 28,000lb (124kN).
Max. speed: 90mph (144km/h).

When at the end of World War I the railways of the world once more began to look to the future, one of the most far-sighted people involved was Sir Vincent Raven of the North Eastern Railway. Raven was Chief Mechanical Engineer, and an enthusiast for electric traction. Moreover, the NER's principal activity was the one it had inherited from its earliest constituent, the Stockton & Darlington Railway—the carriage of minerals in bulk. Railways that do this tend, even today, to be rich and so able to afford costly but remunerative investment such as electrification. The NER was no exception.

One of the company's principal mineral lines, that from Shildon to Newport, had been electrified in 1917 with extremely satisfactory results, and Raven's mind turned towards electric traction for the NER's trunk passenger line from York to Newcastle, part of the East Coast route from London to Edinburgh. A great deal of work was done on this project, including construction of a prototype 2-Co-2 electric locomotive capable of as high a speed—90mph (144km/h)—as was then run on railways anywhere.

No. 13 was built at the company's own Darlington Works in 1921-22; Metropolitan-Vickers supplied the electrical equipment. With six motors it was possible to have three running positions of the controls: all motors in series for starting, two sets of three in parallel and three sets of two in parallel. The 6ft 8in (2,032mm) diameter driving wheels had an unusual spoke arrangement to accommodate the fittings of and

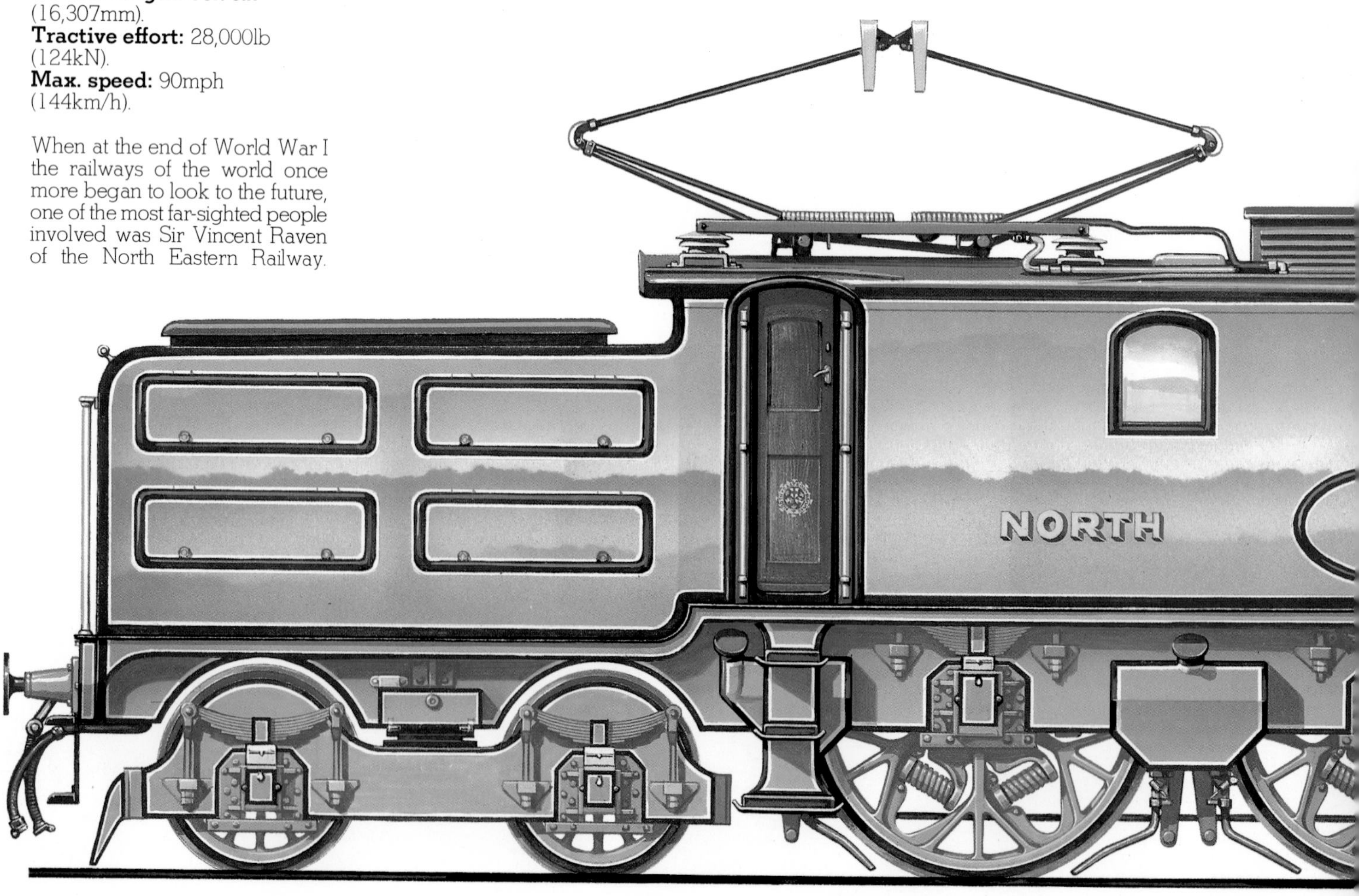

Above: *Swiss Federal Railways' rod-drive electric locomotive No. 12320. Note the buffers and drawgear attached to the bogies rather than to the body of the locomotive.*

near Lucerne to Bellinzona near the Italian frontier was turned over fully to electric traction, the first electrically-hauled train having crossed the mountains the previous year. As regards locomotives for passenger traffic, three prototypes were delivered in 1919 for evaluation. A 1-B-B-1 (No. 12301) and a 1-C-1 (No. 12201) came with electrical equipment by Oerlikon, plus a different and rather simpler 1-B-B-1 (No. 12302) from Brown Boveri. After a brief period of trial the last-named was judged the best and a batch of 39 was ordered, the mechanical parts coming as always from the Swiss Locomotive Works of Winterthur. Numbers ran from 12303 to 12341.

The specification for the "BE 4/6s" called for the haulage of a 300t train at a minimum speed of 31mph (50km/h) up the 1-in-38½ (2.6 per cent) gradient and this was easily met. The articulated design, with small guiding wheels on each bogie, was well suited to the continuous sharp curvature of the line, whilst rheostatic braking equipment (fitted originally only to the last 30) helped with holding trains back when coming downhill. The locomotives were used in pairs on the heaviest trains.

In a long period of satisfactory service, these locomotives were the mainstay of passenger and fast freight operations on one of the most exacting railway routes in the world. Latterly the "Be 4/6s" have been outclassed, as will be seen, by single-unit locomotives with the same number of wheels but five times the power output, but a handful still perform less arduous duties in a useful way. Incidentally, another vital part of the Gotthard propulsion system, the original water turbines (of the Pelton wheel pattern) and generators in the purpose-built power stations at Amsteg and Piotta, still provide some of the current for the mighty train movements over the present day Gotthard line.

---

forces from the spring drive geared to the frame-mounted motors.

Two pantograph current collectors were fitted on the roof in what had by now become the conventional manner, but this was not the final intention. For sections of track in open country, Raven had decided to use a side-mounted third rail because of its cheapness. To protect staff from the high voltage used, and also to prevent problems arising through accumulation of ice, this was to be of the cased under-contact pattern. Trials were made at Strensall, between York and Scarborough. A length of conductor rail was laid, and 4-4-4 tank locomotives used on the line were fitted with the sliding contact equipment.

Above: *No. 13 is seen in the Stockton & Darlington Railway centenary cavalcade, July 1925.*

Normal overhead was to be used in stations where points and crossings would have made the ground-level conductor rail system too complex.

Alas, all this work came to naught, not for technical reasons, but for political ones. In 1923 government action led to amalgamation of the railways of Britain into four main groups. The idea was that the weaker lines could be supported by the stronger ones. So the North Eastern's financial strength went towards supporting its mainly agricultural and weaker partners in the newly-formed London & North Eastern Railway, rather than to improve its own property. So the York-Newcastle electrification was shelved and this great (and rather beautiful) locomotive never fulfilled itself. It was scrapped in 1950.

Left: *Sir Vincent Raven's experimental express electric locomotive built for the North Eastern Railway at their Darlington shops in 1921.*

EASTERN

No.1 B_o-B_o USA: American Locomotive Co (Alco), 1924

Type: Diesel-electric switching locomotive.
Gauge: 4ft 8½in (1,435mm).
Propulsion: Ingersoll-Rand 300hp (224kW) 6-cylinder four-stroke diesel engine and GEC generator supplying current to four nose-suspended traction motors geared to the axles.
Weight: 120,000lb (54.4t).
Max. axleload: 30,000lb (13.6t).
Length: 32ft 6in (9,906mm).

These locomotives can be claimed as the "first commercially-successful diesel-electric locomotives in the world". They were the result of co-operation between three well-known specialist manufacturers; Ingersoll-Rand of Phillips, New Jersey, produced the diesel engine, General Electric of Erie, Pennsylvania, the electric equipment and the American Locomotive Company (Alco) of Schenectady, New York, the locomotive body and running gear. Both the principles of design and the configuration are the same as those used for the majority of today's locomotives. The difference is that for the same size and weight GE today could offer 1,000hp (746kW) instead of 300hp (224kW).

A demonstrator had been built earlier in 1924 and this led to a batch of five locomotives being built later that year for stock; 26 units in all were produced during the years 1924 to 1928. Customers included the Baltimore & Ohio (1), Central of New Jersey (1), Lehigh Valley (1), Erie (2), Chicago & North Western (3), Reading (2), and Delaware, Lackawanna & Western (2). The remainder went to industrial buyers. There were also a few twin-engined models

Nos. 101-103 1-C-C-1 Chile: Chilean Transandine Railway (FCCT), 1925

Type. Electric rack-and-adhesion locomotive.
Gauge: 3ft 3⅜in (1,000mm).
Propulsion: Direct current at 3,000V fed via overhead catenary to four 320hp (239kW) traction motors driving the main wheels by gearing and jackshafts for adhesion, plus two 540hp (403kW) motors driving the pinions for rack working.
Weight: 158,700lb (72t) adhesive, 188,450lb (85.5t) total.
Max. axleload: 26,450lb (12t).
Overall length: 52ft 9in (16,070mm).
Tractive effort: 11,000lb (49kN) adhesion, 22,000lb (98kN) rack.
Max. speed: 25mph (40km/h) adhesion, 12.5mph (20km/h) rack.

Railways connecting the Atlantic with the Pacific have always caught people's imagination, often overshadowing sound financial thinking. Of them all, the original Transandine Railway, built between 1887 and 1908 to connect Argentina with Chile, was both the most spectacular and a case in point. The British company that originally obtained the concession from the two countries did not, however, let enthusiasm for the project carry it away. The deal included a guarantee of a fair but modest profit, but long ago the line was nationalised.

The Transandine Railway provided a metre-gauge line, 159 miles (254km) long, from Mendoza in Argentina to Los Andes in Chile. The summit of La Cumbre, 10,450ft (3,186m) altitude, is also the frontier; on both sides the final stages of the climb—at 1-in-12½ (8 per cent) on the Chilean side—are equipped for rack-and-pinion working using a unique triple rack, an elaboration of the Abt system. There are more tunnels on the Chilean side than on the Argentine, and difficulties encountered in working led to elec-

supplied, generally similar but longer and of twice the power.

Whilst the claim of commercial success was true in the sense that the makers did not lose money, it was not so for the buyers. All these customers had operations for which steam traction could not be used for some extraneous reason such as fire-risk or legislation, and so a more costly form of power was necessary. Amongst them was that famous ordinance whereby steam locomotives were excluded from New York City. Useful experience was gained which eased the general introduction of diesel traction a quarter century later. It says enough, perhaps, of the technical success of these locomotives that, unlike so many firsts, they stood the test of time. Indeed, some were still giving service 35 years later although, like the legendary Irishman's hammer, they had no doubt acquired a few new heads and a few new handles in the meantime. Two units survive, one in the Baltimore & Ohio Railroad Museum at Baltimore, Maryland, and the very first, Central of New Jersey No. 1000, at the National Museum of Transport in St Louis, Missouri.

Alco no longer builds locomotives in the USA, although it does so in Canada. General Electric still produces diesel locomotives, including engines and the mechanical parts, and sells world-wide as well as in the USA.

Below: *The first commercially successful diesel-electric locomotive, used for switching from 1924 until scrapped in the 1950s.*

trification. When completed in 1927 this covered only the highest and most difficult half of the line, that is, the 22½ miles (36km) from Portillo to the summit; in 1942 electrification of the remaining 25 miles (40km) was completed.

The Swiss Locomotive Co. of Winterthur supplied the three original locomotives; Brown Boveri electrical equipment was used. They were designed to haul 150t (165 US tons) up the rack at 9½mph (15km/h).

Several years of closure followed flood damage on the Argentine side in 1937, but relations between Argentina and Chile were never good and, in consequence, traffic and trade between them was not heavy. It says enough that the three original locomotives sufficed to meet all demands on this transcontinental artery for over 35 years.

Right: *Rack locomotive of the Chilean Transandine Railway.*

Ganz 2-B-B-2 France: Paris-Orléans Railway (PO), 1926

Type: Electric express passenger locomotive.
Gauge: 4ft 8½in (1,435mm).
Propulsion: Direct current at 1,500V from overhead wires fed to four 1,200hp (895kW) traction motors mounted on the locomotive frame, with each pair of motors connected to pairs of driving axles by a triangular system of connecting rods.
Weight: 158,690lb (72.0t) adhesive, 290,330lb (131.7t) total.
Max. axleload: 39,670lb (18.0t).
Overall length: 52ft 7½in (16,040mm).
Tractive effort: 39,670lb (176kN).
Max. speed: 75mph (120km/h).

The Paris-Orléans Railway electrified its Paris suburban services from 1899 onwards on the 600V dc third-rail system, and by 1920 it had 20 Bo-Bo locomotives at work on these services. During World War I French railways suffered acutely from shortage of coal, and after the war the government sent a party of engineers to the United States to study recent main-line electrification schemes there, and to report on the possibility of main-line electrification in France. The engineers recommended electrification on the overhead system at 1,500V, and in 1919 a programme of electrification was prepared covering 5,300 miles (8,500km) on the PO, PLM and Midi railways. It was intended that power should be generated mainly by hydro-electric stations in the Massif Central and in the Pyrenees.

In 1923 the PO embarked on its first 1,500V conversion under the programme, the Toulouse main line over the 127 miles (204km) between Paris and Vierzon. For this scheme three types of experimental express locomotive were ordered, representing a wide sample of the technology of the day. Each type had some notable features, but the most remarkable of the three were two locomotives ordered from Ganz of Budapest, and delivered in 1926. They were numbered E401-2.

At this time the Managing Director of Ganz was Kálmán Kandó (1869-1931), a brilliant engineer, who had a great influence on development of three-phase electrification, and later the use of alternating current at industrial frequency. He was less known for his work with dc, but the locomotives which he designed for the PO were as distinctive as any of his three-phase machines. Unfortunately this incursion into dc did not enhance Kandó's reputation.

The wheel arrangement was 2-B-B-2, there being two sets of four-coupled wheels in a rigid frame. Each set of wheels was driven by two motors mounted on the main frame, with a complicated set of rods to connect the motors to the wheels. The system included coupling rods connecting cranks on the armature shafts of each pair of motors, and a triangular arrangement of rods to connect the motor shafts to one of the driving wheels of the pair. These arrangements were necessary to allow for movement of the driving wheels on their springs relative to the main frame. The layout of the rods used on No. E401 was of Kandó's own design, and was used on his three-phase

Class WCG1* C-C India: Great Indian Peninsula Railway (GIP), 1928

Type: Electric locomotive for heavy freight haulage.
Gauge: 5ft 6in (1,676mm).
Propulsion: Direct current at 1,500V supplied via overhead catenary to four 650hp (485kW) motors, geared in pairs to two jackshafts, each of which is connected to three driving axles by connecting rods.
Weight: 275,500lb (125t).
Max. axleload: 46,285lb (21t).
Overall length: 66ft 1in (20,142mm).
Max speed: 50mph (80km/h).

* Indian Railways' classification

The so-called "Crocodile" configuration for an electric locomotive was repeated several times—on standard gauge in Austria or Switzerland and on the narrow gauge in Switzerland also. It is not so generally known that there were also British-built broad-gauge examples, and that they are still running in the Bombay area in India.

In 1929 the Great Indian Peninsula Railway completed electrification of 181 miles (291km) of line connecting the Bombay area with Poona. The ascent of the Western Ghats involved a ruling gradient of 1-in-37 (2.7 per cent), the same as that of the Gotthard main line in Switzerland. Those

Right: *Indian Railways' Class WCG1 C-C electric locomotive on shunting duty in Bombay.*

and 50Hz locomotives. It was the most complicated rod drive used anywhere. The arrangement on No. E402 was simpler.

The electrical equipment was advanced for its day, not least in that the total continuous rating of the four motors was 4,800hp. The motors had forced ventilation and the control system made use of series/series-parallel/parallel combinations, and an unusually large degree (for the day) of field weakening. The appearance of the locomotive was striking, with a central cab flanked by two hoods, which were extraordinarily like the hoods of some American diesels of 30 years later. With the tapered ends and smooth sides of the casing above the 69in (1,750mm) driving wheels with their flailing rods, there was no doubt that these were express engines.

Unfortunately, although the locomotives produced the intended power, they were unreliable in service, to the extent that they were incurring between one and two faults per 100 kilometres. As soon as other express locomotives were available, they were transferred to freight work, where their high power could be put to good effect. It was found that coupling pairs of driving wheels gave better adhesion than the locomotives with individual axle drives. This was significant in the light of the later evolution of the monomotor bogie in France.

In passenger service No. E401 was recorded as averaging 60.6mph (97.5km/h) with 636t between Les Aubrais and Paris, and in freight service maintained between 19mph (30km/h) and 30mph (50km/h) with up to 770t (847 US tons) on a 1-in-100 (1 per cent) gradient. However, this standard was only to be expected, as the specification called for the locomotives to haul 800t at 59mph (95km/h). Despite their indifferent performance, the locomotives were remembered by railwaymen as *Les Belles Hongroises*.

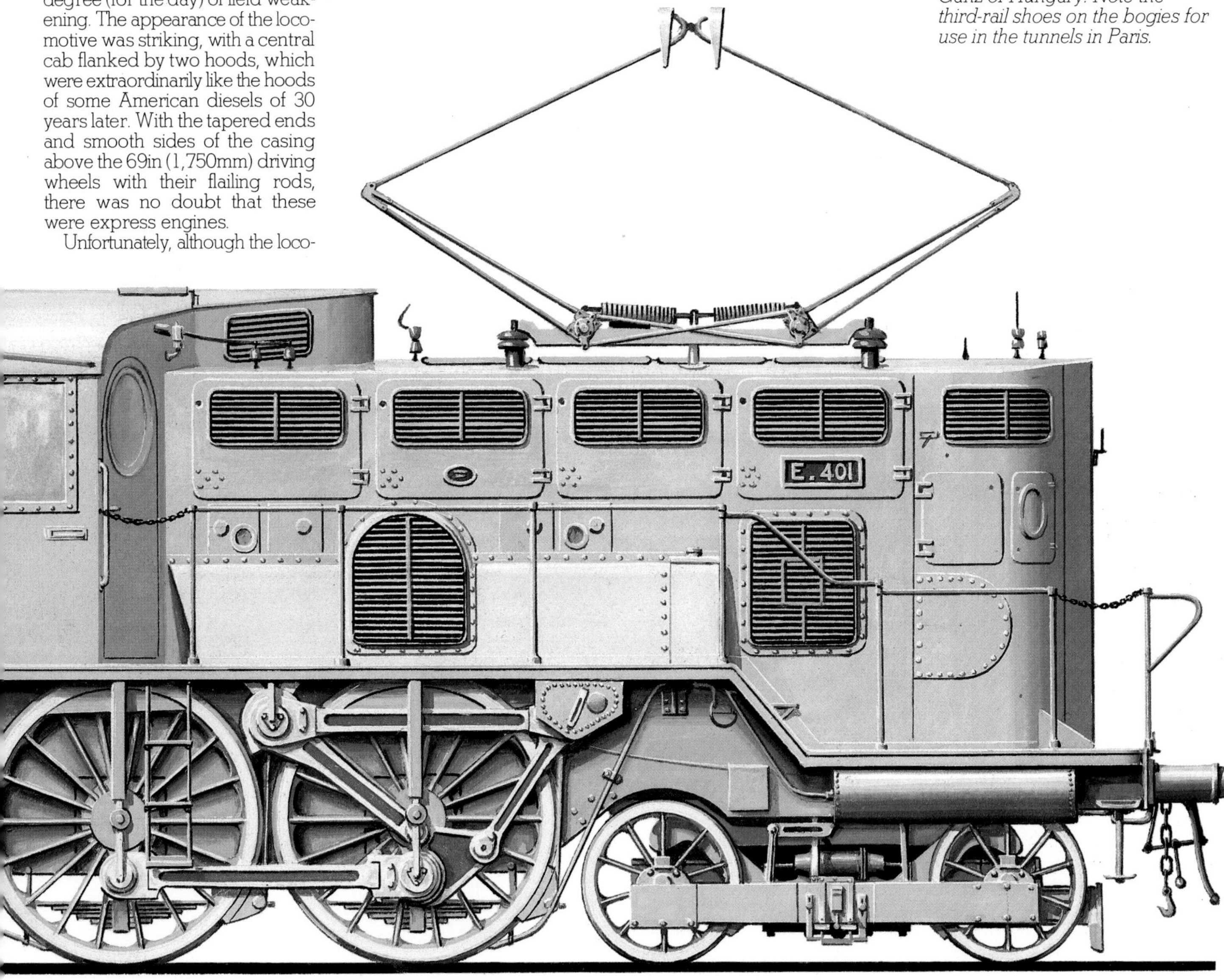

Below: *The unusual lines of Paris-Orléans 2-B-B-2 electric locomotive No. 401 built by Ganz of Hungary. Note the third-rail shoes on the bogies for use in the tunnels in Paris.*

responsible evidently took the view that a proven design was preferable and hence commissioned these distinguished machines, which as regards the mechanical side followed the crocodile locomotives of the Gotthard. An order was placed with the Swiss Locomotive Works of Winterthur for a prototype batch of 10.

The electrical equipment on the other hand, being for direct current, was quite different from that for low-frequency alternating current by which all the Alpine crocodiles worked. Accordingly, Metropolitan-Vickers of Manchester did the electrical work, not only on the 10 Swiss-built engines but also on 31 supplied by the Vulcan Foundry. An advanced feature for the time was the provision of regenerative braking. Six running positions of the controller were provided; the six motors could be grouped in series, in series-parallel or in parallel, and each grouping could be operated with two positions of field strength.

Long and useful lives have followed. Although no longer used on main line work, some of the Indian crocodiles are still in use on shunting work. One is displayed at the Indian Rail Transport Museum in New Delhi.

Right: *An Indian "Crocodile" in ex-works condition at Poona in February 1981.*

Class D 1-C-1

Sweden:
Swedish State Railways (SJ), 1925

Type: Electric mixed-traffic locomotive.
Gauge: 4ft 8½in (1,435mm).
Propulsion: Single-phase current at 15,000V 16⅔Hz fed via overhead catenary and step-down transformer to two 1,250hp (930kW) motors driving the wheels via gearing, jackshaft and connecting rods.
Weight: 112,400lb (51t) adhesive, 165,300lb (75t) total.
Max. axleload: 37,468lb (17t).
Overall length: 42ft 6in (13,000mm).
Tractive effort: 34,600lb (154kN).
Max. speed: 62mph (100km/h).

Sweden is another of those countries poor in coal supplies but rich in water power, in which engineers early on were able to set about electrifying the railway system. Technical restraint was a characteristic of the way it was done, well demonstrated by the fact that this simple locomotive design worked virtually all the traffic. Construction continued over the years from 1925 to 1952, progressive batches being stretched so that the newest (sub-class "Da") show a 30 per cent improvement in tractive effort over the originals, sub-class "Du". Some of the earliest examples had wooden bodies, sub-class "Dg".

Some of the locomotives in the early batches were supplied with (or altered to) a lower gear ratio for freight working, trading maximum speed for increased tractive

Below: *An early woodenbodied version of Swedish State Railways' standard Class D 1-C-1 general-purpose rod-drive electric locomotive.*

Above and left: *Twenty-five years' development of the Swedish standard 1-C-1 electric locomotive is shown in these two pictures. On the left is a preserved example of the earliest version with a wood-panelled body, while above is shown one of the last batch of units to be constructed, a Class Da built in 1950.*

effort; these became respectively 47mph (75km/h) and 46,400lb (206kN). In all 417 Class "D" 1-C-1 locomotives were built, most being still in service.

It might be considered an objection to this 1-C-1 wheel arrangement that the jackshaft, and hence the positioning of the motors, must be unsymmetrical. However, the need to accommodate a single heavy low-frequency transformer corrected the out-of-balance weight distribution which would otherwise have resulted.

The rod-drive seems to have satisfied the Swedes for many years; few people know more about tricky bearings than they, and moreover rod-drive gives a very simple and total form of control over the slipping of individual wheel pairs, otherwise only achieved with some electrical complication. It was notable that SJ was still taking delivery of powerful rod-drive electric locomotives in 1970.

Overall, the electrification system followed that of Germany and Switzerland, although there was one important difference. Instead of having an independent low-frequency generating and distribution system, supplies of electricity were taken from the national grid at normal frequency and converted to low frequency by rotary-convertor substations. These could be set to take a leading current and improve the power factor of electricity supply in Sweden as a whole—in effect, the resulting watt-less kilovolt-amperes are sold back by the railway to the current supplier, a new chapter in the art of profitable disposal of industrial waste.

GPO A1-1A

Great Britain:
His Majesty's Post Office (GPO), 1927

Type: Driverless electric mail carriage.
Gauge: 2ft 0in (610mm).
Propulsion: Direct current at 440V or 150V is fed via a centre conductor rail to two 22hp (16.5kW) traction motors each geared to one driving axle.
Weight: 6,610lb (3t)*.
Max. axleload: 2,204lb (1t).
Overall length: 28ft 0in (8,535mm).
Max. speed: 30mph (48km/h).

*loaded with mail.

For a period during the 1960s, this writer was one of a group of technically-minded people who were asked to take a long look at freight movement on British Railways, then in steep decline. The thought was that modern technology might have something to offer. One of the ideas put forward was to convert major parts of the railway for running unmanned self-propelled automatic freight railcars. Although a bold and fairly costly idea, the economics were superb. Alas, politics are the art of the possible and selling a "zero option" to the trainmen's unions was not considered feasible, although there would have been ample savings to pay off all the staff handsomely. Further development of such a novel scheme was accordingly the subject of a interdict from on high—even though it was pointed out that for 40 years freight of a kind had moved between important BR stations in London in just such a way.

What might have been the foundation of a really effectively competitive British Railways' freight system runs from Paddington Station in London via the Post Office's Mount Pleasant headquarters to Liverpool Street Station and the Eastern District post office on Whitechapel Road. The distance is 3½ miles (5.5km), the gauge is 2ft (610mm) and the whole railway (except at the seven stations) is laid as a double track in a 9ft (2.75m) diameter cast-iron tube tunnel.

Work began in 1914 and when a year or two later the Zeppelins appeared over London, the deep-level tunnels came in useful as a safe store for various national treasures. Progress afterwards was slow and it was not until 1927 that traffic began to flow. Mail was carried in trains formed of either one or two self-propelled railcars. The technology of 50 years ago found no difficulty in producing a safe system, based on electromagnetic relays, of automating the movement of these cars. The system is run under the overall control of a "signalman", if that is the correct term on a railway which, not having any train crews, has no need for signals. Really substantial savings are achieved over the cost of moving mail by road at the snail's pace which is all that is possible for motor vehicles in London. This significant advantage keeps the Post Office Railway viable, as witness the recent renewal of the rolling stock.

Below: *One of the original driverless electric mail carriages of The Post Office underground railway in London.*

Kitson-Still 1-C-1

Great Britain: Kitson & Co Ltd, 1924

Type: Diesel-steam locomotive for local train duties.
Gauge: 4ft 8½in (1,435mm).
Propulsion: Eight double-acting cylinders in two horizontal banks, with diesel action on the side of the pistons and steam on the other; crankshaft connected to driving wheels by gearing and jackshafts, wheels connected by coupling rods; steam supplied by boiler heated either by diesel exhaust gases or by an oil burner.
Weight: 132,160lb (60t) adhesive, 194,880lb (88.4t) total.
Max. axleload: 44,050lb (20t).
Overall length: 39ft (11,890mm).
Tractive effort: 28,000lb (125kN).
Max. speed: 43mph (69km/h).

A diesel engine converts about 35 per cent of the heat energy of the fuel into useful work, but the remaining 65 per cent is thrown away, mainly in heat in the cylinder cooling water and heat in the exhaust gases. Various methods have been employed to recover some of this waste heat, and the Still engine was an example which enjoyed some success for a time in stationary and marine practice. Heat from the cylinder walls and exhaust gases was picked up by water circulating from and to a boiler, and steam collected in the boiler. The pistons were double-acting, with diesel on the side of the pistons and steam on the other. An oil burner was provided in the boiler so that the engine could operate on steam alone; this enabled the engine to start from rest and accelerate to a speed at which the diesel end of the cylinders would fire. The Still principle raised the efficiency of the engine to about 40 per cent which was well ahead of any other contemporary heat engine.

The ability to start from rest on steam alone made the Still engine attractive for locomotive use, as it afforded a means of achieving the high efficiency of the diesel engine without the steam engineers being carried into the mysterious realms of electric and hydraulic transmissions. Patents were taken out by members of the staff of Kitson's of Leeds for applying the Still principle to a locomotive, and a Kitson-Still engine in accordance with these patents was built at the firm's expense in 1924.

This locomotive was of the 1-C-1 or 2-6-2T layout, and it weighed 87 tons. It had eight cylinders arranged in horizontal banks of four on opposite sides of a crankshaft, which was parallel to the axles, and connected to the wheels through gears, a layshaft and coupling rods. The machinery was thus perfectly balanced. The outer ends of the cylinders were diesel and the inner ends steam. The cylinder casting was above the driving wheels,- and above that was the boiler, with a cylindrical firebox for the oil burner. The exhaust gases were led through tubes in the boiler, and the boiler water circulated through the cylinder cooling jackets.

The oil burner raised steam for starting, and at about 5mph fuel was turned on to the diesel ends of the cylinders. In about two revolutions the diesel cylinders reached full power, and steam was then shut off until the next stop, unless required to supplement the diesel output at maximum powers. Between stops the boiler was kept hot by the exhaust gases and cylinder jackets. The locomotive was designed for a maximum speed of 43mph (69km/h) corresponding to 45rpm but as tests proceeded the speed was increased to 55mph (88km/h).

Tests were run intermittently on the LNER for a number of years, and when certain problems had been solved, the locomotive enjoyed considerable success. It made trial trips over various routes of the former North Eastern Railway in Yorkshire. The heaviest load was 400 tons, which the locomotive restarted from a signal stop on a 1-in-33 (3 per cent) gradient. It was reckoned that the weight of fuel consumed was about one-fifth of that of a coal-burning steam locomotive, but what this represented in cost savings depended upon the relative prices of coal and oil. The makers had a particular eye on countries which had oil but no coal.

The maximum horsepower of 700 (522kW) developed at the drawbar was not very high for a locomotive of 87t weight. For commercial use this would need to be improved upon, and a stage had been reached at which further heavy expenditure was required to convert a successful experiment into a production unit. Unfortunately conditions were not favourable. Kitson's finances declined in the industrial depression, and eventually it went into liquidation. In the meantime no orders had come for Kitson-Still locomotives.

By the time British railways were ready for a serious attack on the diesel locomotive, inhibitions about electric and hydraulic transmissions had been overcome, and the Kitson-Still was forgotten.

Right: *The Kitson-Still steam-diesel locomotive as running in later trials during the 1930s.*

Below: *The Kitson-Still locomotive built by Kitson's of Leeds in 1924, using the Still principle of combining diesel and steam propulsion. It is shown as prepared for early trials in the works.*

Class Ae 4/7 2-D$_o$-1

Switzerland: Swiss Federal Railways (SBB), 1927

Type: Electric express passenger locomotive.
Gauge: 4ft 8½in (1,435mm).
Propulsion: Single-phase current at 15,000V 16⅔Hz fed via overhead catenary and step-down transformer to four 769hp (574kW) motors each driving one pair of main wheels through gears and Büchli flexible drives
Weight: 169,710lb (77t) adhesive, 260,070lb (118t) total.
Max. axleload: 42,430lb (19.25t).
Overall length: 55ft (16,760mm).
Tractive effort: 44,100lb (196kN).
Max. speed: 62mph (100km/h).

These superb locomotives, now well into their second half-century, for many years handled the top

Class E432 1-D-1

Italy: Italian State Railways (FS), 1928

Type: Electric express passenger locomotive.
Gauge: 4ft 8½in (1,435mm).
Propulsion: Three-phase alternating current at 3,600V 16⅔Hz fed to two 1,475hp (1,100kW) synchronous traction motors with provision for speed control by pole-changing, driving the four pairs of main wheels direct by means of connecting and coupling rods.
Weight: 156,484lb (71t) adhesive, 207,176lb (94t) total.
Max. axleload: 39,672lb (18t).
Overall length: 45ft 8in (13,910mm).
Tractive effort: 30,856lb (137kN).
Max. speed: 62.5mph (100km/h).

1928 was a critical year for three-phase main-line electrification. Since 1910, when the Class "550" locomotives described earlier began working the Giovi incline, Italian electrification had moved on apace and virtually all of it was three-phase. Most lines of any significance in the Genoa-Turin area were by now electrified and tentacles had stretched south along the Mediterranean coast to reach Pisa and Leghorn. In addition, there were some isolated miles up near the Austrian border and also between Florence and Bologna. The total amounted to some 940 miles (1,500km).

The moment of truth came in 1928 when a proposal to electrify with three-phase between Naples and Foggia was modified to make this line a testbed for direct current electrification. The new system worked so well and was so economical that the three-phase system became instantly obsolete, although the three-phasers fought back bravely but unsuccessfully with another experimental installation (104 miles—166km, from Rome to Sulmona) at high voltage and industrial frequency.

A further result was that these "E432s," of which 40 were built by Breda of Milan, were the last class of main-line three-phase locomotives of any importance built in the world. Compared with the original "E550s," the newer engines had their express passenger status recognised by provision of pony trucks fore and aft and four 64in (1,630mm) driving wheels in place of five of 42in (1,070mm) diameter. Electrical progress now allowed for provision of a larger number of fixed speeds (23, 31, 47 and 63mph—37.5, 50, 75 and 100km/h), by making varying special connections inside and between the two traction motors. "Pole-changing" is the technical term. Some of the class had twin pantograph current collectors instead of the cantilever type more generally fitted—and which were a hall-mark of the three-phase. In fact, the cantilever arrangement allowed the collector bows to be far enough apart to permit operation across inevitable gaps in the double overhead conductor sys-

assignments (including many of the legendary European international trains such as the "Simplon-Orient" expresses) of Swiss Federal Railways. The design was based on that of the extremely successful "Ae 3/6" class of 1921 (3/6 means 3 driving axles out of 6), which were of the 2-Co-1 wheel arrangement; 114 of these were built between 1921 and 1926 and they were way ahead of their time.

When more power was needed it was just a case of splicing in, as it were, another driving wheel, motor and body section. Originally SBB had misgivings over such a long rigid wheelbase, and the fourth pair of driving wheels was, as regards side movement, connected to the small single guiding wheel in the form of a Zara truck. This arrangement was common on Italian steam locomotives and provided some flexibility to otherwise rather rigid wheel arrangements. Later, the worries were found to be unjustified, and a conventional pony truck was substituted. The reason for having a four-wheel bogie at one end and only a two-wheel truck at the other lies in the need to accommodate a heavy low-frequency transformer.

The transmission system was of Swiss origin, known as Büchli after its inventor. The motors drove large gear wheels mounted approximately concentric with and outside the main driving wheels on the side of the locomotive. A lever arrangement transmitted torque to the driving wheels, at the same time allowing for vertical movement of the axles relative to the frames, necessary to cope with small irregularities in the track.

Only a few out of the 127 built (30—Nos. 10973-11002) have regenerative braking and 30 more (Nos. 10931-51 and 11009-17) are equipped for running in multiple. Virtually the whole of the series (Nos. 10901-11027) remain in service.

Left: *Swiss Federal Railways' Class Ae 4/7 locomotive hauling a short freight train past Wadenswil on the shore of Lake Zurich early in 1976.*

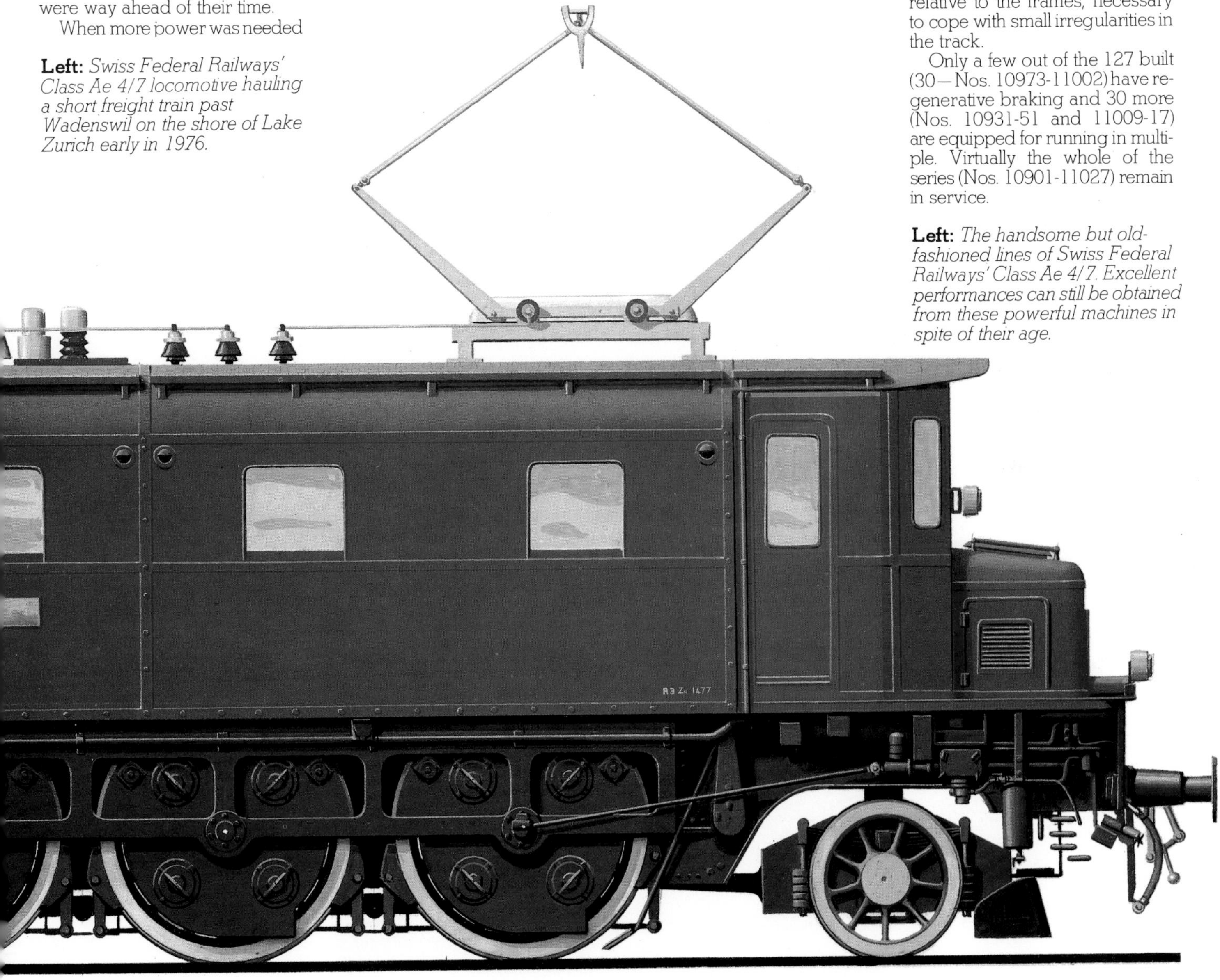

Left: *The handsome but old-fashioned lines of Swiss Federal Railways' Class Ae 4/7. Excellent performances can still be obtained from these powerful machines in spite of their age.*

tem, but the roofs of the "E432" class were long enough to carry two pantographs sufficient distance apart.

During World War II, many railways in Italy were forcibly de-electrified. Re-electrification was usually by dc, but the lines in north-west Italy escaped relatively unscathed and survived as three-phase. The "E432" class also survived intact with them into the 1970s, but conversion to dc and hence extinction of all the three-phase motive power came well before the end of the decade. So ended a heroic chapter in the history of the railway locomotive.

Right: *The FS Class E432 three-phase locomotive.*

No. 9000 2-D$_o$-1

Canada:
Canadian National Railways (CNR), 1929

Type: Main line diesel-electric locomotive.
Gauge: 4ft 8½in (1,435mm).
Propulsion: Beardmore 1,330hp (992kW) four-stroke V12 diesel engine and generator, originally supercharged, supplying direct current to four nose-suspended traction motors geared to the axles.
Weight: 255,644lb (116t) adhesive, 374,080lb (170t) total.
Max. axleload: 63,920lb (29t).
Overall length: 47ft 0½in (14,338mm).
Tractive effort: 50,000lb (222kN).
Max. speed: 75mph (120km/h).

The shape of things to come! These two locomotives—which usually worked coupled back-to-back as a pair—were the first main-line diesel units in North America. They were a joint product of the Canadian Locomotive Co and Westinghouse Electric. From all accounts they worked quite well when they were actually working—keeping time easily with 700 US tons on the "International Limited" between Montreal and Toronto, for example, on a schedule which involved an average speed of 44mph (70km/h) including 13 stops, some lengthy. Running costs were absurdly low, and yet the locomotives were not successful.

The problem lay in the difficulties of maintenance. CN's own maintenance department was almost entirely steam-orientated and so the basic infrastructure was not there. Secondly, the locomotives themselves had all the small faults typical of any unproven piece of equipment. Thirdly, none of the manufacturers involved nor CN had a stock of spare parts worthy of the name—almost all the parts needed had to be specially made to order, and many hand-fitted thereafter, a process

HGe 4/4 B$_o$-B$_o$

Switzerland:
Visp-Zermatt Railway (VZB), 1929

Type: Electric rack-and-adhesion locomotive.
Gauge: 3ft 3⅜in (1,000mm).
Propulsion: Low-frequency alternating current at 11,000V 16⅔Hz fed via overhead catenary and step-down transformer to four 160hp* (120kW) ac traction motors, each geared both directly to a driving axle and (at a subtly different gear ratio) to a rack pinion mounted freely on the same axle.
Weight: 103,590lb (47t).
Max. axleload: 26,450lb (12t).
Overall length: 46ft 3in (14,100mm).
Tractive effort: 30,856lb (137kN).
Max. speed: 28mph (45km/h) adhesion, 12½mph (20km/h) on rack.

*Later increased to 230hp (172kW).

When Edward Whymper's party climbed the Matterhorn so disastrously in 1865, the tiny and fiercely independent high-altitude village of Zermatt came out onto the world stage. Accordingly, a rack-and-adhesion railway 22¼ mile (35½km) long to connect the village to Visp in the Rhone valley was proposed and finally completed in 1891. The ruling gradient on the adhesion sections was 1-in-40 (2.5 per cent) and on the rack sections 1-in-8 (12.5 per cent); curves were as sharp as 3 chains (60m) radius and for many summers little 0-4-2T steam locomotives hauled the tourists up to Zermatt. At other times of the year the Zermatters valued their privacy and visitors had to walk or ride on horseback, no motor cars being permitted.

However, in 1928 a scheme to electrify the line and open it all the year round was put into effect. The 11,000V 16⅔Hz system was adopted in order to match that of the far-off Rhaetian Railway in eastern Switzerland, with which both physical and electrical connection might one day be established—in fact, these things happened in 1930 and 1941, respectively.

Five commendably simple Bo-Bo electric locomotives were supplied by the Swiss Locomotive Works of Winterthur and the Oerlikon company of Zurich. There were no separate motors to drive the rack pinions which were mounted on the adhesion-wheel axles. The pinions were driven by the same appropriate traction motor as the adhesion wheels but at a slightly different and faster rotational speed—the gearing for the rail wheels is 6.2 to 1 and for the rack pinion wheels 5.6 to 1. This compensated for the fact that the rack pinions must clear the rails and so have a smaller effective diameter. Obviously, the rack teeth and the wheel-rim surface must move at the same speed if satisfactory traction is to be established.

Other features were also similar to those of the Rhaetian Railway. Central buffers with screw couplings on each side were standardised and the vacuum brake was used, supplemented by rheostatic braking for use on the main descents, with hand brakes in reserve for an emergency. There was a "deadman" device to permit operation by a single driver. If this was released involuntarily both the rack brakes and the main brakes were applied and the current switched off.

Electric operation was very successful, running times being reduced from 2hr 5min to 1hr 35min, and much heavier trains hauled. The prohibition of motor traffic which is still enforced by the Zermatters—and which makes a visit to the resort such a delight—means that today's problem is that of moving the traffic offering rather than surviving. This local railway is one of the very few in the world which is run at a profit.

All five of the original electric locomotives are still in service, supplemented by another built in 1939, as well as a number of twin articulated railcar trains, in order to handle a passenger traffic flow now counted in millions.

Above: *The mountaineering HGe 4/4 of the Visp-Zermatt Railway (now Brigue-Visp-Zermatt) of 1929.*

Right: *Train ready to leave Zermatt behind locomotive of Class HGe 4/4. "H" denotes a rack loco, "G" narrow gauge, "e" means electric, 4/4 means 4 driven axles out of 4 axles total.*

which was both slow and expensive. No progress in dieselisation could be made until a package appeared which included a solution to these problems. This was shortly to happen, as will be seen.

On the other hand, both the overall technology, and the concept were good, one or two quite basic shortcomings being easily resolved. For example, in 1931 the engine manufacturer had to replace both crankcases with stronger ones nearly a ton heavier. This perhaps underlined the fact that an engine like the Beardmore, which was excellent in a submarine under the watchful eye of highly-qualified "tiffies" (Engine-room Artificer, 1st class, RN), was less satisfactory under railway conditions. Even so, the specific weight of the Beardmore engine at 24.5lb per hp (15kg/kW) had come a long way from the Ingersoll-Rand engines fitted to switchers a few years earlier, which turned the scales at double that figure. This must be considered against the background of present day North American diesel locomotives, which have engines of specific weights only half that of the Beardmore.

After trials with the locomotive as a twin unit, the two "ends" were operated separately, being then renumbered 9000 and 9001. No. 9000 was scrapped in 1939, but during the war No. 9001 found a use in the west as a coastal defence train. Its bodywork was altered to give the appearance of a boxcar, as well as a modicum of armoured protection for the crew. After the war, No. 9001 worked for a short time in the east but was withdrawn in 1947. Even so, 20 years later, virtually all Canadian trains were to be hauled by locomotives of totally similar concept.

Below: *Pioneer diesel-electric main line locomotive built in 1929 for Canadian National Rly.*

Diesel Railcar

Ireland: County Donegal Joint Railways (CDJR), 1931

Type: Trailer-hauling railbus.
Gauge: 3ft 0in (904mm).
Propulsion: Gardner Type L2 74hp (55kW) 6-cylinder diesel engine driving the rear bogie through a mechanical gearbox with four forward speeds and one reverse, a propellor shaft, gearing and—when required—chains coupling the two rear axles.
Weight: 6,720lb (3t) adhesive, 15,680lb (7.1t) total.
Max. axleload: 6,720lb (3t).
Overall length: 28ft 0in (8,534mm).
Max. speed: 40mph (64km/h).

These delightfully economical little vehicles must represent the contribution made by the diesel engine all over the world towards maintaining the sort of little railways that had to think twice before investing in just one rail-spike.

The 3ft gauge County Donegal Railways served a wild and sparsely-populated part of the north-west of Ireland. The system was entirely steam-operated until 1907, when it purchased a four-wheeled petrol-engined vehicle with an open body for use as an inspection car. In 1920 the vehicle needed heavy repairs, and to increase its usefulness it was fitted with an enclosed body seating 10 passengers. In this form it was used occasionally for carrying passengers and mail, but in 1926 the railcar was put into regular service to replace a lightly-loaded steam train.

The experience gained at this time convinced Henry Forbes, the manager of the railway, of the potential of railcars for countering serious competition from motor buses which was already affecting other Irish narrow-gauge lines. From then until his death in 1943, Forbes worked enthusiastically for the extension of railcar services.

Railcars cost less to operate than steam trains, they could be operated by one man, and their acceleration was so good that they could make wayside stops in country areas without seriously affecting their schedules.

By 1930 four more railcars had been acquired, two secondhand from standard-gauge lines and two purpose-built. They were all petrol-engined, but in 1931 railcar No. 7 went into service driven by a 74hp diesel engine. The body was mounted at one end on a bogie which had one axle driven, and at the front, ahead of a projecting bonnet, was a radial axle. The car seated 32 passengers and weighed 7 tons, compared with 5.55 tons for a similar petrol-engined vehicle built in the previous year. No. 7 was the first diesel-engined railcar to enter regular passenger service in the British Isles. A second vehicle of the same type was built in 1931. Usually they worked singly, but at times they worked back-to-back with one or more goods wagons between. Gear changing was then sychronised by hand signals between the drivers.

These two vehicles gave good service for 18 years, and they were followed by 12 further diesel cars, the last of which were mounted on two bogies, and seated 43 passengers. The power unit was at the front, with four wheels connected by coupling rods, and the coach body was hinged to the power unit. These cars prolonged the life of the County Donegal by many years, and one of them ran nearly one million miles. Eventually, however, the line succumbed to road competition, and it closed at the end of 1959. Several of the railcars have been preserved, including Nos. 15 and 16 on the Isle of Man Railway, but unfortunately not No. 7.

Above: *County Donegal petrol railcar No. 10 built in 1932. Note the coupled leading driving wheels and bus-type body.*

Right: *Buses on wheels made the CDJR for many years the only railway in Ireland to be run without a substantial deficit.*

Above: *No. 19, one of the last two CDJR diesel railcars, as built by Walker Bros. of Wigan, England, with Gardner engine.*

Below: *County Donegal Railways' standard diesel railcar. Nos. 12 to 14 were to this style; later units had a full-width cab.*

V40 1-D-1

Hungary:
Royal Hungarian State Railways (MKA), 1933

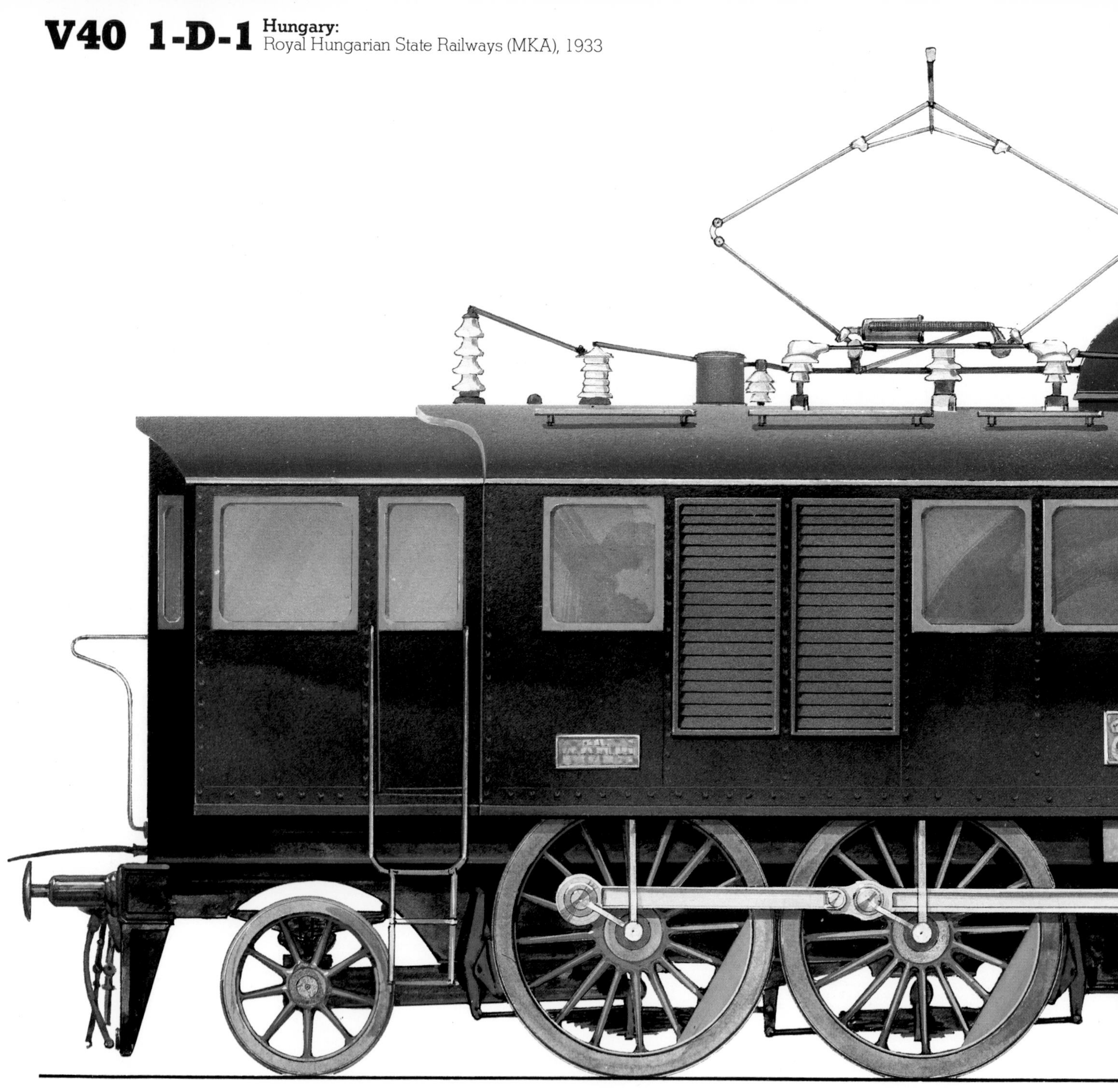

Type: Electric locomotive for express passenger trains.
Gauge: 4ft 8½in (1,435mm).
Propulsion: Single-phase current at 16,000V 50Hz fed via overhead catenary and rotary phase-converter to a single 2,500hp (1,865kW) polyphase motor coupled directly to the driving wheels by connecting rods.
Weight: 154,224lb (70t) adhesive, 215,375lb (97.75t) total.
Max. axleload: 38,556lb (17.5t).
Overall length: 45ft 0in (13,715mm).
Tractive effort: 38,570lb (171kN).
Max. speed: 62.5mph (100km/h).

When electric railways were new, so was electricity supply in general. Hence there was little reason for what was best for the former to be affected by the latter. Later, when electricity supply became generally available, a few far-sighted engineers began to think that it would be best for railways to take their current direct from the mains and supply it to the trains in this form, just like any other customer. One of these prophetic gentlemen was a Hungarian, Dr Kálmán Kandó, who recommended as early as 1917 that this should be the basis of future electrification schemes. In this respect he was some 50 years ahead of the rest of the world, and it is only recently that the essential rightness of the idea has been demonstrated by the fact that virtually all new electrification follows the example he set. Moreover, extensions to older electrification schemes are also commonly carried out using industrial-frequency current, despite the problems of operating a dual system.

Under Kandó's influence a 9 mile (14.5km) trial line was liad out in 1922 north of Budapest and a 1,600hp (1,280kW) trial locomotive of 0-E-0 configuration was built by Ganz & Co. The success achieved led to a loan being raised in Britain and in 1928 work commenced on converting the 118 mile (189km) line connecting Hegyeshalom on the Austrian frontier with Budapest. Twenty-eight locomotives were built jointly by Ganz and by the British company Metropolitan-Vickers. There were to be four 0-F-0s for freight traffic and, as described here, 24 1-D-1s for passenger traffic. Two prototypes of each were delivered in 1932.

Kandó avoided the problems of making traction motors to run on high-frequency single-phase current by converting it to current with an alterable number of phases on the locomotives. So in respect of the very sophisticated internal workings of the locomotives he departed significantly from what is now the world norm. Even so, they correspond in certain principles to what may well become that norm tomorrow. All eight main wheels were coupled directly by massive rodding to a huge polyphase motor of 10ft 6in (3,080mm) diameter, supplied with current at constant frequency but at variable phase by a rotary phase-convertor. As in straight three-phase electrification schemes, but for different reasons, there can only by a certain number of fixed speeds corresponding to the number of phases. In this case the fixed speeds were 15½, 31, 46, and 62mph (25, 50, 75 and 100km/h). Regenerative braking was a built-in feature of the arrangement needing no additional equipment, but the system was a complicated one. For example, the motor had 16 slip-rings to provide electrical access to its innards.

Once some mechanical problems with the running gear had been eliminated, operation was very satisfactory and the locomotives remained in use for many years. The main advantage—that of minimising the cost of the fixed

Below: *Kandó's 2,500hp 1-D-1 standard passenger locomotive as built for the pioneer 50Hz electrification from Budapest to the Austrian frontier in 1932.*

Left: *Royal Hungarian Railways' 1-D-1 50Hz single-phase class V40 locomotive. Twenty-four of these complex machines were supplied from 1932.*

installations—was achieved when one considers that the whole line was supplied by four simple substations. Compare this with the 18 more complex substations needed for 97 miles (155km) of dc electrification on the contemporary Croydon to Brighton electrification.

There is one further advantage of the Kandó system which to some extent compensates for its complications. The power factor of a Kandó locomotive was close to unity or even slightly leading. This is an advantage as it counters the poor power factor (that is, with current flow lagging behind the alternating voltage) which is characteristic of a normal industrial loading. Because there were so few power supplies in the area, Hungarian State Railways had to build their own generating station and supply network, so any savings produced by improving the power factor in this way would accrue to the railway.

So, through the far-sighted genius of one man (who, alas, died in 1931, and so missed seeing his ideas come to fruition) the world's first main-line electrification using single-phase alternating current at industrial frequency came into being, in a country then better known for its agriculture than for heavyweight engineering. Some of the principles may now be changed, but the most obvious has been adopted world-wide in all its detail. This consists of the mast supports for the overhead conductors, with the catenary wire supported by one diagonal and one horizontal rod, another horizontal rod steadying the contact wire. So memorials exist to Kandó and his genius in their tens of thousands, to supplement the one "V40" preserved in the Budapest Transport Museum.

5-BEL Five-car Train

Great Britain: Southern Railway (SR), 1933

Type: Electric multiple-unit Pullman express train.
Gauge: 4ft 8½in (1,435mm).
Propulsion: Direct current at 650V fed via top-contact outside-mounted third rail to two motor coaches each with four 225hp (168kW) nose-suspended motors geared to the axles.
Weight: 277,700lb (126t) adhesive, 557,760lb (253t) total.
Max. axleload: 35,280lb (16t).
Overall length: 347ft 6in (105,920mm).
Max. speed: 75mph (120km/h).

Above: *The "Brighton Belle" could be formed of two five-car sets, as seen here. Note the "4" headcode which indicates a non-stop express train between Victoria and Brighton.*

Although many notable British-built examples existed abroad, it was not until January 1, 1933 that electrically-propelled express passenger trains began running in Britain itself. The Southern Railway and its predecessors had been for many years progessively electrifying the suburban nètwork south of London with excellent results, both financial and technical, and a point had now been reached when it was the turn of the main lines. There had recently been a substantial reduction in the costs involved, since it had become practicable to replace manned substations which had rotating machinery by unattended ones which converted ac to dc using static mercury-arc rectifiers.

If the invisible aspects of the electrification to Brighton, Hove and Worthing represented a bold step forward in technology, the most visible aspect—the trains—had the solid reliability of hardware tested over many years in the fires of day-to-day operation on one of the world's busiest railways. Even so, what the passenger saw was both fine and new.

Very special in the steam service

Below: *A "Brighton Belle" 900hp third class brake-parlour motor coach, of which one was marshalled at each end of a five-car Pullman set.*

AEC Single-unit Railcar

Great Britain: Great Western Railway (GWR), 1933

Type: Diesel-mechanical railcar.
Gauge: 4ft 8½in (1,435mm).
Propulsion: AEC 6-cylinder four-stroke 121hp diesel engine driving the four wheels of one bogie via a mechanical gearbox, a propellor shaft and a drive enclosed in the axleboxes at one end of the driving axles.
Weight: 24,685lb (11.2t) adhesive, 53,780lb (24.4t) total.
Max. axleload: 12,340lb (5.6t).
Overall length: 63ft 1in (19,228mm).
Max. speed: 60mph (96km/h).

If the "Brighton Belle" pointed the way ahead for main-line express passenger trains in Britain, then this modest railcar did the same for the branch-line passenger. Numerous other companies produced lightweight diesel trains, but none stayed the course, and it is from this little vehicle that British Railways' large fleet of diesel-mechanical multiple-unit trains are directly descended.

The Associated Equipment Co (AEC) of Southall, Middlesex, were the main builders of London's buses and it was to them that the GWR went in 1932 for something a bit heftier than a railbus, but based on bus practice. The diesel engine was slung below

between London and Brighton was the all-Pullman "Southern Belle" train and in the new scheme of things this became the "Brighton Belle." One innovation for the Southern (but not for Pullman) was that the three five-car Pullman trains built for this service were of all-steel construction. Each set provided 80 first-class seats and 152 third-class seats. The six first-class Pullman cars (two in each set) were named, not after the customary grand ladies such as *Zenobia* or *Lady Dalziel*, but after the girls next door—*Hazel, Doris, Audrey, Vera, Gwen* and *Mona*.

Apart from World War II, for some 40 years the "Belle" sets provided luxury service several times a day in the even hour over the 52 miles (84km) from London's Victoria Station to Brighton. Eventually they had to be replaced by the more mundane trains running today, but such is the affection in which these trains are held that several survive in museums and as restaurant dining rooms.

Right: *The tail of the Brighton Belle at speed near Wandsworth Common, London. The two five-car sets could muster a respectable 3,600hp between them.*

the underframe and drove the wheels via a longitudinal shaft. An interesting feature was that passengers had a view along the tracks as from an observation car.

Later the same year, three express railcars were delivered, generally similar in appearance, but with two engines and geared for a maximum speed of 75mph (120km/h). There was also a small buffet. During the next few years,

Far left: *GWR diesel railcar No. 1, as built in 1933.*

Left: *A trailer-hauling GWR railcar of the 1940 series.*

other cars followed including No.17, which was for parcels traffic, while No.18 had standard railway drawgear and the ability to haul trailers. Experience gained led to an order for 20, all twin-engined. These later cars all had multiple-unit capability, using vacuum-operated servos. They were distinguished by rather more angular bodywork and were delivered in 1940.

Once the war was over and the upheaval of nationalisation surmounted, the experience was used in the design of several thousand generally similar vehicles supplied to BR from 1953.

Pioneer Zephyr Three-car train

USA: Chicago, Burlington & Quincy Railroad (CB&Q), 1934

Type: High-speed articulated streamlined diesel-electric train.
Gauge: 4ft 8½in (1,435mm).
Propulsion: Electro-Motive Type 201E 600hp (448kW) in-line two-stroke diesel engine and generator feeding two nose-suspended traction motors on the leading bogie.
Weight: 90,360lb (41t) adhesive, 175,000lb (79.5t) total.
Max. axleload: 45,180lb (20.5t).
Overall length: 196ft 0in (59,741mm).
Max. speed: 110mph (177km/h).

On May 25, 1934 the fastest train between Denver and Chicago (1,015 miles—1,624km) was the "Autocrat", timed to do the run in 27hr 45min including 40 stops, an average speed of 37mph (59km/h). On May 26 a brand new stainless steel articulated streamlined self-propelled train reeled off the miles between the two cities in just over 13 hours at an average speed of 78mph (125km/h). As the little train triumphantly ran into its display position at the Century of Progress Exhibition in Chicago, US railroading had changed for ever.

Preparation for this triumph had begun in 1930 when mighty General Motors purchased both the Electro-Motive Company and their engine suppliers, the Winton Engine Co. GM concentrated their efforts on making a diesel engine suitable for rail transport. 'Softly, softly catchee monkey' was their policy and it was with considerable reluctance that after four years work they agreed to let an experimental engine out of their hands for this *Pioneer Zephyr*. The floodlight of publicity that illuminated its triumph could so easily have lit up a disaster—indeed, electrical faults occurring during the trip but bravely corrected by the staff whilst the equipment was still live, indicated that it was a very close-run thing indeed.

In some ways, of course, it was a nonsense. Naturally, the manufacturers pressed the view that

Below: *The observation car at the rear end of the Chicago, Burlington & Quincy Railroad's* Pioneer Zephyr *high-speed diesel-electric trainset, now on display at the Chicago Museum of Science & Industry.*

M-10001 Six-car trainset

USA: Union Pacific Railroad (UP), 1934

Type: Diesel-electric high-speed passenger train.
Gauge: 4ft 8½in (1,435mm).
Propulsion: Electro-Motive 1,200hp (895kW) V-16 two-stroke diesel engine and generator supplying current to four 250hp (187kW) nose-suspended traction motors geared to the axles of the two leading bogies.
Weight: 143,260lb (65t) adhesive, 413,280lb (187.5t) total.
Max. axleload: 35,815lb (16.25t).
Overall length: 376ft 0in (114,605mm).
Max. speed: 120mph (192km/h).*

* Not operated in regular service above 90mph (144km/h).

In February 1934 the famed Union Pacific Railroad only failed by a technicality to be the first in America with a diesel-electric high-speed train. A suitable diesel engine was not quite ready and UP's stunning train had to have a spark-plug engine using distillate fuel. This was the yellow and grey No. M-10000, consisting of three articulated streamlined light-alloy cars weighing including power plant 85t (93½ US tons), in total hardly more than a single standard US passenger car as then existing. The train was built by Pullman Standard and seated 116 passengers in air-conditioned comfort; the leading power car included a 33ft (10m) mail compartment. After a coast-to-coast demonstration tour the train went into service as the "City of Salina" on one of UP's few short-distance daytime inter-city runs, that between Kansas City and Salina.

The success of the principles involved led to the first diesel-

Right: *The original Union Pacific M-10000 three-car self-propelled train in Pullman Works, Chicago, 1934.*

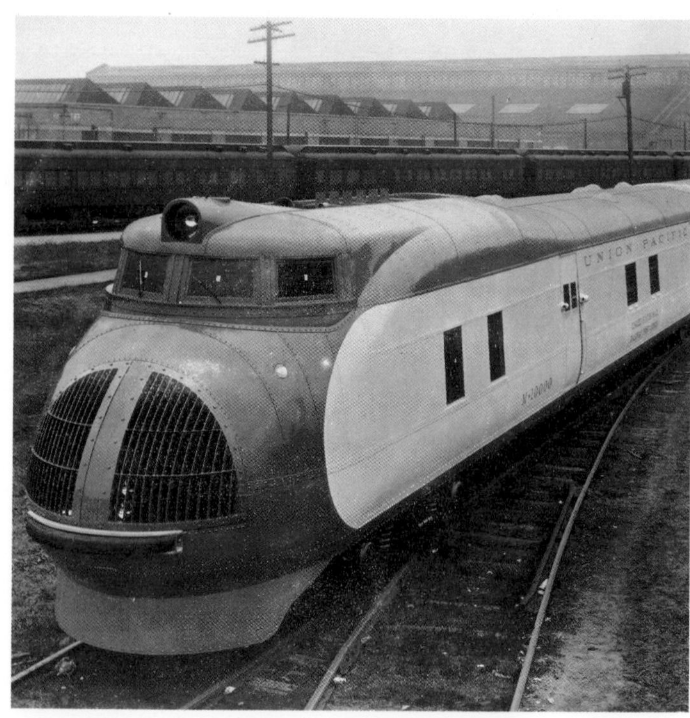

the whole performance was due to diesel traction when it was really due to a different approach to long-distance passenger movement. Various railroads (notably the Chicago, Milwaukee, St Paul & Pacific and Southern Pacific) were quick to demonstrate that equal improvements were possible with steam, at much lower first cost. Of course, once they had been paid for, running costs of the new trains were much lower than with steam, but overall there was little in it. Incidentally, over one-third of the space available was devoted to the carriage of mail and parcels.

Extra comforts such as air-conditioning, radio reception, reclining seats, grill-buffet and observation lounge were very nice, but significantly little has ever been said about the riding of the *Pioneer Zephyr*. One must unkindly suspect, though, that compared with the heavyweight stock the new train replaced, a little was left to be desired. Even so, many other *Zephyr* trains—but never quite as lightly built as the original—were to go into service on the Burlington. It is true that the self-propelled concept was soon dropped in favour of separate locomotives, but the name is still commemorated today with Amtrak's "San Francisco Zephyr" running daily between Chicago and Oakland (San Francisco). The original little 72-seat train—later enlarged to four cars—ran over 3 million miles in traffic and is today enshrined in Chicago's Museum of Science & Industry.

Right: *The leading end of the original* Pioneer Zephyr *train. Note the special headlight with powerful scanning beam, needed as extra warning in the absence of columns of steam and smoke.*

Above: *Six-car diesel-electric train No. M-10001 as supplied to the Union Pacific Railroad in November 1934.*

powered sleeping car train, the articulated six-car M-10001. This train was turned out also by Pullman in November 1934 and this time had a true diesel engine by Electro-Motive in the power car. At first a 900hp V-12 was installed, but later this was replaced by the V-16 engine mentioned above. Behind the power car was a baggage-mail car, then three Pullman sleepers and finally a day coach with buffet. There was accommodation for 124 passengers.

On October 22, 1934, UP set its new train to capture the existing transcontinental record. The then existing coast-to-coast record was a run of 71½ hours by the Atchison, Topeka & Santa Fe route—described vividly by Rudyard Kipling in *Captains Courageous*—achieved by a special train put on in 1906 for railroad tycoon E. H. Harriman. In 1934, 508 miles (817km) from Cheyenne, Wyoming to Omaha, Nebraska were run off at an average speed of 84mph (135km/h) but no fireworks were attempted east of Chicago. To avoid breaking New York City's famous no-smoke law, a vintage 1904 New York Central electric loco (described earlier) had to haul the train the final few miles. In spite of such handicaps and some quite lengthy stops for refuelling and servicing, No. M-10001 lowered the record to a so far unbeaten 57 hours for the 3,260 miles (5,216km) from Oakland Pier opposite San Francisco to Grand Central Terminal, New York.

The impact on the public was tremendous. In the following year the same train went into service as the "City of Portland" running the 2,270 miles (3,652km) between Chicago and Portland, Oregon, cutting 18 hours from the previous best schedule of 58 hours. More importantly, in succeeding years, the demand for travel by these trains was such that at first 11-car and then 17-car streamliners had to be put into service on such trains as the "City of Los Angeles" and "City of San Francisco".

Class E428 2-B$_o$-B$_o$-2 Italy: Italian State Railways (FS), 1934

Type: Electric express passenger locomotive.
Gauge: 4ft 8½in (1,435mm).
Propulsion: Direct current at 3,000V fed via overhead catenary to eight 470hp (350kW) frame-mounted motors geared in pairs to the driving axles through flexible drives.
Weight: 163,103lb (74t) adhesive, 297,533lb (135t) total.
Max. axleload: 36,368lb (16.5t).
Overall length: 62ft 4in (19,000mm).
Tractive effort: 48,500lb (215kN)*.
Max. speed: 93mph (150km/h)*.

*Depending on gear ratio; maximum speed.

As electrification proceeded in Italy, the limitations of the three-phase system induced increasing dissatisfaction amongst those responsible. There were the limited number of fixed speeds, and the complications involved in having to provide twin-insulated conductors above each track. An alternative system used high-voltage direct current, pioneered over long distances by the Chicago, Milwaukee, St Paul & Pacific Railroad of the USA, and experimented with locally on a modest scale over the 63-mile (101km) line between Benevento and Foggia in southern Italy during the late 1920s.

In 1928 the decision was taken that future electrification schemes should be direct current, and by

Left and below: *Italian State Railways' E428 electric locomotive. The pictures show the locomotive finished in a light reddish brown colour. More usual was a khaki shade known as* Isabella *after the colour of the garments of Queen Isabella who unwisely vowed she would eschew clean ones until her army had taken a certain city.*

"Lyntog" Three-car train Denmark: Danish State Railways (DSB), 1935

Type: Articulated diesel-electric express passenger train.
Gauge: 4ft 8½in (1,435mm).
Propulsion: Four Frichs 275hp (205kW) engines and generators, two mounted on each of two end bogies, feeding current to eight nose-suspended traction motors, each geared to one axle.
Weight: 286,520lb (130t).
Max. axleload: 36,366lb (16.5t).
Overall length: 209ft 0in (63,703mm).
Max. speed: 90mph (144km/h).

In the mid-1930s one of the most staid of railway administrations went mad and put on an extraordinary and quite brilliant programme of accelerations in which these diesel-electric trains played a major part. Before the changes were made a traveller from Britain arriving at Esjberg, Denmark, on the excellent ships of the Danish *Det Forende Dampskib Skelskab,* faced a 7½hr 214 mile (342km) journey and a second night in a railway carriage before he reached the capital, including two more sea crossings on train ferries. No less than 2hr 48min was sliced from the timing of this particular run by the new "Englaenderen" express, corresponding amounts taken out of the schedules connecting other towns and cities in Jutland with Copenhagen.

Accounting for 56 minutes of this acceleration was the huge new bridge across that arm of the sea known as the Little Belt, opened by King Christian (a great railway enthusiast) on May 14, 1935. Both the old and the new trains still faced a 1hr 40min crossing of the Great Belt, leaving these well-named (*Lyntog* means 'Lightning Train') diesel expresses responsible for cutting 1hr 50min off a journey of which the rail portion was previously only 4hr 40min. Average rail speeds were almost doubled. The trains were fully articulated, with the power plant mounted on the end bogies. This consisted of four paired and relatively small diesel engine and generator sets, thereby ensuring that a fault which shut down an engine would be unlikely to mean a failure out on the road. At the same time the power plants were arranged so that they could easily be run out from under the train for attention or replacement. High

1934 electric working had begun between Rome and Milan—including the brand new 11½-mile (18.5km) Appennine tunnel, opened on April 12, 1934. There was therefore a requirement for heavy-duty express passenger electric locomotives and these formidable machines were the result.

It is only very recently that it has become possible with static devices to convert high-voltage to low—and since traction motors able to cope with voltages as high as 3,000V are not really practical, it was necessary to connect pairs of 1,500V motors in series. Hence, the eight motors for the four pairs of driving wheels which, although it is not obvious from a cursory glance, are mounted in two separate bogies.

The 241 excellent "E428s" are nearly all still in service, although occupied on less glamorous duties than in their heady early days when it was they rather than Mussolini that made the top Italian trains run to time.

Above: *Italian E428 2-Bo-Bo-2 electric locomotive, later version. The earliest ones did not have the streamlined ends.*

acceleration was ensured by having all the axles motored, again with relatively small motors of 104hp (78kW) each. Seating for 36 first-class and 104 third-class passengers was provided. In addition there was a small dining section seating 12, complete with kitchen/pantry.

The success of these trains led shortly to further orders being placed, this time for four-car sets. The most significant thing was that few changes were made, except those necessary to cater for the extra vehicle in the set. The services initiated by these trains have stood the test of time and those run by their successors could still be found in the timetables until 1982. For some reason recently (the grass always grows greener on the other side of the fence, perhaps!) the Danes, in opposition to the world trend, returned in 1982 to using separate locomotives and new trainsets fitted for push-and-pull working on many main line services.

Left: *Danish State Railways' "Lyntog" diesel-electric train leaving the train ferry after the crossing of the Great Belt.*

Bugatti Single Railcar

France:
State Railway (Etat), 1934

Type: Petrol-mechanical express railcar.
Gauge: 4ft 8½in (1,435mm).
Propulsion: Four 200hp (150kW) Bugatti "Royale" petrol engines driving through hydraulic coupling and cardan shafts the middle two axles of each eight-wheel bogie.
Weight: 35,265lb (16t) adhesive, 70,530lb (32t) total.
Max. axleload: 8,820lb (4t).
Overall length: 73ft 2in (22,300mm).
Max. speed: 99mph (159km/h).

The inter-war years saw perfection of the lightweight internal-combustion-engined railcar, particularly in countries where the cost and availability of coal made a change from steam traction attractive. France was such a country and the dozen or more manufacturers of railcars there included such well-known automobile names as Renault and Michelin.

By the early-1930s, technology had reached a stage at which railcars could not only replace steam on secondary routes, but could improve on the best steam schedules on main lines. This period brought a spectacular new entry into the railcar world. Ettore Bugatti was a famed designer of racing cars; Italian by birth, but now a naturalised Frenchman, he built his cars at Molsheim in Alsace Lorraine. He applied his ingenious brain to the problems of rail traction, starting from the proposition that with a suitably-designed railcar it should be possible to double the speeds then being reached on railways.

Bugatti's first railcar was supplied to the Etat system in 1933, and it bristled with novelties. The shape and proportions of the body suggested speed, for it was only 8ft 10in (2,692mm) high for a length of 73ft 2in (22,300mm), and its ends were brought to horizontal wedges, the shape being determined by wind tunnel tests. The driver was placed in a "conning tower" amidships, with an excellent view of the line ahead (but not immediately ahead!). Four of Bugatti's "Royale" engines of 200hp (150kW), burning a benzol-alcohol fuel, were placed across the body at the centre, the drive being taken to the bogies by cardan shafts along one side. The bogies each had eight wheels mounted in a flexible suspension system which allowed the wheels not only to accommodate vertical irregularities in the track, but also to move laterally to suit the radius of curves. Only the middle axles of each bogie were driven. There

SVT 877 "Flying Hamburger" Two-car Trainset

Germany:
German State Railway (DRG), 1932

Type: High-speed two-car articulated diesel train.
Gauge: 4ft 8½in (1,435mm).
Propulsion: One 410hp (305kW) diesel engine and generator mounted on each outer bogie supplying a dc traction motor on the nearer axle of the middle bogie.
Weight*: 72,290lb (32.8t) adhesive, 206,740lb (93.8t) total.
Max. axleload: 36,150lb (16.4t).
Overall length: 137ft 6in (41,906mm).
Max. speed: 100mph (160km/h).

*The weights apply to the final post-war condition of the train; when built it weighed 171,900lb (78t).

At 08.02 on May 15, 1933 a new era in railway speed began, for at that time the *Fliegender Hamburger* (Flying Hamburger) left Lehrter Station in Berlin on its first 77.4mph (124.5km/h) passenger-carrying journey to Hamburg. That it was the fastest schedule in the world was notable, but that it should have been introduced in Germany was quite remarkable. For, despite the brilliant example set by the Zossen-Marienfelde trials in 1903, Germany had lagged behind other countries in passenger train speeds, and in 1933 the speed limit was only just being raised above 62mph (100km/h).

Diesel railcars were first introduced in Germany in 1915, and during the 1920s their use was extended greatly on local services, but the aim here was a reduction of costs compared with steam operation. The novelty in the *Flying Hamburger* was that diesel propulsion was being used to raise train speeds above the level which was practicable with steam.

The official classification of the new railcar was "SVT877" (*Schnellverkehr*=express service, *Verbrennungs*=internal combustion, *Triebwagen*=railcar), and it was a two-car articulated unit with a 410hp engine mounted on each end bogie. Each engine drove a generator which fed a traction motor on the nearer axle of the articulation bogie. Thus the weight was distributed as evenly as possible. The shape of the vehicles was determined by wind tunnel tests at the Zeppelein Works at Friedrichshafen. The unit was permitted to run at 100mph (160km/h) in traffic, but reached 109mph (175km/h) on test.

There was accommodation for

Above: Flying Hamburger *on display at the German National Railway Museum in Nuremburg.*

98 second-class passengers in the two coaches, and there were also four seats at the small buffet. The livery was a striking combination of mauve and cream. The weight of the unit was stated to be 78t when it appeared, but in the post-war DB diagram book it was given as 93.8t.

The schedule allowed 138 minutes for 178.1 miles (286.5km) on the westbound run, and 140 minutes in the opposite direction. Although much of the journey

was a hydraulic coupling between the engines and the cardan shafts. There was no gearbox, as the characteristics of the engines enabled them to start the car from rest with no more help than the hydraulic coupling.

The total engine power of 800hp (600kW) for a vehicle weighing 32t loaded was exceptional, and enabled the car to accelerate and run at unprecedented rates. There were 48 seats in two saloons. The seat and back-rest were identical, and by a simple movement the back could be slid into the seat position, the seat then becoming the back for facing the opposite direction.

Initial tests demonstrated that the car ran smoothly at speeds up to 107mph (172km/h), but when it entered service between Paris and Trouville-Deauville it was subjected to the normal French speed limit of 75mph (120km/h). Later, as a result of favourable experience, maximum speed was raised to 87mph (140km/h).

Shortly after entering service, the first car carried the French President to Cherbourg at an average speed of 73.3mph (118km/h); following the trip this type of car became known as a *Présidential*. Further cars were delivered to the Etat, and in 1934 the PLM took delivery of a double unit, comprising a power car and trailer permanently coupled. Other versions included a lower-powered lightweight unit and an extra-long car. A total of 76 cars were built up to 1938, of which the État had the largest fleet with 41 sets. One of the 1935 État cars made a demonstration run on the Est from Strasbourg to Paris covering the 311.9 miles (501.8km) at the remarkable average of 88.7mph (142.7km/h).

The cars were little used during World War II, but they made a notable contribution to the revival of express services after the war. SNCF then introduced standard designs of diesel railcar, and the last of the Bugattis was withdrawn in 1958. Fortunately one of them was retained as a service vehicle, and it was eventually restored to its original condition, and placed in the French National Railway Museum at Mulhouse in 1982.

Bugatti cars are remembered as leaders of French railway speed in their early days, and they well merited the name under which the PLM advertised its services operated by them—"Thoroughbreds of the Rail".

Below: *A Bugatti single railcar of the State Railway of France. Note the central conning tower which was the driving position.*

Above: *The combined* Flying Municher *and* Flying Stuttgarter *high-speed diesel electric trains in the Frankenwald near Mt. Lauénstein.*

was on easy gradients and free from speed restrictions, there was one slack to 37mph (60km/h) near the middle of the run, the first 7 miles (11km) out of Berlin were limited to 50mph (80km/h), and at the Hamburg end 17 miles (27km) were limited to 68mph (110km/h).

Although there were a few problems with the train, it averaged 71 per cent availability over the first six months of operation, and this had reached 90 per cent in two years. Timekeeping was good, and the average load was just over half the capacity.

Success of the *Flying Hamburger* led to an order for 13 more two-car units placed in 1934 to operate similar services from Berlin to Cologne, Frankfurt and Munich, and a second service to Hamburg, as well as one from Cologne to Hamburg. When the new cars went into service in 1935, the schedules included a booking from Berlin to Hanover at 82.3mph (132.4km/h), which, with a Berlin to Frankfurt run, were the first runs in the world scheduled at more than 80mph (128.7km/h) start-to-stop.

The high-speed services became increasingly popular, and the next step was a three-car version with two 600hp (448kW) engines, and with the traction motors on the end bogies. One of these sets reached 127mph (205km/h) on test. With these sets the Reichsbahn built up a network of fast services which, for seven years from 1933 to 1940, held the world record for the fastest start-to-stop runs, apart from a short period when the Santa Fe "Super Chief" in the United States was faster.

Fast running in Germany ended early in the war, and the railcars were put into store. After the war they came back into service, but in Federal Germany the main routes were much less suited to high speed than the routes which had radiated from Berlin, and the cars were not able to achieve their pre-war averages. They were withdrawn from service in the late-1950s, by which time some of them had been converted to hydraulic transmission. One power bogie and part of a car body from the first set are preserved in the German National Railway Museum in Nuremberg.

Despite the faith which the old Reichsbahn had in these railcars, large orders for steamlined steam engines had been placed in 1939, and substitution of steam trains for the railcars had to be made from time to time when passengers exceeded the capacity of the cars. It is thus not clear how the pattern of services would have developed had there been no war.

Class E18 1-D$_o$-1 Germany: German State Railway (DRG), 1935

Type: Express passenger electric locomotive.
Gauge: 4ft 8½in (1,435mm).
Propulsion: Alternating current at 15,000V 16⅔Hz supplied through a transformer to four traction motors mounted on the frame, and connected to the axles through flexible drive.
Weight: 172,130lb (78.1t) adhesive, 239,130lb (108.5t) total.
Max. axleload: 43,200lb (19.6t).
Overall length: 55ft 6in (16,920mm).
Tractive effort: 46,300lb (206kN).
Max. speed: 93mph (150km/h).

From 1926 a succession of express passenger locomotives with individual axle drive was built for the growing electrified network of Deutsche Reichsbahn in Bavaria and Saxony. Amongst these was the 3,750hp (2,800kW) Class "E17" 1-Do-1 of 1927, which set the pattern for the layout of several later types of the same wheel arrangement. In 1933, three types of 1-Co-1 locomotive were introduced for the more easily-graded routes, of which the "E04", with a one-hour output of 2,940hp (2,190kW), was notable for its controller with fine gradations and for other electrical refinements. The 1-Do-1 locomotives were limited to 74mph (120km/h) but some of the 1-Co-1s were geared for 83mph (130km/h).

By this time the great revolution in German passenger train speeds was under way, with diesel railcars running at 100mph (160km/h) and steam locomotives at 93mph (150km/h). The next series of electric locomotives, the "E18" 1-Do-1 of 1935, therefore took a major step forward in that its maximum speed was 93mph (150km/h). The specification required the locomotive to be capable of reaching 87mph (140km/h) with a 700t train. To achieve this the continuous power output was increased to 3,800hp (2,840kW) at 76mph (122km/h), compared with 3,080hp (2,300kW) at 60mph (97km/h) in the "E17".

Experience with existing 1-Do-1 locomotives had shown that their riding was steady, despite a firm belief amongst many locomotive engineers that a locomotive with a symmetrical wheelbase was potentially unsteady at speed. The layout of the "E18" therefore followed closely that of the "E17". The electrical equipment was based on that of the "E04" 1-Co-1, with one traction motor per axle and Kleinow flexible drive. Previous German electric locomotives had been angular in shape, but the "E18" had an air-smoothed casing with rounded ends. This fell short of the streamlined shapes of the high-speed railcars and steam engines, but showed clearly that this was a new generation of fast locomotives.

To assist the driver at the higher speeds now contemplated, there was more power operation of controls. Above 44mph (70km/h) greatly increased brake power was available than in the earlier classes. As in the previous types with end carrying axles, those axles were connected to the adjoining driving axles by Krauss-Helmholtz trucks, which made the locomotive flexible but guided it into curves. When the "E18s" were tested at high speed, troubles were encountered with oscillations in the KH trucks. Air cylinders were therefore fitted which could lock the truck so that the driving axle in it had no lateral freedom and the carrying axle had a small amount of individual play. This control came into effect automatically at the trailing end whenever the controller was reversed in direction, and it cured the trouble.

The "E18s" proved to be very successful and plans were approved for construction of 92. By the time work was suspended at the beginning of World War II, 53 had been completed, and after the war they were the mainstay of express passenger workings in West Germany until the new generation of electric locomotives appeared in the 1950s. Two of the locomotives were in Austria at the end of the war, and Austrian Federal Railways retained them. Eight more were built by the Austrians, and for many years they were the fastest express locomotives in that country.

The "E18s" were followed by further locomotives of the same basic dimensions, but designed for normal operation at 112mph (180km/h) and for test running at up to 140mph (225km/h). The continuous power rating was raised to 4,900hp at 112mph (180km/h). Four of these locomotives, Nos. E19.01-4, were built in 1939-40, and until the coming of the "E03" Co-Co locomotives in 1965 they were the most powerful West German express passenger locomotives. They were never exploited to the full, and in the post-war years they worked alongside the "E18s," both classes being limited to 75mph (120km/h) by that time.

Simultaneously with the development of the "E19" series of electric locomotives, the German railway authorities embarked on an extensive assessment of the use of 50Hz industrial frequency current. A line in the Black Forest area, known as the Hollental railway, was converted on this system. It involved gradients as steep as 1-in-20 (5 per cent) and was a severe test. Had the war not intervened, this combination of high-speed locomotive design with cheaper supply systems might have put Germany decades ahead of the rest of the world.

Right: *German Federal Railway's Class E18 1-D-1 electric locomotive No. 118 049-6 passes Aschaffenburg with a relief express from Fulda to Dortmund.*

Below: *The E18 was a classic 1930s electric loco, with independently driven driving wheels in a rigid frame, guided by pony trucks.*

262 BD1 2-C_o-2+2-C_o-2

France:
Paris, Lyons & Mediterranean Railway (PLM), 1937

Type: Twin-unit express passenger diesel-electric locomotive.
Gauge: 4ft 8½in (1,435mm).
Propulsion: In each unit, two 1,025hp (765kW) MAN 6-cylinder four-stroke diesel engines in a common frame, each driving a generator supplying three traction motors mounted on the main frame, with flexible drive to the axles.
Weight: 238,000lb (108t) adhesive, 493,700lb (224t) total.
Max. axleload: 39,670lb (18.0t).
Tractive effort: 70,500lb (314kN).
Max. speed: 81mph (130km/h).

In the mid-1930s the PLM Railway experimented with diesel traction on its Algerian offshoot, and then, in 1935, ordered two large diesel-electric locomotives for its main line from Paris to the Riviera. The specification laid down precise conditions: to haul 450t from Paris to Menton on a schedule which would require maximum speeds of 81mph (130km/h) and a minimum of 53mph (85km/h) on the steepest gradients; to haul 600t trains from Paris to Nice on prevailing schedules; maximum axleload 18t; to cover a mileage of 171,000 (275,000km) in each of the first two years after introduction into service.

To achieve this performance required an engine power of 4,000hp, and this was provided in two ways; first by four MAN 6-cylinder in-line engines, and secondly by two Sulzer 12-cylinder 12LDA 31 double-crankshaft engines. The power available at the rail required a total of six driving axles, and in addition eight carrying axles would be needed to support the total weight. To satisfy these requirements each locomotive was a double 2-Co-2, the two halves being semi-permanently coupled at the centre with a connecting gangway. The bogies had inside frames, like those of a steam locomotive. Each pair of MAN engines had a common casing, with two independent parallel crankshafts, each with its own generator, one at each end of the casing. The twin crankshafts of each Sulzer engine were geared together, and drove a single generator.

The MAN engines developed 1,025hp (765kW) each, giving a total of 4,100hp (3,060kW), of which 300hp (224kW) was absorbed by auxiliaries, leaving 3,800hp (2,835kW) for traction. The Sulzer engines developed 1,900hp (1,420kW) each, with 3,550hp (2,650kW) available for traction. There was a single traction motor for each axle mounted on

Class 11* C

Great Britain:
London, Midland & Scottish Railway (LMS), 1936

Type: Six-coupled diesel-electric shunter (switcher).
Gauge: 4ft 8½in (1,435mm).
Propulsion: One English Electric Type 6K 350hp (260kW) four-stroke 6-cylinder in-line engine and generator supplying two 175hp (130kW) nose-suspended traction motors geared to the outer axles, the axles being connected by cranks and coupling rods.
Weight: 116,260lb (52.7t).
Max. axleload: 38,750lb (17.6t).
Overall length: 28ft 6¾in (8,705mm).
Tractive effort: 30,000lb (133kN).
Max. speed: 30mph (48km/h).

*BR class designation

Above: *British Railways class 08 diesel shunting locomotive based on the LMS 1936 design.*

The first locomotive in the world to be driven by an oil engine was built in England in 1894, and from then onwards numerous firms experimented with internal-combustion locomotives. Some of these were general engineering firms, and some were amongst the smaller steam locomotive builders. By the 1920s several had standard designs of small shunting locomotives, and the first main line or road locomotives were produced by Armstrong-Whitworth of Newcastle-upon-Tyne, an old-established armaments manufacturer which had entered the locomotive field after World War I.

The main line railways still showed little interest, apart from granting facilities for trials of various machines. They bought a few small shunters for use where sparks were dangerous, but in general the steam engine reigned supreme; coal, labour and steam shunting engines were all cheap, and the relatively expensive diesel seemed to have little to commend it. However, in 1932 Armstrong-Whitworth built a demonstration 0-6-0 or C shunter with a single traction motor mounted on the frame, connected to the driving wheels through gearing, a layshaft and connecting rods. The engine was of Armstrong-Sulzer design, with an output of 250hp (187kW). This locomotive was tested by the LNER and GWR in busy marshalling yards, and it created a great impression by its economy and reliability.

In 1933 there came a breakthrough. The LMS, the largest British railway, recognised that diesels might effect some economies, especially in yards where shunting went on round the clock. The company therefore ordered nine locomotives of six different types from five manufacturers. It was an indication of the extent of diesel locomotive activity amongst British builders that all these locomotives were virtually standard models. All had mechanical transmission except for the Armstrong-Whitworth contribution, which was very similar to the earlier demonstrator.

Concurrently, another six-coupled diesel-electric shunter was built by Hawthorn Leslie of Newcastle, incorporating an English Electric engine and equipment. The 300hp (234kW) 6-cylinder in-line engine drove a generator which supplied two traction motors geared to the outer axles; the three axles were connected by coupling rods. The LMS tested this locomotive and bought it.

With the experience gained from these locomotives, the LMS ordered two batches of 350hp (260kW) machines, one batch from Hawthorn Leslie with geared drive and the other from Armstrong-Whitworth with jackshaft drive. The success of these locomotives encouraged the railway to build more. At this point Armstrong-Whitworth gave up locomotive construction, and the LMS therefore produced its own design, in which an English Electric engine and electrical equipment was mounted on a chassis with jackshaft drive from one motor. Thirty of these units were built by Derby Works between 1939 and 1942. In the latter year

the frame, and connected to the axles by a Kleinow quill drive, a well-tried arrangement used in many electric locomotives.

The locomotives were completely enclosed down to rail level in a streamlined casing. In later years the bottom of the casing was cut away slightly.

The MAN-engined machine, No. 262BD1, appeared at the end of 1937, and hauled the first diesel-worked train in France on December 29 of that year. It was at that time the most powerful diesel locomotive outside the United States. No. 262AD1 was completed in April 1938, and for a short time took over from No. 262BD1 the distinction of being the most powerful diesel locomotive, but in July of that year the German firm Henschel completed a double locomotive for Hungary with two 2,200hp (1,640kW) versions of the Sulzer engine fitted to No. 262BD1.

Although they met with various troubles, the two locomotives were soon at work on express trains between Paris and Lyons. By the time they were put into storage in September 1939 they had achieved good mileages, albeit short of the figure laid down in the specification. In January 1945 they returned to service, and helped to relieve the acute post-war locomotive shortage in France. At first they worked between Paris and Lyons, but later they moved to Nice, where they performed some notable work on expresses of up to 750t. They were finally withdrawn from service in 1955, 262AD1 having covered a grand overall total of 985,000 miles, (1,585,000km).

These locomotives were remarkable for their time, and they marked an important step in the development of the main line diesel in Europe. Their significance was obscured by two things—their immobilisation for four years and the post-war electrification of main lines of the SNCF, including the Paris, Lyons & Mediterranean line for which they had been built. As a result of the progress of electrification, no more large diesel locomotives were needed on SNCF until the mid-1960s, by which time the influence of 20 years of post-war development of the electric locomotive masked the significant contribution made to diesel design by these pioneer machines.

Below: *The Paris, Lyons & Mediterranean Railway diesel-electric locomotive No. 262BD1, built in 1937. Two 1,900hp Sulzer engines were provided, one in each half-unit.*

the LMS directors authorised 100 more, but as the long wheelbase which was inherent in the jackshaft drive had proved to be a disadvantage on the sharp curves of some sidings, there was a reversion to the Hawthorn Leslie layout with two geared motors. Twenty of these locomotives were built for the War Department, and then between 1949 and 1952 the order for 100 was executed. In the meantime the other three grouped railways had all built small numbers of very similar locomotives, so that for the first time there was virtually a British standard shunting locomotive.

With this background it was natural that British Railways should adopt a very similar design, and soon after nationalisation, long before it showed any interest in main line diesels, BR embarked on a plan to eliminate steam shunting, for which purpose a total of 1,193 of the 350hp shunters were built, all identical except for a few with different engines for trial purposes.

In a country where railways traditionally designed their own locomotives, the adoption of the Hawthorn Leslie/English Electric design was notable, and it eventually led to construction of the most numerous locomotive class in Britain.

Right: *Netherlands Railways shunting locomotive also based on the pre-war LMS design.*

GG1 $2\text{-}C_o\text{-}C_o\text{-}2$ USA:
Pennsylvania Railroad (PRR), 1934

Type: Heavy-duty express passenger electric locomotive.
Gauge: 4ft 8½in (1,435mm).
Propulsion: Medium-frequency alternating current at 15,000V 25Hz fed via overhead catenary and step-down transformer to twelve 410hp (305kW) traction motors, each pair driving a main axle through gearing and quill-type flexible drive.
Weight: 303,000lb (137t) adhesive, 477,000lb (216t) total.
Max. axleload: 50,500lb (22.9t).
Overall length: 79ft 6in (24,230mm).
Tractive effort: 70,700lb (314kN).
Max. speed: 100mph (160km/h).

Above: *After the demise of the Pennsylvania Railroad and its successor Penn Central, Amtrak took over the GG1s. Here is No. 902 at Paradise, Pennsylvania.*

The Pennsylvania Railroad devised a keystone herald to underline the position it justifiably felt it held in the economy of the USA. The keystone, displayed both front and rear of these superb locomotives, might equally well stand for the position they held in Pennsy's remarkable passenger operations. Since 1928, PRR had been pursuing a long-considered plan to work its principal lines electrically. The statistics were huge; $175 million in scarce depression money were needed to electrify 800 route-miles (1,287km) and 2,800 track-miles (4,505km) on which 830 passenger and 60 freight trains operated daily.

The medium-frequency single-phase ac system with overhead catenary was adopted. The reason lay in the fact that the dc third-rail system used in New York City was not suitable for long-distance operations and, moreover, since 1913 Pennsy had been gaining experience working its Philadelphia suburban services under the wires on 25Hz ac. Only a corporation of colossal stature could have kept such a costly scheme going through the depression years, but by 1934 impending completion of electrification from New York to Washington meant a need for some really powerful express passenger motive power. There were two contenders for the prototype, the first being a 2-Do-2 which was based on the 2-Co-2 "P5a" class already in use. For comparison, a rather plain articulated locomotive of boxcar appearance and 2-Co-Co-2 configuration was borrowed from the neighbouring New York, New Haven & Hartford.

The latter proved superior, but first a further prototype locomotive was built. The main difference was a steamlined casing, which for production members of the class was stylishly improved by the famous industrial designer Raymond Loewy. Between 1935 and 1943, 139 of these "GG1s" were built; only very recently have they been superseded on prime express work.

Some of the "GG1s" were constructed in-house by the railroad's Altoona shops, others by Baldwin or by General Electric. Electrical equipment was supplied

Below: *A Pennsylvania Railroad GG1 passes through Glenolden, Pennsylvania, with the Chesapeake & Ohio Railroad's "George Washington" express.*

Below: *Pennsylvania Railroad Class GG1 electric locomotive in tuscan-red livery. These noble machines could also be seen in black or dark green.*

by both GE and Westinghouse. The philosophy behind the design was the same as that of the railroad—solid, dependable and above all, well tried. For example, the arrangement of twin single-phase motors, the form of drive, and many other systems were essentially the same as had been in use for 20 years on the New Haven. An interesting feature was the continuous cab-signalling system whereby coded track circuits conveyed information regarding the state of the road ahead, which was displayed on a miniature signal inside the "GG1" cabs. It was a remarkable tour-de-force for those days, especially considering that the rails also carried the return traction current.

At this time fortune was smiling on the Pennsy, because low traffic levels during the depression years meant that the physical upheaval of electrification was almost painless, while its completion (there was an extension to Harrisburg, Pennsylvania, in 1939) coincided with the start of the greatest passenger traffic boom ever known, that of World War II. The peak was reached on Christmas Eve 1944 when over 175,000 long-distance passengers used the Pennsylvania Station in New York. It was true that anything that had wheels was used to carry them, but coaches old and new could be marshalled in immense trains which the "GG1s" had no problem at all in moving to schedule over a route which led to most US cities from Florida to Illinois.

In numerical terms, a "GG1" rated at 4,930hp (3,680kW) on a continuous basis, could safely deliver 8,500hp (6,340kW) for a short period. This was ideal for quick recovery from stops and checks. In this respect one "GG1" was the totally reliable equivalent of three or four diesel units 30 or 40 years its junior. It is perhaps telling tales out of school, though, to mention an occasion when brakes failed on a "GG1" and it came through the ticket barrier on to the concourse of Washington Union Station. This was built for people not "GG1s", and the locomotive promptly descended into the basement!

Of the fate of the Pennsylvania Railroad in the post-war years, perhaps the less said the better. It is enough to state that the "GG1" fleet passed piecemeal to the later owners of the railroad, or parts of it—Penn Central, Conrail, Amtrak, and the New Jersey Department of Transportation. At this time it would have been laughable had it not also been tragic how various highly-advertised successors to what were now regarded as relics of a bad past failed to match up to these contemptible museum pieces. But finally, and very recently, the coming of Amtrak's "AEM7" class has put an end to the use of "GG1s" on main-line passenger trains.

Conrail also recently de-electrified the parts of the ex-Pennsylvania lines it inherited on the bankruptcy of Penn Central and so it too had no use for even a handful of "GG1s". Only the New Jersey DoT has—at the time of writing—a humble and, alas, emphemeral operation of suburban trains upon which a few of these noble machines perform. Two as least will survive, though, in museums at Altoona and Strasburg, but no longer will it be possible to see one of these mighty people-movers effortlessly in action at 90mph (144km/h) plus, treating a 20-coach passenger train like a sack of feathers.

Above: *The 10,000hp of two rather shabby GG1s was ample power for a Pennsylvania Railroad freight train in the latter days of that great institution.*

Below: *GG1 No. 4835 restored to Pennsylvania Railroad black livery, ahead of two further GG1s in Amtrak colours, pantographs raised in salute. The fourth loco is a modern E60P unit. A further GG1 is visible on the left.*

4-COR Four-car trainset

Great Britain:
Southern Railway (SR), 1937

Type: Electric express passenger multiple-unit set.
Gauge: 4ft 8½in (1,435mm).
Propulsion: Direct current at 660V fed via side-mounted top-contact third rail to four 275hp (205kW) nose-suspended traction motors geared to the wheels of the outer bogies of each set.
Weight: 130,816lb (59.4t) adhesive, 349,890lb (159t) total.
Max. axleload: 32,704lb (14.8t).
Overall length: 264ft 5in (80,620mm).
Max. speed: 75mph (120km/h).

For many years the Southern Railway claimed to have the most extensive suburban electrification in the world. Its final flowering was the extension in 1937 and 1938 to Portsmouth by two main routes plus a good deal of in-filling. Completion of this ambitious scheme involved electrification of 407 miles (650km) of track. On summer Saturdays more than 120 express trains and 70 stopping trains were to run between

Right: *A Waterloo to Portsmouth express formed of 4-COR and 4-RES units at speed near Clapham Junction, London.*

"Electroliner": Four-car trainset

USA:
Chicago, North Shore & Milwaukee Railroad (North Shore), 1941

Type: High-speed articulated electric interurban train.
Gauge: 4ft 8½in (1,435mm).
Propulsion: Direct current at 550V (600/650V post-World War II) fed via trolley wire and poles (or 600V on third rail on the Loop) to eight 125hp (200kW) Westinghouse nose-suspended traction motors geared to the driving axles of all except the third of the five Commonwealth cast steel bogies.
Weight: 171,030lb (77.6t) adhesive, 210,500lb (95t) total.
Max. axleload: 21,380lb (9.7t).
Overall length: 155ft 4in (47,345mm).
Max. speed: 85mph (136km/h)*

*after World War II

At a time when high-speed electric multiple-unit trains seem set to provide the inter-city transport of the future, it is worth considering that the United States has already developed and discarded a huge network, 18,000 miles (29,000km) in extent, of fast interurban electric trains. Some were faster than others but virtually all have now vanished. Some of the longest lasting, as well as the fastest and best, ran on the Chicago, North Shore & Milwaukee Railroad. On this line, travellers started their journeys at selected stops on the

Below: *The legendary Chicago, North Shore & Milwaukee Railroad* Electroliner *trains consisted of five articulated cars of which the outer two pairs are depicted here. They were financed by employees' pay cuts, staving off closure until 1963.*

London and Portsmouth, and the whole south coast was now served by electric traction from Portsmouth as far as Hastings. The service was on average doubled in frequency, as well as becoming cleaner, and was faster and more reliable. It was railway modernisation of a quality that to us, nearly 50 years later, is totally out of reach.

To work the new services, 193 multiple-unit sets were built, of which 87 were four-car corridor units for the fast services. These could be marshalled to make up eight and twelve car trains, vestibuled throughout; hence the classification "4-COR". Nineteen of the units ("4-RES") included a restaurant car and 13 ("4-BUF") a buffet car.

All the electrical equipment of the two driving motor cars was carried below the underframe, leaving the body free for traffic purposes. The control equipment was electro-pneumatic, but the multiple-unit equipment allowed for older sets with electro-magnetic control to be operated in multiple with the new trains. The driving cabs could be closed off by a hinged vestibule door to provide a through way for passengers when units were coupled together. Air brakes were provided as standard on SR electric stock.

The Portsmouth sets—sometimes affectionately known as "Nelsons"—gave over 30 years of excellent service. Nominal maximum speed was easily exceeded, 90mph (144km/h) often being observed, although at this speed the riding was a trifle lively. More important than speed though was reliability. Constant use of these trains during the period which included World War II and before British Railways had seriously tried its hand at modernisation, gave this writer a totally false impression of the shape of things to come elsewhere. Enough to say then of these trains that at high speeds they might ride like steam-rollers with square wheels, but they never failed to deliver the promises implicit in the timetables. Now they have all gone, except for one motor coach set aside for display in the National Railway Museum at York, and a de-motored but otherwise complete four-car set which is used behind air-braked steam power on the Nene Valley tourist railway near Peterborough.

Above: *This 12-car express electric train bears the headcode "80", indicating that it is on a non-stop run from Waterloo, London, to Portsmouth Harbour.*

famous central loop of Chicago's elevated railway—which meant that trains had to be flexible enough to turn street corners on 90ft (27.5m) radius curves. This was achieved by making the cars articulated as well as rather short. Only a few minutes later they would have to be rolling along at 85mph (135km/h) on the North Shore's excellent main line tracks. In Milwaukee, the trains made their final approach to the city centre terminal on street-car tracks, with all that that involves in control at crawling speeds. It was as if a Bristol to London High Speed Train came on from Paddington Station up Oxford Street and then happily made the right turn into Regent Street!

The famous trains that did all this so spectacularly had some unusual features, not least the fact that the line's employees had agreed to finance improvements to the line, including the "Electroliners" by taking a wage cut! This was because the trains were a last-ditch attempt to hold off abandonment.

St Louis Car built the trains, using electrical equipment from Westinghouse. They seated 146 and boasted a tavern-lounge car. The two "Electroliner" trainsets were scheduled to make the 88-mile (141km) journey from Chicago to Milwaukee and return five times daily from February 9, 1941 until the flexibility of the motor car finally won out. The North Shore's last full day of operation was January 20, 1963.

The "Electroliners" were sold to the Red Arrow lines of the Southeastern Pennsylvania Transportation Authority in Philadelphia. In 1964 they went into service as "Liberty Liners" *Valley Forge* and *Independence Hall,* complete with a vivid maroon, white and grey colour scheme.

EMD E Series A1A-A1A

United States:
Electro-Motive Division, General Motors Corporation (EMD), 1937

Type: Express passenger diesel-electric locomotive; "A" units with driving cab, "B" units without.
Gauge: 4ft 8½in (1,435mm).
Propulsion : Two EMD 567A 1,000hp (746kW) 12-cylinder pressure-charged two-stroke Vee engines and generators, each supplying current to two nose-suspended traction motors geared to the end axles of a bogie.
Weight: "A" unit 212,310lb (96.3t) adhesive, 315,000lb (142.9t) total. "B" units 205,570lb (93.3t) adhesive, 305,000lb (138.4t) total.
Max. axleload: "A" 53,080lb (24.1t), "B" 51,390lb (23.3t).
Overall length*: "A" 71ft 1¼in (21,670mm), "B" 70ft 0in (21,340mm).
Tractive effort: 53,080lb (236kN).
Max. speed: 85mph (137km/h), 92mph (148km/h), 98mph (157km/h), or 117mph (188km/h) according to gear ratio fitted.

Above: *A passenger train of the Gulf, Mobile & Ohio RR hauled by EMD E9 cab unit (leading) and E3 booster unit.*

*Dimensions refer to the E7 variant of 1945

In 1930 the General Motors Corporation made two purchases which were to have dramatic effects on the American locomotive scene. The first was the Winton Engine Co, a firm specialising in lightweight diesel engines. The second was Winton's chief customer, the Electro-Motive Corporation, an organisation established in 1922 to design and market petrol-electric railcars, which had sold some 500 units in 10 years. With the engine-building facility and the expertise acquired in these purchases, EMD was a major partner in the sensational pioneer streamlined trains introduced in 1934, and in the following year the firm produced its first locomotives. There were four Bo-Bo units with rectangular "boxcar" bodies, each powered by two 900hp (670kW) Winton 12-cylinder Vee engines. Pending the completion of its own plant, EMD had to employ other builders to assemble them.

In 1936 EMD moved into its own purpose-built works at La Grange, Illinois, and work commenced on the next locomotives. These were the first of the "E" series, known also as the "Streamline" series. Like the four earlier locomotives, they had two 900hp Winton engines, but the chassis and body were completely new. The body had its main load-bearing strength in two bridge-type girders which formed the sides. The bogies had three axles to give greater stability at high speeds, but as only four motors were needed, the centre axle of each bogie was an idler, giving the wheel arrangement A1A-A1A. The units were produced in two versions, "A" units with a driver's cab and "B" units without. The Baltimore & Ohio was the first purchaser, taking six of each type to use as 3,600hp (2,690kW) pairs. Santa Fe bought eight As and three Bs, and the "City" streamliner roads bought two A-B-B sets for the "City of Los Angeles" and the "City of San Francisco". These latter at 5,400hp were the world's most powerful diesel locomotives when they appeared in 1937. The B&O units were classed "EA" and "EB", the Santa Fe were "E1A" and "E1B", and the City units "E2A" and "E2B".

All these locomotives were an immediate success, not only by their performance but also by their reliability. The reliability was a striking tribute to the quality of the design, for there had been no demonstrator subsequent to the "boxcar" Bo-Bos. In multiple-unit working it was possible for some maintenance to be done on the road on the easier stretches, on which one engine could be shut down. With servicing assisted in this way, remarkable feats of endurance could be achieved. One of the B&O A-B sets gained

Below: *A 2,000hp E9 cab unit supplied to the Chicago, Rock Island & Pacific Railroad and specially painted in the livery of the line's "Rocket" express trains.*

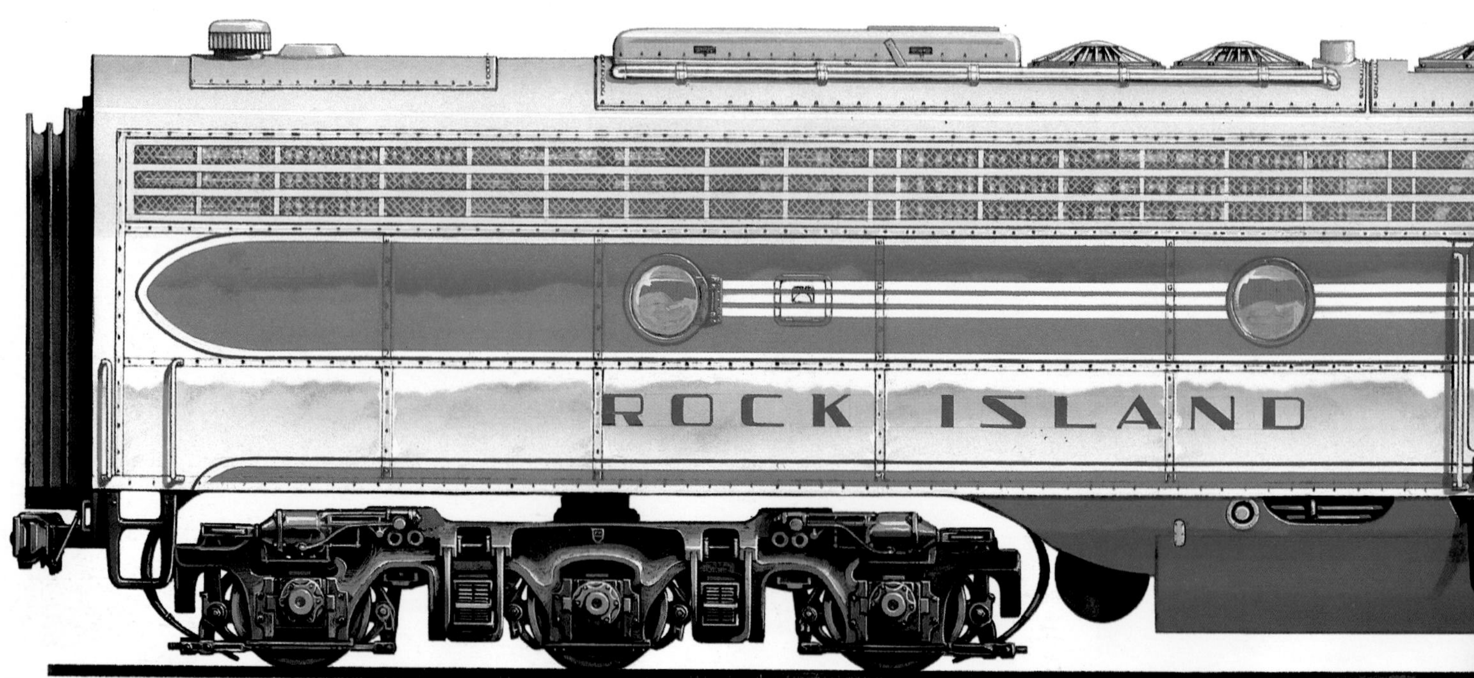

national publicity when it completed 365 continuous days of service between Washington and Chicago, covering 282,000 miles (454,000km) at an average scheduled speed of 56mph (90km/h).

Progress at La Grange was rapid. At 900hp the Winton engine was reaching its limit, and an EMD engine was therefore developed. Designated 567 (the capacity of a cylinder in cubic inches), it was available in three sizes with 8, 12, and 16 cylinders, giving 600, 1,000 and 1,350hp (448, 746 and 1,007kW). Simultaneously La Grange began to manufacture its own generators, motors and other electrical equipment.

The first all-EMD locomotives were an order from Seaboard Air Line for 14A and five B units, which appeared from October 1938 onwards. They had two 1,000hp engines and were operated as 6,000hp three-unit "lash-ups" (in the US jargon). These were the "E4s". "E3" and "E5" followed, the former comprising 18 units for the Sante Fe and the latter 16 for the Burlington.

So far each railroad's order had incorporated some individual variations—hence the different designations—but EMD aimed to gain the maximum benefits from production-line assembly of locomotives, to which end individual variations were to be discouraged. The next series, the "E6", which appeared in the same month in 1939 as the first freight demonstrator, was therefore a standard off-the-shelf unit, with the minimum of options. This was the start of real diesel mass production and 118 units had been built by the time the War Production Board terminated building of passenger locomotives in February 1942.

Construction of passenger locomotives was resumed in February 1945 with the first of the "E7" series. These locomotives benefited from the experience gained from both the "E" and the "F" series freight units. Improvements included a new and larger cooling system for the engine. Externally there was a noticeable difference in that the front of the body was sloped at 80° to the horizontal, as in the "F" series, instead of 70°, as in previous "E" series bodies. Apart from this change, there were few differences in external appearance throughout the range of "E" series, and most of them concerned windows and portholes.

With locomotive fleets rundown by wartime traffic, the railroads were even more eager to acquire passenger diesels, and Electro-Motive Division (as it had now become) settled down to a steady production of "E7s", averaging 10 per month for four years. During this time 428 A units and 82 B units were built, so that the "E7" outnumbered the passenger diesels of all other US makers put together. In general it was roads which had fast passenger services on easy gradients which bought "E7s"; for mountain work the all-adhesion "F" series was favourite.

Amongst "E7" buyers were the Pennsylvania and the New York Central. With 60 and 50 units respectively they had the largest numbers of any owner. On the NYC the most through comparison ever made between steam and diesel was conducted during October 1946. Two twin "E7" locomotives were tested against six of the new "Niagara" 4-8-4 steam engines working between Harmon, New York, and Chicago, 928 miles (1,493km). The "E7s" averaged 28,954 miles in the month and the 4-8-4s 27,221. Average operating costs per mile were $1.11 for the "E7" and $1.22 for the 4-8-4. However, a succession of coal strikes and then some trouble with the alloy steel boilers of the "Niagaras" ensured that the NYC did not allow its lingering love of steam to interpret the results in favour of the 4-8-4s, but the tests were still encouraging to steam enthusiasts in showing how small was the improvement when the best of steam locomotives, intensively used and adequately serviced, were replaced by diesels. But on most roads the margin was much wider, and there was a handsome saving from diesels, quite sufficient to offset the greater capital cost.

In 1953 the 1,125hp (840kW) 567B engine was available, and this was incorporated in the next series, the "E8". By this time most of the principal passenger services were dieselised, so the impact of the "E8" was less spectacular than that of the "E7". By the time the final version appeared, the "E9" with 1,200hp (900kW) 567C engines, the need for passenger diesels had almost been met, and only 144 units were sold between 1954 and 1963, compared with 457 "E8s".

In the 1960s the American passenger train declined rapidly in the face of air and coach competition, and many of the later "Es" had short lives, being traded in against the purchase of new general-purpose locomotives.

The "E" series instituted the general conversion of the American passenger train to diesel operation, and they eventually saw many of the most famous trains out. In their heyday the US had an undisputed world lead in passenger train speeds. Geared for up to 117mph (188km/h), (although few roads operated them above 100mph (160km/h), the "Es" were the fastest diesel locomotives in the world, and yet their construction was rugged and straightforward. In particular they had nose-suspended traction motors, which the heavy North American rails with their close-spaced sleepers seemed able to accept without distress.

In 1980 Amtrak operated the last run of "E" locomotives in multiple and the ranks were very thin by this time. Fortunately the body of the first B&O unit is preserved.

Below: *Early E-series "A" or "cab" unit of the Atchison, Topeka & Santa Fe Railway, 1936.*

EMD "F" Series B_o-B_o

United States:
Electro-Motive Division, General Motors Corporation (EMD), 1939

Type: All-purpose diesel-electric locomotive, "A" units with cab, "B" units without.
Gauge: 4ft 8½in (1,435mm).
Propulsion : One EMD 5,67B 1,500hp (1,120kW) 16-cylinder pressure-charged two-stroke Vee engine and generator supplying current to four nose-suspended traction motors geared to the axles.
Weight: 230,000lb (104.4t) (minimum without train heating steam generator).
Max. axleload: 57,500lb (26.1t).
Overall length*: "A" 50ft 8in (15,443mm), "B" 50ft 0in (15,240mm).
Tractive effort: 57,500lb (256kN).
Max. speed: Between 50mph (80km/h) and 120mph (164km/h) according to which of eight possible gear ratios fitted.

*Dimensions refer to the "F3" variant of 1946

Above: *A single "F" cab unit belonging to the Denver & Rio Grande Western Railroad at the head of a short and now defunct three-car train on the D&RGW's Moffatt Tunnel route.*

The railway locomotive leads a rugged existence, and only the fittest survive. Evolution has thus tended to move in moderate steps, and few successful developments have been sufficiently dramatic to merit the term "revolutionary". One such step was the pioneer four-unit freight diesel, No. 103, produced by the Electro-Motive Division of General Motors in 1939. When that unit embarked on a 83,764-mile (134,780km) demonstration tour on 20 major American railroads, few people, other than EMD's Chief Engineer Richard M. Dilworth, even imagined that it would be possible for the country's railroads to be paying their last respects to steam only 20 years later.

By 1939 EMD had some six years' experience of powering high-speed passenger trains by diesel locomotives tailored to suit the customer's requirements. Their ability to outrun the best steam locomotives had gained them acceptance in many parts of the country, but this was a specialised activity, and even the most diesel-minded motive power officer did not regard the diesel as an alternative to the ten, twelve or sixteen coupled steam locomotive for the heavy grind of freight haulage.

Dilworth had faith in the diesel, and his company shared his faith to the tune of a four-unit demonstrator weighing 912,000lb (414t) and 193ft (58,830mm) in length. Most of the passenger diesels built so far incorporated the lightweight Winton 201 engine, which EMD had acquired, but in 1938 EMD produced its own 567 series of two-stroke Vee engines (numbered from the cubic capacity of the cylinder in cubic inches). The 16-cylinder version was rated at 1,350hp (1,010kW), and this fitted conveniently into a four-axle Bo-Bo layout, with the whole weight thus available for adhesion.

Two such units were permanently coupled, an "A" unit with cab and a "B" or booster unit without; two of these pairs were coupled back-to-back by normal couplings. Multiple-unit control enabled one engineer to control all four units, but they could easily be separated into pairs, or, with a little more work, into 1 + 3. Dilworth reckoned that a 2,700hp pair was the equal of a typical steam 2-8-2 or 2-10-2, and that the full 5,400hp (4,030kW) set could equal any of the largest articulated steam engines. As the combined starting tractive effort of his four units was almost double that of the largest steam engine, his claim had some substance. The demonstrators were geared for a maximum of 75mph (120km/h) but could be re-geared for 102mph (164km/h), producing a true mixed-traffic locomotive.

The units were built on the "carbody" principle, that is, the bodyshell was stressed and formed part of the load-bearing structure of the locomotive. The smooth streamlined casing was in sharp contrast to the Christmas-tree appearance of most large American steam engines, festooned as they were with gadgets. But this was one of the revolutionary ideas demonstrated by No. 103. Bright liveries on the passenger streamliners had attracted great publicity; now there was the possibility of giving the freight locomotive a similar image.

Despite the scepticism of steam locomotive engineers, 20 railroads spread over 35 states responded to EMD's invitation to give No. 103 a trial, and everywhere it went it improved on the best steam performance by a handsome margin. From sea level to 10,240ft (3,120m), from 40°F below zero (−40°C) to 115°F (46°C), the story was the same. Typical figures were an average speed of 26mph (42km/h) over 98 miles (158km) of 1-in-250 grade with 5,400t, compared with 10mph (16km/h) by a modern 4-6-6-4, or an increase of load from 3,800t with a 2-8-4 to 5,100t. The booster units were equipped with steam generators for train heating, and this enabled No. 103 to show its paces on passenger trains. The impression it made on motive power men was profound.

Not least amongst the startling qualities of No. 103 was its reliability. Throughout the 11-month tour no failure occurred, and even when allowance is made for the close attention given by accompanying EMD staff, this was a remarkable achievement.

Below: *A pair of F3s supplied to the Baltimore & Ohio. The left-hand unit is a "cab" or "A" unit, while the right-hand unit has no driving car and is designated "B" or "Booster".*

Production locomotives, designated "FT", followed closely on the heels of the demonstrator, and orders were soon received from all parts of the country. EMD's La Grange Works was tooled-up for quantity production, and over a period of six years 1,096 "FT" units were built, Santa Fe being the biggest customer with 320 units. The War Production Board was sufficiently impressed by the contribution which these locomotives could make to the war effort to allow production to continue with only a short break, despite the use of scarce alloys.

By the end of the war the freight diesel was fully accepted on many railroads, and total dieselisation was already in the minds of some motive power chiefs. The first post-war development was production of the 567B engine rated at 1,500hp (1,120kW) to replace the 1,350hp 567A model. After 104 interim units designated "F2", there came a four-unit demonstrator of the "F3" model, with a larger generator to suit the 1,500hp engine, and a number of other improvements based on six years' experience with the "FTs". Amongst these were automatically-operated cooling fans; the fans fitted to the "FTs" were mechanically-driven through clutches, and had manually-worked shutters. The fireman had a frantic rush to de-clutch the fans and close the shutters when the engine was shut down, particularly in severe cold when the radiators would freeze very quickly.

EMD proclaimed the "F3" as "the widest range locomotive in history", and the railroads seemed to agree, for new sales records were set with a total of 1,807 units sold in little more than two years up to 1949. Railroads took advantage of the scope which the smooth curved shape offered for imaginative colour schemes, and an EMD pamphlet showed 40 different liveries in which these locomotives had been supplied.

Simplicity of maintenance, and improvements in the engine to reduce fuel consumption, were two of EMD's claims for the "F3", and these same claims were repeated for the next model, the "F7", launched in 1949. The main change from the "F3" was in the traction motors and other electrical equipment. With the same engine power, the new motors enabled 25 per cent more load to be hauled up heavy grades. The model was offered with the usual options, including eight different gear ratios.

The "F7" proved to be a best-seller; 49 US roads bought 3,681 "F7s" and 301 "FP7s", the version with train-heating boiler, whilst Canada and Mexico took 238 and 84 respectively. They handled every type of traffic from the fastest passenger trains to the heaviest freight. Measured by sales, the "F7" was the most successful carbody diesel ever. "F7" production ended in 1953, to be replaced by the "F9". The main change was the 567C engine of 1,750hp (1,305kW). By this time the US market for carbody diesels was drying up, as "hood" units gained popularity, and only 175 "F9s" were built over a period of three years.

By the 1960s steam had been replaced totally, and diesel manufacturers were now selling diesels to replace diesels. Trading-in of old models became popular, and trucks in particular could be re-used. Many "Fs" were replaced in this way as the more powerful hood units became more popular, and the decline of passenger traffic helped the process. Nevertheless many units of the "F" series were still to be found at work in 1982, and the Canadian locomotives, in particular, could still be seen on important passenger trains.

The "F" series, more than any other model, showed that improvements in performance and economies in operation could be achieved in all types of traffic by dieselisation, despite the high initial cost compared with steam, and despite uncertainties about the life which could be expected from a diesel locomotive.

Above; *A Gulf, Mobile & Ohio Railroad train leaves Chicago behind a single F unit.*

Right: *F cab and booster units of the Canadian Pacific Railway on a passenger train at London, Ontario, in January 1963.*

Class 1020 C_o-C_o

Austria:
Austrian Federal Railways (OBB), 1941

Type: Electric locomotive for heavy freight traffic.
Gauge: 4ft 8½in (1,435mm).
Propulsion: Alternating current at 15,000V 16⅔Hz fed by overhead catenary and step-down transformer to six 725hp (540kW) nose-suspended traction motors driving to the axles via resilient gearing.
Weight: 264,480lb (120t).
Max. axleload: 44,080lb (20t).
Overall length: 61ft 0in (18,600mm).
Tractive effort: 65,300lb (290kN).
Max. speed: 56mph (90km/h).

These handsome locomotives, with lines which are a pleasant change from the plain box structures normal amongst today's locomotives, were built in large numbers during and after World War II both in Austria and in Germany, while the former country was occupied by the latter. They were a development of the earlier German Class "E93" (now Class "193"). Of 202 constructed, 47 are in service in Austria, two were destroyed in the war and of the remainder some still run in West Germany and a few in East Germany, where they are now designated classes "194" and "254" respectively.

The layout is not strictly that of a normal bogie locomotive, for the

Right: *Austrian Federal Railways No. 1020.41 in original colours at St. Auton on June 2, 1967.*

CC1 C_o-C_o

Great Britain:
Southern Railway (SR), 1941

Type: Electric mixed-traffic locomotive.
Gauge: 4ft 8½in (1,435mm).
Propulsion: Direct current at 660V fed via third-rail or alternatively by an overhead wire to a motor-generator set with flywheel which supplies current to six nose-suspended traction motors each geared to an axle.
Weight: 222,990lb (101.2t).
Max. axleload: 37,296lb (16.9t).
Overall length: 56ft 9in (17,297mm).
Tractive effort: 45,000lb (200kN).
Max. speed: 75mph (120km/h).

From 1932 onwards the Southern Railway extended its third-rail suburban network to main lines, operating passenger services by electric multiple-units. Freight traffic on the SR was in a minority, and the Operating Department was content for freight services, many of which ran at night, to be worked by steam engines which were employed on the remaining non-electrified lines. However, Alfred Raworth, the Chief Electrical Engineer, was anxious to build an electric freight locomotive, and in 1937 he obtained authority to build three. The mechanical parts of all the company's locomotives were the responsiblity of the Chief Mechanical Engineer, and when O. V. S. Bulleid joined the company as CME in 1938, he became involved in the project.

Bulleid argued that the high cost of an electric locomotive could only be justified if it worked passenger trains by day and freight trains by night, and that it had a capacity to work the heaviest passenger and freight trains which the company could envisage. The specification of the engines was thus fixed at the haulage of passenger trains of 475 tons (523 US tons) at 75mph (120km/h) and freight trains of 1,000 tons (1,100 US tons) at 40mph (64km/h). As at this time most British freight trains had no continuous brakes, the engines must be able to stop these trains of 1,000 tons by the engine brakes, aided modestly by the guard's brake van. To achieve this level of braking required an adhesive weight of 100 tons, for which six axles would be needed, giving the wheel arrangement Co-Co.

Above: *British Railways' electric locomotive No. 20001 (ex-Southern Railway CC1) brings HM The Queen from Victoria to Tattenham Corner Station for the races on Derby day.*

Left: *Twenty-four driving wheels! OBB Class 1020 (leading) and Class 1110 Co-Co locomotives.*

couplings and buffers are mounted on the two chassis units, while the cab and main equipment compartment is suspended between them in the manner of a Beyer Garratt steam locomotive, the heavy low-frequency transformer being housed therein. The class is equipped with rheostatic braking and this, combined with the high tractive effort and short rigid wheelbase, makes them very suitable for general service over the heavy grades and sharp curves of Austria's mountain routes. The very orthodox nature of their design and construction has led to this very impressive longevity for, although no longer pressed into service on prime express train work, most of the Austrian examples anyway are still occupied on the heavy freights for which they were designed.

In West Germany, a start was at one time made on re-equipping the Class "194s" so as to enhance their power output, but only a few examples were treated. Apparently the richer nation preferred the extravagant and dubiously economic alternative of scrapping and building again from new.

Left: *Austrian Federal Railways Class 1020 electric locomotive, originally German State Railway Class E94.*

The performance required of the locomotives was not exceptional, but there was a further requirement which was more difficult. Gaps in the third rail could leave even a three-car set momentarily without power. It was therefore essential that the electric locomotives should be able to start a 1,000 ton (1,100 US tons) train and travel a short distance with it, if the engine should happen to stop on a gap in the third rail. It was equally important that when the locomotive passed over a gap in the third rail while pulling hard, there should not be a sudden loss of tractive effort which could cause dangerous jerking of loose-coupled freight wagons. This was a novel problem and a novel solution was devised jointly by Raworth's staff and English Electric. It involved supplying the traction motors through a motor-generator set, one for each bogie, in which a dc generator fed from the third rail drove a 600V generator. The generator was connected in series with the third-rail supply, so that a total of 1,200V was connected across the traction motors. The three conventional traction motors of each bogie were connected in series, so that each took 400V. On each motor-generator shaft was a flywheel weighing 1 ton.

When the engine lost the third-rail supply, the motor-generator continued to turn under the influence of the flywheel. The motor, deprived of its external supply, acted as a generator, and the generator proper continued as before. As the two were connected in series, the traction motors continued to receive a supply at 1,200V until the flywheel slowed down.

Control of the traction motor supply was effected by varying the field strength of the generator, and as the resistances concerned was small, it was possible for each of the 26 positions of the controller to be maintained indefinitely without heating problems (by contrast the contemporary LNER Bo-Bo 1,500V locomotives had only 10 running notches). However, the cost of these advantages was that two heavy electrical machines were running whenever the engine was in use.

The mechanical construction of the locomotive was novel in that there were no pivots to the bogies. The underside of the body carried pads which rested on guides on the top of the bogies. The guides had lips shaped to a circle 9ft (2,743mm) in diameter, and these lips limited the relative movement of the body and bogie to rotation. The absence of pivots left a clear space for the traction motor of the middle bogie axle. All flexibility in the suspension was in the springs of the axle-boxes. This arrangement appeared to violate the rules for the springing of bogie locomotives, but it proved sufficiently acceptable to be used later on 396 diesel-electric locomotives for the SR and BR.

The first locomotive No. CC1, was completed in 1941 and proved that it fulfilled the specification. After testing, it entered freight service, and in February 1942 it spent two weeks hauling an express from London to Portsmouth in substitution for an emu. This was notable as the first time in Britain that a main-line express had been hauled by an electric locomotive.

After the war the locomotives, now two in number, found a niche in working the London to Newhaven boat trains, which had locomotive-hauled coaches on an electrified line otherwise worked by emus. In 1948 they were joined by a third locomotive, and from then until 1969 they divided their work between the boat trains, special passenger trains and freight services. Their BR numbers were 20001-3. By 1969, due to the heavy fall in freight traffic, the SR had a surplus of motive power, so the "flywheel" engines were withdrawn, and their duties taken over by more flexible electro-diesels.

In the meantime BR had built 24 Bo-Bo locomotives with a much simplified version of the flywheel control for the Southern Region, but these also succumbed to electro-diesels after a short life.

Class Ae 4/4 Bo-B

Switzerland:
Berne-Lötschberg-Simplon Railway (BLS), 1944

Type: Electric mixed-traffic mountain locomotive.
Gauge: 4ft 8½in (1,435mm).
Propulsion: Single-phase low-frequency alternating current at 15,000V 16⅔Hz fed via overhead catenary to four 1,000hp (746kW) traction motors driving the axles through a flexible system of discs, shafts and gears.
Weight: 176,320lb (80t).
Max. axleload: 44,080lb (20t).
Overall length: 51ft 2in (15,600mm).
Tractive effort: 52,900lb (236kN).
Max. speed: 78mph (125km/h).

Above: *Simple-looking, but complex in reality, the Ae 4/4 Bo-Bo electric locomotive was introduced in 1944.*

A great leap forward in the art of locomotive building came in 1944 when this small but progessive Swiss railway put into service a deceptively ordinary-looking double-bogie locomotive. The amazing thing was that 4,000hp was offered, when more typically a locomotive of similar size and configuration would offer only half as much.

The early BLS rod-drive locomotives of Class "Be 5/7", built in 1913, have already been discussed. At 2,500hp (1,865kW) they were the most powerful in Europe and for a time handled adequately the heavy traffic on this exacting main line. In 1926 four new 1-Co-Co-1 locomotives (Class "Be 6/8") raised the power available to 4,500hp (3,360kW) but these engines, although effective, had a heavy, complex and consequently expensive basic layout.

Below: *Berne-Lötschberg-Simplon electric locomotive of Class Ae 4/4, which introduced the concept of 1,000hp per axle.*

The idea that even the most important and powerful locomotives should have their wheels arranged in two bogies, just like other vehicles on a railway, was then quite a new one, but many problems had first to be solved. Not least was that of weight in order to keep the axleload down to 20t. A more complex main transformer with a core star-shaped in plan led to a fundamental reduction in the weight of this item (always critical when low frequency current was involved) from 16t to 9½t. Light alloys were also used extensively in the all-welded body.

Reduction of weight brings in problems of providing adequate adhesion, and this was tackled by a combination of mechanical and electrical measures. The voltage was regulated on the high-tension side of the transformer and provided for a much larger number of steps (28) than usual so that slipping of the wheels is less likely to be initiated by a move from one control notch to the next. At the same time the bogies are arranged so that the connection with the body is as near to the ground as possible, so as to minimise transfer of weight from the front wheels of each bogie to the rear when pulling. Mechanical linkages also minimise transfer of weight from the front bogie to the rear and, should slipping occur, an anti-wheelspin brake comes into play. The ancient remedy of sanding gear is also provided. Coming downhill, there is automatic regulation of brake force according to speed to prevent skidding of the wheels when moving slowly, as well as electrical rheostatic (dynamic) braking. Full regenerative braking was rejected because of the extra weight and maintenance involved; by anyone else's standards, the "Ae 4/4s" were already too complex.

Perhaps it says enough to remark that nowadays the majority of high-powered electric (and for that matter diesel-electric) locomotives follow the layout of these path-finding machines. The original four (Nos. 251 to 254) had become eight by 1955; three double units classified "Ae 8/8", which were two "Ae 4/4s" permanently coupled (Nos. 271 to 273), came next, following which in the late-1960s Nos. 253 to 256 were rebuilt to make two further double units (Nos. 274 and 275). The remaining "Ae 4/4s" were equipped for working in multiple, or as push-pull units controlled from a remote driving cab. This was no reflection of any inadequacy on the part of these excellent locomotives, but rather was due to an upsurge in traffic on the Lötschberg route.

A single "Ae 4/4" was rostered to haul 400t (440 US tons) up the 1-in-37 (2.7 per cent) gradients, but this was by no means the end of the matter. A further series, which could handle 630t (693 US tons) on the same climb, was ordered from 1964 onwards, later reclassified "Re 4/4" on account of a high maximum speed. The main difference was abandonment of the single-phase low-frequency ac traction motors so typical of Swiss practice, and their replacement by dc motors fed via solid-state rectifiers. This arrangement is well known for its built-in anti-slipping control but other measures, including water ballast which can be pumped from one end of the locomotive to the other, have enabled the maximum tractive effort to be increased by 33 per cent and power output by 65 per cent as between the old and the new designs. There are now a total of 35 examples of the later class.

Incidentally, the Swiss use their own locomotive classification system, where the figures show the number of driving axles/total number of axles. The capital letter indicates the permissible speed range or usage, while the small letter 'e' indicates an electric locomotive.

Left: *A Berne-Lötschberg-Simplon express for Berne awaits departure from Brig, at the southern end of the Lötschberg railway.*

Below: *A development of the Class Ae 4/4 was this Re 4/4, depicted with a heavy train at Kandersteg in September 1980.*

PA Series A1A-A1A

United States: American Locomotive Company (Alco), 1946

Type: Diesel-electric express passenger locomotive; "A" units with cab, "B" units without.
Gauge: 4ft 8½in (1,435mm).
Propulsion: One Alco 244 2,000hp (1,490kW) 16-cylinder turbocharged four-stroke Vee engine and gearbox, supplying four nose-suspended traction motors geared to the end axles of the bogies.
Weight: 204,000lb (92.6t) adhesive, 306,000lb (138.8t) total.
Max. axleload: 51,000lb (23.1t).
Overall length: "A" unit 65ft 8in (20,015mm), "B" unit 63ft 6in (19,350mm).
Tractive effort: 51,000lb (227kN).
Max. speed: 80mph (129km/h), 90mph (145km/h), 100mph (160km/h), or 117mph (188km/h) according to gear ratio fitted.

Above: *American Locomotive Co's PA-series diesel-electric locomotive. A PA cab unit is followed by a PB booster.*

The American Locomotive Company was mainly a builder of steam locomotives until the end of World War II, but it had already achieved considerable success with diesel shunters (switchers), and in 1940 had produced a 2,000hp (1,490kW) twin-engine passenger locomotive, of which 78 were built before construction ceased during the war. In the following year Alco produced a 1,500hp (1,120kW) road-switcher, but the railroads were not yet accustomed to the idea of a locomotive which could combine two functions. All these locomotives had engines made by specialist firms, but in 1944 Alco produced its own engine, designated the 244, the last two digits indicating the year in which it first ran. It was a turbocharged Vee engine made in two versions, one with 12-cylinders producing 1,500hp (1,200kW) and the other 16 cylinders giving 2,000hp (1,490kW).

With these two engines Alco launched three models in 1945, a 1,500hp "Bo-Bo combination switching locomotive" (in the terminology of the day), a 1,500hp road freight locomotive, and a 2,000hp A1A-A1A passenger locomotive. The first of these was a hood unit, and the others were "cab" or "carbody" units. All three had GE electrical equipment and were marketed as Alco-GE brand. Great emphasis was laid on the fact that 98 per cent of the electrical parts and 96 per cent of the mechanical parts were interchangeable between the three types.

The freight locomotives, the "FA" cab units and the "FB" booster units—note that "cab" is used to denote a locomotive with a driver's (engineer's) cab as well as any locomotive with a totally enclosed body—appeared at the end of 1945, and the passenger locomotives, the "PA" and "PB" series, in September 1946. With high cab windows and a projecting bonnet, both types bore a resemblance to existing EMD and Baldwin designs, but the front and the roof were flatter. The bonnet of the "PA" was quite distinctive. The first units were for the Sante Fe and were finished in a remarkable livery of red, orange and silver, which earned them the nickname of "warbonnets". The three-axle trucks were unusually long, and these combined with the long bonnets to give an appearance of great length, although in fact the locomotives were 5ft (1,525mm) shorter than the corresponding EMD "E" type.

Over the next three years a total of 170 A units and 40 B units were sold, designated "PA1" and "PB1". There was then a pause in production until the "PA2" and "PB2" series appeared in 1950 with the engine uprated to 2,250hp (1,680kW). Finally there came the third version, "PA3" and "PB3", also with the 2,250hp engine, but with a number of detail changes. The last of these was built in 1953, and although a 2,400hp (1,790kW) version was offered, none was built. The day of the carbody was over, and passenger trains were in decline. There was also an export model, which looked very similar but was usually a Co-Co. Some of these were built by Alco licencees in the country concerned.

Below: *Atchison, Topeka & Sante Fe A1A-A1A PA-series diesel-electric locomotive No. 51 supplied by the American Locomotive Co. in 1946.*

The 244 engine had a number of troubles, particularly the 2,000hp version when used intensively on long-distance passenger trains. The "PA" locomotives had several protective devices to prevent damage to the electrical equipment, and at times these were over-protective, giving false warnings. Compared with their EMD competitors, the Alco "PAs" had the simplicity of one engine, whereas the EMD passenger units had two, but the "PAs" never equalled the reliability of the EMD locomotives. Although 16 roads bought them, and used them on the best passenger trains, they were usually outnumbered by EMD units. As passenger traffic declined, the "PAs" were either withdrawn from service or transferred to freight work, often with altered gear ratios. The large GE traction motors could take a heavy overload, and were well suited to freight work. A few "PAs" were re-engined with EMD 1,750hp (1,305kW) engines, but none received the later Alco 251 engine.

The last four "PAs" ended their days in Mexico, having been leased by the Delaware & Hudson to the National Railways (NdeM) in 1978. The "FA" freight series, by contrast, of which a total of 1,072 were built, were still active in the 1980s in the United States, Canada and Mexico.

Above: *A 6,000hp three-unit diesel-electric locomotive formed of Alco PA, PB and PA units in Cajon Pass, California.*

No. 10000 C_o-C_o

Great Britain:
London Midland & Scottish Railway (LMS), 1947

Above: *Ex-LMS Co-Co diesel-electric locomotive No. 10000 at work on the Southern Region with an up express at Basingstoke in May 1953.*

Type: Mixed traffic diesel-electric locomotive.
Gauge: 4ft 8½in (1,435mm).
Propulsion: English Electric 1,600hp (1,200kW) Type 16SVT V-16 turbocharged diesel engine and generator supplying current to six nose-suspended tractiom motors geared to the axles.
Weight: 285,936lb (129.4t).
Max. axleload: 47,824lb (21.7t).
Overall length: 61ft 2in (18,644mm).
Tractive effort: 41,400lb (184kN).
Max. speed: 90mph (144km/h).

The LMS was the first British railway to put diesel locomotives into regular service. It first experimented with diesel shunters in 1932, and by World War II it had adopted 350hp six-coupled machines as standard for its large marshalling yards. However, the 1930s were the high noon of steam in Britain, and there was no interest in main-line diesels. In 1942 there was a change on the LMS; Sir William Stanier was succeeded as Chief Mechanical Engineer by C. E. Fairburn, who had joined the LMS in 1934 as Chief Electrical Engineer after years of experience of electric and diesel traction with English Electric. Under wartime conditions, Fairburn could do no more than arouse interest in the extension of diesel traction, but after his early death his successor, H. G. Ivatt, had the opportunity to develop this interest when English Electric produced a 1,600hp engine, by far the largest diesel engine for rail traction thus far produced in Britain.

Ivatt was interested in innovation, and he was already planning various experiments with steam traction. Among these was construction of two Pacific locomotives which would differ from their predecessors in various details, the changes being directed at reducing maintenance and increasing the annual mileage. He therefore planned to build two diesel-electric locomotives which could be compared with the Pacifics. As the Pacifics could develop up to 2,500hp at the drawbar, twin diesel locomotives of 1,600hp would be needed to make a fair comparison.

There followed a remarkable period of intense activity at Derby Works, in which the first of the locomotives was built in six months. The reason for the hurry was that the LMS was to disappear into the new British Railways at the end of 1947, and Ivatt was determined that the first diesel should legitimately carry the initials "LMS", he having no enthusiasm for nationalisation. The second locomotive followed eight months later when Derby had made up the arrears of other work!

Several layouts were considered, but when English Electric decreed that six traction motors would be needed, the wheel arrangement Co-Co was adopted. The limited height of the British

Below: *London Midland & Scottish Railway No. 10000 as completed at Derby Works shortly before the LMS Company became nationalised.*

loading gauge presented problems which do not arise in other countries, and a novel arrangement was devised to support the pivot of the bogie without it fouling the traction motor of the middle axle. The weight of the body was distributed from a pivot at the centre of an H-shaped frame to four nests of springs at the corner of the H.

It was felt that former steam drivers would be disturbed by the sight of sleepers passing close under them, so the cabs were placed away from the ends, with the view of track partly blocked by a "nose". The resultant styling showed a marked similarity to contemporary EMD styling.

For pioneer locomotives, designed by a steam-orientated staff, Nos. 10000-1 were remarkably successful. But as BR policy was to retain steam traction until electrification, there was little interest in the main-line diesels for some years, and the close comparison with the Pacifics which Ivatt envisaged was never made. Furthermore, the sheer length of the twin unit was a disadvantage on a railway on which some of the longest trains already strained the capacity of platforms at terminal stations. Nevertheless, they demonstrated that 3,200hp of diesel could improve significantly on the work of a single Pacific, and that, barring failures, the diesels could amass tremendous mileages. Sadly, maintained in dirty steam locomotive depots and requiring special attention at a time of acute labour shortage on the railways, the diesels spent a lot of time out of action.

In 1953 they were borrowed by the Southern Region, which had high hopes of alleviating some of its maintenance problems with the unconventional Bulleid Pacifics by the use of its own three diesel locomotives plus the LMS pair. In due course enthusiasm on this region also declined in the face of maintenance problems with the diesels, and all five engines then went to the London Midland Region for the remainder of their lives. Again their fortunes fluctuated. At times they worked the "Royal Scot" and sleeping car trains as a pair, and services from London to Birmingham and Manchester working singly, but they were dogged by heating boiler troubles, and eventually they were confined to freight trains during the train heating season.

In 1955 there was a change of policy on BR, and preparations began for a major conversion to diesel traction. Although the pioneer locomotives continued to yield valuable information for future development, their frequent visits to Derby Works became an increasing nuisance as new diesels were built in quantity, and after long periods out of use they were withdrawn from stock in 1963 and 1966 respectively. Sadly the historical significance of No. 10000 was ignored, and nothing survived of the first main-line diesel to be built or owned by a British railway.

Above: *Just out of the box! No. 10000 at Derby, December 1947.*

Below: *3,200hp for the "Royal Scot"! Nos. 10000 and 10001 in double harness make easy work of a 13-car train on the famous ascent to Shap Summit.*

M-1 2-1 C_o-1-C_o B_o

USA: Chesapeake & Ohio Railway (C&O), 1947

Type: Steam turbo-electric express passenger locomotive.
Gauge: 4ft 8½in (1,435mm).
Propulsion: Coal-fired fire-tube boiler supplying steam at 310psi (21.8kg/cm^2) to a 6,000hp (4,475kW) turbine coupled to two generators, providing current for eight axle-hung motors.
Weight: 508,032lb (230.5t) adhesive, 1,233,970lb (560t) total*.
Max. axleload: 63,475lb (28.8t).
Tractive effort: 98,000lb (436kN).
Overall length: 154ft 1in (46,965mm).
Max. speed: 100mph (160km/h).
*Including tender

Almost since its earliest constituent, the James River Company, got its charter and had George Washington himself as President, the Chessie (as the Chesapeake & Ohio RR has long been affectionately known) has had coal for its life-blood. Small wonder then that it resisted a change to diesel oil as a fuel.

Most electric current is generated by steam-driven turbines and in 1945 there seemed no good reason why locomotives should not with advantage be powered that way. Accordingly, in that year Chessie ordered from Westinghouse Electric and the Baldwin Locomotive Works, three of what were to become the heaviest and largest steam locomotives ever built.

The intention was to use the turbines on a proposed high-speed streamliner to run between Washington and Cincinnati. Mountainous terrain en route gave advantages to a locomotive with a high proportion of its axles powered and this could be arranged to order on any locomotive with electric transmission. Incidentally, the driven axles on the "M-1s" were not the obvious ones; three axles out of the four on each of the central rigid trucks, plus both axles of the rear guiding truck, were the ones motored. The locomotive-type boiler with a grate area of 112sq ft (10.4m^2) was placed so that the firebox was at the leading end, the opposite of normal practice, while right at the front of the engine was a bunker holding some 27t of coal. The

W1 B_o-D_o-D_o-B_o

USA: Great Northern Railway (GN), 1947

Type: Mixed-traffic electric locomotive for mountain grades.
Gauge: 4ft 8½in (1,435mm).
Propulsion: Alternating current at 11,500V 25Hz, fed via overhead catenary to two motor-generator sets supplying direct current to twelve 275hp (205kW) nose-suspended traction motors geared to the axles.
Weight: 527,000lb (239t).
Max. axleload: 43,917lb (20t).
Overall length: 101ft 0in (30,785mm).
Tractive effort: 180,000lb (900kN).
Max. speed: 65mph (104km/h).

The fourth great transcontinental railroad to reach the West Coast of the USA was the Great Northern Railway, built by famed railroad tycoon James J. Hill. The "Big G" crossed the Cascade mountains beneath the Stevens Pass, named after GN's Chief Engineer. After seven years of trouble with a temporary alignment involving 4 per cent grades, the first 2.6 mile (4.2km) Cascade tunnel opened in 1900. In 1909, working through the tunnel was electrified on the three-phase system, the only example in North America. In 1927, three-phase was abandoned and single-phase electrification installed; this time the approach ramps were included, as well as a new Cascade tunnel, at 7.8 miles (12.5km) the longest railway tunnel in America, eliminating the most exposed part

Right: *Great Northern Railway Class W1 Bo-Do-Do-Bo electric locomotive. This machine had no fewer than 24 driving wheels.*

tender at the rear was for water only, no condenser being provided.

The "M-1s" were expensive to run and maintain, offering no serious competition to conventional steam, let alone diesel traction. All three were scrapped in the early 1950s after only a few years' service.

Right and below: *Class M-1 steam-turbine-electric locomotive built for the Chesapeake & Ohio Railroad Company in 1947. Three of these immense machines were built.*

of the route. The scheme covered 73 miles (117km) from Wenatchee to Skykomish, Washington State.

In its principles, this electrification was far ahead of its time, for the single-phase current was converted to dc for use in the traction motors of the locomotives. Of course, solid-state devices for this purpose were still in the future and rotary convertor sets, consisting of synchronous motors coupled to dc generators, had to be used. The technology had been placed in two locomotives constructed in of all places the Ford Motor Works, but equipped electrically by Westinghouse for use on a railroad (the Detroit, Toledo & Ironton) that Henry Ford owned. The GN electrification had four "Y1" 1-C-C-1s and twelve "Z1" 1-D-1s; the latter again heralded the future of US railroading by virtue of their multiple-unit capability. Put another way, they were building blocks from which locomotives of any desired power could be assembled.

The final fling of this little system was purchase of the very large "W1" class, of which two examples were constructed by General Electric in 1947. Modest power, combined with the huge tractive effort possible with all axles motored, was appropriate to a locomotive confined to the mountains. They could be run in multiple both with each other and with the "Y1s" and "Z1s". As with all the GN electric fleet, regenerative braking of trains on the down grades could provide a proportion of the current needed for other trains climbing. The electrification was totally successful but even so, in 1956, after new ventilating equipment had been installed in the second Cascade tunnel, diesels took over. One "W1" was rebuilt as a gas-turbine locomotive for the Union Pacific Railroad, but all the others were scrapped.

Above: *Only two examples of these huge Class W1 electric locomotives were built in 1947. In spite of their vast size, the power output of 3,300hp was only very modest.*

Below: *A Class W1 electric locomotive draws a Great Northern Railway freight train out of the eastern portal of the Cascade tunnel in Washington State, north-western USA.*

No. 18000 A1A-A1A

Great Britain:
British Railways (BR), 1950

Type: Express passenger gas-turbine locomotive.
Gauge: 4ft 8½in (1,435mm).
Propulsion: Brown Boveri 2,500hp (1,865kW) gas turbine and generator feeding four 528hp (394kW) traction motors geared with flexible drive to the two outer axles of each bogie.
Weight: 174,000lb (79t) adhesive, 260,000lb (118t) total.
Max. axleload: 43,000lb (19.5t).
Overall length: 63ft 0in (19,202mm).
Tractive effort: 31,500lb (140kN).
Max. speed: 90mph (144km/h).

Above: *Swiss-built gas-turbine-electric locomotive Brown Boveri No. 18000 in service with an express.*

The aircraft gas turbine made a spectacular entry into the engineering world in the latter days of World War II, and after the war there were high hopes that this mechanically simple machine, with a very high power-to-weight ratio, could replace the more complex diesel engine in various applications. In fact, unostentatiously, development work on industrial gas turbines had been in progress for many years, and a gas-turbine electric locomotive was completed in Switzerland in 1940 by Brown Boveri and the Swiss Locomotive Works (SLM). By the end of the war it had several years of successful running to its credit.

In Britain, after the war, the railways began to make fundamental studies of their future motive power policy, especially in the light of the rapid growth of diesel traction in the United States. The Great Western Railway, maintaining its tradition of being different from other railways, decided that the gas turbine offered the prospect of eventually supplanting the diesel engine, and that it would be worth moving directly to what might be the ultimate motive power. The company therefore ordered a gas turbine electric locomotive from Metropolitan-Vickers, a firm with long experience of electric traction, but one which had also entered the field of aircraft gas turbines quite early. Metro-Vick was to design and build the locomotive, which was to burn diesel oil, and the cost would be shared by the makers and customer.

The GWR technical staff then visited Switzerland to study the work done by Brown Boveri, and they were so impressed that the railway ordered a second gas turbine locomotive from Switzerland. It was to be closely based on the Swiss prototype, adapted to the British loading gauge, and designed to burn heavy Bunker C oil, except at starting when diesel oil would be used. Although ordered in 1946, the locomotive did not reach Britain until February 1950, by which time the former GWR had been the Western Region of British Railways for two years, and BR had adopted the policy of continuing to build steam locomotives until money was available for electrification.

The gas turbine was a 2,500hp unit driving a generator which supplied current to four traction motors. Each bogie had a carrying axle between the motored axles, giving the wheel arrangement A1A-A1A. A heat exchanger transferred part of the heat of the exhaust to the air moving between the compressor and the combustion chamber. Detail work was to Swiss standards, but the locomotive was equipped with a

RDC Single Railcar

USA:
The Budd Company (Budd), 1949

Type: Self-propelled diesel-mechanical railcar.
Gauge: 4ft 8½in (1,435mm).
Propulsion: Two General Motors Type 6-110, six-cylinder 275hp (205kW) diesel engines mounted beneath the floor, each driving the inside axle of one bogie, via longitudinal cardan shafts and gearing.
Weight: 63,564lb (29t) adhesive, 126,728lb (57.5t) total.
Max. axleload: 31,782lb (14.5t).
Overall length: 85ft 0in (25,910mm).
Max. speed: 85mph (136km/h).

Above: *A train of Canadian Pacific RDC railcars leaves Montreal in summer 1958.*

After World War II, the Budd Company made a bid to extend their passenger car-building business using stainless steel construction which had started with the "Pioneer Zephyr" streamline train in 1934 as previously described. By 1948 Budd ranked second in the USA after Pullman and their plan now was to produce not long-distance streamliners but equipment for lesser services—'plug runs', in US vernacular.

To some extent this market had been explored in the 1920s with the gas-electric "doodlebugs" (qv), but something with a more up-to-date aura and still lower costs was needed. Budd's Vice-President for Engineering, Maj-Gen G.M. Barnes, had heard of a new V-6 diesel engine developed by General Motors for tank propulsion. Furthermore, he had had experience of torque-convertor transmission while in the army.

Combined with the weight-saving possibilities of Budd's normal stainless steel construction, a pair of these engines married to two such transmissions would give an excellent self-propelled passenger railcar with an ample power-to-weight ratio of some 8hp/ton. This would provide rapid acceleration from stops and give better than 40mph (64km/h) on a 1-in-50 (2 per cent) grade as well as a maximum speed as high as would be acceptable to the generality of railroad companies. Disc brakes with anti-slide control would also provide superior stopping power. Moreover, the proposal was to produce the car first, then demonstrate it to the railroads, rather than try to sell a mere idea.

Accordingly, in 1949 a demonstrator RDC (Rail Diesel Car) was built and it performed with impressive reliability. In fact, the Budd RDCs sold so well that by 1956 more than 300 were running. The largest fleet was that of Boston & Maine with 64, while RDCs provided a local train service over more than 924 miles (1,478km) from Salt Lake City to Oakland (San Francisco). The longest RDC service was that of the Trans-Australian Railway from Port Piree to Kalgoorlie, 1,008 miles (1,613km). Varying amounts of passenger accommodation could be provided in proportion to mail/parcels space according to customers' requirements, while trains could be made up of any number of RDCs without reducing speed or acceleration, or needing extra crew.

Generally speaking, the Budd cars managed to save their own first cost in less than a year by reducing costs and improving revenue. However, many of these results were obtained against a background of compulsion to provide local passenger services. When this compulsion disappeared, as it had generally in the USA by the 1970s, then not even an RDC could be operated cheaply enough to run the service at a profit. Even so, a large number are still in service more than 33 years after the prototype took to the rails, notably in Canada. No doubt the ever-lasting stainless bodywork and the ease with which replacement engines can be fitted have contributed to this great span, but the main reason for such un-American longevity is the brilliance of execution of the original concept.

Right: *Chicago & North Western Railway RDC railcars at Chicago, summer 1952.*

train heating boiler and vacuum train brakes to meet British requirements. There was a 150hp diesel engine to supply the auxiliaries when the turbine was shut down, and this could move the locomotive at walking pace in depots. The maximum speed was 90mph (145km/h) and the unit was numbered 18000.

After three months of trial running No. 18000 went into service between London Paddington and Plymouth. Various troubles were encountered and overcome, but it was found that the traction motors were better suited to fast running than to the heavy gradients of Devon, and the locomotive was therefore transferred to the Paddington to Bristol route. The combustion chamber proved to be the most troublesome part, as it distorted and cracked. Dynamometer car trials established the performance of the locomotive, and they revealed the fundamental weakness of the gas turbine in this application. The efficiency of the turbine fell off seriously at part-load, and a British locomotive of that period spent only a small proportion of its time working at full load. The overall consumption of oil by weight was therefore little better than the average consumption of coal by a "King" class 4-6-0, although at its best the turbine locomotive was more than twice as efficient as a "King".

The Metro-Vick locomotive, No. 18100, was delivered in December 1951. It had the Co-Co layout, and its gas turbine followed aircraft practice. There was no heat exchanger, which lowered the efficiency, but this was partly compensated by higher gas temperature which increased blade maintenance problems. The turbine output was 3,500hp and the starting tractive effort 60,000lb, which was the highest of any British passenger locomotive of the day, and enabled it to start 600t (672 US tons) on the steepest West Country gradient, compared with 290t (325 US tons) for No. 18000. In due course No. 18100 went into service on the West England route, where its high tractive effort could be utilised. However, as there was only one locomotive of each type, inevitably there was no possibility of recasting timetables to exploit them to the full.

As experience was gained on the Western Region with gas turbine locomotives, other regions of BR were gaining experience with diesel-electrics, and it was clear that both types required further development. However, the diesels had much better fuel consumption than the turbines, and were closer to the stage when series-production could begin. When the GWR ordered the locomotives, the British government was sponsoring development work on a coal-burning gas turbine, but a few years later this was abandoned. So valuable imported oil would have had to be used in any production gas turbines—which was another factor weighing against turbine development.

When in 1955 BR finally embarked on a programme to eliminate steam traction, national enthusiasm for gas turbine had waned. The need for production prototypes was urgent, the capacity of the British rail traction industry was limited, and it was inevitable that diesels should prevail. No. 18000 remained in intermittent service for 10 years, and was nominally booked to work the 09.15 from Paddington to Bristol and the 16.15 back. It was withdrawn from service in December 1960, and after being stored for some years it was returned to the makers, who used it for test purposes. No. 18100 had a shorter career, and in 1958 it was converted to an ac electric locomotive for test work and crew training in preparation for the West Coast electrification.

Below: *Brown Boveri 2,500hp gas-turbine-electric locomotive as ordered by the Great Western Railway but supplied to BR.*

EMD GP Series B_o-B_o

United States:
Electro-Motive Division, General Motors Corporation (EMD), 1949

Type: Diesel-electric road switcher locomotive.
Gauge: 4ft 8½in (1,435mm).
Propulsion : One EMD 567D2 2,000hp (1,490kW) 16-cylinder turbocharged two-stroke Vee engine and generator, supplying current to four nose-suspended traction motors geared to the axles.
Weight: 244,000lb (108.9t) to 260,000lb (116.0t) according to fittings.
Max. axleload: 61,000lb (27.2t) to 65,000lb (29.0t) according to fittings.
Overall length*: 56ft 0in (17,120mm)*.
Tractive effort: 61,000lb (271kN) to 65,000lb (289kN) according to weight.
Max. speed: 65mph (105km/h), 71mph (114km/h), 77mph (124km/h), 83mph (134km/h) or 89mph (143km/h) according to gear ratio fitted.

*Dimensions refer to the GP20 variant of 1959

Above: *General Motors GP9 1,750hp road-switcher unit belonging to the Chesapeake & Ohio Railroad Company.*

For the post-war boom in diesel sales EMD offered a range of models based on three main series. First the "E" series of A1A+A1A express passenger locomotives, secondly the "F" series of Bo-Bo locomotives for freight work, but with optional gear ratios covering passenger work to all but the highest speeds, and thirdly a number of switchers (shunters) and transfer locomotives for work within and between marshalling yards. There was an important difference between the switchers and the other models. In the switchers the structural strength was in the underframe, on which rested the engine, generator and other equipment. The casing or "hood" was purely protective and had no structural strength. The "E" and "F" series, on the other hand, had load-bearing bodies, or "carbodies", which provided an "engine-room" in which maintenance work could be carried out whilst the train was in motion, and which were more satisfactory aesthetically than a hood.

With these models EMD captured about 70 per cent of the North American market. Its ability to do so stemmed from a combination of quality of performance and reliability in the locomotive, low maintenance costs, which were helped by the large number of parts which were common to the different types, and competitive prices made possible by assembly line methods of manufacture. Full benefit of assembly line methods could only be achieved by limiting the number of variants offered to customers, and this, in turn, helped EMD's competitors to pick on omissions from, or weaknesses in, the EMD range by which to hold on to a share of the market. At first EMD's main theme in its diesel sales talk was the benefit accruing from replacing steam by diesel traction, but as its competitors achieved modest success in finding gaps in the EMD range, more and more was that firm concerned with proclaiming the superiority of its products over those of its competitors.

To achieve this superiority some changes were made in the range, of which the most important originated in customer enquiries received before the war for a locomotive which was primarily a switcher, but which could also haul branch line trains, local freights and even local passenger trains. To meet this need a small number of locomotives were built with switcher bodies, elongated to house a steam generator, and mounted on trucks (bogies) of the "F" series; these were "road switchers". Construction was resumed after the war, still on a small scale, and with the design adapted to meet individual customer's requirements.

By 1948 EMD's competitors, particularly Alco, were achieving success with a general purpose hood unit for branch line work. For this application, ability to gain access to the working parts was more important than protection for technicians to work on the equipment on the road, and the hoods also gave the enginemen a much wider field of view. In 1948, therefore, EMD offered a branch line diesel, designated "BL", incorporating the 1,500hp (1,120kW) 567B engine, and other equipment including traction motors from the "F" series. These were accommodated in a small semi-streamlined casing, whose main advantage compared with a carbody was the improved view from the cab. There was, however, a serious snag—the "BL" was too expensive.

EMD then designed a true hood unit for general purpose duties, designated "GP". Richard Dilworth, EMD's Chief Engineer, said that his aim was to produce a locomotive that was so ugly that railroads would be glad to send it to the remotest corners of the system (where a market for diesels to replace steam still existed!), and to make it so simple that the

Right: *The GP 38-2 standard road-switcher 2,000hp diesel electric locomotive as supplied by General Motors (Canada) for the Canadian Pacific rail system.*

price would be materially below standard freight locomotives.

Although the "GP" was offered as a radically new design, many parts were common to the contemporary "F7" series. The power plant was the classic 567 engine, which like all EMD engines was a two-stroke Vee design; this was simplier than a four-stroke but slightly less efficient. Much development work was devoted over the years to improving the efficiency of the EMD engines to meet the competiton of four-stroke engines. The trucks were of the Blomberg type, a fairly simple design with swing-link bolsters, which were introduced in the "FT" series in 1939 and are still, with changes in the springing system, standard in EMD Bo-Bo models in the 1980s. EMD's success with this long-running design is in contrast to the radical changes which have been made in truck design in other countries over that period.

The cab afforded a good view in both directions, the hood gave easy access to the equipment, and, despite the designer's intentions, EMD's stylists produced a pleasing outline. Electrical equipment was simplified from the "F" series, but nevertheless it gave the driver tighter control over the tractive effort at starting, and a more comprehensive overall control to suit the wide range of speeds envisaged.

First production series of the new design was the "GP7", launched in 1949. It was an immediate success, and 2,610 units were supplied between 1949 and 1953 to US roads, plus 112 to Canada and two to Mexico—and this at a time when the "F7" was still selling in record numbers.

In 1954 the next development of the 567 engine, the C series of 1,750hp (1,305kW), was introduced into the range, giving the "GP9". This differed in detail from the "GP7", mainly to bring still further reductions in maintenance. By this time the hood unit was widely accepted, and sales of the "GP" at 4,157 established another record. The "GP" was now America's (and therefore the world's) best selling diesel locomotive.

Below: *A pair of GP-series EMD diesel units, typical freight power for Conrail's huge 17,700-mile (28,485-km) network.*

So far the EMD engines had been pressure-charged by a Roots blower driven mechanically from the engine, but with its competitors offering engines of higher power, EMD now produced a turbocharged version of the 567 engine, 567D2, giving 2,000hp (1,490kW). For customers for whom the extra power did not justify the expense of the turbo-blower, the 567D1 at 1,800hp (1,340kW) was availble. Both these models had a higher compression than their predecessors, which, combined with improvements in the fuel injectors, gave a fuel saving of 5 per cent. These engines were incorporated in the "GP20" and "GP18" series, respectively.

By this time US railroads were fully dieselised, and this, combined with a decline in industrial activity, reduced the demand for diesels. EMD therefore launched its Locomotive Replacement Plan. The company claimed that three "GP20s" could do the work of four "F3s", so it offered terms under which a road traded in four "F3s" against the purchase of three "GP20s", parts being reused where possible. It was claimed that the cost of the transaction could be recovered in three to four years, and the railroad then had three almost new units in place of four older ones with much higher maintenance costs. Despite this, only 260 "GP20s" and 390 "GP18s" were sold over 13 years.

The final phase of "GP" development with the 567 engine came in 1961 with the 567D3 of 2,250hp (1,680kW) in the "GP30." The designation "30" was a sales gimmick, based on there being 30 improvements in the new model; it was claimed that maintenance was reduced by 60 per cent compared with earlier types. The "GP30" was in turn succeeded by the "GP35" of 2,500hp (1,870kW). With trade reviving, and many more early diesels in need of replacement, these models achieved sales of 2,281. At this stage the 567 engine was replaced by the 645 with which the "GP" series remains in full production in the 1980s.

The "GP" series with the 567 engine totalled 10,647 units,or about one-quarter of the total of North American diesels, and it established the hood unit as the norm for all future construction.

Class 9100 2-Do-2

France:
French National Railways (SNCF), 1950

Type: Express passenger electric locomotive.
Gauge: 4ft 8½in (1,435mm).
Propulsion: Direct current at 1,500V from overhead catenary supplied to four 1,330hp (990kW) traction motors connected to the axles through flexible drives.
Weight: 180,730lb (82t) adhesive, 317,380lb (144t) total.
Max. axleload: 45,180lb (20.5t).
Overall length: 59ft 3¾in (18,040mm).
Tractive effort: 50,800lb (226kN).
Max. speed: 87mph (140km/h).

For 25 years the 2-Do-2 locomotive was the most advanced express electric type in France. For the electrification from Paris to Vierzon in 1925-26 the PO Railway built a number of types of express locomotives. All these were in various ways troublesome, particularly in the amount of maintenance required, except for two 2-Do-2 units built in 1925. These were destined to have a major influence on French locomotive practice for 25 years. Nos. E501-2 were designed by Swiss builders Brown Boveri and SLM, and they incorporated a number of features based on contemporary Swiss ac practice.

At this time, many electric locomotives were still driven by clumsy and complex rod drives, and an important feature of Nos. E501-2 was the Büchli drive, a system of links incorporated in the large gear wheel of the traction motor reduction gear between the motor and driving wheels. These allowed for movement of the driving wheels on their springs when they were driven from a motor mounted rigidly on the frame of the locomotive. There was a notable difference between the PO and Swiss machines, in that the former had the Büchli drive at each end of each driving axle, whereas on the Swiss machines it was applied at one end only. French engineers considered this difference to be a major contribution to the small amount of wear which their Büchli drive incurred between overhauls.

After a lengthy test period, 48 further 2-Do-2 locomotives were built between 1933 and 1943; they were numbered E503-50 and became SNCF Nos. 5503-50. The maximum power was 3,520hp (2,625kW). Twenty-three very similar machines were built in 1938 for the Etat Railway electrification from Paris to Le Mans.

For the post-war electrification

Above: *French National Railways' Class 9100 2-Do-2 electric locomotive No. 2D2.9119 enters Dijon Station with a rapide from Paris to Marseilles in 1967.*

of the former PLM main line from Paris to Lyons, a new class of 2-Do-2, the "9101", was built, based on the last of the PO locomotives, but with a number of improvements. The control system was extensively modified by introduction of additional stages of field weakening, made possible by improvements in the compensating windings of the motors. There were considerably more notches on the controller, so that the discontinuity in tractive effort, or "jerk", when a resistance step was cut out was reduced to about one fifth of that with the "5500" class. The extra field weakening improved the whole range of performance at higher speeds. The maximum speed was 87mph (140km/h), an advance of 10km/h on the earlier 2-Do-2s.

The specification for the class required it to haul 900t on the level at 87mph (140km/h), and 1,000t on 1-in-200 (0.5 per cent) at 62mph (100km/h). This requirement had been increased during the design period, following the spectacular tests of the Chapelon 4-8-4 steam locomotive. Although electrification was the logical step for a country with no oil and little coal, and SNCF was fully committed to it, nevertheless the electrical engineers were concerned that their latest product should not be outdone by the older type of motive power. The power output was 4,400hp (3,280kW) continuous and 4,880hp (3,640kW) for one hour. Despite the increase in power, the "9101" class weighed only 3.5t more than the "5500" series.

An initial order for 35 of the new locomotives was placed, and it was expected that a total of 100 would be needed eventually. However, the design was already dated when the class was delivered in 1950. All-adhesion locomotives for express work were well established in Switzerland, and the cumbersome Büchli drive had been rendered unnecessary by improvements in motor design which allowed motors to be fitted on a bogie. When further units were ordered they were of the Co-Co layout.

Nevertheless Class "9101" took a major part in the working of the *Ligne Impériale,* and in Summer 1951 they were working the four fastest schedules in France. The class achieved remarkable standards of reliability, and built up mileage as quickly as their more modern contemporaries. By January 1982 several of the class had exceeded 4.5 million miles (7.25 million km). Withdrawal of this hard-working class of locomotive began in May 1982.

Above: *A Class 9100 2-Do-2 electric locomotive. Note the double current-collecting contact bows provided to cope with the heavy current flows involved.*

Below: *This French National Railways Class 9100 2-Do-2 electric locomotive built in 1950 was the last of a long line with this elegant layout.*

S.N.C.F.

Nos. 10201-3 1-Co-Co-1 Great Britain: British Railways, Southern Region (BR), 1951

Type: Diesel-electric mixed-traffic locomotive.
Gauge: 4ft 8½in (1,435mm).
Propulsion: English Electric 1,750hp (1,305kW) Type 16SVT V-16 four-stroke diesel and generator supplying current to six nose-suspended traction motors geared to the axles.
Weight: 246,950lb (112t) adhesive, 302,400lb (137t) total.
Max. axleload: 41,440lb (19t).
Overall length: 63ft 9in (19,430mm).
Tractive effort: 31,200lb (139kN).
Max. speed: 90 mph (144km/h).

The post-war development plan of the Southern Railway had included introduction of diesel traction on certain routes on which electrification was not justified, and main-line locomotives of 2,500hp were mentioned. Responsibility for diesel locomotives, other than the electrical equipment, rested with the Chief Mechanical Engineer, O. V. S. Bulleid, a strong advocate of steam, who was at this time building large numbers of unconventional Pacific locomotives, and planning even more unconventional steam types. Bulleid was not convinced of the need for diesels, but he believed that the best way to meet competition was to beat it, and he therefore embarked on the design of a large diesel-electric locomotive. As the largest diesel engine then available in Britain was of only 1,600hp, which fell far short of the 2,500hp envisaged, Bulleid had no fear of his Pacifics being outshone.

Three prototype locomotives were approved, and design work began in earnest in 1946. Limitations of axleload on the SR made eight axles inevitable, so Bulleid took the bogie of his electric locomotive as the basis, and added a pair of carrying wheels at one end, this giving the wheel arrangement 1-Co-Co-1. This carrying axle was constrained by two horizontal links to move laterally as if turning about a pivot. Most of the weight was applied to the bogie through central segmental pads, but two additional sliding bearers were provided nearer to the outer ends of the bogies. As in the electric locomotives, the only flexibility in the bogie was in the leaf springs over each axle and their rubber pads. A difference from the electric locomotives was that the couplings and buffers were attached to the bogies instead of the body.

The engine was English Electric's 16-cylinder design, which had already been ordered by the LMS and Egyptian State Railways, and English Electric also supplied the electrical equipment. The body was shaped to the profile of SR postwar passenger stock, and there were numerous access doors, so that, if necessary, the engines and equipment could be withdrawn

Above: *Ex-Southern Railway diesel-electric locomotive No. 10201 at speed on BR's London Midland Region near Kenton, Middlesex, in June 1960.*

Fell 2-D-2 Great Britain: British Railways (BR), 1951

Type: Diesel-mechanical mixed-traffic locomotive.
Gauge: 4ft 8½in (1,435mm).
Propulsion: Four 500hp (370kW) two-stroke Davey Paxman 12-cylinder diesel engines driving a set of four coupled axles through a patented system of hydraulic clutches and constantly-meshing differential gears.
Weight: 170,240lb (77t) adhesive, 268,800lb (122t) total.
Max. axleload: 42,560lb (19.4t).
Overall length: 50ft 0in (15,240mm).
Max. speed: 78mph (125km/h).

At the end of World War II electric transmission was well established in North America as the norm for diesel locomotives, but in Europe there were still engineers who hoped to perfect a hydro-mechanical system. Their aim was higher efficiency and lower weight. Most of this effort was concentrated in West Germany, but one Englishman was active in the field. Lt Col L. F. R. Fell was trained as a steam locomotive engineer, and after an army career joined an aero-engine firm. In his spare time he took out nearly twenty patents for matters concerning diesel engines and mechanical transmissions for locomotives.

Fell favoured a multi-engined locomotive, partly to insure against engine failure and partly for easier maintenance of the smaller engines. In a normal diesel engine horsepower increases with speed, but Fell believed that engine power should remain almost constant over the working speed range of the engine, so that tractive effort would fall as speed increased, as it does in a steam locomotive. His idea, therefore, was to boost the engine with an independent supercharger, so controlled that as engine speed rose the boost fell, keeping power almost constant.

The Fell gearbox not only geared together the engines (four in number in the experimental locomotive to be described) but it also gave a high gear ratio at low speeds for starting, decreasing as speed increased. It made use of differential gears, but whereas in a motor vehicle power is fed in to the planet carrier and is taken out through the sun wheels, in the Fell gearbox an engine was connected to each sun wheel, and the combined power was taken out through the planet carrier. If, with the engine running at steady speed, one rear wheel of a car is brought to rest, the other wheel accelerates to twice its previous speed. The gear ratio between the planet carrier and the sun wheel of the rotating wheel is thereby doubled compared with the condition when both wheels are turning at the same speed. In the Fell system, if one engine of a pair started whilst the other remained at rest, the gear ratio to the planet carrier was doubled compared with the condition when both engines were running.

In a four-engined locomotive, the output from each pair of engines was combined in a third differential and then fed to the wheels. With only one engine running, the gear ratio was four times its value when all four were working. The change in gear ratio took place progressively and smoothly as successive engines were started and connected to their driving shafts.

The LMS had early experience of diesel-electric shunters, and in 1946 it undertook construction of two experimental 1,600hp diesel-electric passenger locomotives. In the following year Fell persuaded H. G. Ivatt, the LMS Chief Mechanical Engineer, to build an engine incorporating his ideas for comparison with the diesel-electrics. The directors of the LMS approved the project shortly before their railway was merged into BR. The locomotive had coupling rods connecting all driving axles; the middle pair of axles were in fact connected by the gearing, and for some time the engine ran with the middle section of the coupling rods removed.

Four 510hp Paxman engines housed under the end "bonnets" provided traction power, and two 150hp engines supplied the superchargers and other auxiliaries. One engine sufficed up to 7mph, two from 7 to 19, three 19 to 27 and four engines from 27 to the maximum speed of 75mph (120km/h). In practice, all four engines were in use for most of the running time. A fluid coupling enabled each engine to idle whilst its output shaft was locked against rotation.

Below: *British Railways' "Fell" 2-D-2 experimental diesel locomotive with mechanical transmission, built in 1951.*

sideways in a workshop which did not have facilities for lifting them through the roof of the locomotive. On a railway on which electric motormen were accustomed to driving positions at the end of vehicles, no projecting "nose" was deemed necessary and the cabs were at the ends.

Work proceeded slowly; the SR was merged into the newly-nationalised British Railways, in which there was little interest in main-line diesels, and in any event post-war austerity made extensive dieselisation of the SR a very distant prospect. Eventually in 1951 the first locomotive, No. 10201, was completed at Ashford Works. By this time the diesel engine had been uprated to an output of 1,750hp for one hour. The locomotive had been optimistically geared for a maximum speed of 110mph (177km/h), but this was soon changed to a more practicable 90mph (144km/h), with a corresponding increase in tractive effort at lower speeds. The locomotive soon established that it was able to work the trains normally hauled by the Bulleid Pacifics, although it fell short of their maximum achievements. But it could work two return trips a day over the 171.8 miles (276km) between London and Exeter, which was more than the steam engines could do at that time. When the second engine No. 10202 appeared, their duties were extended to services between London and Bournemouth.

By this time the railways were in the fifth year of nationalisation, and although BR's policy was to retain steam as the main motive power until electrification was possible, there was a strong feeling in some quarters that main-line diesel locomotives should be given a thorough trial. The completion of the third SR locomotive was therefore delayed pending consideration of improvements which could be made to a design which was already some six years old.

When No. 10203 was at last completed in 1954, the main differences were that the engine had been further uprated to 2,000hp, and that the control system was much improved. In Nos. 10201-2 the driver's controller had eight positions only, and some difficulty was experienced in adjusting the power to control the train speed precisely. In No. 10203 the controller was infinitely variable, an arrangement which became standard for subsequent BR diesel locomotives.

Whereas Nos. 10201-2 could barely equal a Pacific in good form, No. 10203 could better it, and for a time enthusiasm for the diesels ran high on the SR, to the extent that the region borrowed the two LMS locomotives, Nos. 10000-1. Steam locomotive maintenance was at the time at a low ebb on the SR, and the diesels covered workings which could have needed up to 10 steam engines. However, steam maintenace gradually improved, and at the same time the difficulties of servicing diesel locomotives in the crude surroundings of steam locomotive depots became severe, so reliability declined. The SR lost enthusiasm for the new power, and the five locomotives were transferred to the LMR.

Here their fortunes also varied. They took over some of the heaviest duties on the routes from Euston Station, London. Usually the smaller locomotives worked in pairs on long-distance trains, but No. 10203 could not work in multiple, and it proved able to handle trains of up to 500t (560 US tons) on the modest schedules of the period with average speeds of about 55mph (88km/h). They also had periods of working on the former Midland Railway route from London St Pancras.

At their best these locomotives achieved annual mileages unheard of in Britain, but their reliability still varied, and when Derby Works become involved in major dieselisation under the 1955 BR modernisation programme, the pioneer locomotives spent increasingly long periods awaiting repair. The SR locomotives were withdrawn from service in 1963.

Despite their fluctuating fortunes, these locomotives had provided invaluable experience to BR designers, and No. 10203 was the prototype for the first generation of large BR diesel locomotives.

Left: *The Fell diesel locomotive was withdrawn in 1957 after the main gearbox had sustained some accidental damage.*

The locomotive was completed at BR's Derby Works in 1951, and was subjected to a long series of trials on the Midland Division of the London Midland Region. Eventually it went into service, mainly between Derby and Manchester, hauling passenger trains of up to 12 coaches.

In its early years, BR took little interest in main-line diesels, but in 1956, when the modernisation programme was being initiated, dynamometer car trials were conducted with the Fell locomotive to assess its potential. The test report was generally favourable, but only to the extent that with the Fell system "a locomotive could be developed to give a close approach to the required (drawbar) characteristics." In fact the locomotive gave a higher tractive effort than a 2,000hp diesel-electric at speeds between 40 and 60mph (64 and 97km/h), but fell far below at low speed. The maximum tractive effort actually recorded was 29,000lb (129kN) compared with figures of 50,000lb (222kN) which had been obtained with a diesel-electric. The Fell transmission had a higher efficiency than an electric transmission, but this was offset by the much greater power required to drive the auxiliaries in the Fell.

Class Ew B_o-B_o-B_o

New Zealand:
New Zealand Railways (NZR), 1952

Type: Mixed-traffic electric locomotive.
Gauge: 3ft 6in (1,067mm).
Propulsion: Direct current at 1,500V fed via overhead catenary to six 300hp (480kW) nose-suspended traction motors each geared to one axle.
Weight: 167,505lb (76t).
Max. axleload: 27,770lb (12.6t).
Overall length: 62ft 0in (18,900mm).
Tractive effort: 42,000lb (187kN).
Max. speed: 60mph (95km/h).

Mountainous and oil-less New Zealand is one of those countries where electrification would seem to be a natural choice, but in which little has taken place. In 1932, a start was made with electrification at one end of the 428 mile (685km) North Island trunk route from Wellington towards Auckland. Fifty years later, only the 26 miles (42km) as far as Paekakariki had been achieved.

To handle traffic on this short section, English Electric and Robert Stephenson & Hawthorn in 1952 supplied electrical equipment and mechanical parts respectively for seven articulated locomotives of unusual configuration. In contrast, though, their electrical equipment was very conventional and the power output modest in relation to the weight of the locomotive.

The "Ews" are one of those classes best described by what they didn't have rather than what they did. The traction motors were of the elementary axle-hung pattern so there was no flexible drive. There was no electric brake and also, since New Zealand surprisingly follows US rather than British traditions over rolling stock, there was no vacuum exhauster to work the train brakes, as these were fed by air-compressor sets which the system needed anyway. The Bo-Bo-Bo arrangement was excellent for NZR's sharply curved alignments, while arrangement of the six motors could be permutated to give several natural running connections. An absence of external fittings and frills made for a neat and tidy appearance, exceptionally easy on the eye. On the debit side, though, one must compare the "Ews" with some contemporary locomotives of similar wheel arrangement, weight and gauge, built for the Swiss Rhaetian Railway, that could develop 50 per cent more power.

In 1967, diesel locomotives began taking long distance trains through over the electrified lines into Wellington. The "Ews" were then transferred to suburban trains

Above: *A short Ew-hauled passenger train about to pass beneath a diesel-hauled freight.*

Right: *New Zealand Government Railways Class Ew electric loco leaving Wellington station.*

which were confined to the electrified district. And, although electrification of the main part of the Wellington to Auckland trunk is now in progress, the use of very high-voltage ac makes it unlikely that a wider sphere of action will arise for these neat and useful machines.

Class 277* C_o-C_o

Spain:
Spanish National Railways (RENFE), 1952

Type: Electric mixed-traffic locomotive.
Gauge: 5ft 6in (1,668mm).
Propulsion: Direct current at 3,000V fed via overhead catenary and rheostatic control system to six 600hp (447kW) nose-suspended traction motors geared to the axles.
Weight: 264,480lb (120t).
Max. axleload: 44,080lb (20t).
Overall length: 67ft 9½in (20,657mm).
Tractive effort: 69,000lb (307kN).
Max. speed: 68mph (110km/h).

*Originally designated Class 7701.

This class of rather solid-looking electric tractors was one of the very few export successes of the British locomotive industry in Europe. They were intended to serve the electrification of two mountain lines in north-western Spain. The main line from Madrid to the port of Gijon on the Atlantic coast crosses the Cantabrican mountains by a tunnel 1.9 miles (3.1km) long beneath the Pajarks pass at an altitude of 4,170ft (1,271m). The northern ascent to this pass from Ujo (817ft—249m)

Right: *Spanish National Railways' Class 277 Co-Co electric locomotive No. 277-004-8 at Oviedo in September 1975.*

in 39 miles (62km) is exceptionally severe, an additional hindrance in steam days being the existence of 71 tunnels. The ruling grade is 1-in-48 (2.1 per cent). This short section was electrified as early as 1924.

When recovery began after the Civil War, priority was given to extending this electrification back to Leon and on to Gijon, a distance of 108 miles (172km). Furthermore, another mountain line was also electrified, leading from Leon as far as Ponferrada in the direction of Corunna. Hence this order placed with English Electric, the Vulcan Foundry producing mechanical parts for some of the series. Similar locomotives had been supplied to the Santos-Jundiai Railway in Brazil in 1950 and by a fortunate chance the Spanish Purchasing Mission visited the works while the Brazilian locomotives were being erected, so they were used as the basis of the design, many parts being in common.

In accordance with normal dc practice, the running steps in the control system were provided by the usual combination of motor groupings and field weakening, and the locomotives were assisted in their mountain-crossing role by being equipped with both multiple-unit control and regenerative braking. Vacuum brakes were then standard in Spain, so an exhauster system was provided.

A further sale of locomotives built to this basic design—with a few detail differences—was made in 1954 to the Central Railway of India. These in their turn became the basis of the first main line non-steam locomotive class built at Indian Railways' Chitteranjan Works in 1961.

Since then the dc electrification in this area of north-west Spain has been extended to 387 miles (605km) and Class "277" (originally Class 7701) eventually reached 75 in number, the last being delivered in 1959. The whole class was still in service at the time of writing.

Above: *Spanish National Railways Class 277 electric locomotive at La Robla.*

ETR 300 "Settebello" Seven-car train

Italy: Italian State Railways (FS), 1953

Type: De-luxe articulated electric express passenger train.
Gauge: 4ft 8½in (1,435mm).
Propulsion: Direct current at 3,000V fed via overhead catenary to twelve 250hp (187kW) traction motors driving the axles of six of the 10 bogies by gearing and hollow-axle flexible drives.
Weight: 449,620lb (204t) adhesive, 716,300lb (325t) total.
Max. axleload: 37,468lb (17t).
Overall length: 542ft 0in (165,202mm).
Max. speed: 98mph (158km/h).

The day was July 20, 1939 and World War II was barely a month away, when Italian State Railways took a record for long-distance travel by rail which was to stand for over 25 years. The instrument used was a three-car high-speed electric trainset (Class "ETR200") nominally rated at 1,475hp (1,100kW), and the route was from Florence to Milan via the then new 11½-mile (18.4km) Appennine tunnel. The 196 miles (314km) were run off in 1hr 55min, an average speed of 102mph (163km/h). To increase the power available, the line voltage of 3,000 was temporarily increased to over 4,000V and normal speed restrictions were relaxed. The maximum speed recorded was a thrilling 126mph (203km/h)—for those in the know perhaps a little too thrilling, like the rest of the run.

When World War II was over and the worst of the physical destruction in Italy repaired, the expertise that had produced this world-beating train was used to build a new and even better one, this time super-de-luxe as well as fast. And remember that this was a period when austerity ruled the roost elsewhere, particularly on railways.

The "ETR300", *Settebello* or 'Lucky Seven', is a seven-car set seating a mere 160 first-class passengers in considerable comfort. In addition to this, there are spacious observation lounges front and rear, (the driver having been banished to an eyrie upstairs) which seat 11 each. Both driving-observation cars are articulated to another passenger car and these two pairs originally constituted the whole of the revenue-earning accommodation. Style, comfort and decor were luxurious to a

degree which has seldom been approached elsewhere.

There is a separate dining car with 56 seats, and two cars articulated to the dining car in the centre of the train provide kitchen, staff, mail and luggage accommodation plus a small shop. Later, room was found for 30 extra seats, by encroaching on this rather over-ample allowance of space for service use.

Six out of the 10 bogies are motored, each with a pair of 1,500V motors permanently connected in series. Seventeen running notches on the controller are produced by using the motor-pairs in series, series-parallel and parallel, plus field-weakening stages. A hollow-axle flexible drive arrangement is used as the final element in the driving system. Brake force is arranged to lessen automatically as speed reduces.

At a later stage, rheostatic electric braking was added to the system. At the same time new motors with a rated output 28 per cent higher than the originals were substituted. Cab signalling was also fitted and the maximum speed raised theoretically to 125mph (200km/h). In practical terms, though, 100mph (160km/h) was the best permitted out on the line.

It must not be forgotten that there is more to running high-speeds than the trains themselves. That the track has to be improved is obvious, but there are other things as well. The signalling system must provide enough braking distance between the point at which a driver is warned and the place at which he has to stop. Furthermore, if cab signalling is a requirement, then there is a costly ground installation to be provided. Another problem is line capacity. On a busy route (and Rome to Milan is a very busy route indeed), a few trains that run faster than the rest have a quite disproportionate effect on the number of trains that can be run each day.

So, for all these reasons, the new trains were not originally able to better the best pre-war timing of 6 hours for the 392 miles (627km) between Rome and Milan. However, construction of a new *direttissima* railway between Rome and Florence, aligned to permit speeds as high as 156mph (250km/h), has been in progress for some time. The first and southernmost section of 76 miles (122km), over half of which is in tunnel or on bridges and viaducts, was opened in 1977. Although speeds on the new line are still limited to 112mph (180km/h), it was possible then for the *Settebello* schedule between Rome and Milan to be cut to 5hr 35min inclusive of stops at Bologna and Florence. Since then the timings have been eased again and 6 hours or just over is once more the best offered.

There remains just one odd point. In the past the best trains in Britain and France were locomotive-hauled, whereas in Italy they were self-propelled. Now, however, when the best British trains as well as the French are self-propelled, the Italians are going back to locomotives. The Class "E444" Bo-Bos, named "Tortoises" (!), hauling trains of new coaches of a luxury comparable with those of "ETR300", have the same speed potential; that is, a design speed of 125mph (200km/h), but as yet no railway suitably equipped on which to use it.

Left: *The Leading end of an ETR 300* Settebello *train. The wide windows are for the passengers' view, not the driver's.*

Above: *The driver's eyrie is clearly visible above roof level of the leading end in this view of a* Settebello *train.*

Below: *De luxe accommodation for 160 passengers was provided in the seven cars of an Italian ETR 300 trainset.*

Below: *A* Settebello *express train at speed crosses a handsome viaduct on the Rome to Milan trunk route.*

Gas Turbine B_o-B_o-B_o-B_o

United States: Union Pacific Railroad (UP), 1951

Type: Gas-turbine electric freight locomotive.
Gauge: 4ft 8½in (1,435mm).
Propulsion: One 4,500hp (3,360kW) oil-burning gas turbine driving a generator and supplying direct current to eight nose-hung traction motors.
Weight: 551,720lb (250.3t).
Max. axleload: 68,970lb (31.3t).
Overall length: 83ft 6½in (25,464mm).
Tractive effort: 135,000lb (600kN).
Max. speed: 65mph (105km/h).

Above: *Union Pacific Railroad three-unit 8,500hp gas-turbine locomotive. The lead unit has the turbine, the others house auxiliary equipment and fuel.*

Union Pacific is a big railroad; its last three designs of steam engine were all, in some way, the largest or most powerful of their type, and there was a dramatic contrast when the road began to buy off-the-shelf diesels of 1,750hp instead of 6,000hp steam engines. But UP is also a road of contrasts. One main line crosses deserts where coal and water are scarce, but oil is available; this was an obvious line for dieselisation. In other districts, however, the company owns coal mines, and there the economic case for dieselisation was less clear. In particular, any alternative to the diesel which might burn coal was of interest.

In the post-war surge of interest

Trainmaster H-24-66 C_oC_o

United States: Fairbanks Morse & Co (FM), 1953

Type: General-purpose diesel-electric locomotive.
Gauge: 4ft 8½in (1,435mm).
Propulsion: One Fairbanks Morse 38D-12 2,400hp (1,790kW) 12-cylinder turbocharged opposed-piston diesel engine and generator supplying six nose-suspended traction motors geared to the axles.
Weight: 375,000lb (170.1t).
Max. axleload: 62,500lb (28.4t).
Overall length: 66ft 0in (20,120mm).
Tractive effort: 112,500lb (500kN).
Max. speed: 65mph (105km/h), 70mph (113km/h), or 80mph (129km/h) according to gear ratio fitted.

Fairbanks Morse of Beloit, Wisconsin, was an engineering firm which had for a long time supplied general equipment to railroads, such as water stand pipes. In the 1930s the firm developed a specialism, an opposed-piston diesel engine, with two pistons in each cylinder, and two crankshafts connected by gearing. This engine was fitted to a number of railcars, but further railway applications were delayed by the US Navy, which took the total production for four years to power submarines. After the war, FM introduced a range of switcher and transfer locomotives, and then in 1950 it produced the "Consolidation" line of carbody or cab units, with a choice of engines rated at 1,600hp (1,190kW), 2,000hp (1,490kW) or 2,400hp (1,790kW), supplying four traction motors. Twenty-two units with the 2,400hp engine were sold in 1952-53, but the market was changing rapidly, and carbody designs were giving way to the more versatile hood-type road switcher.

Fairbanks Morse acted quickly, and in 1953 produced a 2,400hp hood unit designated "H-24-66" (Hood, 2,400hp, 6 motors, 6 axles). It was mounted on two three-motor three-axle bogies of new design. Compared with its competitors everything about it was big—the dynamic brake power, the train heating boiler (if fitted), the fuel supplies, the tractive effort. Although EMD offered a twin-engined 2,400hp carbody unit, the FM engine was the largest then on the market. With some justification, the firm chose the pretentious name "Trainmaster", and showed the first unit at a Railroad Manufacturers' Supply Association Fair at Atlantic City, where it stole the show. This publicity, combined with the impression made by the four demonstrator units, soon brought orders.

The peak year for Trainmaster production followed all too quickly in 1954, when 32 units were built, but orders then slowed down. Railroads encountered problems with the opposed-piston engine and with the electrical systems. One of the characteristics of EMD service had always been the prompt and thorough attention which was given to faults in the field, but customers found that the smaller FM company could not give such good service. During 1954-55 the firm was still dealing with engine problems, including pistons and bearings, but then came a blow to the future of all FM products.

The Morse family had large holdings in the company, and family feuding cast doubts upon the whole stability of the firm, which led to a takeover by another company. By the time conditions were stable, the diesel market was in the doldrums, and competitors had been busy catching up. One result of this trouble was that Illinois Central decided against

in the gas turbine, General Electric was well placed, with years of successful steam turbine work behind it. As far back as 1904 it had begun work on gas turbines. In 1946, development of a gas turbine for locomotive work was begun, and an experimental locomotive appeared in 1948. The attractions of the gas turbine for locomotives were the high power-to-weight ratio, simple mechanical parts and the ability to use low grade fuel. This turbine burned a heavy oil commonly termed "Bunker C", but already work was in progress on the use of pulverised coal in a turbine.

The gas turbine drove a generator, which supplied direct current to eight traction motors of normal design mounted on four bogies, giving the wheel arrangement Bo-Bo-Bo-Bo. The main frame of the body formed the fuel tank, and a boiler was provided to heat the oil in the tank, as it was too viscous to flow when cold. With a horsepower of 4,500, it was the most powerful internal-combustion locomotive in the world, and it soon attracted the attention of UP, to which it was loaned for trials.

Success of these trials brought a quick response. UP was led by a new President, A. E. Stoddard, a convinced "big engine" man to whom the 4,500hp unit appealed, and 10 were ordered. These where delivered in 1952-53; numbered from 51 to 60, they closely followed the design of No. 50, but had a cab at one end only. They went quickly into freight work between Ogden, Utah, and Green River, Wyoming, where their rated tonnage was 4,890. So successful were they that when only six of them had been delivered, a further 15 were ordered.

Thirteen months after the delivery of the 25th gas turbine, UP was sufficiently enthusiastic to take a second plunge, this time with an order for 15 locomotives (later increased to 30) with an 8,500hp turbine. The new design differed from the previous one in its layout, there being two Co-Co units, one carrying the turbine and generator and the other the control and auxiliary equipment. In addition a converted steam-engine tender was attached as a fuel tank. They took over from the earlier turbines the distinction of being the most powerful internal combustion locomotives in the world—by a considerable margin.

The gas turbine was, by its working cycle, inherently less efficient than a diesel, and the key to its ability to better the diesel in running costs was the use of cheaper fuel. However, this heavy oil brought penalties of corrosion and fouling of the blades, as well as difficulties in handling the viscous fluid. An attempt was made to use liquefied propane gas, but this was expensive and even more difficult to handle than heavy oil. Similarly, blade erosion was the main reason for the attempt to burn coal in a gas turbine being unsuccessful.

Despite the excellent work which the 55 "Big Blows" performed, time was against them. Changes in the petro-chemical industry made Bunker C oil more valuable, whilst developments in diesel locomotives made them more efficient and powerful, and thus more competitive with gas turbines. By the time the turbines needed heavy repairs, UP already had the world's most powerful diesel locomotives in service, and further expenditure on the turbines could not be justified. They were gradually replaced by diesels, and the last of them finished work in December 1969.

Below: *The Union Pacific Bo-Bo-Bo-Bo 4,500hp gas-turbine electric locomotive. An ex-steam locomotive tender adapted as a fuel tank was normally attached when in service.*

Above: *Two Fairbanks-Morse prototype "Trainmaster" Co-Co diesel-electric units coupled together to form a locomotive of 4,800hp, a high figure for diesels of thirty-odd years ago.*

placing an order for 50 to 60 units which it had contemplated, an order which could have changed the whole outlook for the model. In the event a total of 105 were sold to eight US railroads, and a further 22 were built in Canada.

Major users were the Norfolk & Western, which acquired 33 Trainmasters as a result of mergers, and Southern Pacific, which used them extensively on commuter trains. Most of the locomotives ended their days on switching duties, where their high adhesive weight was still appreciated after they had been displaced from main line work by more powerful locomotives from other makers.

A 1,600hp version of the Trainmaster, sometimes known as the "Baby Trainmaster" also failed to achieve satisfactory production, with a total of 58 sales. The opposed-piston engine had failed to make the grade in railway work. The fate of the Trainmaster was sealed when, by three years after its introduction, it had failed to achieve a level of sales which made its production economically viable, but for a time it enjoyed well-earned acclaim.

Class CC7100 C_o-C_o

France: French National Railways (SNCF), 1952

Type: Electric express passenger locomotive.
Gauge: 4ft 8½in (1,435mm).
Propulsion: Direct current at 1,500V from overhead catenary fed to six bogie-mounted traction motors geared to the axles through Alsthom spring drive.
Weight: 235,830lb (107t).
Max. axleload: 39,230lb (17.8t).
Overall length: 62ft 1in (18,922mm).
Tractive effort: 50,700lb (225kN).
Max. speed: 100mph (160km/h).

Above: *French National Railways' Class CC7100 No. CC7135 stands under 1,500V catenary in this wintry railway scene.*

French locomotive design has always been distinctive; much of the distinctiveness has been purely French in origin, but from time to time a foreign influence has been seen. Thus in the development of express passenger locomotives for the main line electrification of the Paris-Orléans Railway (PO), adoption to the Swiss Büchli drive led to a notable series of 2-D-2 locomotives, which bore an external likeness to contemporary Swiss designs. The last 2-Do-2 type, the "9100", was introduced by SNCF as the principal passenger locomotive for the electrification of the former PLM main line to Lyons. However, before those locomotives had been built in the quantity originally intended, another Swiss influence changed the course of French locomotive design.

Until this time, end bogies or pony trucks had been thought essential for fast passenger work, not only to support part of the weight of the locomotive but also to guide it into curves. All-adhesion Bo-Bo locomotives, which constituted the majority of French electrics, were considered suitable only for medium-speed work. Two notable Swiss designs changed the status of the all-adhesion locomotive. In 1946 Swiss Federal Railways introduced the 56t "Re4/4I" Bo-Bo, designed for speeds up to 78mph (125km/h). This class soon attracted attention by its ability to haul trains of 400t at its maximum permitted speed, while, two year earlier the Lötschberg railway had introduced its 80t Bo-Bo, classified "Ae4/4". The success of these classes established the respectability of the double-bogie locomotive for express work, and SNCF commissioned two Bo-Bo machines from Swiss makers, based on the Lötschberg design, together with two Bo-Bo and two Co-Co machines from French builders.

The Co-Co was produced by Alsthom to a specification based on the requirements of the PLM electrification. This called for speeds up to 100mph (160km/h) on the level with 600t, 87mph (140km/h) on the level with 850t, and the ability to start a 600t train on a 1-in-125 (0.8 per cent) gradient and haul it at 75mph (120km/h) on that gradient.

The locomotive has a motor for each axle mounted in the bogie frame, with Alsthom spring drive. The novelty in the bogie was in the pivoting and in the axle guides. The pivots are of Alsthom design, and comprise two vertical links situated mid-way between the pairs of axles on the centre line of the bogie, with their ends resting in conical rubber seatings. Lateral movement of each link is controlled by two horizontal springs. The springs have two effects; when the body of the locomotive swings outward on curves, they provide a restoring force resisting centrifugal action, and when the bogie rotates, the links swing in opposite directions, and exert forces tending to restore the bogie to the straight line. Thus, if the bogie rotates on straight track due to irregularities in the permanent way, the action of the springs tends to damp this motion and discourage the flanges from striking the rails.

Each axlebox is restrained by two horizontal links, which allow vertical movement but not fore-and-aft movement, and they eliminate the wearing surfaces of traditional steam-type axleboxes. End movement of the axles is controlled by stiff springs fitted between the ends of the axles and the axlebox cover plates. These springs reduce the shocks transmitted to the bogie frame when the flanges strike the rails. Extensive use was made of rubber in the pivots of the suspension system, which was unusual at that date.

The electrical equipment was notable for the large number of running notches, made possible by the large amount of field weakening. The clean external lines were enhanced by the two-tone blue livery, set off by light metal beading of the window frames and of the horizontal flashing.

The two locomotives, Nos. CC7001-2, were delivered in 1949 and were subjected to intensive testing on the Paris-Bordeaux main line, which was then the longest electrified line in France. Early in these tests, No. 7001 hauled a train of 170t from Paris to Bordeaux at an average speed of 81.4mph (131km/h), reaching a maximum of 105.6mph (170km/h), which was a world record performance for an electric locomotive and a token of more stirring events to come.

After three years of testing, orders were placed for a further 35 locomotives, differing in detail from Nos. 7001-2. They were delivered in 1952, and are numbered from 7101 to 7135. A further order for 23 brought the class of a total of 60. Compared with Nos. 7001-2 the production units had an increase in maximum power from 4,000hp (2,980kW) to 4,740hp (3,540kW), and the weight increased from 96t to 107t. Compared with the "9100" class

2-Do-2, the adhesive weight had increased from 88t to 107t, but the axleload had fallen from 22t to 17.8t, so that the locomotive was much kinder to the track. Six of the locomotives were fitted with collecting shoes for working on the former PLM line from Culoz to Modane (the Mont Cenis route), which was at that time equipped with third rail current collection.

Electrification from Paris to Lyons was completed in 1952, and the "7100" class then shared with the "9100" 2-Do-2s the heaviest and fastest runs. By the summer of 1954 there were three runs between Paris and Dijon or Paris and Lyons booked at 77.1mph (124km/h) start-to-stop with permissible loads of 650t. Another run from Paris to Dijon was booked at 76.1mph (122.4km/h) with 730t. These were the outstanding speed exploits in Europe at the time—on a railway which 10 years before was devastated by war.

In February 1954 the first very high-speed tests were made with No. CC7121 in standard condition, on a level stretch between Dijon and Beaune. The purpose of the tests was to investigate the effect of high speed on various parameters, including the forces exerted on the rails and the behaviour of the pantograph. With a train of 111t a speed of 151mph (243km/h) was reached, which was a world record for any type of traction, beating the figure of 143mph (230km/h) attained in 1931 in Germany by a curious propellor-driven railcar.

Testing then moved to the former PO railway, where a long stretch of almost straight line was available south of Bordeaux. First the problem of picking up a very heavy current was investigated with two "7100" class locomotives double-heading. With the line voltage boosted by 25 per cent, these two reached 121mph (195km/h) with 714t and 125mph (201km/h) with 617t.

The next target was a speed of 300km/h (185mph), for which purpose No. CC7107 was fitted with gears of higher ratio than normal. The train comprised three coaches weighing 100t, with a streamlined tail attached to the rear vehicle. The target of 300km/h was reached in 21km (13 miles) from the start, and was maintained for 12km (7½ miles), but, very remarkably, speed rose to 330.8km/h (205.6mph) for 2km (1¼ miles), which required an output of 12,000hp (8,950kW). Equally remarkably, the performance was repeated exactly on the following day by an 81t Bo-Bo, No. BB9004, one of the French-built experimental locomotives mentioned earlier. The two locomotives thus became joint world record holders, and as subsequent developments in very high-speed trains have been with railcar-type units, it is likely that this record for locomotives will stand.

The achievement of No. BB9004 was significant; a locomotive costing little more than half a "7100" had achieved the same performance, such was the pace of locomotive development at this time. French activity was then concentrated on four-axle machines, and no more six-axle electric locomotives were built until 1964, by which time design had changed greatly with introduction of the monomotor bogie.

Although the Co-Co locomotives were soon overshadowed by their smaller successors, they took a full share in express work on the former PLM for many years, and in 1982 No. CC7001 became the first French locomotive to cover 8 million km (4.97 million miles), at an overall average of 658km (409 miles) per day.

Above: *French National Railways' Class CC7100 Co-Co 1,500V dc electric locomotive at Paris (Gare de Lyon) in February 1979.*

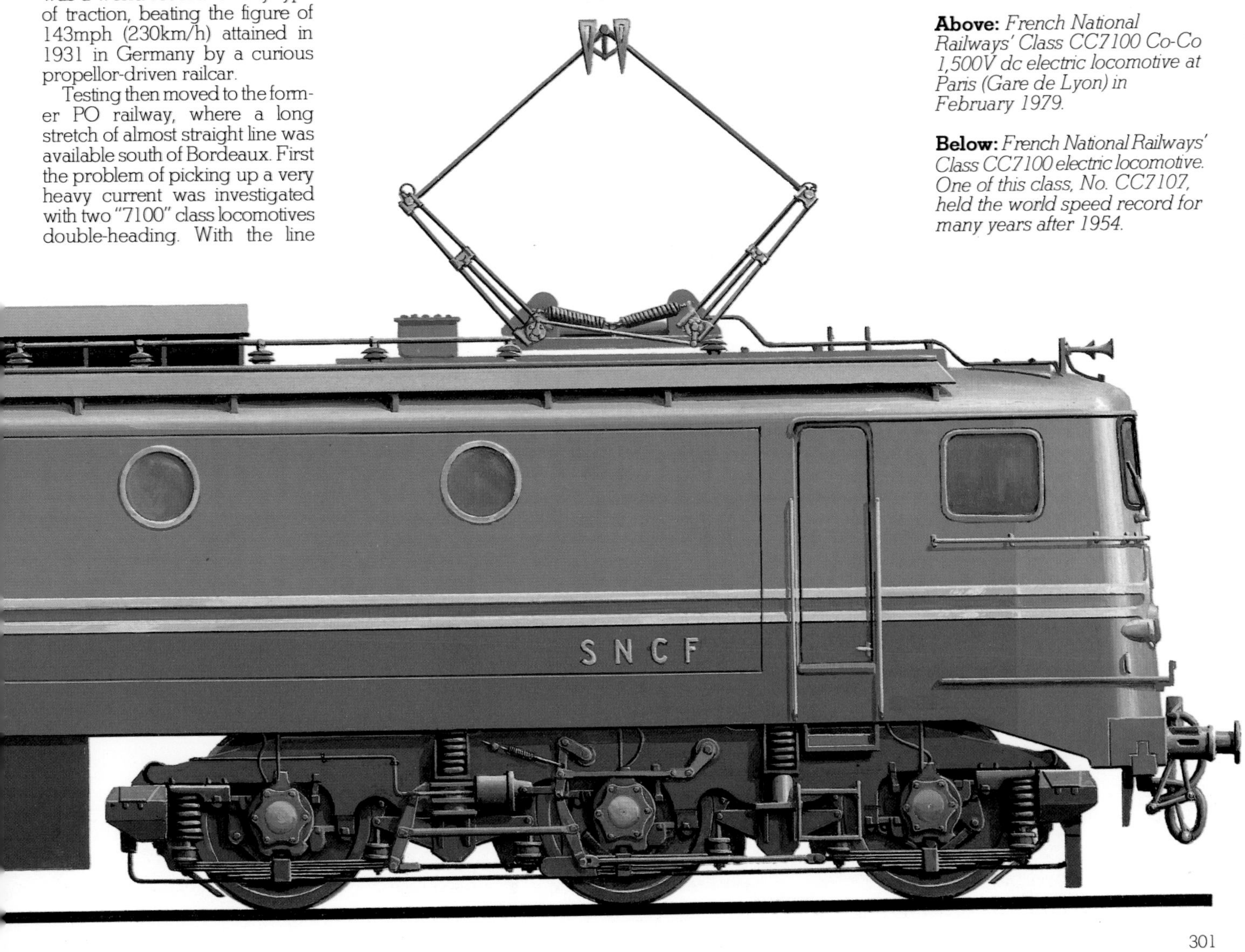

Below: *French National Railways' Class CC7100 electric locomotive. One of this class, No. CC7107, held the world speed record for many years after 1954.*

Class EM2 C_o-C_o

Great Britain: British Railways (BR), 1954

Type: Electric express-passenger locomotive.
Gauge: 4ft 8½in (1,435mm).
Propulsion: Direct current at 1,500V supplied via overhead catenary to six 490hp (366kW) nose-suspended traction motors, one geared to each axle.
Weight: 217,280lb (97t).
Max. axleload: 36,288lb (16.2t).
Overall length: 59ft 4½in (18,000mm).
Tractive effort: 44,600lb (198kN).
Max. speed: 84mph (134km/h).

Seven of these solid reliable machines (inappropriately named after rather flighty Greek godesses) were built in 1958 by British Railways at Gorton Works in order to work the sparse passenger services over the then newly-electrified 70-mile (112km) line across the Pennine Hills from Manchester to Sheffield. Who would then have guessed that the time would come when top luxury international expresses on the continent of Europe would begin their journeys behind one of them?

Before World War II the London & North Eastern Railway put in hand with govenment assistance an ambitious scheme to electrify the busy coal-hauling route from South Yorkshire via the Woodhead tunnel to Manchester. There were major problems with steam haulage over the line but work on the project had to cease with the outbreak of war. Afterwards, a decision to resume was delayed first by nationalisation and later by a state organisation being more cautious (after all, it was someone else's money) and finding it necessary to bore a new 3-mile (4.8km) double-track tunnel for the electric trains. Accordingly, electric traction was not introduced until 1954. The LNER had been intending to re-employ on this project the North Eastern Bo-Bo locomotives already described, but BR discarded them in favour of increasing the fleet of new freight locomotives of dissimilar appearance but similar configuration.

Extravagances over matters like these were accompanied by penny-pinching on more basic things such as reballasting the permanent way, and inevitably the result was an unhappy object lesson in the effects of the heavy unsprung weight of nose-suspended motors on weak track. This did not matter as regards

Above: *Ex-British Railways EM2 class electric locomotive at Hook of Holland, with "Lorelei Express" to Basel, May 1971.*

Class 4E 1-C_o-C_o-1

South Africa: South African Railways (SAR), 1954

Type: Electric mixed-traffic locomotive.
Gauge: 3ft 6in (1,067mm).
Propulsion: Direct current at 3,000V fed via overhead catenary and rheostatic control to six 505hp (377kW) nose-suspended traction motors, each geared with resilient gearwheels to one driving axle.
Weight: 288,960lb (131.1t) adhesive, 347,200lb (157.5t) total.
Max. axleload: 48,160lb (21.85t).
Overall length: 71ft 8in (21,844mm).
Tractive effort: 72,000lb (320kN).
Max. speed: 60mph (97km/h).

It almost says enough about the foresight, continuity and restraint of those who made the decisions about South African Railways' extensive electrification, that after 25 years they had only reached their fourth locomotive class. Even so, these Class "4Es" represented a brief excursion away from plain double-bogie designs by adding to a double six-wheel bogie locomotive guiding pony wheels at the outer ends. Otherwise the same solid, reliable, well-tried technology took great trains effortlessly up the long and severe climb on to the high African central plateau and across the wild Karoo as brings suburban daily-breaders up to London from Sevenoaks or Surbiton.

North British of Glasgow and General Electric of Manchester supplied 40 of these locomotives to South African Railways in 1954 to work traffic on a 149-mile (238km) extension of electrification to Touws River. The new locos represented a 12½ per cent increase in power output over the previous best on the system. A 1,000t (1,100 US tons) freight train could be started and hauled up a 1-in-66 (1.5 per cent) grade at 25mph (40km/h) by these locomotives.

An implicit part of the scheme was a realignment of the notorious climb up the Hex River Pass, so as to improve the gradient from 1-in-40 (2.5 per cent) to this 1-in-66, and the capacity of the locomotives had been designed accordingly. However, construction of the new line was delayed and electric trains had to use the old one, hence double-heading was necessary. Fortunately multiple-unit capability was available and so the second locomotive did not need a second crew. At the end of the steepest portion, the second locomotive could be dispensed with and it was the economical

Below: *South African Railways' Class 4E 1-Co-Co-1 electric locomotive built by North British of Glasgow and General Electric of Manchester in 1954.*

slow-moving mineral trains, but passenger trains hauled by the fine new electric locomotive had to face a semi-permanent speed restriction of 60mph (96km/h) or so over the whole line. And this on a railway region whose steam trains regularly exceeded 100mph (160km/h)!

In 1968, through passenger traffic between Manchester and Sheffield was transferred to another route and so, after what would have been a fair life for a diesel but was barely a moment in time for an electric, the "EM2s" became redundant, other possible routes having been electrified on different systems. Happily a buyer appeared who found the locomotives to his liking and after a few details had been attended to (fitting of electric train heating, air brakes and different vigilance equipment as well as a major overhaul) the "EM2s" have become Netherlands Railways (NS) Class "1500".

The intention was that these locomotives should be an economical stop-gap to cover a temporary power shortage in The Netherlands. It does not, however, seem to have turned out like that; the "EM2s" robust simplicity has found much favour and a further lease of life is now expected. For example, the use of resilient gearwheels to connect the axle-mounted motors to the wheels has ameliorated much of the bad effect on the track of this simple convenient arrangement, whilst still retaining its simplicity. Further simplification has been possible, too, since the original Metropolitan-Vickers electrical equipment provided for regenerative braking, appropriate for the mountain grades of the "EM2s" native heath. For use in the flatlands of Holland the relevant apparatus could be dispensed with, as also could the vacuum-brake exhauster and the electrically-fired steam-heat boiler.

As a postscript, 1981 saw complete closure of the 1,500V dc route from Manchester to Sheffield, apart from a suburban service to Hadfield and Glossop at the Manchester end. As a result, the freight version of the "EM2"—"EM1", later Class "76"—went to the scrap heap.

Above: *British Railways' Class EM2 Co-Co electric locomotive supplied for working between Manchester and Sheffield.*

practice to shunt it into an unmanned siding there. The next suitable train proceeding downhill would then collect a locomotive and use it to assist braking, using the regenerative electric system with which the "4Es" were equipped. Naturally, straight air brakes were provided for the locomotive and vacuum brake equipment for the train. The latter brake is automatically applied should there be an electrical failure during regeneration.

Right: *Class 4E locomotive No. 219. Although railways in South Africa are narrow-gauge, the locomotives are as big and as heavy as any in Europe.*

Class 12000 B_o-B_o

France:
French National Railways (SNCF), 1954

Type: Mixed-traffic electric locomotive.
Gauge: 4ft 8½in (1,435mm).
Propulsion: Alternating current at 25,000V 50Hz passed through transformer and mercury arc rectifier to bogie-mounted traction motors with flexible drive to axles; axles of each bogie geared together.
Weight: 188,660lb (85.6t).
Max. axleload: 47,170lb (21.4t).
Overall length: 49ft 10⅜in (1,5200mm).
Tractive effort: 54,000lb (240kN).
Max. speed: 75mph (120km/h).

Above: *A new era of railway traction was ushered in by these Class 12000 electric locomotives.*

At the end of World War II the standard system for main-line electrification in France was 1,500V dc, but French engineers, like those of a number of other countries, were interested in the possibility of using alternating current at the standard industrial frequency of 50Hz. This offered a number of advantages: 50Hz current could be taken from the public supply at any convenient point and only a small transformer would be needed to reduce the voltage to that required for the overhead wires. As alternating current could be reduced on the locomotives by transformer, the supply could be taken from the overhead at high voltage; the higher the voltage, the smaller the current, and the lighter the overhead wires and their supports. With high voltage, the supply points could be spaced more widely, because voltage drops in the line would be proportionately smaller than with a lower-voltage system.

The second most comprehensive test so far made with electric traction at 50Hz was on the Höllenthal line in West Germany, which happened to be in the French zone of occupation after the war. French engineers thus had an opportunity to study closely this line and the results of ten years' operation of it. They formed a favourable opinion of the system, particularly as a means of electrifying lines with lower traffic densities than had previously been considered economic for electrification. SNCF therefore chose for an experimental ac system the line from Aix-les-Bains to La Roche-sur-Foron in Savoy. This was mainly single track without complicated track layouts, but it had gradients sufficiently severe to test the equipment thoroughly. French and Swiss manufacturers supplied a number of locomotives and motor coaches for this conversion, some to work on ac only and some on both ac and dc.

Success of the Savoy scheme led to a bold step forward—conversion of 188 miles (303km) of the Thionville to Valenciennes route in northern France to electric working at 25,000V 50Hz. Although a secondary route, it carried three express trains and up to 100 freight trains in each direction daily, and it had gradients up to 1-in-90 (1.1 per cent).

The ac traction system in West

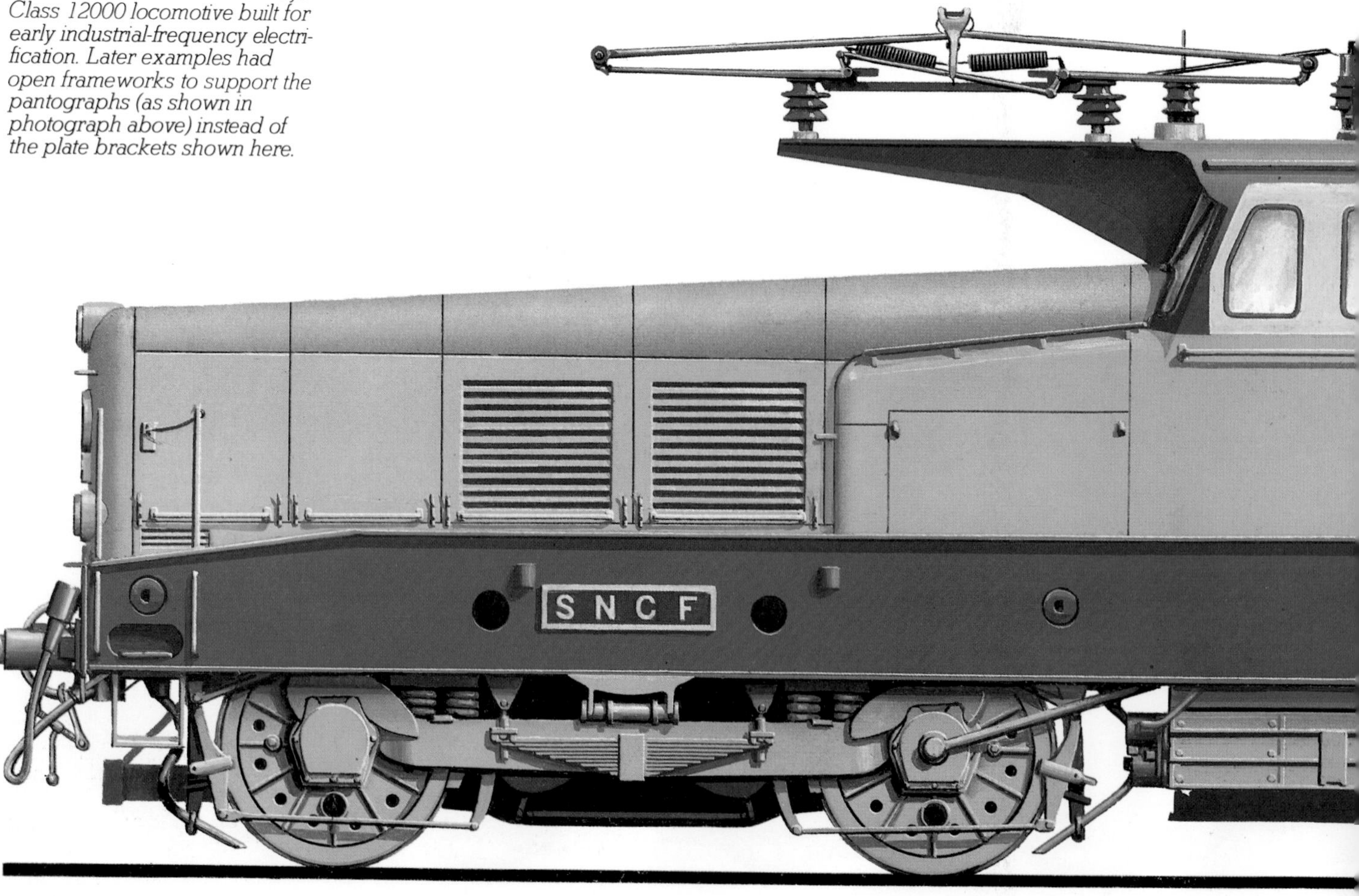

Below: *French National Railways' Class 12000 locomotive built for early industrial-frequency electrification. Later examples had open frameworks to support the pantographs (as shown in photograph above) instead of the plate brackets shown here.*

Germany and Switzerland used current specially generated at 16⅔Hz. A normal type of electric motor as used on dc will operate on ac, but each time the current reverses there are induced effects which tend to upset the working of the commutator. These effects are proportional to the square of the frequency. At 16⅔Hz they can be coped with, but 50Hz is a different proposition, and up to and including the Höllenthal line experiment satisfactory traction motors for this frequency had not been produced, but the target was still worth striving for.

Two main alternatives were available in a 50Hz system: to persevere with 50Hz motors or to convert the supply to some other form on the locomotive for supply to the traction motors. In fact SNCF decided to test four arrangements, conversion to dc by static convertor, direct use of the 50Hz supply, conversion to dc by rotary convertor, and conversion to three-phase by rotary machines.

For this purpose four types of locomotive were designed, two B-Bs for the first two systems and two Co-Cos for the second two. Of these systems the simplest was the second, for as with the 16⅔Hz locomotives in other countries, it involved only a transformer to step down the voltage to a value suitable for the motors, and a tap changer on the transformer to vary the voltage. For the ac to dc conversion by static convertor the Ignitron was selected. This was a form of steel-tank mercury-pool rectifier developed by Westinghouse in the United States. The two types of Co-Co locomotive had heavier equipment involving one or more rotating machines. The four classes were designated "12000", "13000", "14000", and "14100" respectively.

Layout of the locomotives was unusual in that they had centre cabs, an arrangement normally found only on shunting locomotives. The main reason for this was that SNCF had found that 50 per cent of failures of equipment in electric locomotives on the road were in the control equipment. With cabs at both ends of the locomotive, remote control of equipment was unavoidable, but with a central cab, in which the driver could use the same controls for both directions of travel, some of the equipment could be controlled directly. Further advantages were the good all-round view and more protection for the driver in collisions. A conspicuous feature of the locomotives was the platform mounted on the cab roof, and protruding beyond it, to support the pantographs.

Bogies of the B-B locomotives were derived from those of the experimental high-speed B-B machines, Nos. 9003-4, with the axles geared together, but as the new locomotives were intended for lower speeds than Nos. 9003-4, the bogie was shortened and the suspension simplified. For the Thionville line it was sufficient for one of the four classes to be capable of express passenger work, so the "12000s" were geared for 75mph (120km/h), the "13000s" for 65mph (104km/h) and the two C-C types for 37mph (60km/h).

The first of the "12000" class, No. 12001, was delivered in July 1954 and was put to work immediately on passenger and freight trains ranging from 500t to 1,300t. Control of voltage to the motors was by a tap changer on the high-tension side of the transformer as is common in ac practice. On test No. 12006 achieved some remarkable results. It started a train of 2,424t on a gradient of 1-in-100 (1 per cent), with a maximum tractive effort of 38t, or 47 per cent of the adhesive weight. At 8.5km/h the tractive effort was still 33.7t. These were outstanding figures, and the ability of the locomotive to sustain this high tractive effort, just on the point of slipping, but without actually "losing its feet", was considered to be a notable achievement of the Ignitron control in conjunction with the gearing together of the axles on each bogie. The other classes performed well, but not so well as the "12000s", and furthermore the "12000s" proved to be the most reliable.

The other classes were not extended beyond the initial orders, but a total of 148 of Class "12000" were eventually built. The success of the Thionville-Valenciennes scheme led to a major policy decision—that future electrification, except for certain extensions of existing dc routes, would be on ac at 25,000V 50Hz. The first scheme to be affected by this decision was the main line of the former Nord Railway, and this scheme met the Thionville route at its northern extremity. The last of the "12000" class were ordered as part of the Nord scheme.

Before construction of the class was complete, there was a major development in electrical equipment with introduction of the silicon diode rectifier. This was a simpler, more compact and more robust piece of equipment than the ignitron, and well suited to the rough life of equipment on a locomotive. The last 15 of the "12000s" were built with silicon rectifiers, and others have been converted over the years. As the most successful and the most numerous of the four types for the Thionville electrification, these locomotives still dominate traffic on that route.

Experience with these four classes settled finally the type of traction equipment to be used on a future ac lines. Once again, the direct 50Hz motors proved unsatisfactory, whilst the simplicity of the silicon rectifier ruled out decisively any system with rotating machinery.

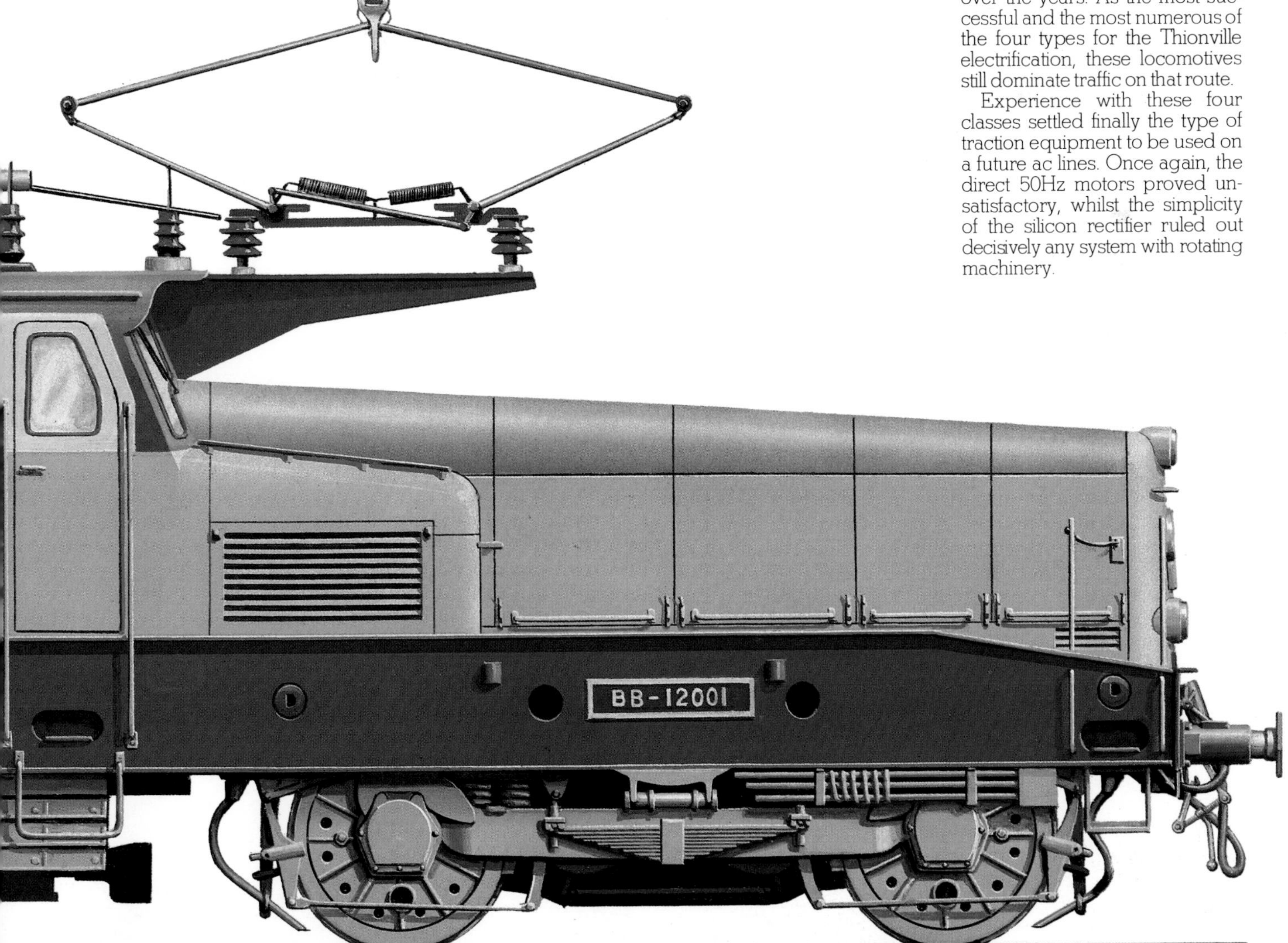

FL9 B_o-A1A

USA: New York, New Haven & Hartford RR (New Haven), 1960

Type: Electro-diesel passenger locomotive.
Gauge: 4ft 8½in (1,435mm).
Propulsion: General Motors 1,750hp (1,350kW) Type 567C V-16 two-stroke diesel engine and generator—or alternatively outside third-rail—feeding current to four nose-suspended traction motors geared to both axles of the leading truck and the outer axles of the trailing one.
Weight: 231,937lb (105.2t) adhesive, 286,614lb (130t) total.
Max. axleload: 57,984lb (26.3t).
Overall length: 59ft 0in. (17,983mm).
Tractive effort: 58,000lb (258kN).
Max. speed: 70mph (112km/h).

These unusual and interesting machines, like a number of others, were the result of that famous ordinance of the City of New York prohibiting the use therein of locomotives which emitted fumes. It occurred like this: the New Haven railroad was in the 1950s considering abandonment of its path-finding single-phase electrification, which dates from as early as 1905, and changing over to diesel traction. The only problem was how to run into New York.

New Haven trains used both the Grand Central terminal (of the New York Central RR) and the Pennsylvania Station. Both routes were equipped with conductor rails (of different patterns) supplying low-voltage direct current. This corresponded closely to the current produced in the generator of a diesel-electric locomotive and it

Mv A1A-A1A

Denmark: Danish State Railways (DSB), 1954

Type: Diesel-electric mixed-traffic locomotive.
Gauge: 4ft 8½in (1,435mm).
Propulsion: General Motors Electro-Motive Division Type 567C 1,700hp (1,268kW) 16-cylinder two-stroke diesel engine and generator supplying current to four nose-suspended traction motors, one geared to each of the outer axles of the two bogies.
Weight: 154,280lb (70t) adhesive, 227,675lb (103.3t) total.
Max. axleload: 38,570lb (17.5t).
Overall length: 62ft 0in (18,900mm).
Tractive effort: 39,700lb (176kN).
Max. speed: 83mph (133km/h).

Danish State Railways were not strangers to diesel-electric motive power—their excellent *Lyntog* or "Lightning" trains had been running since the 1930s. By 1954 the time had come to put a tentative toe in the water and order a small batch of five large modern diesels for main line locomotive-hauled passenger and freight trains. With commendable good sense they settled on more or less standard locomotives of US design produced by General Motors Electro-Motive Division, then almost the only really experienced diesel locomotive builders in the world. They were actually supplied by the Swedish locomotive-building firm of Nydqvist & Holm, better known as Nohab, who had a licence to produce EMD products in Europe. By taking bits out of EMD's comprehensive Meccano set, Nohab were able quickly to put together a suitable package for DSB. The locomotives, classified "Mv" were basically "F" cab units, but with the car body modified so that there was a driving cab at both ends. To reduce the axleload to the lower values appropriate to Europe, six-wheel trucks each with a central unmotored axle were provided. They were the same as those used on EMD's "E" units, but for differences in the springing. Indeed apart from buf-

Right: *General Motors A1A-A1A diesel-electric locomotive built by the Swedish firm of Nydqvist & Holm under licence for Danish State Railways.*

was suggested that a standard General Motors "FP9" passenger cab unit could be modified easily to work as an electric locomotive when required. The ac electrification could then be dismantled, yet trains could continue to run without breaking the law. In fact axleload restrictions led to one quite substantial change—substitution of a three-axle trailing truck for the standard two-axle one; hence a unique wheel arrangement. The end product was designated "FL9" and 60 were supplied between 1956 and 1960. The most obvious evidence of their unique arrangements were the two-position retractable collecting shoes mounted on the trucks, to cater for New York Central's under-contact conductor rail and Long Island RR's top-contact one. Otherwise the presence of additional low-voltage control gear inside the body was the principal technical difference between an "FP9" and an "FL9".

In the event the New Haven changed its mind over dispensing with the electrification, but the "FL9s" still found employment, surviving long enough to be taken over by Amtrak in the 1970s. While they existed, the "FL9s" represented a spark of originality in a country whose locomotives were and are much of a muchness (apart from their livery) from Oregon to Florida or Arizona to Maine.

Below: *New York, New Haven & Hartford Class FL9 Bo-A1A electro-diesel locomotive. These locomotives could run on current drawn from two types of third rail in New York City.*

fers, screw couplings and a Danish Royal Crown on each end, everything was totally trans-Atlantic.

It was Nohab's secret how much they did themselves and how much came over ready-assembled from EMD, but DSB made it clear they liked what they got by ordering a production batch of 54, more or less identical but with uprated engines developing 1,950hp (1,455kW). This was Class "My". Not only that, but other locomotives subsequently ordered followed the same recipe. Next came 45 of the 1,425hp (1,063kW) "MX" class and then, more recently, 46 of 3,300 to 3,900hp (2,462 to 2,910kW) "MZ" class of 1967-79. Locomotives very similar to the "Mv/My" classes went to Norway, Belgium and Hungary, and many other countries and railway administrations were to follow this excellent principle of buying locomotives off-the-shelf from the most experienced people in the business.

Left: *The Norwegian State Railways also had locomotives similar to the Danish Mv and My classes. Here is No. 3.641 at Andalsnes in August 1981.*

V200 B-B

West Germany:
German Federal Railway (DB), 1953

Type: Diesel-hydraulic express passenger locomotive.
Gauge: 4ft 8½in (1,435mm).
Propulsion: Two 1,100hp (820kW) diesel engines each driving the axles of one bogie through Voith hydraulic transmission.
Weight: 162,000lb (73.5t).
Max. axleload: 40,500lb (18.4t).
Overall length: 60ft 7in (18,470mm).
Tractive effort: 52,680lb (234kN).
Max. speed: 87mph (140km/h).

A major discouragement to the development of large diesel locomotives in the 1930s was their great weight in relation to power. By comparison with later diesel-electric locomotives, it can be seen that there were three main contributions to this weight. First the low speed of the engines; secondly heavy electrical equipment; and thirdly body construction based on steam locomotive practice with all the strength in the underframe. Apart from North America, where permissible axle-loads were up to 50 per cent greater than elsewhere, a large diesel locomotive of the 1930s inevitably had several carrying axles because the total weight was well above what was needed for adhesion.

German engineers tackled the first of these factors by developing higher-speed engines, and the second by developing hydraulic transmissions, which were inherently lighter and simpler to control than the electrical type. By 1939 many hydraulic transmissions had been made for shunting locomotives and a 1,400hp (1,040kW) 1-C-1 locomotive had been built in 1937. Further experience was gained from large numbers of locomotives in the power range 130 to 360hp which were built for the German forces.

After World War II construction of diesel-hydraulic locomotives was resumed, and the new Deutsche Bundesbahn began to develop larger units to replace steam traction on routes not scheduled for electrification. A decisive step forward was taken in 1952 with construction of a batch of 10 B-B locomotives of 800 to 1,100hp (600 to 820kW) in which three types of engine were fitted at various times. The transmission was made by Voith, who supplied about 70 per cent of all German hydraulic transmissions, and the weight was kept down to 57t by use of lightweight inside-framed bogies, by careful body design, and by extensive use of welding. The class was originaly known as "V80", later becoming "280", and with a maximum speed of 62mph (100km/h) it was intended for freight and secondary passenger work.

The "V80" design was prepared by Krauss Maffei in conjunction with DB. Although no more locomotives of this class were built, the same firm now produced a design for an express passenger B-B locomotive incorporating two 1,100hp engines, and capable of 87mph (140km/h). Each engine drove the axles of one bogie through a Voith transmission. The main structural members were two steel tubes, and the casing was of a distinctive streamlined form, the upper part tapered to suit the loading gauge. Five prototypes were built in 1953, with three different makes of 1,100hp engine, giving total weights of 70.5 to 73.5t. For the period, this gave a quite remarkable power-to-weight ratio. The class was designated "V200", later becoming Nos. 220.001-5.

After three years of testing, a production batch of 50 locomotives was ordered and delivery

Right: *German Federal Railway Class V200 diesel-hydraulic loco near Lingen in 1976.*

ChS2 Co-Co

USSR:
Soviet Railways (SZD), 1958

Type: Electric express passenger locomotive.
Gauge: 5ft 0in (1,524mm).
Propulsion: Direct current at 3,000V fed via overhead catenary and rheostatic control system to six 828hp (618kW) traction motors driving the axles through Skoda pattern flexible drives and gearing.
Weight: 271,080lb (123t).
Max. axleload: 45,185lb (20.5t).
Overall length: 62ft 1in (18,920mm).
Tractive effort: 70,500lb (314kN).
Max. speed: 100mph (160km/h).

For many years after World War II, the pace of electrification in the USSR was such that locomotive building plants were fully occupied constructing electric locomotives for freight traffic. To obtain motive power for working electric passenger trains the Soviet Union had to look to imports, and fortunately a source was conveniently to hand in one of its satellite countries. This was the world-famous Skoda Works in Pilsen, Czechoslovakia, whose products could compete with any of those of the great industrial nations.

Two prototypes were built in 1958 for trial purposes. Evaluation was satisfactory and production began in 1962. It did not end until 1972, after a quite amazing 944 units had been built of this very plain and straightforward design. Later examples had rheostatic (dynamic) braking as an additional feature and locomotives so fitted are designated "ChS2T" instead of "ChS".

Unusual features were few, but of interest is the glass-fibre bodywork, more or less to European rather than Russian profile. As a result the pantographs have to be mounted on stilts high above the roof to compensate for the fact that the USSR loading gauge is some 2ft (600mm) higher than the European one. Top speed is 100mph (160km/h), but on few lines outside the Moscow to Leningrad trunk is such fast running relevant to day-by-day operation.

Having said that "ChS2T" production ended in 1972, it did in fact continue but with a version so different as to constitute another class, but rather confusingly not so designated. These later examples have a tall steel body, taking advantage of the full height of the SZD loading gauge. Consequently the appearance is completely different, while the electrical equipment offers 30 per cent more installed horsepower.

To add further confusion, similar-looking Skoda locomotives

began in 1956. Three makes of engine could be fitted, but the majority were of Maybach manufacture. The "V200s" proved to be very successful machines, and little trouble was experienced with the transmission equipment for five to six years. In 1960 loadings of trains were increased, and track improvements enabled the locomotives to run greater mileages at their maximum speed. A crop of transmission failures now occurred, which were traced to inadequate lubrication of part of the Voith transmission. This defect was remedied and in 1962 the class averaged 145,000 miles (233,000km) per locomotive on duties which were 30 per cent more onerous than the performance specified for the design. They were capable of hauling 700t on the level at 62mph (100km/h) and a 305t train at a sustained 50mph (80km/h) on a 1-in-100 gradient.

A further batch of 50 locomotives was now built with larger engines of 1,350hp. A number of improvements were made to the design, including the bogies, and the weight was between 78 and 79.5t. These units went into service in 1962. By the early 1980s further electrification had made some of the "V200" series redundant, and several were sold. The remaining units were concentrated in northern Germany.

Although German locomotives were designed with an eye to the export market, few of the twin-engined machines were exported. Their largest application outside West Germany was on the Western Region of British Railways, but those locomotives were built in Britain.

Right: *A Class V200 diesel hydraulic locomotive No. 220 023-6 leaves Aalen with a German Federal Railway Nuremburg to Stuttgart express in Autumn 1969.*

Below: *For use on lines which are not electrified, the German Federal Railway developed powerful diesel-hydraulic locomotives instead of the diesel-electric designs favoured in other countries.*

(classes "ChS4" and "ChS4T") have been built for 25,000V 50Hz lines in the Soviet Union. Quite distinctive in appearance, but belonging to the same family, is a still experimental small batch of double Bo-Bo+Bo-Bo locomotives for the dc lines, with a power output of 10,720hp (8,400kW). These Class "ChS200" machines are geared for 125mph (200km/h) running, ready for the day when such speeds can be offered to SZD's patient customers.

Right: *Czech-built Class ChS2 electric locomotive on trials in the USSR at Kalinin on the October Railway, 1959.*

Class 30* A1A-A1A

Great Britain: British Railways (BR), 1957

Type: Mixed-traffic diesel-electric locomotive.
Gauge: 4ft 8½in (1,435mm).
Propulsion: Mirrlees 1,250hp (933kW) JVST12T 12-cylinder Vee diesel engine and generator supplying direct current to four nose-suspended traction motors geared to the outer axles of the bogies.
Weight: 163,100lb (74t) adhesive, 232,520lb (105.5t) total.
Max. axleload: 40,775lb (18.5t).
Overall length: 56ft 9in (17,297mm).
Tractive effort: 42,800lb (190kN).
Max. speed: 80mph (128km/h).

*As classified in 1968; later, these locos were re-engined and became Class 31.

These low-key machines were some of the very earliest to be supplied under British Railways' so-called pilot scheme for dieselisation, under which a multitude of builders were asked to supply locomotives of various powers and weights. Orders for this programme were placed in late-1955. Brush Engineering of Loughborough based the design on a batch of 25 locomotives supplied to Ceylon in 1953, and in October 1955 No. D5500, the first of an order of 20, was handed over to British Railways.

Originally a Mirrlees 1,250hp (933kW) engine was fitted, but later examples had the more powerful 1,470hp (1,097kW) English Electric 12VV 12-cylinder Vee engine, which later became standard for the whole batch, leading eventually to reclassification as Class "31". One unusual feature of an otherwise very conventional machine was addition of an idle axle between each pair of driving axles to reduce axleload. Steam heating boilers were fitted as well as the usual vacuum train brake equipment. The bogies are one-piece steel castings and they and the underframes were supplied by Beyer Peacock of Manchester.

Although they possessed a quite extraordinarily low power-to-weight ratio of only 11.8hp (8.8kW) per tonne of locomotive weight, the recipe of solid, simple, conventional engineering was in one way successful, for over the years this class proved itself one of the most reliable in the whole of BR's diesel fleet. This in spite of the fact that one disgraced itself by failing when hauling HM The Queen on the first occasion that the Royal Train was entrusted to diesel traction. However, steam came quickly to the rescue and the incident was soon forgotton.

More important was that the class was good enough to be built up to a total of 362 over the years, and that even today well over 200 are still giving good service as Class "31", although withdrawal is proceeding slowly. Even so, it has been thought worthwhile to make improvements to 24 of them (sub-class "31.4") which have been modernised by provision of dual air and vacuum brakes, and electric train-heating equipment.

Right: *British Railways' Class 31 A1A-A1A diesel-electric locomotive at York, September 1982.*

Below: *British Railways' No. D5603 at Oakleigh Park on the Welwyn to King's Cross train.*

Kodama 8-car Trainset

Japan: Japanese National Railways (JNR), 1958

Type: Express passenger electric train.
Gauge: 3ft 6in (1,067mm).
Propulsion: Direct current at 1,500V supplied via overhead catenary to two power cars and then fed to sixteen 135hp (100kW) traction motors, geared to the axles of the two power cars and to those of two adjacent cars.
Weight: 322,560lb (146t) adhesive, 609,280lb (276t) total.
Max. axleload: 21,280lb (9.6t).
Overall length: 546ft 0in (166,420mm).
Max. speed: 75mph (120km/h).

Electrification of the Tokaido line, the most important in Japan and connecting the capital with the city of Osaka, was an opportunity for the railway to take a considerable step forward. It is generally assumed that high speeds cannot be run on narrow-gauge tracks. Of course, the two things are not necessarily interdependent—it is more that heavy well-maintained track is not common on narrow-gauge railways. So far the best achievement had been by steam before 1939 in the island of Java where 70mph (120km/h) was run, but these spectacular Japanese trains—known as *Kodama* or "Echo"—are something else again. The 344 miles (553km) from Tokyo to Osaka were timed in 6hr 50min, an average speed of 50mph (80km/h), certainly a record for any narrow-gauge line.

The two outer cars of each eight-car unit, which look as if they do the work, are in fact mere driving trailers. The main power

Right: *Japanese National Railways' eight-car "Kodama" high-speed electric train.*

cars are the second and seventh; traction motors are provided on the bogies of the power cars and the adjacent cars (the third and sixth). In each of the latter a small buffet is provided. The two centre cars are plain trailers providing 104 second-class seats. The rest of the train provides seating for 321 third-class passengers. Features provided for the benefit of travellers include air coolers fitted on the roof for use in hot weather, drinking water, telephone booths, earphones for receiving radio programmes and even speedometers in the buffet cars. Impressed as the first travellers must have been by 120km/h plus, little did they know that in a few years they would regard such speeds by a train on this route as practically standing still.

Right: *The streamlined nose and conning-tower of a Japanese "Kodama" (Echo) trainset.*

These *Kodama* trains (now Class "481") became the prototypes for a dynasty of high-speed electric self-propelled trains that relatively soon were to provide the majority of express services in Japan on the state-owned narrow-gauge lines. Twelve-car units came soon, as well as sets which could also run on lines electrified with alternating current at standard industrial frequency. Things were further complicated by the fact that different areas of Japan have different standards in this respect —necessitating tri-current power equipment for dc and 50Hz and 60Hz ac. Even so, the challenge was met in providing for this requirement without encroaching on all-important revenue space. In addition to the electric sets, some diesel-hydraulic trains of similar appearance have been built for use on non-electrified lines.

Class 40 1-C_o-C_o-1 Great Britain: British Railways (BR), 1958

Type: Mixed-traffic diesel-electric locomotive.
Gauge: 4ft 8½in (1,435mm).
Propulsion: English Electric 2,000hp (1,480kW) Type SVT V-16 four-stroke turbocharged diesel engine and generator supplying current to six 240hp (180kW) nose-suspended traction motors geared to the main axles.
Weight: 238,032lb (100t) adhesive, 293,132lb (134t) total.
Max. axleload: 29,672lb (18t).
Overall length: 69ft 6in (21,037mm).
Tractive effort: 52,000lb (231kN).
Max. speed: 90mph (145km/h).

After the formation of British Railways in 1948, the controlling body, the Railway Executive, decided that its motive power policy would be based on the use of home-produced fuel. As Britain had little indigenous oil at that time, this implied that steam traction would be retained until electrification was possible. There was an exception in that the use of diesel shunters would be extended, as experience on the LMS had shown marked economies despite the use of imported fuel. The five main-line diesel-electric locomotives which BR acquired from the LMS and SR therefore commanded little interest, although they were used as fully as circumstances permitted, and gave valuable information to BR engineers. The fifth of these locomotives, No. 10203, which was the third of the SR machines, incorporated some important changes from the preceding four, notably in having a 2,000hp engine. This pointed the way ahead, but no immediate steps were taken to incorporate the lessons learned from No. 10203 in an up-to-date design.

By 1955 it was clear that the deteriorating quality of coal, and the difficulty of getting labour for the more disagreeable tasks of steam locomotive maintenance, made a change of policy urgently necessary. The government therefore agreed to a massive modernisation programme, in which several of the busiest main lines from London would be electrified on the overhead system, the SR third-rail system would be extended, and the whole of the remainder of BR would be turned over to diesel traction. Plans were made for a fleet of diesel locomotives which were to be divided into four main groups, numbered in ascending order of power. The highest was Type 4, which embraced locomotives in the power range 2,000 to 2,300hp; a fifth group was added later to include the 3,300hp "Deltic" locomotives.

At this time Britain had one industrial group, English Electric, which could build complete diesel-electric locomotives, including engines and electrical equipment. It had supplied either complete shunting locomotives, or the engines and electrical equipment for them, to each of the four groups before nationalisation, and also the engines and equipment for the five existing main-line diesels. At first English Electric had built diesel locomotives in its works at Preston, but after World War II it made an agreement to sub-contract the assembly of locomotives to a locomotive manufacturer of great historical importance. This company was an amalgamation of Robert Stephenson, Hawthorn Leslie and the Vulcan Foundry, with a continuous record of steam locomotive construction from 1825. In 1955 this company was absorbed into English Electric.

Apart from English Electric, there were firms which could supply diesel engines, supply electrical equipment, or assemble locomotives, but not all three. A scheme was considered for importing some EMD diesels from the USA, to be followed by the granting of licences for several British companies to build to EMD designs, but this was rejected on political grounds. BR then embarked on a pilot scheme of 171 locomotives of 13 different types. Manufacture of these units was spread over a number of companies, to exploit to the full the expertise and capacity of the industry and of BR's workshops.

Not surprisingly, English Electric received the largest share; 40 locomotives were ordered, including 10 of Type 4. Although English Electric was to execute the detailed design, the broad layout was specified by BR. In view of the urgency of the pilot scheme there was no time for more design work than was absolutely necessary. The Co-Co arrangement of the LMS locomotives was ruled out for general use on BR by its high axleload, and the only tried layout with eight axles was that of the SR locomotives. This design was therefore adopted, including the plate frames of the bogies, the axleboxes closely derived from steam practice, and the segmental pads for transmitting body weight to the bogies. By contemporary diesel and electric standards this was a crude arrangement, but it

Above: *British Railways' Class 40 1-Co-Co-1 diesel-electric locomotive No. 40183 at Scarborough in August 1982.*

Right: *An Aberdeen to Edinburgh express, hauled by No. 40151, leaving Montrose. Note the "arrow" warning board indicating a temporary restriction of speed to 40mph (64km/h).*

had been successful so far on the SR units, and it enabled the axle-load to be kept down to 18t.

The general equipment of the locomotives was very similar to the third SR locomotive, No. 10203, but, as on the LMS main-line diesels, it was thought advisable to position the cabs slightly away from the ends to give the enginemen some protection. Doors were provided in the ends to allow a gangway to connect two locomotives working in multiple, but these were little used and were later removed. All locomotive-hauled passenger trains on BR were at this time steam heated, and the new locomotives not only had a boiler and a large water tank, but also scoops for replenishing the tanks from the water-troughs provided for steam engines.

The 10 locomotives were delivered between March and September 1958, and were divided between the East Coast main line from King's Cross to the north and the former Great Eastern line from London Liverpool Street; they were numbered D200 to D209, and until the introduction of a new classification system in 1971 were generally known as "EE Type 4". Their reception was mixed; they suffered from a number of teething troubles, one of which was indicative of a problem which was to plague BR until steam heating was eliminated — the train-heating boiler. Although unable to equal an LNER or BR Pacific at its very best at high speed, the diesels' high starting tractive effort and high adhesive weight gave them an advantage over steam engines at lower speeds.

More importantly, whatever they could do, they could continue to do for long periods day-in, day-out, and it was this ability which gave them a lead over indifferently-maintained and poorly-fuelled steam engines. They soon undertook daily workings which were well beyond the capacity of contemporary British steam, although, as was often demonstrated during the teething troubles of the diesels, steam engines could approach their performance remarkably closely when given special attention.

Before the first 10 locomotives had been delivered, political pressure was applied to BR to accelerate the elimination of steam, and despite the intention to test the pilot-scheme locomotives thoroughly before placing further orders, five more orders had been placed for "EE Type 4" locomotives by 1960, bringing the total to 200 units.

The most important fields of activity of the class were the East Coast and West Coast main lines. On the former they largely replaced the LNER Pacifics until they in turn were displaced by the "Deltic" locomotives and the 2,750hp Brush Type 4s. On the West Coast route they dominated passenger traffic until completion of electrification from Euston to Liverpool and Manchester in 1967, by which time the larger English Electric 2,700hp locomotives were taking over West Coast traffic north of Crewe. The "EE Type 4" machines were then transferred to less demanding duties, largely freight traffic in the north of England. Although various troubles with the class had now been cured, they continued to suffer from cracks in the frames and other troubles associated with the primitive frame and axlebox construction. The locomotives suffered and the track suffered, but overall they became dependable and popular machines. Under the 1971 classification scheme they became Class "40."

Above: *A train of empty hopper wagons leaves York for Morpeth, Northumberland, behind Class 40 No. 40152 in October 1979.*

Below: *Class 40 1-Co-Co-1 No. D312 with a London to Carlisle express, climbing the 1 in 75 (1.33%) past Shap Wells in September 1964.*

In the late-1970s BR's requirement for diesel locomotives declined, and a number of the earlier classes were scheduled for elimination. General withdrawal of Class "40" began in 1980, but was prolonged, and they continued on passenger workings to North Wales each summer when train-heating was not required.

The class was originally painted in standard BR green, which was actually Great Western locomotive green. From 1967 this gradually gave way to BR rail blue, but such was public interest in the class in its latter days that BR repainted one of them in its old livery for working special trains.

The 2,000hp engine fitted to Class "40" was one of a long series of English Electric engines with 10in × 12in (254mm × 305mm) cylinders. The first locomotive application was a six-cylinder version for shunters made in 1934. Subsequently a total of 1,233 engines of this type were supplied to BR and its predecessors between 1934 and 1962. In the late-1930s the development of an engine of Vee-form was undertaken with a two-cylinder test unit, and the first outcome of this work was the 16-cylinder engine fitted to the LMS and SR main-line diesels and to Class "40."

For the BR modernisation programme eight-cylinder and 12-cylinder versions were built. The former was used in a Bo-Bo locomotive of 1,000hp of which 228 were built, and the latter in 309 1,750hp Co-Co locomotives of Class "37." It was Class "37" which was the most direct successor to the pioneer LMS locomotives Nos. 10000-1, but the latter, with a weight of 127½t, were limited in the routes over which they could work, whereas Class "37" weighed between 101t and 105t (according to fittings) and could work very widely over BR. Altogether English Electric had supplied 2,082 diesel engines to BR by 1975, and development of the same family of engines continued under the auspices of GEC.

Class "40" was neither the most powerful nor the most numerous of early BR main-line diesels, but it was the first successful production main-line diesel on the system, and the contribution it made towards acceptance of diesels on a largely steam-operated railway was of great historical importance. The class will be remembered also for the high-pitched whistle of its supercharger, which made it one of the easiest of BR diesels to identify by sound alone.

Class 44 "Peak" 1-C$_o$-C$_o$-1

Great Britain:
British Railways (BR), 1959

Type: Diesel-electric express passenger locomotive.
Gauge: 4ft 8½in (1,435mm).
Propulsion: 2,300hp (1,715kW) Sulzer Type 12LDA28 twin-bank turbocharged diesel engine and generator supplying current to six nose-suspended traction motors geared to the axles with resilient gearwheels.
Weight: 255,360lb (116t) adhesive, 309,120lb (140t) total.
Max. axleload: 42,560lb (19.5t).
Overall length: 67ft 11in (20,701mm).
Tractive effort: 70,000lb (311kN).
Max. speed: 90mph (144km/h).

The famous "Peaks" when new were the highest-powered diesel-electric locomotives supplied to BR. They were the first of a huge and unprecedented order for 147 express passenger locomotives (later increased to 193) with Sulzer twin-bank engines (with two parallel crankshafts in the same crankcase). Most of the latter were made under licence by Vickers Armstrong of Barrow-in-Furness, England. After the first 10, engines rated 200hp (150kW) higher were provided.

Above: *No. 46004 takes a Newcastle to Liverpool express across the King Edward Bridge over the Tyne in April 1977.*

Running gear was similar to that of the Class "40" locomotives already described. This, together with the bodywork, was built at BR's Derby and Crewe works where the locomotives were erected. Electrical equipment for the first 137 engines came from Crompton Parkinson (CP) and for the remainder from Brush Engineering.

Originally the class was numbered D1 to D193, in the prime position in BR's diesel list. Later, the 10 original 2,300hp Sulzer/CP locomotives became Class "44", the 2,500hp Sulzer/CP batch Class "45" and the 2,500hp Sulzer/Brush batch Class "46". All were provided with such usual equipment as an automatic train-heating steam boiler, a vacuum exhauster for train brakes, straight air brakes for the locomotives, multiple-unit control gear and a toilet. Later, the locomotives were fitted for working air-braked trains and (in some cases) heating electrically-heated carriages. The first 10 were named after mountain peaks in Britain; a few others received names of regiments and other military formations.

TEP-60 C$_o$-C$_o$

USSR:
Soviet Railways (SZD), 1960

Type: Diesel-electric express passenger locomotive.
Gauge: 5ft 0in (1,524mm).
Propulsion: Type D45A 3,000hp (2,240kW) turbocharged 16-cylinder two-stroke diesel engine and generator supplying current to six spring-borne 416hp (310kW) traction motors geared to the axles via flexible drives of the Alsthom floating-ring type.
Weight: 284,316lb (129t).
Max. axleload: 47,390lb (21.5t).
Overall length: 63ft 2in (19,250mm).
Tractive effort: 55,750lb (248kN).
Max. speed: 100mph (160km/h).

These powerful single-unit machines form one of the Soviet Union's principal diesel-electric passenger locomotive classes, although at the time of writing they are due to be displaced from the very top assignments by the 4,000hp "TEP-70" class. Production of the "TEP-60" continued for a least 15 years, though the total number built has not been revealed. For many years it has been the only type of Soviet diesel locomotive passed for running at speeds above 140km/h (87mph), although neither the need nor the opportunity for such fast running really exists as yet on the SZD network.

Russian experience with diesel locomotives was minimal (and, as far as it went, totally unsatisfactory) before World War II. Therefore in 1945 the mechanical engineers began with a clean sheet and the early diesels were based very sensibly on US practice. By 1960, however, sufficient confidence had been attained so that original ideas could be incorporated.

A serious weakness in early adaptations of freight locomotives to passenger work was the bad tracking of the bogies. Having regard to SZD aspirations towards faster passenger trains, some electric locomotives had been ordered from Alsthom of France, maker of the bogies for world railway speed record-breaker, French National Railways' Co-Co No. 7107.

Alsthom features were used in the bogies for the "TEP-60" in particular the flexible drive which enabled the traction motors to be spring-borne, and the prototype was able to reach 118mph (189km/h) on test. This was claimed at the time to be a world record for a diesel locomotive and certainly vindicated the restrained wisdom of those responsible for the design. Other features of note in these locomotives included electric braking and the ability to cope with temperatures both hot and cold considerably more extreme than are found in conjunction on other railways.

Right: *Typical Russian diesel locomotives in double harness.*

Although there was 15 per cent more power available than on the Class "40s", the "Peaks" also had very little margin in hand when working to the best steam schedules. But even though one may criticise the design as being unenterprising, with little to offer over and above steam traction, it must be said that this slow-solid approach has paid off in longevity. At the time of writing after more than 20 years, 130 of the original 193 are still in service, while many of their more enterprising successors have taken their brilliant performances with them to the scrapyard.

Right: *A Newcastle to King's Cross relief express passes Brandon, County Durham on Easter Monday, 1978, hauled by Class 46 1-Co-Co-1 No. 46042. Apart from peak periods this class is now mainly confined to freight work.*

Below: *One of the original "Peak" class 1-Co-Co-1 diesel-electric locomotives, now Class 44, depicted in original colours, style and numbering.*

Class 060DA C_o-C_o

Romania: Romanian State Railways (CFR), 1960

Type: Mixed-traffic diesel-electric locomotive.
Gauge: 4ft 8½in (1,435mm).
Propulsion: Sulzer Type 12LDA28 2,300hp (1,690kW) turbocharged twin-bank 12-cylinder diesel engine and generator supplying direct current to six traction motors driving the axles via resilient gearwheels.
Weight: 257,870lb (117t).
Max. axleload: 42,980lb (19.5t).
Overall length: 55ft 9in (17,000mm).
Tractive effort: 64,125lb (285kN).
Max. speed: 62mph (100km/h).

The bulk of the diesel-electric locomotive fleet used by Romanian State Railways is based on six prototypes constructed in Switzerland during 1959. Mechanical parts were built by the Swiss Locomotive Works, the electrical equipment by Brown Boveri, and the diesel engines supplied by Sulzer. There are of the "twin bank" configuration with two parallel rows of cylinders, each driving a separate crankshaft.

The elegant bodywork is typical of Swiss locomotives and is of welded construction. No train heating equipment is included; separate heating vans are used when required.

A 550t freight train can be started by one of these locomotives on the ruling grade (1-in-40—2.5 per cent) of the Brasnov to Bucharest main line and accelerated up to 9mph (14km/h). For heavier loads, the locomotives can be run in multiple. There is no rheostatic or regenerative braking, but the usual straight and automatic air brakes are provided. Automatic detection and correction of wheelslip is a help on these severe grades.

Production of these locomotives has continued in Romania and they are also offered for export.

Class 124 "Trans-Pennine"

Great Britain: British Railways (BR), 1960

Type: Diesel-mechanical express passenger train.
Gauge: 4ft 8½in (1,435mm).
Propulsion: Two 230hp (172kW) Leyland-Albion Type EN602 six-cylinder horizontal diesel engines mounted beneath each of four motor coaches. Each motor drives one bogie through a fluid coupling four-speed Wilson epicyclic gearbox, cardan shafts and gearing.
Weight: 361,455lb (164t) adhesive, 500,310lb (227t) total.
Max. axleload: 23,140lb (10.5t).
Overall length: 395ft 10in (120,650mm).
Max. speed: 75mph (120km/h).

In 1955 British Railways announced a modernisation plan, a central feature of which was replacement of steam traction by diesel and electric. The first aspect of this plan to make an impact on the public was on trains for rural lines and local services. The necessary experience was to hand in a series of diesel-mechanical railcars built for the Great Western Railway between 1933 and 1941, and in a very short time a fleet of self-propelled diesel multiple-unit (DMU) trains eventually totalling 3,740 cars had taken over most local and short-distance trains on non-electrified lines. Although few of these routes actually became viable as a result of the change over, in general expenses fell sharply and revenue rose.

After a few years the same attention was given to shorter-distance express passenger services and outstanding amongst these schemes was the Trans-Pennine services between Liverpool, Manchester, Leeds and Hull. The remarkable trains built in 1960 for this service were the ultimate development of the basic DMU layout, using small multiple underfloor-mounted diesel engines driving the wheels through remotely-controlled mechanical gearboxes.

Above: *A British Railways' Class 124 "Trans-Pennine" diesel-mechanical train set near Selby, Yorkshire, in Autumn 1976.*

For the "Trans-Pennine" sets, formed of six cars, 230hp (172kW) engines were used rather than the 150hp (112kW) more typical of the average DMU. Each set had eight engines mounted in twos under the two end cars and two intermediate cars. There was a buffet/grill, and first-class pass-

Left, right and below: *Romanian State Railways' Class 060DA diesel-electric Co-Co locomotive No. 06204333. These multi-purpose machines of Swiss origin have been produced over a long period, and are used extensively on passenger and freight train workings all over the network. The bright livery is an innovation—a drab green typical of European railway systems was the rule in Romania for many years.*

engers at each end had an observation car ride, looking through wrap-around end windows. Seating was provided for 60 first and 232 second class passengers in main-line comfort. The control system allowed these trains to run in multiple with other DMUs in the area.

The central section of the line is steeply-graded and the relatively high power-to-weight ratio of 8hp (6kW) per tonne could be used to advantage. A steam timing of 3hr 30min for the 128 miles (204km) from Hull to Liverpool was brought down to 2hr 51min. Of this improvement, no less than 5½ minutes was attributable to faster running on the 7.1 mile (11.4km) climb from Huddersfield to Standedge tunnel, mostly at 1-in-96 (1.04 per cent).

Existence of eight independent propulsion systems gave reliability, although one or two were usually "out" on any particular journey which meant a small loss of time. Even so, for some years many people who had previously used their cars to cross the Pennines by indifferent narrow roads "let the train take the strain"—in the words of a BR slogan of more recent days.

Construction of the M62 motorway, however, following the same route, came at a time when these trains were beginning to show their age, and restored the status quo. Loss of patronage led to economy measures such as withdrawal of the buffet cars, extra stops, removal of power equipment from intermediate cars and speed restrictions on track overdue for renewal; it all added up to a 20 minute increase in journey time. This in its turn has led to further loss of patronage and a reorientation of the service, which now consists of locomotive-hauled trains running from North Wales or Liverpool to Leeds and Scarborough and DMUs running from Leeds to Hull.

Right: *A re-formed four-car "Trans-Pennine" set at Hessle near Hull in October 1980.*

TEE Four-car train

Europe:
Trans-Europe Express Organisation (TEE), 1957

Type: High-speed diesel-electric luxury train.
Gauge: 4ft 8½in (1,435mm).
Propulsion: Two Werkspoor 1,000hp (746kW) Type RUHB1616 16-cylinder diesel engines and generators supplying current to four traction motors geared with flexible drive to the outer axles of the power car bogies.
Weight: 176,320lb (80t) adhesive, 506,920lb (230t) total.
Max. axleload: 44,080lb (20t).
Overall length: 318ft 0in (96,926mm).
Max. speed: 87mph (139km/h).

One of the most distinguished men of the rail was a Dutch engineer called F.Q. den Hollander. It was he who in a few short years after World War II transformed mountains of twisted wreckage into the modern Netherlands Railways—an efficient (though small) railway which was and is a model system and which the rest of the world has for so long rightly tried to emulate. Later, den Hollander left his mark on the European scene as the driving force behind creation of a network of high-speed international luxury express routes known still as Trans-Europe-Express or TEE.

It was a firm principle of the operation that frontier delays should be minimal and accordingly it was arranged that all customs and immigration formalities should be conducted aboard while the train was in motion. Furthermore, locomotive changing was eliminated and carriage-shuffling made impossible by making the trains self-propelled and self-contained. Frontier halts measured in hours for regular trains became momentary for the TEEs, a notable example being the 3 minutes allowed in Basle. The objective was to provide an attractive service for business travellers, with the fastest possible timings compatible with smooth riding, air-conditioning and superior cuisine. First class fares plus a supplement were charged. France, West Germany, The Netherlands, Belgium, Italy and Switzerland were the principal partners in the enterprise—as well as, and in spite of a change of gauge, Spain. Admittedly the gauge-changing operation at the Spanish frontier was not absolutely momentary. Each of the partici-

Below: *A Dutch-Swiss TEE near Mörschwil, Switzerland, on the Zurich-Munich "Bavaria" express, October 1972.*

Above: *The power car of the Dutch-Swiss type of diesel-electric high-speed luxury Trans Europe Express set.*

Right: *TEE Dutch-Swiss unit ready to leave Paris Est on the evening "L'Arbaléte" service to Basle in June 1966.*

pants provided trains for different services and the sets described here were jointly owned, provided and developed by Dutch and Swiss enterprise. They include 114 seats, kitchen, and driving positions at both ends, as well as accommodation for customs and immigration staff.

The power car is essentially a powerful locomotive equipped for remote control. In addition to the pair of 1,000hp (746kW) diesel engines for traction, a further 350hp generator set is provided to supply power for train heating, cooking, air-conditioning and lighting. In those days it was not possible to muster all this equipment with a total weight sufficiently low to keep within the permissible axleload, using a pair of two-axle bogies. Hence the two idler axles in the centre of each bogie.

The principal service provided by the Dutch-Swiss TEEs was the "Edelweiss" express once daily each way from Amsterdam via Brussels and Luxembourg to Basle and Zurich. The 656 miles (1,050km) were covered in 9hr 33min including 13 stops at a remarkable average speed of 69mph (110km/h). In 1957, electrification over the whole route was not quite complete; even when it was, four electric supply systems were involved (1,500V dc in The Netherlands, 3,000V dc in Belgium, 25,000V 50Hz in France and 15,000V 16⅔Hz in Switzerland), so diesel traction was the only possible choice. The trains also shared in operating TEE services between Paris, Brussels and Amsterdam.

Developments of economic quadri-current power equipment in due time led to substitution of electric trains but it was not the end of the line for the diesels. A buyer in faraway Canada took three sets which moved from one of the most highly developed areas of the world to one of the least—the Ontario Northland Railway's "Northlander" makes daily 243-mile (388km) runs between Toronto and Timmins, equipped with these ex-TEE trains, serving places so remote that roads have only recently been built.

Below: *Basle to Paris Trans-Europe Express-train passes Culmont-Chalindrey, France, with Dutch-Swiss set, June 1966.*

Class Dm3 1-D+D+D-1

Sweden:
Swedish State Railway (SJ), 1960

Type: Electric locomotive for heavy mineral traffic.
Gauge: 4ft 8½in (1,435mm).
Propulsion: Single-phase low-frequency current at 15,000V 16⅔Hz fed via overhead catenary and step-down transformer to six 1,609hp (1,200kW) motors, driving the wheels by gearing, jackshaft and connecting rods.
Weight: 528,960lb (240t) adhesive, 595,080lb (270t) total.
Max. axleload: 44,080lb (20t).
Overall length: 115ft 8in (35,250mm).
Tractive effort: 210,000lb (932kN).
Max. speed: 47mph (75km/h).

To exploit the vast deposits of iron ore found in the interior of northern Sweden, a railway was needed. It was comparatively easy work to build from the Baltic port of Lulea to the mining area around Kiruna, but the Baltic at this latitude, near to the Arctic circle, freezes over in the winter. Accordingly, the railway was continued further north still as well as westwards, crossing not only the Ofoten mountains but the Arctic circle itself, and what is now the Norwegian frontier, to reach the sheltered port of Narvik, kept free of ice year-round by the friendly Gulf Stream. The iron ore railway from Lulea to Narvik, which began in 1883, extends for a total of 295 miles (473km).

Steam operation was fairly traumatic, especially in winter, because of the heavy loads, the very low temperatures, the mountain gradients, not to speak of continuous darkness. Apart from the mosquitos, in summer things were more pleasant—for example, the lineside tourist hotel at Abisko (with no access except by train!) boasts a north-facing sun verandah to catch the midnight sun!

It is not surprising then that the Lappland iron ore railway was the first important line in Scandinavia to be electrified. Electric working began in 1915 and conversion was completed throughout in 1923. The low-frequency single-phase system was adopted, by then well-proven in Switzerland and elsewhere.

The quality of the iron ore from Kiruna, together with the ease with which it can be won—plus, it must be said, the long-standing neutrality of Sweden, which means that customers are never refused on political grounds—always kept demand high and, in the long term, ever-rising. The problem for the railways, then, has in most years been concerned with the ability to handle the traffic offering.

Below: *A Swedish State Railways Class Dm3 electric locomotive hauls an iron ore train through the forests of Swedish Lappland.*

So far, doubling the line has been avoided by increasing the weight of the trains, and today they are the heaviest in Europe.

It is typical of the Swedish way of railroading that the motive power there today is a modest adaptation of the early standard and essentially simple Class "D" locomotive, already described. The result is this Class "Dm" locomotive of 9,650hp (7,200kW), designed to haul the now legendary ore trains. Loads of up to 5,200t (5,720 US tons) are taken up 1-in-100 (1 per cent) gradients, as well as started in polar temperatures—thereby explaining the need for a tractive effort exceeding 200,000lb (900kN).

One might be puzzled why Swedish State Railways designate this mighty hauler as a sub-class (the "m" in Dm stands for *malm* or iron) of their modest and ubiquitous Class "D" 1-C-1 standard electric locomotive. The reason was that the original Class "Dm" could be said to be two "Ds" with an additional coupled axle substituted for one pony truck on each unit, which also had a cab at only one end. Two units coupled permanently back-to-back originally formed a Class "Dm" locomotive and these were introduced in the late 1940s. Eventually there were 19 twin locomotives plus four owned by Norwegian State Railways (the NSB class is "el 12"). Both the brown Swedish engines and the green Norwegian ones operate indiscriminately over the whole line.

In 1960 still more power was required and three cab-less units (also without pantographs) were built and put in the middle of three existing pairs. By 1970 all the Swedish "Dm" pairs had been converted to triples in this way.

Each individual unit bears a separate number although units are not separated in normal operation. The huge tractive effort available has caused problems with the traditional screw couplings and a start has been made on fitting Russian-pattern automatic knuckle couplers.

As a rod-drive locomotive the "Dm3" was the last of its line. Since 1970 a need for additional power has been met, and history made to repeat itself, by modifying the current standard Swedish high-power Class "Rc4" express passenger locomotive. The alterations include lower gearing, very sophisticated wheel slip control and addition of 10t (12 US tons) of ballast, all in aid of improving tractive effort, while cabs are insulated against arctic temperatures.

Above and below: *Swedish State Railways' Class Dm3 heavy freight locomotive. These mighty haulers are used for the iron ore traffic from Kiruna in northern Sweden to the ice-free port of Narvik situated well north of the Arctic Circle in northern Norway.*

Below: *A 9,600hp three-unit Class Dm3 iron ore locomotive of the Swedish State Railways. The use of rod-drive in a locomotive constructed after 1960 is an unusual feature.*

U25B B_o-B_o United States: General Electric Company (GE), 1960

Type: Diesel-electric road switcher locomotive.
Gauge: 4ft 8½in (1,435mm).
Propulsion: One GE FDL16 2,500hp (1,870kW) four-stroke 16-cylinder Vee engine and generator supplying four nose-suspended traction motors geared to the axles.
Weight: 260,000lb (118.0t).
Max. axleload: 65,000lb (29.5t).
Overall length: 60ft 2in (18,340mm).
Tractive effort: 81,000lb (360kN) with 65mph gear ratio.
Max. speed: 65mph (105km/h), 75mph (121km/h), 80mph (129km/h) or 92mph (148km/h) according to gear ratio fitted.

Above: *General Electric U36C 3,600hp (2,690kW) Co-Co diesel-electric locomotive supplied to the Union Pacific Railroad.*

If, in the 1920s, one had said to an American locomotive engineer: "The diesel-electric locomotive seems to have great potential; which locomotive manufacturer is capable of exploiting it?" he would almost certainly have said "General Electric", for that company was then building on 30 years' experience of electric traction of all sorts by turning out diesel switchers (shunters) incorporating various makes of engine. However, the prophet would have been wrong, for it was the massive resources of General Motors Corporation thrown into its Electro-Motive Division which sparked off, and largely fuelled, the steam-to-diesel revolution in the United States.

GE was thus destined to take a minor part in the overall process, but within the 25 per cent or so of the market which did not fall to EMD, it has always had a major share. When the American Locomotive Company (Alco) embarked seriously on production of road diesels, it made an agreement with GE to use only GE electrical equipment in its products, in return for which GE agreed not to compete with Alco. From 1940 to 1953 both companies benefited from this agreement; Alco profited from the expertise of the biggest firm in the electric traction business, and GE acquired an easy market for products which it was well qualified and equipped to supply. A second manufacturer, Fairbanks Morse, likewise offered GE equipment in its models.

By the early-1950s, total dieselisation of the US railroads was certain, and although Alco was well established in the market, its sales ran a poor second to EMD and were not improving. GE then took the plunge; it quietly terminated its agreement with Alco and embarked on development of its own range of large diesels. Although most of its previous diesels had been small switchers, it had in fact built a 2,000hp (1,490kW) Sulzer-engined unit in 1936, which for 10 years was North America's most powerful single-engined diesel locomotive, and in the post-war years the company had built up an export market in road locomotives.

The essential requirement for GE to enter the home road-diesel market was a large engine. At this time its switchers were fitted with Cooper-Bessemer 6-cylinder in-line and 8-cylinder Vee engines, so the company acquired the rights to develop this engine. Two versions were made, the 8-cylinder developing 1,200hp (895kW) and the 12-cylinder developing 1,800hp (1,340kW).

First outward sign of GE's new venture was a four-unit locomotive, with "cab" or totally-enclosed bodies, two units fitted with the V8 engine and two with the V12. These units were tested on the Erie Railroad from 1954 to 1959, and based on their successful performance the company launched a new series of export models in 1956, designated the "Universal" series. With the experience gained from V8 and V12 engines, GE now embarked on a major step forward, a 16-cylinder version developing 2,400hp (1,790kW). Two of these engines were installed in Bo-Bo hood units, and were tested on the Erie, covering 100,000 miles (160,000km) in 11 months. Although masquerading under the designation "XP24", denoting 2,400hp export test units, these were in fact destined to be the demonstrators of a new model for the home market.

In 1960, seven years after the ending of its partnership with Alco, GE announced its new model, the 2,500hp (1,870kW) "Universal" Bo-Bo, denoted "U25B". Its most obvious sales point was that it had the highest horsepower of any locomotive on

the US market, by 100hp (75kW), but to have any chance of breaking into the EMD/Alco markets, it had to have many attractions which were less obvious, but equally important to customers.

In preparing the design, GE had asked the motive power chiefs of 33 railroads what they liked and disliked in the diesels which they already operated. The costs of operating these units were also analysed, and it was found that repairs accounted for 28.7 per cent of total diesel operating costs. The designers' aim was therefore to improve performance, but at the same time to simplify equipment to make it more reliable and maintenance-free. A major cause of complaint was the air system, both for supplying the engine and for cooling. The incoming air was filtered, and in most contemporary designs the filters needed cleaning at about 2,500 miles (4,000km). Alco designed a self-cleaning mechanical filter. Another complaint was that air for ventilating the equipment compartments commonly passed through the engine compartment, becoming heated and polluted in doing so. On the "U25B" the air from the fan to the equipment compartment passed through ducting in the main frame, well away from the engine. Another simplification was elimination of electrically-controlled shutters to the radiator ventilating system.

In contrast to these changes much of the electrical equipment was well tried, including the traction motors, and roads which operated Alco locomotives would already have many of the parts in stock. However, there was an electrical innovation—use of modular electronic equipment.

Launching of the new model coincided with unfavourable economic conditions on the railroads, and more than a year passed before any orders came in. The first came from Union Pacific, which was always on the lookout for higher-powered locomotives, and other roads which had a specific need for higher power followed. Over a period of six years a total of 478 "U25Bs" were sold, not a great number by EMD standards, but sufficient for GE to displace Alco from second place in the US diesel sales league.

It was already established practice for a US road switcher to be offered both as a four-axle and as a six-axle unit, the latter appealing to railroads which needed more adhesive weight or a slightly lower axleload. The "U25C" therefore appeared in 1963, and added a further 113 units to GE sales. With the spread of the "U" designation, someone referred to "U-boats' and the nickname caught on.

The effect on other manufacturers of GE competition was to spur them to modify their own models. Competition was keen, particularly horsepower competition. GE's 16-cylinder engine and its generator were rated modestly, so that uprating would be possible without major alterations (and more spare parts to stock!), and so in 1966 came the 2,800hp (2,090kW) engine, in the "U28B" and "U28C" models.

UP bought 16 "U25Bs", but then ordered a special model to suit the addiction of its motive power chief, D. S. Neuhart, to very powerful locomotives. Already his road was operating 8,500hp (6,340kW) GE gas turbine locomotives, and the builder now produced a 5,000hp (3,730kW) twin-engined version of the "U25B" mounted on four bogies and weighing 247t; these were the "U50Bs". Later came a simplified Co-Co version of the same power. Neither of these types was entirely successful, and with the coming of standard models of 3,000hp (2,240kW) UP was content to fall into line with other railroads and buy off-the-shelf.

The next landmark in diesel development in the US was the 3,000hp engine, produced by EMD, Alco and GE in 1965-66. The GE models, "U30B" and "U30C", appeared late in 1966, and were followed less than a year later by 3,300hp (2,460kW) versions. In 1969 yet another increase, to 3,600hp (2,690kW), was achieved. The GE decision to use a moderately-rated engine in the first "U-boats" paid good dividends at this time, for whereas GE attained these increases in power by development of the 16-cylinder engine, EMD had to move to 20 cylinders. However, the railroads soon lost their enthusiasm for engines above 3,000hp when they discovered the extra maintenance costs incurred.

In 1976 a further revision of the GE range, known as the "7-series" was accompanied by a change in designation, the 3,000hp Co-Co becoming the "C30-7". With these models GE remains firmly in the US market, and also exports them directly or through overseas associates. There has also been a revival in sales of 3,600hp locomotives.

GE demonstrated that it was possible to compete with EMD. Its models offered some attractive technical alternatives to the EMD products, and by doing so they prevented the larger builder from achieving a monopoly.

Above: *GE U25C Co-Co units belonging to the Lake Superior & Ishpeming RR and leased by the Detroit, Toledo & Ironton.*

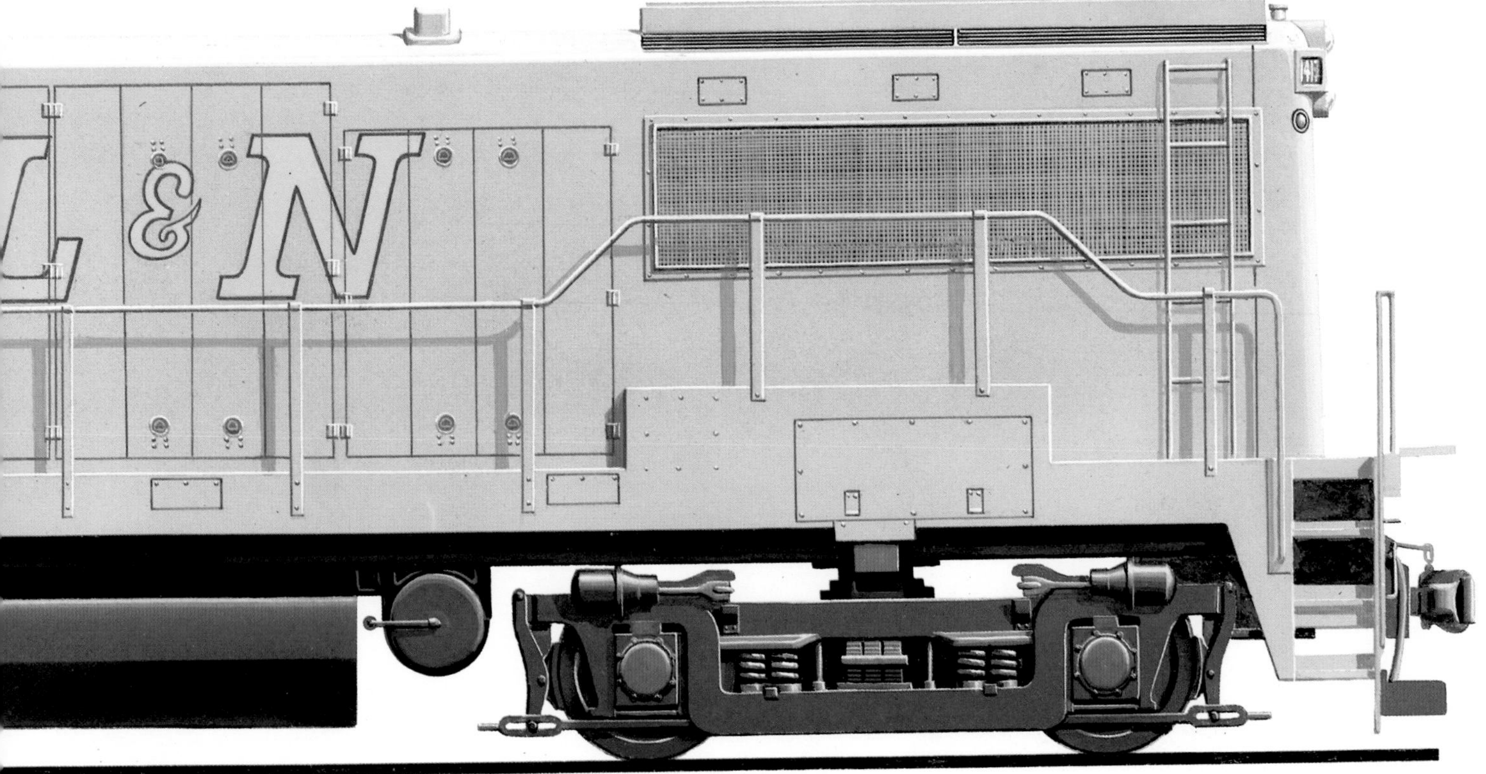

Below: *A four-axle "U-boat" road-switcher of the Louisville & Nashville Railroad.*

Class 47 C_o-C_o

Great Britain: British Railways (BR), 1962

Type: Diesel-electric mixed-traffic locomotive.
Gauge: 4ft 8½in (1,435mm).
Propulsion: Sulzer 2,750hp (2,052kW) 12LDA28C 12-cylinder twin-bank engine and generator supplying direct current to six nose-suspended traction motors geared to the axles.
Weight*: 264,480lb (120t).
Max. axleload*: 44,080lb (20t).
Overall length: 63ft 5in (19,329mm).
Tractive effort: 62,000lb (275kN).
Max. speed: 95mph (152km/h).

*Variations between different sub-groups.

These useful locomotives are the workhorses of BR's diesel fleet and form almost half the total stock of large diesel locomotives of 2,000hp or over. A total of 528 were built between 1962 and 1967 by Brush Engineering and BR's Crewe Works. All have Brush electrical equipment and use the same Sulzer engine—with modest enhancement of power output—as the "Peak" class, but the overall weight was reduced by careful design to the point where the two outer idle axles of the older type could be dispensed with. The engines were built under licence by Vickers-Armstrong of Barrow, England. Originally the "47s" were numbered D1500 to 99 and from D1100 upwards, but renumbering in 1968 to incorporate the class designation brought them into the 47xxx series.

Details vary; the "47.0" group (243 strong) originally had steam

Above: *British Railways' Class 47/0 diesel-electric locomotive No. 47083* Orion *with a freight train at York in September 1981.*

Below: *A relief express hauled by a Class 47 diesel-electric locomotive rounds a curve south of Durham in 1979.*

heating boilers and these run on to include the "471xxx' and "472xx" series. There is a "47.3" sub-class (81 in number) which have no train heating equipment either steam or electric but do include special low-speed control for assisting automatic loading or unloading of merry-go-round coal trains. The 185 "47.4s", which include the "475xx" series, all have electric heating arrangements (and some steam as well). One interesting example of the class, originally No. 47046, has been used as a test bed for a more powerful engine. With a Paxman 3,250hp (2,425kW) 16RK3CT engine fitted in 1975 it became the sole member of sub-class "47.6", later class "47.9" No. 47901. Lastly there is a group fitted for working push-and-pull express trains between Edinburgh and Glasgow; these are renumbered and reclassified "47.4". All the "47s" are equipped with dual brakes for working both air and vacuum-braked trains, automatic wheelslip detectors and correctors as well as an anti-slip brake. The bogies are made from one-piece steel castings.

It must be said that the electric train heating system absorbs power from the engine and affects the amount of power available to haul the train by a noticable amount—several hundred horsepower in fact. In this case the diminution nicely absorbs the amount of power gained by several years of diesel engine development! When considering these locomotives as express passenger power, then, this loss must normally be taken into account. Of course, it is of lesser importance now that most of the prime diesel express passenger assignments in Britain have been taken over by HST125 sets. However, the "47s" equipped for electric train heating have a device whereby, if the full engine power is temporarily needed for traction, the driver can push his controller handle against a spring return which temporarily interrupts the heating supply.

One noticeable thing missing from the Class "47" armoury is multiple-unit capability and this perhaps underlines BR's general philosophy which is (with some exceptions in special cases) to provide a single locomotive of the power needed to haul any given train. It is in complete contrast to the North American principle that diesel units should be building-blocks from which locomotives of any desired power can be assembled.

The experimental Class "47.9", fitted in 1975 with a more powerful engine, spawned in 1976 the BR Class "56". These are a class of Co-Co similar in size, weight and appearance (apart from the style of painting) to the standard "47s" but given 26 per cent more power by installing the same engine as powers No. 47901.

Above: *Before the days of automation, provision was made on locomotives for displaying train reporting numbers. This is no longer needed, hence the group of unevenly set zeros.*

Class 309 "Clacton" Four-car train

Great Britain:
British Railways (BR), Eastern Region, 1962

Type: Electric express-passenger train.
Gauge: 4ft 8½in (1,435mm).
Propulsion: Alternating current at 25,000V 50Hz (and originally at 6,250V 50Hz as well) fed via overhead catenary, step-down transformer and solid-state rectifiers to four 282hp (210kW) nose-suspended traction motors geared to the axles of an intermediate non-driving power car.
Weight: 127,830lb (58t) adhesive, 376,885lb (171t) total.
Max. axleload: 31,960lb (14.5t).
Overall length: 265ft 9in (81,000mm).
Max. speed: 100mph (160km/h), but speed limit of railway 90mph (144km/h).

In the late-1950s, the decision was taken to adopt industrial-frequency as a future standard for British Railways' electrification. A proposed extension of the then new suburban electrification out of London's Liverpool Street Station, using 1,500V direct current, then posed the question whether conversion of these lines to the new standard should be attempted before the extension was begun. To answer this, the branches from Colchester to Clacton-on-Sea and Walton-on-the-Naze were electrified on the new system as a trial. After some traumas, the suburban electrification was converted to ac and in 1961 the gap from its outer limit at Shenfield to Colchester was wired. For the first time then, there was a need for express ac electric sets for the new standard ac system, in order to cover fast London to Clacton trains.

The result was these four-car "Clacton" sets, eight with "griddle" car and seven without, plus eight matching two-car sets to strengthen the trains at peak hours. Four, eight or ten-car trains could be run, vestibuled throughout. Although costly both in weight and expense, one-piece cast-steel Commonwealth bogies were used in order to give good riding. Very adequately-powered traction equipment was provided, with 3,380hp (2,520kW) for a 460 ton (506 US tons) 10-car train. There was automatic changeover between the two voltages, and silicon rectifiers, then quite new, were used. Both electro-pneumatic and ordinary automatic air brakes were provided.

The best working was the "Essex Coast Express" which ran the 70 miles (113km) from Liverpool Street to Clacton in 80 minutes; the hourly interval trains, which made five intermediate stops and shed a unit at Thorpe-le-Soken for Walton, took 8 minutes longer. Of course, the high-speed capability of these units could not be used to full advantage amongst the dense traffic of the Liverpool Street suburban area.

It was clear that these fine trains were really intended for better things; electrification beyond Colchester to Ipswich, Harwich and Norwich then seemed imminent, although this work was actually authorised only in 1982. Since 1962 there has most surprisingly been no futher requirement for high-voltage ac express electric trains (unless you count the APT!) and accordingly the Clacton trains, now all reformed as four-car sets and minus their griddle cars, remain sole examples of their kind in Britain.

Below: *Class 309 electric multiple-unit set at Clacton Station, Essex, forming the "Centenary Express", September 1982.*

Krauss-Maffei C-C

United States:
Denver & Rio Grande Western and Southern Pacific Railroads (D&RGW and SP), 1961

Type: Diesel-hydraulic freight locomotive.
Gauge: 4ft 8½in (1,435mm).
Propulsion: Two 2,000hp (1,500kW) four-stroke pressure-charged 16-cylinder Maybach MD870 engines driving through two Voith three-stage hydraulic transmissions, each geared to the axles of one bogie.
Weight: 330,600lb (150t).
Max. axleload: 55,100lb (25t).
Overall length: 65ft 11⁵⁄₁₆in (20,100mm).
Tractive effort: 90,000lb (400kN).
Max. speed: 70mph (113km/h).

During the 1950s the proportion of the world's single-unit diesel locomotives above 2,000hp (1,500kW) which were fitted with hydraulic transmission rose from 4 per cent to 17 per cent due to vigorous development work in West Germany. In 1960, of the world's major diesel users, the United States alone, with more than half the world's 54,000 diesel locomotives, adhered exclusively to electric transmission. Furthermore, diesel-hydraulics were made in West Germany, and the US had imported no locomotives since the earliest days of railways. There was thus a sensation on both sides of the Atlantic when it was announced that two US railroads, the Denver & Rio Grande Western and Southern Pacific, had each ordered three diesel-hydraulic C-C locomotives from Krauss-Maffei of Munich, and furthermore that they would be 4,000hp (2,980kW) units, which was 1,600hp more than any model a US manufacturer could offer.

D&RGW was the first to approach KM, but to make a viable production run a second order was needed; SP responded. The reasons for this revolutionary step were threefold: diesel-hydraulics gave a much greater horsepower per unit weight than diesel-electrics; German experience showed that with hydraulic transmission adhesion was much improved; and in US experience electrical transmission was the biggest item of repairs in diesels, accounting for up to two-thirds of failures on the road. The improved power-to-weight ratio made it possible to mount two 2,200hp engines in a C-C locomotive.

The engines for the US orders were enlarged versions of the Maybach units used in most German diesel-hydraulics, and were notable for their speed of 1,500rpm, which was almost 50 per cent more than the highest in an American engine. The rating of 2,000hp was the engine output, and after allowing for the losses in the transmission the power was 3,540hp (2,640kW), which was the figure more truly comparable with a US rating (which is power available for traction).

Each engine was connected by a cardan shaft to a Voith gearbox near the outer end of the frame. From this gearbox an inclined cardan shaft led to a final gearbox on the inner end of the bogie, whence a further cardan shaft led to the axles. The gearbox provided for hydro-dynamic braking, and the controls were pneumatic with provision for multiple-unit working.

The first locomotive completed was D&RGW No. 4001. To test the locomotive in Europe under US mountain railroad conditions, the makers arranged for No. 4001 to work for a week on the famous Semmering line in Austria, with gradients of 1-in-40 (2½ per cent). On the steepest gradient the loco-

Above: *12,000 horse-power provided by three Krauss-Maffei diesel-hydraulic units takes a freight over the Rockies on the Rio Grande Denver to Salt Lake City trans-continental route.*

Left: *The later batch of Krauss-Maffei diesel hydraulic locomotives supplied to Southern Pacific were designed as "hood" rather than "cowl" units.*

Below: *Denver & Rio Grande Krauss-Maffei diesel-hydraulic locomotive No. 4003.*

motive started, and hauled at 16mph (26½km/h), a train of 867t. Only once did the wheels slip, and then only slightly, and the dynamic brake was found to work well.

The six units were duly shipped to the US and put to work in 1961. On the D&RGW the locomotives worked in duplicate or triplicate on trains of 4,000t to 7,000t on 1-in-50 (2 per cent) gradients. Although their work was satisfactory, the road decided not to continue with the experiment, and when the locomotives had covered 200,000 miles (320,000km) they were sold to the Southern Pacific. The latter, by contrast, was sufficiently impressed to order 15 more, which were delivered in 1963. With a total of 21 of the German machines, SP was able to assess their economic and technical performance.

The verdict came in 1968; the hydraulic transmission "could provide a reliable means of propulsion with competitive maintenance costs" but the engines suffered from "complexity of construction and inaccessibility for repairs". Air intake problems arose in tunnels, and the pneumatic controls were troublesome. Some modifications were made, but as the diesel-hydraulics came due for heavy repairs they were withdrawn from service.

This was not quite the end of diesel-hydraulics on the SP, for in 1964 Alco built three C-C versions of its Century series fitted with Voith transmission. These showed promise, but the closure of Alco in 1969 ruled out any possibility of further development.

GT3 2-C Great Britain: English Electric Co Ltd, 1960

Type: Direct-drive gas turbine locomotive for mixed traffic.
Gauge: 4ft 8½in (1,435mm).
Propulsion: Double-shaft turbine producing an output of 2,780hp (2,075kW), driving the main wheels direct via gearing and coupling rods.
Weight: 132,720lb (60t) adhesive, 276,416lb (125t) total*
Max. axleload: 44,800lb (20.5t).
Overall length: 68ft 0in (20,726mm).
Tractive effort: 38,000lb (169kN).
Max. speed: 90mph (144km/h).

*Including tender.

Above: *The English Electric Company built this direct-drive gas turbine locomotive in 1960. It was very simple indeed and performed well, and is shown hauling a 12-car train in the northern hills.*

There was great enthusiasm for the gas turbine in post-war Britain, and when the Great Western Railway ordered a gas turbine locomotive from Metropolitan Vickers, it was not surprising that the gas turbine department of English Electric, Metro-Vick's main rival, should embark on the design and manufacture of such a locomotive as a private venture. But there were great differences between the two projects, not least that Metro-Vick delivered its locomotive in five years, whereas EE took as long as fourteen.

The Metro-Vick locomotive conformed to the practice of Brown Boveri of Switzerland and General Electric in the USA, in that the turbine drove a generator from which current was supplied to conventional dc traction motors. EE, on the other hand, took advantage of the capacity of a turbine to transmit a high torque at rest, making direct drive of a locomotive possible, as in some steam turbine locomotives. To effect the necessary direct drive to the wheels, the chassis was made in the form of a 4-6-0 or 2-C steam locomotive.

The turbine rested on the frame ahead of the leading coupled wheels and, unlike those of other gas turbine locomotives, it was a two-shaft machine. The high-pressure end of the turbine drove the compressor, while the low-pressure end was on a separate shaft which was connected to a gearbox mounted on the middle coupled axle. Clutches in the gearbox selected forward or reverse gear as required. Use of two power turbines was essential for direct drive, but it also enabled the unit to be designed with a less unfavourable part-load fuel consumption than the other gas turbine locomotive, thus alleviating one of their great weaknesses. There was a heat exchanger above the turbine, transferring heat from the exhaust gases to the air passing from the compressor to the combustion chamber. The driver's cab was in the conventional steam locomotive position, and there was a six-wheeled tender carrying the train heating steam generator and main fuel tank.

Another unique feature of this design was the extensive developing and testing of individual components before and after they were assembled in the locomotive. For this purpose much use was made of British Railways' Locomotive Testing Station at Rugby, the first time that this plant had been used for outside work of that type. Much ingenuity was displayed in the design, particularly in the

Below: *The 2-C on display at the Institution of Locomotive Engineers Exhibition at Marylebone Goods Yard in 1961.*

Below: *From a casual glance No. GT3 appeared little different from a steam locomotive, yet it had no boiler, no cylinders and no complex transmission system.*

transmission, which was the most novel part. The turbine was an existing type of industrial machine.

The reason for adopting the steam locomotive type of chassis was that it enabled the drive to be taken to an axle which was rigid in the frame, except for movement on its springs. This eliminated a major design problem which would have arisen had the drive been transmitted to wheels on a bogie.

The locomotive was completed in 1960, and after tests in sidings adjoining Rugby Testing Station, it eventually emerged for road trials—and such a sight had never been seen on a British railway, for the early trials were made without the casing in position, to that the turbine, heat exchanger and other components were exposed to view.

In 1961 the locomotive, now decently encased and numbered cryptically GT3, was tested on various parts of the London Midland Region of BR. The climax was a series of runs between Crewe and Carlisle, in which loads of up to 15 coaches (about 450t—490 US tons) were hauled up to Shap Summit at speeds as high as had ever been recorded with steam or with 2,000hp diesels. The performance of the unit was deemed satisfactory, although the turbine never quite reached its designed output of 2,700hp. The tractive effort recorded at starting was 36,000lb (16,500kg), and at speeds between 30 and 80mph (48 and 130km/h) the tractive effort was about equal to that of a rebuilt "Merchant Navy" class 4-6-2 steam locomotive working at a maximum rate which a fireman could sustain, and it was well above that of a 2,000hp diesel.

With the tests concluded, the point was reached at which the experience gained, together with, in this case, 14 years of development work on other types of locomotive, could be incorporated in a production design. There was, however, an essential requirement—money—and this could not be justified unless there was some prospect of orders. BR had withdrawn its two gas turbine locos by this time, and was already testing the experimental second generation diesels in which engines of 2,700 to 2,750hp were installed in a locomotive of less than 120 weight. BR was thus committed to diesels, and was so deeply involved in the problems of dieselisation that it had no interest in alternatives, nor were any export orders forthcoming. Furthermore English Electric's finances were declining, and the time was near when it would join its former rival Metro-Vick in the GEC group. Inevitably, further work on the gas turbine locomotive was cancelled, and GT3 was broken up. There was thus no lasting benefit from 14 years' work.

Above: *Although occasionally featuring in scenes such as the above, the masterpiece in simplicity that was the GT3 never gained recognition.*

Class 55 Deltic C_o-C_o

Great Britain:
British Railways (BR), 1961

Type: High-speed express passenger diesel-electric locomotive.
Gauge: 4ft 8½in (1,435mm).
Propulsion: Two Napier Type 18-25 18-cylinder 1,750hp (1,305kW) "Deltic" two-stroke diesel engines and generators connected in series, feeding current to six nose-suspended traction motors geared to the axles of the two bogies.
Weight: 222,600lb (101t).
Max. axleload: 36,920lb (16.25t).
Overall length: 69ft 6in (21,180mm).
Tractive effort: 50,000lb (222kN).
Max. speed: 100mph (160km/h).

The sad thing about diesel locomotives is that, unlike steam, all the fascinating mechanism is hidden deep within. That is why it is exceptional for what they are like inside to be reflected in what they are called. But on the "Deltics" the mechanism was so very fascinating that its name spilled out into the lay world. In Greek, the capital letter Δ or delta is a triangle which, when inverted, exactly describes the layout of some diesel engines of remarkably high power for their weight and size. They were developed by English Electric's subsidiary Napier soon after World War II for fast motor gun-boats for the Royal Navy. They were to replace engines fuelled by petrol, which presented a serious fire hazard, in action and otherwise.

The advantages of an "opposed piston" engine are well known. Instead of having one piston per cylinder, with a massive cylinder head to take the thrust, there are two pushing against one another. It is not quite two for the price of one, but part way to it. The only problem is that complications arise in making the two opposed thrusts turn a single shaft. In the "Deltic" engine, three banks of double cylinders, each with a pair of opposed pistons and arranged as three sides of a triangle, are connected to a crankshaft at each apex. Each crankshaft is then geared to the central drive shaft of the engine. The result was specific weight of only 6.2lb per hp, (3.8kg/kW), some 2½ times better than contemporary medium-speed conventional diesel engines normally used for traction. There was also perfect balance both of the forces generated and of the reciprocating parts.

English Electric's Traction Division was a main supplier of locomotives to BR, and EE's chairman Lord Nelson realised that by putting this Napier engine on to an English Electric chassis, he had the means to double the power of a typical diesel-electric locomotive. During 1955, in the teeth of opposition from the Traction Division, and at EE's own expense, a prototype was put in hand. During several years' testing the locomotive did everything that might be expected of a machine that had 3,300hp (2,462kW) available compared with the 2,000hp or so of her competitors. Moreover, it proved unexpectedly reliable.

Under BR's modernisation plan, electrification was envisaged from London to the north of England both from Euston and from King's Cross. In the event, the former scheme was the only one put in hand and the Eastern/North Eastern/Scottish Region authorities accordingly sought a stop-gap alternative which would give electrification timings for minimal expenditure. The result was an order in 1959 for 22 of these superb locomotives, a class destined to become a legend in their own lifetime. When built they were by a considerable margin the most powerful single-unit diesel locomotives in the world.

Two separate "Deltic" engine-

Left: *"Deltic" No. 55021 with a King's Cross to Edinburgh express at Ouston Junction, County Durham, in July 1978.*

Below: *A "Deltic" Co-Co diesel-electric locomotive depicted in the original livery applied to these excellent and powerful units when first built.*

and-generator sets were installed, normally connected in series, but in the event of failure the failed engine could be switched out and the locomotive could continue to pull its full load using the other one, but at reduced speed.

Auxiliary equipment on the "Deltics" included an automatic oil-fired steam generator for heating trains. The water tanks for this equipment were originally arranged so they could be filled from steamage water cranes and also—amazingly—at speed from water troughs by means of a scoop! Later, windings were added to the generators to provide for electric heating of the train although this abstracted several hundred horsepower from the output available for traction. Both compressors and vacuum exhauster sets for brake power were provided, as well as cooking facilities and a toilet.

The bogies were standard with the contemporary English Electric 1,750hp Type "3" locomotives (now BR Class "37") and automatic detection and correction of wheelslip was provided for. The controls were also generally similar to other English Electric locomotives, although drivers could not run them exactly the same as other locomotives, because the low angular inertia of a "Deltic" engine precluded heavy-handed throttle movements, which were liable to lead to automatic shutdown. Even so, the possibility of climbing the 1-in-200 (0.5 per cent) gradient to Stoke Summit, north of Peterborough, at a minimum speed of 90mph (144km/h) with a heavy East Coast express was something that earned the total respect of footplatemen. In the old LNER tradition, the "Deltics" were all named—some after race horses that also had won their races and others after English and Scottish regiments. Originally the class was numbered D9000 to D9021; later Nos. D9001 to 21 became Nos. 55001 to 21 and D9000 became No. D55022.

Above: *"Deltic" No. 55010* King's Own Scottish Borderer *under the wires at King's Cross.*

One of the crucial measures in the scheme to acquire the "Deltics" was that the deal should include maintenance at an inclusive price, with penalties to be incurred if, through faults arising, the locomotives were unable to perform an agreed mileage each year. The task of keeping the "Deltic" fleet in running order was simplified because the engines were maintained on a unit-replacement basis. After a few anticipated problems in the first year or so, the "Deltics" settled down to running about 170,000 miles a year, or about 500 miles a day, with a very low failure rate.

After a few improvements to the route, including major track realignments, the "Deltic"-hauled "Flying Scotsman" ran (for example in 1973) from King's Cross to Newcastle, 271 miles (433km) in 3hr 37min and to Edinburgh, 395 miles (632km), in 5hr 30min, average speeds of 74.9 and 71.8mph (119.8 and 114.5km/h) respectively. Such timings as these were applied not just to one or two 'flag' trains but to the service as a whole; they represented substantial gains in time—a 1½ hour acceleration compared with 12 years before between London and Edinburgh, for instance. Teesside customers could have as much as 1¾ hours extra time in London for the same time away from home, compared with what was possible in the pre-"Deltic" era. British Rail reaped their reward in the form of a substantial increase in traffic, and this far more than outweighed the fact that the cost of maintenance of these complex engines was admittedly higher than those of lower specific power output.

Fifteen years and 50 million "Deltic" miles later, electrification seemed as far away as ever, and a further stage of development without it became desirable. In the event, a possible "Super-Deltic" based on two "Deltic" engines of increased power was discarded in favour of the self-propelled High-Speed Trains, with more conventional Paxman engines. It might have been hoped that the existing "Deltics" could be moved on to rejuvenate operations on less important lines, where their low axleload would permit usage. In the end, though, because their engines were expensive to maintain, it was not possible to make a case for keeping them, based on the kind of rather uninspiring arithmetic BR's accountants use in such matters.

So, on January 2, 1982 the last "Deltic"-hauled train ran into King's Cross. Now all that remains are memories of the monumental labours of these fabled machines. Two at least are to be preserved—the prototype in the Science Museum, London, and *King's Own Yorkshire Light Infantry* in the National Railway Museum at York.

Right: *An East Coast express hauled by a "Deltic" in BR standard blue livery rolls southwards through the hills.*

Class 52 "Western" C-C

Great Britain:
British Railways, Western Region (BR), 1962

Type: Diesel-hydraulic express passenger locomotive.
Gauge: 4ft 8½in (1,435mm).
Propulsion: Two 1,350hp (1,000kW) Bristol-Siddeley/ Maybach 12-cylinder Vee-type MD655 "tunnel" engines each driving the three axles of one bogie via a Voith-North British three-stage hydraulic transmission, cardan shaft, intermediate gearbox, further cardan shafts and final-drive gearboxes.
Weight: 242,440lb (110t).
Max. axleload: 40,775lb (18.5t).
Overall length: 68ft 0in (20,726mm).
Tractive effort: 72,600lb (323kN).
Max. speed: 90mph (144km/h).

Above: *Class 52 No. D1005 passes Lostwithiel, Cornwall, with the down "Cornish Riviera Express", in October 1974.*

The episode of the "Western" class diesel-hydraulics was like a glorious but futile last cavalry charge on the part of some army facing inevitable defeat. Of all the companies absorbed into British Railways on January 1, 1948, the Great Western Railway found nationalisation much the hardest to bear. Its own apparently superior standards evolved over more than a century were largely replaced by those emanating from inferior "foreign" (non-GWR) companies. For some time the regional management at Paddington had largely to content itself with words—the General Manager even issued an instruction to the effect that no locomotive of other than GWR design should be rostered for any train on which he was due to travel!

But after a decade had passed, action became possible. Under BR's Modernisation Programme, a thorough trial of diesel hydraulic locomotives was planned on one of the regions, and the Western Region was suitable for this equipment. This was Paddington's chance to do its own thing with locomotives which followed the hallowed Great Western tradition of being as different as possible from anyone else's.

At that time the choice of hydraulic transmission as an alternative to electric for high-power diesels was less radical than it is now. BR's central management had plumped (quite correctly, seen with hindsight) for electric transmission in most of the proposed diesel locomotives, but hydraulic transmission had some great attractions. Since West Germany was the country in which such motive power had developed furthest, German practice was the basis of what was done. In addition to hydraulic-transmission, the German locomotives had high-speed lightweight diesel engines. They revolved at speeds twice those of diesel engines used in other BR locomotives and weighed less than half as much for the same power.

The first class of importance was the 2,000hp B-B "Warship" of 1958, designed to give similar performance to BR's 1-Co-Co-1 Class "40", but weighing 40 per cent less. Sixty-six "Warships" were built, but equality with the

Below: *Class 52 No. 1028* Western Hussar *on humble duty at the head of a five-wagon train of milk tanks.*

rest of BR was not enough. What was wanted was a machine that would run BR's other diesels into the ground.

No. D1000 *Western Enterprise* appeared in late-1961, soon to be followed by 73 more "Western" sisters. The names chosen were mostly evocative and many, like the first, provocative to BR's headquarters at 222 Marylebone Road, London. For example, No. D1001 *Western Pathfinder*, D1019 *Western Challenger*, D1059 *Western Empire*. GWR tradition was also followed in the matter of spelling mistakes—No. D1029 *Western Legionnaire* was at first *Western Legionaire*.

Alas, the locomotives did not cover themselves with Western Glory (D1072). For one thing, the opposition did not allow their lead in power output to be held for long. In the following year came the Brush Class "47" CoCo (described here), with a fraction more power than the "Westerns", for only just over the same weight, and by 1967 the Class "50" diesel-electrics hired from English Electric also matched the diesel-hydraulics for power. Moreover, even by 1963, central management had decided that diesel hydraulics had no real advantage over diesel electrics, of which it had a growing surplus. So some time before the high-speed HST125 trains took over most long-distance passenger services from Paddington in the late-1970s, the "Westerns" had been taken out of service. Withdrawal began with No. 1019 in mid-1973 and all had gone by early-1977. No less than six have survived in preservation but, in contrast, the rival diesel-electric classes "47" and "50" remain virtually intact in normal service.

The "Westerns" had their own kind of good looks, the unusualness of their appearance being enhanced by inside bearings to the wheels. The Maybach engines were also unusual (but invisibly so) in that they were of the tunnel pattern in which the circular crank webs actually form the bearing journals of the crankshafts. Power was transmitted to the wheels via various hydraulic and mechanical transmission boxes connected by numerous cardan shafts. This mechanical complixity was a source of problems with obscure causes but unfortunate results—substitution of hydraulic fluid and mechanical components for electricity as a medium of transmission tended to lower rather than raise as promised reliability and efficiency. Also, there were festoons of electrical circuitry serving the control systems and instrumentation, and these gave the problems to be expected of electrics amongst the oil-mist of a diesel locomotive interior.

The Western Region's mechanical department managed to solve the problems, being especially triumphant when the bad riding which had held down speeds was overcome by altering the bogies (with much simplification) to resemble in principle GWR standard ones dating from Victorian times. Such timings as a 3hr 30min schedule for the 225½ miles (363km) between Paddington and Plymouth then became possible, at last a significant improvement (of 30 minutes) over the best previously achieved with steam.

The reliability problem was eventually solved also by a long and painstaking process of diagnosis, trial and error, and finally by cure of many faults of detail in the design. Alas, by then a decision had already been taken to withdraw the diesel-hydraulic fleet from service prematurely and replace them by the Class "50" diesel-electric locomotives. It then was a case of heaping insult upon injury because (taking 1971 as an example) the "Westerns" were running 15,000 miles per failure while their diesel-electric replacements, the Class "50s", were only managing to achieve an appalling 9,000.

One benefit did arise; some badly needed self-confidence. This quality, previously lacking, was generated on BR by the fact that a foreign import was shown to be very far from the perfect thing it had been cracked up to be, and its designers to be only human like the rest of us.

Above: *British Railways Western Region Class 52 C-C diesel-hydraulic locomotive No. D1012* Western Firebrand *in the red livery originally adopted. Other liveries, including one known as "desert sand", were applied experimentally.*

Below: *Class 52 diesel-hydraulic locomotive No. D1048 with a Birmingham to Paddington express emerges from the short Harbury tunnel between Leamington and Banbury.*

Class 16500 B-B

France:
French National Railways (SNCF), 1962

Type: Mixed-traffic electric locomotive.
Gauge: 4ft 8½in (1,435mm).
Propulsion: Alternating current at 25,000V 50Hz fed through a rectifier (ignitron, excitron or silicon) to a traction motor mounted on each bogie; motor connected to axles through two-speed gearing.
Weight: 156,500lb (71t) to 163,100lb (74t) according to fittings.
Max. axleload: 39,100lb (17.8t) to 40,800lb (18.5t) according to fittings.
Overall length: 47ft 3in (14,400mm).
Tractive effort: Low gear 71,410lb (318kN), high gear 42,320lb (188kN).
Max. speed: Low gear 56mph (90km/h), high gear 93mph (150km/h).

The performance of the Class "12000" B-B locomotives on SNCF's Thionville-Valenciennes line established the superiority of the ignitron over other types of rectifier then available, and it also established the advantage of connecting the axles of a bogie by gearing. Wheelslip develops locally, and rarely do both axles of a bogie begin to slip at the same instant. Coupling the axles enables a locomotive to be worked much nearer to the limit of adhesion than with independent axles, and SNCF engineers reckoned that a 60t locomotive with connected axles could maintain as high a tractive effort as an 85t locomotive with independent axles.

The next electrification after the Thionville-Valenciennes line was the Paris to Lille route of the Northern Region. For this scheme two new types of locomotive were introduced, one of which was a high-speed Bo-Bo geared for 100mph (160km/h). The other was a mixed-traffic B-B machine which introduced another novelty, the monomotor bogie with two-speed gearing. The monomotor bogie had already been tested experimentally and used on two dual-voltage locomotives. As its name implies, each bogie has a single motor mounted above the bogie frame and connected to the axles through gearing and spring drives. Between the small pinion on the motor shaft and the large gear wheel of the reduction gear there is an intermediate gear. Two gear wheels of different sizes are mounted on opposite ends of an arm, and by means of a vertical lever the arm can be rocked to bring one or other of these intermediate gears into mesh; the gear ratio is thereby changed. The changeover can be effected only when the locomotive is stationary. The high-speed gear is the "passenger" gear, and the low-speed is the "freight" setting.

In a monomotor bogie the axles can be brought closer together than in a bogie with two motors situated between the axles, and the whole bogie is more compact. With the motor almost vertically above the centre, the bogie is less susceptible to developing oscillations at speed.

SNCF announced that these locomotives, designated "16500", would weigh only 60t, but in fact they weigh between 71 and 74t. Even so this is low for a locomotive of nearly 3,500hp, capable of developing a starting tractive effort in low gear of 32.4t (318kN).

ELD4 Four-car set

The Netherlands:
Netherlands Railways (NS), 1964

Type: Fast electric passenger train.
Gauge: 4ft 8½in (1,435mm).
Propulsion: Direct current at 1,500V supplied via catenary with twin contact wires to eight 180hp (134kW) nose-suspended traction motors geared to the axles of the bogies of the two intermediate coaches in the set.
Weight: 200,564lb (91t) adhesive, 370,270lb (168t) total.
Max. axleload: 50,695lb (23t).
Overall length: 331ft 7in (101,240mm).
Max. speed: 88mph (140km/h).

Electrification came early to the Netherlands, for it was as long ago as 1924 that electric traction at 1,500V dc was introduced between Amsterdam, The Hague and Rotterdam. The first streamlined stock came in 1934, various features of which set the pattern for the future. Streamlined ends to the sets precluded through access for passengers when units were coupled, but coupling and uncoupling were made painless with automatic couplers which also made all the brake-pipe and electrical connections needed. Amongst these early units there were sets of varying lengths, two- three- four- and five-car and, to suit longer runs then becoming possible under the wires, better facilities were provided on the larger units. Matching diesel-electric sets were built too, and there were also matching travelling post office vans.

The trains were designed to suit a pattern of working appropriate to a small country with a density of population 70 per cent greater than even Britain's, but which had no overwhelming single metropolis such as London. They provided an hourly (or more frequent) pattern of service and gave great emphasis to making journeys possible between all the principal cities without changing trains. Hence those automatic couplers to enable trains to be divided or combined without fuss.

Although the Dutch emerged from World War II facing almost complete destruction of their railways, they very quickly set about restoring not just the status quo, but something very much better, by extending electrification to all important lines in the country. It was decided to continue the use

Below: *Netherlands Railways' four-car electric train set at Amsterdam Station, 1981.*

When the class was introduced, the ignitron was the current type of rectifier on SNCF, and with this regenerative braking could be fitted.

Outwardly the most noticeable difference from the Thionville locomotives was reversion to a completely enclosed rectangular body, the advantages of the centre cab having been outweighed by the limited space for equipment in the end bonnets. A total of 294 of the "16500" class were built, and they were divided between the Northern Region and the subsequent Paris-Strasbourg electrification of the Eastern Region. The first 155 had bogie suspension similar to that of the "7100" class C-C locomotives, with two Alsthom spring-loaded conical pivots. The remaining bogies had swing links at the corners.

During construction of the class a new type of rectifier known as the excitron came into use, and these were fitted to Nos. 16656 to 16750 (and a few others). Finally came the silicon rectifier which was fitted to the last 44, and has since been fitted to others.

Class "16500" fulfilled the designers' intentions that they should be a universal locomotive capable of undertaking, singly or in pairs, every type of duty except the fastest expresses. For these a 100mph (160km/h) version was developed, the "17000" class, and the "8500" dc class and "25500" dual-voltage class were in turn developed from the "17000".

Right: *French National Railways' Class 16500 B-B electric locomotive No. 16506 en route from Paris to Lille.*

of multiple-unit self-propelled trains, with a few international and other trains remaining locomotive hauled. This was in order to give employment during the day to motive-power used for freight, which in the Netherlands moves during the night.

New designs of electric and diesel-electric trains put into service during the 1950s followed the lines of their predecessors, except that they were not articulated and only came in two- and four-car form. They also had bulbous extended fronts, provided not for aesthetic reasons but to give protection to the driver. There are also some units with dual-voltage capability, used for working through between Amsterdam and Brussels on to Belgium's 3,000V dc system.

In the 1960s, further stock was required and these Class "501" units, whilst in appearance very like their immediate predecessors, represent a considerable step forward. Two prototypes appeared in 1961 and the production version in 1964. By a remarkable feat of design, the overall weight of a four-car unit is 23 per cent less than before, while the rate of acceleration is approximately doubled.

Automatic doors are provided and this, combined with better performance, enabled schedules to be cut. One other major difference is that the two end vehicles of each set are driving-trailer cars, the intermediate carriages being non-driving motor cars. Since the trains were built, denser traffic, higher speeds and a bad accident in 1962 have made it seem prudent to instal signalling continuously displayed in the driver's cab, actuated by coded track circuits, for use on the busiest sections.

Right: *The front end of a Dutch electric multiple-unit train showing the automatic coupling which facilitates joining and splitting trains.*

C630 "Century" Co-Co

United States:
Alco Products Incorporated (Alco), 1965

Type: Diesel-electric road-switcher locomotive.
Gauge: 4ft 8½in (1,435mm).
Propulsion: One 16-cylinder four-stroke turbocharged 3,000hp (2,240kW) Alco 251E Vee engine and alternator, supplying three-phase current through rectifiers to six nose-suspended traction motors each geared to one axle.
Weight: 312,000lb (141.5t).
Max. axleload: 52,000lb (23.6t), but could be increased to 61,000lb (27.7t) if desired.
Overall length: 69ft 6in (21,180mm).
Tractive effort: 103,000lb (458kN).
Max. speed: 80mph (129km/h) according to gear ratio.

The old-established American Locomotive Company, long known in the trade as Alco, had pioneered one of the most important types of diesel locomotive, the road switcher, when in 1946 it produced a 1,500hp (1,120kW) A1A+A1A hood unit, the first really successful American diesel to be equally at home on switching (shunting) or freight duties. It incorporated the Alco 244 engine, which had performed well in switchers, but which revealed weaknesses under the more arduous conditions of road working.

The 244 was therefore replaced by a new engine, the 251, which officially displaced the 244 from the Alco range in 1956. It was available in 6-cylinder in-line and 12-cylinder Vee formation, to which were added V16 and V18. At first it was installed in existing designs of locomotives, but in 1963 a new range of road switchers was launched, the "Century" series.

Despite the success of its new engine, the position of Alco at this time was increasingly difficult. From 1940 to 1953 the company had an agreement with General Electric that only GE electrical equipment would be used in Alco locomotives, in return for which GE agreed not to compete with Alco in the diesel locomotive market. In 1953 GE withdrew from the agreement, and began to develop its own range of road switchers, which were launched in 1960. This was formidable competition. With the railroads now fully dieselised, the diesel salesman had to convince potential customers that it would pay them to replace their "first generation" diesels by his latest product.

A very strong selling point in any new model must be reduced maintenance costs, and this point was pressed very strongly in

Right: *A Co-Co road-switcher unit of the Alco C630 design, belonging to the British Columbia Railway, Canada.*

Shin-Kansen Sixteen-car train

Japan:
Japanese National Railways (JNR), 1964

Type: High-speed electric passenger train.
Gauge: 4ft 8½in (1,435mm).
Propulsion: Alternating current at 25,000V 50Hz fed via overhead catenary and step-down transformers and rectifiers to sixty-four 248hp (185kW) motors each driving an axle by means of gearing and flexible drive.
Weight: 2,031,200lb (922t).
Max. axleload: 31,738lb (14.4t).
Overall length: 1,318ft 6in (401,880mm).
Max. speed: 130mph (210km/h).

It took more than 60 years for the promise implicit in the Zossen trials of 1903 (already described) to become reality. Public high-speed trains averaging more than 100mph (160km/h) start-to-stop, with normal running speeds 30 per cent above this, appeared first during 1965, when Japanese National Railways put into full service the new *Shin-Kansen* line from Tokyo westwards to Osaka. The line had been opened in 1964, but a preliminary period of operation at more normal speeds had been deemed prudent.

In spite of the impression they gave, the *Shin-Kansen* (the words simply mean "New Line") trains are quite conventional in a basic sense. The high speed is obtained by having plenty of power; a 16-car train has a continuously-rated installed horsepower as high as 15,870 (11,840kW), while high acceleration is achieved by having every axle motored.

No, the interesting thing is to realise how much can be achieved by using existing railroad state-of-the-art if you begin with a clean sheet. Until 1964, Japanese National Railways used 3ft 6in (1,067mm) gauge exclusively, but their new line was to be totally separate even to the extent of being of different gauge. The investment involved in building a new standard-gauge (1,435mm) railway connecting some of Japan's major cities was very great, but the courage of those who promoted it was fully justified, mainly by a three-fold increase of traffic between 1966 and 1973.

The price of high speed was considerable. Not only are there land costs involved in building new lines into and out of the centres of large cities, but since very flat curves of 125 chain (2,500m) radius are required for this degree of fast running, the engineering works in open country are also very heavy. If you cannot turn quickly to avoid natural obstacles, you have to go through them. Of course, with such high power in relation to weight, gradients on the heavy side (1-in-65—1.5 per cent) are no obstacle.

The principal innovation is the self-signalling system of the trains. Acceleration and deceleration is not only automatic but is also automatically initiated when required, only the final approach to a stop being directly under the motorman's control. There are no lineside signals and all relevant information about the state of the line is passed on to the driving position by coded impulses passing down the main conductor wires. The trains themselves originate signals which set the route ahead, in places where a choice exists. Seismographs in the main control centres automatically stop all trains if an earthquake is recorded.

Originally there were 480 cars arranged in 40 12-car sets, each

Above: *High-speed "Bullet" trains, capable of 130mph (210km/h) speed, of the Japanese National Railways'* Shin-Kansen.

support of the Century range. The makers claimed that a saving in maintenance of up to two-thirds could be expected compared with existing 10 year-old designs.

The new series was designated by three figures, of which the first was the number of axles, all powered; the second and third denoted the engine power, in hundreds of horsepower. The first models launched were "C420", "C424" and "C624", of which the two latter were in the range of power which was most popular at this time. The 16-cylinder turbocharged engine developed 2,600hp (1,940kW), with an output from the generator for traction of 2,400hp (1,790kW); in accordance with US practice it was thus designated a 2,400hp model.

In 1964 a new version of the engine appeared, uprated to 2,750hp (2,050kW) by a combination of increased speed and intercooling. This was the most powerful engine on the US locomotive market. At a time when railroads were increasingly attracted by higher-powered locomotives, this was a strong selling point, but it was only strong enough to sell 135 units in the US.

In 1965 there came another increase in engine speed, raising the power to 3,000hp (2,240kW) for traction. More significantly this model, the "C630", had an alternator generating three-phase ac, which was then rectified for supply to the traction motors. This was the first alternator sold by a US manufacturer, and it led to the general adoption of alternators by other builders.

Finally in 1968 the engine power was raised to 3,600hp (2,690kW), producing the "C636." These increases in power were all achieved with the same 16-cylinder engine. Other variants in the Century range were the "C855" for Union Pacific, a massive Bo-Bo-Bo-Bo with two 2,750hp (2,050kW) engines, and the "C430H", a diesel-hydraulic incorporating two 2,150hp (1,600kW) engines and Voith hydraulic transmission. Neither of these was repeated.

Despite this enterprise, Alco was edged steadily out of second place in the US locomotive market by GE. Major improvements at the Schenectady Works could not save the day. Orders declined and in 1969 the works was closed.

Above: *British Columbia Railway C630 No. 712 at Lillooet, Canada. Note snowplough to cope with the extremely heavy snows of Canadian winters.*

Fortunately for the Alco tradition, the firm's Canadian associate, Montreal Locomotive Works, was in better shape, with continued sales in Canada and Mexico. MLW took over all Alco designs and patents, and in 1982 was still marketing its own versions of the Century series.

Above, left: *A Japanese* Shin-Kansen *train with snow-capped Mount Fuji in the background.*

Below left: *Construction of an entirely new 1.435mm gauge railway was Japan's successful way of cutting journey times.*

12-car train being divided electrically into six two-car units, one of which would have a buffet car, with the bullet-shaped ends and driving cabs placed at the outer ends of the train. In 1970, the 12-car trains were strengthened to 16 including two buffet cars, and train frequency increased from 120 to over 200 both ways daily. The fleet of cars had by then become 1,400, arranged in 87 16-car sets.

In 1970, as soon as success was assured, a national plan was prepared to extend the high-speed passenger network from the 320 miles (515km) of the original line twenty-fold. So far, four *Shin-Kansen* lines have been built—extending the network from Tokyo to Okayama and Hakata, and from Omiya (Tokyo) to Niigata and Morioka, a total of 1,188 miles (1,912km) of standard-gauge line.

The scale of work involved in the mountain regions—not to speak of an 11.6 mile (18.6km) inter-island undersea tunnel—can be seen from the amount of civil engineering work needed. Of the 247 miles (398km) between Okayama and Hakata, 55 per cent is in tunnel, 31 per cent on bridges or viaducts, leaving only 14 per cent as a conventional railway built on the ground. This was partly due to the minimum radius of curvature being increased to 200 chains (4,000m), with a view to raising speed from 130mph (210km/h) to 162mph (260km/h), while at the same time reducing the gradient to 1-in-65 (1.5 per cent). Even though this increase in speed has not yet been realised in public service, the fast hourly *Hikari* trains make the 735-mile (1,176km) overall journey from Tokyo to Hakata in 6hr 40min at an *average* speed of 110mph (176.5km/h). To put this in perspective, a *Shin-Kansen* style journey over the comparable distance between New York and Chicago would more than halve the best current rail time of 18½ hours, to 8¼ hours!

Incidentally the trains built for the Hakata extension provide for raising speed sometime in the future by having installed power increased by 48 per cent to 23,600hp (17,600kW), whilst the extra weight of electrical equipment needed to achieve this is compensated for by building the car bodies in light alloy. Work is now in progress replacing the original trains; on a time basis their lives have been short—but not in relation to the miles run.

WDM2 C_o-C_o

India:
Indian Railways (IR), 1962

Type: Mixed-traffic diesel-electric locomotive.
Gauge: 5ft 6in (1,676mm).
Propulsion: Alco 251D 2,600hp (1,940kW) 16-cylinder Vee diesel engine and generator supplying current to six nose-suspended traction motors geared to the axles.
Weight: 279,910lb (127t).
Max. axleload: 47,385lb (21.5t).
Overall length: 58ft 10in (17,932mm).
Tractive effort: 63,000lb (280kN).
Max. speed: 75mph (120km/h).

In spite of India being a country with little oil and much coal, the railway authorities had decided by 1960 that diesel traction would have advantages. Although with hindsight, it was a decision that might prove to be an expensive

Class 40100 C-C

France:
French National Railways (SNCF), 1964

Type: Express passenger electric locomotive.
Gauge: 4ft 8½in (1,435mm).
Propulsion: Current supply from overhead wires at 1,500V dc, 3,000V dc, 15,000V 16⅔Hz, or 25,000V 50Hz; ac supplies transformed to 1,500V and rectified by silicon rectifiers; current then supplied to two bogie-mounted 2,910hp (2,170kW) traction motors with divided armature windings, allowing series, series/parallel and parallel grouping (parallel not used on 3,000V dc); motor geared to all three axles of the bogie through Alsthom flexible drive.
Weight: 235,830lb (107t).
Max. axleload: 39,300lb (17.8t).
Overall length: 72ft 3¼in (22,030mm).
Tractive effort: 45,000lb (200kN).
Max. speed: 112mph (180km/h).

Through locomotive workings from Paris to Brussels were introduced well back in the days of steam, and were later continued with diesel railcars. Electrification of this route by French and Belgian railways permitted through electric working, but as the French part of the route uses ac at 25,000V 50Hz whilst the Belgians use 3,000V dc, a new type of locomotive was required. At this time, in the early 1960s, a network of *Trans-Europ* expresses had been established, worked by diesel railcars, but SNCF decided to build a small number of locomotives which could work not only into Belgium, but also into other Western European countries, if the TEE trains were ever electrically operated. The requirement was therefore for the locomotives to work on four systems, 1,500V dc (in France and the Netherlands), 3,000V dc (in Belgium and Italy), 15,000V 16⅔Hz (in Austria, West Germany and Switzerland), and 25,000V 50Hz (in France).

Design of the locomotives, the "40100" class, was entrusted to Alsthom, and they were the first of a new generation of electric and diesel classes incorporating monomotor bogies. So far the principle had been applied only to two-axle bogies, and SNCF had not built any six-axle locomotives since 1952. The specification reflected the prevailing ambitious thinking about TEE trains: to haul 210t at 137mph (220km/h) on the level and at 68mph (110km/h) on the 1-in-37 (2.6 per cent) gradients of the Gotthard and Lötschberg routes; to handle 450t at 100mph (160km/h) on the Paris to Brussels route, and at 68mph (110km/h) on the 1-in-70 (1.4 per cent) gradient between Mons and and Quévy in Belgium. These characteristics would enable the locomotive to haul 800t at 100mph (160km/h) between Paris and Aulnoye, and at 77mph (125km/h) on 1-in-200 (0.5 per cent).

The basis adopted for accommodating the four types of current is that the traction motor windings are designed for 1,500V dc. On the ac supplies, the current is transformed to 1,500V and then rectified by silicon rectifiers. On 3,000V the motor windings are connected in pairs in series, whilst on 1,500V dc the motors take the incoming supply directly. Motor control is through starting resistances and there is provision for rheostatic braking.

The weight of this equipment required six axles. To allow for the regrouping of the motors to accept 3,000V, the armature winding of each motor is in two sections. There are four pantographs to suit the characteristics of the four supply systems, and there are

one, they at least went about implementing it in a way that commands admiration. They ignored the temptation succumbed to by so many other "third world" countries, of a big fleet of ready-made diesels, which would have left India for ever in the power of the suppliers. At the same time they recognised that "do-it-yourself" was not possible without assistance from an overseas manufacturer.

In 1961 then, those entrusted with the project looked over the field and decided that the United States firm Alco Products Inc had the best deal to offer. The agreement provided for Alco to supply technical help as well as complete designs to Indian Railways and, at the start, finished parts for locomotive production at a diesel locomotive works to be established in Varanasi (Benares), India. When completed, the covered shops had an area over 20 acres (8Ha) in extent, while the whole factory complex, inclusive of a self-contained township, extended to 550 acres (220Ha).

The first 40 locomotives came over from America early in 1962 in completed form, followed in 1963 by a batch sent over in knocked-down condition. Ten years later production was of the order of 75 units per year and import-content was down from 100 per cent to 25 per cent. The three types which have been or are being produced are the large broad-gauge "WDM2" class (W = broad gauge, D = diesel, M = mixed traffic) described here, a smaller broad-gauge Class "WDM1" and a metre-gauge type, smaller still, Class "YDM4". All three have the Alco 251 engine, the difference being in the number of cylinders—16, 12 and 6 respectively for the three classes.

Alco's designation for the "WDM2" is "DL560" and in many ways it is similar to locomotives in the "Century" series. The six-wheel bogies have had to be modified to allow for the broad gauge, but they are of the familiar unsymmetrical pattern, taking account of the necessarily unsymmetrical arrangement of three nose-suspended traction motors. One change is the installation of a combined compressor-exhauster, provided to cater for vacuum-braked trains. Axleload is also lower than for models produced for the North American market. Although Alco went out of locomotive manufacture in 1969, its Canadian associate, previously the Montreal Locomotive Works but now known as Bombardier, is still very much in business and continues to give support to the Indian enterprise.

A scheme to update the "WDM2" design has been proposed, using an alternator in place of a dc generator and replacing the 16-cylinder engine by a 12-cylinder one developing the same horsepower. However, the advantages of building locomotives to the same good design over a long period very often outweigh any advantage accruing from some technical improvement. A factor which occasionally affects sensible judgements is the need on the part of the engineers concerned to be seen to be abreast of the latest techniques, but those in charge of locomotive development in India have so far shown a sensible contempt for such motives.

Left: *Indian Railways' Class WDM2 standard broad-gauge diesel-electric locomotive No. 17462, built to an Alco design at the railway's own locomotive-building factory at Varanasi.*

interlocks and "feeler" relays to ensure that the dc supplies are not applied to the transformer and that the correct pantograph is in use. The bogies have provision for changing the gear ratio, but unlike the other French two-speed locomotives, this is not simply a matter of moving a lever; changing of the gearwheels is a workshop job. The first four locomotives are geared for a maximum speed of 100mph (160km/h) and the second batch of six for 112mph (180km/h). None has so far been regeared for 220km/h.

Styling of the locomotives was undertaken by an industrial artist, Paul Arzens, who also styled the "CC6500" and "BB15000" electric locomotives, and the "67000" and "72000" diesel-electrics. This was the first of his designs which incorporate a steeply inclined driver's front window to reduce glare from the sun. The other classes have a larger cellular box of steel plates in front of the driver's position to act as a shock-absorber in a collision, but the "40100s" have a smaller structure than the other classes, so that the roof has an overhanging effect. The fluted stainless-steel sides are unique to these locomotives.

The first of the class appeared in 1964. They are based at La Chapelle depot, Paris, and work between Paris, Brussels and Amsterdam. In the event, the international TEE network did not develop further, and the "40100s" have never worked in countries other than France, Belgium and the Netherlands, nor, so far, have the high-speed lines designed for 220km/h running yet materialised.

Six very similar locomotives were built for Belgian National Railways (SNCB) using French electrical equipment in bodies built in Belgium. These locomotives work into West Germany.

Above: *French Railways' quadri-current electric locomotive No. 40101 at full speed.*

Below: *No. 40101 has the capability of running on four types of current—1500 and 3,000V dc, 25,000V 50Hz and 15,000V 16⅔Hz ac. An alternative gear-ratio allows a higher max. speed of 137mph (220km/h) if needed.*

Nos. 111-120 1-E-1 Argentina: Rio Turbio Industrial Railway, 1956

Type: Mineral-hauling gas-fired coal-consuming steam locomotive.
Gauge: 2ft 5½in (750mm).
Propulsion: Gas-producing firebed 26sq ft (2.43m²) in aera generating steam at 228psi (16kg/cm²), which is supplied to a pair of 16½in bore × 17⅜in stroke (420 × 400mm) cylinders, each driving the main wheels directly by connecting and coupling rods.
Weight: 83,700lb (38t). adhesive, 190,529lb (86.5t) locomotive and tender.
Max. axleload: 16,740lb (7.6t).
Overall length: 61ft 7¾in (18,790mm).
Tractive effort: 12,420lb (55.5kN).
Max. speed: 28mph (45km/h).

The many attempts to improve the efficiency of the steam locomotive in the 20th Century fall into two main groups: first, those which involved radical changes in the Stephenson locomotive, such as complex high-pressure boilers or turbine drive; and secondly, those which concentrated on improving the proportions and detailed design of the conventional locomotive. In the second category the work of André Chapelon was outstanding, and his rebuilds developed up to twice the power of the original locomotive, and at the same time used fuel more efficiently.

Above: *A double-shotted train of empty coal hopper wagons prepares to leave the port of Rio Gallegos, Argentina, for the mines at Rio Turbio, hauled by two Porta-Chapelon steam locos.*

QJ "Forward" 1-E-1 China: Railways of the People's Republic (CR), 1956

Type: Steam freight locomotive.
Gauge: 4ft 8½in (1,435mm).
Propulsion: Coal fire burning on a firegrate 73sq ft (6.8m²) in size generating steam at 213psi (15kg/cm²) in a firetube boiler and supplying it via a main steam pipe mounted above the boiler and a superheater to two 25⅝ x 31½in (650 x 800mm) cylinders which drive the main wheels directly through connecting and coupling rods.
Weight: 221,500lb (100.5t) adhesive, 486,080lb (220.5t) total.*
Max. axleload: 44,300lb (20.1t).
Overall length: 86ft 1½in (26,251mm).
Tractive effort: 63,500lb (282kN).
Max. speed: 50mph (80km/h).

*With small tender holding 15t (16.5 US tons) of coal and 7,700gal (35m³-9,620 US gal) of water. With large tender the total weight is increased to 546,592lb (248t), the length to 95ft 9in, (29,180mm) and the coal and water capacity to 21.5t (23.7 US tons) and 11,020gal (50m³-13,775 US gals) respectively.

China began seriously to build steam locomotives after the rest of the world had stopped. Production still continues at a rate approaching one per working day and, not only that, has recently been reprieved indefinitely. In fact, this "QJ" class is currently, at 4,000-strong, the largest class of locomotives in the world, of whatever type of propulsion; it also comprises about a fifth of all the steam locomotives left active in the world.

The reasons for China being out of step with the rest of mankind are plain. Ample indigenous supplies of coal, modest oil reserves and plenty of people to serve a rather labour-intensive form of traction are three of them. More important, perhaps, is the pressing need to keep the capacity of the railways abreast of the rising demands of a rapid industrial growth. This need is best met by continuing with steam locomotives which can be mass-produced in a purpose-built factory for one seventh of the cost, like-for-like, of diesel-electric ones. In Western money, a Chinese steam 2-10-2 costs some £70,000 ($ US105,000), while a diesel of equivalent capacity built in China is priced at £500,000 ($ US800,000). Fuel costs are also now lower with steam than with diesel. A last factor is that the Chinese suffer less pressure to follow the example of neighbouring railway administrations than others. No need to "keep up with the Joneses" if you live by yourself.

The first steps in development of the "QJ" began in 1946 when, after 12 years of struggle, Mao's communist government took over a war-torn and ramshackle railway system. To improve the motive power situation in the long-term, Russian assistance was given in setting up a works at Datong in northern China, to build large freight locomotives. Delays occurred through withdrawal of Russian help and the confusion that resulted, and also because of Mao's "Great Leap Forward", during which embryo locomotive factories were ordered to produce diesel locomotives—Datong's attempt is said to have been called *Sputnik*.

It was 1962 before production of this class (then called *Ho Ping* or "Peace") began at Datong. The design was basically the "Lv" class of 2-10-2 from Russia; some prototypes were built in 1956 at Dalien works in Manchuria. Certain modifications, principally to the boiler, were made in the version for production, which built up

Amongst disciples of Chapelon were several Argentinian engineers, notably Dante Porta. Under the direction of Porta and his colleagues, and with Chapelon's aid, a number of classes were improved beyond recognition, with increases of power of up to 55 per cent despite limitations imposed by the quality of labour compared with France. These rebuilds followed Chapelon's doctrine—increased cross-section of flow throughout the path of the steam, increased steam temperature by redesigning the superheater, and improved blast to increase the steaming rate without restricting the exhaust from the cylinders.

The designs incorporated a number of advances on Chapelon's work, of which the most notable was the gas-producer firebox. In this the firebed is at a comparatively low temperature, and almost all the combustion takes place in the firebox above the fire, air and steam being blown into the firebox under careful control so that almost perfect combustion can be maintained up to the highest rate of steaming. This remedied a major weakness in the normal locomotive boiler—that combustion deteriorates at high rates of steaming, thus reducing the efficiency.

Porta's most spectacular results were achieved on the world's most southerly railway, the Rio Turbio line in Argentina, a 2ft 5½in (750mm) gauge line which carries coal 160 miles (257km) from the Rio Turbio mines to the port of Rio Gallegos on the Atlantic, with grades of 1-in-333 (0.3 per cent) against loaded trains and winds of up to 100mph (160km/h). Light rail limits the axleload to 7½t and the maximum speed is 25 to 28mph (40 to 45km/h).

In 1956, ten 2-10-2 locomotives, based on a design of the Baldwin Locomotive Company, were built for this line in Japan, and Porta later applied his ideas, including the gas-producer firebox, to three of them. As a result, the sustained drawbar horsepower was increased from 700 to 1,200. Despite the poor quality of the coal, which is small for firing in locomotives and has a high ash content, combustion is almost smokeless. The improvements enabled the locomotive to haul 1,700t regularly, and on test as much as 3,000t was hauled on the level, a remarkable achievement for a locomotive weighing 48 tons on a rail gauge little more than half the standard gauge.

In 1964 ten more locomotives were built incorporating Porta's modifications, and one had a circular firebox of his design, arranged to give even more intense combustion by mixing the gases, steam and air in a swirling motion.

Not the least remarkable feature of these engines, is that, for a grate area of 22.5sq ft (2.1m^2), a mechanical stoker is provided; many European and North American grates of twice that size were hand fired, but, although it had not been provided for that purpose, the controlled firing which the stoker permitted was of great help to Porta in his modifications to the firebox.

Porta produced a design for a two-cylinder compound 2-8-0 which was aimed at railways in under-developed countries which had coal but no oil, and in which the railways had difficulty in obtaining skilled labour. However, climbing on the diesel band wagon was already a characteristic of the railways in countries which could have benefitted from Porta's work, aided by countries which made cheap loans available to the third world to aid their own diesel locomotive industry. By the time the crisis in oil prices showed the folly of total dependence on oil, dieselisation had proceeded too far in most countries, and no country has built an engine to the Chapelon/Porta design, although, as recorded later, Porta's ideas are being applied in South Africa at the present time.

Below: *No. 108* André Chapelon, *a modern coal-hauling steam locomotive of the Rio Turbio Industrial Railway.*

Left: *A QJ class 1-E-1 steam locomotive of the Chinese People's Republic Railways steams past Jilin outskirts in October 1980.*

steadily as experience was gained. The 500th "QJ" was built in 1968, the 1,000th in 1970, the 2,000th in 1974 and the 3,000th in 1979, all except the very first at Datong. Datong has also built a number of "JS" or "Construction" class 2-8-2s and a series of mobile diesel-electric generating plants.

The "QJs" are very well-equipped and, apart from having the main steam pipe in trunking above the forward part of the boiler instead of out of sight inside, very much in the North American genre. They have mechanical stokers, exhaust steam injectors, feed water heaters, electric lighting, an air-horn as well as a dragon-scaring steam whistle, and even cooking facilities and a toilet on board. The standard models (numbered with a few exceptions chronologically from QJ 100 upwards) have eight-wheel tenders, but a few in the QJ60xx series have large 12-wheeled versions for use in dry areas.

Though designed for heavy freight movement, these superb locomotives can often be seen on passenger work on heavily-graded mountain lines. With extensive new railway construction going on, it is possible to travel in China on a 1980s railway behind a 1980s steam locomotive. With 2,980hp (2,223kW) available at the wheel-rim—equivalent to say 3,700hp (2,760kW) developed in the cylinders of a diesel engine—an excellent level of performance is available.

Class 103.1 C_o-C_o

West Germany: German Federal Railway (DB), 1970

Type: Express passenger electric locomotive.
Gauge: 4ft 8½in (1,435mm).
Propulsion: Alternating current at 15,000V 16⅔Hz fed through a transformer to six 1,580hp (1,180kW) traction motors mounted on the bogie frames, connected to the axles through spring drive.
Weight: 251,260lb (114t).
Max. axleload: 41,880lb (19.0t).
Overall length: 63ft 11½in (19,500mm).
Tractive effort: 70,000lb (312kN).
Max. speed: 125mph (200km/h).

Above: *A high-speed inter-city train of the German Federal Railway hauled by a Class 103.1 electric locomotive.*

Below: *German Federal Railway's Class 103.1 Co-Co high-speed electric locomotive, introduced in 1970.*

In 1960 Deutsche Bundesbahn began to plan a network of high-speed inter-city trains with which to meet the competition of internal air services. The fast diesel trains in pre-war Germany had operated mainly on routes radiating from Berlin, on which high speeds could be sustained for long distances. In West Germany, however, the principal routes had more frequent stops and speed restrictions, and the ability to reach high speed quickly was thus as important as the ability to sustain it. The specification which was drawn up in 1961 therefore required that a speed of 125mph (200km/h) should be maintained on a gradient of 1-in-200 (0.5 per cent) with 300t, and that the train should be accelerated to this speed in 150 seconds.

In accordance with German practice a number of companies submitted proposals. These in-

VL80T B_o-B_o+B_o-B_o

USSR: Soviet Railways (SZD), 1967

Type: Electric locomotive for heavy freight haulage.
Gauge: 5ft 0in (1,524mm).
Propulsion: Alternating current at 25,000V 50Hz fed via overhead catenary, step-down transformer and silicon rectifiers to eight 790hp (590kW) nose-suspended dc traction motors, each geared to one axle.
Weight: 405,535lb (184t).
Max. axleload: 50,695lb (23t).
Overall length: 107ft 9in (32,840mm).
Tractive effort: 99,500lb (433kN).
Max. speed: 68mph (110km/h).

Soviet Railways' "VL80" series of electric locomotives, one of the most numerous in the world, is the main motive power used for moving heavy freight trains over the USSR's huge 11,600 mile (18,700km) network of industrial-frequency electrification. The letters VL pay tribute to Vladimir Lenin, no less, whose personal enthusiasm for railway electrification has now, many years after his death, had such impressive results.

The eight-axle locomotive has double-bogie units permanently coupled in pairs, and is a favourite for freight work in the USSR. Some 1,500 of Class "VL8" were built for the 3,000V dc lines from 1953 onwards, followed in 1961 by the start of production of the "VL10" class, also for dc lines. For ac lines, the first "VL80s", externally very similar to the "VL10s" began coming into use in 1963 with the class variant "VL80K".

The first "VL80Ks" had mercury-arc rectifiers, but it is difficult to avoid problems when (in lay terms) mercury sloshes around under the influence of vibration and traction shocks. Solid-state silicon rectifiers were soon substituted. The "VL80T" was a modification of the "VL80K" which had rheostatic electric braking, and this has been the main production version of the "VL80" class of which over 2,000 have now been built. After some years of experiment, "VL80" series-production has now changed to a version ("VL80R") with thyristor control and—made painlessly possible by the scope of this system—full regenerative electric braking. This is claimed to reduce current consumption by over 10 per cent.

Experiments are in progress on a "VL80A" version which uses three-phase asynchronous induction motors supplied with variable-frequency current by a solid-state conversion system. Another interesting development, which is obviously very similar to the "VL80A" arrangement theoretically but very different practically, is to use thyristors inside each motor as a substitute for the commutator and brushes. In this way the associated problems of mechanical wear and vulnerability to flashover at the commutators can possibly be avoided. A three-unit version ("VL80S") with 13,100hp (9,780kW) available for hauling 10,000t (11,000 US tons) trains has been produced and

cluded 1-Bo+Bo-1 and A1A+A1A schemes with four motors of 1,250kW (1,675hp), but it was considered that six motors should be fitted to keep the motor weight down, and despite some doubts about its riding qualities, the Co-Co arrangement was chosen.

Four prototypes were ordered in 1963 from Siemens Schuckert and Henschel; delivered in 1965 they were numbered E03.001-4. They made a spectacular entry into service, for in connection with an international transport exhibition in Munich that year they worked a special train twice daily from Munich to Augsburg at an average of 88mph (142km/h) with sustained 200km/h running.

The locomotives followed the pattern already established in DB standard designs, with an ac motor mounted above each axle and fully-sprung drive. Control was by tap changers on the high-tension side of the transformer. Automatic speed control was fitted, with increments of 10km/h on the driver's controller. The motors were of light weight for their power, specially designed for high speed. The one-hour rating was 6,420kW (8,600hp) at 200km/h, and the 10-minute rating was no less than 9,000kW (12,000hp). The locomotives were subjected to a lengthy period of testing, from which it was found that, when employed on heavy expresses running at lower speeds, they suffered from high transformer temperatures, and so larger transformers had to be fitted.

For a time, DB favoured the idea of working the inter-city network by multiple-units, but eventually it was decided that, except for any services which might in the future exceed 200km/h, locomotives would be used, and 145 more of the Co-Co units were ordered. They were delivered from 1970 onwards; under the computerised numbering system then in use they were designated Nos. 103.101-245. They incorporated various improvements to the motors and control equipment which allowed them to work trains of up to 480t at 200km/h. The earlier locomotives had also developed heavy brush and commutator wear when their high-speed motors were subjected to heavy currents at low speeds, and the new machines had an additional tap-changer on the low-tension side of the transformer which made them suitable for working 600t trains at normal speeds.

The body shape of the original locomotives had been determined by wind-tunnel tests, but the resultant curved ends had the effect of making the driver's cab more cramped than in other classes. The last 30 of the new locomotives were 700mm (27½in) longer in the body, to allow for more roomy cabs. Experience with 200km/h running showed that wear on the track and locomotives was greater than had been expected, and it was suspended from 1967. It was not until 1977 that the intended network of *IC-Züge* came into operation. The Class "103" then came fully into its own, for the admission of second-class passengers to these trains had increased the number of coaches above the original proposals.

No. 103.118 is geared for a maximum speed of 155mph (250km/h), and has been used for much high-speed testing. It also has some electrical differences, and has a short-term rating of 14,000hp (10,400kW), making it the most powerful single-unit locomotive in the world.

prototypes have been built of a "VL84" version with increased power.

Also associated with the "VL80s" are the "VL82" series of dual-current locomotives for 3,000 dc and 25,000V 50Hz ac, dating from 1966. Adding together both systems of electrification the overall picture is quite amazing—more electrically-hauled rail freight traffic than the whole of the rest of the world put together, moved on a 28,000 mile (44,800km) network of electrified lines by a fleet of some 4,000 of these massive dc, ac, and dc/ac machines.

Right: *One half of a Soviet Railways' VL82 series Bo-Bo+Bo-Bo dual current electric locomotive.*

Class 73 B_o-B_o

Great Britain: British Railways (BR), 1967

Type: Electro-diesel mixed-traffic locomotive.
Gauge: 4ft 8½in (1,435mm).
Propulsion: Direct-current at 675V fed via an outside third rail, or alternatively generated on the locomotive by an English Electric 600hp (448kW) Type 4 SRKT diesel engine, to four 395hp (295kW) nose suspended traction motors.
Weight: 168,000lb (76t).
Max. axleload: 42,000lb (19t).
Overall length: 53ft 8in (16,358mm)*.
Tractive effort: 42,000lb (187kN).
Max. speed: 90mph (145km/h).

*Buffers extended

Left: *The Honeymoon Special of the Prince and Princess of Wales (note special Charles-Diana headcode) enters Romsey station, Hants, hauled by electro-diesel No. 73142.*

One of the problems of an electrified railway is the need to provide for working over lines which, either permanently or temporarily, have no current supply. With third-rail systems this need is accentuated by the impossibility of providing conductor rails uninterruptedly; BR's Southern Region had solved the problem by electric locomotives which could store energy in fly-wheels to pass trains over short gaps.

As the SR's electrification became more widespread, the use of normal diesel locomotives to cover workings over shorter and shorter portions of a journey became less and less satisfactory. So a powerful electric locomotive

Below: *British Railways Southern Region Class 73 electro-diesel locomotive No. 73142,* Broadlands.

Class ET22 C_o-C_o

Poland: Polish State Railways (PKP), 1972

Type: Electric mixed-traffic locomotive.
Gauge: 4ft 8½in (1,435mm).
Propulsion: Direct current at 3,000V fed via overhead catenary to six 705hp (520kW) traction motors, geared with quill-type flexible drive to the axles.
Weight: 264,480lb (120t).
Max. axleload: 44,080lb (20t).
Overall length: 63ft 1½in (19,240mm).
Tractive effort: 92,568lb (411kN).
Max. speed: 78mph (125km/h).

Poland is a country which, seen from the West, appears as a small (and reluctant) Russian satellite state. Yet its land area and railway mileage—the latter at 15,078 miles (24,125km)—is 30 per cent greater than Britain's, while the population is 40 per cent less. The startling difference is that Polish State Railways (PKP) move seven times as much freight as BR. In fact, apart from the USSR, Poland has more rail traffic than any European country. Poland is also a coal-rich but oil-poor land so, despite relative poverty, 4,438 miles (7,100km) of electrification has been carried out.

Even so, there are some 2,000 diesel locomotives in Poland including shunters (the exact number is not revealed), but it is a sign of the times that—alone in Europe—more than 1,000 steam locomotives continue to contribute their now substantially lower fuel costs (not to speak of zero capital cost) to the economy. But there is no doubt that the electrified network, already carrying over one-third of the country's rail traffic, will be increased.

Heavy density of traffic over many lines still to be electrified means that there is little temptation to depart from the 3,000V dc system adopted in the 1930s. All Polish electric locomotives from the beginning have been of the universal double-bogie pattern, all axles powered, of Bo-Bo or Co-Co wheel arrangement.

These Class "ET22" locomotives are the most common type in Poland and were originally designed for freight traffic. Over 500 have been built by Panstwowa Fabvyka Wagonow (Pafawag) of Wroclaw (mechanical parts) and Kolmex of Warsaw (electrical equipment) since 1971. They follow an anglo-saxon tradition of simplicity introduced to Poland in 1936 with a batch of Bo-Bos from Britain. Hence no frills such as dynamic braking, although some of the units have multiple-unit capability for working heavy trains of coal from Silesia to Gdansk.

Another complication is the use of flexible drive of the quill pattern to ease dynamic loadings and so assist the permanent way to remain permanent. Maximum speed is usefully high and the "ET22s" are equipped for passenger work with electric train heating, a fairly simple matter with medium-voltage dc traction. This is perhaps the reason why some references to

was conceived which carried a modest (but standard) diesel generating plant for movements away from the conductor rail. The result was this versatile group of locomotives (now designated Class "73") of which 42 were built in 1967 following six prototypes of 1962.

Details of interest include provision for multiple-unit operation not only with other electro-diesels, but also with straight electric and diesel-electric trains and locomotives. The weight of the diesel engine and generator, housed at one end of the locomotive, is balanced by a massive buffer beam at the other. Both screw couplings with buffers (for coupling to freight stock) and automatic buck-eye couplers with central buffing plates (for passenger trains) are provided.

The versatility of Class "73" was demonstrated to the world in July 1981, when Charles and Diana, Prince and Princess of Wales, left London for their honeymoon at Romsey, Hampshire, behind No. 73 142 *Broadlands*: 82 miles (131km) of electrified travel down the main line was followed by 5 miles (8km) on a lesser and non-electrified route.

Above: *BR Class 73 electro-diesel. Yellow ends make the locomotive more conspicuous for men working on the track.*

this class designate it "EU22". "E" means electric and "T" means 'Towarowy' or freight, while "U" seems to signify mixed-traffic. Incidentally, Bo-Bo classes are numbered from 01 to (currently) 08, Co-Cos from 20 to 23, and double Bo-Bos from 40 to 42. "P" stands for "Pospiszny" or passenger, and hence a recent 100mph (160km/h) version of the "ET22" is classified "EP23".

The "ET22s" are very successful machines and have extended the once thriving Polish export trade in steam locomotives to include electric, when an order for 23 for Morocco (Class "E-1000") was delivered in 1973.

Right: *No. ET22-112 takes a freight through Lublin, Poland.*

Class 72000 C-C

France: French National Railways (SNCF), 1967

Type: Diesel-electric dual-purpose locomotive.
Gauge: 4ft 8½in (1,435mm).
Propulsion: Société Alsacienne de Constructions Mécaniques 3,550hp (2,650kW) 16-cylinder four-stroke diesel engine and alternator supplying current through silicon rectifiers to two traction motors, one on each bogie; motors connected to the axles through two-speed gearing and spring drive.
Weight: 251,260lb (114t).
Max. axleload: 41,880lb (19t).
Overall length: 66ft 3in (20,190mm).
Tractive effort: Low gear 81,570lb (363kN), high gear 46,300lb (206kN).
Max. speed: Low gear 53mph (85km/h), high 87mph (140km/h).

When SNCF embarked on construction of large main-line diesel locomotives in 1961, it was recognised that a more powerful unit than the 2,650hp Class "68000" would be needed eventually for the heaviest work. So two pairs of twin-engine experimental locomotives were ordered, which could develop up to 4,800hp (3,580kW). However, enthusiasm for the complications of the twin-engine machines was never great, and development of new diesel engines in the range 3,500 to 4,000hp encouraged SNCF in 1964 to invite manufacturers to submit proposals for a powerful single-engine locomotive. Alsthom made a successful submission of a C-C design, based on the AGO16 engine of 3,600hp (2,700kW). "A" denotes the maker, Société Alsacienne de Constructions Mécaniques of Mulhouse, "G" and "O" denote the designers, Grosshaus and Ollier. This engine was a 16-cylinder version of the 12-cylinder engine already fitted to the "68500" series of A1A+A1A locomotives.

Eighteen of the new design were ordered from Alsthom in 1966, and delivery commenced in the following year; the class was allocated numbers from 72001. SNCF was at this period developing a new family of electric locomotives incorporating monomotor bogies, and the "72000s" incorporated various parts in common with the electric units. The bogies followed closely the design recently introduced in the Class "40100" quadricurrent locomotives, with two gear ratios, the maximum speeds in the two settings being 53mph (85km/h) for freight and 87mph (140km/h) for passenger work. The traction motors are identical electrically with those of the "BB8500," "BB17000" and "BB25500" electric locomotives. SNCF estimated that the monomotor bogie saved 9t in weight compared with conventional bogies with individual axle drive, and it enabled the axleload to be kept within the stipulated 18t.

Main innovation in the electrical system was use of an alternator instead of a dc generator. This delivers three-phase current which is rectified by silicon diodes for supply to the dc traction motors. The electrical equipment includes Alsthom's "Superadhesion" system, in which the excitation of the field of the motors is controlled to give an almost direct relationship between motor voltage and current. By this means the tendency for incipient wheelslip to develop

Right: *French National Railways Class 72000 diesel-electric loco.*

Class 68000 A1A-A1A

France: French National Railways (SNCF), 1963

Type: Express passenger diesel-electric locomotive.
Gauge: 4ft 8½in (1,435mm).
Propulsion: CCM-Sulzer 2,650hp (1,980kW) 12LVA24 12-cylinder four-stroke Vee-engine and generator supplying current to four semi-sprung traction motors geared to the end axles of the bogies through spring drive.
Weight: 176,320lb (80t) or 158,690lb (72t) adhesive, 233,620lb (106t) total.
Max. axleload: 44,080lb (20t) or 39,670lb (18t) adjustable.
Overall length: 58ft 9½in (17,920mm).
Tractive effort: 66,140lb (294kN).
Max. speed: 83mph (130km/h).

Above: *A pair of Class 68000 diesel-electric locomotives with an express near Noyelles in 1978.*

During the 1950s, electrification spread rapidly over the busiest main lines in France and many of the most powerful steam engines became available for transfer to non-electrified routes. Until the end of the decade no major steps were taken to introduce large diesel locomotives for the ultimate replacement of these steam engines on routes on which the traffic density was insufficient to justify electrification, and in 1962 only 8 per cent of total tonne-km on SNCF were diesel worked.

By 1960 diesel engines were available which made possible design of locomotives to replace even the largest steam engines, and in 1961 orders were placed for four new types of diesel locomotive, 20 B-Bs of 2,000hp (1,500kW), 18 A1A-A1As of 2,650hp (1,980kW), and two each of two twin-engined machines destined ultimately to have a power of 4,800hp (3,580kW).

It was intended that the 2,650hp Class "68000" should take over the heaviest workings on the routes from Paris to Cherbourg and Basle, pending completion of development of the larger units. The engine is of Sulzer design, produced by Sulzer's French associate, CCM. It is a 16-cylinder unit of Vee-formation, in contrast to the 2,750hp Sulzer engine then being built in large numbers for British Railways, which had twin crankshafts. It was Sulzer's first Vee engine for traction since 1927.

The engine drives a dc generator, which supplies the semi-sprung nose-hung traction motors. The weight of the engine, generator and train boiler made it necessary to have six axles, but only four traction motors were required, so the middle axle of each bogie is an idler. A novel system was applied whereby wedges can be inserted above the springs of the intermediate axles to vary the distribution of weight. On routes on which a 20t axleload is allowed, the intermediate axles carry 13t, but on routes with an 18t limit, the intermediate axles carry 17t. In the latter arrangement, a servo-operated mechanism enables the load on the driving wheels to be increased to 20t at starting, until a speed of 18½mph (30km/h) is

Below: *French National Railways No. 68067 enters Angers with a Paris express in June 1967.*

is greatly reduced, and it is claimed that the effective starting tractive effort can be increased by 15 to 20 per cent.

The body resembles closely those of the corresponding electric classes but has a higher roof to accommodate the engine. The treatment of the ends incorporates cab windows steeply inclined backwards to reduce glare, as introduced on the "40100" class, but the appearance was much altered by restyling of the ends due to inclusion of massive cellular boxes in front of the cab to protect the driver in case of collision.

They were immediately put to work on the Paris to Brittany and Paris to Basle routes, where they enabled modest increases to be made in train speeds over the "68000" class, but consistent with SNCF's target of not developing full power for more than 60 per cent of the run, compared with 67 per cent recorded with the earlier locomotives, and also consistent with supplying electric train heating from the engine power. The class eventually reached a total of 92, and they took over the heaviest work on most non-electrified routes. Ten had modifications made to enable them to run at 100mph (160km/h).

In 1973 No. 72075 was fitted with an SEMT-Pielstick PA 6-280 12-cylinder engine, initially rated at 4,200hp, but increased a year later to 4,800hp (3,580kW), making it the most powerful diesel engine in a locomotive (at least in the Western world). At the end of 1978 the engine was found to be in good condition, and it embarked on a further period of service. This modification increased the weight to 118t. There were no further conversions.

reached. Maximum speed is 83mph (130km/h).

Control equipment is also novel for a diesel locomotive in that it resembles the "notch-up, notch-down, hold" type of controller, already in use on electric locomotives. The driver's controller has four positions, "stop", "run", "faster", "slower". Moving the controller from "stop" to "run" energises the motor circuits with the engine running at idling speed, and engine speed is increased by holding the controller at "faster" against the pressure of a spring until the desired engine speed is reached. Similarly holding the controller at "slower" reduces the engine speed. Body sides are finished with a distinctive chevron design, destined to characterise all subsequent large French diesel locomotives, and the livery is blue and white.

The first 18 Class "68000" locomotives were ordered in 1961 from Cie des Ateliers & Forges de la Loire of St Chamond, and delivery commenced in 1963. A further 18 were ordered in the following year's programme, and eventually the class totalled 82. The first locomotives were put to work between Paris and Mulhouse and Paris and Cherbourg, but it was soon apparent that they could only just equal the everyday work of the "241P" 4-8-2 steam engines on trains of 800t, and then only at the cost of working at full power for a higher proportion of the time than was considered desirable in the interests of reliability.

A second version of the class was introduced late in 1963, fitted with the AGOV12 engine made by Société Alsacienne de Constructions Mécaniques of Mulhouse. This engine is a smaller version of that used in the "72000" class C-C locomotives. Since the appearance of the "72000", the two series of A1A-A1As have been moved to less-demanding duties.

WAM4 C_o-C_o

India:
Indian Railways (IR), 1971

Type: Electric mixed-traffic locomotive.
Gauge: 5ft 6in (1,676mm).
Propulsion: Alternating current at 25,000V 50Hz fed via overhead catenary, step-down transformer and solid-state rectifiers to six 600hp (448kW) nose-suspended traction motors, each geared directly to one of the six axles.
Weight: 249,050lb (113t).
Max. axleload: 41,876lb (19t).
Overall length: 62ft 3in (18,974mm).
Tractive effort: 74,600lb (332kN).
Max. speed: 75mph (120km/h).

When in the 1950s use of industrial-frequency current combined with rectifier locomotives became the world norm, India like most other countries previously wedded to dc systems made the change. Since French developments then led the field, the locomotives supplied at first followed that country's practice, whether built in France or in India. Before long it became apparent that some of their more sophisticated features such as spring-borne traction motors did not suit Indian conditions. The result was the first Indian-designed and Indian-built electric locomotive class, which appeared from the railways' own Chittaranjan Loco Works in 1971.

A feature is the use of the same power bogies as on Indian diesel-electric locomotives. So many electric and diesel-electric loco designers pursue separate and divergent courses, those of British Rail being a notorious example. The fleet of these machines has now reached over 300, rheostatic electric braking and multiple-unit capability being provided on all. Silicon-diode rectifiers and tap-changing on the high tension side of the main transformer are used.

A dual-current series, Class "WCAM1", is also being built, as well as 'WCG2s" for freight traffic on dc lines. Both are similar in appearance to and have many components in common with the "WAM4s". A small group of "WAM4s" have been given a lower gearing for heavy iron-ore trains ("WAM4B"), while a high-speed version is also reported to be under construction.

Class "WAM4" illustrates how sound thinking and a bold approach to self-help have given Indian Railways an enviable foundation on which to build a sound future.

Below: *Indian Railways' Class WAM4 Co-Co 3,600hp electric locomotive built "in-house" at the Chittaranjan Locomotive Works for ac-electrified lines.*

"Virgin" B-B

Spain:
Spanish National Railways (RENFE), 1964

Type: High-speed diesel-hydraulic express passenger locomotive.
Gauge: 5ft 6in (1,668mm).
Propulsion: Two Maybach-Mercedes MD6557 12-cylinder Vee diesel engines of 1,200hp (895kW), each driving a Mekydro K104U hydraulic transmission unit and via cardan shafts and gearing, the main axles.
Weight: 163,100lb (74t).
Max. axleload: 40,775lb (18.5t).
Overall length: 57ft 3in (17,450mm).
Tractive effort: 54,000lb (240kN).
Max. speed: 87mph (140km/h).

Vehicles with less than four wheels are rare in the railway world, except in Spain. There the coaches of the famous "Talgo" trains are not only two-wheeled (the wheel-less end being supported by the next car), but so low-slung that the floors are typically only 14in (356mm) above rail level. This compares with 42in (1,067mm) typically for conventional stock. This gives the "Talgos" excellent stability for fast running on heavily-curved routes. The weight per passenger seat is also low, being only about 672lb (305kg) compared with 1,014lb (460kg) of, say, a British Rail MKIII coach.

In 1964, with many "Talgos" running and planned, Spanish National Railways went to Krauss-Maffei of Munich, West Germany, for a batch of five low-slung matching diesel locomotives. These machines, now officially designated Class "352", were the result. The Spanish share with the British a feeling that locomotives need names, but being a devout nation chose for these names of shrines to the Holy Virgin. Further batches have followed down the years, the next five being virtually identical, except that they were constructed under licence in Spain by Babcock y Wilcox of Bilbao.

Eight more of a stretched version (Class "353") came from Krauss-Maffei in 1969, offering 25 per cent more power than the originals. In 1982, Krauss-Maffei delivered a further eight, with power output increased to 4,000hp (2,980kW), designated Class "354". The last of the original batch, No. 3005 *Virgen de la Bien Aparecida* is interesting in that it originally ran for a time on standard-gauge bogies. This was to haul the "Catalan Talgo" Trans-Europe-Express on the French portion of its journeys between Barcelona and Geneva. The train itself has adjustable axles for a quick change between Spanish broad gauge and French standard gauge.

The locomotives have to have special low drawgear for hauling the "Talgo" sets and, in addition, must provide power for lighting, heating, air-conditioning and cooking on the train. This is taken care of by two 250hp (187kW) diesel-generator sets. The basis of the design was the German Class "V-200" diesel-hydraulics (qv) but modifications were needed to obtain the "Talgo" height of 10ft 9in (3,277mm) overall, compared with that of conventional Spanish trains of 14ft 1in (4,293mm).

The "Talgo" principle has recently been extended to encompass a Paris to Madrid sleeping car express, running the 911 miles (1,458km) in a very creditable 12hr 55min, including gauge change for the carriage units. The most interesting innovation on this and other recent "Talgo" trains is inclusion of a passive tilting system to permit higher speeds on curves.

Right: *A low-slung "Virgin" diesel-hydraulic locomotive of Spanish National Railways,* Virgen Sante Maria, *hauling a Talgo express at Pancorbo on the Miranda to Burgos line.*

Metroliner Two-car Trainset

USA:
Pennsylvania Railroad (PRR), 1967

Type: High-speed electric multiple-unit trainset.
Gauge: 4ft 8½in (1,435mm).
Propulsion: Alternating current at 11,000V 25Hz fed via overhead catenary, step down transformer and rectifiers to eight 300hp (224kW) nose-suspended motors, one geared to each pair of wheels.
Weight: 328,400lb (149t).
Max. axleload: 41,880lb (19t).
Overall length: 170ft 0in (51,816mm).
Max speed: 160mph (256km/h)*.

*Design speed; yet to be achieved in normal service.

In the 1960s, the United States passenger train was at a very low ebb. Most railroads were reporting massive deficits on passenger services as well as a steady loss of traffic. Over long distances the jet airliner had a twenty-fold advantage in time, which hardly affected the time disadvantage between city centre and operational terminal, compared with rail. Over short distances, though, the opposite was the case and there seemed a possibility of the train continuing to compete, were it not for outdated equipment and image.

One such route was the Pennsylvania Railroad's electrified main line between New York, Philadelphia and Washington, now known as the North East Corridor. It was in order to offer better service on this route that these remarkable trains came into being. Possible prototypes had been acquired from the Budd Company of Philadelphia in 1958 ("MP 85") and in 1963 some cars—the Budd *Silverliners*—were acquired on behalf of Pennsy by the City of Philadelphia.

Later in the decade the railroad received some government assistance towards a $22 million scheme for new high-speed self-propelled trains plus $33 million for some improvements to the permanent way; 160mph (256km/h) operation was envisaged.

Orders were placed in 1966 with Budd for 50 (later increased to 61) stainless steel cars to be called *Metroliners*. They drove on all wheels, could attain considerably more than the specified speed and had a fantastic short-term power-to-weight ratio of 34hp per tonne. They also had dynamic braking down to 30mph (48km/h), automatic acceleration, deceleration and speed control using new sophisticated techniques. Full air-conditioning, air-

Below: *Budd Metroliner self-propelled high-speed club car refurbished in Amtrak colours.*

line-type catering, electrically controlled doors and a public telephone service by radio link were provided. The order included parlour cars and snack-bar coaches as well as ordinary day coaches. All had a driving cab at one end, but access between adjacent sets through a cab not in use was possible. They were marshalled semi-permanently in pairs as two-car units. An over-bold decision was taken to begin production straight from the drawing board; for once, with the Pennsylvania Railroad suffering from a terminal sickness, its officers did not insist on the usual Pennsy precaution of building and testing prototypes first. As a result, faults galore again and again delayed entry into public service until after ill-fated Penn Central took over in 1968. A single round-trip daily began at the beginning of 1969 and even then a modification programme costing 50 per cent of the original price of the trains was needed to make them suitable for public service.

Amtrak took over in May 1971 and a year later 14 daily *Metroliner* trips were being run and start-to-stop average speeds as high as 95mph (152km/h) were scheduled. Even so, speeds as high as the announced 150mph were not run in public service, although 164mph (262km/h) was achieved on test; the work done on the permanent way was not sufficient for this, 110mph (176km/h) being the normal limit.

Since then a programme of track work has been carried out over the North East Corridor. At a cost of $2,500 million, this is 75 times as much as the original rather naive proposal, but does include the New York to Boston line. At long last this great work is drawing near to completion, and higher speeds can be envisaged. However, the *Metroliners,* now over 15 years old, have been displaced from the New York-Washington services by "AEM7" locomotives and trains of Amfleet coaches, which are effectively non-powered *Metroliners.* The powered *Metroliners* now work the New York-Philadelphia-Harrisburg route. The original schedule of 2½ hours for the 226 miles (362km) between New York and Washington was never achieved, but (taking 1978 as an example) hourly trains did the run in a very respectable 3 hours (or a minute or two more) with four intermediate stops, an overall average of 75mph (120km/h).

Above: *A New York to Washington train formed of four Metroliner electric cars.*

Below: *A Metroliner express train at speed on the North East Corridor main line.*

"Shao-Shan I" C_o-C_o

China: Railways of the People's Republic, 1969

Type: Electric freight locomotive.
Gauge: 4ft 8½in (1,435mm).
Propulsion: Alternating current at 25,000V 50Hz fed via overhead catenary, step-down transformer and solid state rectifiers to six 940hp (700kW) nose-suspended motors geared to the axles.
Weight: 304,155lb (138t).
Max. axleload: 50,695lb (23t).
Overall length: 66ft 10in (20,368mm).
Tractive effort: 119,100lb (530kN).
Max. speed: 56mph (90km/h).

The Chinese Railway authorities were fortunate in that the dc versus ac question was settled before they began an ambitious programme of electrification, appropriate to a country with ample coal and water-power but little oil. The first scheme to be put in hand was a brand new railway with some amazing engineering running north-south for 422 miles (679km) through mountain country in central China between Baoji and Chengtu. Further schemes both connected to and separate from this original one are now completed or in hand.

When the time came in the late-1950s to consider motive power, French designers had had the most experience in electrification at industrial frequency, and so with commendable good sense orders were placed in France. An early order for locomotives of conventional design was followed in 1972 by a batch of 40 mixed-traffic locomotives of 7,200hp (5,350kW), known as Class "6G". They were of advanced design with thyristor control. But in the meantime an electric locomotive works had been built at Zhouzhou and production of the "Shaoshan I" or "SS1" class had began. The class was named after the birthplace of Chairman Mao, an indication of the part electrification was expected to play in building the future of China.

The "SS1" design was based on the French locomotives supplied in 1960, except that silicon solid-state rectifiers are used instead of the ignitron type of mercury-arc rectifier. Also, in spite of an axleloading on the heavy side, the direct current traction motor drives are of the simple nose-suspended axle-hung pattern. Rheostatic rather than regenerative braking is provided, but multiple-unit capability enables trains of up to 2,400t (2,650 US tons) to be handled on 1-in-30 (3.3 per cent) grades using three "SS1" units, making almost 17,000hp (12,700kW) available. Some 250 of this class have now been built.

Class EF81 B_o-B_o

Japan: Japanese National Railways (JNR), 1968

Type: Electric mixed-traffic locomotive.
Gauge: 3ft 6in (1,067mm).
Propulsion: Direct current at 1,500V or alternating current at 25,000V 50Hz or 60Hz fed via overhead catenary to six 570hp (425kW) nose-suspended traction motors geared direct to the axles of the three bogies. The transformer for the ac current has a fixed ratio and it feeds the normal rheostatic dc control system via solid-state rectifiers.
Weight: 222,610lb (101t).
Max. axleload: 37,470lb (17t).
Overall length: 61ft 0in (18,600mm).
Tractive effort: 43,800lb (195kN) on dc, 40,200lb (179kN) on ac.
Max. speed: 72mph (115km/h).

In recent years the demands for heavy haulage on Japan's 5,270 miles (8,435km) of electrified 3ft 6in (1,067mm) gauge main lines has been met by building a series of locomotive classes of the B-B-B wheel arrangement. Single-current varieties exist for all three current systems used in Japan, that is dc, ac at 50Hz and ac at 60Hz, and also all the permutations for dual current as well as the tri-current type described here. There are also similar locomotives of the B-2-B wheel arrangement, which include a weight distribution system allowing the weight carried on the two outer motor bogies to be varied according to rail-weight limits and adhesion needs. The table sets out the different classes.

Class "EF81" is perhaps the most sophisticated design amongst this plethora of fascinating locomo-

Above: *Class EF electric locomotive at the head of a JNR container train on the Tohoku line, July 1975.*

Below: *Japanese National Railways' Class EF81 twin-current standard B-B-B mixed traffic electric locomotive.*

"SS2" and "SS3" prototypes of modernised and stretched versions of the "SS1" with thyristor control systems have appeared, and it seems that the latter is going into production to cover the demands of electrified routes that will soon exceed 1,250 miles (2,000km) in extent. Now that other than mountain lines are included in the programme, there are plans for electric locomotives capable of speeds up to 75mph (120km/h).

Right: *Chinese People's Railways' 5,640hp (4,200kW) Class SS1 or "Shao-Shan I" standard Co-Co 50Hz ac locomotive for electrified lines.*

tive variety. Complications include automatic control of wheelslip and compensation for load transfer when applying high tractive efforts, but otherwise they are very simple. They have no flexible drive system, neither rheostatic nor regenerative braking, and only the plainest of box-like bodywork. Notable is the relatively high maximum speed for the narrow gauge, although much of Japan's rail passenger traffic is handled by multiple-unit trains—including, as we shall see, overnight sleeping car expresses. Electric train heating is provided for use when passenger trains are hauled.

A total of 156 "EF81s" are in service, construction being in the hands of such well-known names as Hitachi, Mitsubishi and Toshiba. One batch of four have stainless-steel bodyshells, as much of their lives will be spent within the corrosive atmosphere of the 11.6-mile (18.7km) undersea tunnel which connects the main island of Honshu with Kyushu.

Japanese Three-Bogie Electric Locomotives

Date	Class	Type	DC 1500 V	AC 50 Hz	AC 60 Hz	Power hp	Power kW	Weight tonnes	Speed mph	Speed km/h
1960	EF30	B-B-B	●		●	2,410	1,800	96	53	85
1961	EF70	B-B-B			●	3,080	2,300	96	62	100
1961	EF72	B-2-B			●	2,550	1,900	87	62	100
1962	EF63	B-B-B	●			3,420	2,550	108	62	100
1962	EF80	B-B-B	●	●		2,610	1,950	96	65	105
1964	EF64	B-B-B	●			3,420	2,550	108	72	115
1964	EF65	B-B-B	●			3,420	2,550	108	72	115
1965	EF76	B-2-B		●	●	2,550	1,900	90.5	62	100
1965	EF77	B-2-B		●		2,550	1,900	75	62	100
1966	EF66	B-B-B	●			5,230	3,900	101	75	120
1966	EF71	B-B-B		●		3,620	2,700	100.8	62	100
1966	EF78	B-2-B		●		2,550	1,900	81.5	62	100
1968	EF81	B-B-B	●	●	●	3,420	2,550	101	72	115

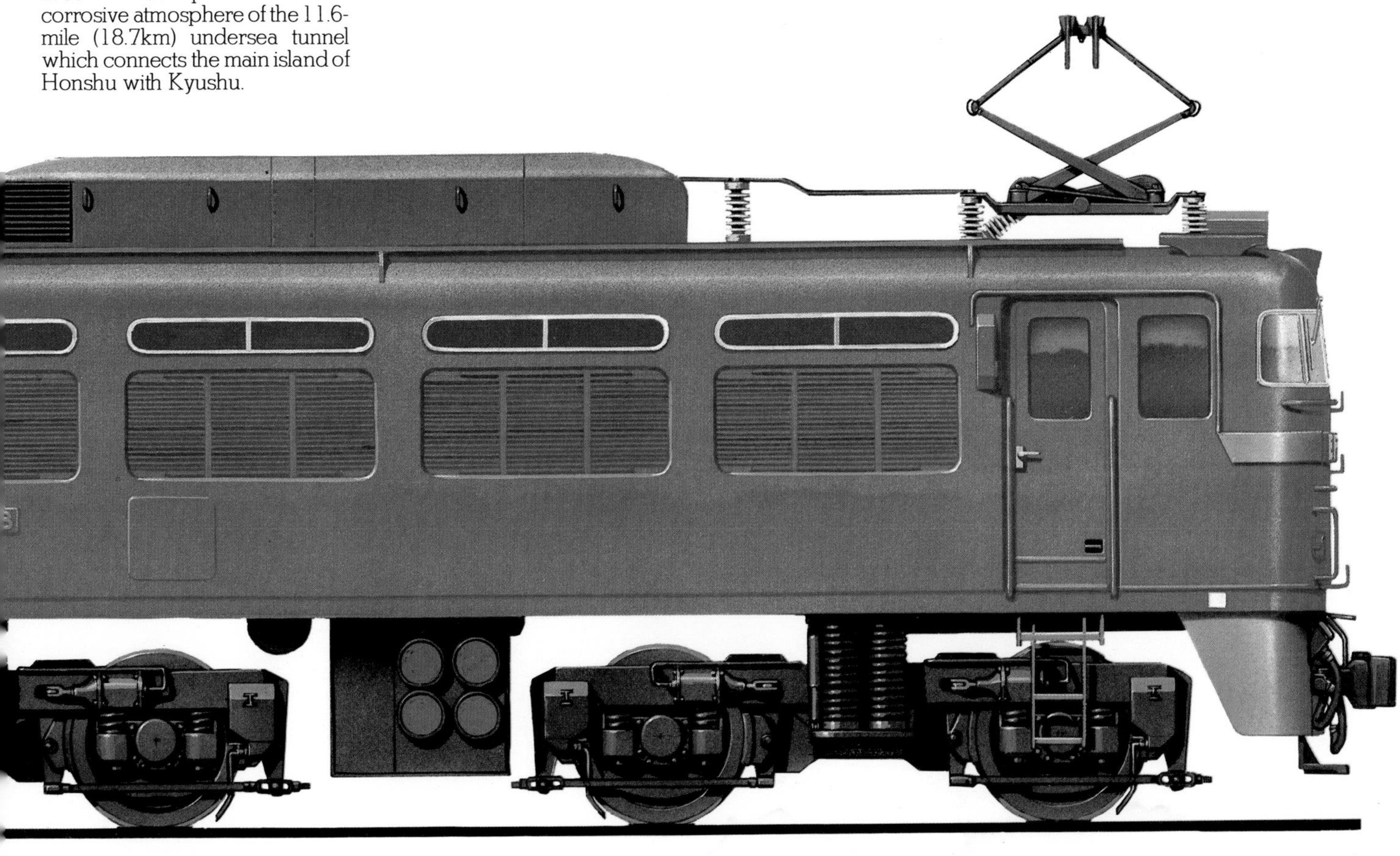

Class DD40AX "Centennial" D_o-D_o

USA:
Union Pacific Railroad (UP), 1969

Type: Diesel-electric locomotive for heavy freight duty.
Gauge: 4ft 8½in (1,435mm).
Propulsion: Two supercharged two-stroke General Motors 16-cylinder Type 645 engines each of 3,300hp (2,460kW) with integral alternators, feeding eight nose-suspended traction motors.
Weight: 545,270lb (247.5t).
Max. axleload: 68,324lb (31t).
Overall length: 98ft 5in (29,997mm).
Tractive effort: 133,766lb (603kN).
Max. speed: 90mph (144km/h).

If one were to choose the world's number one rail line, a fairly likely candidate would be the central section of the first United States transcontinental railroad, known now by the same name—Union Pacific—as it was when opened in 1869. In the days of steam, UP had the largest and most powerful locomotives in the world, the legendary "Big Boys", to haul the heavy and constant flow of freight across the continental divide. Going west, this began with the famous Sherman Hill (named after General Sherman who was in charge of building UP) out of Cheyenne, Wyoming; it consists of some 40 miles (64km) of 1-in-66 (1.5 per cent) grade.

When diesel traction took over, the power of a steam 4-8-8-4 could be matched or exceeded by coupling locomotive units in multiple, but UP management consistently made efforts to find a simpler solution by increasing the power of each unit. It has been described earlier how gas turbines with their increased power-to-weight ratio were used for a time, and how in the end the ability to buy off-the-shelf from diesel locomotive suppliers proved to have an over-riding advantage.

In the late-1960s, the UP operating authorities once again felt that there should be a better solution than having six or even eight locomotives on one train. General Motors had put together a peculiar 5,000hp (3,730kW) locomotive which they called a "DD35", which was essentially a huge booster unit with the works of two standard "GP35" road-switchers mounted on it. The locomotive ran on two four-axle trucks; these were considered to be hard on the track, but being contained in a mere booster unit could not take the leading position in a train where any bad effects of the running gear would be accentuated. Even so, no one was very keen to put the matter to the test. Only a handful of "DD35s" were sold and those only to Union Pacific and Southern Pacific. UP's track was (and is) superb, however, and it was suggested to GM that a "DD35" with a normal cab hood would be useful. The result was the "DD35A", of which 27 were supplied to UP. It was not disclosed how much saving in cost, allowing for an element of custom-building, there was between two "GP35s" and one "DD35A", but in length at least the former's 112ft 4in (34,240mm) compared with the latter's 88ft 2in (26,873mm).

A centenary in a new country is a great event and when during the late-1960s UP considered how to celebrate 100 years of continuous operation, they decided to do it by ordering a class of prime mover which was the most powerful in the world on a single-unit basis. Again, virtually everything except the chassis of the locomotive came off General Motors shelves, but even so the "Centennials" (more prosaically, the "DD40AXs") are a remarkable achievement.

In the same way that the "DD35A" was a double "GP35", the "DD40AX" was a double "GP40". The 16-cylinder engines of the "GP40" (essentially a supercharged version of those fitted to the "GP35") were uprated from 3,000 to 3,300hp (2,240 to 2,460kW), thereby producing a 6,600hp (4,925kW) single-unit locomotive. This was done by permitting an increased rpm. The result was not only the most powerful but also the longest and the largest prime-mover locomotive unit in the world. Forty-seven were built between 1969 and 1971, completion of the first (appropriately No. 6900) being pushed ahead to be ready on centenary day. The locomotives had a full-width cab and incorporated all the recent improvements which GM had introduced in the standard range of diesel locomotives. These included the new Type 645 engine, of uniflow two-stroke design like its long-lived predecessor the Type 567. The same cylinder bore and stroke is common to a 1,750hp (750kW) switcher and the 6,600hp (4,925kW) "Centennial". The generator is basically a brushless alternator, but has built-in silicon diode rectifiers to produce direct current suitable for traction motors. Naturally, the control system includes dynamic braking and wheelslip correction features.

The complex electrical system common to all diesel-electric locomotives was improved in these machines by being concentrated

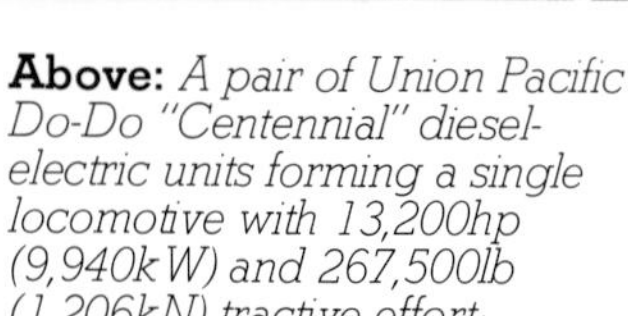

Above: *A pair of Union Pacific Do-Do "Centennial" diesel-electric units forming a single locomotive with 13,200hp (9,940kW) and 267,500lb (1,206kN) tractive effort.*

Below: *Union Pacific DD40AX No. 6900 heads the celebratory "Golden Spike" special, marking 100 years of continuous operation across the continent.*

Above: *Union Pacific Class DD40AX "Centennial". Its genesis as two GP40 units is clear to see from the transverse passage between the two engines.*

in a series of modules which could be isolated, tested and easily replaced if found faulty. In this way, repairs, adjustments or an overhaul could be done under factory conditions. Afterwards this arrangement became standard throughout the whole range of GM locomotives, models with it becoming known as "Dash-2", for example "SD40-2" for an "SD40" with modular electrics.

It could be said that this development proved to be self-destructive to the future of monster diesel-electrics, for a principal advantage of combining two "GP40s" on one chassis was the saving of a lot of electrical control gear. So making the electrics less troublesome made inroads into this advantage, and as a result these diriosaurs are not being repeated, even for Union Pacific. Another factor was the building of the "SD45-2" series with 20-cylinder engines rated at 3,600hp (2,685kW).

After these superb "Centennials", UP once again returned to buying diesel units off-the-shelf like virtually all US railroads and indeed the majority of railways the world over. When a train was called, required power would be calculated on a horsepower per ton basis according to the severity of the route. The most conveniently available units to make up this total horse power would then be coupled up to form the motive power; in these circumstances large special indivisible units are more of a hindrance than a help. Thus the "Big Boys" and the turbines have been superseded, and the "Centennials" submerged by more mundane motive power; even so, the pageant of freight movement up Sherman Hill and across the Divide is still one of the great railway sights of the world.

Below: *Just out of the works. A brand new No. 6900 poses for this Union Pacific Railroad Company photograph.*

Class 92 1-C_o-C_o-1

East Africa:
East African Railways (EAR), 1971

Type: Diesel-electric mixed-traffic locomotive.
Gauge: 3ft 3⅜in (1,000mm).
Propulsion: Alco Type 251F 12-cylinder four-stroke 2,550hp (1,902kW) Vee-type diesel engine and generator supplying direct current to six nose-suspended traction motors geared to the main axles.
Weight: 218,200lb (99t) adhesive, 251,255lb (114.5t) total.
Max. axleload: 36,370lb (16.5t).
Overall length: 59ft 1in (18,015mm).
Tractive effort: 77,000lb (342kN).
Max. speed: 45mph (72km/h).

Above: *A train of empty oil tank wagons en route from Nairobi to Mombasa, hauled by Alco Class 92 diesel-electric.*

Construction of the so-called Uganda Railway was the start of civilisation in what is now called Kenya. Little wood-burning steam engines reached the site of the city of Nairobi in 1895, so beginning the history of a line which for most of its existence has had to struggle to move ever-increasing traffic.

Oil-burning took over from wood in the 1930s, and traffic reached a point where articulated locomotives—the legendary Beyer Garratts—were needed. The efficiency with which traffic was worked by these monsters made what was then called East African Railways a very hard nut indeed for diesel traction to crack. Various studies over the years indicated that there was no case for change, apart from "keeping up with the Joneses", but in the 1960s the administration began to order medium-power units from English Electric of Britain.

By 1970 some progress in dieselisation had been made on peripheral routes, but the main trunk route which climbed steadily from sea level at Mombasa to 9,131ft (2,783m) at Timboroa, en route to Uganda, was still a Garratt stronghold. To find a means of working this traffic economically with diesel traction, EAR went shopping outside Britain, almost for the first time. The result was this Class "92" diesel of Alco design, supplied by the Montreal Locomotive Works. It offered 38 per cent more power than the most powerful diesels then in Kenya.

The Class "92s" were based on the standard Alco product adapted for metre-gauge. To reduce the axleload to a value acceptable on the main line west of Nairobi, not only was it necessary to use six-wheel bogies but an idle pony wheel had to be attached to each bogie also. The arrangement was offered by MLW specially for low axleloads as their

1967 Tube Stock Four-car set

Great Britain:
London Transport (LT), 1967

Type: Electric rapid transit trainset.
Gauge: 4ft 8½in (1,435mm).
Propulsion: Direct current at 600V supplied via third and fourth rails and an automatic control system to eight 140hp (105kW) nose-suspended traction motors.
Weight: 132,250lb (60t) adhesive, 206,075lb (93.5t) total.
Max. axleload: 16,530lb (7.5t).
Overall length: 214ft 5in (65,355mm).
Max. speed: 60mph (96km/h)*.

*Design speed of train. Maximum operational speed is 55mph (88km/h).

When asked the secret of their near perfect lawns, the authorities of King's College, Cambridge, have the maddening answer that there is no problem—just roll, cut and tend them for 400 years. In the same way, London Transport, when asked their recipe for success in introducing automatic operation of a rapid transit underground railway, might suggest having a century of general experience first. The Victoria line, which began its automatic operation in 1968 and was opened throughout from Brixton to Walthamstow in 1971, was the culmination of experience gained in normal operation of underground railways since 1863, of electrification since 1890, and of automatic working since 1963. Public operation of automatic trains began in 1964 on the shuttle service between Woodford and Hainault in east London. Experience was satisfactory, and accordingly the design of new trains needed for the Victoria line project was put in hand.

The main innovation was that once the driver/guard (who was really a 'train-person', since he did not drive) pressed the 'start' button, the train would proceed to the next station without human intervention. Two separate electric pulse systems provide the necessary messages to the control system. There is first a medium-frequency range of pulses which are passed along the running rails and are received continuously by the trains—420 pulses/min means 'go', 270 means 'go slowly', 180 means 'power off' and no signal means 'stop'. In addition there are 'command spots' at appropriate points at which speed-related frequencies in the audio range are picked up by the trains and responded to automatically by the control system within confines of the continuously-received signal.

The cost of installing automatic control was high but there are

"African series" and EAR themselves ordered an even lighter lower-power version (Class "88") for lines with a 12 ton axleload in Tanzania on the same chassis.

In 1976, EAR was divided up among the owning nations, Kenya, Uganda and Tanzania. The Class "92s" went to Kenya, retaining the same classification. Since then a Class "93" Co-Co design of similar power has been imported from General Electric. Advances in design have enabled axleload restrictions to be met without the extra two pairs of pony wheels.

Right: *Kenya Railways' Class 92 locomotive still in the livery and lettering of its former owners, East African Railways, more than a year after the administration was divided.*

Below: *Note how additional pony wheels have been added to the three-axle trucks of this otherwise standard Alco product, in order to spread the load and provide extra guidance and support.*

considerable savings even apart from halving the number of train staff. A 20 per cent increase in average speed means corresponding savings in the number of trains needed for a given frequency of service, whilst automatic operation is also designed to minimise consumption of current for a given average speed.

A few innovations had less-direct relevance to the automatic system, although powerful headlights are there to give the trainman reference points in the tunnels in the absence of signals. In addition, there were wrap-around windscreens, hydraulic handbrakes and rheostatic braking down to 10mph (16km/h).

The trains were arranged in four-car units with two motor cars and two trailers in each. Automatic couplers of the 'Wedgelock' pattern, which also make electrical pneumatic connections at the outer ends, facilitate making up and splitting eight-car trains. City transport under London has come a long way since those tiny locomotive-hauled windowless trains of the City & South London Railway (qv) began operation nearly a century ago.

Right: *An automatically operated tube train enters London's Seven Sisters station.*

RTG Four-car trainset

France: French National Railways (SNCF), 1972

Type: Five-car express passenger gas turbine set.
Gauge: 4ft 8½in (1,435mm).
Propulsion: One Société Française Turbomeca Turmo IIIF 1,150hp (858kW) gas turbine in each end vehicle driving the axles of the outer bogie through Voith hydraulic transmission.
Weight: 143,040lb (64.9t). adhesive, 570,836lb (259t) total.
Max. axleload: 35,760lb (16.2t).
Overall length: 339ft 6 5/16in (128,990mm).
Tractive effort: 26,980lb (120kN).
Max. speed: 112mph (180km/h).

In 1966 SNCF, with no diesel locomotives able to run at more than 87mph (140km/h), studied the problem of designing railcars for non-electrified lines which could equal the performance then being achieved by electric traction, that is, general running at 100mph (160km/h) with speeds of 124mph (200km/h) on suitable stretches. The non-electrified routes often had more speed restrictions than the more generously laid-out electric routes, and the performance contemplated would therefore require a much higher power-to-weight ratio than was being achieved in contemporary diesel railcars to give the required acceleration and speed on gradients.

The French aero-engine industry has scored notable successes with small gas turbines for helicopters, and SNCF saw these turbines as a means of providing the high power required without a significant increase in weight over a diesel railcar. The first experiment was started in 1966. A Turmo III F engine manufactured by Société Française Turbomeca was fitted to the trailer car of a standard two-car diesel set. The output shaft of this engine was connected through reduction gears to the axles of one bogie. The engine was rated at 1,500hp (1,120kW) for aircraft use, but was de-rated to 1,150hp (858kW) for railway use, and it operated on diesel fuel, both for economy in fuel costs and greater safety.

The first trial took place on April 25, 1967, and two months later a speed of 147mph (236km/h) was recorded. The train was driven by the diesel engine below a speed of 20mph (30km/h) with the gas turbine shut down. Fuel consumption was considered acceptable, bearing in mind that there was no other way of obtaining so high a power in so small a space. This set was later designated "TGS" (*Turbine à Gaz Spéciale*).

In 1968, the next step was the ordering of 10 four-car trains for the Paris-Caen-Cherbourg service. In these a 440hp (330kW) diesel engine was fitted in one end coach and a Turmo III F in the other end coach, as in the "TGS", but the coaches were appointed to main line standards with catering facilities and warm-air ventilation. The most important technical difference was that the turbine was connected to the axles through Voith hydraulic transmission, enabling the turbine to be used from rest. These sets

Above: *View of a French National Railways' gas-turbine-powered high-speed five-car train-set for non-electrified lines.*

Below: *The power car of an SNCF RTG train. The powerful gas turbine is accommodated in the small windowless space between the two doors at the leading end.*

Class 132 C_o-C_o

German Democratic Republic: German State Railway (DR), 1975

Type: Diesel-electric express passenger locomotive.
Gauge: 4ft 8½in (1,435mm).
Propulsion: Energomachexport 3,000hp (2,240kW) 16-cylinder Vee-type four-stroke diesel engine with gas-turbine supercharger and alternator feeding current to six nose-suspended traction motors.
Weight: 276,600lb (125.5t).
Max. axleload: 46,285lb (21t).
Overall length: 67ft 8in (20,620mm).
Tractive effort: 146,773lb (326kN).
Max. speed: 75mph (120km/h).

The art of building successful diesel locomotives can only be learnt the hard way—that is, by long, hard and bitter experience. Russian engineers have certainly served their time in this respect ever since, in the 1920s, the legendary Professor Lomosonroff began putting experimental diesel locomotives on the road. Consequently, by the mid-1960s, with thousands of home-built diesel locomotives in service on home rails, the Russian product was good enough to sell abroad. Admittedly there have not yet been sales to administrations which have access to General Motors' products, but it is early days yet. The Russians' adherence to the most successful principle of locomotive building—rugged simplicity—bodes very well for their future prospects.

The first export model was a 2,000hp (1,490kW) double-ended carbody unit. Sales were made to Hungary (Class "M-62"), as classes "T-679.1" and "T679.5" in Czechoslovakia, and "CT-44" in Poland. North Korea also had some and others went to the German State Railway (DR) in the German Democratic Republic, where they became Class "120". All these locomotives were built at the Voroshilovgrad Diesel Locomotive Works and were exported via the Soviet agency Energomachexport. Experience with these modestly-powered machines led to the production of a higher-powered version with dynamic braking known as the "TE-109".

The "TE-109" prototypes were available with two gear ratios for passenger and freight traffic respectively. They used ac-dc transmission with this passenger version as well as convertor equipment to provide a 600kW output of alternating current at 16⅔Hz for train heating. The principal customer was the German Democratic Re-

are designated "ETG" (*Élément à Turbine à Gaz*).

In 1970 the Paris-Caen and Paris-Cherbourg services were taken over by "ETGs", being the first full inter-city service in the world to be operated by gas turbine traction. Caen was reached in 109 minutes at 81.5mph (131km/h). Although the sets were designed for 112mph (180km/h), they have always been limited to 100mph (160km/h) in service.

Success of the "ETGs" created a demand for trains with still more and better accommodation. This was met by building units with longer coaches which could be run in four-coach or five-coach sets, with air-conditioning and other appointments as in the latest locomotive-hauled coaches. The diesel engine was omitted, and there was a Turmo III power unit in each end coach. An additional small Astazou turbine was installed in each power car to provide electric power at all times, the main turbines being run only when required for traction. These trains are the "RTGs" (*Rame à Turbine à Gaz*).

RTGs took over the Cherbourg services in 1972 and were later introduced on cross-country services based on Lyons. A total of 41 sets were built, of which two were later sold to Amtrak in the United States.

Gas turbine trains were a notable success for French engineers, for not only do they perform reliably and at an acceptable cost, but they are environmentally acceptable both to the passengers and to those outside the train. Although no further extensions have been made to these services, they rank as the most successful application of gas turbines to railway passenger services.

Above: *French RTG turbo-train at speed between Tours and Vierzon with a Nantes to Lyons cross-country express.*

Right: *Amtrak turbo-train approaching Chicago. Two sets were supplied from France and several more were built under licence in the USA by Rohr Inc.*

public, which placed an order for 279 at the Leipzig Trade Fair in 1973. There are divided between the passenger Class "132", particulars given above, and Class "131" for freight traffic, the latter having a lower maximum speed of 63mph (100km/h) and a correspondingly higher tractive effort of 77,160lb (34.3kN), but is otherwise indentical. Other "TE-109s" have gone to Bulgaria and Czechoslavakia where they are class "07" and "T-679.2" respectively.

Right: *Class 132 Russian-built diesel locomotive, near Halberstadt, East Germany, in 1978.*

Class 15000 B-B

France: French National Railways (SNCF), 1971

Type: Express passenger electric locomotive.
Gauge: 4ft 8½in (1,435mm).
Propulsion: Alternating current at 25,000V 50Hz from overhead wires, rectified in diodes and thyristors, supplying two 2,960hp (2,210kW) traction motors, one mounted on each bogie and connected to the axles through gearing and spring drives.
Weight: 198,360lb (90t).
Max. axleload: 49,590lb (22.5t).
Overall length: 57ft 4⅛in (17,480mm).
Tractive effort: 64,800lb (288kN).
Max. speed: 112mph (180km/h).

Above: *The dc version of the Class 15000, the Class 7200, is seen at the Gare de Lyon in Paris during 1978.*

Early in its experiments with 25,000V 50Hz ac traction, SNCF recognised that the combination of lines electrified on the new system with its existing network of 1,500V dc lines would make essential the use of dual-voltage locomotives capable of working on both systems. Otherwise the time consumed in changing locomotives, together with the poor utilisation of locomotives which would result from this changing, would nullify much of the economy of the high-voltage system. Dual-voltage machines were therefore included in the experimental ac locomotives, and this was followed by the development of "families" of locomotives, comprising ac, dc and dual-voltage machines incorporating as many common parts as possible. The numbering of these classes was a notable manifestation of Gallic logic, for it was based on the mathematical relationship: (ac + dc) = (dual voltage). Thus the "17000" ac class and the "8500" dc class combined to produce the "25500" dual-voltage class.

Successive phases in the post-war development of the French electric locomotive produced successive families. Thus one group comprised the first all-adhesion four-axle locomotive with individual-axle drive. The next group, one mentioned above, incorporated monomotor bogies with two gear ratios, and silicon rectifiers. The third group, "15000" + "7200" = "22200", moved into the thyristor era, and at a nominal 5,920hp (4,420kW) they are the most powerful French B-B machines. This group is also notable in reverting to a single gear ratio. Class "15000" was intended primarily for express passenger work, and a low-speed gear was unnecessary, but it was hoped that improvements in various aspects of design since the introduction of the two-speed locomotives would enable the thyristor machines to handle freight traffic without provision of a special gear ratio.

It is SNCF's practice to apply new technology experimentally to an existing locomotive or train, retaining as much as possible of the well-proven equipment, so as to concentrate attention on the special equipment under test. Some of the first experiments with thyristors were made with one of the pioneer dual-voltage locomotives, No. 20002, which retained conventional resistance control for dc operation, and silicon diodes for ac traction, but had thyristors for ac regenerative braking. The first application of thyristors to control power circuits was on a multiple-unit train, and in 1971 there appeared the first production units equipped throughout with thyristors, a series of multiple-units, and the Class "15000" B-B locomotives.

Up to this time the standard method of controlling power on French ac locomotives had been by tap-changer on the high-tension side of the transformer. The thyristor offered an elegant alternative to the tap-changer, with the possibility of infinitely-variable control of the voltage applied to the traction motors.

Class "15000" was built to take over principal services on the former Est Railway main line from Paris to Strasbourg, now in the Eastern Region of SNCF. Their introduction followed construction of the "6500" class C-C dc locomotives and the "72000" class C-C diesel-electric locomotives; many parts were common to all three classes, including the main body structure. There is a single traction motor for each bogie, mounted rigidly on top of the bogie frame and connected to the

axles through gearing and Alsthom flexible drives. The body rests on four rubber springs, two at each side of the body and close together. The springs are sandwiches of steel and rubber bonded together. They resist the vertical load by compression, whilst lateral oscillations and rotation of the bogie are resisted by shearing action. This is a remarkably simple and effective suspension.

An important innovation in the "15000s" was the control system, made possible by the comparative simplicity of thyristor circuitry. The driver has two normal methods of controlling speed, constant speed or constant current. With the former the driver sets his controller to the speed required, and he also sets up the value of the current which is not to be exceeded. The control circuits accelerate the locomotive to the speed required, and then vary the current to hold it at that speed, provided that the stipulated maximum current is not exceeded. If, due to a change in gradient, the locomotive attempts to accelerate, current is reduced, and finally, if necessary, regenerative braking is set up. Alternatively the driver can isolate the speed control, and the system holds the current to the pre-selected value, observance of speed being the driver's responsibility.

The "15000s" are designed for 112½mph (180km/h), which is somewhat surprising as 124mph (200km/h) had already been permitted on some parts of SNCF when they were built, but so far on the Eastern Region the limit is 100mph (160km/h). Every effort was made to simplify the design to reduce maintenance costs, and with this in mind the traction motor was modified to make it self-ventilating and so eliminate the need for a forced-ventilation system.

They soon established an excellent reputation, and with 74 in service they dominate the Eastern Region passenger services. Work continued on chopper control for dc locomotives, and for a time C-C locomotive No. 20002, with chopper equipment, ran coupled to standard B-B No. 9252, No. 20002 serving as a current supply to the motors of No. 9252. Next No. 15007 was converted to a dc machine, numbered 7003 to test the equipment for the "7200" class.

In 1976, delivery of the "7200" class began, followed later in the year by the dual-voltage "22200" locomotives. These classes differ only in that the "22200" has an additional pantograph for ac operation, and a transformer and silicon rectifier for converting the ac supply to 1,500V dc. The current is then fed into the same circuits as the dc supply, so that there is only one control system. Both classes closely resemble the "15000s", but are slightly longer in the body, and they have rheostatic braking instead of regenerative.

The "7200" and "22200" classes are allocated to the South-Eastern Region, and have displaced earlier locomotives from the principal services, apart from those worked by TGVs. Their workings include the ac section from Marseilles to Ventimille, on which "22200s" work through from Paris to Ventimille, 695 miles (1,118km). They also work fast freight trains into northern France, a new departure in inter-regional working, which includes running 696 miles (1,120km) from Marseilles to Lille. These are the longest locomotive workings in France, and the high mileage which the locomotives can thereby build up is held to justify the small extra cost of a "22200" compared with a "7200" or "15000."

Although it had been hoped that Class "7200" would be suitable for heavy low-speed freight work, trouble was encountered with overheating of the motors, and the first 35 locomotives were temporarily fitted with bogies geared for 62mph (100km/h). All later locomotives have force-ventilated motors.

For nine months before its gear ratio was changed, No. 7233 was transferred to the South-Western Region, and worked "L' Etendard" between Paris and Bordeaux with considerable running at 125mph (200km/h). Later No. 22278 was tested similarly, thus proving that the classes were suitable for this speed, although designed for 180km/h.

By 1982, orders had been placed for 210 Class "7200" locomotives and 150 of Class "22200." All these locomotives were built by Alsthom, and in due course the firm received an order for 48 similar locomotives for Netherlands Railways. In 1982 also No. 15055 was fitted with synchronous three-phase motors, and No. 15056 was selected for another series of tests with asynchronous motors.

Above: *French National Railways' Class 15000 Bo-Bo No. 15059 is seen near Pringy on the Paris-Strasbourg line with a train of "Corail" carriages.*

Below: *This French locomotive design is produced as depicted for 25,000V ac (Class 15000), for 1,500V dc as Class 7200, and for both as Class 22200.*

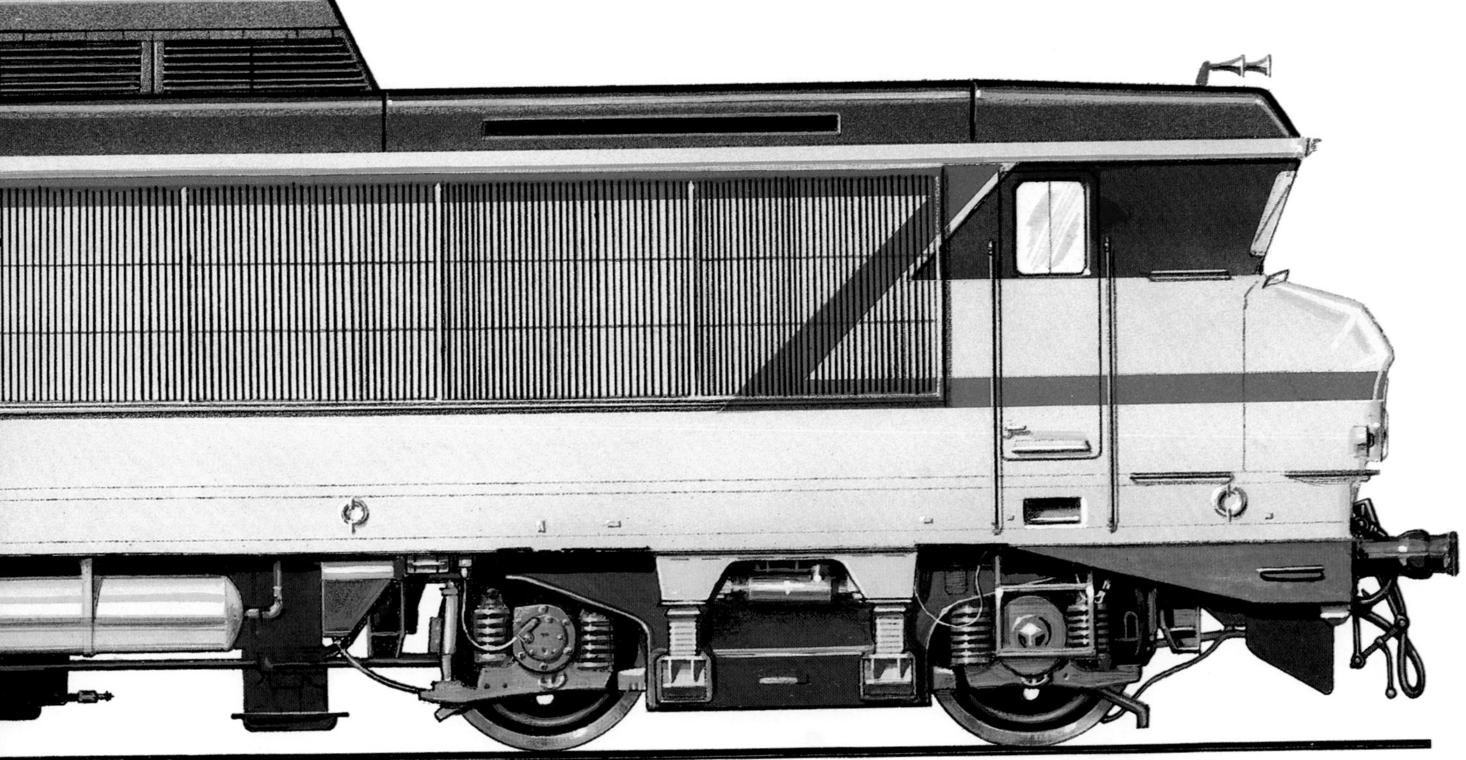

Class Re 6/6 Bo-Bo-Bo

Switzerland:
Swiss Federal Railways (SBB), 1972

Type: Heavy-duty mixed-traffic mountain locomotive.
Gauge: 4ft 8½in (1,435mm).
Propulsion: Low-frequency alternating current at 15,000V 16⅔Hz fed via overhead catenary and step-down transformer to six frame-mounted 1,740hp (1,300kW) motors each driving one axle through a flexible drive system.
Weight: 264,480lb (120t).
Max. axleload: 44,080lb (20t).
Overall length: 63ft 4½in (19,310mm).
Tractive effort: 88,700lb (395kN).
Max. speed: 87mph (140km/h).

Above: *Swiss Federal Railways Class Re 6/6 Co-Co No. 11632 with heavy oil-tanker train on Zürich to Basle line near Effingen, May 1982.*

Ten-thousand horsepower plus in a single locomotive! And no cheating either—all is contained in a single indivisible unit. The story of this Everest amongst locomotives began with the ever increasing demands of traffic on the St Gotthard main line across the Alps.

The original heavy artillery of the Gotthard line was a famous series of rod-drive 1-C-C-1 articulated 'Crocodile' locomotives, of only one-quarter the power of the "Re 6/6" engines. In all 52 were built and a few still survive. In 1931 two rather amazing experimental "Ae 8/14" 1-Bo-1-Bo-1 + 1-Bo-1-Bo-1 twin units appeared, one of which built by Oerlikon brought the power available to 8,800hp (6,560kW), combined with a drawgear-breaking maximum tractive effort of 132,240lb (588kN). The other, by Brown Boveri, was slightly less powerful. These were followed in 1939 by yet another twin locomotive of the same unique wheel arrangement which did offer more than 10,000hp—11,400hp (8,500kW) in fact—as well as 110,200lb (490kN) of tractive effort. However, it was at the cost of a total weight twice that of the "Re 6/6". Experience with these immense machines was such that they were not repeated.

The "Re 4/4" double-bogie locomotives for express passenger work came to SBB in 1946, following the example of the Bern-Lötschberg-Simplon Railway Class "Ae 4/4" (qv) of two years earlier. With hindsight it seems extraordinary that the Swiss did not simply build a lower-geared version of the "Re 4/4" and use it in multiple on the Gotthard. The fact remains, though, that they did not and instead went on seeking a single locomotive unit that would do the job. Hence in 1952 the usual firms—this time in consort—that is Brown Boveri, Oerlikon and the Swiss Locomotive Works, produced a locomotive with six driven axles and all but 1,000hp per axle, classified "Ae 6/6". They used all the know-how gained on the "Ae 4/4" and "Re 4/4" units, but adapting the design for six-wheel instead of four-wheel bogies.

The "Ae 6/6s" were rated at 5,750hp (4,290kW) and 120 were built between 1952 and 1966. Regenerative braking was installed and the maximum speed was 88mph (125km/h). The class ushered in the hitherto almost unheard of practice (for SBB) of naming. Naturally they began with the Swiss Cantons, but soon these ran out and it had to be important towns instead; finally, some of the much mightier successors of the "Ae 6/6s" had to make do with the names of some very small places indeed! The extra power of the "Ae 6/6s" came at the right moment, for an explosion of traffic over the line was about to occur. By the late 1960s, three times the tonnage and over twice the number of trains were passing compared with 1950.

Amongst many measures proposed to cope with the situation was provision of still more powerful locomotives. Something was done quickly by converting existing locomotives to work in multiple—a measure that the Swiss were normally reluctant to take. But in 1972, two single-unit super-power prototypes were delivered by the same consortium. There was no point in providing for haulage of trains above 850t (935 US tons) by a single unit because European wagon couplings were not strong enough to pull heavier loads than this up the Gotthard grades. Larger trains can be hauled but a second locomotive has then to be cut into the centre of the load.

The first two "Re 6/6s" were articulated, but later examples and the production version had the single carbody as described. The haulage capacity was nicely balanced, for an 800t (880 US tons) train could be taken up the 1-in-37 (2.7 per cent) at the line limit of 50mph (80km/h). One of the reasons for adopting the Bo-Bo-Bo wheel arrangement in place of Co-Co was that the length of rigid wheelbase is reduced. This is important on a line like the Gotthard, with almost continuous curvature as sharp as 15 chains (300m) radius. On the other hand, having a rigid body to the locomotive greatly simplified and reduced the cost of the centre bogie, which could align itself with the curves by being allowed sideplay. All three bogies were pivotless and each one was made to run more easily over small irregularities in track alignment by giving its axles lateral movement centralised with springs.

Now in general use on less taxing parts of the Swiss rail system, the "Ae 6/6s" are still a remarkable design, but the "Re 6/6s" are over 80 per cent more powerful within the same weight limitation. In addition to being an excellent freight-hauler for mountain grades, these versatile machines are also suitable for trains running at the highest speeds permitted in Switzerland.

Right: *Swiss Federal Railways Class Re 6/6 Co-Co No. 11630 below Wassen on the Gotthard line with the northbound* Barbarossa *international express on May 24, 1981.*

Below: *Swiss Federal Railways Class Re 6/6 Co-Co. A massive 10,000hp in a single unit!*

EMD SD40-2 Co-Co

United States:
Electro-Motive Division, General Motors Corporation (EMD), 1972

Type: Road switcher diesel-electric locomotive.
Gauge: 4ft 8½in (1,435mm).
Propulsion: One EMD 645E3 3,000hp (2,240kW) 16-cylinder turbocharged two-stroke Vee engine and alternator supplying current through silicon rectifiers to six nose-suspended traction motors.
Weight: 368,000lb (167.0t).
Max. axleload: 61,330lb (27.8t).
Overall length: 68ft 10in (20,980mm).
Tractive effort: 83,100lb (370kN).
Max. speed: 65mph (105km/h).

Above: *Burlington Northern Railroad class SD40-2 road-switcher unit No. 7044, one of nearly 900 supplied to this line.*

For 50 years the Electro-Motive Division of General Motors has dominated the US diesel market, taking 70 to 75 per cent of total orders. The remainder of the market has been shared between the former steam locomotive builders Alco and Baldwin/Lima, a few smaller firms, and latterly GE, but since 1969 only GE has survived. However, the effect has been that EMD has never had a monopoly, and although the company's success has been due very much to its policy of offering a limited number of off-the-shelf models, it cannot ignore specialist needs of its customers. There has thus been steady development and improvement of the EMD models over the years, directed mainly at increasing power, reducing fuel consumption and maintenance costs, and improving adhesion.

Introduction of the "hood" design "GP7" model in 1949 marked the beginning of the end for the "carbody" unit on which EMD had made its reputation. From then onwards nearly all EMD's road locomotives would be general-purpose machines. There was, however, a variant; the four-axle machines inevitably had a heavy axleload, and EMD therefore offered a six-axle version designated "SD", for "Special Duty". Although the axleload was reduced, the total weight of the locomotive was greater than that of a four-axle machine, and it thus appealed also to roads which had a need for maximum adhesion due to climatic conditions. The pattern thus became established of offering four-axle and six-axle variants of each model.

Elsewhere in this book the "GP" series up to "GP35" is discussed. These are the models with the original 567 engine, and corresponding six-axle "SD" models were also built. By the time this engine was pressed to 2,500hp (1,865kW) for traction, it was reaching its limit, and a new engine was produced with the same piston stroke of 10in (245mm), but with the diameter increased from 8.5in (216mm) to 9¹⁄₁₆in (230mm). The cylinder volume became 645cu in, thus giving the engine its designation "645". Like the 567 it is a two-stroke engine, and is available with or without turbocharger. A two-stroke engine requires some degree of pressure-charging to give effective scavenging, and if there is no turbocharger, there is a Roots-type blower driven directly from the engine. There have thus been two lines of development, the turbocharged engine pressed to give successive increases in power, and the engines without turbochargers remaining at 2,000hp (1,490kW), but benefit from mechanical improvements directed at reducing fuel consumption and maintenance costs.

One of the attractions of the diesels which first replaced steam on freight work was that a number of modest-sized units working in multiple under the control of one crew could replace the largest steam engine. These diesels were little bigger than some of the diesel switchers which the roads already operated, and their maintenance was easier than that of overworked steam locomotives which were very demanding of attention and needed good quality fuel to give of their best. The diesels could show a reduction in operating costs, even when their higher capital cost was taken into account.

However, when the possible economies from total dieselisation had been achieved, motive power officers looked for other means of effecting economies. With the problems of diesel maintenance now better understood, an attractive idea was to use a smaller number of larger units to achieve the same total power. This was found to save money both in purchase price and in operating costs. EMD's competitors were first in the field with higher horsepower as a selling point, and it was not until 1958 that EMD marketed a 2,400hp (1,790kW) engine in the "SD24" series with which to match the Fairbanks-Morse Trainmaster of 1953. In 1959 EMD produced its 2,000hp (1,490kW) four-axle model, and from then the horsepower race was on.

The 645 engine was launched in 1965 in two versions, the pressure-charged 645E and the turbocharged 645E3. The 645E was made in 8, 12 and 16 cylinder versions, and the 645E3 with 12, 16 and 20 cylinders. These engines were incorporated in a new range of nine locomotives, which included the "GP40" and "SD40" with the 16-cylinder version of the turbocharged engine, giving 3,000hp (2,240kW), and the "SD45" with the 20-cylinder engine giving 3,600hp (2,690kW). This was the first US engine with 20 cylinders, and it brought EMD firmly into the high horsepower stable, some time after Alco and GE had reached 3,000hp. All these new models incorporated a new design of traction motor,

Right: *An Electromotive SD40-2 road-switcher diesel-electric locomotive, lettered for the Conrail system, a government-financed grouping of bankrupt railroads in eastern USA.*

with improved insulation, and therefore better performance at high power. The six-axle types had a new Flexicoil bogie to give improved riding, and the 3,000hp and 3,600hp engines introduced alternators, instead of generators, to the EMD range. The alternators were more compact than generators, and this assisted the designers in finding space for the larger engines.

With the railroads enthusiastic about high-powered locomotives, the "SD45" was the most popular model in the range, achieving a total of 1,260 sales in six years. The highest-powered four-axle unit in the range, the 3,000hp GP40, achieved sales of 1,201, and for roads which required a six-axle layout, 883 of the "SD40" were supplied.

These models remained standard until the beginning of 1972 when, with competition from GE still keen, a revision was made of the whole range, known as "Dash 2", from the addition which was made to the class designation, for example, "SD40-2". At this stage no further increase in power was offered, and the alterations were directed at improving fuel consumption and simplifying maintenance by eliminating some of the difficulties encountered with existing locomotives. The most important changes were in the electrical control system, which comprises largely plug-in modules of printed circuits which can be changed quickly from stock. Owners of earlier models had encountered difficult in locating electrical faults, and an annunciator was therefore developed which records and stores information about malfunctions in the system.

New high-adhesion trucks were offered in the six-axle models, known as "HT-C" (High Traction, three axle). Adhesion was still a major concern to the railroads, and as orders came in for the "Dash-2" range, two trends became apparent: first, that the extra maintenance costs of the 20-cylinder engine and its large turbocharger and radiators were not justified for 600hp more than the 16-cylinder engine could give, and secondly, that the 3,000hp four-axle locomotive, the "GP40", had given trouble with wheelslip and excessive maintenance of its highly-rated traction motors. The high-power model to emerge as the most popular in the range was therefore the "SD40-2", with 3,000hp transmitted through six axles. By the late-1970s this was established as virtually the standard high-power diesel in the US, with sales approaching 4,000 by the end of the decade. The railroad with the largest number was Burlington Northern with about 900, a quarter of its total locomotive stock.

Concurrently the high cost of maintaining a turbocharger compared with a Roots blower had encouraged railroads to purchase large numbers of "GP38-2" units of 2,000hp for duties for which a 3,000hp locomotive was not required, and sales of this model passed 2,000 by 1980.

EMD now tackled the problem of improving adhesion in four-axle locomotives by a wheelslip detector employing Doppler radar, which is sufficiently sensitive to allow an axle to work safely at the limit of adhesion. Engine development made it possible to offer a 3,500hp (2,610kW) 16-cylinder engine, and in 1980 the company launched the "GP50" with the 3,500hp engine on four axles, so that railroads once again had the choice of a high-power locomotive without the expense of six axles.

Below: *A three-unit SD40-2 combination belonging to Canadian National Railways. Note the modified "safety" cab on the second unit.*

Class Dx C_o-C_o

New Zealand: New Zealand Railways (NZR), 1972

Type: Diesel-electric locomotive for mixed traffic.
Gauge: 3ft 6in (1,067mm).
Propulsion: General Electric (USA) 2,750hp (2,050kW) Type 7FDL-12 twelve-cylinder diesel engine and alternator supplying current via solid-state rectifiers to six nose-suspended traction motors.
Weight: 214,890lb (97.5t).
Max. axleload: 35,925lb (16.3t).
Overall length: 55ft 6in (16,916mm).
Tractive effort: 54,225lb (241kN).
Max. speed: 65mph (103km/h).

New Zealand may be a country with a small population as well as a small-gauge railway system, but its railwaymen have always believed in big powerful locomotives. For example, the legendary New Zealand-built "K" class 4-8-4s were as powerful as anything that ran in the mother country, in spite of an axleload limit only 71 per cent of that in Britain. Similarly, these big "Dx" diesel-electrics have a power output comparable with Britain's standard Class "47s", again within the limits of axleload in proportion as before.

Class "Dx" was the culmination of a dieselisation programme which began in the 1950s—as regards main-line traction units of, say, 750hp plus—with the 40 Class "Dg" A1A-A1A units of 1955. What was called "Commonwealth Preference" in import duties gave British manufacturers a substantial advantage in those days, and the order went to English Electric. The class was lightweight, able to

Left: *New Zealand Railways' Class Dx Co-Co diesel-electric locomotive crosses a trestle viaduct typical of the system, hauling a long freight train.*

Below: *Class Dx Co-Co diesel electric locomotive as supplied by the General Electric (USA) Co.*

ET 403 Four-car train

West Germany: German Federal Railway (DB), 1973

Type: High-speed four-car electric railcar set.
Gauge: 4ft 8½in (1,435mm).
Propulsion: Alternating current at 15,000V 16⅔Hz fed through transformer and thyristors to bogie-mounted traction motors driving each axle of each car, giving a total of 5,150hp. (3,840kW).
Weight: 519,480lb (235.7t).
Max. axleload: 32,400lb (14.7t).
Overall length: 358ft 4in (109,220mm).
Max. speed: 125mph (200km/h).

Following the success of the high-speed international TEE services, the German Federal Railway introduced even faster internal services under the initials "IC" for "Inter-City". These services provided first-class accommodation only in short trains hauled by "103" class electric locomotives. However, use of multiple-unit trains on TEE services had impressed DB engineers with the advantages of this type of train, with all axles powered, both in the greater weight available for adhesion and in the lower forces imposed on the track for a given total power compared with an electric locomotive. In 1973, therefore, three high-speed emu sets were built, with a maximum speed of 125mph (200km/h). Each set normally comprises four coaches, with all axles powered. There are three types of vehicle, of which one variety has a streamlined end with a driver's cab and carries a pantograph. The others are intermediate cars, one of which has catering facilities. From the distinctive shape of the streamlined ends, the sets earned the nickname "Donald Ducks".

The electrical equipment includes many fittings which had already been proved in the "ET420" class suburban stock. Each coach carries a transformer, a rectifier for converting the ac supply to dc, and thyristor chopper equipment both for controlling the voltage to the motors and for regenerative braking. Each coach is thus a self-contained motor coach, except that the electrical supply comes from the vehicle with the pantograph.

Main technical innovation was in the bogies, which incorporate air suspension. By variations of air pressure in the suspension bags, the body can be tilted up to 4° to improve passenger comfort on curves. The bogies have disc and magnetic track brakes. Each axle has an automatic slip-prevention device, and automatic surveillance of axlebox temperature. It was intended that the bogies should run for 600,000km without heavy maintenance, other than correction of tyre profiles.

Post-war DB coaches had been notable for a progressively lighter body weight; the "ET403" units took this reduction a stage further, large extruded aluminium profiles being used for the first time in high-speed stock. The result is an axleloading of 15t, which is much kinder to the track than the 19.5t of the Class "103" locomotives.

The sets were first introduced into regular service in May 1974 on one of the longest internal

run over the light rails of the South Island system, where there was an axleload of only 11t (12 US tons).

Between 1955 and 1967, General Motors came in in a very big way with the 74-strong 1,428hp (1,065kW) Class "Da" as the mainstay of the North Island main lines. There were also the 16 lighter GM "Db" class locomotives for North Island branch lines. In 1968 and 1969 the Japanese firm Mitsubishi delivered 60 Class "Dj" Bo-Bo-Bos for the South Island; this class offered 1,045hp (780kW) for an axleload of 10.9t (12 US tons). As a result of these deliveries the last regular steam-hauled train ran in 1972.

It then became apparent that more powerful locomotives could be used to advantage, and the result was this "Dx" class. Very surprisingly NZR went to a fourth source for these magnificent machines. General Electric of USA —not to be confused with GEC Traction of Britain or its subsidiary

Above: *The "Silver Star" express on the North Island Trunk hauled by a Class Dx.*

General Electric (Australia)—supplied 47 of these units during 1972-75. They are used on crack trains on the North Island trunk line between Wellington and Auckland, both passenger and freight. The design is based on General Electric's standard "U26C" export model.

GEC did not capture the market, though, because subsequent deliveries were from General Motors with both A1A-A1A and Co-Co versions of a similar locomotive (classes "Dc" and "Df" of 67 and 30 units respectively). This in spite of a debate then in full cry concerning the need for railways at all in a country with such modest transport requirements. In the end the verdict was favourable to railways but not to diesels —instead New Zealand Railways is going ahead with a major programme of electrification which will use indigenous forms of energy.

services in West Germany, from Munich to Bremen, 485 miles (781km) with six intermediate stops. These services were well patronised, and on Mondays and Fridays a fifth car was added to each set. They continued until 1979.

By 1979 the definitive pattern of DB's IC services had emerged. After several years in which the service was offered to first-class passengers only, DB had decided that a full-scale network of high-speed services could only be viable if second-class passengers were also carried. Furthermore, after experience with both emu and locomotive operation of these services, DB decided that the greater flexibility of locomotive haulage was preferable.

The "ET403" sets thus became spare, and did not find a definite use until 1982, when the state airline, Lufthansa, sponsored a rail service to connect Düsseldorf with Frankfurt airport, with intermediate stops at Cologne and Bonn, providing a more direct city-to-airport service to connect with important flights from Frankfurt than existing airport-to-airport flights.

Originally the livery was silver grey with a brown band at window level, lined out in orange. For their new duties, they were repainted in a livery of yellow below the windows and white from the windows upwards.

Right: *German Federal Railways high-speed ET 403 train set with body-tilting capability, used now to connect the Ruhr area with Frankfurt Airport.*

Class 87 B_o-B_o

Great Britain:
British Railways (BR), 1973

Type: Mixed-traffic electric locomotive.
Gauge: 4ft 8½in (1,435mm).
Propulsion: Alternating current at 25,000V 50Hz fed via overhead catenary, step-down transformer and solid-state rectifiers to four 1,250hp (932kW) fully spring-borne traction motors, driving the axles by gearing and ASEA hollow-axle flexible drives.
Weight: 182,930lb (83t).
Max. axleload: 45,735lb (20.75t).
Overall length: 58ft 6in (17,830mm).
Tractive effort: 58,000lb (258kN).
Max. speed: 100mph (160km/h).

Although both began almost from scratch after World War II, there could be no greater contrast than between British Rail's ac electric locomotive development story and that of their diesels. Diesel developments followed each other with the consistency of successive pictures in a kaleidoscope, while ac electric locomotives moved through seven related classes all with the same appearance, maximum speed and wheel arrangement.

The first five classes were offerings on the part of five manufacturers to meet a specification for a 100mph (160km/h) locomotive capable of operation on 25,000V or 6,250V 50Hz electrification systems as shown in the table.

All had frame-mounted traction motors with flexible drive. Classes "81" to "84" originally had mercury-arc rectifiers, while Class "85" was fitted with solid-state rectifiers from the start and also had rheostatic braking. In the event, the need for 6,250V operation never arose, although provision was made for it. No steam heating boilers were provided, as electrically-heated sets were provided for all the regular trains on the electrified lines. Separate steam-heating vans were provided for occasions when stock not fitted with electric heaters was hauled by electric locomotives in the winter.

When the complete electric

Original class	Later class	Original quantity	Built by	Electrical equipment by	Present quantity
AL1	81	25	Birmingham Carriage & Wagon	AEI	22
AL2	82	10	Beyer-Peacock	Metropolitan-Vickers	0
AL3	83	15	English Electric		0
AL4	84	10	North British	General Electric	0
AL5	85	40	BR Doncaster	AEI	40

Above: *A Class 87 Bo-Bo electric locomotive at speed with an express train on the West Coast main line.*

Below: *British Railways' latest Class 87 Bo-Bo electric locomotive supplied in 1973-74 for the extension of electric working from north of Crewe to Glasgow.*

Left: *No. 87004 speeds toward Glasgow on a fine winter's day in the northern hills during November 1982.*

service from London to Birmingham, Manchester and Liverpool was introduced, a further 100 locomotives were supplied. These were Class "AL6", later Class "86", which had solid-state silicon rectifiers, rheostatic braking as the prime braking system and —one major simplification—nose-suspended traction motors geared direct to the axles. Not surprisingly, this simple answer was too hard on the permanent way for such dense high-speed traffic and the class is now divided up as follows:

- Class "86.0" in original condition, but with multiple-unit capability added and an 80mph (130km/h) speed limit imposed. Used only for freight traffic. Total 20 locomotives.
- Class "86.1", new bogies with ASEA hollow axle flexible drive. Prototypes for Class "87". Total 3 locomotives.
- Classes "86.2" and "86.3" modified to permit 100mph (160 km/h) running to continue. Fitted with resilient rail wheels and (86.2 only) modified bogie springing. Total 58 of Class "86.2" and 19 of Class "86.3".

The 36 locomotives of Class "87" were supplied for the extension of electric working from Crewe to Glasgow. They were built at BR's Crewe Works with electrical equipment by GEC Traction, into which AEI, English Electric, Metropolitan Vickers and British Thompson-Houston had by now been amalgamated. Power rating had been increased 56 per cent over that of Class "81" for a 4 per cent increase of weight. The ASEA hollow-axle flexible drive, tried out on Class "86.1" was used, and multiple-unit capability was provided. At long last it had not been thought necessary to provide an exhauster for working vacuum-braked trains. All the class carry names, mostly of distinguished people living or dead, and this pleasant practice has now spilled over on to examples of Class "86".

The latest improvement is application of thyristor control, fitted to a Class "87" locomotive re-designated Class "87.1". No. 87101 carries the honoured name of *Stephenson* and no doubt, when the present pause in British electric locomotive development is over, more will be heard of this significant step forward in traction technology.

As regards performance and reliability, it perhaps says enough that this can be entirely taken for granted with these locomotives. Ample power can be drawn from the contact wire for maintaining the maximum permitted speed with the usual loads, while the same locomotives are also suitable for heavier and slower freight trains.

Below: *British Railways' Class 87 Bo-Bo electric locomotive No. 87002, specially prepared and cleaned according to tradition, heading the Royal Train at Norton Bridge between Stafford and Crewe in June 1980.*

Class 381 Nine-car train

Japan:
Japanese National Railways (JNR), 1973

Type: Electric express passenger multiple-unit trainset with tilting mechanism.
Gauge: 3ft 6in (1,067mm).
Propulsion: Direct current at 1,500V or alternating current at 25,000V, 50 or 60Hz, fed from overhead catenary to six motor cars, each with four 160hp (100kW) traction motors geared to the axles.
Weight: 515,760lb (234t) adhesive, 753,802lb (342t) total.
Max. axleload: 21,490lb (9.75t).
Overall length: 628ft 11in (191,700mm).
Max. speed: 75mph (120km/h).

The concept of a tilting train arises from the fact that suitably designed trains can safely run round curves at much higher speeds than are normally comfortable for the passengers. This takes into account the superelevation (otherwise known as "cant" or "banking" applied to the track. The idea was born that a calculated amount of tilt could be added to the cant by servo-mechanisms on the train, and in this way trains could be run much faster, safely and comfortably, without the expensive need to build a new railway. The proposition is so attractive that many railway administrations have acquired experimental tilting trains or coaches but so far only one, Japanese National Railways, has any running in significant numbers.

The Japanese tilting trains (Class 381) are not for high-speed operation, intended to run, say, at 90mph (144km/h) where normal trains run at 75mph (120km/h), but instead to hold 60mph (96km/h) where a normal train would be limited to 50mph (80km/h). The tilt is limited to 5°, compared with the 9° of Britain's APT project, and it is applied when the cars' sensors feel a

Above: *A Japanese National Railways Class 381 electric train with tilting capability on a Hanwa line express, 1978.*

Right: *The tilting abilities of the Class 381 multiple-unit electric trains are used to advantage on mountain lines.*

Class 581 Twelve-car train

Japan:
Japanese National Railways (JNR), 1968

Type: Electric express sleeping-car train.
Gauge: 3ft 6in (1,067mm).
Propulsion: Alternating current at 25,000V 50Hz or 60Hz, or direct current at 3,000V fed via overhead catenary and conversion and control equipment in two power cars to 24 160hp (100kW) traction motors geared to the bogie axles of six of the intermediate sleeping cars in the train.
Weight: 638,720lb (290t) adhesive, 1,218,812lb (553t) total.
Max. axleload: 26,450lb (12t).
Overall length: 816ft 11in (249,000mm).
Max. speed: 100mph (160km/h)*.

*Design speed of train. The maximum permitted speed of the railway is at present 120km/h (75mph)

Above: *Sleeping car express electric multiple-unit train of Japanese National Railways.*

certain transverse acceleration. Being intended for lines with grades up to 1-in-40 (2.5 per cent), ample power is provided with two out of every three cars motored. One out of every two motor cars is a power car with pantographs and control/conversion equipment to cover operation on dc and 50 and 60Hz ac. The normal formation is nine cars, with driving trailers at each end. A nine-car train has 3,200hp (2,400kW) available and this is sufficient to produce 50mph (80km/h) up a 1-in-50 (2 per cent) gradient. Dynamic braking is available for the descent. The combination of higher uphill speeds and higher speeds on sharp curves both uphill and downhill produces worthwhile savings in overall running times. Operation of the original units has been sufficiently successful for JNR's fleet of tilting cars to have risen to over 150 during the last ten years.

The worldwide trend in modern forms of motive power towards self-contained locomotive-less trains took a hold of hitherto unconquered (but not unexplored) territory when Japanese National Railways put into service these very fine electric trains. Previous examples of the provision of sleeping cars in self-propelled trains included Union Pacific's M-10001 train (already described), various long-distance interurban electric trains in the USA and a West German set called the "Komet", which had a brief career in the 1950s. None of these examples led in any way to the idea becoming general practice on the lines concerned.

These handsome trains, however, have now taken over many long-distance overnight workings in Japan. They are also available for day use. Their scope is likely to widen considerably when the 33¾-mile (54km) Seikan tunnel connects the railway system of the Japanese main island of Honshu with that of Hokkaido. Intended eventually for high-speed standard-gauge *Shin-Kansen* trains, the new tunnel (nearly twice as long as its nearest existing rival) is likely to carry only narrow-gauge traffic for some years.

Above: *End doors of a Class 581 train can be opened to give communication between units.*

Below: *A Class 581 driving-trailer sleeping car coupled to a motor non-driving car.*

All berths are longitudinal and separate accommodation is not provided for "green" (first) and "ordinary" class passengers. Instead, there is a higher charge for lower berths compared to that for middle and upper berths. Berth charges do, however, include night attire and washing things, as in Japanese-style hotels. With up to 45 sleeping berths in each narrow-gauge car the designers must be admired for stating that their main objective was to create an impression of spaciousness! The 12-car set includes a dining car seating 40; the remaining 11 cars can sleep 444 or seat 656. The trains are air-conditioned throughout, and it has been said that the sound-proofing is sufficient to reduce noise levels to less than that encountered in locomotive-hauled sleeping cars.

Class Rc4 B_o-B_o

Sweden: Swedish State Railways (SJ), 1975

Type: Electric mixed-traffic locomotive.
Gauge: 4ft 8½in (1,435mm).
Propulsion: Alternating current at 15,000V 16⅔Hz, fed via overhead catenary, step-down transformer and a thyristor control system to four frame-mounted 1,206hp (900kW) traction motors, each driving one axle by gearing and ASEA hollow-axle flexible drive.
Weight: 171,910lb (78t).
Max. axleload: 42,980lb (19.5t).
Overall length: 50ft 11in (15,520mm).
Tractive effort: 65,200lb (290kN).
Max. speed: 84mph (135km/h).

The "Rc" family of electric locomotives, developed by the Allmanna Svenska Elektriska Aktiebolaget (ASEA) organisation initially for Swedish State Railways, bids fair to be the world's most successful electric locomotive design. Basically intended for mixed-traffic, the scope of the design has been developed on the one hand to cope with express passenger traffic at 100mph (160km/h), while on the other a version has been supplied for hauling heavy iron ore trains in the Arctic regions. Abroad, such widely differing customers as Austria, Norway and the USA have ordered "Rc" derivatives.

One of the reasons for this pre-eminence is that the "Rc1" was the world's first thyristor locomotive design, put into service in 1967; ingenuity on the part of other manufacturers is no substitute for years of experience in service.

In 1969, 100 "Rc2s" followed the 20 "Rc1s", and they included improvements to the thyristor control system and more sophisticated electrical filters. These are needed to prevent harmonic ripples produced by the thyristor circuits feeding back into the rails and interfering with signalling currents (which also flow in the same rails) and communication circuits generally. The 10 "Rc3s" of 1970 were "Rc2s" geared for 100mph (160km/h) while 16 units, some of which have rheostatic braking, were supplied to Austria (Class "1043") in 1971-73.

In 1975 came the "Rc4" class, the design of which included a patent system developed by ASEA for countering wheelslip, which automatically reduces the current supplied to any driving motor which begins to creep faster than the others. There are also other improvements such as solid-state instead of rotary convertors for power supply to auxiliary apparatus.

A total of 150 "Rc4s" have

Class E60CP C_o-C_o

USA: National Railroad Passenger Corporation (Amtrak), 1973

Type: High-speed electric express passenger locomotive.
Gauge: 4ft 8½in (1,435mm).
Propulsion: Alternating current at 12,500V 25Hz (or at 12,500V or 25,000V 60Hz) supplied via step-down transformer with thyristor control system to six 1,275hp (951kW) nose-suspended traction motors geared to the axles.
Weight: 387,905lb (176t).
Max. axleload: 48,490lb (22t).
Overall length: 71ft 3in (21,720mm).
Tractive effort: 75,000lb (334kN).
Max. speed: 85mph (137km/h)*.

*In service. Design speed was 120mph (194km/h).

In the 1970s it became urgent to seek a replacement for the legendary "GG1" electric locomotives which worked the New York to Washington express passenger route. This was not so much on account of difficulties with the "GG1s" themselves—they worked as well as ever. It was more the bad image created by having to admit reliance upon motive power almost 50 years old, plus the fact that the "GG1s" were not suitable for a then impending (but now postponed) modernisation of the power supply, involving a change from a special frequency to the normal industrial frequency.

In order to meet the requirements quickly, General Electric, who had not supplied any passenger electric locomotive to US railroads since 1955, modified a coal-hauling Black Mesa & Lake Powell Railroad locomotive in 1972. The changes involved re-gearing, pro-

Above: *Amtrak E60P electric locomotive at Newark, New Jersey, with New York-Miami "Silver Star" train, June 1982.*

been supplied to Swedish State Railways, plus another 15 with modifications produced for Norway (Class "el.16"), but ASEA's greatest success occurred in the USA. The National Railroad Passenger Corporation (better known as Amtrak) had had the problem of finding motive power to replace the superb but now ageing "GG1" class of 1934 (already described). The new engines were required for use on the New York-Philadelphia-Washington main line, electrified at 12,500V 25Hz. Various substitutes fielded by US industry (which had built very few high-speed electric locomotives since the "GG1s") and one from France were disappointing, but a modified "Rc4" sent over on trial—"our little Volvo", Amtrak's motive power men called her—proved to be just what the doctor ordered. Accordingly, a fleet of 47 was proposed.

Rather than fight the "Buy American" lobby in the USA, ASEA sensibly licensed General Motors Electro-Motive Division to build, using ASEA parts, what are now known as Class "AEM7". The "AEM7s" have stronger bodies, 25 per cent more power, and multi-current capability to cover future conversions to 25,000V 60Hz, with a certain amount of 12,500V 60Hz in areas with close clearances. This is in addition to 12,500V 25Hz capability. Maximum speed is much higher at 125mph (200km/h), while the weight has risen by 17 per cent. This is no detriment, since very high axleloads are catered for in the USA by the use of heavy rail, closely spaced sleepers and deep ballast.

The six iron-ore haulers of 1977 (Class "Rm") had ballasting to raise the axleload to 50,700lb (23t), automatic couplers, lower gearing, rheostatic braking and multiple-unit capability, as well as better heating and more insulation in the cab.

Below: *A Swedish Class Rc4 "universal" electric locomotive with thyristor control system.*

vision for supplying auxiliary power to the train and (for some of the units) oil-fired steam-heating boilers. The 27 locomotives supplied in 1973 ran well except that the riding at high speeds left something to be desired. So, in the event, the "GG1s" had to be retained to cater for this requirement.

Some "E60CPs" were found employment on lesser duties, others were disposed of to other users; it was left for locomotives of Swedish design and possessing excellent riding qualities, to displace the old faithfuls.

Right: *The E60P locos can use either the original Pennsylvania RR supply at 25Hz, or the proposed 50Hz.*

Class X C_o-C_o

Australia:
Victorian Railways (VicRail), 1966

Type: Diesel-electric mixed-traffic locomotive.
Gauge: 5ft 3in (1,600mm) and 4ft 8½in (1,435mm).
Propulsion: General Motors Type 16-567E 1,950hp (1,455kW) Vee 16-cylinder two-stroke diesel engine and generator supplying current to six nose-suspended traction motors geared to the axles.
Weight: 255,665lb (116t).
Max. axleload: 42,980lb (19.5t).
Overall length: 60ft 3in (18,364mm).
Tractive effort: 64,125lb (285kN).
Max. speed: 84mph (134km/h).

It is well known that Australia has a serious railway gauge problem, the various states having in the early days gone their own ways in this respect. The state of Victoria and its neighbour South Australia were the two which opted for a 5ft 3in (1,600mm) broad gauge. In steam days this meant different designs of locomotive, but with diesels the differences can be minimal, confined almost wholly to the appropriate wheelsets.

These Class "X" diesels of Victorian Government Railways are a case in point because, now that standard-gauge has put a tentacle into the state (notably to connect Melbourne to the Trans-Australian railway as well as over the trunk route from Sydney), they provide haulage over both gauges.

The locomotives are a typical General Motors product—like virtually all VicRail's diesel locomo-

Left: *"X" class diesel-electric locomotive No. X49 arrives in Melbourne with the "Southern Aurora" express from Sydney.*

Class 2130 C_o-C_o

Australia:
Queensland Railways (QR), 1970

Type: Diesel-electric mineral-hauling locomotive.
Gauge: 3ft 6in (1,067mm).
Propulsion: General Motors Type 16-645E 2,200hp (1,640kW) 16-cylinder Vee two-stroke diesel engine and alternator feeding via solid-state rectifiers six nose-suspended traction motors geared to the axles.
Weight: 215,050lb (98t).
Max. axleload: 35,850lb (16.3t).
Overall length: 59ft 3in (18,060mm).
Tractive effort: 64,500lb (287kN).
Max. speed: 50mph (80km/h).

Queensland's 6,206 mile (9,930km) railway system has been extended recently to serve various mining operations, and so has rather surprisingly moved into the premier place as regards mileage amongst the Australian state and national administrations. Furthermore, in spite of being mostly laid on narrow-gauge, QR also holds the top place in load hauling. The locomotives that achieve this record are these Class "2130" diesel-electrics. The 11 machines which form the "2130" class are, like 57 per cent of the QR fleet, of General Motors design but built (or at any rate, assembled, under licence) by Clyde Engineering. They also follow US practice in being used as building blocks to form a tractive effort of the power desired.

The most heroic use for these excellent machines is their employment as two groups of three on the newly built Goonyella line to haul 148-wagon coal trains weighing 11,140t (12,250 US tons) and carrying 8,700t (9,130 US tons) of coal. As the drawgear of the train is not strong enough to take the tractive effort of all six locomotives,

Above: *A 6,600 horsepower couplage of QR Class 2130 diesel electric units.*

Below: *Queensland Railways' Class 2130 diesel-electric locomotive, supplied in 1970.*

tives—and were assembled by GM's Australian licensee, Clyde Engineering Pty of Sydney, New South Wales. This standardisation gives an advantage in that most of the diesel fleet can be run in multiple regardless of class.

Soon after the first six "Xs" had been delivered, Clyde began offering GM's new 645 series engine and this was used for a subsequent batch of 18 supplied in 1970. The power output could thus be increased to 2,600hp (1,940kW) without weight penalty. These were then the most powerful units on the system, but subsequently axleload limits have been raised to 22.5t (24.8 US tons) on certain lines. Hence a further batch of GM Co-Co units (the "C" class) supplied with an installed power of 3,300hp (2,460kW).

One requirement for all Victorian locomotives that possibly defeated General Motors' ability to supply off-the-shelf was provision of sets of pneumatically-operated token exchange equipment. Under British-style operating rules, some physical token of authority is needed to be on any particular section of single line. The token (or staff) has to be exchanged for another when passing from one section to the next. The places where this happens often do not coincide with the train's stopping places and the exchange apparatus enables this to be done at speed. Modern electrical methods of signalling are slowly doing away with this picturesque operation, but for the moment it continues and locomotives however modern have to be equipped to cope.

Right: *Victorian Railways' Class "X" Co-Co diesel-electric locomotive No. X45* Edgar. B. Brownbill, *built in 1970.*

Left: *Note the alternative of automatic couplings or link-and-screw with buffers on these Class 2130 locos.*

the second group is cut into the centre of the train. These mid-train units are remotely controlled from the lead units without any cable connections between them, by a system of US origin widely-used in North America and known as Locotrol.

The Locotrol system involves a special vehicle marshalled next to the group of units in the centre of the train. This vehicle operates on the principle of sensing the drawbar pull and applying power to the units it controls accordingly. Safety is ensured by having the brakes of the whole train under the control of the driver in the leading unit. Six of the locomotives (Nos. 2135 to 40) are fitted out for use as lead units, with air-conditioned cabs and Locotrol equipment.

The "2130" class is part of a group of generally similar diesel locomotives, 57 in number, all of General Motors origin and numbered in the 21xx and 22xx series, as befits their rating of 2,000hp-plus. The only non-General Motors units of this order of power on the system are the 16 Class "2350" of 2,350hp (1,735kW) supplied by English Electric and used on lines with an axleload limit of 15t. This high-power fleet may be the summit of diesel development in Queensland because plans are afoot to begin electrification of some heavily-used lines.

DF4 'East Wind IV' C_o-C_o

China:
Railways of the People's Republic (CR), 1969

Type: General-purpose diesel-electric locomotive.
Gauge: 4ft 8½in (1,435mm).
Propulsion: 3,600hp (2,686kW) Type 16-240-Z 16-cylinder Vee-type four-stroke diesel engine and alternator supplying current via solid-state rectifiers to six traction motors geared to the axles.
Weight: 304,155lb (138t).
Max. axleload: 50,695lb (23t).
Overall length: 62ft 2½in (21,100mm).
Tractive effort: 76,038lb (338kN).
Max. speed: 75mph (120km/h).

Above: *An "East Wind IV" diesel-electric locomotive of the Chinese Railways near Peking in November 1980.*

Diesel locomotive production in China started off quite incredibly badly in the 1960s when, in response to Chairman Mao's call for a 'Great Leap Forward', the various locomotive works, 'aiming high', set out to design and build their own, unhampered by any previous experience. The result was disaster, but when sanity returned it was rightly felt important not to respond by putting the nation into the hands of some foreign country.

The immediate solution was for steam building to continue and for a slow-but-sure diesel-electric development programme to be put in hand. There were some imports of main line diesel-electric locomotives, notably 50 of 4,000hp (2,985kW) from Alsthom of France during the early-1970s and 20 of 2,100hp (1,567kW) from Electroputere of Romania, in 1975, but home-building also began in earnest, and this is the most common type.

The DF4 is a general-purpose locomotive, of which versions exist for both passenger (numbered 2001 upwards) or freight traffic (numbered 0001 upwards). It is not often used in multiple, being the most powerful in China with a single engine and consequently having adequate power to haul trains of the size normally run. Its appearance is neat and there is a cab at both ends. The engine, the ac/dc transmission and the mechanical parts are wholly Chinese-made and developed from a prototype built in 1969. Series production is now in hand at the Talien (Dairen) Works. Incidentally, the type number of the engine, 16240, indicates the number of cylinders (16) followed by their bore in millimetres (240mm—9.45in). It is delightful to note that, with a frankness unmatched amongst the world's railway mechanical departments, the weights are officially specified as being within plus or minus 3 per cent. It is thought that about 450 had been produced by the end of 1981.

Beijing B-B

China:
Railways of the People's Republic (CR), 1971

Type: Diesel-hydraulic express passenger locomotive.
Gauge: 4ft 8½in (1,435mm).
Propulsion: Type 12240Z 3,300hp (2,462kW) 12-cylinder four-stroke Vee diesel engine driving the four axles through a hydraulic torque-converter system.
Weight: 202,770lb (92t).
Max. axleload: 50,695lb (23t).
Overall length: 54ft 2in (16,505mm).
Tractive effort: 52,257lb (232kN).
Max. speed: 75mph (120km/h).

In parallel with diesel-electric progress, diesel-hydraulic locomotive development has also been pursued in China. With some experience gained with 30 class "NY6" 4,300hp (3,208kW) and "NY7" 5,400hp (4,028kW) locomotives imported from Henschel of West Germany, the February 7th Locomotive Works at Peking (Beijing) produced in 1971 some prototypes of a rather smaller locomotive for passenger work. These are known as the "BJ" or "Beijing" class. Full production began in 1975 and by the end of 1981 about 150 were in service, numbered BJ3001 upwards.

These compact-looking locomotives have more haulage capacity than would appear. The powerful engine is matched by high tractive effort, due to the high axleloading. For example, on a really steep gradient of 1-in-30 (3.3 per cent), a load of 600t (660 US tons) can be hauled at the very respectable speed in the circumstances of 15mph (24km/h). A low-level connection to transmit tractive effort from the bogies to the body helps improve performance by reducing weight transfer from one axle to another. The hydraulic transmission incorporates two torque convertors, one for starting and one for running at normal speeds. Either can be used to drive one or both bogies and the system can also be used as a hydrokinetic brake to give dynamic braking. A twin-engine version is under development and so highly is the performance and reliability of the "BJ" class regarded that its designers now have sufficient confidence to offer it for export.

Left: *Compact Chinese Railways "Beijing" class diesel-hydraulic locomotive No. BJ3062 standing at Peking main station in October 1980.*

Right: *A "Beijing" class diesel-hydraulic locomotive of Chinese Railways at the head of the daily tourist train from Peking to the Great Wall of China.*

Class Dr 13 C-C

Finland:
Finnish State Railways (VR), 1963

Type: Diesel-electric mixed-traffic locomotive.
Gauge: 5ft 0in (1,524mm).
Propulsion: Two Tampella-MGO Type V-16 BHSR 1,400hp (1,030kW) Vee 16-cylinder diesel engines and generators supplying current to two large traction motors, one mounted on each bogie. Each motor drives the three axles of its bogie via gearing with two alternative gear ratios.
Weight: 218,200lb (99t).
Max. axleload: 36,370lb (16.5t).
Overall length: 60ft 11in (18,576mm).
Tractive effort: 62,373lb (277kN).
Max. speed: 87mph (140km/h) high gear, 62mph (100km/h) low gear.

Above: *Finnish State Railways Class Dr 13 C-C diesel-electric locomotive.*

Two prototypes of these unusual-looking locomotives were obtained in 1963 from Alsthom of France; they contained many typical features of that famous firm's products. Later a production batch of 52 was built (or certainly assembled) under licence in Finland. Lokomo and Valmet, both of Tampere, shared the order and 48 out of the original 54 are still in service.

The design was based on engines of modest power output which were available in Finland, two being used to provide the desired output. The running gear and electrical equipment, however, followed original principles, which had been adopted for both electric and diesel-electric locomotives then recently introduced in France. The bogies were of the monomotor pattern, each with one large traction motor mounted above the wheels in the centre of the bogie. The wheels were driven by gearing which had the unusual feature of alternative ratios. The higher of these was suitable for express passenger work, while the other was appropriate for heavy freight haulage. A change-over between the two has to wait, of course, until the locomotive is stationary.

While these interesting machines have served VR well, it is clear that future diesel development in Finland is likely to be overshadowed by electrification.

Class 6E B_o-B_o

South Africa:
South African Railways (SAR), 1969

Type: Electric mixed traffic freight locomotive.
Gauge: 3ft 6in (1,067mm).
Propulsion: Direct current at 3,000V fed via overhead catenary and rheostatic controls to four 835hp (623kW) nose-suspended motors geared to the driving axles.
Weight: 195,935lb (88.9t).
Max. axleload: 49,040lb (22.25t).
Overall length: 50ft 10in (15,494mm).
Tractive effort: 70,000lb (311kN).
Max. speed: 70mph (112km/h).

The first important electrification scheme in South Africa came as early as 1925, when a steeply-graded section of the Durban to Johannesburg main line between Estcourt and Ladysmith was placed under the wires. The Class "1E" locomotives supplied—the original group came from Switzerland—were direct ancestors of Class "6E" with the same wheel arrangement and mechanical configuration. Fifty-five years of progress has resulted in increases of 77 per cent in tractive effort, 208 per cent in power output, and 180 per cent in maximum permitted speed at a cost of only 31 per cent in weight and 16 per cent in overall length. It is typical of electric traction, though, that many of the "1Es" remain in service on humble but still arduous duties after half-a-century of work.

A country that combines prosperous development and great

Left: *South African Railways' famous "Blue Train" near Fountains Pretoria, hauled by two specially painted electric locomotives.*

Class 9E C_o-C_o

South Africa:
South African Railways (SAR), 1978

Type: Electric mineral-hauling locomotive.
Gauge: 3ft 6in (1,067mm).
Propulsion: Alternating current at 50,000V 50Hz fed via overhead catenary, step-down transformer with thyristor control to six nose-suspended 910hp (680kW) traction motors geared to the wheels.
Weight: 370,270lb (168t).
Max. axleload: 61,712lb (28t).
Overall length: 69ft 4in (21,132mm).
Tractive effort: 121,000lb (538kN).
Max. speed: 56mph (90km/h).

It is said that the only work of man on Earth visible from the moon is the Great Wall of China, but a likely further candidate must be the 529-mile (846km) line from Sishen in the centre of South Africa to a new Atlantic port at Saldanha Bay. Not only would it have been noticed by a moon-bound earth-watcher on account of the rapidity with which it appeared, but is conspicuousness would have been enhanced by the featureless semi-desert nature of the most of the route.

Although built by the South African government's Iron & Steel Industrial Corporation (ISCOR) for moving iron ore for shipment, South African Railways operate the line, and the scale of operations is such that some unprecedented equipment has been needed. In virtually uninhabited country, electric power supplies are far apart and hence a nominal voltage twice that normally used nowadays was specified. The result is that there are only six substations for the entire route, the contact wire itself acting as a main transmission line. The 25 locomotives built for the railway (after a period of diesel operation) were designed by GEC Traction in Great Britain but built in South Africa by Union Carriage & Wagon. They normally operate in threes, so making up a 16,350hp (12,200kW) unit capable of starting as well as hauling a 20,000t (22,000 US tons) load on the ruling gradient—against loaded trains—of 1-in-250 (0.4 per cent). They can also operate (but at reduced speed) when the voltage drops as low as 25,000, which can happen in certain conditions, say 45 miles (70km) from the nearest substation.

One delightful feature of a harsh operation in the harshest of environments is the motor scooter provided in a special cabinet below the locomotive running board. This enables someone to inspect both sides of a 200-wagon train almost 1½ miles (2.3km)

Right: *South African Railways' Class 9E 50,000V electric locomotive, as used on the Sishen to Saldanha Bay line.*

mineral riches with non-existent oil supplies is well-suited to electrification. Both the scale of electric operation and its rate of development in South Africa are indicated by the fact that the "6E/6E1" fleet already approaches 1,000 in number, while 850 of their very similar immediate predecessors, classes "5E" and "5E1," were built between 1955 and 1969. South Africa's growing industrial capability is also shown by the fact that while the 172 "1Es" (and the similar "2Es") were wholly built in Europe, only the earlier examples of Class "5E" and none of the "6Es" were built abroad.

All the classes mentioned, and this is especially impressive for half-a-century ago, are capable not only of regenerative braking but also of working in multiple. This whole concept of railroading, using exclusively tractors with the same two bogies as most other vehicles but coupling up as many of them as are needed to haul the train was far ahead of its time. Five or six locomotives running in multiple can often be seen.

Above: *The striking matching livery of the locomotive and carriages of the prestigious and luxurious "Blue Train", running three times a week between Johannesburg and Cape Town.*

Below: *South African Railways' standard 5E/6E series Bo-Bo locomotives, depicted here in the special "Blue Train" colours, are now fast approaching the amazing total of 2,000 in number.*

long, returning reasonably quickly to the locomotive after the round trip. Other comforts provided for the crew include full air-conditioning, a toilet and a refrigerator, as well as a hotplate for cooking. The unusual appearance is due to the roof having to be lowered to accommodate the large insulators and switchgear needed for the high voltage.

The control system is of advanced design, using thyristors. The position of the driver's main control lever is arranged to determine not external physical things such as resistance values or transformer tapping, but instead the actual value of the traction motor currents and therefore the individual torque applied to each pair of wheels. This gives a much more direct control over the movement of the train. There are five systems of braking: straight air on the locomotive, normal air braking for the train, vacuum brakes (on some units) for occasional haulage of ordinary SAR rolling stock, a handbrake and electrical braking. The latter, which is rheostatic rather than regenerative, can hold a full 20,000t (22,000 US tons) train to 34mph (55km/h) on a 1-in-167 (0.6 per cent) downgrade. It is thought that this operation is the only one in the world where trains of this weight are operated using other than North American designs of equipment.

F40PH B_o-B_o

United States:
Electro-Motive Division, General Motors Corporation (EMD), 1976

Type: Diesel-electric passenger locomotive.
Gauge: 4ft 8½in (1,435mm).
Propulsion: One EMD 645E3 3,000hp (2,240kW) 16-cylinder turbocharged two-stroke Vee engine and alternator supplying current through silicon rectifiers to four nose-suspended traction motors geared to the axles.
Weight: 232,000lb (105.2t).
Max. axleload: 58,000lb (26.3t).
Overall length: 52ft 0in (15,850mm).
Tractive effort: 68,440lb (304kN).
Max. speed: 103mph (166km/h).

Above: *A push-pull commuter train hauled by F40PH No. 4120 of New Jersey Transit passes Harrison, New Jersey.*

The last of the EMD passenger "carbody" diesels was built at the end of 1963, and with passenger traffic declining rapidly, the need for special passenger locomotives seemed to have disappeared. Both EMD and its competitors offered a train-heating steam generator as an optional extra on certain "hood" units, and this met the needs of the railroads which required replacements for ageing "E" or "F" series units.

In 1968, with the railroads' enthusiasm for high-power diesels at its climax, the Atchison, Topeka & Santa Fe Railway proposed to buy from EMD some 20-cylinder 3,600hp (2,690kW) Co-Co locomotives geared for high speed to operate its premier passenger services. The railroad asked that the locomotives should be given a more acceptable appearance for passenger work, and that the body should have less air resistance at speed than a normal hood unit. The outcome was the "cowl", a casing shaped like an angular version of the old carbody, but differing from it in that the casing does not carry any load. The cowl extends ahead of the cab, giving the front of the cab more protection against the weather than a normal hood.

The model was designated "FP45", and was very similar in its equipment to the "SD45" road switcher. Another variant had a shorter frame resulting from the omission of the steam generator; it was designated "F45".

In 1971 the National Railroad Passenger Corporation (Amtrak) took over most of the non-commuter passenger services in the US, and in 1973 took delivery of its first new locomotives to replace the old "E" and "F" series. By this

Below: *An F40PH belonging to Ontario's GO Transit brings a rake of striking double-deck cars through Scarborough, Ont.*

time, enthusiasm for engines above 3,000hp had declined, so the Amtrak units were similar to the "FP45" but with a 16-cylinder 3,000hp (2,240kW) engine. A total of 150 were delivered in 1973-74. They were equipped with two steam generators mounted on skids, which could easily be replaced by two diesel-alternators when steam-heated stock was replaced by electrically-heated vehicles. In view of the similarity to the "SD40s", these locomotives were classified "SDP40".

For a time all was well, but then an alarming series of derailments occurred to the trailing bogies of "SDP40s" whilst negotiating curves. No explanation could be found, but it was clear that the track had been spread or rails turned over by excessive lateral forces. The bogies were only slightly different from those of other EMD "Dash-2" three-axle bogies, but it was the only part of the locomotive on which suspicion could fall.

In the meantime, for shorter-distance routes on which the coaches were already electrically-heated, Amtrak had ordered a four-axle 3,000hp (2,240kW) locomotive, with an alternator for supplying three-phase current at 60Hz for train services driven by gearing from the engine crankshaft. This model is designated "F40PH", and deliveries began in March 1976 when the problem of the "SDP40" derailments was acute. As the well-tried Blomberg truck fitted to the "F40PH" had given no cause for criticism, Amtrak decided that the Co-Co locomotives should be rebuilt as "F40PHs". The frame could be shortened by 16ft, as the steam generator was no longer needed. The "F40PHs" built new had a 500kW alternator, which drew a maximum of 710hp from the engine, but for the transcontinental "Superliner" trains an 800kW alternator and larger fuel tanks were needed, so that the "F40PHs" obtained by rebuilding are 4ft longer than the others.

In the fact the rebuilding was nominal, for it cost nearly 70 per cent of the price of a new locomotive, and in effect the "SDP40s" were scrapped when only four to five years old. Amtrak now has a fleet of 191 "F40PH" locomotives.

Many US commuter services are the responsibility of transit authorities, some of whom operate their own trains. A number of these operators bought a shortened version of the unhappy "SD40F", in which the steam generator was replaced by an alternator. This is the "F40C", and in this application the engine is uprated to 3,200hp (2,390kW). At the moderate speeds of commuter services, no trouble has been experienced with derailments, but nevertheless when further locomotives were required the transit authorities ordered the four-axle "F40PH", in some cases with the engine uprated to 3,200hp.

Below: *Amtrak's standard passenger locomotive is this F40PH "Cowl" Bo-Bo unit built by General Motors' Electro-Motive Division. The F40PHs displaced most of the vintage "F" and "E" series locomotives from Amtrak's principal long-distance trains in the late 1970s.*

Below: *An F40PH Bo-Bo diesel-electric locomotive belonging to Amtrak arrives at Chicago Union Station with a short train composed of "Amfleet" passenger cars.*

Class 1044 B_o-B_o

Austria:
Austrian Federal Railways (OBB), 1974

Type: Electric express passenger locomotive.
Gauge: 4ft 8½in (1,435mm).
Propulsion: Low-frequency alternating current at 15,000V 16⅔Hz fed via overhead catenary, step-down transformer with thyristor control system to four 1,765hp (1,317kW) traction motors driving the axles through Brown Boveri spring drives and gearing.
Weight: 185,140lb (84t).
Max. axleload: 46,285lb (21t).
Overall length: 52ft 6in (16,000mm).
Tractive effort: 70,600lb (314kN).
Max. speed: 100mph (160km/h).

Above: *Austrian Federal Railways class 1044 electric locomotive No. 1044.83 leaving Seefeld, Tirol, in September 1982.*

Austrian locomotives were in the past distinctive almost to the point of quaintness, whether steam or electric. But since the German occupation, during which standard German types were imposed, the Federal Railways locomotives have been capable but otherwise as conventional as could be. Only 62 out of 406 electric locomotives supplied since the war were not Bo-Bos, and of these 50 were Co-Cos and the others rod-drive switchers.

Most of the 406 also came from the Austrian state-owned locomotive-building firm of Simmering-Graz-Pauker (SGP) of Vienna and Graz, but an exception was a batch of 10 thyristor-controlled locomotives (Class "1043") imported from Sweden between 1971 and 1973. Satisfactory experience with these led to the thought that Austrians had been building electric locomotives a lot longer than these northerners. The result was this Class "1044", of which two prototypes were completed by SGP in 1974. Orders for a further 96 have followed.

Their high-speed capability is only relevant to a tiny proportion of the Austrian rail network, but high tractive effort and surefootedness, the key to operations in the mountains, are special features. Accordingly, the new locomotives were designed to complement

Left: *Innsbruck locomotive depot in foreground; note Class 1020 Co-Co locos on siding. A Class 1044 Bo-Bo locomotive is leaving the station.*

No. 12 B-B

Great Britain:
Romney, Hythe & Dymchurch Railway (RH&DR), 1983

Type: Locomotive for local passenger haulage.
Gauge: 1ft 3in (381mm).
Propulsion: Perkins Type 6.3544 120hp (90kW) diesel engine driving all four axles direct via two-speed bi-directional gearbox and torque converter, drop-down gearbox, longitudinal cardan shafts and gearing.
Weight: 13,225lb (6t).
Max. axleload: 3,310lb (1.5t).
Overall length: 21ft 0in (6,400mm).
Tractive effort: 6,000lb (27kN).
Max. speed: 25mph (40km/h).

Above: *Romney, Hythe & Dymchurch Railway B-B diesel mechanical locomotive in the maker's works, 1983. The machine is named after the founder of the school whose pupils travel daily behind the locomotive.*

This minute locomotive already plays a vital role in local light rail transport and may well play a bigger one in the future. Ever since it was opened in 1927, the 13 mile (21km) Romney, Hythe & Dymchurch Railway has claimed the title of "Smallest Public Railway in the World". A few years ago the claim became a degree firmer when a contract was obtained from local government to carry some 200 pupils to and from school each day.

Steam traction—however attractive as part of the RH&DR's normal tourist-railway operations—was quite uneconomic for the school train. Accordingly, with the assistance of a local government grant, a diesel locomotive was designed and built for the railway by the firm of TMA Engineering of Birmingham.

Sufficient tractive effort to handle a 200-passenger train was required and to obtain this a major ingredient was the Twin-Disc transmission. This was based on that used for many years on British

the stepless thyristor control with other measures, to bring adhesion up to values that only a very few years ago were thought beyond the bounds of possibility.

One measure taken is to provide linkage so that the tractive effort from each bogie is transmitted to the body as near to rail level as possible. This avoids weight transfer from one wheelset to another when either bogie applies tractive force to the body. Transverse forces imposed on the bogies by constant changes of curvature in the mountains are ameliorated by giving the axles spring-controlled sideplay.

Although some problems have arisen, leading to a temporary cessation of production, their effectiveness means that one of these locomotives (and they are often employed in pairs) can, for example, be rostered to take 550t (605US tons) up the 1-in-32½ (3.1 per cent) ascent to the Arlberg tunnel on the trunk route from Switzerland to Salzberg and Vienna. The amazing one-hour output of 7,075hp (5,278kW) that makes such feats possible shows how far ac traction using double-bogie four-axle locomotives has come since the New York, New Haven & Hartford Railroad put their first Baldwin-Westinghouse Bo-Bo on the rails in 1905, with a rated power output of 1,420hp (1,060kW).

Right: *Head-on view of Austrian Federal Railways Class 1044 Bo-Bo locomotive at Innsbruck station with Vienna-Basle Trans-Alpine express, Autumn 1980.*

Railways' diesel-mechanical trains and therefore, hopefully, the long build-up of experience so gained will lead to reliability. The shape of the locomotive has been designed to give the driver a good look-out both ways as well as protection in the event of a level-crossing collision. The cab is heated, sound-proofed, equipped with radio for signalling purposes, and has reversible seats with duplicate instrumentation for each direction. Vacuum brake equipment is provided to work the train brakes, using an off-the-shelf exhauster and other fittings of automotive origin.

To some, of course, the introduction of diesel traction to this famous piece of railway showbiz is as if the *Folies Bergére* decided to dress its equally famous girls in denim overalls. So to that extent a question mark must stand over the use of this acquisition. But perhaps the most interesting thing about it is that a combination of this locomotive and a rake of standard RH&DR light-alloy passenger carriages could now offer a way of providing a low-key rapid-transit system.

Such a system might bear a similar relationship to what is now called LRT (Light Rapid Transit) as LRT does to a full metro system. An LRT—effectively what used to be called trams, but mainly, or wholly confined to reserved tracks—has perhaps one-third the capacity of a hypothetical metro and achieves half the average speed, but only costs one-seventh of its grander rival. A Romney-style VLRT (Very Light Rail Transit) might provide half the capacity, and a very little lower speed, all for one-quarter the cost of LRT.

Above: *The cab end of RH&DR locomotive No. 12. Within an axleload limit of 1.5t and an overall height of 6ft 6in (2m), haulage capability has been provided for handling trains with a load of 200 passengers.*

Class Ge 4/4 B₀-B₀

Switzerland:
Furka-Oberalp Railway (FOB), 1979

Type: Electric mixed-traffic mountain locomotive.
Gauge: 3ft 3⅜in (1,000mm).
Propulsion: Low-frequency alternating current at 11,000V 16⅔Hz fed via overhead catenary and step-down transformer with thyristor control to four 570hp (425kW) traction motors with both series and independent field windings. Connection to the wheels is through gearing and Brown Boveri spring drives.
Weight: 110,220lb (50t).
Max. axleload: 27,550lb (12.5t).
Overall length: 42ft 6½in (12,960mm).
Tractive effort: 40,050lb (178kN).
Max. speed: 56mph (90km/h).

Above: *Furka-Oberalp rack-and-adhesion motor luggage vans, Class De 4/4, used for working trains on 1-in-9 (11 per cent) grades.*

'To The Clouds By Rail' wrote Cecil J. Allen, King of railway journalists, referring to Switzerland's remarkable mountain railways. Nearer the clouds than most of those which crossed Alpine passes was the Furka-Oberalp Railway reaching, with rack-and-pinion assistance on 1-in-9 (11 per cent) gradients, 7,085ft (2,160m) at the Furka tunnel and 6,668ft (2,033m) at Oberalp Passhoehe. The ascents to the former were a little too close to the clouds in winter. Which leads to these neat locomotives with such remarkable properties for their size, which were acquired in connection with an amazing project to convert the line into an all-weather route open all year.

The project was construction of a 9¾ mile (15.5km) Furka base tunnel running from Oberwald (4,480ft—1,366m) to Realp (5,045ft —1,538m) to avoid the difficult section. These stations were the termini of the winter shuttle services from Brig and Andermatt respectively. Work started in 1973 and traffic began to pass on June 25, 1982; the estimates were overun by three times in cost and one-and-a-half times in contruction time.

There were to be motor-car shuttle trains through the tunnel as well as additional trains coming up from Brig. To work this traffic the FO management wondered whether the extra expense of rack-equipped motive power could be avoided, by working with adhesion on the rack sections concerned which had a lesser gradient of 1-in-11 (9 per cent). They were encouraged in this by the performance of four-axle locomotives (Class "Ge 4/4 II") recently supplied to the connecting Rhaetian Railway. On test they had produced 50 per cent adhesion, that is a drawbar pull of 25t, and in addition they could manage the equally unprecedented speed for the Swiss metre-gauge of 56mph (90km/h). This would be useful now that the FO at last had acquired straight track in the tunnel—the only possible place for high speed on its 62½ miles (100km) of route. Hence Nos. 81 *Uri* and 82 *Wallis*, supplied in 1979, and lent to the Rhaetian Railway when acquired until the tunnel was ready.

Adhesion, that all important quantity for a rack-less mountain railway, was maximised on these locomotives by step-less thyristor control and low-level traction bars connecting the bogies to the body, as in the Austrian Class "1044". In addition, to minimise the effect of drawbar pull causing weight transfer from the front to the rear bogie, there is an electrically-con-

Below: *Class Ge 4/4 adhesion-only Bo-Bo locomotive used for working car-carrying trains through the new Furka tunnel.*

trolled compensation system with two stages of adjustment. Wheel-creep, indicating the imminence of slipping, is also detected automatically and the appropriate motor current adjusted to correct the situation. Friction (and wear) is reduced by a flange-lubricating system and, in addition, rheostatic braking is provided. Finally, it is a pleasure to find accompanying all this superb technology provision of rectractable rail brushes for clearing and cleaning the rail heads of leaves and other detritus.

The locomotives can haul loaded car trains weighing 350t (385 US tons) on the 1-in-37 (2.7 per cent) grade in the tunnel. On 1-in-11 (9 per cent) grades, on which other motive power uses the rack for traction, some 75t (88 US tons) could in principle be hauled by adhesion alone. This does not sound a lot, but lightweight FO carriages weigh a mere 12t empty although carrying up to 48 passengers.

Although trains are worked by adhesion alone on gradients as steep as 1-in-11 (9 per cent) on other mountain railways in Switzerland, for the moment it seems that this will not occur on the Furka-Oberalp. The fleet of De4/4 rack-and-adhesion motor luggage vans has been increased to cater for the increase in regular traffic anticipated as a result of opening the new tunnel.

Right: *End view of FO rack-and-adhesion motor luggage van. Note the central buffer with screw couplings on each side.*

HST 125 ten-car train

Great Britain: British Railways (BR), 1978

Type: Diesel-electric high-speed train.
Gauge: 4ft 8½in (1,435mm).
Propulsion: One supercharged two-stroke Paxman Valenta 12RP200L Vee-type 12-cylinder engine of 2,250hp (1,680kW) with integral alternator in each of two driving motor luggage vans, each engine feeding current to sets of four traction motors mounted in the bogie frames.
Weight: 308,560lb (140t) adhesive, 844,132lb (383t) total.
Max. axleload: 38,570lb (17.5t).
Overall length: 720ft 5in (219,584mm).
Max. speed: 125mph (200km/h).

These superb diesel-electric trains, the fastest in the world with that system of propulsion, marked a great step forward in the long history of the British express passenger train and, in addition, represent the first real original and countrywide success story of Britain's nationalised rail system in the passenger field.

As with most other success stories, the main ingredient of this triumph was the technical restraint of the trains involved, representing as they did a development of existing equipment rather than the result of beginning with a clean sheet of paper. The disastrous experiences at the time of writing with the Advanced Passenger Train—a clean-sheet-of-paper design if ever there was one—are a case in point.

If, then, the technology of the HST was just an update—except possibly for bogie suspension—then so much more impressive is the somersault in operational thinking. Ever since Liverpool & Manchester days, long distance trains had had detachable locomotives, not only because the locomotives were liable to need more frequent (and messier) attention than the carriages, but also because they could then haul more than one type of train at different times of the day. The argument was that if the obvious disadvantages of self-propelled trains with fixed formation could be accepted, then the problems of giving them the ability to run at 125mph (200km/h) were much reduced. The power units themselves were simplified, since the need to haul other types of trains was non-existent. Things like vacuum brake equipment, slow running gear and much else was just not required and their space, cost and weight would all be saved.

As well as disadvantages, self-propelled trains have advantages. For example, HSTs can run into a London terminus and leave again after a minimum interval for servicing (in 1983 as little as 18 minutes). At the same time there is no question of trapping its locomotive against the buffer stops until another locomotive is attached at the opposite end. Annual mileages in the quarter-million region can be the rule rather than the exception. And to counter the argument that the locomotives that handled the day trains would be needed for sleeping car expresses at night, there is still the point that, for example, now that Newcastle to London is only a 3-hour ride, the need for sleeping car accommodation is much reduced.

The plan was originally for 132 HST trains intended to cover the principal non-electrified routes of British Railways with a network of 125mph (200km/h) trains. The routes in question were those between London (Paddington and King's Cross) and the West of England, South Wales, Yorkshire, the North East, Edinburgh and Aberdeen, as well as the North-East to South-West cross-country axis via Sheffield, Derby and Birmingham. Modifications to the plan since it was first drawn up have reduced this number to 95, providing a dense and comprehensive service of high speed diesel trains which has no precedent nor as yet any imitators worldwide.

The improvement in running time over routes where there is an adequate mileage available for running at maximum speed can approach as much as 20 per

Above: *British Rail's prototype High Speed Train. This unit still holds the world's speed record for diesel traction at 143mph (230km/h).*

Below: *One of these power car-luggage vans at each end of an HST 125 set provides a total of 4,500hp for high-speed operation.*

Above: *An HST 125 train set, made up temporarily to eleven cars, raises a dust of powdery snow on an East Coast main line express working.*

cent. For example, the shortest journey time for the 268 miles (428km) from King's Cross to Newcastle is 2hr 54min (in 1983) compared with the 3hr 35min applicable during 1977 for trains hauled by the celebrated "Deltic" diesel locomotives. Coupled with a substantial improvement in passenger comfort, this acceleration has led to a gratifyingly increased level of patronage. A particular point is that the HSTs are not first-class only, or extra-fare trains, but available to all at the standard fare.

The design of the train was based on a pair of lightweight Paxman Valenta V-12 diesel engines each rated at 2,260hp (1,680kW) and located in a motor-baggage car at each end of the train. The specific weight of these engines is about half that of other conventional diesel engines in use on BR and the design is very compact. This led to the motor cars of the units being built within 154,000lb (70t) overall weight, and it was also possible to provide baggage accommodation within the vehicle's 58ft 4in (17,792mm) length. Compare this with the "Peak" (Class "44") diesel locomotives of 20 years earlier (already described), where a unit of similar power output was so heavy it needed *eight* axles to carry it. The lower axleloads of the HST trains were also important because raising the speed of trains has a progressively destructive effect on the track.

The MkIII carriages of the trains were the result of some 10 years development from British Railways' Mk1 stock, standard since the 1950s. In spite of the addition of air-conditioning, sophisticated bogies, soundproofing, automatic corridor doors, and a degree of luxury hardly ever before offered to second-class passengers, the weight per seat *fell* by around 40 per cent. One factor was adoption of open plan seating—allowing four comfortable seats across the coach instead of three—and another was the increase in length from a standard of around 64ft (19,507mm) to 75ft 6in (23,000mm). This represented two additional bays of seating.

Particularly noticeable to the passenger is the superb ride at very high speeds over track whose quality is inevitably sometimes only fair. This is the result of the application of some sophisticated hardware evolved for the APT train, using air suspension. Including refreshment vehicles, some of the HST trains have seven passenger cars and others eight. For a period some of those on the East Coast route had nine, but this was only a temporary expedient, as maintenance installations had been designed round the standard formations.

The concept of the HST was to provide a super train service on the existing railway, without rebuilding, replacing or even electrifying it. This meant being able to stop when required at signals within the warning distances which were implicit in the existing signalling system and, accordingly, the braking system—with disc brakes on all wheels—includes sophisticated wheelslip correction.

A complete prototype train was built and tested; this train reached 143mph (230km/h) on one occasion, a world record for diesel traction. Even so, there were aggravating problems with minor details of the production trains when they first went into service. Two things, however, mitigated the effects; first, a failure of one power car still left the other to drive the train at a more modest but still respectable pace. The second factor was the will to win through at all levels on the part of the staff, engendered by the possession of a tool which was not only a world-beater in railway terms but capable of beating airliners and motor cars as well.

Class 120 B_o-B_o

West Germany: German Federal Railway (DB), 1979

Type: Mixed-traffic electric locomotive.
Gauge: 4ft 8½in (1,435mm).
Propulsion: Alternating current at 15,000V 16⅔Hz from overhead wires rectified by thyristors and then inverted by thyristors to variable-frequency three-phase ac for supply to four 1,880hp (1,400kW) induction traction motors with spring drive.
Weight: 185,140lb (84t).
Max. axleload: 46,280lb (21t).
Overall length: 63ft 0in (19,200mm).
Tractive effort: 76,440lb (340kN).
Max. speed: 100mph (160km/h).

Above: *The stylish lines of the Class 120 German Federal Railway electric locomotive is matched by its equally advanced electric circuits.*

The relative merits of the three types of traction motors, dc, single-phase ac and three-phase ac, were well understood at the turn of the century, but the choice of motor in early electrification schemes was determined more by considerations of supply and control than by the characteristics of the motors. The commutator motors (dc and single-phase ac) proved to be the most adaptable to the control equipment available, and three-phase motors were little used. Recently, however, new control systems using thyristors have revived the three-phase motor, because it is now possible to exploit efficiently and economically its inherent qualities.

Three-phase motors are of two types: synchronous, in which the frequency is directly tied to the supply frequency, and asynchronous or induction motors. It is the latter which have excellent traction characteristics. In this motor, three-phase current is supplied to poles located round the inside of the stator, producing a "rotating" magnetic field. The rotor carries closed turns of conductors, and as the magnetic field rotates relative to the rotor, currents are induced in the rotor conductors. Due to these currents, forces act on the conductors (the normal "motor" effect), and these cause the rotor to turn. The torque thereby exerted on the rotor shaft depends upon the difference between the rotor speed and the speed of rotation of the field. This difference is expressed as the "slip" (not to be confused with normal wheelslip).

It can be shown that the speed of the rotor is proportional to the frequency of the current supplied to the motor, to the slip, and inversely to the number of poles. Under steady running conditions, slip is only one or two per cent of the speed, so varying the slip does not offer much scope for speed control. In early three-phase systems, the frequency of the supply to the motor was the frequency of the mains supply, and was fixed. The only way of varying the speed of the motor was thus by changing the number of poles. Even by regrouping the poles by different connections, it was only possible to get three or four steady running speeds. It was this limitation on speed control which hindered development of three-phase traction.

It was only possible to vary the frequency of the current supplied to the motors by the use of rotating machinery. This was done in several installations by a rotary converter, but the advantages of the three-phase motor were then offset by the disadvantages of an additional heavy rotating machine.

The development of thyristors opened up a new future for the induction motor. By their ability to switch current on and off quickly and very precisely, thyristors can be used to "invert" dc to ac by interrupting a dc supply. By inverting three circuits with an interval of one third of a "cycle" between each, a three-phase ac supply can be produced, and it is relatively simple to vary the frequency of this supply within wide limits. This is the key to controlling the speed of an induction motor by varying the frequency of the current supplied to it. Furthermore, this variation can be "stepless', that is, it can be varied gradually without any discontinuities.

In any motor control system the effects of "steps" or sudden changes in motor current are important because they can institute wheelslip. With thyristor control, three-phase motors can be worked much nearer to the limit of adhesion than can other types because not only is wheelslip less likely to develop, but also it is self-correcting. If a pair of wheels loses its grip on the rails, it accelerates slightly, thereby reducing the slip, and, in turn, reducing the torque which it transmits. This reduces the tendency for the wheels to lose their grip, so that wheelslip is self-correcting.

Below: *German Federal Railway's Class 120 Co-Co prototype electric locomotive with advanced three-phase transmission system.*

If the train begins to accelerate on a down gradient, the rotor accelerates, and "overtakes" the speed of the rotating field. Motor slip changes direction, and the motor exerts a braking rather than a driving torque, that is, the motor becomes a three-phase alternator. If provision is made for the current generated to be fed back into the overhead line, or to resistances, the induction motor provides electric braking quite simply.

Various experiments with induction motors were made in Europe in the 1960s and 1970s, both for electric locomotives and for diesel-electrics. Although all the systems had the common aim of supplying variable-frequency three-phase current to the traction motors by the use of thyristors, the circuitry varies between manufacturers.

In 1971, the West German locomotive manufacturer Henschel built, as a private venture, three 2,500hp (1,865kW) diesel locomotives with induction motors, using an electrical system produced by Brown Boveri (BBC). The basis of the BBC system is that the incoming supply is first changed to direct current at 2,800V, this voltage being closely controlled. This dc supply is fed into the inverter circuits, which feed variable-frequency three-phase ac to the traction motors. Deutsche Bundesbahn acquired the locomotives, and they were extensively tested and then put into regular service. In 1974 one of them had its diesel engine removed and replaced by ballast, and the locomotive was coupled permanently to an electric test coach equipped with pantograph, transformer and rectifier, from which direct current at 2,800V was supplied to the inverters on the locomotive.

Experience with this experimental unit encouraged DB to order five four-axle locomotives using equipment developed from the experimental work, and they appeared in 1979. The specification called for the locomotive to haul passenger trains of 700t at 100mph (160km/h), fast freights of 1,500t at 62mph (100km/h), and heavy freights of 2,700t at 50mph (80km/h); this performance was achieved in a locomotive weighing only 84t. Full advantage was taken of the good adhesion of the induction motors, for the continuous rating is 7,500hp (5,600kW), making them the most powerful four-axle locomotives in the world. The omission of commutators and brushes from the motors enables their weight to be reduced, and in these locomotives the motors are 65 per cent lighter than corresponding DB single-phase motors. Maintenance is also simplified. The single-phase supply from the overhead is rectified to dc at 2,800V, and is then inverted to three-phase ac at a frequency which can vary from zero to 125Hz.

Above: *An end of DB No. 120.001-3. The last number is a check digit, used when entering locomotive identities into a computer.*

Early testing revealed a number of problems, and particular attention had to be given to the effect of the inverter circuits on signalling and telephone systems, and the general effect of thyristor control on the overhead supply (technically, the "harmonics" caused). Extensive tuning of the circuitry was necessary. The body suspension is by Flexicoil springing, as in other modern DB types, and it was necessary to reduce the stiffness of this springing to control bogie oscillations.

With these problems under control, the locomotives were tested on trains of various loads, and one of them was also subjected to high-speed trials hauling one test coach. It reached 143.5mph (231km/h), thus beating the previous world record for induction motor traction set up in 1903 in the Zossen-Marienfelde trials in Germany with high speed motor coaches. Another remarkable feat was to accelerate from rest to 124mph (200km/h) in 30 seconds. One of the locomotives was tested on the Lötschberg route in Switzerland where, in severe weather conditions, it performed almost as well on the 1-in-37 (2.7 per cent) gradients as a lower-speed BLS locomotive designed specifically for work on heavy gradients.

These results are promising, but three-phase traction is not cheap, and some time will elapse before DB can assess whether it offers economic advantages over its well-tried and highly standardised single-phase equipment. Nevertheless, the induction motor is the most promising new development in electric traction.

LRC B_o-B_o Canada: Via Rail Canada (Via), 1982

Type: High-speed diesel-electric locomotive for matching train with tilting mechanism.
Gauge: 4ft 8½in (1,435mm).
Propulsion: Alco Type 251 16-cylinder 3,900hp (2,910kW) turbocharged four-stroke diesel engine and alternator feeding via rectifiers four nose-suspended direct current traction motors geared to the axles.
Weight: 185,135lb (84t).
Max. axleload: 46,285lb (21t).
Overall length: 66ft 5in (202,692mm).
Max. speed: 125mph (200km/h)*.

*Design speed of train; track limitations at present reduce this to 80mph (128km/h).

Having as its designation carefully chosen letters that read the same in English or French—Light, Rapid, Comfortable or *Leger, Rapide, Confortable* respectively—the designers had to have pointed out to them the letter L might in French just as well stand for *Lourd* or 'heavy'. The fact that an LRC passenger car weighs "only" 57 per cent more than, for example, an HST car of the same capacity in Britain does lend some sharpness to the point made. Similarly the LRC locomotive weighs 20 per cent more than the HST power car. Even so, LRC is an impressive creation, although the many years which have passed in development have seen as many (or more) setbacks and premature entries into service as Britain's APT. Even so, the new trains were due to go into service between Montreal and Toronto in September 1981. A scheduled time of 3hr 40min was originally intended for the 337 miles (539km), 45 minutes better than that offered by their best predecessors, the lightweight "Turbo-trains" in the late-1970s. But by July 1982 the best offered in the timetable was 4hr 25min, with an ominous note "Timings subject to alterations, journeys may be extended by up to 55 minutes", indicating a possible need to substitute conventional equipment.

This note reflects the fact that the LRC trains had to be withdrawn during the Canadian winter of 1981-82, having suffered from fine dry powdery snow getting inside sophisticated equipment. That the improvement in timings has been so relatively modest is due to the effects of heavy freight traffic on the existing track and the speed limits consequently imposed on the LRC. Two sets leased by the USA operator Amtrak have also not given satisfaction, and they have recently been returned to the makers.

Even so, LRC is a well thought out concept with a fourteen-year period of development behind it. An "active" tilting system allowing 8½° of tilt, ½° less than BR's APT, is combined with an advanced level of comfort of passengers. Ample power is available from the locomotives (which, incidentally, do not tilt) for both traction and substantial heating/air-conditioning requirements. One unique detail is the provision of outside loudspeakers so that announcements can be made to intending passengers on station platforms. The current order for Via Rail Canada provides for 22 locomotives and 50 cars. At the present time, however, problems with the cars have led to a surplus of motive power; LRC locomotives have been noted coupled to non-tilting stock on the Toronto to Chicago "International Limited".

Right: *The Canadian LRC train developed by Bombardier is shown under test in prototype form with a single coach during 1978, and* **(below)** *as a series-production unit in full Via Rail Canada livery in 1982. The train attains its objective by having sophisticated tilting capability—up to 8½°—a low profile and a low centre of gravity. Propulsion is conventional diesel-electric.*

Below: *The LRC diesel-electric locomotive, production version, decked out in the handsome livery of VIA Rail Canada.*

XPT Eight-car train

Australia: New South Wales Public Transport Commission, 1981

Type: High-speed diesel-electric passenger train.
Gauge: 4ft 8½in (1,435mm).
Propulsion: Paxman 2,000hp (1,490kW) "Valenta" 12-cylinder Vee diesel engine and alternator supplying through solid-state rectifiers to four dc traction motors geared to the axles with hollow-axle flexible drive.
Weight: 156,485lb (71t) adhesive, 826,500lb (375t) total.
Max. axleload: 39,675lb (18t).
Overall length: 590ft 2in (179,870mm).
Max. speed: 100mph (160km/h).

The HST125 development in Britain (already described) is so successful and remarkable that one wonders whether others might not consider adopting it. One organisation that has done just this is the railway administration of the Australian State of New South Wales. Their Express Passenger Train or "XPT", however, has certain differences to take account of conditions met 'down-under'. First, there are only five passenger cars per train instead of seven, eight or even nine in Britain. Although the Paxman Valenta engines are down-rated by 10 per cent, the overall power-to-weight ratio is increased and this, combined with lower gearing (a 125mph maximum speed would be meaningless on Australian alignments), gives increased acceleration to recover from stops and slacks. Preliminary experiments led to bogie modifications to suit rather different permanent way and there are improvements to the ventilation systems to cater for a hotter and dustier external environment. The passenger cars are built of corrugated stainless steel, matching other modern Australian passenger stock, notably that of the "Indian-Pacific" Trans-Australian Sydney to Perth express.

The new train silenced many critics by pulverising the Australian rail speed record with 144mph (183km/h) attained near Wagga-Wagga in August 1981. Early in 1982, the XPTs went into service with a daily trip on three routes out of Sydney. Best time-saving achieved was that of 1hr 46min over the 315 miles (504km) between Sydney and Kempsey.

It says enough of the experience gained that an inital order for 10 power cars and 20 trailers to make up four seven-car trains (with two spare power cars) was augmented in April 1982 by an order for four power cars and 16 trailers to form six eight-car trains. In addition, Victorian Railways decided in February 1982 to purchase three "XPT" sets for the Melbourne-Sydney service.

Above and below: *The Australian version of the British HST 125 high-speed diesel-electric train. These sets, built for the New South Wales Public Transport Commission in 1981 by Clyde Engineering of Sydney, for rail passenger services within the state, will shortly extend their activities to include Sydney to Melbourne inter-state expresses.*

ER 200 Fourteen-car train

USSR: Soviet Railways (SZD), 1975

Type: High-speed electric train.
Gauge: 5ft 0in (1,524mm).
Propulsion: Direct current at 3,000V fed via overhead catenary to forty-eight 288hp (215kW) traction motors driving the axles of the 12 intermediate cars of the train with gearing and flexible drives.
Weight: 1,586,880lb (720t) adhesive, 1,829,320lb (830t) total.
Max. axleload: 33,060lb (15t).
Overall length: 1,220ft 6in (372,000mm).
Max. speed: 125mph (200km/h).

Above: *The leading driving trailer car of the Soviet Railways' high-speed experimental 14-coach ER 200 electric passenger train.*

This, Soviet Railways' first high-speed electric self-propelled train, was built in 1975 at the Riga Carriage Works. The intention was to provide high-speed service over the 406 miles (650km) between Moscow and Leningrad. This was the line for which the Czar, when asked to choose a route, picked up (so legend has it) a ruler and ruled a line. Hence there was no need for tilting, just adequate power—in this case 13,834hp (10,320kW). In addition, adequate braking, rheostatic above 22mph (35km/h) and electromechanical disc brakes below that speed. An electromagnetic rail brake is provided for emergency use.

Electrically, the 14 cars of the train are divided into six two-car powered units, each with 128 seats, plus, at each end, a driving trailer car. Each of these has seats for 24, a buffet section and luggage space. An 'Autodriver' system automatically responds to transponder units at track level which set the speed to be maintained between particular points.

It has been reported that "ER 200" travelled between Moscow and Leningrad in 3hr 50min (an average speed of 106mph (170km/h) on a test carried out in 1980, but entry into public service at anything like these speeds has not yet taken place. No doubt Soviet Railways is not yet convinced—in an uncompetitive situation—of either the need or the desirability for high-speed trains. In the meantime SZD customers have to accept times on this route of 7 hours or more.

Fairlie B-B

Wales: Festiniog Railway (FR), 1979

Type: Steam locomotive for tourist railway.
Gauge: 1ft 11¾in (600mm).
Propulsion: Atomised oil fuel burnt in two fireboxes within a single boiler shell, generating steam at 1,600psi (10.6kg/cm^2) which is fed to twin 9in bore × 14in stoke (229 × 356mm) cylinders on each of two bogies, the wheels of which are driven directly by connecting and coupling rods.
Weight: 88,640lb (40t).
Max. axleload: 22,040lb (10t).
Overall length: 30ft 6in (9,297mm).
Tractive effort: 9,140lb (41kN).
Max. speed: 25mph (40km/h).

The majority of railway power units in the world (and in this book) run on two four-wheel bogies with all four axles driven. No exception to this rule is this Fairlie steam locomotive built in 1979 for and by an historic narrow-gauge tourist line in North Wales, called the Festiniog Railway. In fact, back in the mid-nineteenth century Fairlie steam locomotives were the first to use this now almost universal B-B wheel arrangement. Also very unusual nowadays is the fact that the locomotive was built "in-house" at the railway's own Boston Lodge Works. The end result is a modernised version of the last one built there in 1879, 100 years before.

Although the line is operated for pleasure travellers rather than for serious customers, the specification is a severe one. Trains of up to 12 cars seating up to 500 passengers need to be hauled up gradients up to 1-in-80 (1.25 per cent), with curves as sharp as 2¼ chains (45m) radius and all within a 22,040lb (10t) axleload limitation.

The use of oil as fuel for a steam locomotive might seem an extravagance, but a high proportion of that used is obtained cheaply as waste and residues. There were problems with coal-burning because of setting fire to forest plantations, while the use of steam propulsion in this day and age is essential because of the customer-drawing qualities of steam locomotives. The waste oil happily gives the authentic "coaly" smell demanded by the public.

The Fairlie design involves raising steam in a patent double boiler with twin fire-boxes and smokeboxes at both ends. The steam is then fed via two throttles—arranged so that the two handles can be moved either together or singly—and two main steam pipes complete with flexible joints to the two motor bogies. The driver and fireman have to stand in restricted space, one each side of the boiler.

Above: *Fairlie B-B steam locomotive on Porthmadog train near Blaenau Ffestiniog. Note vintage carriages and slate tip in the background.*

A drawback of the Fairlie design is the complexity of the boiler. But once this is accepted the advantages of being able to run out the power bogies easily from under the locomotive for repair or attention are considerable. Some concession is made on *Iarll Merionnydd (Earl of Merioneth)*—one of the titles of the Duke of Edinburgh—to the approaching 21st century with an electronic speedometer in the cab. An electric headlamp at each end is also a welcome innovation.

Class 26 2-D-2 South Africa: South African Railways (SAR), 1982

Type: Mixed-traffic steam locomotive.
Gauge: 3ft 6in (1,067mm).
Propulsion: Coal-fired gas-producer firebox with grate area of 70sq ft (6.5m²) generating superheated steam at 225psi (15.75kg/cm²) in a fire-tube boiler and supplying it to two 24x28in (610x711mm) cylinders, driving the four main axles direct by means of connecting and coupling rods.
Weight: 167,505lb (76t) adhesive, 506,920lb (230t) total.
Max. axleload: 43,640lb (19.8t).
Overall length: 91ft 6½in (27,904mm).
Tractive effort: 47,025lb (209kN).
Max. speed: 60mph (96km/h).

Many people regard steam locomotives as the only proper motive power, any other kind being *ersatz* to some degree. Yet at the same time we are aware of steam's drawbacks—its low thermal efficiency, its labour-intensiveness and its dirtiness. Of course, the low thermal efficiency can be countered by use of less costly fuels—in some countries oil costs four (or more) times coal for the same heat content and this more than cancels out the better efficiency of diesel vis-a-vis steam. At the same time the amount of fuel wasted by a steam locomotive can be reduced by relatively small improvements, and since the dirt connected with steam operation represents waste, less waste auto-

Above and below: *Views of the rebuilt South African Railways Class 25 steam locomotive, now known variously as Class 26,* Red Devil *after its colour, or* L.D. Porta *after the Argentinian who evolved the proposal.*

Class 20 2-D-1+1-D-2 Rhodesia: Rhodesian Railways (RR), 1954

Type: Beyer-Garratt steam freight locomotive.
Gauge: 3ft 6in (1,067mm).
Propulsion: Coal fire with a grate area of 63.1sq ft (5.9m²) in a fire-tube boiler generating steam at 200psi (14kg/cm²) which is supplied to two pairs of 20in bore by 26in stroke (508 × 600mm) cylinders, each pair driving the main wheels of its respective unit directly by connecting and coupling rods.
Weight: 369,170lb (167.5t) adhesive, 503,614lb (228.5t) total.
Max. axleload: 38,019lb (17.25t).
Overall length: 95ft 0½in (28,969mm).
Tractive effort: 69,330lb (308kN).
Max. speed: 35mph (56km/h).

Most railways in Africa were built to open up newly-developed colonies. Traffic expectations were not great, and the lines were often constructed cheaply to a narrow gauge, with light rails, and with severe curvature. As the colonies developed, and particularly when their mineral resources became important, the railways faced the problem of acquiring larger locomotives which would be suited to existing gauge and curvature. The solution for many lay in articulated or hinged locomotives, particularly if there was a limited axleload.

The type of articulated locomotive most popular in Africa was the Garratt, a British design which originated in 1907, and which reached its highest state of development in the 1950s. In this design the boiler is mounted on a frame suspended by pivots from two rigid units which carry the fuel bunker and water tanks. As there are no wheels under the boiler, it can have a large diameter and deep firebox, and the whole boiler unit is more accessible than in a normal rigid locomotive. Each end unit can have as many axles as the curvature of the line permits, six or eight driving axles being the norm.

The largest user of Garratts was South African Railways with 400, but Rhodesia Railways, now the National Railways of Zimbabwe, came second. This system bought 250 of them between 1926 and 1958 from Beyer Peacock of Manchester, 200 of them coming after World War II. They constituted half the total steam locomotives built for the railway. The last and largest were 61 4-8-2+2-8-4 machines built between 1954 and 1958. The engines have an axleload of 17t, made possible by installation of heavy rail on parts of the system, and their total weight put them near the top of the Garratt league table. They are equipped with every device for reducing maintenance costs and fuel consumption, and for increasing availability. They are notable in being the only Rhodesian Garratts to be stoker fired.

As with other African railways, Rhodesia Railways succumbed to the charms of the diesel salesmen, who could offer not only machines which were much more economical in fuel than steam engines, but also low-interest loans, which some Western governments would make available to third-world countries to assist their own diesel manufacturers. 1980 was thus set as the date for the dieselisation of the whole Rhodesian system.

However, the combination of the tremendous increase in the cost of oil from 1973 onwards with the difficulties caused by imposition of sanctions against Rhodesia following UDI, made the railway authorities review their policy. The country had large supplies of coal but no oil, so that imported oil cost thirty times as much as coal. Even though the diesel had three times the efficiency of a steam engine, this still left fuel costs for the diesel ten times as great as for steam. Furthermore, whereas many wearing parts of the steam engines could be manufactured locally, the diesels required specialised parts which only the makers could supply, and sanctions had cut these supplies. Plans for dieselisation were therefore halted, and replaced by a long-term target of electrification. In the meantime, in

matically means less pollution too.

This "Red Devil" (named *L.D. Porta* after the Argentinian engineer who was responsible for the basics of the system) is an attempt to produce a steam locomotive for the 21st century by rebuilding a "25NC" 4-8-4, a class built by Henschel and North British in 1953. The principal change is in the method of burning the coal, which is now gasified before being burnt; the other alterations are more in the nature of the fine tuning. All were carried out in South African Railways' Salt River Workshops at Cape Town, at very modest cost.

The first big change is that now less than half the air needed for combustion enters the firebox through the fire itself, the amount of reduction being set by smaller and exactly calculated openings between the bars of the grate. This change cuts down waste by eliminating fire-throwing when the locomotive is working hard.

Steam is also fed into the hot firebed from the sides. This comes from the auxiliaries and from the exhaust side of the main cylinders. It reacts chemically with the hot coal to produce cleanly combustible water gas, while at the same time the reaction is one which absorbs rather than produces heat. So the temperature of the firebed does not reach the level at which fusion takes place and clinker forms. The air passing through the hot (but not too hot) firebed makes producer gas and it is this mixture of gases which burns cleanly, using the air entering through openings in the side of the firebox. The existing mechanical stoker is retained; the hard labour of running steam power is reduced both when putting the fuel in and when taking the residues out.

Other improvements made include increased superheat (with consequent provision of improved cylinder lubrication), better draughting and a feed-water heater, all of which contribute to a further improvement in thermel efficiency. Adding this to the contribution made by the avoidance of unburnt fuel in the residues of combustion gives the startling result of one-third less fuel burnt for a given output. The maximum power output is increased, whilst both the quantity and the difficulty of disposal of the residues is considerably reduced. The result is a machine that can really look its diesel brethren in the eye in respect of such important matters as availability and cleanliness, and really wipe the floor with them when it comes to fuel costs in South African conditions.

Below: *The* Red Devil *ready to go forth and re-conquer the rails of South Africa.*

Above: *For a country with ample coal supplies and no oil it makes sense to continue with steam traction. Many of the Beyer-Garratt locomotives of National Railways of Zimbabwe such as this Class 20 2-D-1 + 1-D-2 machine have been rebuilt and fully modernised.*

1978, a scheme was initiated for rehabilitating 87 of the remaining Garratts, many of which had already been laid aside.

Although locomotives had never been built in the country, there was an engineering firm which could undertake major work on locomotive parts, beyond the capacity of the railway workshops. The work included renewal of fireboxes and, surprisingly, replacement of friction bearings by roller bearings, together with a thorough overhaul of all other working parts.

The locomotives concerned were 18 light branch line 2-6-2+2-6-2s of Class "14A," 35 4-6-4+4-6-4s of classes "15" and "15A" (these had been the principal passenger engines before dieselisation), 15 heavy 2-8-2+2-8-2 of Class "16A", and 19 of the largest 4-8-2+2-8-4s of classes "20" and "20A." As a symbol of their revivification, many of the locomotives were given names. The first rehabilitated engines emerged in June 1979 and the scheme was completed in 1982.

The locomotives are largely employed in the south-western part of the country near the coalfields, and they work between Gwelo, Bulawayo and Victoria Falls. They are intended to have a life of at least 15 years, but whether electrification will be sufficiently advanced by that time for them to be released remains to be seen. In the meantime, Zimbabwe has the largest steam locomotives still in operation in the world, many of which are as good as new. There must be other African countries which have coal but no oil wondering if their hasty replacement of steam was really wise.

TGV Ten-car trainset

France: French National Railways (SNCF), 1981

Type: High-speed articulated multiple-unit electric train.
Gauge: 4ft 8½in (1,435mm).
Propulsion: In each of two motor coaches, current taken from overhead wires at either 1,500V dc or 25,000V 50Hz (or, in a few cases 15,000V 16⅔Hz) supplied through rectifiers and/or chopper control to six 704hp (525kW) traction motors mounted on the coach body and geared to the axles through spring drive; two motors on each bogie of the power car and two on the adjoining end bogie of the articulated set.
Weight: 427,575lb (194t) adhesive, 841,465lb (381.8t) total.
Max. axleload: 35,480lb (16.1t).
Overall length: 656ft 9½in (200,190mm).
Max. speed: 162mph (260km/h) initially, 186mph (300km/h) ultimately.

Above: *French National Railways' (TGV) holds the world speed record of 236mph (380km/h) for a conventional train.*

When, in 1955, two French electric locomotives separately established a world record of 205.7mph (331km/h) in the course of tests to measure various parameters on the locomotive and track, it seemed an esoteric exercise, far removed from everyday train running, which at that time was limited in France to 87mph (140km/h). But 21 years later two French test trains had between them exceeded 186mph (300km/h) on 223 test runs, and construction had commenced of 236 miles (380km) of new railway laid out for 300km/h running.

The main line of the former PLM railway connects the three largest cities in France, and has the heaviest long-distance passenger traffic in the country. Post-war electrification increased traffic still further, and by the 1960s congestion was severe. In an effort to overcome the problem of interleaving fast passenger trains and slower freights, traffic was arranged in "flights", with a succession of passenger trains at certain times of day and a succession of freights at others. The case for additional line capacity was very strong, and in 1966 serious study of a possible new route began. This line would not only relieve the existing route, but by taking advantage of French research into higher speeds, it would win traffic from air and road.

It was clear that a great advantage would accrue if the line could be dedicated solely to passenger traffic. The canting of curves on a line carrying mixed traffic at different speeds is always a compromise, and technology had reached a stage at which considerable increases in passenger train speeds were possible, but not those of freight trains. The axleloads of freight vehicles reach 20t and those of electric locomotives 23t, but if the axleloading on the new line could be limited to about 17t, it would be much easier to maintain the track in a suitable condition for very high speeds.

One outcome of the 1955 test running was that in 1967 limited running at 124mph (200km/h) was introduced on the Paris-Bordeaux line of the South Western Region, but further testing beyond that speed was made by railcar sets. The first experimental gas turbine train was run up to 147mph (236km/h), and one of the production gas turbine sets made 10 runs above 155mph (250km/h), but it was the experimental very-high-speed gas turbine set which pointed the way ahead. Designated at first TGV001 (but later changed to TGS when TGV was applied to the electric version) this was the first French train specifically designed to run at 186mph (300km/h), and it made 175 runs in which 300km/h was exceeded, with a maximum of 197mph (317km/h). A special high-speed electric motor coach was also built, and this reached 192mph (309km/h).

The project for a new line to relieve traffic on the Paris-Lyons section was initially based on using gas turbine trains similar to TGV001. To avoid the tremendous expense of a new entry into Paris, the existing route from Paris Gare de Lyon would be used for 18.6 miles (30km), and from there to the outskirts of Lyons there would be a completely new line, connected to existing lines at two intermediate points to give access to Dijon and to routes to Lausanne and Geneva in Switzerland. Substantial state aid would be needed to finance the project, but it was predicted that both SNCF and the State would reap a satisfactory return on the investment.

Before the project received ministerial approval, the oil crisis of 1973 caused a radical change of plan, and gas turbine propulsion was abandoned in favour of electrification at 25,000V 50Hz. As the new route would be used solely by very fast passenger trains, it was possible to have much steeper gradients than on a conventional railway. The "kinetic energy" or energy of movement of a vehicle depends on the *square* of the speed, and the

faster a train is travelling, the smaller is the loss of speed due to "rushing" a given gradient. On the new line, maximum gradient is 1-in-28.5 (3.5 per cent), or four times as steep as the gradients on the existing route. By adoption of steep gradients the cost of the line has been reduced by about 30 per cent compared with a conventional railway. The longest gradient on the new line will reduce speed from 162mph (260km/h) to 137mph (220km/h).

Orders for the electric version of the TGV (*Train à Grande Vitesse*) were placed in 1976, and delivery began two years later. Although the design of the train follows that of the gas turbine version, the equipment is completely different, but it incorporates well-proven parts wherever possible. Each train comprises two end power cars flanking an eight-car articulated rake of trailers; that is, the adjoining ends of coaches are carried on a common bogie. To transmit the maximum power of 8,450hp (6,300kW) requires 12 motored axles, so in addition to the four axles of the motor coach, the end bogie of the articulated set also has motors. As the existing lines on which the trains work are electrified at 1,500V dc, the sets can operate on this system also, and six are equipped to work on 15,000V $16\frac{2}{3}$Hz in Switzerland. For ac working there is one transformer in each motor coach, with a separate thyristor rectifier for each motor, to reduce the risk of more than one motor being out of action at once. The same thyristors work as choppers for control of the motor voltage on dc.

The sets have a new type of bogie developed directly from the gas turbine train. As the new line is used only by "TGVs", the curves are canted to suit these trains, and no tilting of the coach bodies on curves is needed. The traction motors are mounted on the body of the motor coach, with a flexible drive to the axles. By this means the unsprung mass of the bogie is unusually low, and the forces exerted on the track at 300km/h are less than with an electric locomotive at 200km/h.

There are no lineside signals on the new line, the driver receiving signal indications in the cab. The permitted speed is displayed continuously in front of the driver, and he sets his controller to the speed required. The control system maintains speed automatically. There are three braking systems, all of which are controlled by the one driver's brake valve: dynamic, disc and wheel tread. The dynamic brake uses the traction motors as generators, feeding energy into resistances. During braking the motors are excited from a battery, so that failure of the overhead supply does not affect the braking. The dynamic brake is effective from full speed down to 3km/h. In normal service applications the disc brakes are half applied, and wheel tread brakes are applied lightly to clean the wheel treads. For emergency braking all systems are used fully. The braking distance from 162mph (260km/h) is 3,500m. Most of the 87 trains have first and second-class accommodation; six are first-class only and three others are exclusively mail carriers.

Above: *The TGV trains can run on lines electrified at 1,500V dc as well as on the 25,000V ac Paris to Lyons high-speed line. This TGV is speeding across the plain of Alsace.*

The trains were built by Alsthom, the motor coaches at Belfort and the trailers at La Rochelle. Initial testing was done on the Strasbourg-Belfort line, where 260km/h was possible over a distance. As soon as the first part of the new line was ready, testing was transferred, and one of the sets was fitted with larger wheels than standard to allow tests above the normal speeds. On February 26, 1981 a new world record of 236mph (380km/h) was established.

Services over the southern section of the new line began in September 1981, and passenger carryings soon showed an increase of 70 per cent. The northern section was due for opening in September 1983, with a scheduled time of 2 hours for the 266 miles (426km) from Paris to Lyons. In 1983 also the maximum speed was due to be raised from 260km/h to 270km/h (168mph).

Apart from some trouble with damage to the overhead wires at maximum speed, which necessitated a restriction to 124mph (200km/h) for a period, the new trains have worked very well. Riding on the new line is very good, but the sets are not so smooth when running on conventional lines.

The Paris-Sud-Est line is a remarkable achievement, for which the detailed planning and construction required only 10 years, and was completed to schedule. It seems also likely to become a financial success earlier than expected. Other new high-speed routes are being planned.

Below left: *A power-car of the French National Railways' TGV. All wheels, as well as those of the adjacent bogie of the next coach, are powered.*

ETR 401 Pendolino Four-car train

Italy:
Fiat Ferroviaria Savigliano SpA (Fiat), 1976

Type: High-speed electric train with body-tilting mechanisms.
Gauge: 4ft 8½in (1,435mm).
Propulsion: Direct current at 3,000V fed via overhead catenary to eight 335hp (250kW) motors, two on each car, each driving one axle with longitudinal cardan shafts and gearing.
Weight: 177,422lb (80.5t) adhesive, 354,845lb (161t) total.
Max. axleload: 23,145lb (10.5t).
Overall length: 340ft 2½in (103,700mm).
Max. speed: 156mph (250km/h).

Italy was the second country to put tilting trains into service, Japan being the first with the Class "381" trains described elsewhere in this book. The project was financed by Fiat. High-speed is provided for with ample power in relation to the train's weight, plus three independent systems of braking. Dynamic braking, using the motors as dynamos is for normal use, with conventional electro-pneumatic air brakes for application at low speeds. In addition there is an electro-magnetic rail brake which, of course, acts independently of the adhesion between wheel and rail. Because of the effects of high speed vehicles on the track, the axleload has been limited to the low figure given above.

But most of the interest arises out of the high tilting capability of the train, which seats 170 passengers and permits a tilt of up to 9°. The tilt is positively actuated and is controlled by a combination of accelerometers and gyroscopes. The pantograph current collector is mounted on a framework attacted to one of the bogie bolsters, so that it is not affected by the tilting.

Operation has been successful up to a point. The train has gone into regular service over the 185 mile (298km) Trans-Appennine route between Rome and Ancona. Only over a short length of the journey is its speed capability utilised, but the tilting mechanism is used to full effect on the sharp curves of the line in the mountains.

Below: *The 15.20 Ancona express ready to depart from Rome on April 19, 1978. It is formed of the impressive looking experimental ETR 401 tilting high-speed train.*

An acceleration of 45 minutes (or 25 per cent) over the best previous time for the journey was theoretically possible, but prudence has dictated that the actual improvement should be half that. However, lingering doubts would appear to have precluded any further adoption of the tilting principle, and the Fiat train remained until recently (when some similar *Basculante* trainsets based on the Fiat example were supplied to Spanish National Railways) the sole example of this principle in public service outside Japan.

Right: *The Fiat "Pendolino" train demonstrates its undoubted agility in tilting (up to 9° is possible). This train is currently in commercial service on Italian State Railways.*

Class 58 C_o-C_o

Great Britain:
British Railways (BR), 1982

Type: Diesel-electric freight locomotive.
Gauge: 4ft 8½in (1,435mm).
Propulsion: One GE (Ruston) RK3ACT 3,300hp (2,460kW) 12-cylinder four-stroke turbocharged Vee engine and alternator, generating three-phase current which is supplied through rectifiers to six nose-suspended traction motors geared to the axles.
Weight: 286,520lb (130t).
Max. axleload: 47,750lb (21.7t).
Overall length: 62ft 9in (19,130mm).
Tractive effort: 59,100lb (263kN).
Max. speed: 80mph (129km/h).

Dieselisation of non-electrified lines of British Railways was completed in 1968, and from then onwards no new diesel locomotives were needed until, in 1973, BR was warned to expect a large increase in coal traffic due to the oil crisis. Work began forthwith on designing a new class of locomotive, to be more powerful than the existing 2,580hp (1,925kW) Class "47", and with a maximum speed of 80mph (129km/h) to give much better performance on heavy freight trains at low speeds than the 95mph (153km/h) Class "47."

The most common diesel engines on BR are the family derived from the pre-war English Electric shunter. This engine first appeared as a main line unit in 1947, developing 1,600hp (1,190kW) from 16 cylinders. By 1973 the engine had been uprated to 3,520hp (2,625kW), although for reliability BR decided to rate it at 3,250hp (2,425kW).

As BR could not produce a new design from its own resources in the time available, a contract was placed with Brush Electrical Machines to design a locomotive based on that builder's Class "47," but incorporating the English Electric-type engine and ac transmission. This work was done jointly by Brush and Electroputere of Romania, with whom Brush had an agreement for technical co-operation. As Electroputere could deliver the locomotives sooner than BR's Doncaster Works, the first 30 were ordered from Romania.

The first of these locomotives, designated Class "56," appeared in 1976. BR regarded them as an interim design, produced with the minimum of new design work to meet an urgent need, and it was soon decided that only 135 would be built. Further construction would be to a completely new design, Class "58", to be capable of hauling 1,000t on the level at 80mph (129km/h).

Class "58" was much influenced by design work which had been done by BR on a 2,500hp (1,865kW) locomotive which BR's workshop subsidiary, British Rail Engineering, hoped to sell abroad. Great emphasis had been laid on reducing the cost of this locomotive, and in its severely restricted financial condition BR was glad to have a locomotive cheaper than a Class "56."

The most obvious change in Class "58" is that it is a "hood" unit, with the structural strength in the underframe (Class "56" has a stressed bodyshell inherited from Class "47"). The massive underframe should have an indefinite life, whereas the thin panels of the stressed bodies corrode easily. The hood construction gives easier access to equipment and simplifies

Right: *British Railways' new Class 58 freight locomotive.*

the division of the body into air-tight compartments. Most of the equipment is in sub-assemblies which are bolted to the underframe, and can be replaced from stock. The cabs are self-contained, and can be disconnected, unbolted, and replaced in a few days, whereas on earlier BR diesels repairs to a damaged cab can take months. Access is from a cross-passage between the cab and the machinery compartments, so that the cab has no outside door to admit draughts. The layout of the controls is new for BR, and they can be operated whilst the driver is leaning out of the cab window.

The engine is a new model in the long line descended from the English Electric units of 1947. Compared with the engine in Class "56," the speed has been increased from 900rpm to 1,000rpm, and a new and simpler turbocharger is fitted. As a result it has been possible to reduce the number of cylinders from 16 to 12, and yet to rate the engine 50hp higher than the Class "56" engine, at 3,300hp (2,460kW).

Amongst other duties, these locomotives will be used on "merry-go-round" coal trains which discharge their loads at power stations whilst in motion, and for this purpose they are fitted with an automatic slow-speed control to hold the speed accurately at 1mph (1.6km/h).

Simplification in the design has produced a reduction of about 13 per cent in the cost of a Class "58" compared with a Class "56," and further economies will result from reduced maintenance costs. An initial order for 30 was placed with BREL's Doncaster Works, and the first was delivered in December 1982, wearing new colours based on the current livery of BR "Speedlink" freight wagons.

Class 370 "APT-P" Train

Great Britain: British Railways (BR)

Type: High-speed electric passenger train.
Gauge: 4ft 8½in (1,435mm).
Propulsion: Alternating current at 25,000V 50Hz fed via overhead catenary, step-down transformer and thyristor-based control system to four body-mounted 1,000hp motors in two power cars, driving the wheels through longitudinal shafts and gearing.
Weight: 297,540lb (135t) adhesive, 1,014,942lb (460.6t) total.
Max. axleload: 37,248lb (16.9t).
Overall length: 963ft 6in (293,675mm).
Max. speed: 150mph (240km/h).

Above: *The driving end of British Railways' Advanced Passenger Train, production-prototype version, "APT-P". The power cars were situated in mid-train and also had tilting capability.*

Although the final outcome of this project, one of the most far-sighted and ambitious passenger train developments ever begun, is still in the future, it is fair to say that up to now it has also been one of the most painful. The saga began in the 1960s when British Railways set its much-enlarged Research Department at Derby to do a thorough study of their most fundamental problem, the riding of flanged wheels on rails. Out of this emerged the possiblity of designing vehicles which could run smoothly at higher speeds than previously permitted over sharply-curved track with the usual imperfections. To keep the passengers comfortable, the trains would tilt automatically when negotiating curves which would have to stay canted or banked only for normal speeds.

Several railways have done or are doing this, notably those of Japan, Italy and Canada. The Canadian LRC train (described previously) is the only one which approaches the ambitiousness of the British scheme—in the others the body tilt is purely a passive response to the sideways forces encountered. In the APT, body-tilting is achieved in a much more sophisticated and positive manner, each coach adjusting its tilt response to curvature by sensing movement of the coach ahead. The amount of body tilt can rise to as much as 9°, which means that at full tilt one side of the car can be 16in (400mm) higher than the other. The result would be a train which could provide the high average speeds that the future would seem to demand if railways are to remain in business for journeys over 200 miles, without the hugh capital investment involved in building new lines for them. For example, 105mph (167km/h) or 3h 50min between London and Glasgow is very close to 103mph (165km/h) envisaged in France over a similar distance from Paris to Marseilles, using the new purpose-built railway between Paris and Lyons. Put another way, the British solution—if it had succeeded—would have equalled the French for a cost of only one-fifth.

At this point one must say that the body-tilting is only part of this advanced concept—a new and fundamentally improved suspension system with a self-steering feature in the bogies contributed even more to a package which looked like being a winner. A formal submission for funds to develop the project was made in December 1967. In 1973 after some delay, a four-car experimental prototype powered by a gas turbine was authorised and in 1975 was brought out into the world after early testing in secret on BR's test track near Nottingham. APT-E as it was called managed 151mph (242km/h) run-

Below: *The futuristic lines of British Railways' Advanced Passenger Train did not, alas, presage a successful future for these magnificent examples of carriage-building skills.*

ning between Reading and Swindon and, more impressive, ran from London to Leicester (99 miles—158km) in just under the hour. These favourable experiences led to the authorising of three 14-car "production prototype" trains, the two central cars of each train being non-tilting and non-driving power cars, providing 8,000hp (5,970kW) for traction. The two halves of the train were isolated from one another and each had to have its own buffet/restaurant car; 72 first-class and 195 second-class seats were provided in each half.

Electric propulsion was chosen because there was no diesel engine available with a suitable power-to-weight ratio, and a gas turbine was now considered too extravagant in fuel consumption after the recent trebling in price of oil. Moreover, the envisaged first use for APT trains was now on the longer electric journeys out of Euston to Glasgow, Liverpool and Manchester. One innovation was the solution to the problem of braking from very high speeds above 155mph (250km/h). The hydro-kinetic (water turbine) brake was adopted, giving a reasonable braking distance of 2,500yd (2,290m) from full speed, with 2,000yd (1,830m) possible in emergency. Disc brakes provided braking force at speeds too low for the hydro-kinetic brakes to be effective.

The first APT-P train was completed in 1978, but there was a series of tiresome small defects including one that caused a derailment at over 100mph (160km/h). This meant that, although the 4hr 15min Glasgow to London service (average speed 94mph—151km/h), which it was intended to provide at first, had been printed in the public timetables for several years, it was not until late-1981 that public service actually began. Even then, only one complete Glasgow-to-London and back public run was made. A combination of further small defects, unprecedently severe weather and impending serious industrial action, led BR to take the train out of public service, although tests continue. It all happened in a blaze of unfortunate publicity, which mattered less than the fact that authorisation by the government of a series-production version (APT-S) was deferred indefinitely.

A series of options now presented themselves. Because it was not economic to provide continuous cab signalling, the APT trains were in the end limited to the speed of the HST already described. Accordingly, one might envisage an electric version of the latter train, very simply obtained by replacing diesel alternator sets with the necessary electrical equipment. Some faster running round curves might well be possible without any of the complications of tilting, but it is the tilting and riding mechanism of the APT which has been its most successful feature. An alternative proposal is a simpler or "utility" 125mph APT (APT-U) with no 150mph capability, no articulation (which saves money on maintenance facilities), and no hydro-kinetic brake.

Above: *An Advanced Passenger Train propelled by a diesel locomotive is shown to the crowds watching the cavalcade of railway motive power at Rainhill in May 1979.*

Below: *British Railways' Advanced Passenger Train demonstrates its tilting capability during a high-speed test run on the London-Glasgow West Coast main line in 1981.*

Index

Bold figures refer to subjects mentioned in captions to illustrations

D

E

F

G

H

I

J

K

L

M

N

O

P

Q

R

S

T

U

V

W

X

Y

Z

Picture Credits

The publishers wish to thank the following organisations and individuals who have supplied photographs for this book. Photographs have been credited by page number. Some references have, for reasons of space, been abbreviated, as follows:
AAR=Colourviews. AC=Arthur Cook. BBC=BBC Hulton Picture Library. BH=Brian Hollingsworth. BS=Brian Stephenson. CG=C.Gammell. CV=Colourviews Birmingham. GFA=Geoffrey Freeman-Allen. HB=Hugh Ballantyne. JJ=Jim Jarvis. MARS=Mechanical Archive and Research Services. PNWA=Peter Newark's Western Americana.

Page 20: top, B Stephenson; bottom, BBC Hulton Picture Library. **21:** CV; right, R Bastin. **22:** B Stephenson. **23:** top, C Gammell; bottom, N Trotter. **24:** left, B Stephenson; top right, B Hollingsworth; bottom right, CV. **25:** GFA; bottom, D Cross; top, Robert Barton. **26:** left, Robert Barton; top right, Union Pacific RR; bottom right, B Stephenson. **28:** top, CV; bottom, CV. **29:** top, Science Museum/CV; bottom, CV. **30:** top, Science Museum; bottom, AAR. **31:** top, PNWA; bottom, PNWA. **32:** Science Museum/CV. **34:** top, R Bastin; bottom, PNWA. **35:** AAR. **37:** J Adams. **39:** Science Museum/CV. **40:** CV. **41:** CV. **42:** top, Swiss Federal Railways; bottom, CV. **43:** left, CV; right, O Bamer. **44:** top, CV; centre, VR/Henry; bottom, Science Museum. **45:** CV. **46:** AAR. **47:** J Winkley. **48:** top, CV; bottom, CV. **49:** CV. **50:** VR. **51:** J Dunn. **52:** CV. **53:** GFA. **55:** M Whitehouse. **56:** CV. **57:** CV. **58:** CV. **59:** top, CV; bottom, CV. **60:** DB Museum, Nurnberg. **61:** DB Museum, Nurnberg. **63:** top, CV, bottom, AAR. **64:** top, AAR; centre, Strasburg RR; bottom, Strasburg RR. **65:** Strasburg RR. **66-67:** GFA. **67:** CV. **68:** top, Italian State Railways; bottom, GFA. **70:** VR. **72:** VR. **73:** CV. **74:** top, D Cross; bottom, GFA. **75:** D Cross. **76:** CV. **76-77:** J Winkley. **77:** top left, CV; top right, CV. **78:** Colour-rail. **79:** top, CV; bottom, CV. **80-81:** CV. **81:** top, CV; bottom, JM Jarvis. **82-83:** Colour-rail/RM Quinn. **84:** CV. **85:** top, CV; bottom, CV. **86:** CV. **87:** CV. **88:** top, CV; bottom, CV. **89:** top, CV; bottom, VR. **90:** top, Staatsbibliotek Berlin; centre, MARS. **90-91:** GFA. **91:** CV. **92:** bottom, Swiss Federal Railways. **92-93:** K Mills. **93:** bottom, M Whitehouse. **94:** CV. **96:** CV. **97:** top, Novosti Press Agency; bottom, Italian State Railways. **98:** top, Colour-rail/RM Quinn; centre, CV; bottom, Colour-rail/RM Quinn. **99:** top, Archiv Triebl; bottom, CV. **100:** top, CV; bottom, Swedish State Railways. **101:** Swedish State Railways/MARS. **102:** top, JM Jarvis; bottom, GFA. **103:** CV. **104:** CV. **104-105:** CV. **105:** LG Marshall. **106:** CV. **107:** CV. **108:** CV. **108-109:** GFA. **109:** D Cross. **110:** CV. **110:** CV. **112:** VR. **112-113:** top, C Gammell; bottom, CV. **113:** GFA. **114:** top, J Winkley; bottom, R Bastin. **115:** R Bastin. **116:** D Cross. **117:** R Bastin. **118:** Victorian Government Railways. **118-119:** Colour-rail/RM Quinn. **119:** top, CV, centre, GFA; bottom, Finnish State Railways. **120:** J Winkley. **121:** CV. **122:** Burlington Northern. **123:** CV. **124:** Southern Railway System/MARS. **125:** CV. **126:** JM Jarvis. **127:** top, GFA; bottom, AAR. **128:** South Australian Railways. **129:** top, D Cross; bottom, South Australian Railways. **130:** K Cantlie. **131:** top, C Gammell; bottom, D Cross. **132:** top, CV; bottom, CV. **133:** CV. **134:** CV. **134:** CV. **136:** top, JM Jarvis; centre, JM Jarvis. **136-137:** GFA. **137:** top, GFA; bottom, Canadian Pacific. **138:** top, CV; centre, CV; bottom, Colour-rail/HN James. **139:** top, CV; bottom left, CV; bottom right, CV. **140:** top, Bundarchiv; bottom, Norwegian State Railways. **141:** Norwegian State Railways. **142:** C Gammell. **142-143:** AAR. **144:** top, AAR; bottom, CV. **144:** GFA. **145:** CV. **146:** D Cross. **147:** top, CV; bottom, CV. **148:** CV. **149:** top, GFA; bottom, CV. **149:** British Columbia Railway/MARS. **151:** British Columbia Railway/ MARS. **152:** Canadian National Railways/MARS. **153:** CV. **154-155:** Chicago & North Western/MARS. **155:** Colour-rail. **157:** top, CV; bottom, CV. **158:** C Gammell. **159:** top, JM Jarvis; bottom, JM Jarvis. **160:** top, CV; bottom, J Dunn. **161:** top, CV; bottom, SAR. **162:** top, CV; bottom, GFA. **163:** top, D Cross; bottom, GFA. **164:** CV. **165:** Union Pacific RR. **166:** JM Jarvis. **167:** top, JM Jarvis; bottom, GFA. **168:** GFA. **169:** left, Santa Fe RR; right, GFA. **170:** CV. **171:** D Cross. **172:** JM Jarvis. **173:** top, GFA; bottom, JM Jarvis. **174:** top, VR/Fenino; bottom, VR. **175:** VR. **176:** top, K Yoshitani; bottom, C Gammell. . **177:** K Yoshitani. **178:** Colour-rail/R Hill. **179:** top, CV; bottom, C Gammell. **180:** B Stephenson. **181:** C&O RR/MARS. **182:** top, R Bastin; centre, CV; bottom, M Whitehouse. **183:** top, CV; bottom, VR. **184:** top, CV; centre, R Ziel; bottom, J Westwood. **185:** top, J Westwood; bottom, R Ziel. **186:** Colour-rail/RM Quinn. **187:** top, CV; bottom, Colour-rail/RM Quinn. **188:** Canadian Pacific. **189:** CV. **190:** top, D Cross; bottom, CV. **191:** Colour-rail/J Dewing. **192:** top, South African Railways/MARS; bottom, CV. **193:** C Gammell. **194:** top, CV; centre, CV; bottom, CV. **195:** CV. **196:** top, CV; bottom, Colour-rail/JG Dewing. **197:** top, CV; bottom, RENFE/MARS. **198:** top, B Hollingsworth; bottom, C Gammell. **199:** top, R Gillard; bottom, CV. **204:** J Winkley. **205:** top, South African Railways; bottom left, P Robinson; right, GFA. **206:** General Electric. **207:** top, BH; bottom left, Victorian Government Railways; bottom right, DB. **208:** top, CG; bottom, R Barton. **209:** top, P Robinson; bottom left, Swedish State Railways; bottom right, K Yoshitani. **210:** Union Pacific. **210-211:** SNCF. **211:** bottom left, JJ; bottom right, J Winkley. **212:** Panama Canal Company. **212-213:** SNCF. **213:** top right, P Robinson. **216:** top, BBC; bottom, J Winkley. **217:** top, Deutsches Museum, Munich; bottom, JJ. **220-221:** Gornergratbahn. **223:** J Winkley. **225:** via MARS. **226:** JJ. **227:** top, Panama Canal Company, BH. **228:** Colour-rail. **229:** top, JJ; bottom, BBC. **230:** BH. **232:** JJ. **233:** J Winkley. **234:** Colour-rail. **235:** BS. **236:** BS. **237:** R Bastin. **238:** Swiss Federal Railways. **239:** top, Swiss Federal Railways, bottom. **241:** BH. **242:** LG Marshall. **243:** JJ. **244:** Swedish State Railways. **245:** top, JJ; bottom, Post Office. **247:** National Railway Museum. **248-249:** JJ. **250-251:** AC. **252:** top, CG; bottom, CV. **253:** AC. **255:** BH. **256:** top, Colour-rail; bottom, Oxford Publishing Co. **257:** top, BS; bottom, Oxford Publishing Co. **258:** top, J Winkley; bottom, Union Pacific RR. **259:** top, J Winkley; bottom, Union Pacific RR. **260:** Italian State Railways. **261:** top, Italian State Railways; bottom, Danish State Railways. **262:** AC. **263:** GFA. **265:** BS. **266:** CG. **267:** CG. **268:** top, AMTRAK; bottom, BH. **270:** AMTRAK. **270:** CG. **271:** BS. **272:** CG. **273:** AT&SF. **274:** Emery Gulash. **275:** top, J Winkley; bottom, CG. **276:** top, BS; bottom, CG. **277:** J Whiteley. **278:** BLS. **279:** R Bastin. **280-281:** AT&SF. **282-283:** JJ. **284:** Burlington Northern RR. **285:** top, GFA; centre, Burlington Northern RR; bottom, Burlington Northern RR. **286:** top, CV; bottom, CG. **287:** top, Oxford Publishing Co: bottom, JJ. **288:** BH. **289:** J Winkley. **290:** BS. **291:** SNCF. **292:** D Cross. **293:** Colour-rail. **294:** top, CV; bottom, via MARS. **295:** top, NZGR; bottom, J Winkley. **296-297:** Italian State Railways. **298:** BH. **299:** Fairbanks-Morse. **300:** SNCF. **301:** R Bastin. **302:** BS. **303:** top, Colour-rail; bottom, SAR. **304:** SNCF. **306:** Danish State Railways. **307:** J Winkley. **308:** BS. **309:** top, BS; centre, J Whiteley; bottom, J Westwood. **310:** top, D Cross; bottom, M Kashima. **311:** top, BS; bottom, M Kashima. **312:** top, J Winkley; bottom, P Robinson. **313:** top, P Robinson; bottom, D Cross. **314-315:** top, P Robinson; bottom, J Westwood. **316:** J Winkley. **317:** top left, J Westwood; top right, Romanian State Railways; bottom, P Robinson. **318-319:** BS. **320:** Swedish State Railways. **321:** top, ASEA; bottom, JJ. **322:** J Winkley. **323:** BH. **324:** top, HB; bottom, P Robinson. **325:** left, HB; right, CG. **326:** Southern Pacific RR. **327:** Denver & Rio Grande RR. **328:** top, Colour-rail; bottom, JJ. **329:** Colour-rail. **330:** P Robinson. **331:** top, CV; bottom, BS. **332:** top, D Cross; bottom, BS. **333:** R Bastin. **334:** J Westwood. **335:** top, SNCF; bottom, MARS. **336:** top, P Cook; bottom, Koyusha. **337:** top, P Cook; centre, Japanese Information Service; bottom, K Yoshitani. **338:** JJ. **339:** GFA. **340:** Dr Hedley. **341:** JJ. **342:** DB. **343:** J Westwood. **344-345:** top, BR; bottom, BS. **346:** top, SNCF; bottom, BS. **347:** top, SNCF; bottom, CG. **348:** AMTRAK. **349:** top, J Winkley; centre & bottom, AMTRAK. **350:** H Kawai. **351:** CV. **352:** top, Union Pacific RR; bottom, J Winkley. **353:** Union Pacific RR. **354:** J Winkley. **355:** top, HB; bottom, London Transport. **356-357:** top, SNCF; bottom, BS. **358:** R Bastin. **359:** SNCF. **360-361:** BS. **362:** J Winkley. **363:** CV. **364:** NZGR. **365:** top, NZGR; bottom, DB. **366:** top, R Bastin; bottom, J Winkley. **367:** HB. **368:** top, K Yoshitani; bottom, H Kawai. **369:** top, H Kawai; bottom, Kazunori. **370:** CV. **371:** AMTRAK. **372:** top, HB; bottom, Queensland Government Railways. **373:** top, Victorian Government Railways; bottom, Queensland Government Railways. **374:** top, CG; bottom, JJ. **375:** top, Finnish State Railways; bottom, CG. **376-377:** South African Railways. **378:** top, CV; bottom, CV. **379:** J Winkley. **380:** top & centre, J Whiteley; bottom, Romney, Hythe & Dymchurch Railway. **381:** top, Austrian State Railways; bottom, RH&DR. **382:** FOB. **383:** AC. **384:** R Bastin. **385:** BS. **386-387:** DB. **388-389:** Via Rail. **390:** NSW Railways. **391:** top, J Dunn; bottom, N Gurley. **392:** HB. **393:** top, SAR; bottom, Colour-rail. **394-395:** SNCF. **395:** CV. **396:** top, Italian State Railways. **397:** bottom, BR. **398-399:** BR.

gardening in small spaces

gardening in small spaces

Rachel de Thame

Dedication

For my parents, Ghita and Michael Cohen, who, a long time ago, showed a little girl the beauty of plants

GARDENING IN SMALL SPACES
First published in Great Britain by BBC Worldwide Limited, Woodlands, 80 Wood Lane, London W12 0TT
North American edition © 2002 by Winding Stair Press

NATIONAL LIBRARY OF CANADA CATALOGUING IN PUBLICATION DATA

De Thame, Rachel
Gardening in small spaces

North American ed.
Includes index.
First published in Great Britain under title: Small town gardens.
ISBN 1-55366-267-9

1. Gardening. I. Title. II. Title: Small town gardens.

SB473.D475 2002 635.9'67 C2002-900542-6

Winding Stair Press
An imprint of Stewart House Publishing Inc.
290 North Queen Street, #210
Etobicoke, Ontario, M9C 5K4 Canada
1-866-574-6873
www.stewarthouse.com

Executive Vice President and Publisher: Ken Proctor
Director of Publishing and Product Acquisition: Joe March
Production Manager: Ruth Bradley-St-Cyr
North Americanization: Alison Maclean and Laura Brady
Commisioning Editor: Vivien Bowler
Project Editor: Khadija Manjlai
Copy-editor: Ruth Baldwin
Art Editor: Lisa Pettibone
Designer: Andrew Barron & Collis Clements Associates

This book is available at special discounts for bulk purchases by groups or organizations for sales promotions, premiums, fundraising and educational purposes. For details, contact: Peter March, Stewart House Publishing Inc., Special Sales Department, 195 Allstate Parkway, Markham, Ontario L3R 4T8. Toll free 1-866-474-3478.

1 2 3 4 5 6 07 06 05 04 03 02

Printed and bound in France by Imprimerie Pollina s.a.

Previous page: Cool tones and restrained planting bring serenity to a tiny courtyard.

Acknowledgements

Creating a new series is always a group undertaking, and the *Small Town Gardens* team is second to none, but the impetus, as always, comes from the top.

My thanks to Jane Root for her total commitment to gardening on the BBC, and Owen Gay for igniting the spark that became *Small Town Gardens*; Abigail Harvey, an inspirational series producer and Julia Murkin, the producer, who indefatigably held it all together, headed a team that worked tirelessly on the series; directors Paul O'Connor and David Wheeler; researchers Russell Jordan, Adelle Martins and especially Anna Maynard for her meticulous help in compiling the plant directory for this book; and an excellent group of cameramen, soundmen, editors, office-based researchers and backroom staff.

The series could not have been made without the garden designers who participated so enthusiastically in this adventure in garden design. Thanks to Douglas Coltart, Paul Cooper, Will Giles, Bunny Guinness, Cleve West and Stephen Woodhams; and, of course, the garden owners – Gillian and Julian Herbert, Carol and Richard Hughes, Rose and Nick Painter, Andrea and David Purdie, Ruthanne and Jack Reid and Gill and Chris Short – who all had to contend with muddy footprints, unsociable filming hours and provide gallons of tea.

Thanks also to the following for allowing us to film at their gardens and nurseries: Ian Hamilton, Finlay at Little Sparta, George Anderson at the Royal Botanic Gardens, Edinburgh, the Duke and Duchess of Devonshire at Chatsworth House, John Carter at Rowden Gardens, the Abbey Gardens, Tresco, Angus White at Architectural Plants, Anthony Paul and the Hannah Peschar Sculpture Garden, Beth Chatto, John Humphries at Sutton Place, Marina Christopher and John Coke at Green Farm Plants, Raymond Blanc at Le Manoir aux Quat' Saisons and Annie Huntington at the Old Rectory Gardens. Finally, thanks also to all the contractors and gardeners – the unsung heroes of the team – who helped us to meet the deadline.

At BBC Worldwide, thanks are due to Robin Wood, Viv Bowler for her patience and encouragement, Khadija Manjlai for guiding me through the book-writing process so painlessly, the meticulous Ruth Baldwin for her copy-editing, Bea Thomas for her impeccable picture research and Andrew Barron, whose design work brought the book to life. Thanks are also due to Jonathan Buckley for his flawless photographer's eye and Dan Welldon for the excellent photographs of the Paisley garden.

Those who offered encouragement from the outset include Rosemary Alexander and Simon Pyle at the English Gardening School, and Tony Laryea and Colette Foster at Catalyst Television, who took a chance on a new girl. Thanks also to Annie Sweetbaum, Hilary Murray-Watts and all at Arlington Enterprises for their unfailing care and commitment; Luigi Bonomi at Sheil Land Associates for his expert guidance on my first foray into book writing; Ghita Cohen, for reading every word of the manuscript, spurring me on when I began to flag and never being too busy to listen to my concerns; Simon Cohen for his valuable contribution to the picture research; and James Gladwin for his much-needed technical support.

And, finally, thanks to my husband, Gerard, for his constant love, support, encouragement and unerring good judgement, and most especially to my children, Lauren and Joseph, for their infinite patience.

contents

introduction

Private gardens cover more than a million acres in this country; most of this vast space is composed not of large rural gardens but small urban plots. From the air it immediately becomes clear just how much of the land in our cities is turned over to tiny gardens. Add up all the little green squares and rectangles, the pots perched on rooftops and balconies, and you have a true picture of the strength of our national obsession – and I don't mean football. If Napoleon were describing our nation today, he'd have to substitute the word 'gardeners' for 'shopkeepers'.

Those of us who live willingly or otherwise in towns and cities are no less keen than country folk to have our own patch of green. In fact, such is the strength of the desire to grow plants and humanize urban spaces by surrounding ourselves with living things that we cram them into every available nook and cranny. The most inhospitable basement wells in front of old terraced houses receive almost no light, yet we won't give up trying to make something grow, and rightly so. If that is your only outdoor space, you should make the best of it, and you can be assured there is something that will thrive there, however difficult the conditions.

Eighty per cent of gardeners have plots that are less than 18m (60ft) long, with town gardens being even smaller. Yet the traditional gardening press seems to give a disproportionate amount of attention to large rural gardens with acres of bowling-green lawn and swathes of herbaceous perennials billowing in endless borders. It's all very lovely, and we can certainly take inspiration from such gardens, but what we need is information relevant to our own modest back yards. There are no restrictions as to what you can do in a small city garden, only perceived restrictions. If you want to devote the space to vegetables, go ahead. If you yearn to recreate the Amazon jungle on a housing estate, go for it.

Small spaces, far from being a problem, can actually prove advantageous. Having a limited area forces you to hone the design, to get rid of distracting elements and consider carefully practical aspects such as storage, lighting and irrigation. Gardeners with small plots quickly become adept at weeding out plants that aren't earning their keep, and moving or pruning others to suit the specific conditions. In a tiny garden you can't afford to have areas that look tatty or past their best; being fussy about the plants you buy and where you place them makes you a very selective shopper.

The most adventurous steps in domestic garden design often occur in city gardens, with cutting-edge modern and minimalist gardens becoming increasingly popular with ordinary homeowners. Whether this is

because town dwellers are more adventurous or because it's harder to break away from traditional styles in the country is debatable, but size restrictions can actually help to create a really strong design statement. Confined by a clear boundary, the design cannot become diluted, as is often the case in larger gardens through simply having a large space that needs filling, or an ancient rockery, border or topiary hedge that no one dare touch.

The majority of people living in cities are doing so, I'm pleased to say, because they want to. Towns are invigorating places in which to dwell and bring up children. Watching people on the move in cities that never sleep and revelling in the buzz that pervades modern urban spaces are often the reasons why people enjoy living in them. If you find you're trying to block it all out, perhaps you should consider a move. It is a misconception that towns and gardens are incompatible; on the contrary, having a bit of green space, somewhere to escape from the inevitable pressures that go with urban living, can be crucial to our quality of life.

Most of us will never own a large garden, and many of us choose to remain in the city all our life. Small urban plots are the gardening reality for the majority of us. This book recognizes that fact, and aims to show that having this sort of garden should not be regarded as a disadvantage. With careful planning and clever design, city gardens can outdo the rural equivalents in originality and ingenuity. Above all, this book is a celebration of small town gardens and the joy they give to millions of gardeners and non-gardeners alike.

Above left: Lushly planted evergreens bring a touch of the exotic to the heart of the city.

Above right: Simplicity and symmetry combine to create a sleekly modern style that is perfectly suited to a small urban garden.

Opposite left: An eclectic mixture of objects brings individuality to a corner with a seaside theme.

Opposite middle: Architectural plants heightened with bright colour are packed into this small space.

Opposite right: Gently flowing water brings a sense of calm to a Japanese-influenced garden.

plotting *and* planning

Starting work on a new garden, or changing the style of an existing one is an exciting time. Small town plots have just as much potential as large country gardens and can be anything you want them to be; many of the most interesting developments in garden design are happening in unlikely urban environments. The first step is to decide on a look that's right for you, your family and your lifestyle, and then put it into practice. Lack of space need not restrict your imagination, so make bold choices and you'll reap the benefits in the future.

Left: Limiting the colour palette to shades of green can bring coherence to a small space.

Opposite: The restraint shown in this formal geometric design results in an intensely satisfying garden, proving that less is indeed more.

Take a cool hard look at your garden. Is it the best it could be? Is it what you want? Could it be improved? Many of us delay doing something about the exterior space until the interior is finished, but the effort and expense of improving the garden is disproportionate to the amount of pleasure we then get from using it. Tackling your outside space should not be an afterthought; it's well known that a beautiful garden is a major factor in helping to sell a property, as well as adding considerably to the value of a house or flat. It's a fact that good gardens get noticed and add to our quality of life.

Having decided to make improvements, the starting point is to assess your garden carefully. Which direction does it face? Is there any area that gets full sun or is it all in permanent shade? Are there any existing trees and – unless they are protected, in which case you need permission in order to touch them – are they contributing anything to the garden? If there are none, would adding a tree improve the garden? Think long term; tiny saplings can quickly cast a lot of shade. There are many more questions you need to answer: is the garden overlooked? Could something be done to improve your privacy? What about storage, a greenhouse, a water feature, growing vegetables? Look critically at the boundaries, the garden floor, and the access into the garden from the house.

Your garden can be anything you want it to be, and deciding on a style is one of the best parts of planning a new garden. If you yearn for tropical climes but live in, say, the northern part of the UK, you can still have an exotic feel to the garden. Landlocked seaside lovers can bring a taste of marine life to the city, and a corner of Japan can come to you, complete with bamboo, bonsai and boulders, wherever you live. Whether you have a penchant for traditional soft curves, formal box parterres or concrete and sleek lines, it can all be achieved in a small town garden.

Of course there are practicalities to consider. Before doing anything else, make a list of what you actually need, then move on to what you really want. If you have three boys under five, it will frustrate everybody if your minimalist garden has nowhere to store dayglo plastic cars, bikes and footballs. We all reach an age when stooping to deal with weeds becomes more difficult, so raised beds and low-maintenance planting are the perfect answer. There are solutions to most problems, without having to compromise the look of the garden; what's needed is clever design.

Not all of us can call on the services of a garden designer, though we can draw inspiration from seeing examples of their work. With thought and imagination we can do a lot to improve our own gardens. Be realistic about your budget and cut your coat

to fit your cloth. Where possible, employ the services of professionals to deal with the aspects of remaking the garden that you find daunting; many garden landscaping companies offer a design service. However, there is a surprising amount that can be done by keen, fit and enthusiastic amateurs. Use one of the new three-dimensional computer programs to help you visualize your design, or work on paper; there are many good books on garden design to help you. When in doubt, the best approach is to keep it simple.

Once you've chosen a style, taken careful measurements and drawn up a plan, the next step will be to clear the garden. It's liberating to get rid of outdoor clutter: just as clearing out an interior boxroom filled with junk can be a cathartic experience, so can removing a tired lawn or overgrown shrubs from the garden. Being unsentimental about the garden requires a different way of thinking. If you're used to saving any plant that shows the smallest sign of being alive, it will be hard to throw out those that are perfectly healthy but are no longer right for the garden. By all means incorporate anything that could work in a different position – even mature shrubs can recover from a move if it is done carefully – then give away what you cannot use. Be aware that the design will be compromised if you attempt to salvage everything.

Installing the hard landscaping elements of the garden can be both terrifying and exciting. When all around you is a sea of mud, it's tempting to wonder why you ever embarked on such a project and suddenly you miss that scrappy bit of weedy turf you called a lawn. Forge ahead, however; this part of the overhaul imperceptibly reaches a turning point when you can really see the design beginning to emerge. Be flexible – this is the stage when changes can still be made, and you never know what obstacles or advantages you may discover while work is in progress.

With the bones of the garden in place, it's time to flesh it out. For me the most worthwhile stage of the transformation is getting the plants in, but some groundwork needs to be done to give them the best possible chance in life. Any form of building work will have a detrimental effect on the structure of the soil, and the gardens of newly built houses often have rubble barely concealed just beneath the surface. You may be forced to skim off soil that has been badly contaminated with cement mixture and other detritus, and import fresh topsoil from elsewhere. Buy from a reliable supplier and, if possible, pay them a visit first to see exactly what you're getting.

Even if your existing soil is worth keeping, it will still benefit hugely from an injection of goodness. Work in plenty of organic material in the form of well-rotted farmyard manure –

Left: The flower-filled borders and gentle curves of traditional garden style can soften the hard lines of the urban environment.

which can be bought ready-bagged from garden centres – or good garden compost. Many town gardens have heavy clay soil which, though fertile, is stiff and sticky in the winter and parched and cracked in summer. Improve the drainage by incorporating horticultural grit with the manure or compost. Improving the soil structure is a long-term investment; putting in expensive plants without preparing the ground properly first could be a costly mistake.

Once you're ready to start planting, get the big structural plants in first. When drawing up the plan of the garden, you will probably have decided on their final positions, but the smaller plants may still need to be arranged. Most designers use some sort of block planting technique, placing several plants of the same type together to create drifts or geometric chunks for maximum effect. Avoid bitty planting with dozens of different varieties packed together. It's often a case of less is more. Lay out all the plants in their positions before planting and move things around until they look right. Remember to stand back from large plants once you've dropped them into the planting hole to check that they're facing the right way: many individual specimens have a definite front and back.

Some fixed accessories, such as recessed lighting and water features, will have gone in at the building stage. The fun part – dressing the garden – adds finishing touches, such as containers, furniture and movable lights, and is much like arranging objects in the home. Choose well-made items that add to the overall design statement. Don't feel you have to fill every corner of the garden. The space around things is often just as important in terms of visual success.

One of the biggest bonuses of a small plot is that it's not unrealistic or too expensive to have a change when you fancy something completely different. Fashions move on in garden design as in everything else. Think of the garden as a constantly evolving space; living plants never remain the same, so neither does the look of a garden. You should play an active part in altering your outdoor space. Put your own imprint on it and make it something unique that reflects your tastes and the way in which you live today.

Above left: A patchwork of contrasting gravels, sempervivums and *Solierolia solierolii* (mind-your-own-business) add interest to the garden floor.

Above right: Incorporating the needs of children is what family gardens are all about.

Opposite left: Children will love quirky features such as these pod chairs, but water is strictly for older kids.

Opposite middle: A mulch of coloured glass beads sets off a collection of contrasting grasses to perfection.

Opposite right: Swirls of pebbles introduce shape and texture underfoot.

the family garden

Gardens are for families and the best spaces fulfil the needs of parents and children. Adults need somewhere to relax, entertain friends and indulge a love of gardening. Kids, from toddlers to teenagers, deserve a flexible space in which to play in safety and allow their imagination full rein. It's a lot to pack in. Combining the needs of the whole family in a restricted space is not easy, but with planning and clever design you can create a beautiful garden from a potential battlefield.

Left: Interesting designs at ground level will catch the eye of a small child.

Opposite: A child's sand-pit becomes an attractive focal point rather than being hidden away in the corner of the garden.

Modern family life is hectic; both parents may be working and time spent together as a family is precious. Ensuring the garden is a family-friendly space that works for everyone will help us enjoy to the full our time with the children. Small children and small gardens are not the most compatible combination; kids need space to run around and expend some of that boundless energy, and space is the one thing lacking in small gardens. This doesn't mean that the majority of children's other needs cannot be met in a small plot, and on the plus side, gardens designed with children in mind are usually fun, friendly spaces. Keep a sense of humour and use clever design solutions to make the garden a success for the entire family.

Some of my best memories as a parent are of events that have happened in our city garden: the howls of laughter and hysterical whoops as the children run through a sprinkler on a hot day; their uncontrollable giggles when pretending not to want to get 'caught' by the hose while fully dressed. I can still picture my children in straw hats, sitting drawing in the shade, finding that frogs had invaded the outsize paddling pool, and enjoying birthday parties that rapidly got out of control. These are the things that make having a garden such a valuable part of life. To exclude our children from enjoying to the full the outdoor space, however small, is to deny pleasure to them and to us.

The problems arise when you crave a super-smart minimalist garden. Although you dearly love your children, how can you combine the two when they're so clearly at odds? There are really two ways to approach this mismatch. You could turn over the garden completely to the needs of your young family when they need it most; after all, in retrospect the years of swinging on a rope and making perfume from your prize blooms are all too fleeting. Some of the purpose-built play structures are attractive enough, and even better when custom made. Playhouses, sandpits, climbing frames, goalposts, swings and slides don't have to be made from garish plastic, and can all be dismantled once they're outgrown. Well-designed storage is a necessity for large items, such as bikes and paddling pools. Once the children reach a certain age (often signalled by a desire to hide in their bedrooms day and night with their friends), it's time to get rid of all the childish clutter and start again, this time to please yourself.

Alternatively, if you cannot wait that long to get your garden back, you will have to share it from the start. Employ ingenious methods to combine the needs of adults and children, and find ways to conceal all the practical stuff that goes with a modern childhood. Again, the key to success lies in providing sufficient storage: if it's easy at the end of the day to sweep away the detritus of play, there will be fewer areas of contention. Gardens should feed a child's

Opposite: Vivid colours, eye-catching plants, child-friendly accessories and a soft play surface combine to make a stimulating space for the very young.

Right: A deep layer of bark chippings provides a soft surface beneath this shady play area.

Below: The paraphernalia of play can be successfully incorporated into the smallest spaces; here, it forms the basis of the entire design.

imagination, and hide-and-seek can be played in the smallest spaces if there are 'secret' corners or large shrubs to conceal a little person. When incorporating pieces of sculpture or large structures, try to choose items that could metamorphose in a child's mind to become the deck of a ship, a car, or a fairy castle.

Wherever possible, include water in the design. Choose a more naturalistic pond to encourage wildlife; you'll find that frogs and damselflies will appear from nowhere overnight. In a modern space, imaginative ways with flowing water can fascinate children, but do bear in mind that kids love to get wet. How will the design of the feature stand up to the wear and tear of children's play and, above all, is it safe?

Planting should also be child-friendly. A surprising number of plants are highly poisonous, and are best avoided while children are at the stage when everything goes into their mouths. Laburnum, aconitum and yew are all toxic. Check with your nurseyman when buying plants that might tempt small fingers and explain to your children that birds can safely eat red berries that will give *them* a bad tummy ache. A lawn is undoubtedly the most comfortable play surface, but once the games become more boisterous and the tricycles are swapped for mountain bikes, it will need a fastidious gardener to keep it looking good. Choose brightly coloured, scented and even humorous plants to stimulate all the children's senses. Popping open the mouths of snapdragons and stroking the kitten-soft leaves of *Stachys lanata* can keep a child happy for hours. Wherever you can, give children a small corner of the garden to grow their own plants: the excitement of watching a seed germinate, develop and finally flower has instilled a love of plants and gardens in generations of youngsters. It's an experience that city-dwelling children shouldn't be denied.

a family garden *designed by* Cleve West

Left: Anthony Paul's woodland garden in Surrey, a source of inspiration for Cleve West.

Opposite: Raised beds constructed from heavy granite setts give a sense of permanence and solidity to the garden.

A larger-than-average town garden with stately, mature trees and dappled shade, this plot sounded idyllic on paper; the reality was more of a battlefield. The owners of this garden in Harborne on the outskirts of Birmingham barely used the majority of their leafy exterior, and were scared to venture beyond the boundaries of the tiny patio outside the back door. It wasn't a bad case of agoraphobia that prevented them from enjoying the garden to the full, but fear of being hit by a football in full flight, or some other low-flying missile. The owners' four young sons and their friends had turned the garden into a scene from *The Lord of the Flies.*

The garden was long and rectangular with a pleasant prospect and not badly overlooked by the neighbours' windows. There were several existing large trees, with spreading canopies overhanging the plot. North-facing, this garden was blessed with only intermittent periods of sunshine and, for the most part, the space was in dappled or full shade. This is a problem only if you crave the sun and are desperate to grow sun-loving plants. In many ways the garden – though unstructured – certainly had plenty of potential.

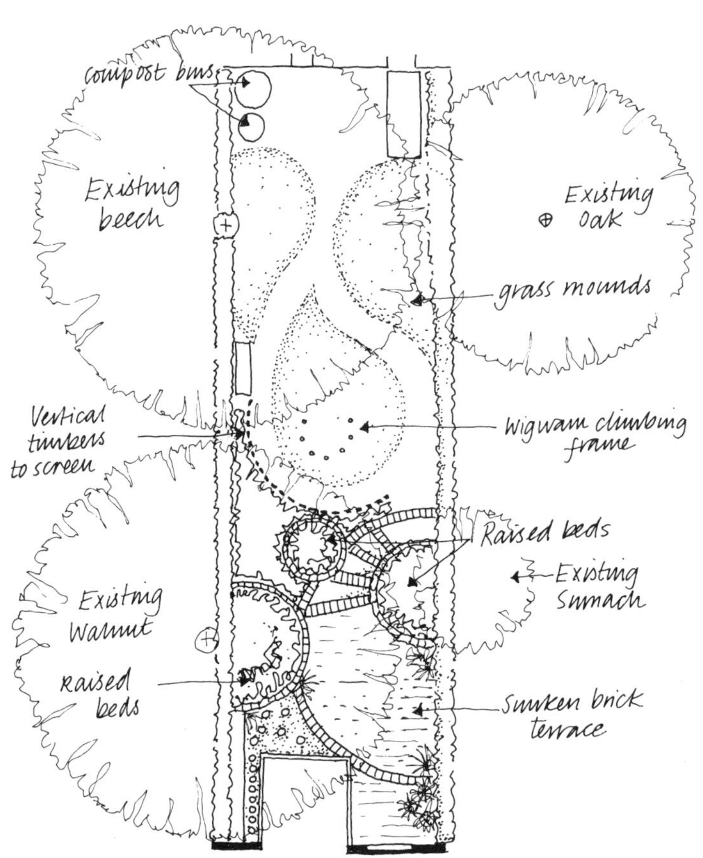

The vast majority of the space was entirely taken up by a worn and patchy lawn, which was strewn with bikes and assorted footballs. Some attempt had been made to introduce a variety of plants, but many were unsuitable for the shady conditions and others were languishing in pots. Towards the rear of the garden was an old, neglected climbing-frame. At the end

Left: A simple but highly practical timber frame ensures the children's bikes stay off the lawn.

Opposite: Sound and movement are introduced in the form of a child-safe water feature.

nearest the house an extremely cramped patio area sat directly outside the doors of the glazed kitchen extension. For a reasonably sized garden, there was little space to sit or to entertain, few areas suitable for planting and insufficient storage for the ever-expanding belongings of four lively lads.

This project needed a designer with vision – someone who could bring out the potential in a promising site while dealing effectively with the practical problems. Enter multi-award-winning Cleve West (see Designers' Biographies, page 122), one of our most innovative young designers, renowned for his imaginative and solidly built gardens. Cleve frequently collaborates with his business partner, Johnny Woodford, to create atmospheric, uncluttered spaces, incorporating spectacular organic sculptures. He likes his gardens to have a sense of quiet strength and permanence, to feel as if they have been there for some time and are simply continuing to evolve.

Having spent time chatting to the owners, getting to know what their priorities were, and watching their children kick a ball about, Cleve – a keen football fan himself – measured up carefully before heading back to his studio to get his ideas down on paper. The resulting design worked with the existing overhanging trees to create a garden that would instantly become at one with its surroundings. Cleve chose to work with curved shapes, interlocking a series of circles and gently sweeping lines. He got rid of the dull flat space and divided the garden into two main areas, using different levels to add structural variety. The section nearest to the house was to become a sunken terrace, with plenty of space for the adults to sit out, enjoy the garden and entertain without being terrorized by the kids. This area was much larger than the original patio, taking up more than one-third of the garden. A tall physical barrier would divide this part of the plot from a generous area of lawn, which would fill the remainder of the garden. The design incorporated plenty of large beds for planting, to satisfy the owners' desire to grow a much wider selection of plants. While Cleve discussed the plan with his clients, footballs thwacked rythmically into the plants covering the fence, emphasizing the need to move fast to regain some territory.

Work began as soon as possible. While the plot was being cleared, several of the existing shade-loving plants were salvaged. They were potted up until they could be repositioned in the finished garden. The entire plot was then landscaped to form gentle undulating mounds beneath the lawn. By getting away from a traditional flat bowling-green swathe, Cleve made the lawn more interesting for imaginative play. The area nearest the house was excavated to make a clear distinction

This project needed a designer with vision – someone who could bring out the potential in a promising site while dealing effectively with the practical problems.

between the lower sunken terrace and the grass area beyond. These two levels were to be linked by a series of wide curved steps. Once the surface of the ground had been scooped and moulded to fit Cleve's design, the hard landscaping could begin. A master of grounded, solid gardens, Cleve likes to use heavy materials and had chosen a mixture of granite setts, bricks – some of them recycled – and timber. The terrace was paved using red bricks in a simple herringbone design. This was edged with larger blue engineering bricks, which followed the curve of the terrace's rounded shape. The walls of the circular raised beds were built with row upon row of heavy granite setts. Each row was simply bedded on to a layer of soil. No mortar was needed to secure them; the weight of the setts themselves was sufficient to compact the soil and make the structure really solid. Each new row of setts was slightly set back from those in the row below, so the walls gently tapered inwards as they ascended. Occasionally Cleve left a gap in the wall, in which to plant a fern or some ivy.

The beds slowly reached the required height, but Cleve had a couple of changes in mind. On one side of the garden the heights were looking too uniform, so he decided that another tier should be added to the larger bed. The other change was a little more drastic. Since finalizing the design Cleve had felt it could be improved upon by introducing water into the garden. After a quick discussion with the owners – though the work was now well under way – it was agreed to include water in the design. The circular bed in the prime position near the steps was soon adapted to become a unique water feature.

This was to be a covered feature; the constant drop of foliage from the surrounding trees would have resulted in many hours being spent collecting leaves from the surface of even a small area of open water. A large, circular, pre-fabricated plastic pool was hidden below the rim of the raised bed. It contained the water and an electric pump, and was covered with metal mesh. This mesh supported the centrepiece – a large coil of heavy rusted chain, wound into a ball around a simple fountain-head and placed in the middle of the grid. Around the chain ball concentric circles of gravel and *Soleirolia soleirolii* (commonly known as mind-your-own-business) rayed from the centre out to the edge of the bed. The mixture of colours – the dark grey of the gravel, the speckled orange of the rusty chain and the vivid green of the planting – were a subtle but stunning combination.

When the water was turned on, it bubbled gently through the top of the ball, bringing the restful sound of babbling water to the terrace. Whether Cleve intended a surrealist pun on the words 'ball and chain' when he

Left: Coils of rusted chain glisten on a bed of *Soleirolia soleirolii* and gun-metal-grey gravel.

came up with this design is unclear, but the result is simple, witty and – almost perversely – very soothing.

The steps linking the two levels of the garden were built while Cleve was away from the site. On his return, he found a problem. Although beautifully made, the treads of each step had been carefully covered in crazy paving. At times a designer has to become a diplomat. Cleve tactfully pointed out to the man who had just constructed the steps that the crazy paving was beautifully done, but completely out of character with the rest of the garden and not part of the original design. It would have to go. To Cleve's relief, the man immediately agreed that he didn't like it either, and happily started to lever up the broken slabs. Disaster averted, the treads could now be filled with granite setts, as per the original spec.

During Cleve's initial meeting with the owners, they had joked that what was needed was a 'Berlin Wall' between them and the more raucous children's activities. Cleve took them at their word. To everyone's astonishment enormously tall telegraph poles began to appear and were fixed on their ends one after the other about 12 cm (5 in) apart, like sentries on guard. The introduction of a feature of this scale is always something of a shock, but Cleve persevered, convinced that this bold wall of poles would tie the whole design together. The wall continued from one side of the garden to the point at which the steps reached the lawn. Once in place the poles were stained matt black and their tops were cut to size; they now tapered down in a swooping curve towards the centre and up again slightly on the other side. As well as protecting other garden users from projectiles, this feature immediately became a piece of sculpture on the grand scale when viewed from a distance. And if you look at the garden through the gaps between the poles as you walk slowly by, the effect is like watching the flickering frames of an old silent movie.

After the existing hedges were tidied up, turf was laid over the newly shaped upper section of the garden, sweeping over the large central mound and down again into the surrounding 'valley'. Another sculptural structure was constructed atop the mound. This was a hybrid of different ideas and inspirations.

Left: Interlocking circular beds are echoed in the sweep of the steps up to the lawn and the dramatic curve of the wall of poles.

Solid poles were rammed into the ground in a semi-circle and tied together at the top to form an open-sided wigwam. At the apex a large, decorative coil of rope was nailed down, echoing the shape of the ball of chain on the water feature. Swags of the same rope were then strung between the poles. This structure could be climbed like a climbing-frame; it could be the rigging of a ship, a spider's web, a goalpost or, of course, a wigwam. Rather spookily, Cleve later found out that some of the family's ancestors were Native Americans.

With the garden construction complete, the planting could begin. The soil in the raised beds was extremely dry and sandy. It needed beefing up with plenty of organic material, so lashings of compost and well-rotted manure were added to improve the soil structure and help retain moisture. Cleve's design called for large swathes of single-variety planting – nothing fussy in this garden. To give height to the back of a bed, he planted a leycesteria with deep reddish-purple bracts. A sweep of *Rodgersia aesculifolia* on one side of the terrace was mirrored on the other by a group of *Acanthus spinosus* with large glossy leaves. Some of the salvaged plants found new homes: our native fern *Dryopteris filix-mas*, which is a tough customer, was planted in the dry shade nearest the house, and a *Carex pendula* was given pride of place next to the water feature. Towering, pure white *Agapanthus africanus* 'Albus' were planted in tall containers and placed on the terrace. Cleve very much hoped that the new garden would inspire the owners, already on the verge of becoming keen gardeners, to take up the trowel and add to the planting as they became more confident. This garden is certainly an ideal environment for bulbs, many of which would thrive in the semi-shady conditions.

The moment the family were able to start using the garden, they began to make it their own. Despite the highly innovative design details, this garden instantly felt comfortable. It is rare for a newly built garden to acquire such atmosphere and a real sense of permanence so quickly. Above all, Cleve's design succeeds in keeping all the family members happy. The adults can enjoy relative peace and quiet and absolute protection from flying objects. A long, low wall, constructed from sleepers and placed along the boundary on one side of the terrace, provides informal seating for entertaining. The owners plan to do plenty of this now that plates and glasses are no longer in constant danger of being knocked over, while the children can play as wildly as they please, without constant censure from their parents.

From an overgrown shady plot – the stage for many scenes of family strife – Cleve has created an imaginative yet calm garden that feels solid enough to last for ever.

Left: Small, shady basements can be given the minimalist treatment.

Below left: Alternatively fill the space with planting; either way the pale walls add brightness.

Opposite left: Low box hedges contain a palette of vivid greens heightened with small splashes of white.

Opposite right: Perfect partners for shade: *Dryopteris marginalis* and *Asplenium scolopendrium*.

dealing *with* **shade**

Shady gardens, like the one in the case study, are usually seen as a problem, but in many respects they can be a blessing. Once you accept the limitations on the range of plants you can grow and have come to terms with losing the real sun-lovers, you can appreciate the benefits. Gardens have a completely different atmosphere in the shade. Their gentle ambience and total absence of garish flower colour create elegant and peaceful spaces, and on those – albeit rare – sweltering summer days you'll appreciate the cooler air.

Losing out on a full quota of sunshine doesn't mean the garden will look boring. There is a wonderful range of plants that insists on shady places in order to do well. Many shrubs grow in woodland conditions in nature and will thrive if you can create a similar environment in your shady garden. Some of the best mid-height plants with strong structural leaf shapes – such as Rodgersias and Rheums – are also shade-lovers; these look their best planted *en masse* to fill the mid-storey. Beneath them perennials, such as *Helleborus orientalis*, *Geranium phaeum* and a host of hostas and ferns, thrive. Many bulbs are also happiest in shady spots, giving a wealth of blooms throughout the year. The flowers of shade-loving plants tend to be subtle, but are no less lovely for that. These soft, pale tones glow in low light levels, shimmering in a rich sea of contrasting foliage.

Determine the type of shade in your own garden before you purchase a single plant. If you have a courtyard garden enclosed on all sides, or a basement lower than street level, it's most likely in full shade. Gardens in the lee of a large tree will be subjected to dry shade, one of the most difficult conditions to deal with. The roots of a mature tree are thirsty and hungry, and will compete for available moisture and nutrients. Rain may have trouble filtering through a dense canopy, as will sunlight. Lawns will have difficulty surviving these conditions, but there are many plants that will do surprisingly well; it's just a question of making a considered choice.

Smaller trees often result in dappled shade. This type of shade is much easier to deal with and enlarges considerably the range of suitable plants. Your garden may have semi-shade conditions, with full sun for part of the day before it disappears entirely behind your house

or another building; this is particularly common in town gardens. Such a variance from one extreme to another makes selecting plants a potential minefield. Depending on the amount of full sun, and the time of day in which this occurs, you may even have success with real sun-lovers – silver-leaved beauties, such as lavender, *Helichrysum italicum* and santolina. If the sunny periods are shorter than their optimum growing conditions would dictate, sun-loving perennials will survive but become leggy in their search for better light during the shady part of the day. It's very much a case of choosing varieties that tolerate a bit of both. Trial and error will then narrow the selection down to the best plants for your garden.

A good design trick for a shady plot is to choose bright reflective surfaces to make the most of the available light by bouncing it around the garden. Paint walls in pale colours or use shiny metallic materials. Mirrors can also be used to brighten a dark corner. What you choose to put on the garden floor can make a huge difference to a shady garden. Pale Portland stone, light-coloured gravel and galvanized metal will instantly lift the area and are perfect for courtyard gardens. It may be best, however, to avoid using pale gravel under large trees – it soon becomes covered in green moss or algae, which is difficult to remove. Plants with variegated leaves will also lift dark areas. A surprising number tolerate low light conditions. *Euonymus fortunei* 'Silver Queen' is a perfect, low-growing evergreen for the front of a border, and there are numberous hostas that will fit the bill.

It's impossible to reorientate your garden, and there is little you can do about large trees, so accept what you have to work with. Keep water features small if they are to be positioned near overhanging trees. Removing fallen leaves from the water will soon become a chore.

Most gardeners with shady plots crave the sun-loving plants that will sooner or later fail miserably in their gardens. Far better to grow some of the wonderful plants that will not only survive but thrive in the conditions, and treat the shade as an advantage. It's time to see the light and create something that gardeners with parched sunny plots can only dream of. Lush, verdant and dreamlike, shady gardens have a bright future.

Left: Lawns can work just as successfully in a modern space as in a more traditional garden.

Opposite: A swirl of cobble stones, as in this design by Maggy Howarth, transforms a humble path into a work of art.

the garden floor

One of the main strengths of Cleve's design for the family garden in Harborne was his imaginative use of landscaping materials. The combination of brickwork and granite setts formed the backbone of the design. Yet what we put on the garden floor is often the most neglected part of the garden. Time and money are lavished on plants, pots and water features, while what lies beneath our feet is ignored.

Look at any photograph of an attractive small garden, then cover the ground space with your hand: you'll find that in most cases the floor is what holds the entire design together. The garden floor is often the largest single element in a garden. For a design to be successful as a whole, you need to start with the base level before you can work upwards. What you choose is likely to require a considerable financial investment and will affect the whole atmosphere of the garden. Don't rush to make a decision. Do your research first, visit other gardens to see what works and scour the latest magazines and design books. Your choice will probably be with you for a while.

Just a few years ago, the number of options in garden surface materials was limited. There was the obvious lawn, stone slabs (if you were lucky), concrete paving stones (usually in the form of crazy paving), brick and gravel. Today things couldn't be more different. Innovation in garden flooring has made it the most exciting growth area in the world of garden design. For every style and theme of garden there is something to go on the ground that will enhance that particular space, and the range is expanding all the time.

Many of us like the feel of something soft underfoot that is also a safe play surface for children. Lawns have had a bad press recently, and it's true that in small city gardens they're not always the best choice. All too often shady town gardens are held hostage to a tiny scrap of tatty old turf. Grass will never grow successfully in the shade, particularly the dry shade found under the crown of large trees or right next to shade-making buildings. If your garden has similar conditions, don't bother trying to grow a lawn. It's rare to find a small town garden in full sun, but many are blessed with sun for at least part of the day and these plots are more likely to sustain a reasonable patch of grass.

If you do decide to have all or part of the garden turfed, keeping the shape simple is invariably the best plan. Fiddly convoluted shapes are much too fussy in a large garden and look ridiculous in a small one. Choose a simple oval in informal gardens, and rectangular shapes where the design is symmetrical. It's a misconception that lawns look inappropriate in a modern design – they can be incorporated in the most minimalist

Opposite: Panels of timber decking give this garden a strong geometric structure, softened by a subtly toned woodstain and an abundance of foliage plants.

Right: Illuminated glass blocks inset into a lawn make a change from traditional paviours, and look stunning after dark.

garden very successfully, particularly when the rest of the planting is spare. Lawns don't always have to be curved: straight-sided shapes often work best in an urban environment.

Careful ground preparation and using the correct grass mix are the keys to success with lawns. If you have children, forget the bowling-green look and use a tougher, utility-type seed mix or turf. Whether you use seed or buy rolls of turf will depend on your budget and how quickly you need to get the job done. Seed is much cheaper and you can be sure of exactly what you're getting, but you may not be able to use the lawn properly for at least five months. Turf certainly looks good almost immediately, but it too needs a couple of months to come fully into growth. Do buy turf from a reputable supplier and, if possible, ask to see it first: it's all too easy to end up with a bit of weedy meadow.

Having a lawn doesn't preclude the use of other materials. Most designs will incorporate a terrace, steps or a path. But in many circumstances a lawn simply isn't suitable; far better to choose a hard landscaping surface. Here there need be no limit to your creativity and in a small space you can revel in making a real statement with the garden floor. From the most traditional-looking design to cutting-edge modernity, there is a surface for every garden.

Stone, granite and gravel are endlessly practical, adaptable and the longest-lasting materials. Brick is still one of the most flexible choices, with a range of sizes and colours available. Concrete has taken on a new image and looks fantastic in modern gardens. Some of the new, reconstituted stone products make complex designs with paving and cobbles simplicity itself to construct, and not beyond the average pocket. Timber gives instant warmth and texture to a garden and is now no longer restricted to simple strip decking. The most exciting development is the widening range of materials that designers are using. Plastic and rubber surfaces, once strictly for commercial use, are finding their way into the domestic garden. Galvanized metal and crushed glass are reflective surfaces that bring maximum light into dark city gardens.

With so many options, it's getting harder to make a choice, and sometimes the answer is to use a couple of different surfaces. Combining two or more contrasting materials is all part of the art of garden creativity. But avoid the temptation to use a bit of everything. In a small garden things can quickly look cluttered; as in all areas of design, a little goes a long way.

Above left: Strong shapes, bold colours and an exciting use of materials combine to great effect.

Above right: The soft fronds of grasses and sedums are silhouetted against a movable screen.

Opposite left: A geometric grid of contrasting flooring materials is softened by an ethereal collection of grasses.

Opposite right: Pared-down style calls for pared-down lighting.

the modern garden

Small spaces need big ideas, and town gardens lend themselves extremely well to modern style. A clean, minimalist approach suits the cityscape. Straight lines, geometric shapes and the use of metal, glass and concrete echo and enhance the shapes we see all around us. We've become braver in our interior design. Now it's time to shake things up outside and create an unbroken link between the internal and external living space. Revel in the urban – you choose to live in the city because it's colourful and lively, so don't block it out, celebrate it.

Left: The silvery metallic sheen of a light fitting that is small, simple and stunning.

Opposite: Blurring the boundaries between the interior and exterior unifies the living space, transforming the garden into an extra room.

Recent years have seen huge strides in accessible and attainable modern garden design. The groundwork was done in the twentieth century, and now in the twenty-first it is possible for owners of average small plots to chuck out their chintzy gardens and try something new. Small town gardens are especially suited to being at the forefront of this quiet revolution. The smaller scale lends itself particularly well to modern style, and it's somehow less daunting to be brave in an urban environment. Indeed, with the frantic pace of life in the city, it's often beneficial to have a clean, minimalist space in which to escape and unwind. It's worth bearing in mind that some of the latest hi-tech materials are expensive and if you have acres to redesign, you may need a second mortgage.

Now that modern garden design has gone mainstream and is no longer the preserve of the few, even the most traditional gardener should consider a fresh approach. Modern doesn't have to mean empty; it's perfectly possible to have curves, flowers, even a lawn, and retain the sleek lines and calm atmosphere of a modern space. Minimalist designs are more likely to be very sparing with planting and colour, which is a bonus if you have little time to spend tending plants. Making the minimalist style work with small children is tricky, but with clever design it can be done.

Good modern garden design is often linked closely to the house; a seamless transition from one living space to the next has given rise to the outdoor room. Planning your garden so that it functions like another room of the house means that more thought will be given to how you like to spend your time outside. The result is not just a place to grow plants, but a plant-filled environment that fulfils a range of leisure functions for the family and their friends. Plants do not cease to be important in a minimal scheme. On the contrary, when less is more, the plants you choose really have to earn their keep. Single specimens, prominently displayed, attract far more attention than a conglomeration of shrubs.

All too often town gardens are dreary, dark and depressing; a light and airy modern scheme can open up the area, creating the illusion of a larger space. The use of pale colours and reflective surfaces bounces light into those shady corners. Cramped basement and courtyard gardens in particular are greatly improved with this type of treatment. Get rid of your cluttered old garden and enjoy the breath of fresh air that comes with a new approach.

a modern garden *designed by* Stephen Woodhams

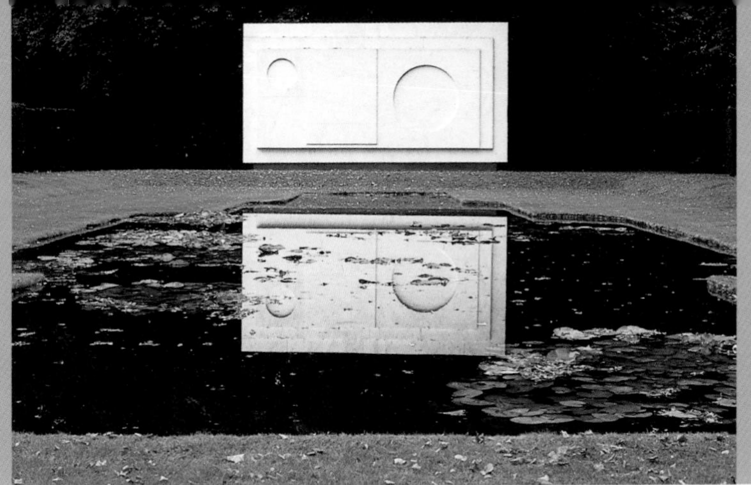

Left: The Ben Nicholson sculpture at Sutton Place in Surrey, Stephen Woodhams's inspirational garden.

Opposite: Link the outdoor space to the interior by unifying colours. Here, the blue of the French doors is reflected in the parasol and walls, and contrasted by the pale blue of the decking.

The owners of this terraced house in Hackney, east London, love the bustle of modern life in the city. They have ripped out walls, stripped off the veneer of age, and dragged their typical Edwardian home firmly into the twenty-first century. When work began on the garden, the interior of the house was still unfinished but well on the way to becoming a sleek, modern, open-plan space, with plenty of metal surfaces, timber floors and seamless expanses of petrol-blue walls. Although modern, the space was approachable, practical and child-friendly. The same couldn't be said of the garden, which was completely overgrown, filled with weeds, a collection of dead or dying plants in pots and a peppering of discarded plastic toys.

This garden was particularly small and irregularly shaped, a rectangle with one straight end that abutted the newly built glazed extension to the house. At the bottom end of the garden, the fence was built at an angle, resulting in one side of the plot being much shorter than the other. On the practical side, this plot would have to work as a family garden, where storage space would be needed for tools and the plethora of toys and bikes that growing toddlers accumulate. There was also a really keen desire to incorporate some sort of safe water feature in the finished garden.

Both the owners work in the visual arts and have a bold approach to design. They wanted to achieve the same sort of strong design

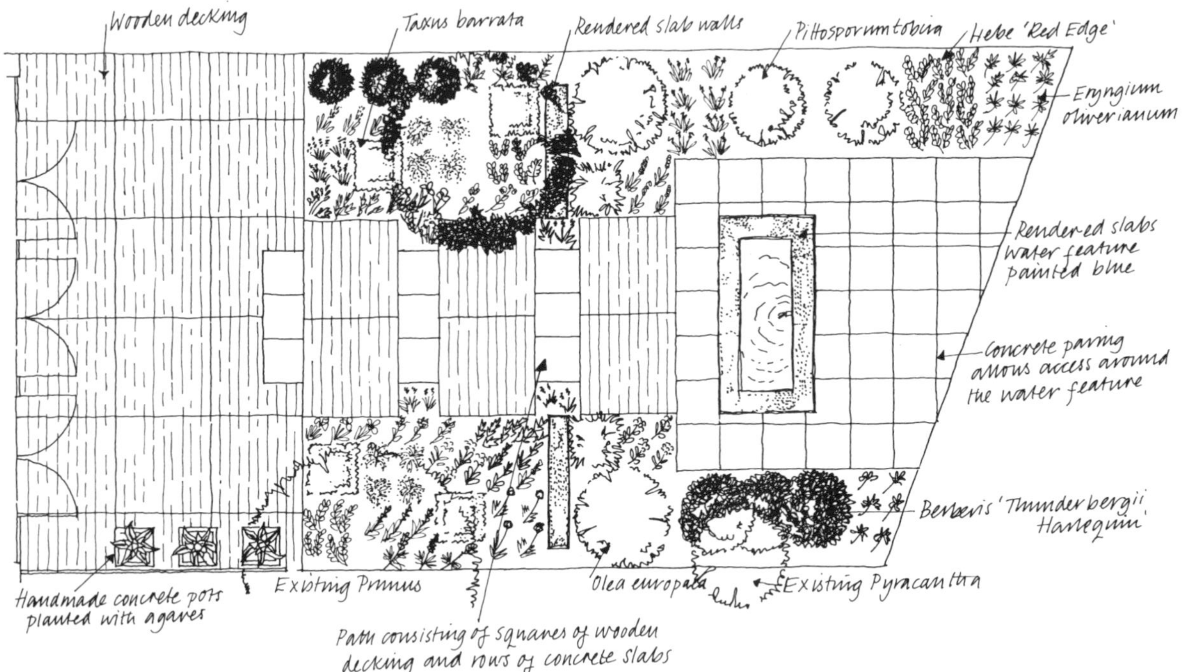

Left: *Festuca glauca* nestles at the base of a wall.

Opposite: The satisfying symmetry of the minimalist water feature forms an impressive focal point at the end of the garden.

statement in the garden that they were developing in the house. Apart from an old *Prunus cerasifera* 'Nigra', the crown of which they had previously reduced, there was nothing in the garden they wanted to keep. It's always exciting for a designer to work with brave clients, and we were able to match them with award-winning Stephen Woodhams (see Designers' Biographies, page 122), who is renowned for his sleek, spare and spectacular gardens. Stephen's first visit to the site was productive and positive. Ideas flowed freely among this creative group of people, and Stephen could see from what had been achieved in the house that his clients were open to contemporary ideas. They were also keen to develop their gardening knowledge further, and to grow a wide range of plants. This wasn't to be a minimalist garden in terms of planting.

Having discussed and measured the garden and considered the brief, Stephen went back to the studio to work on the plan. The fruit of his labour was a deceptively simple symmetrical design. He succeeded brilliantly in creating an outdoor room, linked both visually and physically to the new extension. The floor of the garden was to be raised to match exactly the interior floor level, and the petrol-blue paint colour would be continued unbroken on to the exterior surfaces. By creating seamless connections between the inside and the outside spaces, he had magically enlarged both areas. The garden was to be divided into three sections, using subtle changes in materials at ground level and low rendered walls to give form and structure to the design. All too often small spaces are treated as one area, but by splitting even the tiniest garden into distinct sections it is possible to create the illusion of extra space and achieve a far more interesting result.

The garden was quickly cleared of rubbish and the ground levelled. Carefully chosen hard landscaping materials were installed; simple wooden fence panels with an unusual horizontal construction instantly modernized the boundary abutting the house. Directly outside the extension the first section of the garden was covered with wooden decking in individual rectangular sections. The strips of timber were laid widthways across the garden to exaggerate the size of the space. The decking was given a wash of colour in a soft greyish-blue to look like faded denim and tone with the deeper blue of the main theme colour. The decking narrowed one-third of the way down the garden, becoming a wide path, and the timber panels were interspersed with square concrete paving slabs. These would lead the eye down the length of the garden to the main focal point.

Once the garden floor was complete, the vertical structural elements could be installed. It was extremely exciting to see these structures metamorphose from flat, two-dimensional

Stephen's design managed to fulfil exactly the owners' brief and provide that extra-special ingredient that shows in the work of a top garden designer.

details on paper to three-dimensional reality. A pair of low, free-standing walls were built two-thirds of the way down the garden to break up the length of the space. When painted blue, these proved to be one of the most successful aspects of the design, providing structure and a dramatic backdrop to the planting. The main focal point – a third large rectangular wall – was constructed towards the end of the garden. This dominated the plot, gave the illusion that the space was in fact a perfect rectangle and provided a visual full stop. Cleverly, however, the garden did not end at this point: Stephen had concealed behind the wall a simple wooden shed, taking care of all the toys and clutter with one brilliant storage solution.

This wall was more than a strong vertical statement – the addition of a single spout and a slim raised pool to the front of the wall created the much-wanted water feature. The result was minimal in design, powerful in effect and, above all, safe, thanks to a metal grid fixed just centimetres below the water surface. The water was pumped up to the spout before falling again in a single stream back into the pool. During the construction of the water feature a point was reached when the walls had been rendered but remained unpainted. At this stage it looked so attractive that there was some discussion between Stephen and the owners about the possibility of leaving it in its raw state rather than painting it as he had planned. As Stephen explained, 'One has, of course, to be open to the possibility of changing the design from time to time – you never know what ideas can crop up during the work.' But in this instance he stuck to his guns, feeling that his original instincts were correct, and the results show how that clarity of vision can make the difference between so-so and stunning.

With the hard landscaping completed, the planting could begin. In addition to the prunus, Stephen had decided to retain a mature pyracantha towards the rear of the garden. In early autumn the brilliant orange berries would provide a stunning contrast to the petrol-blue walls. He felt that some height was also needed on the opposite side of the garden, to balance the existing tree, and a semi-mature *Acer japonica*, with complementary plummy-coloured foliage, was the first plant to go in. Vertical accents were also provided by a pair of slender olive trees. These specimens had not been standardized to leave bare trunks, but retained their feathered lower branches, which appeared right from the base. Though not hardy in exposed areas, these should be perfectly happy in a sheltered London town garden. Their silvered leaves catch the light as they twirl in the slightest breeze, and they may even produce olives.

Other architectural plants soon followed. A pair of matching bamboos – *Fargesia*

Left: A trio of *Agave america* in tall containers create a strong vertical accent, and raise the spiky leaves out of the reach of children.

Opposite: An array of foliage shapes and textures and a palette of greens contrast with the intense blue of the walls.

murieliae 'Simba' – were placed just behind the two low walls, the stems arching gracefully into view and showing off to perfection the bright green foliage against the vivid blue paintwork. Several purple-leaved *Berberis thunbergii* 'Harlequin', with wine-red foliage speckled with cream, were added to tone with the acer and provide some height next to the fence. Stephen's planting scheme for the beds flanking the wide central path followed the geometric theme of the garden as a whole. A diverse range of plants was planted in blocks of varying heights and textures. This avoided uniformity and was unconventional in not banking the plants from highest at the back of the bed to lowest at the front.

Solid cubes of box contrasted with silvery domes of *Santolina chamaecyparissus* 'Lambrook Silver' and the strappy foliage of *Iris sibirica* 'Silver Edge'. Foliage colour ranged from deep plums and dark greens to vivid lime-green and silver-grey, and with the addition of *Helichrysum italicum* subsp. *serotinum* (the curry plant) and *Artemisia* 'Powis Castle' the garden will always be scented. Subtle flower colour in soft blues, mauves and purple – toning with the blue walls – will be provided by the irises and *Lavandula angustifolia* 'Hidcote' in early summer, the spires of *Aconitum carmichaelii* 'Arendsii' and shrubby *Caryopteris* × *clandonensis* 'Worcester Gold' taking over the show in the early autumn. Finally, spiky hummocks of *Festuca glauca* were placed at the front of the beds, where the concrete slabs cut into the decking.

Finishing touches were added to bring the whole garden together. Beautifully designed lights with metal half-domes punctuated the front of the water feature and the low blue walls. A decorative mulch of paddle stones was spread among the planting, covering any bare soil. This mulch will in future help to prevent weeds from germinating and to retain moisture in the soil, cutting down the need for watering. Stephen then added three identical tall containers to the terrace area, and planted each one with an *Agave americana*. These instantly added a strong architectural element, and were tall enough to prevent their spiny leaves from getting near a small child's eyes.

Stephen's design managed to fulfil exactly the owners' brief and provide that extra special ingredient that shows in the work of a top garden designer. It achieves the near-impossible task of providing a modern but not minimalist garden. This is a wonderfully sleek space, continuing unbroken the design themes developed in the house. But there is still colour and scent, there is a wide range of plants, and there is an awareness of the practical needs of younger members of the family. It is a thoroughly modern garden – and one that works.

Left: The feathered petals of *Tulipa* 'Black Parrot' glow with rich intensity in the spring sunshine.

Opposite: *Papaver somniferum's* crêpe-paper flowers range from pale lilac to deep mauve and this lovely crushed raspberry pink.

colour *in* planting *and in* landscape features

Stephen Woodhams's scheme for the Hackney garden shows how colour can be employed to stunning effect in an exterior space. The use of colour is an intensely personal thing: it can alter mood, stir up strong emotions and be the cause of harmony or disagreements. Most people have very particular ideas about what they like or dislike when it comes to colour in the garden. What makes one person love the combination of orange and pink, when others can barely tolerate anything more colourful than the addition of a little white to highlight a palette of green foliage?

Where colour combinations are concerned, ideas of good taste are no longer so cut and dried. The old adage that 'blue and green should never be seen' is now regularly ignored in garden design. Painted walls and furniture in various shades of blue and bluish-greens are particularly popular and, when placed against a backdrop of green foliage, create one of the best combinations. The blending of soft pastel shades, so often seen in the blowsy borders of country gardens, is being challenged, particularly in urban gardens, by the use of intense, sometimes clashing, hues. Cities give us the incentive to be brave when putting colours together, and in the increasingly adventurous world of garden design it seems appropriate to be less inhibited in our use of colour.

However, that doesn't mean we should ignore some basic rules. In towns we are surrounded by a kaleidoscope of colour. Bearing in mind that anything visible from the garden constitutes part of the view, it seems wise to consider this when planning our gardens. Much of the background will probably be in the neutral tones of brick, stone, glass and other building materials, as well as the various greens and browns of trees and large shrubs. But your neighbours may have painted their garden shed bright purple, or an overlooking block of flats may have vivid scarlet panels (as does one not far from my own house). These things need to be addressed; ignoring them will not make them disappear from your view, and the best option is to tackle them head on.

If screening isn't possible because of the size and dominance of the feature, it may be best to give in gracefully and design a colour scheme for your own garden that links with,

Left: Black furniture and accessories stand out against the warmth of a wall painted the colour of ripe papaya flesh.

and is complemented by, the immediate surroundings. Choose plants that echo the colours in the environment around you. These don't have to be identical – it's often better to use subtle tones, blending and softening the overall effect. Pick shrubs with mauve flowers, such as lilacs, to grow near the purple shed, and weave varieties of clematis through the branches to give a second burst of flowers.

If the view is relatively neutral, and the impact won't be too great for your neighbours, you can be brave, choose dominant colours and make your own plot stand out. The power of colour is often in the contrast between two or more. A series of concrete walls, rendered and painted in burnt orange and petrol-blue, juxtaposed one against the other, would be the most fantastic backdrop for evergreen foliage interspersed with groups of vivid tangerine *Tulipa* 'Prinses Irene' followed by clumps of *Iris sibirica* and vibrant orange crocosmias and kniphofias. All will be well until the neighbours paint their pergola pink!

When designing the garden, choose the colour and finish of any hard landscaping elements first. There are several things that might affect your choice. In the smallest spaces tie in the exterior colours to those of the interior of the house. Having a unifying theme to all the living areas will allow a seamless flow as you move from one space into the next, giving the illusion of spaciousness. This method of linking the atmosphere of the room directly to the garden is particularly effective in small modern homes, where we often refer to the garden as an outdoor room. If a chrome and glass kitchen/dining area opens straight on to the garden, re-use those materials, and others that echo them, in the terrace and choose planting to complement them.

A complementary colour doesn't have to be a matching one; as usual, there are alternatives and choices to be made. An exact colour match will create the smoothest and most obvious link to the house; a similar shade or tone of the original will unconsciously link the two. But just as effective is a complete contrast, carefully chosen to bring out the best in the interior shade. Very dark brown, the colour of bitter chocolate, is currently

Left: The traditional style of a small terrace is enlivened with a lilac wall.

Below left: A white border is the height of restrained elegance.

Below right: The adage 'blue and green should never be seen' doesn't apply to gardens.

fashionable when combined with pale, pepperminty aqua, dark wenge wood veneers and brushed chrome. Plenty of contrasts here, but the strength of the overall combination lies in how the different colours and textures of the materials used in a scheme bring out the best in one another.

Fashion is as fickle in plant colours as it is in anything else. Current trends have included a penchant for black and near-black plants. The black grass *Ophiopogon planiscapus* 'Nigrescens' has sold like hot cakes from garden centres, but needs careful placing and a contrasting background to be seen effectively. *Tulipa* 'Queen of Night' is a deliciously deep shade, as close to a black tulip as we have been able to produce. Both of these examples work brilliantly with the vibrant contrast of acid green euphorbias to set them off perfectly.

In a small space a good way to approach the choice of a colour theme is to choose one dominant colour, then add a couple of tones of that colour and something to act as a sharp contrast. Remember that, whatever else you choose, green foliage will probably be providing the main bulk of colour in the garden. Of course, foliage doesn't come only in green – you could have an area of plants with bronze, red and purple leaves, or an entire section of silver and grey-leaved plants. But most of us like to combine and contrast different foliage colour with a range of greens to add interest and variety to the planting.

Left: A design by Paul Cooper incorporates screens that can be illuminated with different colours and images for a constantly changing effect.

Opposite: Subtle lighting creates a welcoming glow for a twilight meal, and highlights a piece of sculpture.

lighting: *the* garden at night

Lighting can often look out of place in a large expanse of country garden. The restraint imposed by lack of space, however, actually seems to enhance the use of lighting in small city gardens. Look up at the night sky: in large cities the sky is never velvety black as it is out in the country. The warm amber glow is caused by the reflection of millions of lights from towns that never sleep. This is something city dwellers are all familiar with; it takes a visit to the countryside to remind us just how dark the dark can be. Lighting the exterior space at night is something townies are comfortable with, whereas in the country a luminous garden stands out like a sore thumb.

The use of light is a compelling part of modern garden design. City gardens with minimal planting schemes often come to life with just a couple of expertly placed lights. The small town garden and lighting were made for each another. Illuminating the garden will increase the amount of time you'll spend out there: the garden becomes a true extension of the home, with summer days out of doors drifting into balmy nights. With the addition of a heater, this continental café-life need not end with the sudden drop in temperature in the autumn.

But lighting outside needs as much thought as we give it within our homes. Think carefully about the positioning of each light-fitting. Planning on paper is a start, but the placing may need to be adjusted several times to get exactly the right effect. Don't be tempted to blast the whole area with wattage; subtlety speaks volumes and (as is so often the case) less is frequently more. The aim is not to illuminate the garden to look like the land of the midnight sun, but to create intriguing shadows and soft, mysterious tones, and to highlight special features so that they look even more striking.

The range of different forms of exterior lighting has never been better, with increasingly imaginative alternatives appearing all the time. It's no longer as straightforward as sticking a spotlight on a stake into the ground. There are still plenty of traditional-looking lanterns and porch lights available, but some of the innovations for modern and minimalist garden lighting are among the most thought-provoking and ground-breaking of all areas of contemporary garden design.

Clever use of lighting among the plants can be especially effective. The intense green of illuminated leaves stands out against the night and, when lit from below, the branches of shrubs and small trees create a sculptural tracery as effective as any piece of art. Keep the light source soft; harsh spotlights can create really 'hot' areas and looming dark shadows. Be adventurous: conceal lighting in the crown of trees, wrap tiny fairy lights

Left: Spotlights glow through gravel to mark the edge of a path.

Opposite: Dress the garden for special occasions. Here, a box ball is draped with fairy-light netting.

around topiary and thread spotlights through dark corners of the borders to create hidden areas of magical illumination. You can also buy coloured lights to shine among your plants or for use underwater. By all means give them a try, but the garden can quickly resemble a stage or film set. Unless there's a particular effect you're after, you may prefer not to re-create a *son et lumière* show in your own garden.

Don't use exterior lighting solely for effect. It's obviously sensible to make sure steps and passageways are well lit. Security lighting is often neglected, but it could make all the difference in deterring an opportunistic intruder, and is particularly useful in gardens outside basement flats.

It's worth mentioning that as a responsible city dweller you should consider the neighbours when choosing where to place lights. Remember that in a small town environment what we do affects other people around us. The constant glare of an upward-facing spotlight could be very unpleasant for someone on the receiving end, and the cause of a long-running disagreement. There are many companies offering a complete lighting service, planning and installing everything from start to finish, but at a price.

Alternatively, scan magazines, search the pages of design books and manufacturers' catalogues and design your own scheme. When it comes to the practicalities, however, it's unwise to try to save money by trying to do it yourself: electricity is strictly for the experts.

Of course, lighting up the night isn't solely reliant on electric power. Solar-powered lights are becoming increasingly popular and are much more environmentally friendly, harnessing the power of the sun and storing it to use later in the day. Oil lanterns are long-lasting and give a lovely light. But for the ultimate romantic atmosphere, candlelight is still the best. Storm lanterns are large, producing plenty of light, and practical when it's a bit breezy. Nightlights dotted about randomly between the plants, or lined up like a battalion of tiny torches, are exquisitely pretty, bringing a fairytale atmosphere to any garden.

Above left: Water droplets glisten in the sunlight.

Above middle: A sleek, modern fountain is attached to a turquoise blue wall.

Above right: The serenity of a circular pool of still water.

Opposite left: Lead is fashioned into an elegant water feature, topped with a gilded ball.

Opposite middle: Vivid blue walls flank a mirrored waterfall to spectacular effect.

Opposite right: A tiered sculpture forms a tower of flowing water.

the water garden

Water is the elixir of life, and incorporating this element into our garden designs brings vitality, movement, sound and serenity. A garden without water can often feel as if something is missing, and it's now so easy to install any sort of feature, from the simplest pond in a pot to a scaled-down version of the extravaganzas at Chatsworth House. Small spaces are no less able to benefit from the positive sensations that water instils, so be bold in your plans and bring its benefits into your own town garden.

Left: Even a small water feature can add movement to the garden.

Opposite: Bubbling water breaks up the still surface of a long narrow rill.

Below left: A tiny courtyard is entirely filled with slate slabs over water.

We are all aware of the importance of water in our life; it is essential to our survival, important to our wellbeing and a crucial part of our recreation. We human beings seem to be drawn to water, perhaps as a result of spending the first nine months of our existence in liquid. Watch babies gurgling in the bath, children splashing in puddles and the scene at the local swimming pool or on the beach. Throughout life water sustains, fascinates and delights us.

Bringing water into a garden often makes it seem complete. For many of us the pleasures of gardening encompass a collection of ideal pursuits – being outside, enjoying the weather or the passing of the seasons, tending plants, entertaining friends, watching our children play or simply relaxing – and water enhances most of these experiences. Water is also extremely sensuous: who can resist the temptation to draw their hand through the silken surface of a still pool?

Small gardens are perfectly suited to the introduction of water. Often the whole design can be planned around water. But even if you install just the simplest of water features in a pot, you can enjoy watching the light playing on the surface, try a couple of the wide selection of aquatic plants and encourage more wildlife into your patch.

There are many artists working with water to create sculptures that shimmer with its movement, but you can produce similar effects in your own garden. Build a free-standing mirrored wall with a concealed length of plastic pipe fixed to the top edge. The resulting sheets of water slipping down the glassy surface can be hypnotic to watch. Pump water through a group of slender hollow tubes cut off at different levels like organ pipes and it will gently flow back down the sides, creating a quiet but effective display.

Sometimes the gentlest features are the most effective. Still pools bring serenity and a calming atmosphere into a garden, and work particularly well in formal or symmetrical spaces, whether traditional or modern in style. Moving water can take many forms, from the simplest single water spout to an elaborate tiered fountain. Movement brings different pleasures and can create a huge

Above: A canal of dark still water crosses the width of a lushly planted garden.

Right: Circular planters float on a pond, with an illuminated Perspex fountain creating a strong focal point.

Opposite: The smooth sheen of water slides over a glass sphere by Allison Armour-Wilson.

range of visual effects. It can be exhilarating – the sparkling water droplets of a fine spray can appear to effervesce in sunlight, and the foamy bubbles created by a jet of water hitting a still pool beneath produce turmoil on the calm surface. But movement can also be soothing: the gentle sheen of water falling in an unbroken sheet down a glass or polished metal surface is mesmerizing. The sounds that these various types of movement create can be as varied as the visual effects.

Children are particularly drawn to water, though it seems to bring out the playful side in all of us. It's a challenge to design a water feature that will be both stunning and safe for the kids. But if you do introduce a water feature – no matter how small – into a garden with small children, it is imperative that you put safety before sensation. Luckily there are some good ways to make a water garden safe as well as attractive. Place a metal grid just below or level with the surface of the water. Choose a simple gurgling pebble pool or a smooth object with water slipping over its surface: both will fascinate children. But if you want to have more movement, make sure the water from a wall fountain or spout falls into a covered reservoir.

a water garden, *designed by* **Paul Cooper**

Left: The spectacular water cascade at Chatsworth in Derbyshire.

Opposite: Although smaller in scale, the water curtain in Henley also sparkles with movement.

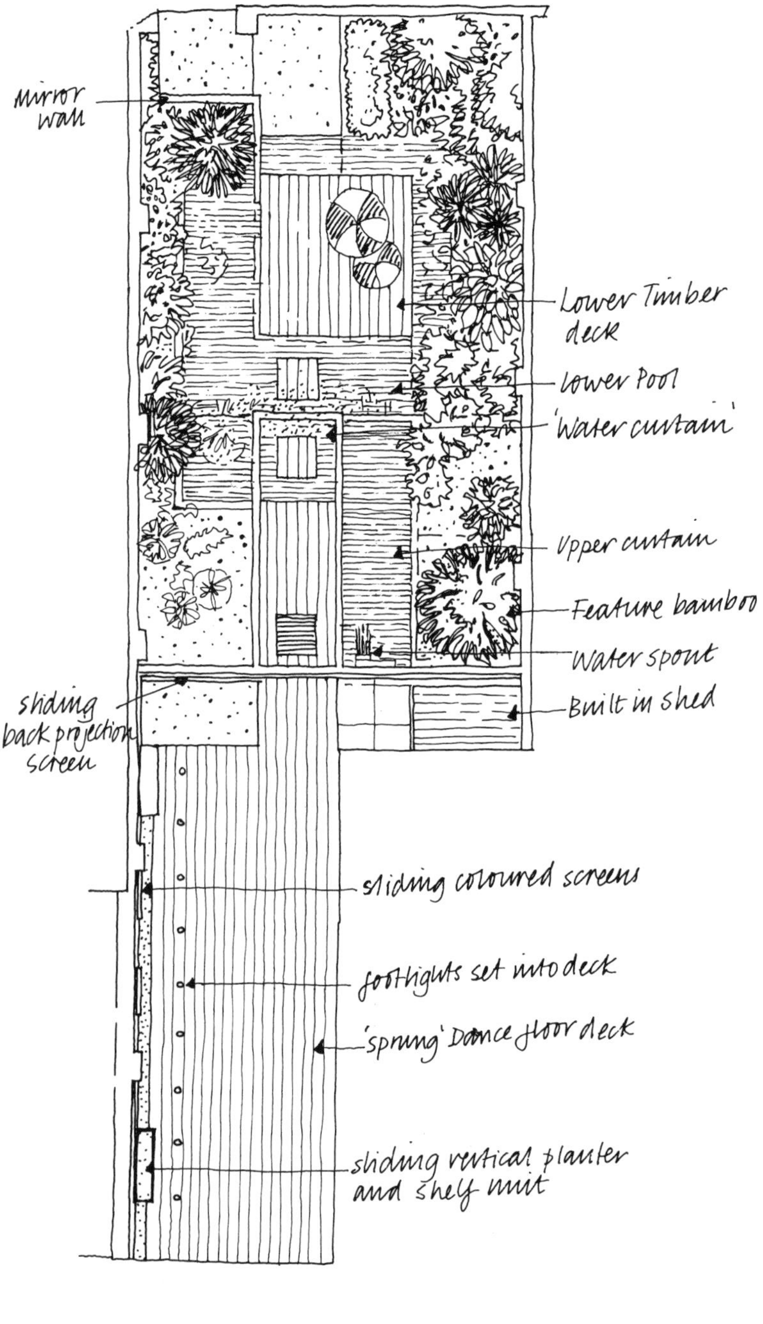

Mirror wall
Lower Timber deck
Lower Pool
'Water curtain'
Upper curtain
Feature bamboo
Water spout
Built in shed
sliding back projection screen
sliding coloured screens
footlights set into deck
'spring' Dance floor deck
sliding vertical planter and shelf unit

Sometimes the problems that affect your garden are completely beyond your control. The small town garden in picturesque Henley-on-Thames chosen for this case study was already quite pretty, if rather conventional, and contained some well-established plants. The problem lay not within the garden, but outside its boundaries. Just over the wall at the bottom of the garden there used to be an orchard. Today a vast supermarket car park, and beyond that the enormous supermarket itself, have taken the place of billowing blossom and luscious fruits. The sound of car ignitions and the beeping of juggernauts reversing to deliver their goods was constant, and with the supermarket open all hours, there was little respite from the noise.

Visually the supermarket could be thought an eyesore. But the garden owners had decided not to dwell on the negative aspects, but to try to appreciate the vitality and hustle and bustle of city life. As a bonus, a mature sycamore tree screened out much of the view, and the garden was a couple of metres higher than the level of the car park. This meant that although the garden afforded a clear view of people pushing trolleys to their cars, the people themselves were unable to see into the garden.

This plot was typical of many small gardens in Britain, tucked behind a late Victorian terraced house with no direct access from the road. At the rear, however, a narrow passageway

Left: Contrasting materials are combined to add interest and variety to a small space.

Opposite: Movable brightly coloured screens glide smoothly on wheels along a track, giving maximum flexibility.

ran along the back of all the gardens in the street. The shape of the garden was rectangular, with one corner notched out by the kitchen conversion, which protruded from the back of the house. This created a narrower strip of rather shady garden outside the kitchen door. The owners were keen to improve their plot, and had an interest in plants – though the tatty scrap of lawn suggested otherwise – but were desperately in need of inspiration. At present this was a traditional-looking garden, and rather dull for a lively young couple with plenty of interests. One of them is a keen dancer and jokingly suggested incorporating a dance area. The other was particularly keen on the attractive, low-level, red-brick walls that surrounded the garden and didn't want them hidden by climbing plants. They both agreed that something had to be done about the noise so that they could really start to enjoy their under-used garden.

It was accepted that getting rid of the source of the din was impossible and what was needed was some form of distraction. The pleasant burbling and splashing sounds of moving water would draw attention away from the traffic noise, so it seemed a good idea to try to incorporate some sort of water feature in the new garden.

This couple would be fun clients to work with; they, and the garden, needed a designer who would deal with the noise issue, loved working with water and could come up with something unusual with an extra twist. Paul Cooper (see Designers' Biographies, page 122) was without question the man for the job. A highly respected, cutting-edge designer with a string of awards to his name, Paul regularly produces ideas that no one else would think of. Strongly visual, his gardens are pure theatre. Sometimes they resemble a sculptural installation, the entire space becoming a work of art. Above all Paul's work is imbued with a sense of humour and a certain irreverence.

At the first meeting, various thoughts about how to deal with the noise problem were bandied about. Paul agreed that the use of water would be ideal as a distraction and suggested that he might introduce two or more different water sounds. It all seemed very promising and, after listening to the owners' wish list and taking measurements of the plot, Paul headed for his studio.

This plot was typical of many small gardens in Britain, tucked behind a late Victorian terraced house with no direct access from the road.

Following a period of contemplation, and a visit to the remarkable water gardens at Chatsworth House for further inspiration, Paul was ready to unveil the finished design, He had produced a three-dimensional working model rather than the usual flatplan. This was wise, given the complexity of the design; the clients were expecting water, but what they got was much more than your average water feature. The garden was to be transformed: the design made the most of the vertical plane, and many unusual features would guide the eye upwards. With this much excitement crammed into a small space, who would notice a car park?

The garden was to be divided into two main sections. A properly sprung deck would create a dance floor outside the kitchen, which could also be furnished with a table and chairs to double as an eating area. A large part of the section furthest from the house would be entirely covered with water, which would in turn be covered by metal grids, to give the impression of quite literally walking on water. Specimen plants were to be placed in gravel-covered beds between the two sections. Another smaller area of decking was positioned towards the end of the garden, surrounded by further beds packed with planting.

The details of Paul's design made it utterly unique. This was to be primarily a water garden, and Paul had succeeded in introducing the different sounds of running water he had spoken about in the initial meeting. Water was to flow from a minimal wall fountain on the back of the shed wall into the top pool. It then flowed over three narrow slabs of slate, spaced equally along the length of the wider lower pool, from where it was pumped back up to the wall fountain. But there was a trick up Paul's sleeve. A simple wooden vertical structure was to be constructed where the two sections of the garden met. At first sight this was simply a contemporary-looking pergola, something to stretch the garden up towards the sky. But at the end of the structure Paul had devised a water curtain, and when it was turned on, a sheet of water fell in fine threads of liquid to the pool below. It was a magical effect, particularly when the sunlight caught the water or when the wind blew the curtain to

Left: The vertical vegetable garden is filled with ornamental cabbages and parsley.

Opposite: A strategically placed mirror sets off the white-bloomed stems of *Rubus thibetanus* 'Silver Fern'.

one side. Interaction between the garden and the user is an important aspect of Paul's work. Here you had a choice either to walk around the side of the curtain to avoid getting wet or to go straight through it. On a hot day the second option would be a deliciously cooling experience, and a sure-fire hit with children.

However, it was with some of the other design elements that Paul had really given his imagination full rein. Vertical sliding screens in different colours were fitted with wheels that ran along a narrow runner at the base of the wall surrounding the dance floor. These could be moved at will to produce constantly changing effects. A large white divider turned out to be a back-projection screen. This could completely block the supermarket from view while the house owners were dining outdoors, and at night images of paintings, landscapes, flowers or family holiday photos could transport them anywhere in the world. But the biggest surprise for the unsuspecting visitor was an industrial electric fan set into the decking beneath a grille just at the point where the two sections of the garden met. The motor was to be linked to a movement sensor which switched itself on as someone walked over the grille, providing a sudden whoosh of air and possibly causing the same effect the subway vent had on Marilyn Monroe's famous white dress.

The weedy lawn was the first thing to go, but the tedious work of excavating the site was slowed by lack of proper access to the garden. It took several days to dig down to the necessary level entirely by hand, with many barrow-loads of soil to go in the skip. Once the profile of the land was correctly shaped, brick retaining walls could be built to create strong sides to the pond areas. Large sheets of butyl pond-liner were laid over a thick bed of sand to stop sharp objects from puncturing the liner. The remaining walls and red-brick pond edges were completed before any excess liner was trimmed away.

The sprung dance floor was installed directly on top of the existing paviours, using layers of rubber sandwiched between them and the timber decking. At the end of the garden the rest of the decking formed the square terrace, which was to be bordered on two sides by water. On the back wall of the kitchen a small

but perfectly formed shed was built. This would house garden tools and bikes, which were supported vertically by hooks in order to save space. This was also the place for the switches and controls for the water pumps and the electric fan. A low-level wall continued from the back of the shed – which was painted a fresh, clear turquoise – on to which a beautifully sleek water spout was fixed.

The vertical structure in the centre of the garden was constructed entirely from exterior-grade marine ply to ensure longevity, and the pipes to carry the water to the water curtain were run up to the top along grooves in the timbers. The curtain 'rail' was simply a length of plastic pipe, drilled at regular intervals along its length, which was then fixed to the horizontal beam at the end of the structure.

Pumps were installed in each pond to circulate the water, one in the higher pond and three in the lower – including one to pump the water up to the curtain. It was crucial to the success of the garden that the pumps were correctly balanced. At one stage the water pressure was too great in the top pool, causing water to gush over the slates – which were fixed at three points at the edge of the top pool – into the lower pond. But with a bit of fine-tuning, the correct levels were achieved and it was time to move on.

With all the workings of the water garden in place, the metal grids could be lowered on to the ponds. These were made from galvanized steel and were incredibly heavy. It took several men to cut them to shape, spray the cut ends with protective anti-rust galvanizing spray and lay them slowly in place. But before they could go down, there was an important job to do.

Paul wanted to bring in something living to soften the hard lines of the grilles and had chosen a couple of aquatic plants. *Iris versicolor* 'Kermesina' is an American water iris with stunning deep purple flowers in June or July and slender, strap-like leaves. As a contrast, *Schoenoplectus lacustris* subsp. *tabernaemontani* 'Zebrinus' has spiky leaves, striped like a zebra, as well as an unpronounceable name. They were both planted in plastic baskets, which were filled with aquatic compost, topped up with a thick layer of gravel and gently lowered into the pond.

The complex landscaping and mechanics of Paul's design were complete; it was time to get the plants in. A magnificent bamboo, *Phyllostachys nigra*, was given pride of place next to the wall fountain, its foliage contrasting wonderfully with the blue wall. To set it off perfectly, a layer of pale gravel was raked around its base. Three large *Elaeagnus* × *ebbingei* were planted by the end wall to

Opposite: Water splashes over the slates into the lower pool.

Right: A smooth arc of water flows from the wall fountain.

provide a dense protective shield from the noise beyond. A ghostly *Rubus thibetanus* 'Silver Fern' was also positioned at the end of the garden, this time directly in front of an acrylic mirror. This had the effect of beefing up the number of white-bloomed stems and gave the illusion that the planting area had doubled in size. The leaves of *Berberis* × *media* 'Red Jewel' toned perfectly with the brick walls, and the pure white, cheery flowers of *Anemone* × *hybrida* 'Honorine Jobert' danced above a group of thymes that Paul had planted beneath another metal grid. They would soon fill out to cover the walkway with a carpet of fragrant foliage.

Paul encouraged the owners to put their own stamp on the garden immediately. The movable screens around the dance floor needed painting and Paul insisted they choose the colours themselves. The results were just as he had hoped – modern, slightly off-the-wall tones, so to speak, that justified his faith in their good taste. A couple of large square terracotta containers had been purchased to dress the gravel area between the dance floor and the water. Again, on Paul's suggestion, the owners were to choose the planting combination. Once more, the result was a brilliant success: the reddish leaves of *Panicum virgatum* 'Squaw' and the maroon-toned, squirrel-tailed flowers of *Pennisetum alopecuroïdes* 'Hameln' mingled with *Sedum* 'Ruby Glow', which spilled over the edge in the most ravishing, slightly dishevelled fashion.

As a final touch Paul created a vertical vegetable garden on another movable screen near the dance floor. Young seedlings could be nurtured beneath a protective Perspex cover, and a row of herbs was ready for picking just by the kitchen door.

One of the main advantages of having a small garden is that the total effect of a scheme is not diluted, as it often can be when lost within a large space. Paul's cutting-edge design for this small town garden is totally uncompromising in its clarity of vision. It reflects his own sense of humour and the open minds of the owners, and is absolutely crammed with originality. Everyone agreed that this was more than a garden: it was a total sensory experience.

Left: The sound of moving water can be gently soothing.

Opposite: A greater volume of water will screen out unwanted noise as it splashes on to a still pool.

noise *and* pollution

As the owners of the garden in Henley soon discovered, noise pollution is a major problem for city dwellers; creating your own urban paradise is hard when you can't hear yourself think. The constant drone of traffic is something you become so accustomed to that when you are somewhere really quiet, the silence is almost tangible. Other familiar urban noises – the din of building sites, circling police helicopters, pubs emptying at night, reversing lorries and screeching motorbike couriers – impinge even on the background growling of the cars. Those of us who live in towns need to find some respite from the unrelenting cacophony of sounds. The garden is the perfect place to bring some serenity back into your life, but to do that it's imperative to try to create a calm, if not quiet, atmosphere.

Planting a living barrier to act as a buffer against undesirable noise is sometimes advised, and a screening of densely foliaged hedges or shrubs is often suggested. It's questionable whether plants have any measurable physical effect in noise reduction, and unlikely that they can actually 'absorb' it. But they give the psychological impression of doing just that. Perhaps the feeling of separateness and protection that a screen of greenery gives helps to foster the illusion that the sound is deadened.

It's generally a far better plan to use distraction: create your own pleasing sounds within the garden and the exterior noise won't be so obvious. Water is perfect for this – the soothing effect of a gently flowing wall fountain can transport you to a citrus-filled, Mediterranean courtyard; the sparkling sound of water cascading from a spout into a pool below may remind you of the surf; and the bubbling of a pebble fountain conjures up images of a rural brook. Unfortunately, many water features are more reminiscent of a flushing lavatory or an irritating running tap, thereby adding to the unwanted sounds. Some adjustment to the water outlet or the rate of flow is usually all that's needed to resolve the problem.

City noise can add to the stress of urban life, but there is another form of pollution that affects town dwellers in particular: atmospheric pollution, from traffic fumes and industrial activity, is ultimately a far more sinister threat. Trees provide a vital lifeline for towns, and Britain's cities are thankfully far greener than many equivalents abroad, but things could still be improved. Our urban trees are such a vital resource that many are safeguarded by protection orders. However, those that are not are frequently cut down without any plan to plant a replacement and in this way the number of trees is gradually depleted. I feel that if you can incorporate a tree in your garden – and many are suitable for even very small gardens – you almost have a duty to do so. This is simply forward-

thinking good sense. Trees absorb carbon dioxide and produce oxygen – they are the lungs of a city and therefore future generations depend on us to keep planting young saplings now.

Some plants can suffer quite badly from the effects of pollution, but luckily there are others that will thrive in the heart of the big smoke. The London plane often springs to mind when city trees are mentioned, but of course it's far too large for most domestic gardens and is primarily a street tree. The hawthorn family is pollution-tolerant, and *Crataegus laevigata* 'Paul's Scarlet', with its clusters of rosy-red flowers, is a good choice for a small space. Alternatively, members of the prunus, pyrus and malus families are also excellent contenders for gardens on busy main roads. Hollies are tough plants for this situation, and *Ilex* × *altaclerensis* 'Belgica Aurea' has a compact, columnar shape with cream edges to the glossy green leaves and plenty of scarlet berries in the autumn.

For something a little smaller, try a lilac: *Syringa vulgaris* 'Madame Lemoine' is a popular variety, with plumes of headily scented, white flowers towards the end of tspring. Buddleias are also pollution-tolerant and will attract butterflies into your garden. Smaller still are the evergreen skimmias. *Skimmia* × *confusa* 'Kew Green' has fragrant white flowers atop its dark green leaves. Other good evergreens include members of the elaeagnus, euonymus and sarcococca families. If it's perennials you're after, there is a wide selection to choose from. One of my favourites is *Astrantia major* 'Hadspen Blood', with diminutive but devastatingly attractive plummy-red flowers. As a bonus it will also cope with the semi-shade conditions found in many town gardens.

Left: Vertical timber structures give architectural 'bones' to a small garden.

Opposite: A metal arch smothered with clematis brings the atmosphere of a traditional English country garden to the heart of the city.

using *the* vertical

Small gardens can be incredibly restrictive in terms of useful space. A regular trick of top designers is to extend the garden by using the vertical dimension: the area above ground level is so often completely forgotten. It helps to think of your garden in three-dimensional terms – not as a flat piece of ground, but as a space that includes the air above it. If you can't spread out, you can at least go up.

On a practical note, it's wise to check the local planning regulations on erecting structures in the garden. You probably won't need planning permission, but there may be restrictions relating to the height of walls and other structural elements. In any case, it is simply good manners to show a certain amount of neighbourly awareness when constructing anything that may affect those around you.

Paul Cooper found myriad ways of using the vertical space in the Henley garden. You may prefer to use just one, but this is still preferable to restricting the design of the garden to the horizontal plane. One of the most traditional ways of adding height is with a pergola, usually a simple timber structure consisting of upright and crossing beams. This can be updated, as it was in Henley, by a very slight alteration to the design. Rose arches and tripods are also ways to incorporate vertical wooden features. These are all wonderful supports for climbers, if it is your aim to make the most of the airspace for growing plants, and are often attractive design elements in their unadorned state.

Stone columns add stature to a garden and work well in a formal space, but there's no reason (other than the restriction of cost) that these couldn't be made of Perspex or galvanized sheet steel. Updating a classic feature in this way gives you all the benefits of a style that has lasted thousands of years, with a modern twist. Other metals can also be crafted into beautiful structures. Copper, which is best treated with varnish or lacquer, can be fashioned into an obelisk to create height in the middle of a border or stand alone as a feature sculpture. Water features can also be used to extend the space vertically. Wall-spouts, water sculptures and fountains can all add interest at eye level. Tall containers of varying heights can be constructed to stand in a shallow pond and be filled with planting.

Varying the planting levels is one of the best ways to liven up a garden. Raised beds are the simplest way to achieve this, but the effect will be more interesting if you can introduce several different heights and shapes of bed, juxtaposed one against the other. Build up one section of the garden in this way and you will avoid the uniformity that often goes with borders at ground level backed by a wall or fence. You can also create outdoor shelving systems to hold an assortment of containers.

Fill small pots with a collection of alpines so that you can enjoy their ravishing flowers at close quarters without having to bend down. Alternatively, use larger pots and cram them with cheerful annuals for a full-on blast of colour. Place trailing plants on the higher shelves and allow them to cascade down the side. This type of tiered planting is particularly good for edible plants when positioned outside the kitchen door. Use it for growing herbs and small salad crops, such as rocket. Pop the dwarf tomato 'Tumbler' into a pot at the top of the stack where the fruits can hang over the edge.

Climbing plants are perfect for guiding the eye upwards. In a small space you may want to avoid anything too vigorous. *Solanum jasminoïdes* 'Album' is a beautiful plant, smothered in starry white flowers at the end of summer. But if you don't want your climber to reach more than 6m (20ft) up the back wall of the house, it's best avoided. With such a wide range of climbing plants, there is something for every eventuality. There are many good climbers for shade: a huge diversity of ivies, the stalwart self-clinging *Hydrangea anomala* subsp. *petiolaris*, *Clematis* 'Nelly Moser', which retains the dusky pink of its saucer-shaped blooms far better in the shade, and *Rosa* 'Madame Alfred Carrière', with its softly shaped white flowers. *Euonymous* 'Silver Queen' is best known as a good, low-growing, evergreen filler, but this variegated beauty – tolerant of sun or shade – will also snake its way up a conveniently placed wall to form a compact covering of foliage.

There are so many good climbers for sunny walls that it will be hard to make your choice. Most roses and wisterias prefer a position in full sun, and also partial to basking in the heat is the honeysuckle *Lonicera periclymenum* 'Graham Thomas', which releases the full intensity of its sweet scent on summer evenings. Clematis push their heads up into the light, but prefer some cool shade at their feet. *Passiflora caerulea*, the passion flower, is currently a fashionable plant and its exotic looks are perfect for a garden with a tropical feel. Wall shrubs make good vertical interest plants; *Ceanothus griseus* var. *horizontalis* 'Yankee Point' is a compact variety, which will fan itself out against a low wall if given a few judicious nips and tucks.

Above left: With a purpose-built compost bin, mini greenhouse and cloche, functional items can become a pleasure to look at.

Above right: Vegetables are not only tasty but beautiful too.

Opposite left: A reclaimed brick barbecue provides a permanent outdoor cooking area.

Opposite right: The dusky bloom of black grapes.

the **edible garden**

Nowadays we are all increasingly aware of the importance of knowing where what we eat comes from. Living in a city is no barrier to growing your own edible plants. The trick in a small space is knowing how to combine the practical with the visual, to create a garden that provides tasty produce and a beautiful space in which to relax. It's so rewarding to eat what you have grown yourself and picked only moments before. Once you've experienced the freshness and flavour of home-grown fruit and vegetables, there's no turning back.

Left: Vines can fruit well in a sunny sheltered spot.

Below: Herbs thrive in a raised bed on a rooftop garden.

Opposite: Simple metal containers overflow with Tomato 'Tumbler' and Strawberry 'Eros'.

What could be nicer than stepping out of your back door and harvesting a lettuce still dripping with dew from your own garden? A quick rinse and the leaves are ready to eat, fresh, crisp and sweet. This might seem like a dream to town gardeners, but historically city dwellers devoted whatever meagre space they had outside their houses entirely to growing edible plants; only the very rich could afford to waste space on ornamental plants. Today we are turning once again to making our gardens productive as well as beautiful, and there are many ways to make the most of a limited space.

One option is to incorporate edibles throughout, designing a flower garden specifically to include fruit and vegetables among the ornamental plants. Alternatively, try a twist on the traditional potager; this name for an ornamental vegetable garden is derived from the French word *potage*, meaning 'soup'. As well as providing the ingredients for a soup, these kitchen gardens resembled one, the mixture of different vegetables, salads and fruits all jostling for space in one place. Potagers were often laid out on formal lines, with small box hedges marking the divisions between the beds. This created individual planting compartments to be filled with a vast range of vegetables and herbs. The result was both practical and decorative, the colourful mix of varieties and symmetry of the designs making them very easy on the eye.

Even if the garden is primarily an ornamental one, edible plants can still be grown very successfully among the shrubs and perennials. Plant parsley as an edging to a flower bed, and include ruby chard in a 'hot' planting scheme for its stunning blood-red stems. The feathery

Left: A herb border containing artemisia, mentha, *Anthriscus cerefolium*, lovage and a selection of thymus makes a decorative and aromatic edging.

Opposite: A variety of galvanized metal pots containing herbs and ornamentals are within easy reach of the kitchen.

foliage of bronze-leaved fennel looks wonderful grown with herbaceous perennials and grasses, and the glaucous blue of certain types of cabbage is a rare and highly prized leaf colour in any plant. Fan-trained fruit trees can clothe a wall as attractively as any climber, smothered with blossom in spring and heavy with fruit by the autumn.

For a movable feast, plant salads, vegetables and herbs in containers. Choose pots that suit the style of the garden – galvanized metal for sleek modern spaces, terracotta or timber Versailles planters in more traditional plots. Don't forget the space above ground level: some varieties of dwarf tomato are particularly well suited to growing in hanging baskets, provided they're not allowed to dry out. Higher still, why not grow vegetables on roof gardens: use large planters, keep them well watered by installing a simple irrigation system and they'll thrive in the good light. Window-boxes make excellent mini vegetable plots: plant fast-growing rocket or 'Little Gem' lettuces, or pack the box with a selection of herbs for easy access outside a kitchen window. Strawberries – particularly little wild strawberries – are a perfect fruit for small areas and look lovely all year round. They can be grown in special terracotta towers, in purpose-made self-assembly stacking pots, or individually dotted around ornamental plants.

The best thing about incorporating edibles in a small garden is their flexibility. If you fancy a complete change next year, grow a different range of vegetables or salads, which will also help to avoid the build-up of soil-borne diseases. Get the bones of the garden right with structural evergreen planting to hold the design together and then play with the vast range of varieties available. Above all, enjoy the delicious results!

CASE STUDY

an edible garden *designed by* Bunny Guinness

Left: A corner of the potager at the Old Rectory in Sudborough, Bunny's inspiration for the edible small garden.

Opposite: Strategically placed willow arches backed with mirror panels hint at areas of garden beyond, waiting to be explored.

At first sight this garden in St Albans in Hertfordshire seemed to have very little going for it. It formed an awkward L-shape tacked on as an afterthought to a newly built house. Like many recent building projects, the house was squeezed on to a plot that had once been part of someone else's back garden. There was a steeply raised area banked up along one side of the property, creating an uncomfortably narrow passageway against the wall of the house. This side of the garden was dominated by a row of semi-mature leylandii trees backing on to wooded common land. The result was a dark, useless space with a few rather forlorn-looking shrubs dotted about. The other arm of the L-shape formed the main part of the garden and was accessed from the house by patio doors. This area linked with the passageway and was covered for the most part in crazy paving, with some shrubs and a couple of large conifers tucked into the edges of the garden.

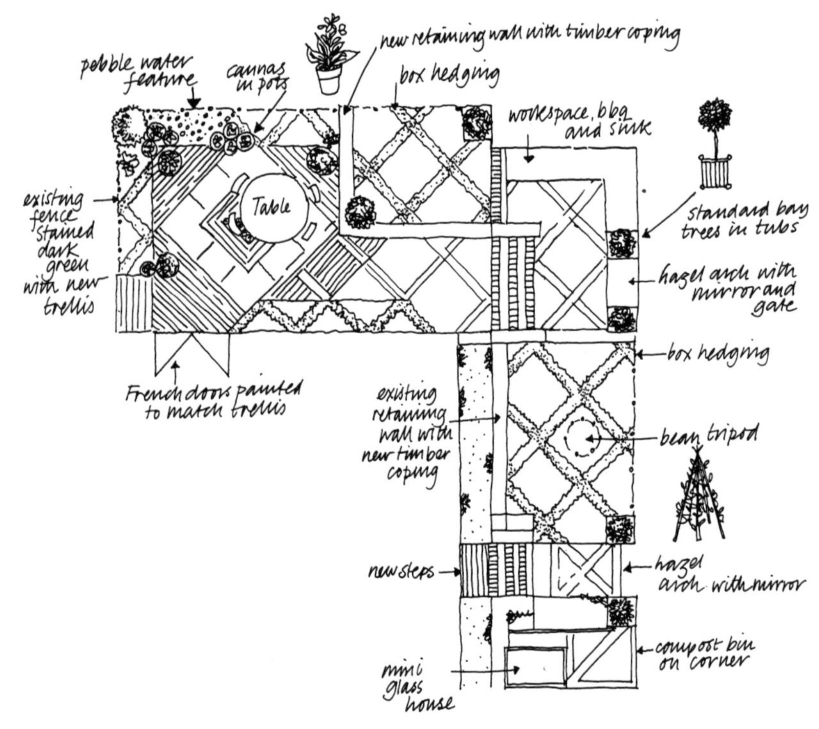

The neighbouring buildings and gardens created additional problems: a tall blue pergola on the other side of the fence was clearly visible, and there was the potential problem of being overlooked if too many of the taller plants were removed. The owners are keen cooks and the tatty old barbecue had seen plenty of action. The brief here was to create a garden that brought this love of food and cookery to the fore by making the space productive in terms of vegetables and herbs. In addition, it had to be an attractive, child-friendly space for entertaining friends and family, with room to indulge the barbecue bug and party well into the night.

This was a demanding brief for any designer. It needed someone who could come up with a visually attractive solution for this awkward plot, while having a real understanding of the practical aspects of growing edible plants and the needs of children and a sociable couple who love to cook. Enter Bunny Guinness (see Designers' Biographies, page 122), who, as a five-times gold medal-winning designer at the Chelsea Flower Show, mother of two, keen cook and all-round super-gardener, was just the person for the job.

Left: Changes of level draw the eye to the built-in outdoor kitchen area.

Opposite left: Carved pineapple finials provide the finishing touch.

Opposite below: Wavy trellis topped with woven willow is a novel twist on a conventional design.

Bunny had several meetings with the owners, discussing their particular requirements, and getting to know their likes and dislikes. The garden was carefully measured and photographed, and Bunny went off to let it all sink in before commencing work on the design. What she came up with is an incredibly imaginative use of a difficult space. The design, a contemporary take on the traditional potager, addresses all the problems and has found effective solutions. Bunny combined ornamental plants with edibles, reshaped existing trees and gave the whole garden structure a framework of diagonal lines in the form of paving detail and low box hedging criss-crossing the small space.

The first step was to clear the garden. The leylandii trees were the first to go. Once they were down, the small plot immediately opened up, metres of space were gained and light flooded in. One is often reluctant to make such drastic changes to a garden, not least because it involves killing plants. But being ruthless is often the only way to bring out the true potential of a space; sometimes you just have to take a deep breath and do it. One of the two large conifers was also removed, but the other, in the opposite corner of the garden, was transformed from a conical shape into a standard by having all its lower branches stripped away. This was a clever way of retaining the height of the tree, to provide screening from the neighbours' upper windows, while clearing the space beneath the newly formed crown. The result was a more formally shaped tree that fitted in perfectly with the style of the new garden.

Clearing can be extremely therapeutic, and lifting the crazy paving, which came up easily, was a cathartic experience. Landscaping the plot followed. The top of the raised area to the side of the house was levelled and steps cut into it to give the appearance of widening the restrictive passageway and to allow access on to the raised space. To the rear of the house a large, mid-height raised bed was created, butting up to the existing raised section in the corner of the L-shape. In this way a series of interesting changes of level was developed, making maximum use of the available space.

Plenty of thought went into the choice of landscaping materials. Large, square stone paving slabs were laid diagonally across the garden, divided by narrow rows of stone setts. These lines of setts were picked up exactly in the lines formed by the tiny box plants that would soon grow together to form solid dividing hedges. A coping of wood was added, raising the height of the existing retaining walls of the raised area and creating a useful place to sit. Panels of unusual trellis, constructed with wavy strips of wood and painted Bunny's favourite shade of blue, quickly went up around the boundary.

Although at first sight this is a garden rooted in traditional style, much of the detail is thoroughly modern.

Above right: Among the edibles, companion planting of marigolds will attract beneficial insects that help to control unwanted pests.

But the *pièce de résistance* was the outdoor kitchen, designed for serious entertaining and constructed by a master craftsman in a deceptively simple, rusticated style from blocks of heavy oak; the worktops were solid enough to last a lifetime. A state-of-the-art gas barbecue hob was concealed until needed under a lift-up worktop. Set into the unit was a chunky drawer for storing cooking implements, and a deep sink for rinsing off freshly harvested salad leaves. Bunny dressed the area with terracotta pots containing herbs, to be picked as needed during cooking.

Bunny's eye for detail is second to none, and the decorative touches she introduced made the garden instantly recognizable as a 'Bunny Guinness garden'. Finials in the shape of pineapples were added to the tops of the posts connecting the trellis panels and were repeated on the corners of the Versailles planters. They were originally designed to be painted gold, replicating gilding with gold leaf, but Bunny decided after experimenting with one finial that she preferred them in their natural state. A lion's-head mask that acted as a spout for the wall-fountain was gilded and glowed triumphantly through a wreath of ivy. The water falls from the mask on to a small basin at ground level, lined with plaster casts of fossil ammonites. The ammonite detail is picked up in other parts of the garden, with some embedded into the soil around the base of one of the standard bay trees, the gaps filled with gravel to act as a decorative mulch.

To create the illusion of extra space beyond the boundary, Bunny placed woven willow arches at two strategic points on the raised side of the garden. The first, directly opposite the kitchen door, invites you to step up to the little terraced area; the other, near the outdoor kitchen, elongates the sight line across the widest part of the garden. The backs of the arches were filled in with mirror panels, accentuating the illusion of infinite space beyond. Although at first sight this is a garden rooted in traditional style, much of the detail is thoroughly modern. The sides of the Versailles planters are made of galvanized metal, and the wavy trellis gives a modern twist to a classic design. This individual

combination of traditional and contemporary style is what makes the garden so successful and utterly unique.

With the landscaping finished, the garden had become a blank sculptural canvas and planting could commence, bringing Bunny's design to life. First to go in was the structural backbone planting. The crossing rows of small box plants were planted 20 cm (8 in) apart and the tops were trimmed immediately to encourage them to bush out from the base. *Buxus sempervirens* was chosen, which is faster-growing and less susceptible to disease than the dwarf form, *Buxus sempervirens* 'Suffruticosa'. Several standard clipped bays were placed strategically around the garden, with one taking pride of place on the front corner of the new raised bed, creating a visual full stop.

Finally, the sections could be filled in with vegetables. We planted late in the season, so used small, ready-grown, individual plants; an increasingly wide selection is available as plug plants from garden centres in the spring. But for a better range of varieties, and to cut costs considerably, the owners plan to raise the majority themselves from seed next year. To facilitate this and to give protection to tender vegetables, such as aubergines and peppers, Bunny designed an ingenious mini-greenhouse to stand against the wall at the end of the garden, next to an equally attractive compost bin. In a small space everything in it is on show, so it should be beautiful as well as functional. The ingenuity of the greenhouse design is in its flexibility: large doors open by folding into smaller sections, which prevents them from blocking the passageway to the back gate, and the lid can be raised to increase ventilation when necessary in hot weather.

In the bed to the side of the house a tower of French beans gave height to the central area. Each surrounding compartment created by the box divisions was planted with a different vegetable or salad crop. Since this potager constitutes the entire garden, the varieties were chosen for their decorative qualities, as well as for taste, and were arranged to be pleasing to the eye. The blood-red stems of a ruby chard contrasted with the glaucous bluish-green of brassica foliage. Contrast was also to be found in the variation of heights, texture and leaf shapes, with curly-leaved parsley next to purple sage and baby leeks. In the future it will be wise for the owners to rotate the plants in each section, just as you would in a conventional vegetable garden, to prevent the build-up of disease-causing organisms in the soil.

To prevent gaps forming once a crop had been harvested, Bunny suggested the use of cut-and-come-again salads, where you remove from the lettuce only what you need for that

Opposite: A mulch of decorative ammonites and gravel surrounds the base of a standard bay tree.

Left: The same triangular shape is echoed in the low box hedges that divide the beds into planting compartments.

meal, leaving the main plant *in situ* to grow on. In compartments that had been cleared completely, ornamental bedding could be introduced: French marigolds look jolly, and their strong scent is a great deterrent to unwanted pests and an attractant to beneficial insects, so using them as companion planting is both decorative and useful. In the winter, when the range of vegetables grown would be greatly depleted, winter-flowering pansies and violas would add colour and happily take the place of the harvested vegetables. Colour and interest in the beds needn't be confined to the plants: terracotta rhubarb forcers and glazed mini-cloches were introduced for practical and decorative purposes.

Ornamental plants were also added to the borders surrounding the paved area. Towering cannas planted around the wall-fountain brought a touch of the exotic to the garden, and clouds of pink-flowered cosmos would go on blooming for months above frothy green foliage. Ivy was introduced beneath the large conifer, where a tough plant was needed to survive the dry shade. More ivy was added to climb through the trellis around the lion's-head mask, where it would soften the edges in no time at all. Other climbers were incorporated, including a pre-existing fruiting grapevine and the evergreen *Clematis armandii*, which would be smothered with scented white flowers in early spring and thrive in the semi-shady conditions found in parts of the garden.

The beauty of the planting in this garden lies in its great flexibility. Within the long-term framework of box hedging the plants can be changed year by year to include any combination of edible and ornamental plants. Should the owners decide to have a complete change, the garden could easily be completely turned over to flowering plants, using annuals within the compartments, or perennials if a more permanent scheme is preferred. The colour theme can also be changed on a whim – one year hot, spicy shades can predominate, the next icy cool white and blue, altering entirely the atmosphere of the space.

In practical terms the garden fulfils the brief exactly. I joined the party the first time that guests were invited and the garden looked beautiful and functioned perfectly on every level. Entertaining was easy-going and comfortable, with people perched informally on the walls and steps, as well as using the seating area. Plates overflowed with freshly picked corn-on-the-cob dripping with butter and sizzling meat barbecued with home-grown herbs. Candles flickered and glasses of wine were passed back and forth in a space that felt far from cramped. The garden was filled with the scent of aromatic plants, children traced the shape of the fossils in the pool of water and happy laughter filled the air. From the most unpromising of plots has emerged a beautiful garden that really works.

Left: Introduce a touch of the Mediterranean with a fruiting vine.

Opposite: The perfect setting for dining al fresco amid lush planting.

entertaining *in the* garden

One of the greatest pleasures of having a garden is being able to share it with others, and Bunny Guinness's scheme certainly enhanced that pleasure. Enjoyable memories of endless summer evenings spent with family and friends can sustain us through a long hard winter, and with the advent of effective outdoor heaters there's no reason not to be able to party all night on New Year's Eve. Socializing outside makes the experience far more relaxed and informal, and of course it's the perfect opportunity to show off all the hard work you've done in the garden and talk plants with other keen gardeners.

Cooking outdoors instantly turns into something more exciting than just providing a meal. Keen barbecue cooks treat the whole experience as a performance, with much heated discussion about recipes for marinades, optimum cooking temperatures and the virtues of charcoal versus gas barbecues. In view of the pleasure gained from entertaining in the garden, it makes sense to consider all the practicalities when planning the layout, particularly in a small garden where space is always at a premium.

You need to consider how much cooking you like to do, whether you are happy to buy the occasional disposable barbecue, or if you want a state-of-the-art outdoor kitchen. Whatever your requirements, choose something that will fit in with the overall style of the garden – plenty of sleek metal in a modern garden, and a recycled brick barbecue in a traditional plot. In small town gardens the usual advice to position the cooking area near the kitchen door is irrelevant as every part of the garden will be close enough. So you can be led by other design considerations and select the spot where it will look most pleasing, or be least obtrusive, depending on your preference.

Seating is equally important; guests will feel much more comfortable if there is somewhere to sit down. If you have an area of lawn, this will never be a problem as rugs and cushions can be scattered where needed and food can be served picnic-style. In gardens with a hard landscaped floor, incorporate perching places in the design – the edges of raised beds, pools and steps are all perfect for informal chatting. Furniture becomes vital, however, when you want to provide a sit-down meal, and where you position the dining area will have some bearing on the atmosphere that is created. Placing a table beneath the lower branches of a mature tree will provide a hint of rural life and dappled shade from midday sun. Tucking the table next to a boundary, rather than right in the middle of the garden, may help to avoid a sense of exposure. It's hard to relax while being watched by the neighbours.

Left: Tall trellis panels help screen an unsightly wall.

Below left: A mirror is positioned above a still pool, doubling its length and reflecting an attractive view.

Opposite: This seating area is shielded from neighbouring buildings by small-squared trellis and a row of slender trees in containers.

boundaries *and* screens

In small town gardens we are all too aware of what surrounds us at close quarters; the boundaries are always there to remind us of the limits of our domain. Walls and fences are often neglected, and in a large garden with banks of mature shrubs you can get away with that, but in a small plot they are so visible that the best plan is to turn them into a feature. Create something so attractive that to hide it with climbers is almost a sin.

For city gardeners the main preoccupation is dealing with the neighbours. Providing a sense of privacy can be difficult when flats and houses are packed together, but gardens should help us to feel separate from the bustle of life going on around us. Creating an oasis of calm amid the turmoil isn't easy, and trying to block out the world around you completely is a mistake. Better to accept that you will probably be able to see and be seen by other residents to some extent, and improve those areas within your own domain that you can change. Boundaries are often subject to local by-laws and regulations, and these need to be checked before deciding on the height. It's tempting to make them as high as possible, but that can result in a space that feels dark and claustrophobic. If your plot has an attractive view or local feature – and many town gardens do – find a way to include it; you could consider incorporating 'windows' in the wall or fence to frame the view.

There are many options available to us when choosing a boundary, and the range is increasing all the time. If you have old brick walls, try to keep them, unless they really don't work with a sleek, modern design. You can always raise walls that are too low by adding trellis or woven willow panels. Boring brick can be rendered to give a smooth or

textured finish and painted in blocks of bright colour. Fencing, trellis and other wooden boundaries come in myriad styles and are perfect if you want to grow twining climbers, such as ivy or clematis. Living boundaries are often neglected in town gardens, with rows of dull privet giving hedges a bad name, but a careful choice of plant makes a hedge a really attractive option in the right place.

Living willow and bamboo screens can be planted along a conventional fence to soften the hard edges, or form a living space divider. Dividing up the plot is a technique used in large gardens all the time, but it's just as effective in a small space, giving the illusion that there is much more to the garden than meets the eye. The best dividers form screens that allow glimpses of what lies beyond, rather than solid barriers. For a traditional effect, that old favourite, wrought iron, can look particularly attractive, especially when it supports climbing roses, clematis or honeysuckle. In modern spaces low walls of glass bricks are really effective, particularly when used in conjunction with imaginative lighting effects at night.

Mirrors can also help give the illusion of added space. A little goes a long way, but when positioned behind a feature plant they can double the effect it creates. By reflecting light they can lift dark corners and, when strategically placed in false doorways and arches, extend the garden into the land of make-believe. Walls covered in sheets of galvanized metal and beaten copper and zinc are still at the cutting edge of boundary design. These shiny reflective (but not mirrored) surfaces are perfect for a state-of-the-art minimalist garden and would be particularly effective in an enclosed shady courtyard.

Above left: The graceful fronds of *Stipa gigantea* are silhouetted against the chimney pots.

Above right: A subdued palette of colours works perfectly in this traditionally styled terrace garden.

Opposite left: Make the most of every available space to bring greenery into your environment.

Opposite middle: Tall, galvanized metal containers are filled with sun-loving plants.

Opposite right: Timber decking is the perfect flooring for rooftop gardens.

the **roof garden**

There is a garden for every location and the most inhospitable of conditions. Roof-top and balcony gardens present a range of problems to overcome, not least exposure to the elements and lack of privacy. But it is possible to create something special in the most unpromising places and the result can be a unique, high-rise, inner-city paradise. There is a perverse pleasure in solving design problems, so look for the potential, be imaginative and create an oasis among the rooftops.

Left: Design details are all-important in a small garden.

Opposite: An oasis of calm nestles among the urban rooftops.

Such is our love of plants and gardens that we strive to create outdoor space wherever we can. If you've nowhere to garden at ground level but have a bit of flat roof, you can go up in the world. Properly constructed roof gardens add value to your property and are now a common sight in our cities, where the rooftop landscape is often punctuated by hints of foliage and flashes of colour. Budget permitting, even water features can be introduced. In design terms, the sky's the limit.

Gardening under an open sky is exciting, and roof-garden design has come on in leaps and bounds; an eclectic collection of mismatched pots on a bitumen surface is no longer acceptable. The design can encompass any of the style elements found in ground-level gardens, from the soft, traditional and flower-filled, to oriental Zen-like calm, to sleek and slinky modernity. If the roof terrace connects directly to one of the rooms in the house or flat, consider linking the two in terms of style; this will give a sense of continuity and spaciousness.

Many city dwellers have access not to a terrace or flat roof, but to a balcony. Tower blocks constructed in the sixties and seventies are now becoming fashionable and sought-after properties; it's time to update and make the best use of their balconies, some of which can be quite large. With a thoughtful choice of accessories, the balcony can become a really useful extension of the flat. The plants will have to be chosen carefully as high winds can howl around the top floors of tall blocks. There are several practicalities to address before you bring a single plant on to the roof. Paving and soil-filled planters are heavy, so it's vital you get a structural engineer to check the strength of the roof itself and the loading it will bear. Also, give some thought to the watering: it can be a chore to have to water a large number of containers up to twice daily in hot weather: small pots in particular dry out rapidly in high summer. Far better to think ahead at the outset and install an automatic watering system. This can be linked to a timer to continue the watering when you're not around.

Problems of exposure can take two forms. The first is the literal sense: plants can be buffeted by the elements, and without protection from sun, wind and rain, only the toughest survive. But over-exposure can also refer to the sense of openness and vulnerability you feel if overlooked by all and sundry. On high roof gardens this won't be a problem – you can simply enjoy the view below. But many city roofs will be lower than neighbouring flats and office blocks, and it's hard to relax and enjoy the garden when you feel you're being watched. If you are overlooked by taller neighbouring buildings, consider erecting some sort of screening.

Left: Sleek modern design fits perfectly with the geometric shapes of the inner-city landscape.

Opposite: Using a different approach, an abundance of flowers and verdant foliage softens the view of high-rise towers.

Trellis is ideal because it allows wind to pass through it. Trying to block out anything stronger than a slight breeze with a physical barrier could be dangerous unless the barrier is extremely firmly fixed. Panels of strengthened frosted glass or Perspex would make an effective contemporary screen. Whatever you choose to surround the edge of the roof, make sure it's high enough to provide a safe barrier.

A wide range of different floorings can be suitable for roof gardens. Paving slabs look great, but may be too heavy for some roofs. Timber decking, ranging from the simplest strip flooring to highly decorative patterns, is an excellent choice. Some of the newest plastic and rubber surfaces are both lightweight and practical. Combining two or more materials is particularly effective, but avoid an over-complicated pattern.

The hard landscaping is a backdrop to the planting, and plants on roofs need containers. Using really large planters provides one of the most effective planting solutions and creates a similar effect to planting in beds on the ground. In this way plants can be grouped in swathes, with drifts of contrasting leaf and flower colour, texture and shape flowing into one another. If you do choose individual containers, you can group collections of unmatched small pots together, creating an informal, eclectic effect. Alternatively, substantially sized containers can provide strong sculptural shapes, and the increased amount of compost they hold means you can grow a wide range of large plants. Use three or more identical pots together for the strongest design statement.

In the relative shelter of the town most plants thrive in roof gardens, but in cooler parts of the country more exposed roofs can suffer from high winds and exposure, so your choice of plants should take that into account. In cooler areas it's wise to position a row of really tough, wind-resistant plants around the roof edge. This should take the worst bite out of the weather and help to shelter less rugged plants, which can then be placed within this protective barrier.

a roof garden *designed by* Douglas Coltart

Left: The dramatic setting of Ian Hamilton Finlay's garden, Little Sparta, is an inspiration for Douglas Coltart.

Opposite: A rill of water follows the edge of the decking, which is punctuated by up-lighters and softened with the red-tinged foliage of *Sorbus reducta*.

When the potential of a new garden is under assessment, some sites sound more promising than others. Freezing temperatures, howling winds and total lack of protection from the rain, closely followed by periods of full, glaring sun, didn't sound great. But when you added the words 'building site', it seemed downright depressing. Yes, this roof terrace in Paisley on the outskirts of Glasgow had its fair share of problems. Complete exposure to the extreme weather conditions, a building site for a new housing development right on its doorstep, which would mean new neighbours with a full view of the terrace, and all directly under the flight path from Glasgow airport. Why, you may ask, would anyone want to build a roof garden here?

But it wasn't all doom and gloom. The terrace was on the second floor of an attractive Victorian listed building constructed of local grey stone. A reminder of the textile industry in the Paisley area at the time, this had been the wages office, where hundreds of workers collected their pay at the end of a hard week. The building had recently been renovated and

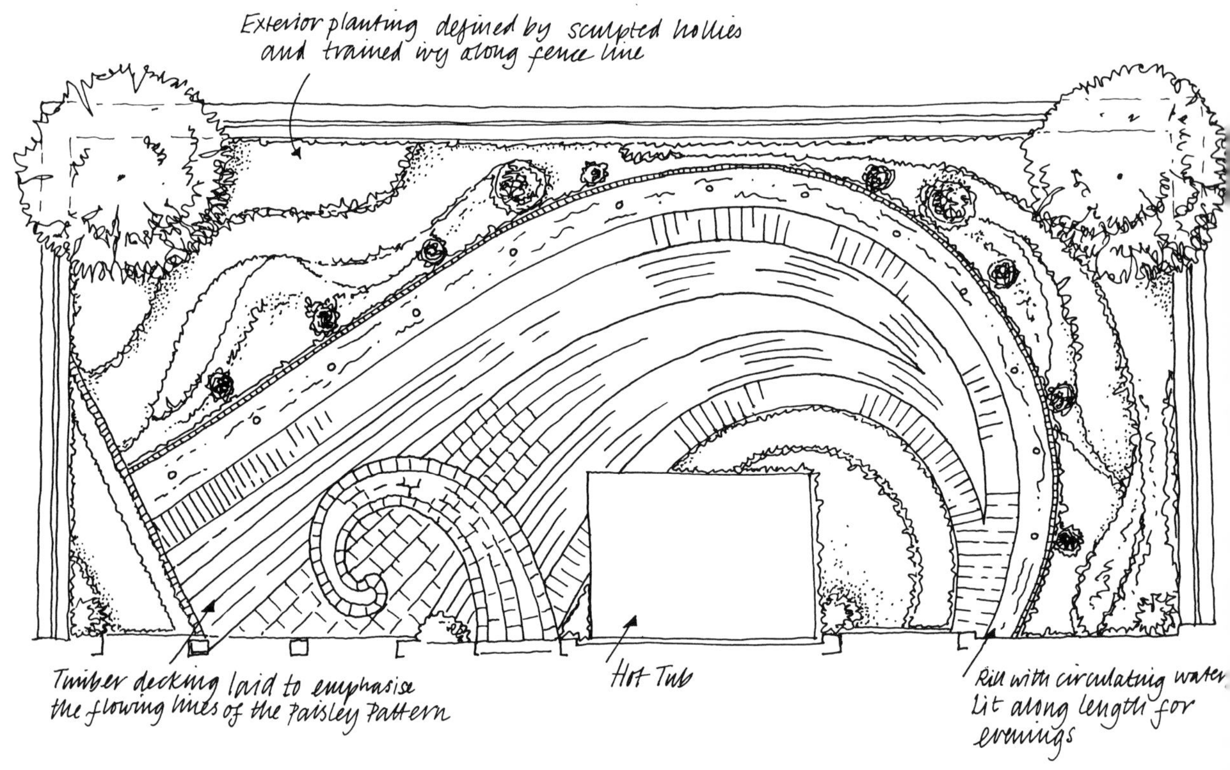

Left: A Paisley swirl inspired by the location of the roof garden is cleverly incorporated into the timber floor.

Opposite left: Steel balls give the design a space-age touch.

Opposite right: Sturdy, wind-resistant plants are enclosed by the metal railings.

the owners of the bleak roof terrace had created a lovely flat. A canal, on which a pair of swans drifted, followed by their adolescent cygnets, flowed gently alongside the property.

The terrace itself was a generous size, a perfect rectangle with simple railings edging the roof. An attempt had been made to do something with the space. A motley collection of pots contained some severely wind-burnt conifers, struggling to survive in bone-dry compost. The owners were eager to get maximum use from their terrace. A sociable couple with a grown-up daughter, they were particularly keen on using the outside space for entertaining. However, their previous attempts had been hampered by the weather. On one occasion a glass-topped metal table was blown off the roof and flew into the canal; had it landed a few metres further away, the consequences could have been lethal. Smaller items, such as paddling pools, were always being whisked away. Although the owners wanted the garden to have plenty of greenery, they didn't have time to do too much in the way of plant maintenance. As a final twist, there was a further stipulation: the design had to incorporate their dream luxury item – a hot tub.

This garden would need a designer with plenty of ingenuity, a practical mind to deal with the not inconsiderable problems, and a sense of humour. Douglas Coltart (see Designers' Biographies, page 122) fitted the bill exactly; he is a lecturer and garden designer, and made his first television appearances on the BBC programme *The Beechgrove Garden*. As an added bonus, this multi-award-winning designer is a local boy, who understands the worst of the Scottish weather. Douglas is inspired in his work by his native landscape; his own garden is surrounded on all sides by gently rolling hills. His first thoughts on seeing the roof terrace were how to integrate the distant views of the hills beyond Glasgow and incorporate some of the history of the area. After a discussion with the owners, measurements and photographs were taken and Douglas could begin shaping his ideas into a design.

When embarking on a new roof terrace, the first priority is to have it checked over by a structural engineer. Calculations were made based on the strength of the building, and the

This garden would need a designer with plenty of ingenuity, a practical mind to deal with the not inconsiderable problems, and a sense of humour.

amount of loading it would bear. Douglas could then work out exactly how much weight he could add to the roof. Generally, how the load is distributed is as important as the actual weight – small areas of heavy weight can be more problematic than the same load spread evenly over a large area. In his original design Douglas wanted large, square planters in each corner of the terrace for the trees he hoped to include in the plan. However, these were immediately vetoed by the engineer because they would place too great a concentration of weight on small sections of the roof.

As Douglas was dealing with a listed building, permission had to be sought to develop the terrace. This was granted, with the proviso that nothing be fixed to the side wall of the building, which meant that another part of the original design, a sail-shaped canopy, had to go. But Douglas was undeterred, and after further alterations he presented the owners with a beautiful finished design.

Taking as his inspiration the famous Paisley swirls found in Victorian textile designs, Douglas planned to cover the terrace with contrasting wooden decking, cut and shaped into the curved lines so familiar in Paisley patterns. The widest curve would sweep across the roof, de-emphasizing the rectilinear shape of the terrace. The hot tub was to be positioned near the door that opened on to the roof from the living area of the flat; in this way it was just a short dash back into the warmth after enjoying a mid-winter soak.

At last, following all the preliminaries, work could commence. The terrace had been covered in dull concrete slabs, and the original plan, and cheaper option, was to build the decking directly on top of them. But weight restrictions meant that the slabs would have to come up. The surface underneath was in good order and the timber frame supporting the decking could be constructed. This was to be a floating frame without any fixings on to the roof surface so that the waterproofing wasn't compromised in any way. The finished height of the deck would be higher than that of the previous paved surface, making the transition from interior to exterior more comfortable. Douglas needed the extra height to allow him to include a water rill in the design.

Left: The graceful curve of decking sweeps across the rectangular space.

Opposite: A collection of contrasting grasses will tolerate the harsh weather conditions.

Introducing water into a roof garden is a delightful idea that is rarely carried out. But if the work is done carefully to ensure there are no leakages, water features really add something to gardens above ground level. The sweeping curve of the rill was constructed below the surface of the deck and lined with black butyl liner. This was disguised with vertical, cross-cut timber pieces, which formed a little dividing wall between the water and the raised planting area. On the deck side an edging of short timber sections was laid along the rill. Simple and stunning light-fittings were installed along the timber edging at regular intervals. These were flush with the surface of the deck and could be walked on.

On the other side of the terrace the same pieces of edging timber followed the shape of the deck. Here Douglas had inserted steel balls into some of the pieces so that half of each sphere protruded. These were painted with silver metallic paint to give a matt finish, and looked like giant ball-bearings. This simple idea gave the design a space-age touch and brought something unique, tactile and playful to the garden.

The centre of the decked area was brought to life by the subtle swirl of the Paisley motif. Douglas created the pattern using the same cross-cut pieces of timber and inserted them vertically into the surrounding horizontally laid decking. Once complete, the deck was almost too attractive to hide with garden furniture. The hot tub, which had been craned in from the roadside, was installed and, though large enough to make its presence felt, looked integral to the overall design.

Douglas chose to create large, raised planting beds from fibreglass, rather than using individual containers for the plants. This would give the garden a similar look to a ground-level plot. The planting beds were constructed to be deep enough for the roots of the plants, some of which were quite large, to be able to get a firm hold. The base of the beds was given a layer of lightweight pea-gravel to improve drainage, and this was topped up with 6 cubic metres of compost mixture, a blend of multi-purpose and soil-based compost. This last ingredient was particularly important to give real substance to the mix for long-term planting, and to support the larger plants. These large beds would retain moisture far better than small containers, but at this point an automatic watering system was installed to ensure that the soil need never dry out.

The planting in this garden had to fulfil certain objectives. Given the planning restriction on increasing the height of the boundary, it was important to introduce plants that could provide a sense of protection

and privacy from prying eyes, and to choose varieties that could cope with the worst vagaries of the weather. Structural specimens were the first to go in. The only plants to have individual pots were a series of three Japanese flowering cherries. *Prunus* 'Amanogawa' has a fastigiate growth habit; that is to say, it grows straight up in a narrow, columnar shape. In spring the trees will be smothered in pale pink blossom, and in autumn their foliage will turn to shades of gold. Douglas positioned them at intervals along the side of the building, to break up the long expanse of wall, and to give them some protection from the elements.

Bearing in mind the extreme weather conditions, he could then begin the rest of the planting. Two young *Sorbus vilmorinii* trees, related to the British native rowan, were placed, one in each corner on the terrace. Their delicate foliage is composed of small leaflets that allow the wind to pass through easily. With the additional benefit of clusters of deep pink berries that ripen to the palest blush pink, this robust tree is a star performer in any small garden. Continuing the theme of protection, it was Douglas's plan to create a weather-resistant barrier of holly and ivy, which was planted around the perimeter railing. These would also help screen the terrace for privacy, but were shaped to allow glimpses of the canal and the more attractive views. In conjunction with some other tough customers – *Viburnum davidii*, *Elaeagnus ebbingei* and an assortment of conifers – a protective outer screen was formed. Within the screen, a gentler microclimate would allow less resilient plants to thrive. Douglas didn't want his clients to miss out on the 'pretties' that would be impossible to grow without the improved conditions.

Opposite: A young *Sorbus vilmorinii* adds extra height to the planting scheme.

Right: *Hosta* 'Halycon', *Festuca glauca* and *Convolvulus cneorum* stand up to the rain.

A low hedge of *Sorbus reducta* gave added protection to a group of *Verbascum* 'Helen Johnson', the unusually subtle colour of the verbascum flowers picked up beautifully in the soft flesh-toned berries of the sorbus. Douglas's planting scheme was well thought out: he chose plants to create stunning colour combinations, with contrasting and complementary foliage sizes, shapes and textures, and a smattering of scented plants. *Nepeta* × *faassenii* and the fleshy leaves of *Hosta* 'Halcyon' backed a row of tufty *Festuca glauca* planted along the edge of the water rill, to create a bluish-green haze. *Convolvulus cneorum* and *Leymus arenarius* added flecks of silver foliage to an area of deep plummy-red *Heuchera* 'Palace Purple', *Hebe* 'Purple Queen' and *Sedum* 'Bertram Anderson'. (Be warned, though, as *Leymus arenarius* is an aggressive grower, as Douglas pointed out to the owners; an alternative suggestion would be *Salix lanata* or *Lavandula* 'Sawyers Variety'.)

With so many difficulties to contend with, this roof terrace was a tall order for any designer. Rising to the occasion, Douglas produced an impressive design that addressed the problems and came up with practical solutions that also look beautiful. He took as his inspiration the history of the building and the local area. His design is a real garden, not just a collection of pots on a rooftop, and is a masterpiece of soft curves in a hard urban landscape. Finally, his skill in choosing appropriate plants means that they will have a good chance of surviving all that the Paisley sky can throw at them.

As a finishing touch, heavy timber furniture and a patio gas heater were purchased to make the garden fit for the owners' friends. A couple of nights after the garden was completed, the party was in full swing. Gentle lighting illuminated the skein of water in the rill, and most guests enjoyed a leisurely meal, blissfully warm beneath the heater. But a small group of brave souls drank to a successfully completed garden from the bubbling cauldron of the hot tub.

Left: Rectangular, galvanized steel containers mulched with slate are simple and stunning in a modern space.

Opposite: Painted terracotta pots are home to a series of box balls.

containers

Roof gardens, like the one in the case study, couldn't exist without some form of container for the planting, but the addition of pots makes any garden seem complete. Container gardening is one of the most satisfying forms of gardening. Creating miniature gardens in a pot is an art in itself, and experimenting with different recipes for planting combinations is infinitely enjoyable.

Above all, container gardening gives you flexibility. You can think long term and plant large tubs with small, slow-growing trees, such as olives or clipped bays. Or you can fill them with annuals, ringing the changes with every season. Small containers are relatively light and easy to move around, so alter the colours and planting combinations whenever you please and you can enjoy a new garden every week. Plant up pots with plenty of bulbs – remembering to think ahead – and you can have a constantly changing rotation of flowers, from the earliest *Iris reticulata* and crocuses, through narcissi and tulips to alliums and nerines. There isn't a season that cannot be brightened up with bulbs.

The range of different container types is growing all the time. Nowadays the pot itself is often the highlight of the scheme, with the planting – if there is any – simply icing on the cake. In a very small space just two or three carefully chosen, stunning containers can provide the focal point for the whole garden. There is a style of pot suitable for every type of garden, from the most traditional to the sleekest modern space, and the range of materials is rapidly expanding.

Most familiar is the warmth of terracotta, which is available in myriad designs, from the very simplest unadorned shapes to elaborately decorated urns festooned with swags of fruit and ribbon bows. Don't confine terracotta to traditional-looking gardens; when simple shapes are chosen, it can look just as effective in a modern space. If you want to introduce colour, terracotta and timber tubs are both suitable for painting. Wooden tubs, such as Versailles containers, have been used in gardens for centuries. This is a timeless style, which can be updated by combining the timber with an unexpected material, such as galvanized steel, to make up the side panels.

The ball finials that top each corner of the container can be made from metal too.

Galvanized metal containers have become increasingly popular and are the obvious choice for minimalist gardens. However, they can look equally good planted with formally trained topiary. Many garden centres stock a selection, but for something really original try commissioning your own design. Ceramic pots come in a wonderful range of coloured glazes and textured finishes, but do check that they are frost-resistant and have holes for drainage in the bottom. Concrete is perfect for really solid-looking containers for modern gardens, and is growing in popularity with designers.

With containers it is certainly true that size matters. In small gardens it's often assumed that you should stick to small plants and small pots. But filling a little space with diminutive accessories can accentuate the smallness because it's what your eye expects to see. Better to distract from the lack of area by using a few well-chosen, substantial pieces which give a sense of scale and solidity that will exaggerate the size of the space. If you do prefer to use small pots, choosing one design, repeated in either identical or differing sizes, will help to avoid a cluttered feel.

Planting up containers couldn't be simpler. Place broken crocks over the drainage holes and part-fill with a mixture of multi-purpose compost and soil-based compost, which adds weight and helps to retain moisture. Stir in a few handfuls of horticultural grit and, if desired, some ready-wetted moisture-retaining gel. Position your plants, ensuring that there is enough space between the soil surface and the rim of the container to allow for watering. Fill around the plants with more of the compost mixture, firming with your fingers to prevent any air pockets being left below the surface. Give the pot a really good water and don't allow it to dry out subsequently. Remember that once in a container, the plant is totally reliant on you for its needs. Apart from consistent watering, it will need regular feeding with a slow-release fertilizer. For long-term plantings it's advisable to remove some of the old compost every year and replace it with fresh.

Left: The success of this seaside-inspired garden owes much to the weather-beaten appearance of the planters and the wind-blown grasses.

braving *the* **elements**

The roof garden in Paisley suffered from unpredictable weather, but conditions in many parts of the world make Scotland seem positively balmy. Plants manage to survive in some of the most inhospitable places on Earth. In order to cope with these extremes, an extraordinary diversity of plant life has evolved that is adapted for specific areas. For many centuries enthusiastic plant collectors were mesmerized by the beauty of the plants they found abroad, and, as a result, many thousands of species have been introduced into this country. Today keen gardeners are equally captivated, and determined to include in their own gardens many plants that originated in far-flung parts of the world.

All too often we are seduced by an unusual specimen in the garden centre and, before we know it, it's in the boot of the car and on its way home. More often than not, this turns out to be an expensive mistake. Plants invariably fail to thrive when their requirements are not met. There's more to this than feeding and watering: every plant has physical characteristics that suit it perfectly to its native environment. If we can't provide the same conditions, or at least something fairly similar, the plant will sicken and eventually die.

On the plus side, even if your garden has particularly difficult conditions, there is bound to be a selection of plants that will thrive. The trick is to do your homework before you go shopping, know your garden and take a list of suitable plants with you. Sometimes even a very small garden has areas offering quite different growing conditions, which will enable you to grow a wider range of plants. No matter what the aspect, all urban gardens are affected to some degree by pollution. Some plants are unaffected by this, others yearn for cleaner air. Again, it's a question of being selective.

Town gardens are often fortunate in being sheltered, and can be several degrees warmer than those just outside the city. But coastal town gardens and roof gardens can suffer from extreme conditions just as difficult as those found out of town. There is a certain amount you can do to improve problem sites. Windy and exposed gardens can sometimes be protected with physical barriers, but take care not to create a worse problem, with wind being forced up and over a solid barrier only to eddy around on your side. Planting a screening of plants is often more effective. In this way you form a sheltered microclimate within the screen.

Sometimes it's possible to take measures to protect a plant that might not otherwise survive. Using a greenhouse is one way of manipulating a plant's environment: for example, to overwinter citrus plants that may

Left: The vibrant foliage of *Hakonechloa macra* 'Alboaurea' will thrive on a shady roof.

Right: In the stark beauty of this exposed position, phormiums and grasses can withstand a battering by the elements.

otherwise succumb to persistent frosts. Exotic-looking tender plants can be left *in situ* in the garden and wrapped with horticultural fleece or bubble wrap to protect them from low temperatures. A final top layer of an attractive material, such as a roll of woven grass or willow, will help to stop them looking too much of an eyesore in the winter garden. Glass or Perspex cloches do the same job for smaller plants.

In sheltered town gardens in warmer areas many plants, such as olives, that you would not attempt to leave outside in colder areas, can survive the winter happily without protection. Others need just a bit of help. Dahlia corms can be left in the ground, but as insurance you could spread a thick, insulating layer of mulch over the surface of the soil above. If you leave the tops on perennial grasses over the winter instead of cutting them back in late autumn, they will protect themselves.

Full sun can be a blessing; there is an enormous range of sun-loving plants. On the other hand, you'll miss out on the gentle charms of shade-lovers, and have to deal with all the problems that go with drought. Hose-pipe bans can mean death to plants that are not specially adapted to survive dry conditions. Luckily, there are many that are perfectly content in the sun. Leaf shape and colour are often good indicators of a plant's preferred growing conditions. Silvery foliage is covered in hundreds of tiny, soft hairs that prevent water evaporation and is found on plants adapted to cope with low water levels or well-drained soils. Narrow leaves, such as those on lavender, are also an indication that the plant will tolerate full sun: the reduced surface area helps to conserve moisture. (Shade-loving plants often have large, rounded foliage to make the most of the limited light they receive.) Succulents work in a different way, storing water within their fleshy leaves.

Some of these adaptations are also helpful for plants struggling with exposed, windy sites, which can also quickly have a drying effect on plants. In addition, plants with divided leaves or leaflets are less likely to suffer physical damage in high winds. In coastal areas plants have to cope with drying, salt-laden winds. Tough plants, such as *Atriplex halimus* and eryngiums, are needed here. Nature often provides clues to help you select the best plants for your own garden. A plant's form – its natural shape – is also the result of evolutionary necessity. Low mounded or hummock-forming plants are often simply trying to get out of the wind. Spiky or thorny shrubs may have been fending off hungry herbivores. Growing plants that will thrive in your particular garden conditions, rather than giving in to momentary temptation, is the way to hassle-free gardening and a collection of healthy plants.

Above left: *Fatsia japonica* is the perfect easy-to-grow plant for the tropical look.

Above right: *Canna striata*, *Lobelia cardinalis* and *Dahlia* 'Bednall Beauty' make a striking tableau of contrasts.

Opposite left: Verdant planting surrounds a small statue.

Opposite middle: Gold is the unifying theme in this grouping that includes the spotted laurel *Aucuba japonica* and the bamboo *Phyllostachys vivax* 'Aureocaulis'.

Opposite right: Emerald fronds add delicacy to an exotic garden.

the **exotic garden**

Lack of space need not restrict your imagination. Go where the fancy takes you. If you dream about windswept beaches, then plan a seaside garden in the middle of the city centre. Perhaps the deep blue of the Mediterranean sky and the silvery leaf of an olive tree evoke happy memories. Why not recreate that atmosphere in the suburbs? One of the benefits of town gardening is that temperatures are often milder and the gardens more sheltered, enabling you to grow a wide range of exotic-looking plants. So indulge that fantasy and bring your dreams to your own back yard.

Left: Ferns are perfect to fill the understorey in a shady spot.

Opposite: A dazzling colour combination that really packs a punch includes *Canna* 'Striata' and 'Durban', *Lobelia cardinalis*, *Dahlia* 'Bednall Beauty' and *Lysimachia* 'Firecracker'.

England may be green and pleasant in abundance, but it can also be drizzly and cold, with that distinctive low blanket of thick, greyish cloud, which has been likened to living inside a Tupperware box. Sometimes you yearn to be transported to a hot and sunny climate, with a blue sky that stretches into space. One way of achieving this is to get on a plane and head for the tropics; the other is to bring a little taste of it to your own home.

Turning your temperate garden into an exotic paradise will cheer you on the dullest day and remind you of holidays abroad. But how do you define an exotic garden? For most of us this term conjures up images of palm trees, dense green vegetation and hot flower colours. But 'exotic' can refer to any type of garden in which the planting is significantly different from the traditional English style, and that usually means evoking the atmosphere of a warmer climate.

The lush tropical style is probably the most popular form of exotic gardening, with sales of Tasmanian tree ferns (*Dicksonia antarctica*) and Chusan palms (*Trachycarpus fortunei*) rocketing through the roof. This Amazonian look is typified by the use of abundant evergreen planting, often incorporating architectural plants with large structured leaves that are far hardier than they appear. But exotic can also mean an arid landscape or a dry river bed. Planting spiky succulents, such as *Agave americana*, and sculptural plants, such as *Cordyline australis*, will bring a suggestion of the desert to the centre of town. The Mediterranean garden is an exotic style that we are more familiar with – by planting rosemary and lavender among gravel and adding an olive tree in a pot you can almost see the azure of a Provençal sky. All these garden styles are achievable in a small town garden; perhaps the best plan is to choose the look that inspires you.

Whichever style you opt for, all exotic gardens have one thing in common: the plants are the dominant factor. The success of the garden will depend not only on design and landscaping, but also on the type of plants that go into it. These are the main elements and will define the feel you are trying to achieve. It's important to stick to the theme of the garden: if you succumb to sentimentality and include *Rosa* 'Constance Spry', you will dilute the overall effect.

Colour is one of the ways to suggest the type of exotic garden you want. The hot, fiery reds and oranges of *Canna* 'Durban' and *Crocosmia* 'Lucifer' or *C.* × *crocosmiiflora* 'Star of the East' are perfect for the tropical feel. Soft blues and mauves and the golden glow of sunflowers evoke the Mediterranean look. Above all, look at the colour of the foliage: fresh, lush greens are the most important component of humid,

Opposite: Long strap-like leaves and bright orange flowers of *Crocosmia masoniorum* arch gracefully over a clump of solenostemon.

Right: The exotic beauty of *Canna indica*.

jungle-like gardens, and silvery-greys the prime colours of plants from arid conditions.

It's important before you buy a plant that you ascertain whether or not it's hardy in your part of the country. Garden stalwarts, such as *Fatsia japonica*, *Phormium tenax* and hostas, are typical of plants that give the desired exotic effect without needing any special treatment. An urban plot can be the perfect location for a garden with a tropical feel. The climate is usually far milder in the centre of large cities; warmer temperatures and sheltered locations give tender plants a more friendly welcome than the harsher conditions found out of town. However, even this may not be enough to see some plants through a bad winter, and they may need a little extra help.

Wrapping tender plants is the best way to give them the protection they need. Pack straw among the leaves and stems to protect the crown, which is generally the most vulnerable part, and then gently envelop the whole plant in a layer of bubble wrap or horticultural fleece. When in doubt, check the requirements of a specific plant in a good reference book. Small specimens can be protected with glass or plastic bell-cloches. Orange trees and other citrus plants can either be brought into a cool greenhouse over the winter or left *in situ* and wrapped up. Olives should be able to cope with an occasional drop in temperature without being wrapped if the garden is sheltered. In the worst-case scenario, you might need to move your most delicate specimens to a more sheltered part of the garden or a cold greenhouse. Look after your more vulnerable plants carefully and you'll be rewarded with a garden that many visit only in their dreams.

an exotic garden *designed by* Will Giles

Left: The glorious Abbey Gardens in Tresco – Will Giles's inspirational garden.

Opposite: The back door opens on to a lushly planted scene, with *Dicksonia antarctica* fronds at the base of the steps.

It can be difficult, when your garden is pretty enough already, to alter it just because you fancy a change. The temptation to stick with what you know, the safe and the familiar, can be too strong to fight. But if you do have a burning desire to be surrounded by a completely different atmosphere when you're in the garden, it's time to steel yourself and go for it.

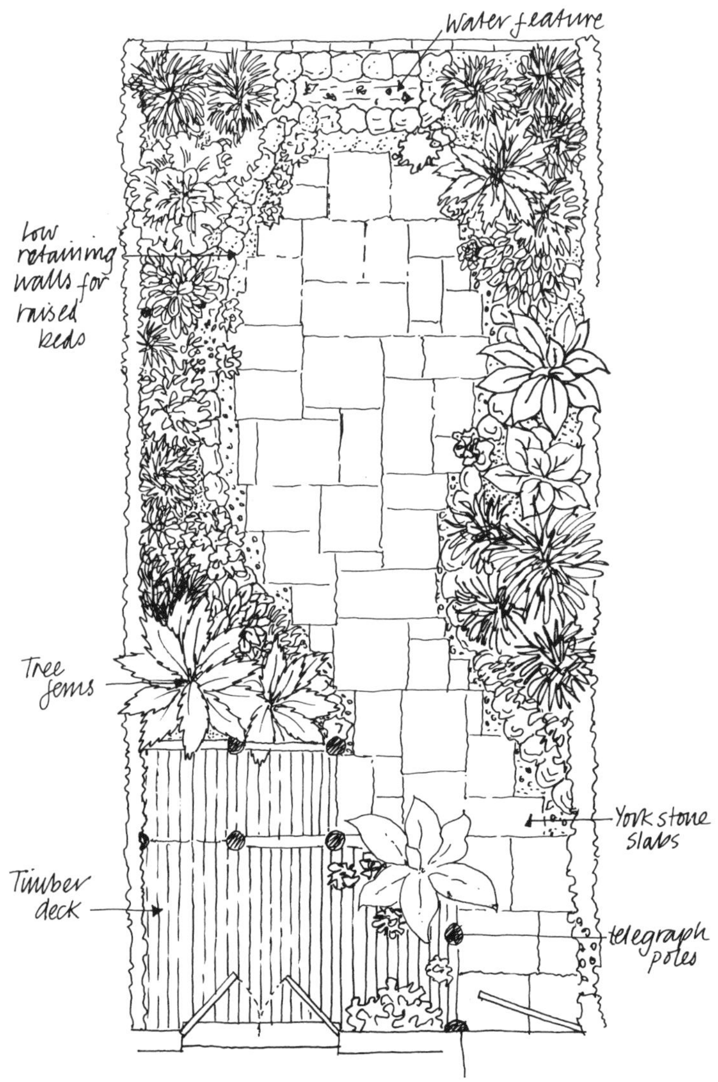

Our small town garden in the shadow of Alexandra Palace in north London was certainly a pleasant spot. Tucked behind an attractive row of Victorian brick houses, with good light and an abundance of pretty plants, the narrow, rectangular plot already had plenty of good points. However, there were some problems the owners wanted to address: the steep steps into the garden were potentially unsafe, an old shed and an unused coal house had outgrown their usefulness, and the storage facilities needed improvement now that the owners' small son was beginning to accumulate more toys. They couldn't wait to replace the tiny, threadbare lawn and crazy-paving path, and create a proper area for entertaining. But the main problem was that the garden simply didn't speak to them. It was uninspiring and average and the owners were bored with it. They wanted instead to be thrilled by their garden every time they stepped outside.

Knowing that you want a change is almost half the battle; knowing what you want to replace it with is the next stage, and putting it into practice the final part. The owners had already accomplished the first stage and they had some strong ideas about the second. Both of them were fed up with traditional English

Left: The Abyssinian banana, *Ensete ventricosum* 'Maurelii'.

Opposite: The vertical rock wall forms a dramatic focal point at the end of the garden.

garden style, and one in particular was a keen traveller who had previously spent much time abroad in warmer climes. She was determined to invoke those happy memories, and the atmosphere of warmth and sunshine that she remembered, in this quiet corner of London. An unusual yet safe water feature was also on their wish list. Thus they reached the third part of the puzzle: how – or more precisely who – could help them achieve that taste of the exotic?

Will Giles (see Designers' Biographies, page 122) is totally immersed in his passion for exotic gardening. His background as an illustrator and his love of plants give him an incredible knack for grouping them together to create stunning planting combinations. He uses the wide variety of textures, colours and shapes in exotic-looking hardy and tender plants to tremendous effect. With customary modesty, Will would not describe himself as designer specifically, though he has created a ravishing, exotic-style garden in Norfolk. He is primarily a craftsman with plants, inspired by numerous trips to far-flung parts of the world, ranging from the Amazon jungle to the deserts of Arizona, and is an expert in how to care for tender plants in a temperate climate such as that of the UK.

However, Will does himself a disservice in playing down his skills as a designer, for his talents are not confined to planting alone, as we were to discover. After a productive first meeting with his clients, and taking careful notes and measurements, Will had some very clear ideas immediately about how the garden might eventually look. Although he admired many of the existing plants, he knew they wouldn't fit into the tropical theme he had in mind, so he advised the owners to give away some of the best specimens.

By the next meeting, Will had devised a simple but stunning design, which, typically – coming from an illustrator – was so beautifully drawn and coloured that it constituted a work of art in itself. Will had paid particular attention to the poor access into the garden: he wanted to provide a platform that people could step on to comfortably from the kitchen. From here you could enjoy a first glimpse of the garden and possibly sit out on balmy evenings. His design for a raised timber deck continued the level of

The design was for a satisfyingly simple structure with a real feeling of solidity.

the kitchen floor directly into the garden, giving a seamless entry into the exotic oasis before you.

Beneath this platform Will had created extra room for storage and taken care to leave clear the entry to an existing storage area under the ground floor of the house, which was accessed by a small door. To add to this rather inadequate space, he planned to make better use of a narrow passageway at the side of the house to store the larger garden tools, barbecue and toys. Feeling the garden needed some sort of focal point, Will decided to build a vertical rockery: this wall would take pride of place at the end of the plot and would incorporate moving water, as the owners had requested. The central area was to be paved to provide a large space for entertaining and tricycle races.

Will's priority when creating this garden was to keep the hard landscaping simple so that it would form a backdrop to set off the spectacular planting to best advantage. The entire perimeter of the garden was to be lushly planted with tropical-looking plants. One of the owners works in lighting design and Will was keen to make use of his expertise in creating the lighting effects for the finished garden. The plan was to illuminate the strongly architectural planting and make the steps down from the deck safe to use at night. Once the design had been agreed with the owners, it was time to commence work. The dilapidated shed and old coal bunker were the first things to go, and immediately the space doubled in size. Climbers were hacked back, plants removed and the remaining bits of turf skimmed from the surface of the soil. Finally, the site was levelled in preparation for the hard landscaping.

The supports for the timber deck were installed against the back wall of the house. This was constructed using telegraph poles for the uprights and Tanalised wood for the decking and balustrades. The design was for a satisfyingly simple structure with a real feeling of solidity. Generous steps were fixed to the front of the platform and followed the front edge of the deck, rather than going straight out into the garden.

Will had specified York stone slabs for the paved area in the centre of the plot, but cost restrictions meant that a cheaper alternative had to be found. Reconstituted stone slabs in a warm honey tone were a good substitute and worked well with the large quantity of Derbyshire stone that was brought in directly from the quarry for the rest of the construction. The low retaining walls for the raised beds around the sides of the garden were constructed from randomly sized pieces of stone, and the beds were filled with a mixture of topsoil, multi-purpose compost, well-rotted manure and horticultural grit.

Left: *Trachycarpus fortunei*, the Chusan Palm, brings a touch of the tropics to North London.

Opposite: The golden-stemmed bamboo, *Phyllostachys vivax* 'Aureocaulis'.

Concrete breeze-blocks were used to support the stones that would form the vertical rock wall at the end of the garden. Local planning regulations stipulated that a height restriction of only 2m (6½ft) applied to permanent structures on boundaries, but luckily the view over the top of the wall was – for a city garden – not unattractive. The fence on either side of the rock wall was covered with a pair of bamboo screens to provide an appropriately tropical backdrop to the planting. Trellis was used in other places to give uniformity to the boundaries.

Will's spectacular water feature could now be constructed; this was to be the linchpin of the whole design. The rocks were placed randomly one above the other to create the effect of a natural rock-face. Water was to be pumped to the top of the wall, where it had several concealed outlets between the stones. The pressure from the pump was kept low so that the water spilled over the rocks and ran in rivulets down the face, collecting in any small grooves and gullies and creating a glistening sheen of gently falling liquid rather than a cascading waterfall. The water finally reached a large but shallow reservoir at the base, also formed by rocks of varying sizes. Here a range of aquatic plants – such as the tender water hyacinth *Eichhornia crassipes*, which floats on the water surface – would thrive. But planting wasn't restricted to the pool. Ferns and sempervivums were tucked into gaps between the rocks wherever a small quantity of soil would give them a foothold, and mosses and lichens will doubtless move in before long.

When it comes to plants, Will is a hard man to hold back. He is profoundly affected by places such as the incredible Tresco Abbey Gardens on the Isles of Scilly, garnering inspiration every time he visits the largest collection of exotics in the British Isles, which flourish in the warm Gulf Stream climate. For the Alexandra Palace garden Will had carefully considered the orientation of the plot and selected plants specifically for its sunnier and shadier areas.

The prime position in the shadier section near the house was to be taken by a pair of tree ferns (*Dicksonia antarctica*), one large and one small. These tremendous specimens were planted at the base of the new steps, with a group of hostas at their feet. This gives an instant impression of the exotic as you enter the garden, and your shoulders brush the giant fronds when you descend the steps. At the sunnier end, an enormous 2.5m (8ft) tall Chusan palm (*Trachycarpus fortunei*) had to be dragged through the house before it could be installed in the far corner of the plot. A bank of black-stemmed bamboo (*Phyllostachys nigra*) was planted in front of the bamboo-screened fence on either side of the rock water wall. In this way the

boundaries of the garden began to blur, and in time the mature specimens will completely enclose the end of the plot, while remaining soft and airy in appearance, the foliage rustling with every breath of wind. Among the other structural plants was a second variety of bamboo, this time *Phyllostachys vivax* 'Aureocaulis' with pale gold stems, and the spiky-leaved *Cordyline australis*. An *Aucuba japonica* 'Crotonifolia', one of the common spotted laurels that look so ordinary when planted *en masse* outside blocks of flats, went in opposite the Chusan palm. Here it became a key plant rather than merely background dressing, fulfilling its true destiny by forming a crucial part of an exotic planting scheme.

Beneath these statuesque plants, which created the backbone of the garden, an understorey of rodgersias, ferns – such as *Polystichum setiferum* and *Adiantum venustum* – and a host of hostas soon filled in the gaps. Flashes of brilliant colour were brought in with the addition of scarlet-flowered cannas, and clumps of mind-your-own-business (*Soleirolia soleirolii*) were dotted among the rocks at the front of the raised beds. A selection of climbers was added to the garden boundaries to increase the impression of enveloping lush vegetation. The vine (*Vitis coignetiae*) and the passion flower (*Passiflora caerulea*) were far better candidates for this garden than roses and honeysuckle.

Will's planting strategy for exotic gardens involves creating a framework of sturdy, evergreen architectural plants, such as the Chusan palm and bamboos, aucubas, fatsias and choisyas. He then uses tender plants, such as codiaeums, to put meat on the bones and add splashes of colour. These are often plants that we would think of as houseplants, but

Left: Water slips gently over the rock face, which is interplanted with ferns and studded with lights at night.

Opposite: The new raised deck improves the access into the garden, adds an interesting change of level and extra storage space beneath.

Will treats them as summer bedding, planting them out once the threat of frost is past and digging them up again in late autumn. In sheltered town gardens, some of the plants that would normally be taken inside can safely be left outside for the winter. Cannas may be left *in situ*, but when the foliage has faded should be cut to the base and the crown of the plant covered with a protective layer of thickly applied mulch – such as composted bark, straw or garden compost – to act as an insulating blanket.

The owners of this garden will probably have to do some basic plant protection each year to ensure the survival of their highly prized specimens. The prime candidate for special treatment is the purple Abyssinian banana (*Ensete ventricosum* 'Maurelii') that Will popped in a pot in the front corner of the deck. This banana is unlikely to overwinter successfully in the British climate and should be brought in for the winter months. A sheltered spot will help prevent the spectacular large leaves from shredding in the wind.

When all the plants were in place, the furniture and containers chosen and the work completed, it was time to road-test the new garden with a special outdoor meal on a late summer evening. With the improved access and plenty of room for people to move around the space – which made serving food and drinks far safer – the garden functioned perfectly. The water-wall really came into its own at night. Small candles were placed all over it, on ridges and under overhangs where the water wouldn't be able to drench them. These sparkled in the darkness, illuminating from behind the glassy water droplets. The sound of the gently tinkling water and the flickering of the flames gave this area a magical quality. This contrasted well with the dramatic shapes and silhouettes of the larger plants, which, when lit from below, gave presence and stature to the garden.

The owners were delighted with their unrecognizable north London plot. The great strength of Will's design was its deceptive simplicity in what was primarily a garden where plants came first. He had succeeded beyond expectation in transforming a dull urban space into a lush, exotic paradise that was full of warmth, atmosphere and, above all, the stunning, large-leaved plants that he adores. It would be hard to find a more dramatic transformation than this tropical oasis in the shadow of Alexandra Palace.

Left: Timber is combined with galvanized steel grids to form gently rising steps.

Opposite: A wrought-iron circular staircase and brick steps provide access to a small courtyard garden.

changes *of* level

Town gardens often have a complex arrangement of levels: many have a garden below street level at the front of the house and a plot behind the house at basement level. So, just as Will Giles did in the case study, the first question to consider is whether you are entering the garden in the right place. By creating an additional access from a first-floor drawing-room – perhaps a simple, timber-decked structure, or an elaborate wrought-iron balcony and staircase if the garden style is to be traditional. you might get much more enjoyment from your back garden. Opt for industrial metal grids or rubber floorings to step out into a modern urban retreat, no matter what the date of your house.

Lack of storage space is a massive problem in small town gardens, and sticking an ugly shed in one of the bottom corners is usually the answer. By building a raised platform, as Will Giles did in his exotic garden, it's often possible to kill several birds with one stone. You gain another point of entry into the garden, a new vantage point from which to enjoy the view, a terrace for entertaining – and some, or all, of the space below can be used for storing tools, a lawnmower and all the children's clutter. Raised platforms in other areas of the garden, and a series of inter-linking raised walkways can also conceal hidden storage areas and are imaginative ways to make the most of the limited space.

Introducing another level in this way can really liven up a dull rectangular space, adding another dimension to the plot. In a small garden the confines of the boundaries are only too obvious, so by changing the levels and introducing extra space in the form of cubed metres, you side-step the restrictions that lack of square metres imposes. But adding different levels to the garden needn't be confined to building raised areas: the alternative is to create further levels by digging down. Some of the best contemporary gardens have had the original ground profile of the space radically altered, yet we are often reluctant to make such a dramatic change.

Gardens on a steeply sloped site are prime candidates for this treatment; slopes are notoriously difficult to deal with and restrict the design possibilities. Far better to cut into the base of the slope and level off the top to

Opposite: Numerous changes of level turn a boring rectangular space into a garden full of structural interest.

Right: The problem of a sloping front garden is dealt with by creating squared-off tiers and planting low box hedges to give a stepped effect.

create two – or more – distinct areas. Even if your garden is as level as a snooker table, you should still consider getting in the digger. Carve out a central recessed section and create an intimate outdoor 'room' below ground level, furnished with comfortable seating, good lighting and a few well-chosen plants.

Altering the level of the planting also adds interest, versatility and plenty of extra growing space in small gardens. Create tiered or stepped beds and plant with eye-catching feature specimens or trailing plants that will drape themselves over the sides of the beds. Even lawns can be split into stepped sections. This is hugely effective but can mean a lot of extra work in terms of maintenance.

When thinking of changes of level, don't overlook the steps themselves. Even the humble garden step can be a distinctive design statement. There is a vast range of possible materials, styles, shapes and sizes to choose from, but do start with the basic premise that they should, above all, be safe. Reputable contractors will be *au fait* with the dos and don'ts of step-building, and if you plan to build them yourself, make sure you familiarize yourself with the rules too. Don't necessarily assume that the steps have to run in a straight line; it's often far more effective to break up the descent with a series of turns or curves. Steps can also vary in width – though, ideally, not in height – so think of all the possible permutations before resolving what will bring your garden to life.

Left: A mirrored obelisk by Allison Armour-Wilson reflects the elegant green and white planting scheme.

Opposite: Don't be afraid of colour when furnishing your garden.

furnishings *and* decorations

The hard work is done, the plot is landscaped, the water feature is burbling and the plants are getting used to their new environment. All that remains is the enjoyable task of dressing the finished garden. This is the time to choose furniture, extra containers, statuary, sculpture and – heaven forbid – gnomes.

The first priority for most people is to be able to start really using their new garden, and this means acquiring some furniture so that you can relax and enjoy that first drink, or get the neighbours over to show off your state-of-the-art back yard. Your choice of table and chairs will depend on space, the style of the garden and the number of people you want to be able to seat. Furniture made from hardwoods, such as teak and iroko, are extremely desirable, if pricy, and weather to a soft silvery-grey. But do make sure they come from sustainable managed sources before you buy: you don't want to improve your corner of the world at the expense of someone else's. Timber furniture comes in a huge range of styles, to suit everything from the most blowsy garden to sleek modernism.

Wrought- or cast-iron furniture – often in Regency or Victorian style, and usually painted – can work well with formal gardens or those with a traditional feel. Metals are also being used in modern outdoor furniture, though for something really unusual you might have to commission your own pieces. There are many furniture designers who specialize in producing unique outdoor furniture, and some of their sculptural creations are nothing less than works of art. Cutting-edge design is what's required for a state-of-the-art, minimalist urban space, so let your eye be your guide and go as strong as you dare.

There may be extras that will enhance your use of the garden and give you a plot for all seasons and all weathers. If you do have that rare thing, a small town garden with plenty of sun, you may need to invest in a parasol or an awning to protect you from the full force of the rays. Most of us, however, will be more likely to require one of the new gas patio heaters, many of which are free-standing and, depending on size, can be easily moved around the garden as needed. The benefit of being able to extend the long summer days

late into the night and to enjoy Guy Fawkes Night, Hallowe'en and even New Year's Eve outside makes these a worthwhile investment.

In a small space you will probably already have given plenty of consideration to containers, and may have incorporated them as an integral part of the design, but you may find that the finished garden looks incomplete without the addition of a few more. However, avoid the temptation to dilute the style of the garden by importing even a couple of pots that don't tie in with the general theme. It doesn't take much to detract from the design principles that make the garden work as a whole.

Any extra touches are really the icing on the cake. In a small space it's all too easy to clutter the place up with something bought on a whim. If you want to include statuary, one strong piece will have far more impact if it stands alone. Reconstituted stone is far cheaper than the real thing and, once aged, looks just as effective. Sculpture can bring a garden to life, and is often the inspiration for the whole design, but again, unless you want your garden to be a backdrop for a collection of art, a little goes a long way. Sundials, birdbaths and armillary spheres can all contribute to a small space if placed sympathetically. Mirrored, glass and ceramic objects can be stunning when used sparingly, and for a different look in a formal garden try gilding a simple object – perhaps a sphere – to catch the sun or glow warmly in a shady corner backed by a curtain of ivy.

designers' biographies

On graduating with a degree in landscape architecture, **Douglas Coltart** worked in the private and public sectors before taking up lecturing and freelance design work. His exhibitions and displays at flower shows in the UK have earned him several awards, including two RHS gold medals, two silver medals and two silver-gilt medals for displays in marquees. Douglas's contemporary approach to garden design combines an innovative use of space and materials with imaginative plantings. He set up his own garden design consultancy in 1999, and his work to date includes not only garden designs, but also the design of civic areas and parkland regeneration plans. Douglas is a full member of The UK Society of Garden Designers.

Paul Cooper was formerly a lecturer in art and design at the University of Lancaster and a successful sculptor before turning to garden design in 1984. He has won RHS bronze, silver and gold medals and the Sword of Excellence for the Best Garden at the Chelsea Flower Show. His controversial Cool and Sexy garden at Chelsea in 1994 firmly established him as one of the most thought-provoking of contemporary designers and his innovative domestic gardens have attracted attention for their use of unconventional materials and theatrical effects. He regularly features on television and radio, his work has appeared in various publications and he has written a book, *The New Tech Garden* (Mitchell Beazley, 2001).

Will Giles has been potty about plants, especially exotics, since he was seven. On being told there was no money in gardening, he studied art history and design at Great Yarmouth School of Art and then graduated from Norwich Art School to become an illustrator specializing in botanical subjects. Trips to far corners of the world in the eighties rekindled his love for plants, and in 1986 he was asked to open his garden for the National Garden Scheme. In April 2000 his first book, *The New Exotic Garden* (Mitchell Beazley), was published. He contributes to a weekly gardening phone-in on Radio Norfolk and writes for various magazines and online gardening forums. Ironically, his latest commission is for The Sea Front Partnership in Great Yarmouth, where he is redesigning the Golden Mile, totally in exotica.

Bunny Guinness completed a degree in horticulture and a post-graduate course in landscape architecture, before working for a range of architectural firms and corporations, designing commercial and private outdoor spaces. She then set up her own practice in 1986 and won five gold medals at Chelsea Flower Show (1994–99). The majority of her work is now on private gardens in the UK and further afield, ranging from stately homes to low-budget, inner-city gardens. She has published three books: *Family Gardens*, *Garden Transformations* and *Garden Workshop* (all published by David & Charles). She is a regular panel member of BBC Radio 4 *Gardener's Question Time* and has co-authored a book of the programme (Orion, 2000). She has appeared in several television programmes, including *Gardener's Garden* and Carol Vorderman's *Better Gardens*, where her garden won best garden in the series award, and has her own website: www.bunnyguinness.com.

Cleve West became interested in gardening when injury forced him to retire from a promising athletic career. Taught by garden designer and published author John Brookes at the Royal Botanic Gardens in Kew, Cleve formed his own landscape company in 1986. Since then he has won three RHS Gold Medals and other awards (with sculptor Johnny Woodford) for innovation for his show gardens, has appeared on *Gardeners' World* and written articles for magazines. He now runs his own London-based design practice – where his attention to the use of space is complemented by bold forms and textural foliage offset by seasonal colour – with a separate partnership with Johnny Woodford (Woodford-West) for show gardens and special projects. He also writes regularly for www.dig-it.co.uk and contributes several features on his organic allotment for the RHS's magazine *The Garden*.

Widely recognized as one of London's most exciting florists, **Stephen Woodhams** is quickly gaining international praise for his work in flower arranging and garden design. Having trained at the Royal Horticultural Society at Wisley, where he gained an RHS Certificate with honours, Stephen went on to form his own floral and landscape design company, Woodhams Ltd. He has written two books: *Flower Power* (Quadrille Publishing, 1998) and *Portfolio of Contemporary Gardens* (Quadrille Publishing, 1999); he makes regular lectures and television appearances, and has been featured in many interior and lifestyle magazines in the UK and internationally.

plant directory

Acer palmatum 'Sango-kaku'
Coral bark maple
The young stems of this deciduous shrub or small tree are bright coral red. The delicate foliage is apple green in spring and summer, often tinged red at the edges, turning in the autumn to shades of butter yellow. A plant with year-round appeal.
Height 6 m (20ft) × spread 5m (16ft)
Sun or partial shade; fully hardy

Alchemilla mollis
Lady's mantle
This perennial has wonderful, softly hairy, rounded leaves which trap raindrops in their shallow centres. The frothy sprays of acid-green flowers are borne through the summer. Remove these before they set seed unless you want the plant to spread all over the garden.
Height 30cm (1ft) × spread 25cm (10in)
Sun or partial shade; fully hardy

Anemone × hybrida 'Honorine Jobert'
Tall herbaceous perennial with clumps of palm-shaped leaves towards the base. Sends up slender stems bearing single white flowers, tinged with pink on the reverse, the centres with a ring of golden stamens.
Height 1.2m (4ft) × spread 1.2m (4ft)
Sun or partial shade; fully hardy

Asplenium scolopendrium
Hart's tongue fern
An evergreen fern with shiny, strap-like leaves. These bright green fronds have slightly frilled edges. An excellent garden fern with a strongly architectural shape.
Height 60cm (2ft) × spread 60cm (2ft)
Full or partial shade; fully hardy

Berberis thunbergii atropurpurea
A deciduous shrub with compact growth and wine-red leaves. Useful for introducing a touch of purple foliage to contrast with green-leaved plants.
Height 60cm (2ft) × spread 75cm (2½ ft)
Sun or partial shade; fully hardy

Betula utilis var. *jacquemontii* 'Silver Shadow'
Birch
This elegant tree is blessed with gleaming white bark. The foliage colours yellow in autumn before falling. Stunning when planted in front of an evergreen hedge. A vigorous grower, so not for the smallest spaces.
Height 18m (60ft) × spread 10m (33ft)
Sun to semi-shade; fully hardy

Cerinthe major 'Purpurascens'
This winter annual (illustrated left, page 125) has become increasingly fashionable, but it deserves a place in teh garden simply because it's so beautiful, the leaves have a glaucous bloom and the pendulous purple flowers are surrounded by blue bracts. Flowering well until the frosts, it might self-seed and the resulting seedlings will overwinter in milder positions. Sow seeds in autumn, or wait until spring in more exposed positions.
Height 60cm (2ft) × spread 30cm (1ft)
Sun or semi-shade

Choisya ternata
Mexican orange blossom
Reliable evergreen shrub (illustrated right, page 124) with a neat growth habit and attractive glossy green foliage. Citrus-scented, pure white flowers appear in late spring or early summer, sometimes with a second flush in late autumn. Frequently seen, but no less desirable for that.
Height 2.5m (8ft) × spread 2.5m (8ft)
Full sun or light shade; fully hardy

Corydalis flexuosa
This perennial (illustrated above and left, page 124) is unusual in being dormant during the summer months. A mound of delicate filigree foliage appears towards the end of the year, and in spring and early summer long-lasting, electric-blue flowers tinged with purple hover like butterflies above the leaves.
Height 30cm (1ft) × spread 30cm (1ft). Partial shade

Crataegus persimilis 'Prunifolia'
An unusual member of the hawthorn family, this tree has a rounded shape with glossy green leaves and white flowers in spring. The foliage turns to fiery shades in autumn, when the tree is also covered in scarlet berries – the effect is dazzling.
Height 8m (26ft) × spread 10m (33ft)
Sun or partial shade; fully hardy

Crocosmia 'Lucifer'
This cormous perennial is a wonderful foliage plant with strap-like leaves. The summer flowers, borne on

arching stems, are spectacularly scarlet, though not long-lasting. Best as a large clump within the border.
Height 1.1m (3½ft) × spread 8cm (3in)
Sun or partial shade; frost hardy

Dicksonia antarctica
Tasmanian tree fern
Once a rarity in the northern hemisphere, this plant is now hugely popular. The shaggy, reddish-brown trunk is actually a mass of roots, both living and dead. Large fronds spray out from the top of the trunk in a dramatic fashion. An evergreen in mild climates, perfect for the jungle look.
Height 6m (20ft) × spread 4m (13ft), though likely to be smaller
Partial or full shade; frost hardy

Euonymus fortunei 'Emerald Gaiety'
Compact evergreen variegated shrub. The bright green leaves have white margins and will lighten a drab corner. This easy-going, adaptable plant will even climb if planted at the base of a wall, and also makes good ground cover between larger shrubs.
Height 1m (3ft) × spread 1.5m (5ft)
Sun, semi-shade or full shade; fully hardy

Euphorbia polychroma
A herbaceous perennial with dark green leaves and acid-yellow, long-lasting flowers from mid-spring to early summer. A euphorbia with a neat growing habit, which makes it perfect for a small space.
Height 40cm (16in) × spread 60cm (2ft)
Full sun or light dappled shade; fully hardy

Fatsia japonica
This evergreen shrub is the stalwart of many gardens. The palm-shaped leaves are a glossy mid-green; autumnal sprays of creamy-white flowers are followed by black berries. An excellent architectural plant.
Height 2m (6½ft) × spread 4m (13ft)
Full sun or semi-shade; frost hardy to half-hardy

Geranium 'Rozanne'
This is a brand new variety with a compact shape smothered in violet-blue flowers from June right through to the first frosts; removing the spent blooms will encourage further flowering. This herbaceous perennial spreads but is not invasive and may be grown in a container. As an added bonus, the foliage develops rich autumnal tints.
Height 50cm (20in) × spread 1m (3ft)
Full sun; fully hardy

Hakonechloa macra 'Alboaurea'
This perennial grass forms rounded mounds of slender golden leaves striped thinly with green. Perfect for adding a touch of brightness to a shady spot. Excellent at the front of a border or in a container.
Height 35cm (14in) × spread 40cm (16in)
Partial shade; fully hardy

Helleborus × hybridus
Clump-forming perennial (illustrated right, page 125), hybrid of *Helleborus orientalis* and other species. Excellent plant for woodland-type conditions in dappled shade. Large, long-lasting, leathery leaves set off the saucer-shaped flowers, which come in a range of colours, including white, pale green, buff pink and dusky deep purple, sometimes with speckled markings.
Height 45cm (1½ft) × spread 45cm (1½ft)
Shade; fully hardy

Heuchera micrantha var. *diversifolia* 'Palace Purple'
This clump-forming perennial has deep burgundy-red, heart-shaped leaves, pinky-purple on the underside with a metallic sheen on the upper face. Salmon-pink flowers appear atop slender stems in early summer, but this is a plant grown primarily for its foliage.
Height 45cm (1½ft) × spread 60cm (2ft)
Sun or partial shade; fully hardy

Hosta 'Halcyon'
Perennial with clump-forming habit, grown for its large, overlapping, heart-shaped, grey-blue, fleshy leaves. Understated lavender-grey flowers are produced on tall stems in mid-summer. Although hostas are excellent architectural plants, providing good ground cover, they are also loved by slugs and snails, so they need protection.
Height 40cm (16in) × spread 70cm (28in)
Full or partial shade; fully hardy

Iris sibirica
This perennial is often associated with water, but it is unfussy about growing conditions and copes with well-drained or damp soil. Produces slender, upright

sheaves of foliage and small but show-stopping flowers in rich bluish-purple. A truly elegant plant.
Height 1m (3ft) × spread 10cm (4in)
Sun or partial shade; fully hardy

Phormium tenax
New Zealand flax
A clump-forming, evergreen perennial with strap-like, slender leaves and flowers held on towering stems in late summer. A strongly architectural plant. Many hybrids are available, some of them more compact, with tints of red or gold in the foliage.
Height 2m (6½ft) × spread 1.5m (5ft)
Full sun; frost hardy

Phyllostachys nigra
This black-stemmed bamboo has a clump-forming habit. On young growth the stems are green, turning inky-black after a couple of years. The canes sway and the evergreen foliage rustles in the slightest breeze.
Height 3–5m (10–16ft) × spread 2–3m (6½–10ft)
Sun or dappled shade; fully hardy

Prunus × subhirtella 'Autumnalis Rosea'
Deciduous winter-flowering cherry with a spreading shape. The dark green leaves turn yellow in autumn, after which the tree is periodically smothered in tiny, semi-double, palest pink flowers during mild spells through the winter. Often covered with blossom on Christmas Day.
Height 8m (26ft) × spread 8m (26ft)
Sun or partial shade; fully hardy

Rodgersia pinnata 'Superba'
A clump-forming perennial with dramatic, palm-shaped leaves, which are purplish-bronze when young and deeply veined. The plumes of bright pink flowers are not to everyone's taste: remove them if you think they detract from the foliage. An excellent mid-storey plant.
Height 1.2m (4ft) × spread 75cm (2½ft)
Sun or partial shade; fully hardy

Rosa 'Penny Lane'
Recently introduced climbing rose, named Rose of the Year in 1998. Smothered in nicely shaped champagne through palest blush-pink flowers. Repeats well, often still producing its scented blooms in December. Good disease resistance.
Height 3m (10ft) × spread 2.5m (8ft)
Sun or light semi-shade; fully hardy

Rosa 'Princess of Wales'
Compact floribunda rose, with trusses of pure white scented flowers and dark green foliage. Incredibly floriferous, it repeats well until late autumn. Excellent rose for a small garden.
Height 80cm (2ft 8in) × spread 60cm (2ft)
Prefers full sun or light semi-shade; fully hardy

Sarcococca hookeriana var. *digyna* 'Purple Stem'
Good evergreen shrub for tough places. Tolerant of shade, neglect and atmospheric pollution. The young stems and the leaf stalks on the narrow green leaves are tinged with purple. An understated plant until the winter, when clusters of tiny but very fragrant flowers will scent the garden.
Height 1.5m (5ft) × spread 2m (6½ft)
Full or partial shade; fully hardy

Sorbus vilmorinii
This elegant deciduous tree is a relative of the rowan. The foliage is composed of delicate-looking leaflets that are tougher than they appear and colour well in autumn. White flowers appear in late spring and are followed in autumn by clusters of rosy-pink berries that fade gradually almost to white.
Height 4m (13ft) × spread 5m (16ft)
Sun; fully hardy

Stipa arundinacea
This wonderful evergreen perennial grass forms clumps of arching foliage which change in colour from brown to olive green and rusty oranges, looking good all year. Stems bearing a haze of soft flowers pick up the slightest breeze from late summer to mid-autumn.
Height 1m (3ft) × spread 1.2m (4ft)
Sun or partial shade; frost hardy

Trachycarpus fortunei
Chusan palm
A single-stemmed evergreen palm with numerous fan-shaped leaves. The thick, trunk-like, fibrous stem has a shaggy appearance. Perfect for a touch of the exotic.
Height 10m (33ft) × spread 2.5m (8ft), usually shorter
Sun or dappled shade; frost hardy

Index

Page numbers in *italic* refer to illustrations

Picture credits

BBC Worldwide would like to thank the following for providing photographs and for permission to reproduce copyright material. While every effort has been made to trace and acknowledge all copyright holders, we would like to apologize should there have been any errors or omissions.

The following abbreviations have been used:

GPL Garden Picture Library
HGL Harpur Garden Library
JB Jonathan Buckley
DW Don Welldon
l left, r right, c centre, b bottom

Page 1 JB/Bunny Guinness; **p2** HGL/Luciano Giubbilei,; **p5**, **6**, JB; **p7** BBC Radio Times/Mark Harrison; **p8** l GPL/Ron Sutherland; p8 r Clive Nichols/Stephen Woodhams; **p9** l JB/Green & Cade; p9 c JB/ Stephen Woodhams, p9 r & **p10** l JB/ John Tordoff; **p11** Hugh Palmer; **p13** JB; **p14** l Marianne Majerus; p14 r JB; **p15** l Derek St Romaine; p15 c Clive Nichols; p15 r & **p16** l GPL/Jacqui Hurst; **p17** HGL/ Michael Balston; **p18** Colin Philp; **p19** l HGL/Simon Fraser; p19 r GPL/ Clive Nichols; **p20** GPL/Michael Paul; **p21**, **22**, **23**, **24** & **25** JB/Cleve West; **p26** l & r Marianne Majerus; **p27** l Hugh Palmer/Colin Livingstone; p27 r Marianne Majerus; **p28** Clive Nichols/Bradley-Hole; **p29** Andrew Lawson/Maggy Howarth; **p30** GPL/Ron Sutherland; **p31** Liz Eddison; **p32** l Chris Maton; p32 r JB/Paul Cooper; **p33** l David Spero; p33 r & **p34** l JB/Stephen Woodhams; **p35** HGL/Luciano Giubbilei; **p36** GPL/Clive Boursnell; **p37**, **38**, **39**, **40** & **41** JB/Stephen Woodhams; **p42** Emap Active; **p43** Marianne Majerus; **p44** Marianne Majerus/Sarah Crisp; **p45** l Marianne Majerus/Bunny Guinness; p45 c Clive Nichols; p45 r Marianne Majerus; **p46** Marianne Majerus/Paul Cooper; **p47** HGL/Lucian Giubbilei; **p48** Clive Nichols/Garden & Security Lighting; **p49** Marianne Majerus; **p50** l & c JB/Paul Cooper; p50 r GPL/John Glover; **p51** l, r & **52** l Marianne Majerus/ Allison Armour-Wilson, p52 c Marianne Majerus/David Stevens; p52 r GPL/Ron Sutherland; **p53** Chris Maton; **p54** l JB/Declan Buckley; p54 r Marianne Majerus/Paul Cooper; **p55** Marianne Majerus/ Allison Armour-Wilson; **p56** GPL/Clay Perry; **p57**, **58**, **59**, **60**, **61**, **62** & **63** JB/Paul Cooper; **p64** Marianne Majerus/Robin Cameron Don; **p65** GPL/Stephen Wooster; **p66** Marianne Majerus/George Carter; **p67** HGL/ Judith Sharpe; **p68** JB/Bunny Guinness; **p69** l GPL/Juliette Wade; p69 r & **p70** l JB/Bunny Guinness; p70 r Marianne Majerus/Barbara Schwartz; **p71** GPL/Juliet Greene; **p72** GPL/Eric Crichton; **p73** JB/ Green & Cade; **p74** Andrew Lawson; **p75**, **76**, **77**, **78**, **79** & **80** JB/Bunny Guinness; **p81** GPL/Ron Sutherland; **p82** t Andrew Lawson/James Aldridge; p82 b HGL/Barbara Thomas; **p83** GPL/Steven Wooster; **p84** l Marianne Majerus; p84 r HGL; **p85** l Andrew Lawson; p85 c HGL/Dan Pearson; p85 r & **p86** l DW; **p87** GPL/Stephen Wooster; **p88** Marianne Majerus/ Michele Osborne; **p89** HGL/ Henrietta Parsons; **p90** Andrew Lawson/Ian Hamilton Finlay; **p91**, **92**, **93**, **94**, **95**, **96** & **97** DW; **p98** Derek St Romaine/Wynniatt-Husey Clarke; **p99** HGL/Jonathan Baillie; **p100** Marianne Majerus/Ruth Collier; **p101** l Rachel de Thame; p101 r Marianne Majerus/Michele Osborne; **p102** l JB/Will Giles; p102 r Marianne Majerus/Will Giles; **p103** l Marianne Majerus/John Sarbutt; p103 c JB/Will Giles; p103 r & **p104** l JB/Maurice Green; **p105** & **106** Marianne Majerus/Will Giles; **p107** JB; **p108** Andrew Lawson; **p109**, **110**, **111**, **112**, **113**, **114** & **115** JB/Will Giles; **p116** Marianne Majerus/Paul Cooper; **p117** Marianne Majerus/Jill Billington; **p118** HGL/ Tim Ruval; **p119** GPL/Marianne Majerus; **p120** Marianne Majerus/ Allison Armour-Wilson; **p121** GPL/ Lynn Brotchie; **p123**, **124** & **125** Rachel de Thame.